BUTTERWORTHS COMMERCIAL LAW HANDBOOK

Editor

GWYNETH PITT
Lecturer in Law, Leeds University

BUTTERWORTHS
LONDON
1989

United Kingdom	Butterworth & Co (Publishers) Ltd, 88 Kingsway, LONDON WC2B 6AB and 4 Hill Street, EDINBURGH EH2 3JZ
Australia	Butterworths Pty Ltd, SYDNEY, MELBOURNE, BRISBANE, ADELAIDE, PERTH, CANBERRA and HOBART
Canada	Butterworths Canada Ltd, TORONTO and VANCOUVER
Ireland	Butterworth (Ireland) Ltd, DUBLIN
Malaysia	Malayan Law Journal Sdn Bhd, KUALA LUMPUR
New Zealand	Butterworths of New Zealand Ltd, WELLINGTON and AUCKLAND
Puerto Rico	Equity de Puerto Rico, Inc, HATO REY
Singapore	Malayan Law Journal Pte Ltd, SINGAPORE
USA	Butterworth Legal Publishers, AUSTIN, Texas; BOSTON, Massachusetts; CLEARWATER, Florida (D & S Publishers); ORFORD, New Hampshire (Equity Publishing); ST PAUL, Minnesota; and SEATTLE, Washington

All rights reserved. No part of this publication may be reproduced or transmitted in any form or by any means (including photocopying and recording) without the written permission of the copyright holder except in accordance with the provisions of the Copyright Act 1956 (as amended) or under the terms of a licence issued by the Copyright Licensing Agency Ltd, 33-34 Alfred Place, London, England WC1E 7DP. The written permission of the copyright holder must also be obtained before any part of this publication is stored in a retrieval system of any nature. Applications for the copyright holder's written permission to reproduce, transmit or store in a retrieval system any part of this publication should be addressed to the publisher.

Warning: The doing of an unauthorised act in relation to a copyright work may result in both a civil claim for damages and criminal prosecution.

© Butterworth & Co (Publishers) Ltd 1989
Reprinted 1990

A CIP Catalogue record for this book is available from the British Library.

ISBN 0 406 54722 X

Printed and bound in Great Britain by
Biddles Ltd, Guildford and King's Lynn

PREFACE

Commercial law is very much a statute-based subject. In recent years, as in other areas of the law, the pace of legislative change has quickened, in part to meet higher social expectations and in part as a result of our membership of the European Economic Communities. The purpose of this compilation is to provide students and practitioners of commercial law with the basic tools in a convenient and comprehensive form. This collection has the advantages of providing the materials in an up-to-date format and at a considerable saving on the cost of purchasing these items individually.

The book is divided into five sections: Contracts for the Supply of Goods; Consumer Credit; Consumer Protection; International Trade, and European Materials. Within each section statutes are arranged chronologically, followed by relevant statutory instruments. Most statutes are reproduced in full: where there are omissions, they are indicated and explained. The annotations are based on the LEXIS format and give the sources of amendments and repeals. As several statutes, notably the Consumer Credit Act 1974, contain many enabling provisions, details of orders and regulations made under the authority of the statute are given where appropriate. It is hoped that this feature will provide a useful source of reference.

The law is stated as at 1 May 1989, although prospective amendments are included where available. Legislation which applies to Scotland or Northern Ireland only is omitted, but legislation included applies to Northern Ireland unless otherwise indicated.

Since there are many views on what should be included within the rubric 'commercial law', some readers will find omissions or inclusions which they regard as inexplicable. It is impossible to satisfy everyone, but their comments would be welcome for consideration in the future. Finally, I would like to thank the staff at Butterworths, and especially LEXIS the computer, for their assistance in preparing this book.

Gwyneth Pitt

CONTENTS

Preface iii

SECTION I   CONTRACTS FOR THE SUPPLY OF GOODS

	para
Factors Act 1889	[1]
Law Reform (Frustrated Contracts) Act 1943	[16]
Hire Purchase Act 1964 (Part III)	[19]
Misrepresentation Act 1967	[22]
Supply of Goods (Implied Terms) Act 1973	[27]
Torts (Interference with Goods) Act 1977	[36]
Unfair Contract Terms Act 1977	[56]
Civil Liability (Contribution) Act 1978	[77]
Sale of Goods Act 1979	[86]
Supply of Goods and Services Act 1982	[150]

SECTION II   CONSUMER CREDIT

Consumer Credit Act 1974	[171]
Consumer Credit (Exempt Agreements) (No 2) Order 1985 (SI 1985 No 757) (as amended)	[362]

SECTION III   CONSUMER PROTECTION

Trading Stamps Act 1964	[371]
Trade Descriptions Acts 1968–72	[382]
Unsolicited Goods and Services Acts 1971–5	[422]
Fair Trading Act 1973 (Parts I and III)	[432]
Consumer Protection Act 1987	[453]
Consumer Arbitration Agreements Act 1988	[511]
Consumer Transactions (Restrictions on Statements) Order 1976 (SI 1976 No 1813) (as amended)	[520]
Consumer Protection (Cancellation of Contracts Concluded away from Business Premises) Regulations 1987 (SI 1987 No 2117) (as amended)	[525]
Control of Misleading Advertisements Regulations 1988 (SI 1988 No 915)	[538]

SECTION IV   INTERNATIONAL TRADE

Bills of Lading Act 1855	[549]
Marine Insurance Act 1906	[553]
Uniform Laws of International Sales Act 1967	[646]

Carriage of Goods by Sea Act 1971 . . . . . . [658]
Civil Jurisdiction and Judgments Act 1982 . . . . . [665]

SECTION V EUROPEAN MATERIALS

European Convention on Products Liability in regard to Personal
   Injury and Death . . . . [735]
EC Directive on Misleading Advertising 84/450/EEC . . . [755]
EC Directive on Product Liability 85/374/EEC . . . . [765]
EC Directive on Contracts Negotiated away from Business Premises
   EC 85/577/EEC . . . . [788]
EC Directive on Consumer Credit 87/102/EEC . . . . [799]

Index

SECTION I
CONTRACTS FOR THE SUPPLY OF GOODS

FACTORS ACT 1889
(c 45)

ARRANGEMENT OF SECTIONS

Preliminary

Section		Para
1	Definitions	[1]

Dispositions by Mercantile Agents

2	Powers of mercantile agent with respect to disposition of goods	[2]
3	Effect of pledges of documents of title	[3]
4	Pledge for antecedent debt	[4]
5	Rights acquired by exchange of goods or documents	[5]
6	Agreements through clerks, etc	[6]
7	Provisions as to consignors and consignees	[7]

Dispositions by Sellers and Buyers of Goods

8	Disposition by seller remaining in possession	[8]
9	Disposition by buyer obtaining possession	[9]
10	Effect of transfer of documents on vendor's lien or right of stoppage in transitu	[10]

Supplemental

11	Mode of transferring documents	[11]
12	Saving for rights of true owner	[12]
13	Saving for common law powers of agent	[13]
16	Extent of Act	[14]
17	Short title	[15]

An Act to amend and consolidate the Factors Acts [26 August 1889]

GENERAL NOTE
This Act extends to Northern Ireland.
This Act saved by the Hire-Purchase Act 1964.

Preliminary

1. Definitions

For the purposes of this Act—

(1) The expression "mercantile agent" shall mean a mercantile agent having in the customary course of his business as such agent authority either to sell goods, or to consign goods for the purpose of sale, or to buy goods, or to raise money on the security of goods.

(2) A person shall be deemed to be in possession of goods or of the documents of title to goods, where the goods or documents are in his actual custody or are held by any other person subject to his control or for him or on his behalf.

(3) The expression "goods" shall include wares and merchandise.

(4) The expression "document of title" shall include any bill of lading, dock warrant, warehouse-keeper's certificate, and warrant or order for the delivery

of goods, and any other document used in the ordinary course of business as proof of the possession or control of goods, or authorising or purporting to authorise, either by endorsement or by delivery, the possessor of the document to transfer or receive goods thereby represented.

(5) The expression "pledge" shall include any contract pledging, or giving a lien or security on, goods, whether in consideration of an original advance or of any further or continuing advance or of any pecuniary liability.

(6) The expression "person" shall include any body of persons corporate or unincorporate. [1]

Dispositions by Mercantile Agents

2. Powers of mercantile agent with respect to disposition of goods

(1) Where a mercantile agent is, with the consent of the owner, in possession of goods or of the documents of title to goods, any sale, pledge, or other disposition of the goods, made by him when acting in the ordinary course of business of a mercantile agent, shall, subject to the provisions of this Act, be as valid as if he were expressly authorised by the owner of the goods to make the same; provided that the person taking under the disposition acts in good faith, and has not at the time of the disposition notice that the person making the disposition has not authority to make the same.

(2) Where a mercantile agent has, with the consent of the owner, been in possession of goods or of the documents of title to goods, any sale, pledge, or other disposition, which would have been valid if the consent had continued, shall be valid notwithstanding the determination of the consent: provided that the person taking under the disposition has not at the time thereof notice that the consent has been determined.

(3) Where a mercantile agent has obtained possession of any documents of title to goods by reason of his being or having been, with the consent of the owner, in possession of the goods represented thereby, or of any other documents of title to the goods, his possession of the first-mentioned documents shall, for the purposes of this Act, be deemed to be with the consent of the owner.

(4) For the purposes of this Act the consent of the owner shall be presumed in the absence of evidence to the contrary. [2]

3. Effect of pledges of documents of title

A pledge of the documents of title to goods shall be deemed to be a pledge of the goods. [3]

4. Pledge for antecedent debt

Where a mercantile agent pledges goods as security for a debt or liability due from the pledgor to the pledgee before the time of the pledge, the pledgee shall acquire no further right to the goods than could have been enforced by the pledgor at the time of the pledge. [4]

5. Rights acquired by exchange of goods or documents

The consideration necessary for the validity of a sale, pledge, or other disposition, of goods, in pursuance of this Act, may be either a payment in cash, or the delivery or transfer of other goods, or of a document of title to goods, or of a negotiable security, or any other valuable consideration; but where goods are pledged by a mercantile agent in consideration of the delivery or transfer of other goods, or of a document of title to goods, or of a negotiable security, the pledgee shall acquire no right or interest in the goods so pledged in excess of the value of the goods, documents, or security when so delivered or transferred in exchange. [5]

6. Agreements through clerks, etc

For the purposes of this Act an agreement made with a mercantile agent through a clerk or other person authorised in the ordinary course of business to make contracts of sale or pledge on his behalf shall be deemed to be an agreement with the agent. [6]

7. Provisions as to consignors and consignees

(1) Where the owner of goods has given possession of the goods to another person for the purpose of consignment or sale, or has shipped the goods in the name of another person, and the consignee of the goods has not had notice that such person is not the owner of the goods, the consignee shall, in respect of advances made to or for the use of such person, have the same lien on the goods as if such person were the owner of the goods, and may transfer any such lien to another person.

(2) Nothing in this section shall limit or affect the validity of any sale, pledge, or disposition, by a mercantile agent. [7]

DISPOSITIONS BY SELLERS AND BUYERS OF GOODS

8. Disposition by seller remaining in possession

Where a person, having sold goods, continues, or is, in possession of the goods or of the documents of title to the goods, the delivery or transfer by that person, or by a mercantile agent acting for him, of the goods or documents of title under any sale, pledge, or other disposition thereof, or under any agreement for sale, pledge, or other disposition thereof, to any person receiving the same in good faith and without notice of the previous sale, shall have the same effect as if the person making the delivery or transfer were expressly authorised by the owner of the goods to make the same. [8]

9. Disposition by buyer obtaining possession

Where a person, having bought or agreed to buy goods, obtains with the consent of the seller possession of the goods or the documents of title to the goods, the delivery or transfer, by that person or by a mercantile agent acting for him, of the goods or documents of title, under any sale, pledge, or other disposition thereof, or under any agreement for sale, pledge, or other disposition thereof, to any person receiving the same in good faith and without notice of any lien or other right of the original seller in respect of the goods, shall have the same effect as if the person making the delivery or transfer were a mercantile agent in possession of the goods or documents of title with the consent of the owner.

[For the purposes of this section—
  (i) the buyer under a conditional sale agreement shall be deemed not to be a person who has bought or agreed to buy goods, and
  (ii) "conditional sale agreement" means an agreement for the sale of goods which is a consumer credit agreement within the meaning of the Consumer Credit Act 1974 under which the purchase price or part of it is payable by instalments, and the property in the goods is to remain in the seller (notwithstanding that the buyer is to be in

possession of the goods) until such conditions as to the payment of instalments or otherwise as may be specified in the agreement are fulfilled.] [9]

NOTES
Words in square brackets added by the Consumer Credit Act 1974, s 192(3)(a), Sch 4, para 2.
Commencement: 19 May 1985.
Commencement order: SI 1983 No 1551.

10. Effect of transfer of documents on vendor's lien or right of stoppage in transitu

Where a document of title to goods has been lawfully transferred to a person as a buyer or owner of the goods, and that person transfers the document to a person who takes the document in good faith and for valuable consideration, the last-mentioned transfer shall have the same effect for defeating any vendor's lien or right of stoppage in transitu as the transfer of a bill of lading has for defeating the right of stoppage in transitu. [10]

SUPPLEMENTAL

11. Mode of transferring documents

For the purposes of this Act, the transfer of a document may be by endorsement, or, where the document is by custom or by its express terms transferable by delivery, or makes the goods deliverable to the bearer, then by delivery. [11]

12. Saving for rights of true owner

(1) Nothing in this Act shall authorise an agent to exceed or depart from his authority as between himself and his principal, or exempt him from any liability, civil or criminal, for so doing.

(2) Nothing in this Act shall prevent the owner of goods from recovering the goods from an agent or his trustee in bankruptcy at any time before the sale or pledge thereof, or shall prevent the owner of goods pledged by an agent from having the right to redeem the goods at any time before the sale thereof, on satisfying the claim for which the goods were pledged, and paying to the agent, if by him required, any money in respect of which the agent would by law be entitled to retain the goods or the documents of title thereto, or any of them, by way of lien as against the owner, or from recovering from any person with whom the goods have been pledged any balance of money remaining in his hands as the produce of the sale of the goods after deducting the amount of his lien.

(3) Nothing in this Act shall prevent the owner of goods sold by an agent from recovering from the buyer the price agreed to be paid for the same, or any part of that price, subject to any right of set-off on the part of the buyer against the agent. [12]

13. Saving for common law powers of agent

The provisions of this Act shall be construed in amplification and not in derogation of the powers exercisable by an agent independently of this Act. [13]

NOTE
Ss 14–15 repealed by the Statute Law Revision Act 1908.

16. Extent of Act
This Act shall not extend to Scotland. [14]

NOTES
Repealed with savings by virtue of the Factors (Scotland) Act 1890.

17. Short title
This Act may be cited as the Factors Act 1889. [15]

LAW REFORM (FRUSTRATED CONTRACTS) ACT 1943
(c 40)

An Act to amend the law relating to the frustration of contracts [5 August 1943]

GENERAL NOTE
This Act does not extend to Northern Ireland

1. Adjustment of rights and liabilities of parties to frustrated contracts

(1) Where a contract governed by English law has become impossible of performance or been otherwise frustrated, and the parties thereto have for that reason been discharged from the further performance of the contract, the following provisions of this section shall, subject to the provisions of section two of this Act, have effect in relation thereto.

(2) All sums paid or payable to any party in pursuance of the contract before the time when the parties were so discharged (in this Act referred to as "the time of discharge") shall, in the case of sums so paid, be recoverable from him as money received by him for the use of the party by whom the sums were paid, and, in the case of sums so payable, cease to be so payable:

Provided that, if the party to whom the sums were so paid or payable incurred expenses before the time of discharge in, or for the purpose of, the performance of the contract, the court may, if it considers it just to do so having regard to all the circumstances of the case, allow him to retain or, as the case may be, recover the whole or any part of the sums so paid or payable, not being an amount in excess of the expenses so incurred.

(3) Where any party to the contract has, by reason of anything done by any other party thereto in, or for the purpose of, the performance of the contract, obtained a valuable benefit (other than a payment of money to which the last foregoing subsection applies) before the time of discharge, there shall be recoverable from him by the said other party such sum (if any), not exceeding the value of the said benefit to the party obtaining it, as the court considers just, having regard to all the circumstances of the case and, in particular,—

    (*a*) the amount of any expenses incurred before the time of discharge by the benefited party in, or for the purpose of, the performance of the contract, including any sums paid or payable by him to any other party in pursuance of the contract and retained or recoverable by that party under the last foregoing subsection, and

    (*b*) the effect, in relation to the said benefit, of the circumstances giving rise to the frustration of the contract.

(4) In estimating, for the purposes of the foregoing provisions of this section, the amount of any expenses incurred by any party to the contract, the court

may, without prejudice to the generality of the said provisions, include such sum as appears to be reasonable in respect of overhead expenses and in respect of any work or services performed personally by the said party.

(5) In considering whether any sum ought to be recovered or retained under the foregoing provisions of this section by any party to the contract, the court shall not take into account any sums which have, by reason of the circumstances giving rise to the frustration of the contract, become payable to that party under any contract of insurance unless there was an obligation to insure imposed by an express term of the frustrated contract or by or under any enactment.

(6) Where any person has assumed obligations under the contract in consideration of the conferring of a benefit by any other party to the contract upon any other person, whether a party to the contract or not, the court may, if in all the circumstances of the case it considers it just to do so, treat for the purposes of subsection (3) of this section any benefit so conferred as a benefit obtained by the person who has assumed the obligations as aforesaid.

2. Provision as to application of this Act

(1) This Act shall apply to contracts, whether made before or after the commencement of this Act, as respects which the time of discharge is on or after the first day of July, nineteen hundred and forty-three, but not to contracts as respects which the time of discharge is before the said date.

(2) This Act shall apply to contracts to which the Crown is a party in like manner as to contracts between subjects.

(3) Where any contract to which this Act applies contains any provision which, upon the true construction of the contract, is intended to have effect in the event of circumstances arising which operate, or would but for the said provision operate, to frustrate the contract, or is intended to have effect whether such circumstances arise or not, the court shall give effect to the said provision and shall only give effect to the foregoing section of this Act to such extent, if any, as appears to the court to be consistent with the said provision.

(4) Whether it appears to the court that a part of any contract to which this Act applies can properly be severed from the remainder of the contract, being a part wholly performed before the time of discharge, or so performed except for the payment in respect of that part of the contract of sums which are or can be ascertained under the contract, the court shall treat that part of the contract as if it were a separate contract and had not been frustrated and shall treat the foregoing section of this Act as only applicable to the remainder of that contract.

(5) This Act shall not apply—

(a) to any charterparty, except a time charterparty or a charterparty by way of demise, or to any contract (other than a charterparty) for the carriage of goods by sea; or

(b) to any contract of insurance, save as is provided by subsection (5) of the foregoing section; or

(c) to any contract to which [section 7 of the Sale of Goods Act 1979] (which avoids contracts for the sale of specific goods which perish before the risk has passed to the buyer) applies, or to any other contract for the sale, or for the sale and delivery, of specific goods, where the contract is frustrated by reason of the fact that the goods have perished.

NOTES
Sub-s (3) does not apply to agreements deemed to be frustrated under s 32(1) of the Aircraft and Shipbuilding Industries Act 1977: see s 32(2) of that Act.
Sub-s (5): amended by the Sale of Goods Act 1979, s 63, Sch 2, para 2.

3. Short title and interpretation

(1) This Act may be cited as the Law Reform (Frustrated Contracts) Act 1943.

(2) In this Act the expression "court" means, in relation to any matter, the court or arbitrator by or before whom the matter falls to be determined. [18]

HIRE-PURCHASE ACT 1964
(c 53)

An Act to amend the law relating to hire-purchase and credit-sale, and, in relation thereto, to amend the enactments relating to the sale of goods; to make provision with respect to dispositions of motor vehicles which have been let or agreed to be sold by way of hire-purchase or conditional sale; to amend the Advertisements (Hire-Purchase) Act 1957; and for purposes connected with the matters aforesaid. [16 July 1964]

GENERAL NOTE
Part III of this Act is printed in full as substituted by the Consumer Credit Act 1974, s 192(3)(a), Sch 4, para 22. This reproduced existing provisions with changes of terminology. The rest of this Act was repealed by the Consumer Credit Act 1974, except for s 37 (short title, commencement and extent).
This Act does not extend to Northern Ireland.

PART III
[TITLE TO MOTOR VEHICLES ON HIRE-PURCHASE OR CONDITIONAL SALE]

27. Protection of purchasers of motor vehicles

[(1) This section applies where a motor vehicle has been bailed or (in Scotland) hired under a hire-purchase agreement, or has been agreed to be sold under a conditional sale agreement, and, before the property in the vehicle has become vested in the debtor, he disposes of the vehicle to another person.

(2) Where the disposition referred to in subsection (1) above is to a private purchaser, and he is a purchaser of the motor vehicle in good faith without notice of the hire-purchase or conditional sale agreement (the "relevant agreement") that disposition shall have effect as if the creditor's title to the vehicle has been vested in the debtor immediately before that disposition.

(3) Where the person to whom the disposition referred to in subsection (1) above is made (the "original purchaser") is a trade or finance purchaser, then if the person who is the first private purchaser of the motor vehicle after that disposition (the "first private purchaser") is a purchaser of the vehicle in good faith without notice of the relevant agreement, the disposition of the vehicle to the first private purchaser shall have effect as if the title of the creditor to the vehicle had been vested in the debtor immediately before he disposed of it to the original purchaser.

(4) Where, in a case within subsection (3) above—

(a) the disposition by which the first private purchaser becomes a purchaser of the motor vehicle in good faith without notice of the relevant agreement is itself a bailment or hiring under a hire-purchase agreement, and

(b) the person who is the creditor in relation to that agreement disposes of the vehicle to the first private purchaser, or a person claiming under him, by transferring to him the property in the vehicle in pursuance of a provision in the agreement in that behalf,

the disposition referred to in paragraph (b) above (whether or not the person to whom it is made is a purchaser in good faith without notice of the relevant agreement) shall as well as the disposition referred to in paragraph (a) above, have effect as mentioned in subsection (3) above.

(5) The preceding provisions of this section apply—

(a) notwithstanding anything in [section 21 of the Sale of Goods Act 1979] (sale of goods by a person not the owner), but

(b) without prejudice to the provisions of the Factors Act (as defined by [section 61 (1) of the said Act of 1979]) or of any other enactment enabling the apparent owner of goods to dispose of them as if he were the true owner.

(6) Nothing in this section shall exonerate the debtor from any liability (whether criminal or civil) to which he would be subject apart from this section; and, in a case where the debtor disposes of the motor vehicle to a trade or finance purchaser, nothing in this section shall exonerate—

(a) that trade or finance purchaser; or

(b) any other trade or finance purchaser who becomes a purchaser of the vehicle and is not a person claiming under the first private purchaser,

from any liability (whether criminal or civil) to which he would be subject apart from this section.] [19]

NOTES
Commencement: 19 May 1985.
Commencement order: SI 1983 No 1551.
Substituted by the Consumer Credit Act 1974, s 192(3)(a), Sch 4, para 22.
Sub-s (5): amended by the Sale of Goods Act 1979, s 63, Sch 2, para 4.
S 61(1) of the said Act of 1979: ie Sale of Goods Act 1979.

28. Presumptions relating to dealings with motor vehicles

[(1) Where in any proceedings (whether criminal or civil) relating to a motor vehicle it is proved—

(a) that the vehicle was bailed or (in Scotland) hired under a hire-purchase agreement, or was agreed to be sold under a conditional sale agreement, and

(b) that a person (whether a party to the proceedings or not) became a private purchaser of the vehicle in good faith without notice of the hire-purchase or conditional sale agreement (the "relevant agreement"),

this section shall have effect for the purposes of the operation of section 27 of this Act in relation to those proceedings.

(2) It shall be presumed for those purposes, unless the contrary is proved, that the disposition of the vehicle to the person referred to in subsection (1) (b) above (the "relevant purchaser") was made by the debtor.

(3) If it is proved that that disposition was not made by the debtor, then it shall be presumed for those purposes, unless the contrary is proved—
  (a) that the debtor disposed of the vehicle to a private purchaser purchasing in good faith without notice of the relevant agreement, and
  (b) that the relevant purchaser is or was a person claiming under the person to whom the debtor so disposed of the vehicle.

(4) If it is proved that the disposition of the vehicle to the relevant purchaser was not made by the debtor, and that the person to whom the debtor disposed of the vehicle (the "original purchaser") was a trade or finance purchaser, then it shall be presumed for those purposes, unless the contrary is proved,—
  (a) that the person who, after the disposition of the vehicle to the original purchaser, first became a private purchaser of the vehicle was a purchaser in good faith without notice of the relevant agreement, and
  (b) that the relevant purchaser is or was a person claiming under the original purchaser.

(5) Without prejudice to any other method of proof, where in any proceedings a party thereto admits a fact, that fact shall, for the purposes of this section, be taken as against him to be proved in relation to those proceedings.] [20]

NOTES
Commencement: 19 May 1985.
Commencement order: SI 1983 No 1551.
Substituted by the Consumer Credit Act 1974, s 192(3)(a), Sch 4, para 22.

29. Interpretation of Part III

[(1) In this Part of this Act—
  "conditional sale agreement" means an agreement for the sale of goods under which the purchase price or part of it is payable by instalments, and the property in the goods is to remain in the seller (notwithstanding that the buyer is to be in possession of the goods) until such conditions as to the payment of instalments or otherwise as may be specified in the agreement are fulfilled;
  "creditor" means the person by whom goods are bailed or (in Scotland) hired under a hire-purchase agreement or as the case may be, the seller under a conditional sale agreement, or the person to whom his rights and duties have passed by assignment or operation of law;
  "disposition" means any sale or contract of sale (including a conditional sale agreement), any bailment or (in Scotland) hiring under a hire-purchase agreement and any transfer of the property in goods in pursuance of a provision in that behalf contained in a hire-purchase agreement, and includes any transaction purporting to be a disposition (as so defined), and 'dispose of' shall be construed accordingly.
  "hire-purchase agreement" means an agreement, other than a conditional sale agreement, under which—
  (a) goods are bailed or (in Scotland) hired in return for periodical payments by the person to whom they are bailed or hired, and
  (b) the property in the goods will pass to that person if the terms of the agreement are complied with and one or more of the following occurs—
    (i) the exercise of an option to purchase by that person,
    (ii) the doing of any other specified act by any party to the agreement,
    (iii) the happening of any other specified events; and

"motor vehicle" means a mechanically propelled vehicle intended or adapted for use on roads to which the public has access.

(2) In this Part of this Act "trade or finance purchaser" means a purchaser who, at the time of the disposition made to him, carries on a business which consists, wholly or partly,—

(a) of purchasing motor vehicles for the purpose of offering or exposing them for sale, or
(b) of providing finance by purchasing motor vehicles for the purpose of bailing or (in Scotland) hiring them under hire-purchase agreements or agreeing to sell them under conditional sale agreements,

and "private purchaser" means a purchaser who, at the time of the disposition made to him, does not carry on any such business.

(3) For the purposes of this Part of this Act a person becomes a purchaser of a motor vehicle if, and at the time when, a disposition of the vehicle is made to him; and a person shall be taken to be a purchaser of a motor vehicle without notice of a hire-purchase agreement or conditional sale agreement if, at the time of the disposition made to him, he has no actual notice that the vehicle is or was the subject of any such agreement.

(4) In this Part of this Act the "debtor" in relation to a motor vehicle which has been bailed or hired under a hire-purchase agreement, or, as the case may be, agreed to be sold under a conditional sale agreement, means the person who at the material time (whether the agreement has before that time been terminated or not) either—

(a) is the person to whom the vehicle is bailed or hired under that agreement, or
(b) is, in relation to the agreement, the buyer, including a person who at the time is, by virtue of section 130 (4) of the Consumer Credit Act 1974 treated as a bailee or (in Scotland) a custodier of the vehicle.

(5) In this Part of this Act any reference to the title of the creditor to a motor vehicle which has been bailed or (in Scotland) hired under a hire-purchase agreement, or agreed to be sold under a conditional sale agreement, and is disposed of by the debtor, is a reference to such title (if any) to the vehicle as, immediately before that disposition, was vested in the person who then was the creditor in relation to the agreement.] [21]

NOTES
Commencement: 19 May 1985.
Commencement order: SI 1983 No 1551.
Substituted by the Consumer Credit Act 1974, s 192(3)(a), Sch 4, para 22.

MISREPRESENTATION ACT 1967
(c 7)

ARRANGEMENT OF SECTIONS

Section		Para
1	Removal of certain bars to rescission for innocent misrepresentation	[22]
2	Damages for misrepresentation	[23]
3	Avoidance of certain provisions excluding liability for misrepresentation	[24]

Section	Para
5 Saving for past transactions	[25]
6 Short title, commencement and extent	[26]

An Act to amend the law relating to innocent misrepresentations and to amend sections 11 and 35 of the Sale of Goods Act 1893 [22 March 1967]

1. Removal of certain bars to rescission for innocent misrepresentation

Where a person has entered into a contract after a misrepresentation has been made to him, and—

    (*a*) the misrepresentation has become a term of the contract; or
    (*b*) the contract has been performed;

or both, then, if otherwise he would be entitled to rescind the contract without alleging fraud, he shall be so entitled, subject to the provisions of this Act, notwithstanding the matters mentioned in paragraphs (*a*) and (*b*) of this section. [22]

2. Damages for misrepresentation

(1) Where a person has entered into a contract after a misrepresentation has been made to him by another party thereto and as a result thereof he has suffered loss, then, if the person making the misrepresentation would be liable to damages in respect thereof had the misrepresentation been made fraudulently, that person shall be so liable notwithstanding that the misrepresentation was not made fraudulently, unless he proves that he had reasonable ground to believe and did believe up to the time the contract was made that the facts represented were true.

(2) Where a person has entered into a contract after a misrepresentation has been made to him otherwise than fraudulently, and he would be entitled, by reason of the misrepresentation, to rescind the contract, then, if it is claimed, in any proceedings arising out of the contract, that the contract ought to be or has been rescinded, the court or arbitrator may declare the contract subsisting and award damages in lieu of rescission, if of opinion that it would be equitable to do so, having regard to the nature of the misrepresentation and the loss that would be caused by it if the contract were upheld, as well as to the loss that rescission would cause to the other party.

(3) Damages may be awarded against a person under subsection (2) of this section whether or not he is liable to damages under subsection (1) thereof, but where he is so liable any award under the said subsection (2) shall be taken into account in assessing his liability under the said subsection (1). [23]

3. [Avoidance of provision excluding liability for misrepresentation]

[If a contract contains a term which would exclude or restrict—

    (*a*) any liability to which a party to a contract may be subject by reason of any misrepresentation made by him before the contract was made; or
    (*b*) any remedy available to another party to the contract by reason of such a misrepresentation,

that term shall be of no effect except in so far as it satisfies the requirement of reasonableness as stated in section 11(1) of the Unfair Contract Terms Act 1977; and it is for those claiming that the term satisfies that requirement to show that it does.] **[24]**

NOTES
Commencement: 1 February 1978.
Substituted by the Unfair Contract Terms Act 1977, s 8(1).
S 4 amended the Sale of Goods Act 1893 ss 11 and 35. The amendments are incorporated in the Sale of Goods Act 1979.

5. Saving for past transactions

Nothing in this Act shall apply in relation to any misrepresentation or contract of sale which is made before the commencement of this Act. **[25]**

6. Short title, commencement and extent

(1) This Act may be cited as the Misrepresentation Act 1967.

(2) This Act shall come into operation at the expiration of the period of one month beginning with the date on which it is passed.

(3) ...

(4) This Act does not extend to Northern Ireland. **[26]**

NOTES
Sub-s (3): applies to Scotland only.

SUPPLY OF GOODS (IMPLIED TERMS) ACT 1973
(c 13)

ARRANGEMENT OF SECTIONS

HIRE-PURCHASE AGREEMENTS

Section		Para
8	Implied terms as to title	[27]
9	[Bailing or hiring by description]	[28]
10	Implied undertakings as to quality or fitness	[29]
11	Samples	[30]
12	Exclusion of implied terms and conditions	[31]
14	Special provisions as to conditional sale agreements	[32]
15	Supplementary	[33]

MISCELLANEOUS

17	Northern Ireland	[34]
18	Short title, citation, interpretation, commencement, repeal and saving	[35]

An Act to amend the law with respect to the terms to be implied in contracts of sale of goods and hire-purchase agreements and on the exchange of goods for trading stamps, and with respect to the terms of conditional sale agreements: and for connected purposes [18 April 1973]

NOTES
Ss 1–7 repealed by the Sale of Goods Act 1979, s 63(2), Sch 3.

Hire-purchase agreements

8. Implied terms as to title

[(1) In every hire-purchase agreement, other than one to which subsection (2) below applies, there is—
- (a) an implied condition on the part of the creditor that he will have a right to sell the goods at the time when the property is to pass; and
- (b) an implied warranty that—
  - (i) the goods are free, and will remain free until the time when the property is to pass, from any charge or encumbrance not disclosed or known to the person to whom the goods are bailed or (in Scotland) hired before the agreement is made, and
  - (ii) that person will enjoy quiet possession of the goods except so far as it may be disturbed by any person entitled to the benefit of any charge or encumbrance so disclosed or known.

(2) In a hire-purchase agreement, in the case of which there appears from the agreement or is to be inferred from the circumstances of the agreement an intention that the creditor should transfer only such title as he or a third person may have, there is—
- (a) an implied warranty that all charges or encumbrances known to the creditor and not known to the person to whom the goods are bailed or hired have been disclosed to that person before the agreement is made; and
- (b) an implied warranty that neither—
  - (i) the creditor; nor
  - (ii) in a case where the parties to the agreement intend that any title which may be transferred shall be only such title as a third person may have, that person; nor
  - (iii) anyone claiming through or under the creditor or that third person otherwise than under a charge or encumbrance disclosed or known to the person to whom the goods are bailed or hired, before the agreement is made;

will disturb the quiet possession of the person to whom the goods are bailed or hired.] [27]

NOTES
    Commencement: 19 May 1985.
    Commencement order: SI 1983 No 1551.
    Substituted by the Consumer Credit Act 1974, s 192(3)(a), Sch 4, para 35.

9. [Bailing or hiring by description]

[(1) Where under a hire-purchase agreement goods are bailed or (in Scotland) hired by description, there is an implied condition that the goods will correspond with the description, and if under the agreement the goods are bailed or hired by reference to a sample as well as a description, it is not sufficient that the bulk of the goods corresponds with the sample if the goods do not also correspond with the description.

(2) Goods shall not be prevented from being bailed or hired by description by reason only that, being exposed for sale, bailment or hire, they are selected by the person to whom they are bailed or hired.] [28]

NOTES
Commencement: 19 May 1985.
Commencement order: SI 1983 No 1551.
Substituted by the Consumer Credit Act 1974, s 192(3)(*a*), Sch 4, para 35.

10. Implied undertakings as to quality or fitness

[(1) Except as provided by this section and section 11 below and subject to the provisions of any other enactment, including any enactment of the Parliament of Northern Ireland or the Northern Ireland Assembly, there is no implied condition or warranty as to the quality or fitness for any particular purpose of goods bailed or (in Scotland) hired under a hire-purchase agreement.

(2) Where the creditor bails or hires goods under a hire-purchase agreement in the course of a business, there is an implied condition that the goods [supplied under the agreement] are of merchantable quality, except that there is no such condition—

  (*a*) as regards defects specifically drawn to the attention of the person to whom the goods are bailed or hired before the agreement is made; or
  (*b*) if that person examines the goods before the agreement is made, as regards defects which that examination ought to reveal.

(3) Where the creditor bails or hires goods under a hire-purchase agreement in the course of a business and the person to whom the goods are bailed or hired, expressly or by implication, makes known—

  (*a*) to the creditor in the course of negotiations conducted by the creditor in relation to the making of the hire-purchase agreement, or
  (*b*) to a credit-broker in the course of negotiations conducted by that broker in relation to goods sold by him to the creditor before forming the subject matter of the hire-purchase agreement,

any particular purpose for which the goods are being bailed or hired, there is an implied condition that the goods supplied under the agreement are reasonably fit for that purpose, whether or not that is a purpose for which such goods are commonly supplied, except where the circumstances show that the person to whom the goods are bailed or hired does not rely, or that it is unreasonable for him to rely, on the skill or judgment of the creditor or credit-broker.

(4) An implied condition or warranty as to quality or fitness for a particular purpose may be annexed to a hire-purchase agreement by usage.

(5) The preceding provisions of this section apply to a hire-purchase agreement made by a person who in the course of a business is acting as agent for the creditor as they apply to an agreement made by the creditor in the course of a business, except where the creditor is not bailing or hiring in the course of a business and either the person to whom the goods are bailed or hired knows that fact or reasonable steps are taken to bring it to the notice of that person before the agreement is made.

(6) In subsection (3) above and this subsection—

  (*a*) "credit-broker" means a person acting in the course of a business of credit brokerage.
  (*b*) "credit brokerage" means the effecting of introductions of individuals desiring to obtain credit—

    (i) to persons carrying on any business so far as it relates to the provision of credit, or

(ii) to other persons engaged in credit brokerage.] [29]

NOTES
Commencement: 19 May 1985.
Commencement order: SI 1983 No 1551.
Substituted by the Consumer Credit Act 1974, s 192(3)(a), Sch 4, para 35.
Sub-s (2): amended by the Supply of Goods and Services Act 1982, s 17(1).

11. Samples

[Where under a hire-purchase agreement goods are bailed or (in Scotland) hired by reference to a sample, there is an implied condition—
  (a) that the bulk will correspond with the sample in quality; and
  (b) that the person to whom the goods are bailed or hired will have a reasonable opportunity of comparing the bulk with the sample; and
  (c) that the goods will be free from any defect, rendering them unmerchantable, which would not be apparent on reasonable examination of the sample.] [30]

NOTES
Commencement: 19 May 1985.
Commencement order: SI 1983 No 1551.
Substituted by the Consumer Credit Act 1974, s 192(3)(a), Sch 4, para 35.

12. Exclusion of implied terms and conditions

[(1) An express condition or warranty does not negative a condition or warranty implied by this Act unless inconsistent with it.]

(2)–(9) ... [31]

NOTES
Commencement: 19 May 1985.
Commencement order: SI 1983 No 1551.
Sub-s (1): substituted by the Consumer Credit Act 1974, s 192(3)(a), Sch 4, para 35.
Sub-ss (2)–(9): repealed by the Unfair Contract Terms Act 1977, s 31(4), Sch 4.
S 13 repealed by the Unfair Contract Terms Act 1977, s 31(4), Sch 4.

14. Special provisions as to conditional sale agreements

[(1) [Section 11(4) of the Sale of Goods Act 1979] (whereby in certain circumstances a breach of a condition in a contract of sale is treated only as a breach of warranty) shall not apply to [a conditional sale agreement where the buyer deals as consumer within Part I of the Unfair Contract Terms Act 1977 . . . .]

(2) In England and Wales and Northern Ireland a breach of a condition (whether express or implied) to be fulfilled by the seller under any such agreement shall be treated as a breach of warranty, and not as grounds for rejecting the goods and treating the agreement as repudiated, if (but only if) it would have fallen to be so treated had the condition been contained or implied in a corresponding hire-purchase agreement as a condition to be fulfilled by the creditor.] [32]

NOTES
Commencement: 19 May 1985.
Commencement order: SI 1983 No 1551.
Substituted by the Consumer Credit Act 1974, s 192(3)(a), Sch 4, para 36; first amendment made by the Sale of Goods Act 1979, s 63, Sch 2, para 16; second amendment made by the Unfair Contract Terms Act 1977, s 31(3), Sch 3; words omitted repealed by the Statute Law (Repeals) Act 1981, Sch 1, Part XII.

15. Supplementary

[(1) In sections 8 to 14 above and this section—

"business" includes a profession and the activities of any government department (including a Northern Ireland department), [or local or public authority];

"buyer" and "seller" includes a person to whom rights and duties under a conditional sale agreement have passed by assignment or operation of law;

"condition" and "warranty", in relation to Scotland, mean stipulation, and any stipulation referred to in sections 8 (1) (*a*), 9, 10 and 11 above shall be deemed to be material to the agreement.

"conditional sale agreement" means an agreement for the sale of goods under which the purchase price or part of it is payable by instalments, and the property in the goods is to remain in the seller (notwithstanding that the buyer is to be in possession of the goods) until such conditions as to the payment of instalments or otherwise as may be specified in the agreement are fulfilled;

. . .

"creditor" means the person by whom the goods are bailed or (in Scotland) hired under a hire-purchase agreement or the person to whom his rights and duties under the agreement have passed by assignment or operation of law; and

"hire-purchase agreement" means an agreement, other than a conditional sale agreement, under which—

(*a*) goods are bailed or (in Scotland) hired in return for periodical payments by the person to whom they are bailed or hired, and

(*b*) the property in the goods will pass to that person if the terms of the agreements are complied with and one or more of the following occurs—

(i) the exercise of an option to purchase by that person,
(ii) the doing of any other specified act by any party to the agreement,
(iii) the happening of any other specified event.

(2) Goods of any kind are of merchantable quality within the meaning of section 10 (2) above if they are as fit for the purpose or purposes for which goods of that kind are commonly bought as it is reasonable to expect having regard to any description applied to them, the price (if relevant) and all the other relevant circumstances; and in section 11 above "unmerchantable" shall be construed accordingly.

(3) In section 14 (2) above "corresponding hire-purchase agreement" means, in relation to a conditional sale agreement, a hire-purchase agreement relating to the same goods as the conditional sale agreement and made between the same parties and at the same time and in the same circumstances and, as nearly as may be, in the same terms as the conditional sale agreement.

(4) Nothing in sections 8 to 13 above shall prejudice the operation of any other enactment including any enactment of the Parliament of Northern Ireland or the Northern Ireland Assembly or any rule of law whereby any condition or warranty, other than one relating to quality or fitness, is to be implied in any hire-purchase agreement.] [33]

NOTES
Commencement: 19 May 1985.
Commencement order: SI 1983 No 1551.
Substituted by the Consumer Credit Act 1974, s 192(3)(*a*), Sch 4, para 36.

Sub-s (1): definition "business" amended, and words omitted repealed by the Unfair Contract Terms Act 1977, s 31(3), (4), Sch 4.
S 16 amends the Trading Stamps Act 1964, s 4 and the amendments have been incorporated on the text of that Act. It also amends the Trading Stamps Act (Northern Ireland) 1965, s 4 (not reproduced in this book).

MISCELLANEOUS

17. Northern Ireland

(1) It is hereby declared that this Act extends to Northern Ireland.

(2) ... [34]

NOTES
Commencement: 18 May 1973.
Sub-s (2): repealed by the Northern Ireland Constitution Act 1973, s 41(1), Sch 6, Part I.

18. Short title, citation, interpretation, commencement, repeal and saving

(1) This Act may be cited as the Supply of Goods (Implied Terms) Act 1973.

(2) ...

(3) This Act shall come into operation at the expiration of a period of one month beginning with the date on which it is passed.

(4) ...

(5) This Act does not apply to contracts of sale or hire-purchase agreements made before its commencement. [35]

NOTES
Commencement: 18 May 1973.
Sub-s (2): repealed by the Sale of Goods Act 1979, s 63(2), Sch 3.
Sub-s (4): repeals ss 17-20, 29(3)(c) of the Hire-Purchase Act 1965, the Hire-Purchase (Scotland) Act 1965 and the Hire-Purchase Act (Northern Ireland) 1966.

TORTS (INTERFERENCE WITH GOODS) ACT 1977
(c 32)

ARRANGEMENT OF SECTIONS

PRELIMINARY

Section		Para
1	Definition of "wrongful interference with goods"	[36]

DETENTION OF GOODS

2	Abolition of detinue	[37]
3	Form of judgment where goods are detained	[38]
4	Interlocutory relief where goods are detained	[39]

DAMAGES

5	Extinction of title on satisfaction of claim for damages	[40]
6	Allowance for improvement of the goods	[41]

Section		Para
	LIABILITY TO TWO OR MORE CLAIMANTS	
7	Double liability	[42]
8	Competing rights to the goods	[43]
9	Concurrent actions	[44]
	CONVERSION AND TRESPASS TO GOODS	
10	Co-owners	[45]
11	Minor amendments	[46]
	UNCOLLECTED GOODS	
12	Bailee's power of sale	[47]
13	Sale authorised by the court	[48]
	SUPPLEMENTAL	
14	Interpretation	[49]
15	Repeal	[50]
16	Extent and application to the Crown	[51]
17	Short title, etc	[52]

SCHEDULES

Schedule 1—Uncollected Goods
    Part I—Power to Impose Obligation to Collect Goods .. .. [53]
    Part II—Notice of Intention to Sell Goods .. .. [54]
Schedule 2—Transitional .. .. [55]

An Act to amend the law concerning conversion and other torts affecting goods
[22 July 1977]

PRELIMINARY

1. Definition of "wrongful interference with goods"

In this Act "wrongful interference", or "wrongful interference with goods", means—

    (*a*) conversion of goods (also called trover),
    (*b*) trespass to goods,
    (*c*) negligence so far as it results in damage to goods or to an interest in goods,
    (*d*) subject to section 2, any other tort so far as it results in damage to goods or to an interest in goods.

[and references in this Act (however worded) to proceedings for wrongful interference or to a claim or right to claim for wrongful intereference shall include references to proceedings by virtue of Part I of the Consumer Protection Act 1987 (product liability) in respect of any damage to goods or to an interest in goods or, as the case may be, to a claim or right to claim by virtue of that Part in respect of any such damage.] [36]

NOTES
    Commencement: 1 June 1978 (England & Wales); 1 January 1981 (Northern Ireland).
    Commencement orders: SI 1978 No 627, 1980 No 2024.
    Words in square brackets added by the Consumer Protection Act 1987, s 48, Sch 4, para 5.

DETENTION OF GOODS

2. Abolition of detinue

(1) Detinue is abolished.

(2) An action lies in conversion for loss or destruction of goods which a bailee has allowed to happen in breach of his duty to his bailor (that is to say it lies in a case which is not otherwise conversion, but would have been detinue before detinue was abolished). [37]

NOTES
Commencement: 1 June 1978 (England & Wales); 1 January 1981 (Northern Ireland).
Commencement order: SI 1978 No 627, 1980 No 2024.

3. Form of judgment where goods are detained

(1) In proceedings for wrongful interference against a person who is in possession or in control of the goods relief may be given in accordance with this section, so far as appropriate.

   (2) The relief is—
- (a) an order for delivery of the goods, and for payment of any consequential damages, or
- (b) an order for delivery of the goods, but giving the defendant the alternative of paying damages by reference to the value of the goods, together in either alternative with payment of any consequential damages, or
- (c) damages.

   (3) Subject to rules of court—
- (a) relief shall be given under only one of pargraphs (a), (b) and (c) of subsection (2),
- (b) relief under paragraph (a) of subjection (2) is at the discretion of the court, and the claimant may choose between the others.

(4) If it is shown to the satisfaction of the court that an order under subsection (2) (a) has not been complied with, the court may—
- (a) revoke the order, or the relevant part of it, and
- (b) make an order for payment of damages by reference to the value of the goods.

(5) Where an order is made under subsection (2) (b) the defendant may satisfy the order by returning the goods at any time before execution of judgment, but without prejudice to liability to pay any consequential damages.

(6) An order for delivery of the goods under subsection (2) (a) or (b) may impose such conditions as may be determined by the court, or pursuant to rules of court, and in particular, where damages by reference to the value of the goods would not be the whole of the value of the goods, may require an allowance to be made by the claimant to reflect the difference.

For example, a bailor's action against the bailee may be one in which the measure of damages is not the full value of the goods, and then the court may order delivery of the goods, but require the bailor to pay the bailee a sum reflecting the difference.

(7) Where under subsection (1) or subsection (2) of section 6 an allowance

is to be made in respect of an improvement of the goods, and an order is made under subsection (2) (*a*) or (*b*), the court may assess the allowance to be made in respect of the improvement, and by the order require, as a condition for delivery of the goods, that allowance to be made by the claimant.

(8) This section is without prejudice—
- (*a*) to the remedies afforded by section 133 of the Consumer Credit Act 1974, or
- (*b*) to the remedies afforded by sections 35, 42 and 44 of the Hire-Purchase Act 1965, or to those sections of the Hire-Purchase Act (Northern Ireland) 1966 (so long as those sections respectively remain in force), or
- (*c*) to any jurisdiction to afford ancillary or incidental relief. [38]

NOTES
Commencement: 1 June 1978 (England & Wales); 1 January 1981 (Northern Ireland).
Commencement orders: SI 1978 No 627, 1980 No 2024.

4. Interlocutory relief where goods are detained

(1) In this section "proceedings" means proceedings for wrongful interference.

(2) On the application of any person in accordance with rules of court, the High Court shall, in such circumstances as may be specified in the rules, have power to make an order providing for the delivery up of any goods which are or may become the subject matter of subsequent proceedings in the court, or as to which any question may arise in proceedings.

(3) Delivery shall be, as the order may provide, to the claimant or to a person appointed by the court for the purpose, and shall be on such terms and conditions as may be specified in the order.

(4) The power to make rules of court under section [84 of the Supreme Court Act 1981] or under section 7 of the Northern Ireland Act 1962 shall include power to make rules of court as to the manner in which an application for such an order can be made, and as to the circumstances in which such an order can be made; and any such rules may include such incidental, supplementary and consequential provisions as the authority making the rules may consider necessary or expedient.

(5) The preceding provisions of this section shall have effect in relation to county courts as they have effect in relation to the High Court, and as if in those provisions references to rules of court and to section [84] of the said Act of [1981] or section 7 of the Northern Ireland Act 1962 included references to county court rules and to [section 75 of the County Courts Act 1984] or [Article 47 of the County Courts (Northern Ireland) Order 1980]. [39]

NOTES
Commencement: 1 June 1978 (England & Wales); 1 January 1981 (Northern Ireland).
Commencement orders: SI 1978 No 627, 1980 No 2024.
Sub-s (4): amended by the Supreme Court Act 1981, s 152 (1), Sch 5.
Sub-s (5): first and second amendments made by the Supreme Court Act 1981, s 152 (1), Sch 5; third amendment made by the County Courts Act 1984, s 148(1), Sch 2, para 64; final amendment made by the County Courts (Northern Ireland) Order 1980, SI 1980 No 397, art 68 (2), Sch 1, Part II.

DAMAGES

5. Extinction of title on satisfaction of claim for damages

(1) Where damages for wrongful interference are, or would fall to be, assessed on the footing that the claimant is being compensated—
- (a) for the whole of his interest in the goods, or
- (b) for the whole of his interest in the goods subject to a reduction for contributory negligence,

payment of the assessed damages (under all heads), or as the case may be settlement of a claim for damages for the wrong (under all heads), extinguishes the claimant's title to that interest.

(2) In subsection (1) the reference to the settlement of the claim includes—
- (a) where the claim is made in court proceedings, and the defendant has paid a sum into court to meet the whole claim, the taking of that sum by the claimant, and
- (b) where the claim is made in court proceedings, and the proceedings are settled or compromised, the payment of what is due in accordance with the settlement or compromise, and
- (c) where the claim is made out of court and is settled or compromised, the payment of what is due in accordance with the settlement or compromise.

(3) It is hereby declared that subsection (1) does not apply where damages are assessed on the footing that the claimant is being compensated for the whole of his interest in the goods, but the damages paid are limited to some lesser amount by virtue of any enactment or rule of law.

(4) Where under section 7 (3) the claimant accounts over to another person (the "third party") so as to compensate (under all heads) the third party for the whole of his interest in the goods, the third party's title to that interest is extinguished.

(5) This section has effect subject to any agreement varying the respective rights of the parties to the agreement, and where the claim is made in court proceedings has effect subject to any order of the court. **[40]**

NOTES
Commencement: 1 June 1978 (England & Wales); 1 January 1981 (Northern Ireland).
Commencement orders: SI 1978 No 627, 1980 No 2024.

6. Allowance for improvement of the goods

(1) If in proceedings for wrongful interference against a person (the "improver") who has improved the goods, it is shown that the improver acted in the mistaken but honest belief that he had a good title to them, an allowance shall be made for the extent to which, at the time as at which the goods fall to be valued in assessing damages, the value of the goods is attributable to the improvement.

(2) If, in proceedings for wrongful interference against a person ("the purchaser") who has purported to purchase the goods—
- (a) from the improver, or
- (b) where after such a purported sale the goods passed by a further purported sale on one or more occasions, on any such occasion,

it is shown that the purchaser acted in good faith, an allowance shall be made on the principle set out in subsection (1).

For example, where a person in good faith buys a stolen car from the improver and is sued in conversion by the true owner the damages may be reduced to reflect the improvement, but if the person who bought the stolen car from the improver sues the improver for failure of consideration, and the improver acted in good faith, subsection (3) below will ordinarily make a comparable reduction in the damages he recovers from the improver.

(3) If in a case within subsection (2) the person purporting to sell the goods acted in good faith, then in proceedings by the purchaser for recovery of the purchase price because of failure of consideration, or in any other proceedings founded on that failure of consideration, an allowance shall, where appropriate, be made on the principle set out in subsection (1).

(4) This section applies, with the necessary modifications, to a purported bailment or other disposition of goods as it applies to a purported sale of goods.

[41]

NOTES
Commencement: 1 June 1978 (England & Wales); 1 January 1981 (Northern Ireland).
Commencement order: SI 1978 No 627, 1980 No 2024.

LIABILITY TO TWO OR MORE CLAIMANTS

7. Double liability

(1) In this section "double liability" means the double liability of the wrongdoer which can arise—
  (a) where one of two or more rights of action for wrongful interference is founded on a possessory title, or
  (b) where the measure of damages in an action for wrongful interference founded on a proprietary title is or includes the entire value of the goods, although the interest is one of two or more interests in the goods.

(2) In proceedings to which any two or more claimants are parties, the relief shall be such as to avoid double liability of the wrongdoer as between those claimants.

(3) On satisfaction, in whole or in part, of any claim for an amount exceeding that recoverable if subsection (2) applied, the claimant is liable to account over to the other person having a right to claim to such extent as will avoid double liability.

(4) Where, as the result of enforcement of a double liability, any claimant is unjustly enriched to any extent, he shall be liable to reimburse the wrongdoer to that extent.

For example, if a converter of goods pays damages first to a finder of the goods, and then to the true owner, the finder is unjustly enriched unless he accounts over to the true owner under subsection (3); and then the true owner is unjustly enriched and becomes liable to reimburse the converter of the goods.

[42]

NOTES
Commencement: 1 June 1978 (England & Wales); 1 January 1981 (Northern Ireland).

Commencement orders: SI 1978 No 627, 1980 No 2024.

8. Competing rights to the goods

(1) The defendant in an action for wrongful interference shall be entitled to show, in accordance with rules of court, that a third party has a better right than the plaintiff as respects all or any part of the interest claimed by the plaintiff, or in right of which he sues, and any rule of law (sometimes called jus tertii) to the contrary is abolished.

(2) Rules of court relating to proceedings for wrongful interference may—
   (a) require the plaintiff to give particulars of his title,
   (b) require the plaintiff to identify any person who, to his knowledge, has or claims any interest in the goods,
   (c) authorise the defendant to apply for directions as to whether any person should be joined with a view to establishing whether he has a better right than the plaintiff, or has a claim as a result of which the defendant might be doubly liable,
   (d) where a party fails to appear on an application within paragraph (c), or to comply with any direction given by the court on such an application, authorise the court to deprive him of any right of action against the defendant for the wrong either unconditionally, or subject to such terms or conditions as may be specified.

(3) Subsection (2) is without prejudice to any other power of making rules of court.

NOTES
Commencement: 1 June 1978 (England & Wales); 1 January 1981 (Northern Ireland).
Commencement orders: SI 1978 No 627, 1980 No 2024.

9. Concurrent actions

(1) This section applies where goods are the subject of two or more claims for wrongful interference (whether or not the claims are founded on the same wrongful act, and whether or not any of the claims relates also to other goods).

(2) Where goods are the subject of two or more claims under section 6 this section shall apply as if any claim under section 6 (3) were a claim for wrongful interference.

(3) If proceedings have been brought in a county court on one of those claims, county court rules may waive, or allow a court to waive, any limit (financial or territorial) on the jurisdiction of county courts in [the County Courts Act 1984] or the County Courts [(Northern Ireland) Order 1980] so as to allow another of those claims to be brought in the same county court.

(4) If proceedings are brought on one of the claims in the High Court, and proceedings on any other are brought in a county court, whether prior to the High Court proceedings or not, the High Court may, on the application of the defendant, after notice has been given to the claimant in the county court proceedings—
   (a) order that the county court proceedings be transferred to the High Court, and
   (b) order security for costs or impose such other terms as the court thinks fit.

NOTES
Commencement: 1 June 1978 (England & Wales); 1 January 1981 (Northern Ireland).
Commencement orders: SI 1978 No 627, 1980 No 2024.
Sub-s (3): first amendment made by the County Courts Act 1984, s 148(1), Sch 2, para 65; second amendment made by the County Courts (Northern Ireland) Order 1980, SI 1980 No 397, art 68 (2), Sch 1, Part II.

CONVERSION AND TRESPASS TO GOODS

10. Co-owners

(1) Co-ownership is no defence to an action founded on conversion or trespass to goods where the defendant without the authority of the other co-owner—

(a) destroys the goods, or disposes of the goods in a way giving a good title to the entire property in the goods, or otherwise does anything equivalent to the destruction of the other's interest in the goods, or

(b) purports to dispose of the goods in a way which would give a good title to the entire property in the goods if he was acting with the authority of all co-owners of the goods.

(2) Subsection (1) shall not affect the law concerning execution or enforcement of judgments, or concerning any form of distress.

(3) Subsection (1) (a) is by way of restatement of existing law so far as it relates to conversion.

NOTES
Commencement: 1 June 1978 (England & Wales); 1 January 1981 (Northern Ireland).
Commencement orders: SI 1978 No 627, 1980 No 2024.

11. Minor amendments

(1) Contributory negligence is no good defence in proceedings founded on conversion, or on intentional trespass to goods.

(2) Receipt of goods by way of pledge is conversion if the delivery of the goods is conversion.

(3) Denial of title is not of itself conversion.

NOTES
Commencement: 1 June 1978 (England & Wales); 1 January 1981 (Northern Ireland).
Commencement orders: SI 1978 No 627, 1980 No 2024.
Sub-s (1): excluded by Banking Act 1979, s 47.

UNCOLLECTED GOODS

12. Bailee's power of sale

(1) This section applies to goods in the possession or under the control of a bailee where—

(a) the bailor is in breach of an obligation to take delivery of the goods or, if the terms of the bailment so provide, to give directions as to their delivery, or

(b) the bailee could impose such an obligation by giving notice to the bailor, but is unable to trace or communicate with the bailor, or

(c) the bailee can reasonably expect to be relieved of any duty to safeguard the goods on giving notice to the bailor, but is unable to trace or communicate with the bailor.

(2) In the cases in Part I of Schedule 1 to this Act a bailee may, for the purposes of subsection (1), impose an obligation on the bailor to take delivery of the goods, or as the case may be to give directions as to their delivery, and in those cases the said Part I sets out the methods of notification.

(3) If the bailee—
 (a) has in accordance with Part II of Schedule 1 to this Act given notice to the bailor of his intention to sell the goods under this subsection, or
 (b) has failed to trace or communicate with the bailor with a view to giving him such a notice, after having taken reasonable steps for the purpose,

and is reasonably satisfied that the bailor owns the goods, he shall be entitled, as against the bailor, to sell the goods.

(4) Where subsection (3) applies but the bailor did not in fact own the goods, a sale under this section, or under section 13, shall not give a good title as against the owner, or as against a person claiming under the owner.

(5) A bailee exercising his powers under subsection (3) shall be liable to account to the bailor for the proceeds of sale, less any costs of sale, and—
 (a) the account shall be taken on the footing that the bailee should have adopted the best method of sale reasonably available in the circumstances, and
 (b) where subsection (3) (a) applies, any sum payable in respect of the goods by the bailor to the bailee which accrued due before the bailee gave notice of intention to sell the goods shall be deductible from the proceeds of sale.

(6) A sale duly made under this section gives a good title to the purchaser as against the bailor.

(7) In this section, section 13, and Schedule 1 to this Act,
 (a) "bailor" and "bailee" include their respective successors in title, and
 (b) references to what is payable, paid or due to the bailee in respect of the goods include references to what would be payable by the bailor to the bailee as a condition of delivery of the goods at the relevant time.

(8) This section, and Schedule 1 to this Act, have effect subject to the terms of the bailment.

(9) This section shall not apply where the goods were bailed before the commencement of this Act. [47]

NOTES
Commencement: 1 January 1978.
Commencement order: SI 1977 No 1910.

13. Sale authorised by the court

(1) If a bailee of the goods to which section 12 applies satisfies the court that he is entitled to sell the goods under section 12, or that he would be so entitled if he had given any notice required in accordance with Schedule 1 to this Act, the court—

(a) may authorise the sale of the goods subject to such terms and conditions, if any, as may be specified in the order, and

(b) may authorise the bailee to deduct from the proceeds of sale any costs of sale and any amount due from the bailor to the bailee in respect of the goods, and

(c) may direct the payment into court of the net proceeds of sale, less any amount deducted under paragraph (b), to be held to the credit of the bailor.

(2) A decision of the court authorising a sale under this section shall, subject to any right of appeal, be conclusive, as against the bailor, of the bailee's entitlement to sell the goods, and gives a good title to the purchaser as against the bailor.

(3) In this section "the court" means the High Court or a county court, and a county court shall have jurisdiction in the proceedings if the value of the goods does not exceed the county court limit. [48]

NOTES
Commencement: 1 January 1978.
Commencement order: SI 1977 No 1910.

SUPPLEMENTAL

14. Interpretation

(1) In this Act, unless the context otherwise requires—

"county court limit" means the [amount which for the time being is the county court limit for the purposes of section 15 of the County Courts Act 1984], or in Northern Ireland the current amount mentioned in [Article 10(1) of the County Courts (Northern Ireland) Order 1980],

"enactment" includes an enactment contained in an Act of the Parliament of Northern Ireland or an Order in Council made under the Northern Ireland (Temporary Provisions) Act 1972, or in a Measure of the Northern Ireland Assembly,

"goods" includes all chattels personal other than things in action and money,

"High Court" includes the High Court of Justice in Northern Ireland.

(2) References in this Act to any enactment include references to that enactment as amended, extended or applied by or under that or any other enactment. [49]

NOTES
Commencement: 1 January 1978.
Commencement order: SI 1977 No 1910.
Sub-s (1): first amendment made by the County Courts Act 1984, s 148(1), Sch 2, para 66; second amendment made by the County Courts (Northern Ireland) Order 1980, art 68 (2), Sch 1, Part II.

15. Repeal

(1) The Disposal of Uncollected Goods Act 1952 is hereby repealed.

(2) In England and Wales that repeal shall not affect goods bailed before the commencement of this Act.

(3) ... [50]

NOTES
Commencement: 1 January 1978.
Commencement order: SI 1977 No 1910.
Sub-s (3): applies to Scotland only.

16. Extent and application to the Crown

(1) ...

(2) This Act, except section 15, extends to Northern Ireland.

(3) This Act shall bind the Crown, but as regards the Crown's liability in tort shall not bind the Crown further than the Crown is made liable in tort by the Crown Proceedings Act 1947. [51]

NOTES
Commencement: 1 January 1978.
Commencement order: SI 1977 No 1910
Sub-s (1): applies to Scotland only.

17. Short title, etc

(1) This Act may be cited as the Torts (Interference with Goods) Act 1977.

(2) This Act shall come into force on such day as the Lord Chancellor may by order contained in a statutory instrument appoint, and such an order may appoint different dates for different provisions or for different purposes.

(3) Schedule 2 to this Act contains transitional provisions. [52]

NOTES
Commencement: 1 January 1978 (sub-ss (1),(2)); 1 June 1978 (sub-s (3),—(England & Wales); 1 January 1978 (Northern Ireland).
Commencement orders: SI 1977 No 1910, 1978 No 627, 1980 No 2024.

SCHEDULES

SCHEDULE 1

Section 12

UNCOLLECTED GOODS

PART I

Power to Impose Obligation to Collect Goods

1.—(1) For the purposes of section 12 (1) a bailee may, in the circumstances specified in this Part of this Schedule, by notice given to the bailor impose on him an obligation to take delivery of the goods.

(2) The notice shall be in writing, and may be given either—
  (a) by delivering it to the bailor, or
  (b) by leaving it at his proper address, or
  (c) by post.

(3) The notice shall—
  (a) specify the name and address of the bailee, and give sufficient particulars of the goods and the address or place where they are held, and
  (b) state that the goods are ready for delivery to the bailor, or where combined with a notice terminating the contract of bailment, will be ready for delivery when the contract is terminated, and
  (c) specify the amount, if any, which is payable by the bailor to the bailee in respect of the goods and which became due before the giving of the notice.

(4) Where the notice is sent by post it may be combined with a notice under Part II of this Schedule if the notice is sent by post in a way complying with paragraph 6 (4).

(5) References in this Part of this Schedule to taking delivery of the goods include, where the terms of the bailment admit, references to giving directions as to their delivery.

(6) This Part of this Schedule is without prejudice to the provisions of any contract requiring the bailor to take delivery of the goods.

Goods accepted for repair or other treatment

2. If a bailee has accepted goods for repair or other treatment on the terms (expressed or implied) that they will be re-delivered to the bailor when the repair or other treatment has been carried out, the notice may be given at any time after the repair or other treatment has been carried out.

Goods accepted for valuation or appraisal

3. If a bailee has accepted goods in order to value or appraise them, the notice may be given at any time after the bailee has carried out the valuation or appraisal.

Storage, warehousing, etc.

4.—(1) If a bailee is in possession of goods which he has held as custodian, and his obligation as custodian has come to an end, the notice may be given at any time after the ending of the obligation, or may be combined with any notice terminating his obligation as custodian.

(2) This paragraph shall not apply to goods held by a person as mercantile agent, that is to say by a person having in the customary course of his business as a mercantile agent authority either to sell goods or to consign goods for the purpose of sale, or to buy goods, or to raise money on the security of goods.

Supplemental

5. Paragraphs 2, 3 and 4 apply whether or not the bailor has paid any amount due to the bailee in respect of the goods, and whether or not the bailment is for reward, or in the course of business, or gratuitous.

NOTES
Commencement: 1 January 1978.
Commencment order: SI 1977 No 1910.

PART II

Notice of Intention to Sell Goods

6.—(1) A notice under section 12 (3) shall
   (a) specify the name and address of the bailee, and give sufficient particulars of the goods and the address or place where they are held, and
   (b) specify the date on or after which the bailee proposes to sell the goods, and
   (c) specify the amount, if any, which is payable by the bailor to the bailee in respect of the goods, and which became due before the giving of the notice.

(2) The period between giving of the notice and the date specified in the notice as that on or after which the bailee proposes to exercise the power of sale shall be such as will afford the bailor a reasonable opportunity of taking delivery of the goods.

(3) If any amount is payable in respect of the goods by the bailor to the bailee, and became due before giving of the notice, the said period shall be not less than three months.

(4) The notice shall be in writing and shall be sent by post in a registered letter, or by the recorded delivery service.

7.—(1) The bailee shall not give a notice under section 12 (3), or exercise his right to sell the goods pursuant to such a notice, at a time when he has notice that, because of a dispute concerning the goods, the bailor is questioning or refusing to pay all or any part of what the bailee claims to be due to him in respect of the goods.

(2) This paragraph shall be left out of account in determing under section 13 (1) whether a bailee of goods is entitled to sell the goods under section 12, or would be so entitled if he had given any notice required in accordance with this Schedule.

Supplemental

8. For the purposes of this Schedule, and of section 26 of the Interpretation Act 1889 in its application to this Schedule, the proper address of the person to whom a notice is to be given shall be—
   (a) in the case of a body corporate, a registered or principal office of the body corporate, and
   (b) in any other case, the last known address of the person. [54]

NOTES
Commencement: 1 January 1978.
Commencement order: SI 1977 No 1910.

Section 17

SCHEDULE 2
Transitional

1. This Act shall not affect any action or arbitration brought before the commencement of this Act or any proceedings brought to enforce a decision in the action or arbitration.

2. Subject to paragraph 1, this Act applies to acts or omissions before it comes into force as well as to later ones, and for the purposes of the Limitation Act 1939, the Statute of Limitations (Northern Ireland) 1958, or any other limitation enactment, the cause of action shall be treated as having accrued at the time of the act or omission even if proceedings could not have been brought before the commencement of this Act.

3. For the purposes of this Schedule, any claim by way of set-off or counterclaim shall be deemed to be a separate action, and to have been brought on the same date as the action in which the set-off or counterclaim is pleaded. [55]

NOTES
Commencement: 1 June 1978 (England & Wales); 1 January 1981 (Northern Ireland).
Commencement orders: SI 1978 No 627, 1980 No 2024.

UNFAIR CONTRACT TERMS ACT 1977
(c 50)

ARRANGEMENT OF SECTIONS

Part I
Amendment of Law for England and Wales and Northern Ireland

Introductory

Section		Para
1	Scope of Part I	[56]

Avoidance of liability for negligence, breach of contract, etc.

2	Negligence liability	[57]
3	Liability arising in contract	[58]
4	Unreasonable indemnity clauses	[59]

Section		Para
	Liability arising from sale or supply of goods	
5	"Guarantee" of consumer goods	[60]
6	Sale and hire-purchase	[61]
7	Miscellaneous contracts under which goods pass	[62]
	Other provisions about contracts	
9	Effect of breach	[63]
10	Evasion by means of secondary contract	[64]
	Explanatory provisions	
11	The "reasonableness" test	[65]
12	"Dealing as consumer"	[66]
13	Varieties of exemption clause	[67]
14	Interpretation of Part I	[68]

PART III
PROVISIONS APPLYING TO WHOLE OF UNITED KINGDOM

Miscellaneous

26	International supply contracts	[69]
27	Choice of law clauses	[70]
28	Temporary provision for sea carriage of passengers	[71]
29	Saving for other relevant legislation	[72]

General

31	Commencement; amendments; repeals	[73]
32	Citation and extent	[74]

SCHEDULES

Schedule 1—Scope of sections 2 to 4 and 7	[75]
Schedule 2—"Guidelines" for Application of Reasonableness Test	[76]

An Act to impose further limits on the extent to which under the law of England and Wales and Northern Ireland civil liability for breach of contract, or for negligence or other breach of duty, can be avoided by means of contract terms and otherwise, and under the law of Scotland civil liability can be avoided by means of contract terms [26 October 1977]

GENERAL NOTE
This Act is printed in full with the following exceptions: s 18 (which amends the Misrepresentation Act 1967, s 3 and is incorporated in the text of that Act); Part II (ss 15–25) (which applies to Scotland only); s 30 (repealed) and Schs 3–4 (amendments and repeals).

PART I
AMENDMENT OF LAW FOR ENGLAND AND WALES AND NORTHERN IRELAND

Introductory

1. Scope of Part I

(1) For the purposes of this Part of this Act, "negligence" means the breach—

(a) of any obligation, arising from the express or implied terms of a contract, to take reasonable care or exercise reasonable skill in the performance of the contract;

(b) of any common law duty to take reasonable care or exercise reasonable skill (but not any stricter duty);

(c) of the common duty of care imposed by the Occupiers' Liability Act 1957 or the Occupiers' Liability Act (Northern Ireland) 1957.

(2) This Part of this Act is subject to Part III; and in relation to contracts, the operation of sections 2 to 4 and 7 is subject to the exceptions made by Schedule 1.

(3) In the case of both contract and tort, sections 2 to 7 apply (except where the contrary is stated in section 6 (4)) only to business liability, that is liability for breach of obligations or duties arising—
- (a) from things done or to be done by a person in the course of a business (whether his own business or another's); or
- (b) from the occupation of premises used for business purposes of the occupier;

and references to liability are to be read accordingly [but liability of an occupier of premises for breach of an obligation or duty towards a person obtaining access to the premises for recreational or educational purposes, being liability for loss or damage suffered by reason of the dangerous state of the premises, is not a business liability of the occupier unless granting that person such access for the purposes concerned falls within the business purposes of the occupier.]

(4) In relation to any breach of duty or obligation, it is immaterial for any purpose of this Part of this Act whether the breach was inadvertent or intentional, or whether liability for it arises directly or vicariously. [56]

NOTES
Commencement: 1 February 1978.
Sub-s (3): amended by the Occupiers' Liability Act 1984, s 2.

Avoidance of liability for negligence, breach of contract, etc

2. Negligence liability

(1) A person cannot by reference to any contract term or to a notice given to persons generally or to particular persons exclude or restrict his liability for death or personal injury resulting from negligence.

(2) In the case of other loss or damage, a person cannot so exclude or restrict his liability for negligence except in so far as the term or notice satisfies the requirement of reasonableness.

(3) Where a contract term or notice purports to exclude or restrict liability for negligence a person's agreement to or awareness of it is not of itself to be taken as indicating his voluntary acceptance of any risk. [57]

NOTES
Commencement: 1 February 1978.

3. Liability arising in contract

(1) This section applies as between contracting parties where one of them deals as consumer or on the other's written standard terms of business.

(2) As against that party, the other cannot by reference to any contract term—
- (a) when himself in breach of contract, exclude or restrict any liability of his in respect of the breach; or
- (b) claim to be entitled—

(i) to render a contractual performance substantially different from that which was reasonably expected of him, or
(ii) in respect of the whole or any part of his contractual obligation, to render no performance at all,

expect in so far as (in any of the cases mentioned above in this subsection) the contract term satisfies the requirement of reasonableness. **[58]**

NOTES
Commencement: 1 February 1978.

4. Unreasonable indemnity clauses

(1) A person dealing as consumer cannot by reference to any contract term be made to indemnify another person (whether a party to the contract or not) in respect of liability that may be incurred by the other for negligence or breach of contract, except in so far as the contract term satisfies the requirement of reasonableness.

(2) This section applies whether the liability in question—
   (a) is directly that of the person to be indemnified or is incurred by him vicariously;
   (b) is to the person dealing as consumer or to someone else. **[59]**

NOTES
Commencement: 1 February 1978.

Liability arising from sale or supply of goods

5. "Guarantee" of consumer goods

(1) In the case of goods of a type ordinarily supplied for private use or consumption, where loss or damage—
   (a) arises from the goods proving defective while in consumer use; and
   (b) results from the negligence of a person concerned in the manufacture or distribution of the goods,

liability for the loss or damage cannot be excluded or restricted by reference to any contract term or notice contained in or operating by reference to a guarantee of the goods.

(2) For these purposes—
   (a) goods are to be regarded as "in consumer use" when a person is using them, or has them in his possession for use, otherwise than exclusively for the purposes of a business; and
   (b) anything in writing is a guarantee if it contains or purports to contain some promise or assurance (however worded or presented) that defects will be made good by complete or partial replacement, or by repair, monetary compensation or otherwise.

(3) This section does not apply as between the parties to a contract under or in pursuance of which possession or ownership of the goods passed. **[60]**

NOTES
Commencement: 1 February 1978.

6. Sale and hire-purchase

(1) Liability for breach of the obligations arising from—

(a) [section 12 of the Sale of Goods Act 1979] (seller's implied undertakings as to title, etc);
(b) section 8 of the Supply of Goods (Implied Terms) Act 1973 (the corresponding thing in relation to hire-purchase)

cannot be excluded or restricted by reference to any contract term.

(2) As against a person dealing as consumer, liability for breach of the obligations arising from—
(a) [section 13, 14 or 15 of the 1979 Act] (seller's implied undertakings as to conformity of goods with description or sample, or as to their quality or fitness for a particular purpose);
(b) section 9, 10 or 11 of the 1973 Act (the corresponding things in relation to hire-purchase),

cannot be excluded or restricted by reference to any contract term.

(3) As against a person dealing otherwise than as consumer, the liability specified in subsection (2) above can be excluded or restricted by reference to a contract term, but only in so far as the term satisfies the requirement of reasonableness.

(4) The liabilities referred to in this section are not only the business liabilities defined by section 1 (3), but include those arising under any contract of sale of goods or hire-purchase agreement. [61]

NOTES
Commencement: 1 February 1978.
Sub-ss (1), (2): amended by the Sale of Goods Act 1979, s 63, Sch 2, para 19.

7. Miscellaneous contracts under which goods pass

(1) Where the possession or ownership of goods passes under or in pursuance of a contract not governed by the law of sale of goods or hire-purchase, subsections (2) to (4) below apply as regards the effect (if any) to be given to contract terms excluding or restricting liability for breach of obligation arising by implication of law from the nature of the contract.

(2) As against a person dealing as consumer, liability in respect of the goods' correspondence with description or sample, or their quality or fitness for any particular purpose, cannot be excluded or restricted by reference to any such term.

(3) As against a person dealing otherwise than as consumer, that liability can be excluded or restricted by reference to such a term, but only in so far as the term satisfies the requirement of reasonableness.

[(3A) Liability for breach of the obligations arising under section 2 of the Supply of Goods and Services Act 1982 (implied terms about title etc in certain contracts for the transfer of the property in goods) cannot be excluded or restricted by references to any such term.]

(4) Liability in respect of—
(a) the right to transfer ownership of the goods, or give possession; or
(b) the assurance of quiet possession to a person taking goods in pursuance of the contract,

cannot [(in a case to which subsection (3A) above does not apply)] be excluded or restricted by reference to any such term except in so far as the term satisfies the requirement of reasonableness.

(5) This section does not apply in the case of goods passing on a redemption of trading stamps within the Trading Stamps Act 1964 or the Trading Stamps Act (Northern Ireland) 1965. **[62]**

NOTES
Commencement: 4 January 1983 (sub-s (3A)); 1 February 1978 (remainder).
Sub-ss (3A), (4): amended by the Supply of Goods and Services Act 1982, s 17(2), (3).

Other provisions about contracts

9. Effect of breach

(1) Where for reliance upon it a contract term has to satisfy the requirement of reasonableness, it may be found to do so and be given effect accordingly notwithstanding that the contract has been terminated either by breach or by a party electing to treat it as repudiated.

(2) Where on a breach the contract is nevertheless affirmed by a party entitled to treat it as repudiated, this does not of itself exclude the requirement of reasonableness in relation to any contract term. **[63]**

NOTES
Commencement: 1 February 1978.

10. Evasion by means of secondary contract

A person is not bound by any contract term prejudicing or taking away rights of his which arise under, or in connection with the performance of, another contract, so far as those rights extend to the enforcement of another's liability which this Part of this Act prevents that other from excluding or restricting.
[64]

NOTES
Commencement: 1 February 1978.

Explanatory provisions

11. The "reasonableness" test

(1) In relation to a contract term, the requirement of reasonableness for the purposes of this Part of this Act, section 3 of the Misrepresentation Act 1967 and section 3 of the Misrepresentation Act (Northern Ireland) 1967 is that the term shall have been a fair and reasonable one to be included having regard to the circumstances which were, or ought reasonably to have been, known to or in the contemplation of the parties when the contract was made.

(2) In determining for the purposes of section 6 or 7 above whether a contract term satisfies the requirement of reasonableness, regard shall be had in particular to the matters specified in Schedule 2 to this Act; but this subsection does not prevent the court or arbitrator from holding, in accordance with any rule of law, that a term which purports to exclude or restrict any relevant liability is not a term of the contract.

(3) In relation to a notice (not being a notice having contractual effect), the requirement of reasonableness under this Act is that it should be fair and reasonable to allow reliance on it, having regard to all the circumstances obtaining when the liability arose or (but for the notice) would have arisen.

(4) Where by reference to a contract term or notice a person seeks to restrict

liability to a specified sum of money, and the question arises (under this or any other Act) whether the term or notice satisfies the requirement of reasonableness, regard shall be had in particular (but without prejudice to subsection (2) above in the case of contract terms) to—

    (*a*) the resources which he could expect to be available to him for the purpose of meeting the liability should it arise; and

    (*b*) how far it was open to him to cover himself by insurance.

(5) It is for those claiming that a contract term or notice satisfies the requirement of reasonableness to show that it does. [65]

NOTES

Commencement: 1 February 1978.

12. "Dealing as consumer"

(1) A party to a contract "deals as consumer" in relation to another party if—

    (*a*) he neither makes the contract in the course of a business nor holds himself out as doing so; and

    (*b*) the other party does make the contract in the course of a business; and

    (*c*) in the case of a contract governed by the law of sale of goods or hire-purchase, or by section 7 of this Act, the goods passing under or in pursuance of the contract are of a type ordinarily supplied for private use or consumption.

(2) But on a sale by auction or by competitive tender the buyer is not in any circumstances to be regarded as dealing as consumer.

(3) Subject to this, it is for those claiming that a party does not deal as consumer to show that he does not. [66]

NOTES

Commencement: 1 February 1978.

13. Varieties of exemption clause

(1) To the extent that this Part of this Act prevents the exclusion or restriction of any liability it also prevents—

    (*a*) making the liability or its enforcement subject to restrictive or onerous conditions;

    (*b*) excluding or restricting any right or remedy in respect of the liability, or subjecting a person to any prejudice in consequence of his pursuing any such right or remedy;

    (*c*) excluding or restricting rules of evidence or procedure;

and (to that extent) sections 2 and 5 to 7 also prevent excluding or restricting liability by reference to terms and notices which exclude or restrict the relevant obligation or duty.

(2) But an agreement in writing to submit present or future differences to arbitration is not to be treated under this Part of this Act as excluding or restricting any liability. [67]

NOTES

Commencement: 1 February 1978.

14. Interpretation of Part I

In this Part of this Act—

"business" includes a profession and the activities of any government department or local or public authority;

"goods" has the same meaning as in [the Sale of Goods Act 1979]:

"hire-purchase agreement" has the same meaning as in the Consumer Credit Act 1974;

"negligence" has the meaning given by section 1 (1);

"notice" includes an announcement, whether or not in writing, and any other communication or pretended communication; and

"personal injury" includes any disease and any impairment of physical or mental condition.

NOTES
Commencement: 1 February 1978.
Amended by the Sale of Goods Act 1979, s 63, Sch 2, para 20.

PART III

PROVISIONS APPLYING TO WHOLE OF UNITED KINGDOM

Miscellaneous

26. International supply contracts

(1) The limits imposed by this Act on the extent to which a person may exclude or restrict liability by reference to a contract term do not apply to liability arising under such a contract as is described in subsection (3) below.

(2) The terms of such a contract are not subject to any requirement of reasonableness under section 3 or 4 . . .

(3) Subject to subsection (4), that description of contract is one whose characteristics are the following—

(a) either it is a contract of sale of goods or it is one under or in pursuance of which the possession or ownership of goods passes; and

(b) it is made by parties whose places of business (or, if they have none, habitual residences) are in the territories of different States (the Channel Islands and the Isle of Man being treated for this purpose as different States from the United Kingdom).

(4) A contract falls within subsection (3) above only if either—

(a) the goods in question are, at the time of the conclusion of the contract, in the course of carriage, or will be carried, from the territory of one State to the territory of another; or

(b) the acts constituting the offer and acceptance have been done in the territories of different States; or

(c) the contract provides for the goods to be delivered to the territory of a State other than that within whose territory those acts were done.

NOTES
Commencement: 1 February 1978.
Sub-s (2): words omitted apply to Scotland only.

27. Choice of law clauses

(1) Where the proper law of a contract is the law of any part of the United Kingdom only by choice of the parties (and apart from that choice would be the

law of some country outside the United Kingdom) sections 2 to 7 and 16 to 21 of this Act do not operate as part of the proper law.

(2) This Act has effect notwithstanding any contract term which applies or purports to apply the law of some country outside the United Kingdom, where (either or both)—
  (a) the term appears to the court, or arbitrator or arbiter to have been imposed wholly or mainly for the purpose of enabling the party imposing it to evade the operation of this Act; or
  (b) in the making of the contract one of the parties dealt as consumer, and he was then habitually resident in the United Kingdom, and the essential steps necessary for the making of the contract were taken there, whether by him or by others on his behalf.

(3) ... [70]

NOTES
Commencement: 1 February 1978.
Sub-s (3): applies to Scotland only.

28. Temporary provision for sea carriage of passengers

(1) This section applies to a contract for carriage by sea of a passenger or of a passenger and his luggage where the provisions of the Athens Convention (with or without modification) do not have, in relation to the contract, the force of law in the United Kingdom.

(2) In a case where—
  (a) the contract is not made in the United Kingdom, and
  (b) neither the place of departure nor the place of destination under it is in the United Kingdom,
a person is not precluded by this Act from excluding or restricting liability for loss or damage, being loss or damage for which the provisions of the Convention would, if they had the force of law in relation to the contract, impose liability on him.

(3) In any other case, a person is not precluded by this Act from excluding or restricting liability for that loss or damage—
  (a) in so far as the exclusion or restriction would have been effective in that case had the provisions of the Convention had the force of law in relation to the contract; or
  (b) in such circumstances and to such extent as may be prescribed, by reference to a prescribed term of the contract.

(4) For the purposes of subsection (3) (a), the values which shall be taken to be the official values in the United Kingdom of the amounts (expressed in gold francs) by reference to which liability under the provisions of the Convention is limited shall be such amounts in sterling as the Secretary of State may from time to time by order made by statutory instrument specify.

(5) In this section,—
  (a) the references to excluding or restricting liability include doing any of those things in relation to the liability which are mentioned in section 13 or section 25 (3) and (5); and
  (b) "the Athens Convention" means the Athens Convention relating to the Carriage of Passengers and their Luggage by Sea, 1974; and

(c) "prescribed" means prescribed by the Secretary of State by regulations made by statutory instrument;

and a statutory instrument containing the regulations shall be subject to annulment in pursuance of a resolution of either House of Parliament. [71]

NOTES
Commencement: 1 February 1978.

29. Saving for other relevant legislation

(1) Nothing in this Act removes or restricts the effect of, or prevents reliance upon, any contractual provision which—

    (a) is authorised or required by the express terms or necessary implication of an enactment; or

    (b) being made with a view to compliance with an international agreement to which the United Kingdom is a party, does not operate more restrictively than is contemplated by the agreement.

(2) A contract term is to be taken—

    (a) for the purposes of Part I of this Act, as satisfying the requirement of reasonableness; and

    (b) ...

if it is incorporated or approved by, or incorporated pursuant to a decision or ruling of, a competent authority acting in the exercise of any statutory jurisdiction or function and is not a term in a contract to which the competent authority is itself a party.

(3) In this section—

    "competent authority" means any court, arbitrator or arbiter, government department or public authority;

    "enactment" means any legislation (including subordinate legislation) of the United Kingdom or Northern Ireland and any instrument having effect by virtue of such legislation; and

    "statutory" means conferred by an enactment. [72]

NOTES
Commencement: 1 February 1978.
Sub-s (2): words omitted apply to Scotland only.

General

31. Commencement; amendments; repeals

(1) This Act comes into force on 1st February 1978.

(2) Nothing in this Act applies to contracts made before the date on which it comes into force; but subject to this, it applies to liability for any loss or damage which is suffered on or after that date.

(3) The enactments specified in Schedule 3 to this Act are amended as there shown.

(4) The enactments specified in Schedule 4 to this Act are repealed to the extent specified in column 3 of that Schedule. [73]

NOTES
Commencement: 1 February 1978.

32. Citation and extent

(1) This Act may be cited as the Unfair Contract Terms Act 1977.

(2) Part I of this Act extends to England and Wales and to Northern Ireland; but it does not extend to Scotland.

(3) . . .

(4) This Part of this Act extends to the whole of the United Kingdom. **[74]**

NOTES
   Commencement: 1 February 1978.
   Sub-s (3): applies to Scotland only.

SCHEDULES
SCHEDULE 1

Section 1 (2)

SCOPE OF SECTIONS 2 TO 4 AND 7

1. Sections 2 to 4 of this Act do not extend to—
   (*a*) any contract of insurance (including a contract to pay an annuity on human life);
   (*b*) any contract so far as it relates to the creation or transfer of an interest in land, or to the termination of such an interest, whether by extinction, merger, surrender, forfeiture or otherwise;
   (*c*) any contract so far as it relates to the creation or transfer of a right or interest in any patent, trade mark, copyright [or design right], registered design, technical or commercial information or other intellectual property, or relates to the termination of any such right or interest;
   (*d*) any contract so far as it relates—
      (i) to the formation or dissolution of a company (which means any body corporate or unincorporated association and includes a partnership), or
      (ii) to its constitution or the rights or obligations of its corporators or members;
   (*e*) any contract so far as it relates to the creation or transfer of securities or of any right or interest in securities.

2. Section 2 (1) extends to—
   (*a*) any contract of marine salvage or towage;
   (*b*) any charterparty of a ship or hovercraft; and
   (*c*) any contract for the carriage of goods by ship or hovercraft;
but subject to this sections 2 to 4 and 7 do not extend to any such contract except in favour of a person dealing as consumer.

3. Where goods are carried by ship or hovercraft in pursuance of a contract which either—
   (*a*) specifies that as the means of carriage over part of the journey to be covered, or
   (*b*) makes no provision as to the means of carriage and does not exclude that means,
then sections 2 (2), 3 and 4 do not, except in favour of a person dealing as consumer, extend to the contract as it operates for and in relation to the carriage of the goods by that means.

4. Section 2 (1) and (2) do not extend to a contract of employment, except in favour of the employee.

5. Section 2 (1) does not affect the validity of any discharge and indemnity given by a person, on or in connection with an award to him of compensation for pneumoconiosis attributable to employment in the coal industry, in respect of any further claim arising from his contracting that disease. **[75]**

NOTES
Commencement: 1 February 1978.
Para 1: in sub-para (c) the reference to a trade mark includes reference to a service mark, by virtue of the Patents, Designs and Marks Act 1986, s 2(3), Sch 2, Part I, and words in square brackets prospectively added by the Copyright, Designs and Patents Act 1988, s 303(1), Sch 7, para 24, as from a day to be appointed.

SCHEDULE 2
Sections 11(2), 24(2)
"GUIDELINES" FOR APPLICATION OF REASONABLENESS TEST

The matters to which regard is to be had in particular for the purposes of sections 6 (3), 7 (3) and (4), 20 and 21 are any of the following which appear to be relevant—

(a) the strength of the bargaining positions of the parties relative to each other, taking into account (among other things) alternative means by which the customer's requirements could have been met;

(b) whether the customer received an inducement to agree to the term, or in accepting it had an opportunity of entering into a similar contract with other persons, but without having to accept a similar term;

(c) whether the customer knew or ought reasonably to have known of the existence and extent of the term (having regard, among other things, to any custom of the trade and any previous course of dealing between the parties);

(d) where the term excludes or restricts any relevant liability if some condition is not complied with, whether it was reasonable at the time of the contract to expect that compliance with that condition would be practicable;

(e) whether the goods were manufactured, processed or adapted to the special order of the customer. [76]

NOTES
Commencement: 1 February 1978.

CIVIL LIABILITY (CONTRIBUTION) ACT 1978
(c 47)

ARRANGEMENT OF SECTIONS

PROCEEDINGS FOR CONTRIBUTION

Section		Para
1	Entitlement to contribution	[77]
2	Assessment of contribution	[78]

PROCEEDINGS FOR THE SAME DEBT OR DAMAGE

3	Proceedings against persons jointly liable for the same debt or damage	[79]
4	Successive actions against persons liable (jointly or otherwise) for the same damage	[80]

SUPPLEMENTAL

5	Application to the Crown	[81]
6	Interpretation	[82]
7	Savings	[83]
8	Application to Northern Ireland	[84]
10	Short title, commencement and extent	[85]

An Act to make new provision for contribution between persons who are jointly or severally, or both jointly and severally, liable for the same damage and in

certain other similar cases where two or more persons have paid or may be required to pay compensation for the same damage; and to amend the law relating to proceedings against persons jointly liable for the same debt or jointly or severally, or both jointly and severally, liable for the same damage
[31 July 1978]

PROCEEDINGS FOR CONTRIBUTION

1. Entitlement to contribution

(1) Subject to the following provisions of this section, any person liable in respect of any damage suffered by another person may recover contribution from any other person liable in respect of the same damage (whether jointly with him or otherwise).

(2) A person shall be entitled to recover contribution by virtue of subsection (1) above notwithstanding that he has ceased to be liable in respect of the damage in question since the time when the damage occurred, provided that he was so liable immediately before he made or was ordered or agreed to make the payment in respect of which the contribution is sought.

(3) A person shall be liable to make contribution by virtue of subsection (1) above notwithstanding that he has ceased to be liable in respect of the damage in question since the time when the damage occurred, unless he ceased to be liable by virtue of the expiry of a period of limitation or prescription which extinguished the right on which the claim against him in respect of the damage was based.

(4) A person who has made or agreed to make any payment in bona fide settlement or compromise of any claim made against him in respect of any damage (including a payment into court which has been accepted) shall be entitled to recover contribution in accordance with this section without regard to whether or not he himself is or ever was liable in respect of the damage, provided, however, that he would have been liable assuming that the factual basis of the claim against him could be established.

(5) A judgment given in any action brought in any part of the United Kingdom by or on behalf of the person who suffered the damage in question against any person from whom contribution is sought under this section shall be conclusive in the proceedings for contribution as to any issue determined by that judgment in favour of the person from whom the contribution is sought.

(6) References in this section to a person's liability in respect of any damage are references to any such liability which has been or could be established in an action brought against him in England and Wales by or on behalf of the person who suffered the damage; but it is immaterial whether any issue arising in any such action was or would be determined (in accordance with the rules of private international law) by reference to the law of a country outside England and Wales. [77]

NOTES
Commencement: 1 January 1979.

2. Assessment of contribution

(1) Subject to subsection (3) below, in any proceedings for contribution under section 1 above the amount of the contribution recoverable from any person

shall be such as may be found by the court to be just and equitable having regard to the extent of that person's responsibility for the damage in question.

(2) Subject to subsection (3) below, the court shall have power in any such proceedings to exempt any person from liability to make contribution, or to direct that the contribution to be recovered from any person shall amount to a complete indemnity.

(3) Where the amount of the damages which have or might have been awarded in respect of the damage in question in any action brought in England and Wales by or on behalf of the person who suffered it against the person from whom the contribution is sought was or would have been subject to—

(a) any limit imposed by or under any enactment or by any agreement made before the damage occurred;
(b) any reduction by virtue of section 1 of the Law Reform (Contributory Negligence) Act 1945 or section 5 of the Fatal Accidents Act 1976; or
(c) any corresponding limit or reduction under the law of a country outside England and Wales;

the person from whom the contribution is sought shall not by virtue of any contribution awarded under section 1 above be required to pay in respect of the damage a greater amount than the amount of those damages as so limited or reduced. [78]

NOTES
Commencement: 1 January 1979.

PROCEEDINGS FOR THE SAME DEBT OR DAMAGE

3. Proceedings against persons jointly liable for the same debt or damage

Judgment recovered against any person liable in respect of any debt or damage shall not be a bar to an action, or to the continuance of an action, against any other person who is (apart from any such bar) jointly liable with him in respect of the same debt or damage. [79]

NOTES
Commencement: 1 January 1979.

4. Successive actions against persons liable (jointly or otherwise) for the same damage

If more than one action is brought in respect of any damage by or on behalf of the person by whom it was suffered against persons liable in respect of the damage (whether jointly or otherwise) the plaintiff shall not be entitled to costs in any of those actions, other than that in which judgment is first given, unless the court is of the opinion that there was reasonable ground for bringing the action. [80]

NOTES
Commencement: 1 January 1979.

SUPPLEMENTAL

5. Application to the Crown
Without prejudice to section 4(1) of the Crown Proceedings Act 1947 (indemnity and contribution), this Act shall bind the Crown, but nothing in this Act shall be construed as in any way affecting Her Majesty in Her private capacity (including in right of Her Duchy of Lancaster) or the Duchy of Cornwall.

NOTES
Commencement: 1 January 1979.

6. Interpretation
(1) A person is liable in respect of any damage for the purposes of this Act if the person who suffered it (or anyone representing his estate or dependants) is entitled to recover compensation from him in respect of that damage (whatever the legal basis of his liability, whether tort, breach of contract, breach of trust or otherwise).

(2) References in this Act to an action brought by or on behalf of the person who suffered any damage include references to an action brought for the benefit of his estate or dependants.

(3) In this Act "dependants" has the same meaning as in the Fatal Accidents Act 1976.

(4) In this Act, except in section 1(5) above, "action" means an action brought in England and Wales.

NOTES
Commencement: 1 January 1979.

7. Savings
(1) Nothing in this Act shall affect any case where the debt in question became due or (as the case may be) the damage in question occurred before the date on which it comes into force.

(2) A person shall not be entitled to recover contribution or liable to make contribution in accordance with section 1 above by reference to any liability based on breach of any obligation assumed by him before the date on which this Act comes into force.

(3) The right to recover contribution in accordance with section 1 above supersedes any right, other than an express contractual right, to recover contribution (as distinct from indemnity) otherwise than under this Act in corresponding circumstances; but nothing in this Act shall affect—
    (a) any express or implied contractual or other right to indemnity; or
    (b) any express contractual provision regulating or excluding contribution;
which would be enforceable apart from this Act (or render enforceable any agreement for indemnity or contribution which would not be enforceable apart from this Act).

NOTES
Commencement: 1 January 1979.

8. Application to Northern Ireland

In the application of this Act to Northern Ireland—

(a) the reference in section 2(3)(b) to section 1 of the Law Reform (Contributory Negligence) Act 1945 or section 5 of the Fatal Accidents Act 1976 shall be construed as a reference to section 2 of the Law Reform (Miscellaneous Provisions) Act (Northern Ireland) 1948 or Article 7 of the Fatal Accidents (Northern Ireland) Order 1977;

(b) the reference in section 5 to section 4(1) of the Crown Proceedings Act 1947 shall be construed as a reference to section 4(1) of that Act as it applies in Northern Ireland;

(c) the reference in section 6(3) to the Fatal Accidents Act 1976 shall be construed as a reference to the Fatal Accidents (Northern Ireland) Order 1977;

(d) references to England and Wales shall be construed as references to Northern Ireland; and

(e) any reference to an enactment shall be construed as including a reference to an enactment of the Parliament of Northern Ireland and a Measure of the Northern Ireland Assembly. **[84]**

NOTES
Commencement: 1 January 1979.
S 9, which deals with consequential amendments and repeals, is omitted, as are Sch 1 and 2 which set out the amendments and repeals.

10. Short title, commencement and extent

(1) This Act may be cited as the Civil Liability (Contribution) Act 1978.

(2) This Act shall come into force on 1 January next following the date on which it is passed.

(3) . . . **[85]**

NOTES
Commencement: 1 January 1979.
Sub-s (3): applies to Scotland only.

SALE OF GOODS ACT 1979
(c 54)

ARRANGEMENT OF SECTIONS

Part I
Contracts to which Act Applies

Section		Para
1	Contracts to which Act applies	[86]

Part II
Formation of the Contract

Contract of sale

2	Contract of sale	[87]
3	Capacity to buy and sell	[88]

Section		Para
	Formalities of contract	
4	How contract of sale is made	[89]
	Subject matter of contract	
5	Existing or future goods	[90]
6	Goods which have perished	[91]
7	Goods perishing before sale but after agreement to sell	[92]
	The price	
8	Ascertainment of price	[93]
9	Agreement to sell at valuation	[94]
	Conditions and warranties	
10	Stipulations about time	[95]
11	When condition to be treated as warranty	[96]
12	Implied terms about title, etc	[97]
13	Sale by description	[98]
14	Implied terms about quality or fitness	[99]
	Sale by sample	
15	Sale by sample	[100]

Part III

Effects of the Contract

Transfer of property as between seller and buyer

16	Goods must be ascertained	[101]
17	Property passes when intended to pass	[102]
18	Rules for ascertaining intention	[103]
19	Reservation of right of disposal	[104]
20	Risk prima facie passes with property	[105]

Transfer of title

21	Sale by person not the owner	[106]
22	Market overt	[107]
23	Sale under voidable title	[108]
24	Seller in possession after sale	[109]
25	Buyer in possession after sale	[110]
26	Supplementary to sections 24 and 25	[111]

Part IV

Performance of the Contract

27	Duties of seller and buyer	[112]
28	Payment and delivery are concurrent conditions	[113]
29	Rules about delivery	[114]
30	Delivery of wrong quantity	[115]
31	Instalment deliveries	[116]
32	Delivery to carrier	[117]
33	Risk where goods are delivered at distant place	[118]
34	Buyer's right of examining the goods	[119]
35	Acceptance	[120]
36	Buyer not bound to return rejected goods	[121]
37	Buyer's liability for not taking delivery of goods	[122]

Section		Para

Part V
Rights of Unpaid Seller Against the Goods

Preliminary

38	Unpaid seller defined	[123]
39	Unpaid seller's rights	[124]

Unpaid seller's lien

41	Seller's lien	[125]
42	Part delivery	[126]
43	Termination of lien	[127]

Stoppage in transit

44	Right of stoppage in transit	[128]
45	Duration of transit	[129]
46	How stoppage in transit is effected	[130]

Re-sale etc by buyer

47	Effect of sub-sale etc by buyer	[131]

Rescission: and re-sale by seller

48	Rescission: and re-sale by seller	[132]

Part VI
Actions for Breach of the Contract

Seller's remedies

49	Action for price	[133]
50	Damages for non-acceptance	[134]

Buyer's remedies

51	Damages for non-delivery	[135]
52	Specific performance	[136]
53	Remedy for breach of warranty	[137]

Interest, etc

54	Interest, etc	[138]

Part VII
Supplementary

55	Exclusion of implied terms	[139]
56	Conflict of laws	[140]
57	Auction sales	[141]
59	Reasonable time a question of fact	[142]
60	Rights etc enforceable by action	[143]
61	Interpretation	[144]
62	Savings: rules of law etc	[145]
63	Consequential amendments, repeals and savings	[146]
64	Short title and commencement	[147]

Schedules

Schedule 1—Modification of Act for Certain Contracts	[148]
Schedule 4—Savings	[149]

An Act to consolidate the law relating to the sale of goods [6 December 1979]

Part I
Contracts to which Act Applies

1. Contracts to which Act applies

(1) This Act applies to contracts of sale of goods made on or after (but not to those made before) 1 January 1894.

(2) In relation to contracts made on certain dates, this Act applies subject to the modification of certain of its sections as mentioned in Schedule 1 below.

(3) Any such modification is indicated in the section concerned by a reference to Schedule 1 below.

(4) Accordingly, where a section does not contain such a reference, this Act applies in relation to the contract concerned without such modification of the section. **[86]**

NOTES
Commencement: 1 January 1980.
Sub-s (1) derived from the Sale of Goods Act 1893, s 63; sub-s (2) derived from the Misrepresentation Act 1967, s 5, the Criminal Law Act 1967, s 12(1), the Supply of Goods (Implied Terms) Act 1973, s 18(5), the Consumer Credit Act 1974, s 192(4) and the Unfair Contract Terms Act 1977, s 31(2).

Part II
Formation of the Contract
Contract of sale

2. Contract of sale

(1) A contract of sale of goods is a contract by which the seller transfers or agrees to transfer the property in goods to the buyer for a money consideration, called the price.

(2) There may be a contract of sale between one part owner and another.

(3) A contract of sale may be absolute or conditional.

(4) Where under a contract of sale the property in the goods is transferred from the seller to the buyer the contract is called a sale.

(5) Where under a contract of sale the transfer of the property in the goods is to take place at a future time or subject to some condition later to be fulfilled the contract is called an agreement to sell.

(6) An agreement to sell becomes a sale when the time elapses or the conditions are fulfilled subject to which the property in the goods is to be transferred. **[87]**

NOTES
Commencement: 1 January 1980.
This section derived from the Sale of Goods Act 1893, s 1.

3. Capacity to buy and sell

(1) Capacity to buy and sell is regulated by the general law concerning capacity to contract and to transfer and acquire property.

(2) Where necessaries are sold and delivered to a minor or to a person who by reason of mental incapacity or drunkenness is incompetent to contract, he must pay a reasonable price for them.

(3) In subsection (2) above "necessaries" means goods suitable to the condition in life of the minor or other person concerned and to his actual requirements at the time of the sale and delivery. **[88]**

NOTES
Commencement: 1 January 1980.
This section derived from the Sale of Goods Act 1893, s 2.

Formalities of contract

4. How contract of sale is made

(1) Subject to this and any other Act, a contract of sale may be made in writing (either with or without seal), or by word of mouth, or partly in writing and partly by word of mouth, or may be implied from the conduct of the parties.

(2) Nothing in this section affects the law relating to corporations. **[89]**

NOTES
Commencement: 1 January 1980.
This section derived from the Sale of Goods Act 1893, s 3.

Subject matter of contract

5. Existing or future goods

(1) The goods which form the subject of a contract of sale may be either existing goods, owned or possessed by the seller, or goods to be manufactured or acquired by him after the making of the contract of sale, in this Act called future goods.

(2) There may be a contract for the sale of goods the acquisition of which by the seller depends on a contingency which may or may not happen.

(3) Where by a contract of sale the seller purports to effect a present sale of future goods, the contract operates as an agreement to sell the goods. **[90]**

NOTES
Commencement: 1 January 1980.
This section derived from the Sale of Goods Act 1893, s 5.

6. Goods which have perished

Where there is a contract for the sale of specific goods, and the goods without the knowledge of the seller have perished at the time when the contract is made, the contract is void. **[91]**

NOTES
Commencement: 1 January 1980.
This section derived from the Sale of Goods Act 1893, s 6.

7. Goods perishing before sale but after agreement to sell

Where there is an agreement to sell specific goods and subsequently the goods, without any fault on the part of the seller or buyer, perish before the risk passes to the buyer, the agreement is avoided. **[92]**

NOTES
Commencement: 1 January 1980.
This section derived from the Sale of Goods Act 1893, s 7.

The price

8. Ascertainment of price

(1) The price in a contract of sale may be fixed by the contract, or may be left to be fixed in a manner agreed by the contract, or may be determined by the course of dealing between the parties.

(2) Where the price is not determined as mentioned in subsection (1) above the buyer must pay a reasonable price.

(3) What is a reasonable price is a question of fact dependent on the circumstances of each particular case. **[93]**

NOTES
Commencement: 1 January 1980.
This section derived from the Sale of Goods Act 1893, s 8.

9. Agreement to sell at valuation

(1) Where there is an agreement to sell goods on the terms that the price is to be fixed by the valuation of a third party, and he cannot or does not make the valuation, the agreement is avoided; but if the goods or any part of them have been delivered to and appropriated by the buyer he must pay a reasonable price for them.

(2) Where the third party is prevented from making the valuation by the fault of the seller or buyer, the party not at fault may maintain an action for damages against the party at fault. **[94]**

NOTES
Commencement: 1 January 1980.
This section derived from the Sale of Goods Act 1893, s 9.

Conditions and warranties

10. Stipulations about time

(1) Unless a different intention appears from the terms of the contract, stipulations as to time of payment are not of the essence of a contract of sale.

(2) Whether any other stipulation as to time is or is not of the essence of the contract depends on the terms of the contract.

(3) In a contract of sale "month" prima facie means calendar month. **[95]**

NOTES
Commencement: 1 January 1980.
This section derived from the Sale of Goods Act 1893, s 10.

11. When condition to be treated as warranty

(1) ...

(2) Where a contract of sale is subject to a condition to be fulfilled by the seller, the buyer may waive the condition, or may elect to treat the breach of the

condition as a breach of warranty and not as a ground for treating the contract as repudiated.

(3) Whether a stipulation in a contract of sale is a condition, the breach of which may give rise to a right to treat the contract as repudiated, or a warranty, the breach of which may give rise to a claim for damages but not to a right to reject the goods and treat the contract as repudiated, depends in each case on the construction of the contract; and a stipulation may be a condition, though called a warranty in the contract.

(4) Where a contract of sale is not severable and the buyer has accepted the goods or part of them, the breach of a condition to be fulfilled by the seller can only be treated as a breach of warranty, and not as a ground for rejecting the goods and treating the contract as repudiated, unless there is an express or implied term of the contract to that effect.

(5) ...

(6) Nothing in this section affects a condition or warranty whose fulfilment is excused by law by reason of impossibility or otherwise.

(7) Paragraph 2 of Schedule 1 below applies in relation to a contract made before 22 April 1967 or (in the application of this Act to Northern Ireland) 28 July 1967. **[96]**

NOTES
Commencement: 1 January 1980.
This section derived from the Sale of Goods Act 1893, s 11, as amended by the Misrepresentation Act 1967.
Sub-ss (1), (5): apply to Scotland only.

12. Implied terms about title, etc

(1) In a contract of sale, other than one to which subsection(3) below applies, there is an implied condition on the part of the seller that in the case of a sale he has a right to sell the goods, and in the case of an agreement to sell he will have such a right at the time when the property is to pass.

(2) In a contract of sale, other than one to which subsection (3) below applies, there is also an implied warranty that—
    (a) the goods are free, and will remain free until the time when the property is to pass, from any charge or encumbrance not disclosed or known to the buyer before the contract is made, and
    (b) the buyer will enjoy quiet possession of the goods except so far as it may be disturbed by the owner or other person entitled to the benefit of any charge or encumbrance so disclosed or known.

(3) This subsection applies to a contract of sale in the case of which there appears from the contract or is to be inferred from its circumstances an intention that the seller should transfer only such title as he or a third person may have.

(4) In a contract to which subsection (3) above applies there is an implied warranty that all charges or encumbrances known to the seller and not known to the buyer have been disclosed to the buyer before the contract is made.

(5) In a contract to which subsection (3) above applies there is also an implied warranty that none of the following will disturb the buyer's quiet possession of the goods, namely—
    (a) the seller;

(b) in a case where the parties to the contract intend that the seller should transfer only such title as a third person may have, that person;
(c) anyone claiming through or under the seller or that third person otherwise than under a charge or encumbrance disclosed or known to the buyer before the contract is made.

(6) Paragraph 3 of Schedule 1 below applies in relation to a contract made before 18 May 1973. **[97]**

NOTES
Commencement: 1 January 1980.
This section derived from the Sale of Goods Act 1893, s 12, as amended by the Supply of Goods (Implied Terms) Act 1973.

---

13. Sale by description

(1) Where there is a contract for the sale of goods by description, there is an implied condition that the goods will correspond with the description.

(2) If the sale is by sample as well as by description it is not sufficient that the bulk of the goods corresponds with the sample if the goods do not also correspond with the description.

(3) A sale of goods is not prevented from being a sale by description by reason only that, being exposed for sale or hire, they are selected by the buyer.

(4) Paragraph 4 of Schedule 1 below applies in relation to a contract made before 18 May 1973. **[98]**

NOTES
Commencement: 1 January 1980.
This section derived from the Sale of Goods Act 1893, s 13, as amended by the Supply of Goods (Implied Terms) Act 1973.

---

14. Implied terms about quality or fitness

(1) Except as provided by this section and section 15 below and subject to any other enactment, there is no implied condition or warranty about the quality or fitness for any particular purpose of goods supplied under a contract of sale.

(2) Where the seller sells goods in the course of a business, there is an implied condition that the goods supplied under the contract are of merchantable quality, except that there is no such condition—
   (a) as regards defects specifically drawn to the buyer's attention before the contract is made; or
   (b) if the buyer examines the goods before the contract is made, as regards defects which that examination ought to reveal.

(3) Where the seller sells goods in the course of a business and the buyer, expressly or by implication, makes known—
   (a) to the seller, or
   (b) where the purchase price or part of it is payable by instalments and the goods were previously sold by a credit-broker to the seller, to that credit-broker,

any particular purpose for which the goods are being bought, there is an implied condition that the goods supplied under the contract are reasonably fit for that purpose, whether or not that is a purpose for which such goods are commonly supplied, except where the circumstances show that the buyer does not rely, or that it is unreasonable for him to rely, on the skill or judgment of the seller or credit-broker.

(4) An implied condition or warranty about quality or fitness for a particular purpose may be annexed to a contract of sale by usage.

(5) The preceding provisions of this section apply to a sale by a person who in the course of a business is acting as agent for another as they apply to a sale by a principal in the course of a business, except where that other is not selling in the course of a business and either the buyer knows that fact or reasonable steps are taken to bring it to the notice of the buyer before the contract is made.

(6) Goods of any kind are of merchantable quality within the meaning of subsection (2) above if they are as fit for the purpose or purposes for which goods of that kind are commonly bought as it is reasonable to expect having regard to any description applied to them, the price (if relevant) and all the other relevant circumstances.

(7) Paragraph 5 of Schedule 1 below applies in relation to a contract made on or after 18 May 1973 and before the appointed day, and paragraph 6 in relation to one made before 18 May 1973.

(8) In subsection (7) above and paragraph 5 of Schedule 1 below references to the appointed day are to the day appointed for the purposes of those provisions by an order of the Secretary of State made by statutory instrument.

NOTES
Commencement: 1 January 1980.
This section derived from the Sale of Goods Act 1893, ss 14, 62 (1A), as amended by the Supply of Goods (Implied Terms) Act 1973.

Sale by sample

15. Sale by sample

(1) A contract of sale is a contract for sale by sample where there is an express or implied term to that effect in the contract.

(2) In the case of a contract for sale by sample there is an implied condition—
- (*a*) that the bulk will correspond with the sample in quality;
- (*b*) that the buyer will have a reasonable opportunity of comparing the bulk with the sample;
- (*c*) that the goods will be free from any defect, rendering them unmerchantable, which would not be apparent on reasonable examination of the sample.

(3) In subsection (2) (*c*) above "unmerchantable" is to be construed in accordance with section 14 (6) above.

(4) Paragraph 7 of Schedule 1 below applies in relation to a contract made before 18 May 1973.

NOTES
Commencement: 1 January 1980.
Sub-ss (1), (2) derived from the Sale of Goods Act 1893, s 15; sub-s (3) derived from the Sale of Goods Act 1893, s 62 (1A).

Part III

Effects of the Contract

Transfer of property as between seller and buyer

16. Goods must be ascertained

Where there is a contract for the sale of unascertained goods no property in the goods is transferred to the buyer unless and until the goods are ascertained.

[101]

NOTES
Commencement: 1 January 1980.
This section derived from the Sale of Goods Act 1893, s 16.

17. Property passes when intended to pass

(1) Where there is a contract for the sale of specific or ascertained goods the property in them is transferred to the buyer at such time as the parties to the contract intend it to be transferred.

(2) For the purpose of ascertaining the intention of the parties regard shall be had to the terms of the contract, the conduct of the parties and the circumstances of the case. [102]

NOTES
Commencement: 1 January 1980.
This section derived from the Sale of Goods Act 1893, s 17.

18. Rules for ascertaining intention

Unless a different intention appears, the following are rules for ascertaining the intention of the parties as to the time at which the property in the goods is to pass to the buyer.

Rule 1.—Where there is an unconditional contract for the sale of specific goods in a deliverable state the property in the goods passes to the buyer when the contract is made, and it is immaterial whether the time of payment or the time of delivery, or both, be postponed.

Rule 2.—Where there is a contract for the sale of specific goods and the seller is bound to do something to the goods for the purpose of putting them into a deliverable state, the property does not pass until the thing is done and the buyer has notice that it has been done.

Rule 3.—Where there is a contract for the sale of specific goods in a deliverable state but the seller is bound to weigh, measure, test, or do some other act or thing with reference to the goods for the purpose of ascertaining the price, the property does not pass until the act or thing is done and the buyer has notice that it has been done.

Rule 4.—When goods are delivered to the buyer on approval or on sale or return or other similar terms the property in the goods passes to the buyer:—
   (a) when he signifies his approval or acceptance to the seller or does any other act adopting the transaction;
   (b) if he does not signify his approval or acceptance to the seller but retains the goods without giving notice of rejection, then, if a time has been fixed for the return of the goods, on the expiration of that time, and, if no time has been fixed, on the expiration of a reasonable time.

Rule 5.—(1) Where there is a contract for the sale of unascertained or future goods by description, and goods of that description and in a deliverable state are unconditionally appropriated to the contract, either by the seller with the assent of the buyer or by the buyer with the assent of the seller, the property in the goods then passes to the buyer; and the assent may be express or implied, and may be given either before or after the appropriation is made.

(2) Where, in pursuance of the contract, the seller delivers the goods to the buyer or to a carrier or other bailee or custodier (whether named by the buyer or not) for the purpose of transmission to the buyer, and does not reserve the right of disposal, he is to be taken to have unconditionally appropriated the goods to the contract. **[103]**

NOTES
Commencement: 1 January 1980.
This section derived from the Sale of Goods Act 1893, s 18.

19. Reservation of right of disposal

(1) Where there is a contract for the sale of specific goods or where goods are subsequently appropriated to the contract, the seller may, by the terms of the contract or appropriation, reserve the right of disposal of the goods until certain conditions are fulfilled; and in such a case, notwithstanding the delivery of the goods to the buyer, or to a carrier or other bailee or custodier for the purpose of transmission to the buyer, the property in the goods does not pass to the buyer until the conditions imposed by the seller are fulfilled.

(2) Where goods are shipped, and by the bill of lading the goods are deliverable to the order of the seller or his agent, the seller is prima facie to be taken to reserve the right of disposal.

(3) Where the seller of goods draws on the buyer for the price, and transmits the bill of exchange and bill of lading to the buyer together to secure acceptance or payment of the bill of exchange, the buyer is bound to return the bill of lading if he does not honour the bill of exchange, and if he wrongfully retains the bill of lading the property in the goods does not pass to him. **[104]**

NOTES
Commencement: 1 January 1980.
This section derived from the Sale of Goods Act 1893, s 19.

20. Risk prima facie passes with property

(1) Unless otherwise agreed, the goods remain at the seller's risk until the property in them is transferred to the buyer, but when the property in them is transferred to the buyer the goods are at the buyer's risk whether delivery has been made or not.

(2) But where delivery has been delayed through the fault of either buyer or seller the goods are at the risk of the party at fault as regards any loss which might not have occurred but for such fault.

(3) Nothing in this section affects the duties or liabilities of either seller or buyer as a bailee or custodier of the goods of the other party. **[105]**

NOTES
Commencement: 1 January 1980.
This section derived from the Sale of Goods Act 1893, s 20.

Transfer of title

21. Sale by person not the owner

(1) Subject to this Act, where goods are sold by a person who is not their owner, and who does not sell them under the authority or with the consent of the owner, the buyer acquires no better title to the goods than the seller had, unless the owner of the goods is by his conduct precluded from denying the seller's authority to sell.

(2) Nothing in this Act affects—
> (a) the provisions of the Factors Acts or any enactment enabling the apparent owner of goods to dispose of them as if he were their true owner;
> (b) the validity of any contract of sale under any special common law or statutory power of sale or under the order of a court of competent jurisdiction. **[106]**

NOTES
> Commencement: 1 January 1980.
> This section derived from the Sale of Goods Act 1893, s 21.

22. Market overt

(1) Where goods are sold in market overt, according to the usage of the market, the buyer acquires a good title to the goods, provided he buys them in good faith and without notice of any defect or want of title on the part of the seller.

(2) This section does not apply to Scotland.

(3) Paragraph 8 of Schedule 1 below applies in relation to a contract under which goods were sold before 1 January 1968 or (in the application of this Act to Northern Ireland) 29 August 1967. **[107]**

NOTES
> Commencement: 1 January 1980.
> This section derived from the Sale of Goods Act 1893, s 22.

23. Sale under voidable title

When the seller of goods has a voidable title to them, but his title has not been avoided at the time of the sale, the buyer acquires a good title to the goods, provided he buys them in good faith and without notice of the seller's defect of title. **[108]**

NOTES
> Commencement: 1 January 1980.
> This section derived from the Sale of Goods Act 1893, s 23.

24. Seller in possession after sale

Where a person having sold goods continues or is in possession of the goods, or of the documents of title to the goods, the delivery or transfer by that person, or by a mercantile agent acting for him, of the goods or documents of title under any sale, pledge, or other disposition thereof, to any person receiving the same in good faith and without notice of the previous sale, has the same effect as if the person making the delivery or transfer were expressly authorised by the owner of the goods to make the same. **[109]**

NOTES
Commencement: 1 January 1980.
This section derived from the Sale of Goods Act 1893, s 25(1). Cf Factors Act 1889, s 8.

25. Buyer in possession after sale

(1) Where a person having bought or agreed to buy goods obtains, with the consent of the seller, possession of the goods or the documents of title to the goods, the delivery or transfer by that person, or by a mercantile agent acting for him, of the goods or documents of title, under any sale, pledge, or other disposition thereof, to any person receiving the same in good faith and without notice of any lien or other right of the original seller in respect of the goods, has the same effect as if the person making the delivery or transfer were a mercantile agent in possession of the goods or documents of title with the consent of the owner.

(2) For the purposes of subsection (1) above—
  (*a*) the buyer under a conditional sale agreement is to be taken not to be a person who has bought or agreed to buy goods, and
  (*b*) "conditional sale agreement" means an agreement for the sale of goods which is a consumer credit agreement within the meaning of the Consumer Credit Act 1974 under which the purchase price or part of it is payable by instalments, and the property in the goods is to remain in the seller (notwithstanding that the buyer is to be in possession of the goods) until such conditions as to the payment of instalments or otherwise as may be specified in the agreement are fulfilled.

(3) Paragraph 9 of Schedule 1 below applies in relation to a contract under which a person buys or agrees to buy goods and which is made before the appointed day.

(4) In subsection (3) above and paragraph 9 of Schedule 1 below references to the appointed day are to the day appointed for the purposes of those provisions by an order of the Secretary of State made by statutory instrument.

NOTES
Commencement: 1 January 1980.
Sub-ss (1), (2) derived from the Sale of Goods Act 1893, s 25(2), as amended by the Consumer Credit Act 1974, Sch 4, para 4. Cf Factors Act 1889, s 9.

26. Supplementary to sections 24 and 25

In sections 24 and 25 above "mercantile agent" means a mercantile agent having in the customary course of his business as such agent authority either—
  (*a*) to sell goods, or
  (*b*) to consign goods for the purpose of sale, or
  (*c*) to buy goods, or
  (*d*) to raise money on the security of goods.

NOTES
Commencement: 1 January 1980.
This section derived from the Factors Act 1889, s 1(1).

Part IV

Performance of the Contract

27. Duties of seller and buyer

It is the duty of the seller to deliver the goods, and of the buyer to accept and pay for them, in accordance with the terms of the contract of sale. [112]

NOTES
Commencement: 1 January 1980.
This section derived from the Sale of Goods Act 1893, s 27.

28. Payment and delivery are concurrent conditions

Unless otherwise agreed, delivery of the goods and payment of the price are concurrent conditions, that is to say, the seller must be ready and willing to give possession of the goods to the buyer in exchange for the price and the buyer must be ready and willing to pay the price in exchange for possession of the goods. [113]

NOTES
Commencement: 1 January 1980.
This section derived from the Sale of Goods Act 1893, s 28.

29. Rules about delivery

(1) Whether it is for the buyer to take possession of the goods or for the seller to send them to the buyer is a question depending in each case on the contract, express or implied, between the parties.

(2) Apart from any such contract, express or implied, the place of delivery is the seller's place of business if he has one, and if not, his residence; except that, if the contract is for the sale of specific goods, which to the knowledge of the parties when the contract is made are in some other place, then that place is the place of delivery.

(3) Where under the contract of sale the seller is bound to send the goods to the buyer, but no time for sending them is fixed, the seller is bound to send them within a reasonable time.

(4) Where the goods at the time of sale are in the possession of a third person, there is no delivery by seller to buyer unless and until the third person acknowledges to the buyer that he holds the goods on his behalf; but nothing in this section affects the operation of the issue or transfer of any document of title to goods.

(5) Demand or tender of delivery may be treated as ineffectual unless made at a reasonable hour; and what is a reasonable hour is a question of fact.

(6) Unless otherwise agreed, the expenses of and incidental to putting the goods into a deliverable state must be borne by the seller. [114]

NOTES
Commencement: 1 January 1980.
This section derived from the Sale of Goods Act 1893, s 29.

30. Delivery of wrong quantity

(1) Where the seller delivers to the buyer a quantity of goods less than he contracted to sell, the buyer may reject them, but if the buyer accepts the goods so delivered he must pay for them at the contract rate.

(2) Where the seller delivers to the buyer a quantity of goods larger than he contracted to sell, the buyer may accept the goods included in the contract and reject the rest, or he may reject the whole.

(3) Where the seller delivers to the buyer a quantity of goods larger than he contracted to sell and the buyer accepts the whole of the goods so delivered he must pay for them at the contract rate.

(4) Where the seller delivers to the buyer the goods he contracted to sell mixed with goods of a different description not included in the contract, the buyer may accept the goods which are in accordance with the contract and reject the rest, or he may reject the whole.

(5) This section is subject to any usage of trade, special agreement, or course of dealing between the parties. [115]

NOTES
Commencement: 1 January 1980.
This section derived from the Sale of Goods Act 1893, s 30.

31. Instalment deliveries

(1) Unless otherwise agreed, the buyer of goods is not bound to accept delivery of them by instalments.

(2) Where there is a contract for the sale of goods to be delivered by stated instalments, which are to be separately paid for, and the seller makes defective deliveries in respect of one or more instalments, or the buyer neglects or refuses to take delivery of or pay for one or more instalments, it is a question in each case depending on the terms of the contract and the circumstances of the case whether the breach of contract is a repudiation of the whole contract or whether it is a severable breach giving rise to a claim for compensation but not to a right to treat the whole contract as repudiated. [116]

NOTES
Commencement: 1 January 1980.
This section derived from the Sale of Goods Act 1893, s 31.

32. Delivery to carrier

(1) Where, in pursuance of a contract of sale, the seller is authorised or required to send the goods to the buyer, delivery of the goods to a carrier (whether named by the buyer or not) for the purpose of transmission to the buyer is prima facie deemed to be a delivery of the goods to the buyer.

(2) Unless otherwise authorised by the buyer, the seller must make such contract with the carrier on behalf of the buyer as may be reasonable having regard to the nature of the goods and the other circumstances of the case; and if the seller omits to do so, and the goods are lost or damaged in course of transit, the buyer may decline to treat the delivery to the carrier as a delivery to himself or may hold the seller responsible in damages.

(3) Unless otherwise agreed, where goods are sent by the seller to the buyer by a route involving sea transit, under circumstances in which it is usual to

insure, the seller must give such notice to the buyer as may enable him to insure them during their sea transit; and if the seller fails to do so, the goods are at his risk during such sea transit. [117]

NOTES
Commencement: 1 January 1980.
This section derived from the Sale of Goods Act 1893, s 32.

33. Risk where goods are delivered at distant place

Where the seller of goods agrees to deliver them at his own risk at a place other than that where they are when sold, the buyer must nevertheless (unless otherwise agreed) take any risk of deterioration in the goods necessarily incident to the course of transit. [118]

NOTES
Commencement: 1 January 1980.
This section derived from the Sale of Goods Act 1893, s 33.

34. Buyer's right of examining the goods

(1) Where goods are delivered to the buyer, and he has not previously examined them, he is not deemed to have accepted them until he has had a reasonable opportunity of examining them for the purpose of ascertaining whether they are in conformity with the contract.

(2) Unless otherwise agreed, when the seller tenders delivery of goods to the buyer, he is bound on request to afford the buyer a reasonable opportunity of examining the goods for the purpose of ascertaining whether they are in conformity with the contract. [119]

NOTES
Commencement: 1 January 1980.
This section derived from the Sale of Goods Act 1893, s 34.

35. Acceptance

(1) The buyer is deemed to have accepted the goods when he intimates to the seller that he has accepted them, or (except where section 34 above otherwise provides) when the goods have been delivered to him and he does any act in relation to them which is inconsistent with the ownership of the seller, or when after the lapse of a reasonable time he retains the goods without intimating to the seller that he has rejected them.

(2) Paragraph 10 of Schedule 1 below applies in relation to a contract made before 22 April 1967 or (in the application of this Act of Northern Ireland) 28 July 1967. [120]

NOTES
Commencement: 1 January 1980.
Sub-s (1) derived from the Sale of Goods Act 1893, s 35, as amended by the Misrepresentation Act 1967.

36. Buyer not bound to return rejected goods

Unless otherwise agreed, where goods are delivered to the buyer, and he refuses to accept them, having the right to do so, he is not bound to return them to the seller, but it is sufficient if he intimates to the seller that he refuses to accept them. [121]

NOTES
Commencement: 1 January 1980.
This section derived from the Sale of Goods Act 1893, s 36.

37. Buyer's liability for not taking delivery of goods

(1) When the seller is ready and willing to deliver the goods, and requests the buyer to take delivery, and the buyer does not within a reasonable time after such request take delivery of the goods, he is liable to the seller for any loss occasioned by his neglect or refusal to take delivery, and also for a reasonable charge for the care and custody of the goods.

(2) Nothing in this section affects the rights of the seller where the neglect or refusal of the buyer to take delivery amounts to a repudiation of the contract.

NOTES
Commencement: 1 January 1980.
This section derived from the Sale of Goods Act 1893, s 37.

PART V
RIGHTS OF UNPAID SELLER AGAINST THE GOODS
Preliminary

38. Unpaid seller defined

(1) The seller of goods is an unpaid seller within the meaning of this Act—

    (*a*) when the whole of the price has not been paid or tendered;
    (*b*) when a bill of exchange or other negotiable instrument has been received as conditional payment, and the condition on which it was received has not been fulfilled by reason of the dishonour of the instrument or otherwise.

(2) In this Part of this Act "seller" includes any person who is in the posistion of a seller, as, for instance, an agent of the seller to whom the bill of lading has been indorsed, or a consignor or agent who has himself paid (or is directly responsible for) the price.

NOTES
Commencement: 1 January 1980.
This section derived from the Sale of Goods Act 1893, s 38.

39. Unpaid seller's rights

(1) Subject to this and any other Act, notwithstanding that the property in the goods may have passed to the buyer, the unpaid seller of goods, as such, has by implication of law—

    (*a*) a lien on the goods or right to retain them for the price while he is in possession of them;
    (*b*) in case of the insolvency of the buyer, a right of stopping the goods in transit after he has parted with the possession of them;
    (*c*) a right of re-sale as limited by this Act.

(2) Where the property in goods has not passed to the buyer, the unpaid

seller has (in addition to his other remedies) a right of withholding delivery similar to and co-extensive with his rights of lien or retention and stoppage in transit where the property has passed to the buyer. **[124]**

NOTES
Commencement: 1 January 1980.
This section derived from the Sale of Goods Act 1893, s 39.
S 40 applies to Scotland only.

Unpaid seller's lien

41. Seller's lien

(1) Subject to this Act, the unpaid seller of goods who is in possession of them is entitled to retain possession of them until payment or tender of the price in the following cases:—
- (a) where the goods have been sold without any stipulation as to credit;
- (b) where the goods have been sold on credit but the term of credit has expired;
- (c) where the buyer becomes insolvent.

(2) The seller may exercise his lien or right of retention notwithstanding that he is in possession of the goods as agent or bailee or custodier for the buyer. **[125]**

NOTES
Commencement: 1 January 1980.
This section derived from the Sale of Goods Act 1893, s 41.

42. Part delivery

Where an unpaid seller has made part delivery of the goods, he may exercise his lien or right of retention on the remainder, unless such part delivery has been made under such circumstances as to show an agreement to waive the lien or right of retention. **[126]**

NOTES
Commencement: 1 January 1980.
This section derived from the Sale of Goods Act 1893, s 42.

43. Termination of lien

(1) The unpaid seller of goods loses his lien or right of retention in respect of them—
- (a) when he delivers the goods to a carrier or other bailee or custodier for the purpose of transmission to the buyer without reserving the right of disposal of the goods;
- (b) when the buyer or his agent lawfully obtains possession of the goods;
- (c) by waiver of the lien or right of retention.

(2) An unpaid seller of goods who has a lien or right of retention in respect of them does not lose his lien or right of retention by reason only that he has obtained judgment or decree for the price of the goods. **[127]**

NOTES
Commencement: 1 January 1980.
This section derived from the Sale of Goods Act 1893, s 43.

Stoppage in transit

44. Right of stoppage in transit

Subject to this Act, when the buyer of goods becomes insolvent the unpaid seller who has parted with the possession of the goods has the right of stopping them in transit, that is to say, he may resume possession of the goods as long as they are in course of transit, and may retain them until payment or tender of the price. **[128]**

NOTES
Commencement: 1 January 1980.
This section derived from the Sale of Goods Act 1893, s 44.

45. Duration of transit

(1) Goods are deemed to be in course of transit from the time when they are delivered to a carrier or other bailee or custodier for the purpose of transmission to the buyer, until the buyer or his agent in that behalf takes delivery of them from the carrier or other bailee or custodier.

(2) If the buyer or his agent in that behalf obtains delivery of the goods before their arrival at the appointed destination, the transit is at an end.

(3) If, after the arrival of the goods at the appointed destination, the carrier or other bailee or custodier acknowledges to the buyer or his agent that he holds the goods on his behalf and continues in possession of them as bailee or custodier for the buyer or his agent, the transit is at an end, and it is immaterial that a further destination for the goods may have been indicated by the buyer.

(4) If the goods are rejected by the buyer, and the carrier or other bailee or custodier continues in possession of them, the transit is not deemed to be at an end, even if the seller has refused to receive them back.

(5) When goods are delivered to a ship chartered by the buyer it is a question depending on the circumstances of the particular case whether they are in the possession of the master as a carrier or as agent to the buyer.

(6) Where the carrier or other bailee or custodier wrongfully refuses to deliver the goods to the buyer or his agent in that behalf, the transit is deemed to be at an end.

(7) Where part delivery of the goods has been made to the buyer or his agent in that behalf, the remainder of the goods may be stopped in transit, unless such part delivery has been made under such circumstances as to show an agreement to give up possession of the whole of the goods. **[129]**

NOTES
Commencement: 1 January 1980.
This section derived from the Sale of Goods Act 1893, s 45.

46. How stoppage in transit is effected

(1) The unpaid seller may exercise his right of stoppage in transit either by taking actual possession of the goods or by giving notice of his claim to the carrier or other bailee or custodier in whose possession the goods are.

(2) The notice may be given either to the person in actual possession of the goods or to his principal.

(3) If given to the principal, the notice is ineffective unless given at such time and under such circumstances that the principal, by the exercise of reasonable diligence, may communicate it to his servant or agent in time to prevent a delivery to the buyer.

(4) When notice of stoppage in transit is given by the seller to the carrier or other bailee or custodier in possession of the goods, he must re-deliver the goods to, or according to the directions of, the seller; and the expenses of the re-delivery must be borne by the seller. [130]

NOTES
Commencement: 1 January 1980.
This section derived from the Sale of Goods Act 1893, s 46.

Re-sale etc by buyer

47. Effect of sub-sale etc by buyer

(1) Subject to this Act, the unpaid seller's right of lien or retention or stoppage in transit is not affected by any sale or other disposition of the goods which the buyer may have made, unless the seller has assented to it.

(2) Where a document of title to goods has been lawfully transferred to any person as buyer or owner of the goods, and that person transfers the document to a person who takes it in good faith and for valuable consideration, then—
  (a) if the last-mentioned transfer was by way of sale the unpaid seller's right of lien or retention or stoppage in transit is defeated; and
  (b) if the last-mentioned transfer was made by way of pledge or other disposition for value, the unpaid seller's right of lien or retention or stoppage in transit can only be exercised subject to the rights of the transferee. [131]

NOTES
Commencement: 1 January 1980.
This section derived from the Sale of Goods Act 1893, s 47.

Rescission: and re-sale by seller

48. Rescission: and re-sale by seller

(1) Subject to this section, a contract of sale is not rescinded by the mere exercise by an unpaid seller of his right of lien or retention or stoppage in transit.

(2) Where an unpaid seller who has exercised his right of lien or retention or stoppage in transit re-sells the goods, the buyer acquires a good title to them as against the original buyer.

(3) Where the goods are of a perishable nature, or where the unpaid seller gives notice to the buyer of his intention to re-sell, and the buyer does not within a reasonable time pay or tender the price, the unpaid seller may re-sell the goods and recover from the original buyer damages for any loss occasioned by his breach of contract.

(4) Where the seller expressly reserves the right of re-sale in case the buyer should make default, and on the buyer making default re-sells the goods, the original contract of sale is rescinded but without prejudice to any claim the seller may have for damages. [132]

NOTES
Commencement: 1 January 1980.
This section derived from the Sale of Goods Act 1893, s 48.

PART VI

ACTIONS FOR BREACH OF THE CONTRACT

Seller's remedies

49. Action for price

(1) Where, under a contract of sale, the property in the goods has passed to the buyer and he wrongfully neglects or refuses to pay for the goods according to the terms of the contract, the seller may maintain an action against him for the price of the goods.

(2) Where, under a contract of sale, the price is payable on a day certain irrespective of delivery and the buyer wrongfully neglects or refuses to pay such price, the seller may maintain an action for the price, although the property in the goods has not passed and the goods have not been appropriated to the contract.

(3) ...

NOTES
Commencement: 1 January 1980.
This section derived from the Sale of Goods Act 1893, s 49.
Sub-s (3): applies to Scotland only.

50. Damages for non-acceptance

(1) Where the buyer wrongfully neglects or refuses to accept and pay for the goods, the seller may maintain an action against him for damages for non-acceptance.

(2) The measure of damages is the estimated loss directly and naturally resulting, in the ordinary course of events, from the buyer's breach of contract.

(3) Where there is an available market for the goods in question the measure of damages is prima facie to be ascertained by the difference between the contract price and the market or current price at the time or times when the goods ought to have been accepted or (if no time was fixed for acceptance) at the time of the refusal to accept.

NOTES
Commencement: 1 January 1980.
This section derived from the Sale of Goods Act 1893, s 50.

Buyer's remedies

51. Damages for non-delivery

(1) Where the seller wrongfully neglects or refuses to deliver the goods to the buyer, the buyer may maintain an action against the seller for damages for non-delivery.

(2) The measure of damages is the estimated loss directly and naturally resulting, in the ordinary course of events, from the seller's breach of contract.

(3) Where there is an available market for the goods in question the measure

of damages is prima facie to be ascertained by the difference between the contract price and the market or current price of the goods at the time or times when they ought to have been delivered or (if no time was fixed) at the time of the refusal to deliver.

NOTES
Commencement: 1 January 1980.
This section derived from the Sale of Goods Act 1893, s 51

52. Specific performance

(1) In any action for breach of contract to deliver specific or ascertained goods the court may, if it thinks fit, on the plaintiff's application, by its judgment or decree direct that the contract shall be performed specifically, without giving the defendant the option of retaining the goods on payment of damages.

(2) The plaintiff's application may be made at any time before judgment or decree.

(3) The judgment or decree may be unconditional, or on such terms and conditions as to damages, payment of the price and otherwise as seem just to the court.

(4) . . .

NOTES
Commencement: 1 January 1980.
This section derived from the Sale of Goods Act 1893, s 52.
Sub-s (4): applies to Scotland only.

53. Remedy for breach of warranty

(1) Where there is a breach of warranty by the seller, or where the buyer elects (or is compelled) to treat any breach of a condition on the part of the seller as a breach of warranty, the buyer is not by reason only of such breach of warranty entitled to reject the goods; but he may—

   (a) set up against the seller the breach of warranty in diminution or extinction of the price, or
   (b) maintain an action against the seller for damages for the breach of warranty.

(2) The measure of damages for breach of warranty is the estimated loss directly and naturally resulting, in the ordinary course of events, from the breach of warranty.

(3) In the case of breach of warranty of quality such loss is prima facie the difference between the value of the goods at the time of delivery to the buyer and the value they would have had if they had fulfilled the warranty.

(4) The fact that the buyer has set up the breach of warranty in diminution or extinction of the price does not prevent him from maintaining an action for the same breach of warranty if he has suffered further damage.

(5) . . .

NOTES
Commencement: 1 January 1980.
This section derived from the Sale of Goods Act 1893, s 53.
Sub-s (5): applies to Scotland only.

Interest, etc

54. Interest, etc

Nothing in this Act affects the right of the buyer or the seller to recover interest or special damages in any case where by law interest or special damages may be recoverable, or to recover money paid where the consideration for the payment of it has failed. [138]

NOTES
Commencement: 1 January 1980.
This section derived from the Sale of Goods Act 1893, s 54.

Part VII

Supplementary

55. Exclusion of implied terms

(1) Where a right, duty or liability would arise under a contract of sale of goods by implication of law, it may (subject to the Unfair Contract Terms Act 1977) be negatived or varied by express agreement, or by the course of dealing between the parties, or by such usage as binds both parties to the contract.

(2) An express condition or warranty does not negative a condition or warranty implied by this Act unless inconsistent with it.

(3) Paragraph 11 of Schedule 1 below applies in relation to a contract made on or after 18 May 1973 and before 1 February 1978, and paragraph 12 in relation to one made before 18 May 1973. [139]

NOTES
Commencement: 1 January 1980.
This section derived from the Sale of Goods Act 1893, s 55.

56. Conflict of laws

Paragraph 13 of Schedule 1 below applies in relation to a contract made on or after 18 May 1973 and before 1 February 1978, so as to make provision about conflict of laws in relation to such a contract. [140]

NOTES
Commencement: 1 January 1980.

57. Auction sales

(1) Where goods are put up for sale by auction in lots, each lot is prima facie deemed to be the subject of a separate contract of sale.

(2) A sale by auction is complete when the auctioneer announces its completion by the fall of the hammer, or in other customary manner; and until the announcement is made any bidder may retract his bid.

(3) A sale by auction may be notified to be subject to a reserve or upset price, and a right to bid may also be reserved expressly by or on behalf of the seller.

(4) Where a sale by auction is not notified to be subject to a right to bid by or on behalf of the seller, it is not lawful for the seller to bid himself or to employ

any person to bid at the sale, or for the auctioneer knowingly to take any bid from the seller or any such person.

(5) A sale contravening subsection (4) above may be treated as fraudulent by the buyer.

(6) Where, in respect of a sale by auction, a right to bid is expressly reserved (but not otherwise) the seller or any one person on his behalf may bid at the auction. [141]

NOTES
Commencement: 1 January 1980.
This section derived from the Sale of Goods Act 1893, s 58.
Section 58 applies to Scotland only.

59. Reasonable time a question of fact

Where a reference is made in this Act to a reasonable time the question what is a reasonable time is a question of fact. [142]

NOTES
Commencement: 1 January 1980.
This section derived from the Sale of Goods Act 1893, s 56.

60. Rights etc enforceable by action

Where a right, duty or liability is declared by this Act, it may (unless otherwise provided by this Act) be enforced by action. [143]

NOTES
Commencement: 1 January 1980.
This section derived from the Sale of Goods Act 1893, s 57.

61. Interpretation

(1) In this Act, unless the context or subject matter otherwise requires,—

"action" includes counterclaim and set-off, and in Scotland condescendence and claim and compensation;

"business" includes a profession and the activities of any government department (including a Northern Ireland department) or local or public authority;

"buyer" means a person who buys or agrees to buy goods;

"contract of sale" includes an agreement to sell as well as a sale;

"credit-broker" means a person acting in the course of a business of credit brokerage carried on by him, that is a business of effecting introductions of individuals desiring to obtain credit—

(a) to persons carrying on any business so far as it relates to the provision of credit, or

(b) to other persons engaged in credit brokerage;

. . .

"delivery" means voluntary transfer of possession from one person to another;

"document of title to goods" has the same meaning as it has in the Factors Acts;

"Factors Acts" means the Factors Act 1889, the Factors (Scotland) Act 1890, and any enactment amending or substituted for the same;

"fault" means wrongful act or default;

"future goods" means goods to be manufactured or acquired by the seller after the making of the contract of sale;
"goods" includes all personal chattels other than things in action and money, and in Scotland all corporeal moveables except money; and in particular "goods" includes emblements, industrial growing crops, and things attached to or forming part of the land which are agreed to be severed before sale or under the contract of sale;
"plaintiff" includes pursuer, complainer, claimant in a multiplepoinding and defendant or defender counter-claiming;
"property" means the general property in goods, and not merely a special property;
"quality", in relation to goods, includes their state or condition;
"sale" includes a bargain and sale as well as a sale and delivery;
"seller" means a person who sells or agrees to sell goods;
"specific goods" means goods identified and agreed on at the time a contract of sale is made;
"warranty" (as regards England and Wales and Northern Ireland) means an agreement with reference to goods which are the subject of a contract of sale, but collateral to the main purpose of such contract, the breach of which gives rise to a claim for damages, but not to a right to reject the goods and treat the contract as repudiated.

(2) ...

(3) A thing is deemed to be done in good faith within the meaning of this Act when it is in fact done honestly, whether it is done negligently or not.

(4) A person is deemed to be insolvent within the meaning of this Act if he has either ceased to pay his debts in the ordinary course of business or he cannot pay his debts as they become due ....

(5) Goods are in a deliverable state within the meaning of this Act when they are in such a state that the buyer would under the contract be bound to take delivery of them.

(6) As regards the definition of "business" in subsection(1) above, paragraph 14 of Schedule 1 below applies in relation to a contract made on or after 18 May 1973 and before 1 February 1978, and paragraph 15 in relation to one made before 18 May 1973. **[144]**

NOTES
Commencement: 1 January 1980.
This section derived from the Sale of Goods Act 1893, ss 14(3), 62(2)–(4).
Sub-ss (1) and (2): words omitted apply to Scotland only.
Sub-s (4): words omitted repealed by the Insolvency Act 1985, s 235, Sch 10, Part III, and the Insolvency Act 1986, s 437, Sch 11.

62. Savings: rules of law etc

(1) The rules in bankruptcy relating to contracts of sale apply to those contracts, notwithstanding anything in this Act.

(2) The rules of the common law, including the law merchant, except in so far as they are inconsistent with the provisions of this Act, and in particular the rules relating to the law of principal and agent and the effect of fraud, misrepresentation, duress or coercion, mistake, or other invalidating cause, apply to contracts for the sale of goods.

(3) Nothing in this Act or the Sale of Goods Act 1893 affects the enactments

relating to bills of sale, or any enactment relating to the sale of goods which is not expressly repealed or amended by this Act or that.

(4) The provisions of this Act about contracts of sale do not apply to a transaction in the form of a contract of sale which is intended to operate by way of mortgage, pledge, charge, or other security.

(5) ... [145]

NOTES
Commencement: 1 January 1980.
This section derived from the Sale of Goods Act 1893, s 61.
Sub-s (5): applies to Scotland only.

63. Consequential amendments, repeals and savings

(1) Without prejudice to section 17 of the Interpretation Act 1978 (repeal and re-enactment), the enactments mentioned in Schedule 2 below have effect subject to the amendments there specified (being amendments consequential on this Act).

(2) The enactments mentioned in Schedule 3 below are repealed to the extent specified in column 3, but subject to the savings in Schedule 4 below.

(3) The savings in Schedule 4 below have effect. [146]

NOTES
Commencement: 1 January 1980.

64. Short title and commencement

(1) This Act may be cited as the Sale of Goods Act 1979.

(2) This Act comes into force on 1 January 1980. [147]

NOTES
Commencement: 1 January 1980.

SCHEDULES

SCHEDULE 1

Section 1

MODIFICATION OF ACT FOR CERTAIN CONTRACTS

Preliminary

1.—(1) This Schedule modifies this Act as it applies to contracts of sale of goods made on certain dates.

(2) In this Schedule references to sections are to those of this Act and references to contracts are to contracts of sale of goods.

(3) Nothing in this Schedule affects a contract made before 1 January 1894.

Section 11: condition treated as warranty

2. In relation to a contract made before 22 April 1967 or (in the application of this Act to Northern Ireland) 28 July 1967, in section 11(4) after "or part of them," insert "or where the contract is for specific goods, the property in which has passed to the buyer,".

Section 12: implied terms about title, etc

3. In relation to a contract made before 18 May 1973 substitute the following for section 12:—

12. Implied terms about title, etc
In a contract of sale, unless the circumstances of the contract are such as to show a different intention, there is—

    (a) an implied condition on the part of the seller that in the case of a sale he has a right to sell the goods, and in the case of an agreement to sell he will have such a right at the time when the property is to pass;

    (b) an implied warranty that the buyer will have and enjoy quiet possession of the goods;

    (c) an implied warranty that the goods will be free from any charge or encumbrance in favour of any third party, not declared or known to the buyer before or at the time when the contract is made.

Section 13: sale by description

4. In relation to a contract made before 18 May 1973, omit section 13(3).

Section 14: quality or fitness (i)

5. In relation to a contract made on or after 18 May 1973 and before the appointed day, substitute the following for section 14:—

14. Implied terms about quality or fitness

(1) Except as provided by this section and section 15 below and subject to any other enactment, there is no implied condition or warranty about the quality or fitness for any particular purpose of goods supplied under a contract of sale.

(2) Where the seller sells goods in the course of a business, there is an implied condition that the goods supplied under the contract are of merchantable quality, except that there is no such condition—

    (a) as regards defects, specifically drawn to the buyer's attention before the contract is made; or

    (b) if the buyer examines the goods before the contract is made, as regards defects which that examination ought to reveal.

(3) Where the seller sells goods in the course of a business and the buyer, expressly or by implication, makes known to the seller any particular purpose for which the goods are being bought, there is an implied condition that the goods supplied under the contract are reasonably fit for that purpose, whether or not that is a purpose for which such goods are commonly supplied, except where the circumstances show that the buyer does not rely, or that it is unreasonable for him to rely, on the seller's skill or judgment.

(4) An implied condition or warranty about quality or fitness for a particular purpose may be annexed to a contract of sale by usage.

(5) The preceding provisions of this section apply to a sale by a person who in the course of a business is acting as agent for another as they apply to a sale by a principal in the course of a business, except where that other is not selling in the course of a business and either the buyer knows that fact or reasonable steps are taken to bring it to the notice of the buyer before the contract is made.

(6) Goods of any kind are of merchantable quality within the meaning of subsection (2) above if they are as fit for the purpose or purposes for which goods of that kind are commonly bought as it is reasonable to expect having regard to any description applied to them, the price (if relevant) and all the other relevant circumstances.

(7) In the application of subsection (3) above to an agreement for the sale of goods under which the purchase price or part of it is payable by instalments any reference to the seller includes a reference to the person by whom any antecedent negotiations are conducted; and section 58(3) and (5) of the Hire-Purchase Act 1965, section 54(3) and (5) of the Hire-Purchase (Scotland) Act 1965 and section 65(3) and (5) of the Hire-Purchase Act (Northern Ireland) 1966 (meaning of antecedent negotiations and related expressions) apply in relation to this subsection as in relation to each of those Acts, but as if a reference to any such agreement were included in the references in subsection (3) of each of those sections to the agreements there mentioned.

Section 14: quality or fitness (ii)

6. In relation to a contract made before 18 May 1973 substitute the following for section 14:—

14. Implied terms about quality or fitness
(1) Subject to this and any other Act, there is no implied condition or warranty about the quality or fitness for any particular purpose of goods supplied under a contract of sale.

(2) Where the buyer, expressly or by implication, makes known to the seller the particular purpose for which the goods are required, so as to show that the buyer relies on the seller's skill or judgment, and the goods are of a description which it is in the course of the seller's business to supply (whether he is the manufacturer or not), there is an implied condition that the goods will be reasonably fit for such purpose, except that in the case of a contract for the sale of a specified article under its patent or other trade name there is no implied condition as to its fitness for any particular purpose.

(3) Where goods are bought by description from a seller who deals in goods of that description (whether he is the manufacturer or not), there is an implied condition that the goods will be of merchantable quality; but if the buyer has examined the goods, there is no implied condition as regards defects which such examination ought to have revealed.

(4) An implied condition or warranty about quality or fitness for a particular purpose may be annexed by the usage of trade.

(5) An express condition or warranty does not negative a condition or warranty implied by this Act unless inconsistent with it.

Section 15: sale by sample

7. In relation to a contract made before 18 May 1973, omit section 15(3).

Section 22: market overt

8. In relation to a contract under which goods were sold before 1 January 1968 or (in the application of this Act to Northern Ireland) 29 August 1967, add the following paragraph at the end of section 22(1):—
"Nothing in this subsection affects the law relating to the sale of horses."

Section 25: buyer in possession

9. In relation to a contract under which a person buys or agrees to buy goods and which is made before the appointed day, omit section 25(2).

Section 35: acceptance

10. In relation to a contract made before 22 April 1967 or (in the application of this Act to Northern Ireland) 28 July 1967, in section 35(1) omit "(except where section 34 above otherwise provides)".

Section 55: exclusion of implied terms (i)

11. In relation to a contract made on or after 18 May 1973 and before 1 February 1978 substitute the following for section 55:—

55. Exclusion of implied terms
(1) Where a right, duty or liability would arise under a contract of sale of goods by implication of law, it may be negatived or varied by express agreement, or by the course of dealing between the parties, or by such usage as binds both parties to the contract, but the preceding provision has effect subject to the following provisions of this section.

(2) An express condition or warranty does not negative a condition or warranty implied by this Act unless inconsistent with it.

(3) In the case of a contract of sale of goods, any term of that or any other contract exempting from all or any of the provisions of section 12 above is void.

(4) In the case of a contract of sale of goods, any term of that or any other contract exempting from all or any of the provisions of section 13, 14 or 15 above is void in the case of a consumer sale and is, in any other case, not enforceable to the extent that it is shown that it would not be fair or reasonable to allow reliance on the term.

(5) In determining for the purposes of subsection (4) above whether or not reliance on any such term would be fair or reasonable regard shall be had to all the circumstances of the case and in particular to the following matters—

    (*a*) the strength of the bargaining positions of the seller and buyer relative to each other, taking into account, among other things, the availability of suitable alternative products and sources of supply;

    (*b*) whether the buyer received an inducement to agree to the term or in accepting it had an opportunity of buying the goods or suitable alternatives without it from any source of supply;

    (*c*) whether the buyer knew or ought reasonably to have known of the existence and extent of the term (having regard, among other things, to any custom of the trade and any previous course of dealing between the parties);

    (*d*) where the term exempts from all or any of the provisions of section 13, 14 or 15 above if some condition is not complied with, whether it was reasonable at the time of the contract to expect that compliance with that condition would be practicable;

    (*e*) whether the goods were manufactured, processed, or adapted to the special order of the buyer.

(6) Subsection (5) above does not prevent the court from holding, in accordance with any rule of law, that a term which purports to exclude or restrict any of the provisions of section 13, 14 or 15 above is not a term of the contract.

(7) In this section "consumer sale" means a sale of goods (other than a sale by auction or by competitive tender) by a seller in the course of a business where the goods—

    (*a*) are of a type ordinarily bought for private use or consumption; and

    (*b*) are sold to a person who does not buy or hold himself out as buying them in the course of a business.

(8) The onus of proving that a sale falls to be treated for the purposes of this section as not being a consumer sale lies on the party so contending.

(9) Any reference in this section to a term exempting from all or any of the provisions of any section of this Act is a reference to a term which purports to exclude or restrict, or has the effect of excluding or restricting, the operation of all or any of the provisions of that section, or the exercise of a right conferred by any provision of that section, or any liability of the seller for breach of a condition or warranty implied by any provision of that section.

(10) It is hereby declared that any reference in this section to a term of a contract includes a reference to a term which although not contained in a contract is incorporated in the contract by another term of the contract.

(11) Nothing in this section prevents the parties to a contract for the international sale of goods from negativing or varying any right, duty or liability which would otherwise arise by implication of law under sections 12 to 15 above.

(12) In subsection (11) above "contract for the international sale of goods" means a contract of sale of goods made by parties whose places of business (or, if they have none, habitual residences) are in the territories of different States (the Channel Islands and the Isle of Man being treated for this purpose as different States from the United Kingdom) and in the case of which one of the following conditions is satisfied:—

    (*a*) the contract involves the sale of goods which are at the time of the conclusion of the contract in the course of carriage or will be carried from the territory of one State to the territory of another; or

    (*b*) the acts constituting the offer and acceptance have been effected in the territories of different States; or

(c) delivery of the goods is to be made in the territory of a State other than that within whose territory the acts constituting the offer and the acceptance have been effected.

Section 55: exclusion of implied terms (ii)

12. In relation to a contract made before 18 May 1973 substitute the following for section 55:—

55. Exclusion of implied terms
Where a right, duty or liability would arise under a contract of sale by implication of law, it may be negatived or varied by express agreement, or by the course of dealing between the parties, or by such usage as binds both parties to the contract.

Section 56: conflict of laws

13.—(1) In relation to a contract on or after 18 May 1973 and before 1 February 1978 substitute for section 56 the section set out in sub-paragraph (3) below.

(2) In relation to a contract made otherwise than as mentioned in sub-paragraph (1) above, ignore section 56 and this paragraph.

(3) The section mentioned in sub-paragraph (1) above is as follows:—

56. Conflict of laws
(1) Where the proper law of a contract for the sale of goods would, apart from a term that it should be the law of some other country or a term to the like effect, be the law of any part of the United Kingdom, or where any such contract contains a term which purports to substitute, or has the effect of substituting, provisions of the law of some other country for all or any of the provisions of sections 12 to 15 and 55 above, those sections shall, notwithstanding that term but subject to subsection (2) below, apply to the contract.

(2) Nothing in subsection (1) above prevents the parties to a contract for the international sale of goods from negativing or varying any right, duty or liability which would otherwise arise by implication of law under sections 12 to 15 above.

(3) In subsection (2) above "contract for the international sale of goods" means a contract of sale of goods made by parties whose places of business (or, if they have none, habitual residences) are in the territories of different States (the Channel Islands and the Isle of Man being treated for this purpose as different States from the United Kingdom) and in the case of which one of the following conditions is satisfied:—

(a) the contract involves the sale of goods which are at the time of the conclusion of the contract in the course of carriage or will be carried from the territory of one State to the territory of another; or
(b) the acts constituting the offer and acceptance have been effected in the territories of different States; or
(c) delivery of the goods is to be made in the territory of a State other than that within whose territory the acts constituting the offer and the acceptance have been effected.

Section 61(1): definition of "business" (i)

14. In relation to a contract made on or after 18 May 1973 and before 1 February 1978, in the definition of "business" in section 61(1) for "or local or public authority" substitute "local authority or statutory undertaker".

Section 61(1): definition of "business" (ii)

15. In relation to a contract made before 18 May 1973 omit the definition of "business" in section 61(1). **[148]**

NOTES
Commencement: 1 January 1980.

Paras 2, 3, 5, 6, 8, 11–14 derived from the Sales of Goods Act 1893, ss 11–14, 22, 55, 56, 62. Sch 2 (consequential amendments) and Sch 3 (repeals) are omitted.

SCHEDULE 4

Section 63

SAVINGS

Preliminary

1. In this Schedule references to the 1893 Act are to the Sale of Goods Act 1893.

Orders

2. An order under section 14 (8) or 25 (4) above may make provision that it is to have effect only as provided by the order (being provision corresponding to that which could, apart from this Act, have been made by an order under section 192 (4) of the Consumer Credit Act 1974 bringing into operation an amendment or repeal making a change corresponding to that made by the order under section 14 (8) or 25 (4) above).

Offences

3. Where an offence was committed in relation to goods before 1 January 1969 or (in the application of this Act to Northern Ireland) 1 August 1969, the effect of a conviction in respect of the offence is not affected by the repeal by this Act of section 24 of the 1893 Act.

1893 Act, section 26

4. The repeal by this Act of provisions of the 1893 Act does not extend to the following provisions of that Act in so far as they are needed to give effect to or interpret section 26 of that Act, namely, the definitions of "goods" and "property" in section 62 (1), section 62 (2) and section 63 (which was repealed subject to savings by the Statute Law Revision Act 1908).

Things done before 1 January 1894

5. The repeal by this Act of section 60 of and the Schedule to the 1893 Act (which effected repeals and which were themselves repealed subject to savings by the Statute Law Revision Act 1908) does not affect those savings, and accordingly does not affect things done or acquired before 1 January 1894.

6. In so far as the 1893 Act applied (immediately before the operation of the repeals made by this Act) to contracts made before 1 January 1894 (when the 1893 Act came into operation), the 1893 Act shall continue so to apply notwithstanding this Act. **[149]**

NOTES
Commencement: 1 January 1980.
Ss 24, 26, 60, 62(1), (2), 63, Schedule of the 1893 Act: ie Sale of Goods Act 1893.

SUPPLY OF GOODS AND SERVICES ACT 1982
(c 29)

ARRANGEMENT OF SECTIONS

PART I

SUPPLY OF GOODS

Contracts for the transfer of property in goods

Section	Para
1 The contracts concerned	[150]

Section		Para
2	Implied terms about title, etc	[151]
3	Implied terms where transfer is by description	[152]
4	Implied terms about quality or fitness	[153]
5	Implied terms where transfer is by sample	[154]

Contracts for the hire of goods

6	The contracts concerned	[155]
7	Implied terms about right to transfer possession, etc	[156]
8	Implied terms where hire is by description	[157]
9	Implied terms about quality or fitness	[158]
10	Implied terms where hire is by sample	[159]

Exclusion of implied terms, etc

11	Exclusion of implied terms, etc	[160]

PART II

SUPPLY OF SERVICES

12	The contracts concerned	[161]
13	Implied term about care and skill	[162]
14	Implied term about time for performance	[163]
15	Implied term about consideration	[164]
16	Exclusion of implied terms, etc	[165]

PART III

SUPPLEMENTARY

17	Minor and consequential amendments	[166]
18	Interpretation: general	[167]
19	Interpretation: references to Acts	[168]
20	Citation, transitional provisions, commencement and extent	[169–70]

An Act to amend the law with respect to the terms to be implied in certain contracts for the transfer of the property in goods, in certain contracts for the hire of goods and in certain contracts for the supply of a service; and for connected purposes. [13 July 1982]

PART I

SUPPLY OF GOODS

Contracts for the transfer of property in goods

1. The contracts concerned

(1) In this Act a "contract for the transfer of goods" means a contract under which one person transfers or agrees to transfer to another the property in goods, other than an excepted contract.

(2) For the purposes of this section an excepted contract means any of the following:—

    (*a*) a contract of sale of goods;
    (*b*) a hire-purchase agreement;
    (*c*) a contract under which the property in goods is (or is to be) transferred in exchange for trading stamps on their redemption;

(d) a transfer or agreement to transfer which is made by deed and for which there is no consideration other than the presumed consideration imported by the deed;

(e) a contract intended to operate by way of mortgage, pledge, charge or other security.

(3) For the purposes of this Act a contract is a contract for the transfer of goods whether or not services are also provided or to be provided under the contract, and (subject to subsection (2) above) whatever is the nature of the consideration for the transfer or agreement to transfer. **[150]**

NOTES
Commencement: 4 January 1983.

2. Implied terms about title, etc

(1) In a contract for the transfer of goods, other than one to which subsection (3) below applies, there is an implied condition on the part of the transferor that in the case of a transfer of the property in the goods he has a right to transfer the property and in the case of an agreement to transfer the property in the goods he will have such a right at the time when the property is to be transferred.

(2) In a contract for the transfer of goods, other than one to which subsection (3) below applies, there is also an implied warranty that—

(a) the goods are free, and will remain free until the time when the property is to be transferred, from any charge or encumbrance not disclosed or known to the transferee before the contract is made, and

(b) the transferee will enjoy quiet possession of the goods except so far as it may be disturbed by the owner or other person entitled to the benefit of any charge or encumbrance so disclosed or known.

(3) This subsection applies to a contract for the transfer of goods in the case of which there appears from the contract or is to be inferred from its circumstances an intention that the transferor should transfer only such title as he or a third person may have.

(4) In a contract to which subsection (3) above applies there is an implied warranty that all charges or encumbrances known to the transferor and not known to the transferee have been disclosed to the transferee before the contract is made.

(5) In a contract to which subsection (3) above applies there is also an implied warranty that none of the following will disturb the transferee's quiet possession of the goods, namely—

(a) the transferor;

(b) in a case where the parties to the contract intend that the transferor should transfer only such title as a third person may have, that person;

(c) anyone claiming through or under the transferor or that third person otherwise than under a charge or encumbrance disclosed or known to the transferee before the contract is made. **[151]**

NOTES
Commencement: 4 January 1983.

3. Implied terms where transfer is by description

(1) This section applies where, under a contract for the transfer of goods, the transferor transfers or agrees to transfer the property in the goods by description.

(2) In such a case there is an implied condition that the goods will correspond with the description.

(3) If the transferor transfers or agrees to transfer the property in the goods by sample as well as by description it is not sufficient that the bulk of the goods corresponds with the sample if the goods do not also correspond with the description.

(4) A contract is not prevented from falling within subsection (1) above by reason only that, being exposed for supply, the goods are selected by the transferee. **[152]**

NOTES
Commencement: 4 January 1983.

4. Implied terms about quality or fitness

(1) Except as provided by this section and section 5 below and subject to the provisions of any other enactment, there is no implied condition or warranty about the quality or fitness for any particular purpose of goods supplied under a contract for the transfer of goods.

(2) Where, under such a contract, the transferor transfers the property in goods in the course of a business, there is (subject to subsection (3) below) an implied condition that the goods supplied under the contract are of merchantable quality.

(3) There is no such condition as is mentioned in subsection (2) above—
  (a) as regards defects specifically drawn to the transferee's attention before the contract is made; or
  (b) if the transferee examines the goods before the contract is made, as regards defects which that examination ought to reveal.

(4) Subsection (5) below applies where, under a contract for the transfer of goods, the transferor transfers the property in goods in the course of a business and the transferee, expressly or by implication, makes known—
  (a) to the transferor, or
  (b) where the consideration or part of the consideration for the transfer is a sum payable by instalments and the goods were previously sold by a credit-broker to the transferor, to that credit-broker,
any particular purpose for which the goods are being acquired.

(5) In that case there is (subject to subsection (6) below) an implied condition that the goods supplied under the contract are reasonably fit for that purpose, whether or not that is a purpose for which such goods are commonly supplied.

(6) Subsection (5) above does not apply where the circumstances show that the transferee does not rely, or that it is unreasonable for him to rely, on the skill or judgment of the transferor or credit-broker.

(7) An implied condition or warranty about quality or fitness for a particular purpose may be annexed by usage to a contract for the transfer of goods.

(8) The preceding provisions of this section apply to a transfer by a person who in the course of a business is acting as agent for another as they apply to a transfer by a principal in the course of a business, except where that other is not transferring in the course of a business and either the transferee knows that fact

or reasonable steps are taken to bring it to the transferee's notice before the contract concerned is made.

(9) Goods of any kind are of merchantable quality within the meaning of subsection (2) above if they are as fit for the purpose or purposes for which goods of that kind are commonly supplied as it is reasonable to expect having regard to any description applied to them, the price (if relevant) and all the other relevant circumstances. [153]

NOTES
Commencement: 4 January 1983.

5. Implied terms where transfer is by sample

(1) This section applies where, under a contract for the transfer of goods, the transferor transfers or agrees to transfer the property in the goods by reference to a sample.

(2) In such a case there is an implied condition—
   (a) that the bulk will correspond with the sample in quality; and
   (b) that the transferee will have a reasonable opportunity of comparing the bulk with the sample; and
   (c) that the goods will be free from any defect, rendering them unmerchantable, which would not be apparent on reasonable examination of the sample.

(3) In subsection (2)(c) above "unmerchantable" is to be construed in accordance with section 4(9) above.

(4) For the purposes of this section a transferor transfers or agrees to transfer the property in goods by reference to a sample where there is an express or implied term to that effect in the contract concerned. [154]

NOTES
Commencement: 4 January 1983.

Contracts for the hire of goods

6. The contracts concerned

(1) In this Act a "contract for the hire of goods" means a contract under which one person bails or agrees to bail goods to another by way of hire, other than an excepted contract.

(2) For the purposes of this section an excepted contract means any of the following:—
   (a) a hire-purchase agreement;
   (b) a contract under which goods are (or are to be) bailed in exchange for trading stamps on their redemption.

(3) For the purposes of this Act a contract is a contract for the hire of goods whether or not services are also provided or to be provided under the contract, and (subject to subsection (2) above) whatever is the nature of the consideration for the bailment or agreement to bail by way of hire. [155]

NOTES
Commencement: 4 January 1983.

7. Implied terms about right to transfer possession, etc

(1) In a contract for the hire of goods there is an implied condition on the part of the bailor that in the case of a bailment he has a right to transfer possession of the goods by way of hire for the period of the bailment and in the case of an agreement to bail he will have such a right at the time of the bailment.

(2) In a contract for the hire of goods there is also an implied warranty that the bailee will enjoy quiet possession of the goods for the period of the bailment except so far as the possession may be disturbed by the owner or other person entitled to the benefit of any charge or encumbrance disclosed or known to the bailee before the contract is made.

(3) The preceding provisions of this section do not affect the right of the bailor to repossess the goods under an express or implied term of the contract.

[156]

NOTES
Commencement: 4 January 1983.

8. Implied terms where hire is by description

(1) This section applies where, under a contract for the hire of goods, the bailor bails or agrees to bail the goods by description.

(2) In such a case there is an implied condition that the goods will correspond with the description.

(3) If under the contract the bailor bails or agrees to bail the goods by reference to a sample as well as a description it is not sufficient that the bulk of the goods corresponds with the sample if the goods do not also correspond with the description.

(4) A contract is not prevented from falling within subsection (1) above by reason only that, being exposed for supply, the goods are selected by the bailee.

[157]

NOTES
Commencement: 4 January 1983.

9. Implied terms about quality or fitness

(1) Except as provided by this section and section 10 below and subject to the provisions of any other enactment, there is no implied condition or warranty about the quality or fitness for any particular purpose of goods bailed under a contract for the hire of goods.

(2) Where, under such a contract, the bailor bails goods in the course of a business, there is (subject to subsection (3) below) an implied condition that the goods supplied under the contract are of merchantable quality.

(3) There is no such condition as is mentioned in subsection (2) above—
    (*a*) as regards defects specifically drawn to the bailee's attention before the contract is made; or
    (*b*) if the bailee examines the goods before the contract is made, as regards defects which that examination ought to reveal.

(4) Subsection (5) below applies where, under a contract for the hire of goods, the bailor bails goods in the course of a business and the bailee, expressly or by implication, makes known—

(a) to the bailor in the course of negotiations conducted by him in relation to the making of the contract, or
(b) to a credit-broker in the course of negotiations conducted by that broker in relation to goods sold by him to the bailor before forming the subject matter of the contract,

any particular purpose for which the goods are being bailed.

(5) In that case there is (subject to subsection (6) below) an implied condition that the goods supplied under the contract are reasonably fit for that purpose, whether or not that is a purpose for which such goods are commonly supplied.

(6) Subsection (5) above does not apply where the circumstances show that the bailee does not rely, or that it is unreasonable for him to rely, on the skill or judgment of the bailor or credit-broker.

(7) An implied condition or warranty about quality or fitness for a particular purpose may be annexed by usage to a contract for the hire of goods.

(8) The preceding provisions of this section apply to a bailment by a person who in the course of a business is acting as agent for another as they apply to a bailment by a principal in the course of a business, except where that other is not bailing in the course of a business and either the bailee knows that fact or reasonable steps are taken to bring it to the bailee's notice before the contract concerned is made.

(9) Goods of any kind are of merchantable quality within the meaning of subsection (2) above if they are as fit for the purpose or purposes for which goods of that kind are commonly supplied as it is reasonable to expect having regard to any description applied to them, the consideration for the bailment (if relevant) and all the other relevant circumstances. **[158]**

NOTES
Commencement: 4 January 1983.

10. Implied terms where hire is by sample

(1) This section applies where, under a contract for the hire of goods, the bailor bails or agrees to bail the goods by reference to a sample.

(2) In such a case there is an implied condition—
(a) that the bulk will correspond with the sample in quality; and
(b) that the bailee will have a reasonable opportunity of comparing the bulk with the sample; and
(c) that the goods will be free from any defect, rendering them unmerchantable, which would not be apparent on reasonable examination of the sample.

(3) In subsection (2)(c) above "unmerchantable" is to be construed in accordance with section 9(9) above.

(4) For the purposes of this section a bailor bails or agrees to bail goods by reference to a sample where there is an express or implied term to that effect in the contract concerned. **[159]**

NOTES
Commencement: 4 January 1983.

Exclusion of implied terms, etc

11. Exclusion of implied terms, etc

(1) Where a right, duty or liability would arise under a contract for the transfer of goods or a contract for the hire of goods by implication of law, it may (subject to subsection (2) below and the 1977 Act) be negatived or varied by express agreement, or by the course of dealing between the parties, or by such usage as binds both parties to the contract.

(2) An express condition or warranty does not negative a condition or warranty implied by the preceding provisions of this Act unless inconsistent with it.

(3) Nothing in the preceding provisions of this Act prejudices the operation of any other enactment or any rule of law whereby any condition or warranty (other than one relating to quality or fitness) is to be implied in a contract for the transfer of goods or a contract for the hire of goods. [160]

NOTES
Commencement: 4 January 1983.
1977 Act: the Unfair Contract Terms Act 1977.

PART II
SUPPLY OF SERVICES

12. The contracts concerned

(1) In this Act a "contract for the supply of a service" means, subject to subsection (2) below, a contract under which a person ("the supplier") agrees to carry out a service.

(2) For the purposes of this Act, a contract of service or apprenticeship is not a contract for the supply of a service.

(3) Subject to subsection (2) above, a contract is a contract for the supply of a service for the purposes of this Act whether or not goods are also—
  (a) transferred or to be transferred, or
  (b) bailed or to be bailed by way of hire,
under the contract, and whatever is the nature of the consideration for which the service is to be carried out.

(4) The Secretary of State may by order provide that one or more of sections 13 to 15 below shall not apply to services of a description specified in the order, and such an order may make different provision for different circumstances.

(5) The power to make an order under subsection (4) above shall be exercisable by statutory instrument subject to annulment in pursuance of a resolution of either House of Parliament. [161]

NOTES
Commencement: 4 July 1983.
Commencement order: SI 1982 No 1770.

13. Implied term about care and skill

In a contract for the supply of a service where the supplier is acting in the course of a business, there is an implied term that the supplier will carry out the service with reasonable care and skill. **[162]**

NOTES
Commencement: 4 July 1983.
Commencement order: SI 1982 No 1770.

14. Implied term about time for performance

(1) Where, under a contract for the supply of a service by a supplier acting in the course of a business, the time for the service to be carried out is not fixed by the contract, left to be fixed in a manner agreed by the contract or determined by the course of dealing between the parties, there is an implied term that the supplier will carry out the service within a reasonable time.

(2) What is a reasonable time is a question of fact. **[163]**

NOTES
Commencement: 4 July 1983.
Commencement order: SI 1982 No 1770.

15. Implied term about consideration

(1) Where, under a contract for the supply of a service, the consideration for the service is not determined by the contract, left to be determined in a manner agreed by the contract or determined by the course of dealing between the parties, there is an implied term that the party contracting with the supplier will pay a reasonable charge.

(2) What is a reasonable charge is a question of fact. **[164]**

NOTES
Commencement: 4 July 1983.
Commencement order: SI 1982 No 1770.

16. Exclusion of implied terms, etc

(1) Where a right, duty or liability would arise under a contract for the supply of a service by virtue of this Part of this Act, it may (subject to subsection (2) below and the 1977 Act) be negatived or varied by express agreement, or by the course of dealing between the parties, or by such usage as binds both parties to the contract.

(2) An express term does not negative a term implied by this Part of this Act unless inconsistent with it.

(3) Nothing in this Part of this Act prejudices—
  (a) any rule of law which imposes on the supplier a duty stricter than that imposed by section 13 or 14 above; or
  (b) subject to paragraph (a) above, any rule of law whereby any term not inconsistent with this Part of this Act is to be implied in a contract for the supply of a service.

(4) This Part of this Act has effect subject to any other enactment which defines or restricts the rights, duties or liabilities arising in connection with a service of any description. **[165]**

NOTES
Commencement: 4 July 1983.
Commencement order: SI 1982 No 1770.
1977 Act: the Unfair Contract Terms Act 1977.

PART III

SUPPLEMENTARY

17. Minor and consequential amendments

...   [166]

NOTES
Commencement: 4 January 1983.
Sub-s (1): amends the Supply of Goods (Implied Terms) Act 1973, s 10(2).
Sub-ss (2), (3): amend the Unfair Contract Terms Act 1977, s 7. The amendments are incorporated in the text of these Acts.

18. Interpretation: general

(1) In the preceding provisions of this Act and this section—

"bailee", in relation to a contract for the hire of goods means (depending on the context) a person to whom the goods are bailed under the contract, or a person to whom they are to be so bailed, or a person to whom the rights under the contract of either of those persons have passed;

"bailor", in relation to a contract for the hire of goods, means (depending on the context) a person who bails the goods under the contract, or a person who agrees to do so, or a person to whom the duties under the contract of either of those persons have passed;

"business" includes a profession and the activities of any government department or local or public authority;

"credit-broker" means a person acting in the course of a business of credit brokerage carried on by him;

"credit brokerage" means the effecting of introductions—

    (a) of individuals desiring to obtain credit to persons carrying on any business so far as it relates to the provision of credit; or

    (b) of individuals desiring to obtain goods on hire to persons carrying on a business which comprises or relates to the bailment of goods under a contract for the hire of goods; or

    (c) of individuals desiring to obtain credit, or to obtain goods on hire, to other credit-brokers;

"enactment" means any legislation (including subordinate legislation) of the United Kingdom or Northern Ireland;

"goods" include all personal chattels (including emblements, industrial growing crops, and things attached to or forming part of the land which are agreed to be severed before the transfer or bailment concerned or under the contract concerned), other than things in action and money;

"hire-purchase agreement" has the same meaning as in the 1974 Act;

"property", in relation to goods, means the general property in them and not merely a special property;

"quality", in relation to goods, includes their state or condition;

"redemption", in relation to trading stamps, has the same meaning as in the Trading Stamps Act 1964 or, as respects Northern Ireland, the Trading Stamps Act (Northern Ireland) 1965;
"trading stamps" has the same meaning as in the said Act of 1964 or, as respects Northern Ireland, the said Act of 1965;
"transferee", in relation to a contract for the transfer of goods, means (depending on the context) a person to whom the property in the goods is transferred under the contract, or a person to whom the property is to be so transferred, or a person to whom the rights under the contract of either of those persons have passed;
"transferor", in relation to a contract for the transfer of goods, means (depending on the context) a person who transfers the property in the goods under the contract, or a person who agrees to do so, or a person to whom the duties under the contract of either of those persons have passed.

(2) In subsection (1) above, in the definitions of bailee, bailor, transferee and transferor, a reference to rights or duties passing is to their passing by assignment, operation of law or otherwise. [167]

NOTES
Commencement: 4 January 1983 (so far as it relates to Part I); 4 July 1983 (so far as it relates to Part II).
Commencement order: SI 1982 No 1770.

19. Interpretation: references to Acts

In this Act—
"the 1973 Act" means the Supply of Goods (Implied Terms) Act 1973;
"the 1974 Act" means the Consumer Credit Act 1974;
"the 1977 Act" means the Unfair Contract Terms Act 1977; and
"the 1979 Act" means the Sale of Goods Act 1979. [168]

NOTES
Commencement: 4 January 1983 (so far as it relates to Part I); 4 July 1983 (so far as it relates to Part II).
Commencement order: SI 1982 No 1770.

20. Citation, transitional provisions, commencement and extent

(1) This Act may be cited as the Supply of Goods and Services Act 1982.

(2) The transitional provisions in the Schedule to this Act shall have effect.

(3) Part I of this Act together with section 17 and so much of sections 18 and 19 above as relates to that Part shall not come into operation until 4 January 1983; and Part II of this Act together with so much of sections 18 and 19 above as relates to that Part shall not come into operation until such day as may be appointed by an order made by the Secretary of State.

(4) The power to make an order under subsection (3) above shall be exercisable by statutory instrument.

(5) No provision of this Act applies to a contract made before the provision comes into operation.

(6) This Act extends to Northern Ireland but not to Scotland. [169–170]

NOTES
Commencement: 13 July 1982.

SECTION II
CONSUMER CREDIT

CONSUMER CREDIT ACT 1974
(c 39)

ARRANGEMENT OF SECTIONS

Part I
Director General of Fair Trading

Section		Para
1	General functions of Director	[171]
2	Powers of Secretary of State	[172]
4	Dissemination of information and advice	[173]
6	Form etc of applications	[174]
7	Penalty for false information	[175]

Part II
Credit Agreements, Hire Agreements and Linked Transactions

8	Consumer credit agreements	[176]
9	Meaning of credit	[177]
10	Running-account credit and fixed-sum credit	[178]
11	Restricted-use credit and unrestricted-use credit	[179]
12	Debtor-creditor-supplier agreements	[180]
13	Debtor-creditor agreements	[181]
14	Credit-token agreements	[182]
15	Consumer hire agreements	[183]
16	Exempt agreements	[184]
17	Small agreements	[185]
18	Multiple agreements	[186]
19	Linked transactions	[187]
20	Total charge for credit	[188]

Part III
Licensing of Credit and Hire Businesses

Licensing principles

21	Businesses needing a licence	[189]
22	Standard and group licences	[190]
23	Authorisation of specific activities	[191]
24	Control of name of business	[192]
25	Licensee to be a fit person	[193]
26	Conduct of business	[194]

Issue of licences

27	Determination of applications	[195]
28	Exclusion from group licence	[196]

Renewal, variation, suspension and revocation of licences

29	Renewal	[197]
30	Variation by request	[198]
31	Compulsory variation	[199]
32	Suspension and revocation	[200]
33	Application to end suspension	[201]

Miscellaneous

34	Representations to Director	[202]
35	The register	[203]
36	Duty to notify changes	[204]
37	Death, bankruptcy etc of licensee	[205]

Section		Para
39	Offences against Part III	[206]
40	Enforcement of agreements made by unlicensed trader	[207]
41	Appeals to Secretary of State under Part III	[208]

Part IV
Seeking Business

Advertising

43	Advertisements to which Part IV applies	[209]
44	Form and content of advertisements	[210]
45	Prohibition of advertisement where goods etc not sold for cash	[211]
46	False or misleading advertisements	[212]
47	Advertising infringements	[213]

Canvassing etc

48	Definition of canvassing off trade premises (regulated agreements)	[214]
49	Prohibition of canvassing debtor-creditor agreements off trade premises	[215]
50	Circulars to minors	[216]
51	Prohibition of unsolicited credit-tokens	[217]

Miscellaneous

52	Quotations	[218]
53	Duty to display information	[219]
54	Conduct of business regulations	[220]

Part V
Entry into Credit or Hire Agreements

Preliminary matters

55	Disclosure of information	[221]
56	Antecedent negotiations	[222]
57	Withdrawal from prospective agreement	[223]
58	Opportunity for withdrawal from prospective land mortgage	[224]
59	Agreement to enter future agreement void	[225]

Making the agreement

60	Form and content of agreements	[226]
61	Signing of agreement	[227]
62	Duty to supply copy of unexecuted agreement	[228]
63	Duty to supply copy of executed agreement	[229]
64	Duty to give notice of cancellation rights	[230]
65	Consequences of improper execution	[231]
66	Acceptance of credit-tokens	[232]

Cancellation of certain agreements within cooling-off period

67	Cancellable agreements	[233]
68	Cooling-off period	[234]
69	Notice of cancellation	[235]
70	Cancellation: recovery of money paid by debtor or hirer	[236]
71	Cancellation: repayment of credit	[237]
72	Cancellation: return of goods	[238]
73	Cancellation: goods given in part-exchange	[239]

Exclusion of certain agreements from Part V

74	Exclusion of certain agreements from Part V	[240]

Section		Para

Part VI
Matters Arising During Currency of Credit or Hire Agreements

75	Liability of creditor for breaches by supplier	[241]
76	Duty to give notice before taking certain action	[242]
77	Duty to give information to debtor under fixed-sum credit agreement	[243]
78	Duty to give information to debtor under running-account credit agreement	[244]
79	Duty to give hirer information	[245]
80	Debtor or hirer to give information about goods	[246]
81	Appropriation of payments	[247]
82	Variation of agreements	[248]
83	Liability for misuse of credit facilities	[249]
84	Misuse of credit-tokens	[250]
85	Duty on issue of new credit-tokens	[251]
86	Death of debtor or hirer	[252]

Part VII
Default and Termination

Default notices

87	Need for default notice	[253]
88	Contents and effect of default notice	[254]
89	Compliance with default notice	[255]

Further restriction of remedies for default

90	Retaking of protected hire-purchase etc goods	[256]
91	Consequences of breach of s 90	[257]
92	Recovery of possession of goods or land	[258]
93	Interest not to be increased on default	[259]

Early payment by debtor

94	Right to complete payments ahead of time	[260]
95	Rebate on early settlement	[261]
96	Effect on linked transactions	[262]
97	Duty to give information	[263]

Termination of agreements

98	Duty to give notice of termination (non-default cases)	[264]
99	Right to terminate hire-purchase etc agreements	[265]
100	Liability of debtor on termination of hire-purchase etc agreement	[266]
101	Right to terminate hire agreement	[267]
102	Agency for receiving notice of rescission	[268]
103	Termination statements	[269]

Part VIII
Security

General

105	Form and content of securities	[270]
106	Ineffective securities	[271]
107	Duty to give information to surety under fixed-sum credit agreement	[272]
108	Duty to give information to surety under running-account credit agreement	[273]
109	Duty to give information to surety under consumer hire agreement	[274]
110	Duty to give information to debtor or hirer	[275]
111	Duty to give surety copy of default etc notice	[276]
112	Realisation of securities	[277]
113	Act not to be evaded by use of security	[278]

Section		Para
	Pledges	
114	Pawn-receipts	[279]
115	Penalty for failure to supply copies of pledge agreement, etc	[280]
116	Redemption period	[281]
117	Redemption procedure	[282]
118	Loss etc of pawn-receipt	[283]
119	Unreasonable refusal to deliver pawn	[284]
120	Consequence of failure to redeem	[285]
121	Realisation of pawn	[286]
	Negotiable instruments	
123	Restrictions on taking and negotiating instruments	[287]
124	Consequences of breach of s 123	[288]
125	Holders in due course	[289]
	Land mortgages	
126	Enforcement of land mortgages	[290]

PART IX

JUDICIAL CONTROL

Enforcement of certain regulated agreements and securities

127	Enforcement orders in cases of infringement	[291]
128	Enforcement orders on death of debtor or hirer	[292]

Extension of time

129	Time orders	[293]
130	Supplemental provisions about time orders	[294]

Protection of property pending proceedings

131	Protection orders	[295]

Hire and hire-purchase etc agreements

132	Financial relief for hirer	[296]
133	Hire-purchase etc agreements: special powers of court	[297]
134	Evidence of adverse detention in hire-purchase etc cases	[298]

Supplemental provisions as to orders

135	Power to impose conditions, or suspend operation of order	[299]
136	Power to vary agreements and securities	[300]

Extortionate credit bargains

137	Extortionate credit bargains	[301]
138	When bargains are extortionate	[302]
139	Reopening of extortionate agreements	[303]
140	Interpretation of sections 137 to 139	[304]

Miscellaneous

141	Jurisdiction and parties	[305]
142	Power to declare rights of parties	[306]

Northern Ireland

143	Jurisdiction of county court in Northern Ireland	[307]
144	Appeal from county court in Northern Ireland	[308]

Section		Para
	PART X	
	ANCILLARY CREDIT BUSINESSES	
	Definitions	
145	Types of ancillary credit business	[309]
146	Exceptions from section 145	[310]
	Licensing	
147	Application of Part III	[311]
148	Agreement for services of unlicensed trader	[312]
149	Regulated agreements made on introductions by unlicensed credit-broker	[313]
150	Appeals to Secretary of State against licensing decisions	[314]
	Seeking business	
151	Advertisements	[315]
152	Application of sections 52 to 54 to credit brokerage etc	[316]
153	Definition of canvassing off trade premises (agreements for ancillary credit services)	[317]
154	Prohibition of canvassing certain ancillary credit services off trade premises	[318]
155	Right to recover brokerage fees	[319]
	Entry into agreements	
156	Entry into agreements	[320]
	Credit reference agencies	
157	Duty to disclose name etc of agency	[321]
158	Duty of agency to disclose filed information	[322]
159	Correction of wrong information	[323]
160	Alternative procedure for business consumers	[324]
	PART XI	
	ENFORCEMENT OF ACT	
161	Enforcement authorities	[325]
162	Powers of entry and inspection	[326]
163	Compensation for loss	[327]
164	Power to make test purchases etc	[328]
165	Obstruction of authorised officers	[329]
166	Notification of convictions and judgments to Director	[330]
167	Penalties	[331]
168	Defences	[332]
169	Offences by bodies corporate	[333]
170	No further sanctions for breach of Act	[334]
171	Onus of proof in various proceedings	[335]
172	Statements by creditor or owner to be binding	[336]
173	Contracting-out forbidden	[337]
	PART XII	
	SUPPLEMENTAL	
	General	
174	Restrictions on disclosure of information	[338]
175	Duty of persons deemed to be agents	[339]
176	Service of documents	[340]
177	Saving for registered charges	[341]
178	Local Acts	[342]
	Regulations, orders, etc	
179	Power to prescribe form etc of secondary documents	[343]
180	Power to prescribe form etc of copies	[344]

Section		Para
181	Power to alter monetary limits etc	[345]
182	Regulations and orders	[346]
183	Determinations etc by Director	[347]

Interpretation

184	Associates	[348]
185	Agreement with more than one debtor or hirer	[349]
186	Agreement with more than one creditor or owner	[350]
187	Arrangements between creditor and supplier	[351]
188	Examples of use of new terminology	[352]
189	Definitions	[353]

Miscellaneous

190	Financial provisions	[354]
191	Special provisions as to Northern Ireland	[355]
192	Transitional and commencement provisions, amendments and repeals	[356]
193	Short title and extent	[357]

SCHEDULES

Schedule 1—Prosecution and Punishment of Offences	[358]
Schedule 2—Examples of Use of New Terminology	
Part I—List of Terms	[359]
Part II—Examples	[360]

An Act to establish for the protection of consumers a new system, administered by the Director General of Fair Trading, of licensing and other control of traders concerned with the provision of credit, or the supply of goods on hire or hire-purchase, and their transactions, in place of the present enactments regulating moneylenders, pawnbrokers and hire-purchase traders and their transactions, and for related matters [31 July 1974]

PART I

DIRECTOR GENERAL OF FAIR TRADING

1. General functions of Director

(1) It is the duty of the Director General of Fair Trading ("the Director")—

    (*a*) to administer the licensing system set up by this Act;

    (*b*) to exercise the adjudicating functions conferred on him by this Act in relation to the issue, renewal, variation, suspension and revocation of licences, and other matters;

    (*c*) generally to superintend the working and enforcement of this Act, and regulations made under it, and

    (*d*) where necessary or expedient, himself to take steps to enforce this Act, and regulations so made.

(2) It is the duty of the Director, so far as appears to him to be practicable and having regard both to the national interest and the interests of persons carrying on businesses to which this Act applies and their customers, to keep under review and from time to time advise the Secretary of State about—

    (*a*) social and commercial developments in the United Kingdom and elsewhere relating to the provision of credit or bailment or (in Scotland) hiring of goods to individuals, and related activities; and

(b) the working and enforcement of this Act and orders and regulations made under it. **[171]**

NOTES
Commencement: 31 July 1974.

2. Powers of Secretary of State

(1) The Secretary of State may by order—
   (a) confer on the Director additional functions concerning the provision of credit or bailment or (in Scotland) hiring of goods to individuals, and related activities, and
   (b) regulate the carrying out by the Director of his functions under this Act.

(2) The Secretary of State may give general directions indicating considerations to which the Director should have particular regard in carrying out his functions under this Act, and may give specific directions on any matter connected with the carrying out by the Director of those functions.

(3) The Secretary of State, on giving any directions under subsection (2), shall arrange for them to be published in such manner as he thinks most suitable for drawing them to the attention of interested persons.

(4) With the approval of the Secretary of State and the Treasury, the Director may charge, for any service or facility provided by him under this Act, a fee of an amount specified by general notice (the "specified fee").

(5) Provision may be made under subsection (4) for reduced fees, or no fees at all, to be paid for certain services or facilities by persons of a specified description, and references in this Act to the specified fee shall, in such cases, be construed accordingly.

(6) An order under subsection (1) (a) shall be made by statutory instrument and shall be of no effect unless a draft of the order has been laid before and approved by each House of Parliament.

(7) References in subsection (2) to the functions of the Director under this Act do not include the making of a determination to which section 41 or 150 (appeals from Director to Secretary of State) applies. **[172]**

NOTES
Commencement: 31 July 1974.

NOTES
Section 3, which amends the Tribunals and Inquiries Act 1971, is omitted.

4. Dissemination of information and advice

The Director shall arrange for the dissemination, in such form and manner as he considers appropriate, of such information and advice as it may appear to him expedient to give to the public in the United Kingdom about the operation of this Act, the credit facilities available to them, and other matters within the scope of his functions under this Act. **[173]**

NOTES
Commencement: 31 July 1974.

NOTES
Section 5, which amends the Fair Trading Act 1973, is omitted.

6. Form etc of applications

(1) An application to the Director under this Act is of no effect unless the requirements of this section are satisfied.

(2) The application must be in writing, and in such form, and accompanied by such particulars, as the Director may specify by general notice, and must be accompanied by the specified fee.

(3) After giving preliminary consideration to an application, the Director may by notice require the applicant to furnish him with such further information relevant to the application as may be described in the notice, and may require any information furnished by the applicant (whether at the time of the application or subsequently) to be verified in such manner as the Director may stipulate.

(4) The Director may by notice require the applicant to publish details of his application at a time or times and in a manner specified in the notice. **[174]**

NOTES
Commencement: 31 July 1974.

7. Penalty for false information

A person who, in connection with any application or request to the Director under this Act, or in response to any invitation or requirement of the Director under this Act, knowingly or recklessly gives information to the Director which, in a material particular, is false or misleading, commits an offence. **[175]**

NOTES
Commencement: 31 July 1974.

PART II

CREDIT AGREEMENTS, HIRE AGREEMENTS AND LINKED TRANSACTIONS

8. Consumer credit agreements

(1) A personal credit agreement is an agreement between an individual ("the debtor") and any other person ("the creditor") by which the creditor provides the debtor with credit of any amount.

(2) A consumer credit agreement is a personal credit agreement by which the creditor provides the debtor with credit not exceeding [£15,000].

(3) A consumer credit agreement is a regulated agreement within the meaning of this Act if it is not an agreement (an "exempt agreement") specified in or under section 16. **[176]**

NOTES
Commencement: 1 April 1977.
Commencement order: SI 1977 No 325, art 2(1), and Sch 3, para 1, to this Act.
Sub-s (2): amended by SI 1983 No 1878, art 4, Schedule, Part II as from 20 May 1985.

9. Meaning of credit

(1) In this Act "credit" includes a cash loan, and any other form of financial accommodation.

(2) Where credit is provided otherwise than in sterling, it shall be treated for the purposes of this Act as provided in sterling of an equivalent amount.

(3) Without prejudice to the generality of subsection (1), the person by whom goods are bailed or (in Scotland) hired to an individual under a hire-purchase agreement shall be taken to provide him with fixed-sum credit to finance the transaction of an amount equal to the total price of the goods less the aggregate of the deposit (if any) and the total charge for credit.

(4) For the purposes of this Act, an item entering into the total charge for credit shall not be treated as credit even though time is allowed for its payment. [177]

NOTES
Commencement: 1 April 1977.
Commencement order: SI 1977 No 325, art 2(1), and Sch 3, para 1, to this Act.

10. Running-account credit and fixed-sum credit

(1) For the purposes of this Act—
  (a) running-account credit is a facility under a personal credit agreement whereby the debtor is enabled to receive from time to time (whether in his own person, or by another person) from the creditor or a third party cash, goods and services (or any of them) to an amount or value such that, taking into account payments made by or to the credit of the debtor, the credit limit (if any) is not at any time exceeded; and
  (b) fixed-sum credit is any other facility under a personal credit agreement whereby the debtor is enabled to receive credit (whether in one amount or by instalments).

(2) In relation to running-account credit, "credit limit" means, as respects any period, the maximum debit balance which, under the credit agreement, is allowed to stand on the account during that period, disregarding any term of the agreement allowing that maximum to be exceeded merely temporarily.

(3) For the purposes of section 8 (2), running-account credit shall be taken not to exceed the amount specified in that subsection ("the specified amount") if—
  (a) the credit limit does not exceed the specified amount; or
  (b) whether or not there is a credit limit, and if there is, notwithstanding that it exceeds the specified amount,—
    (i) the debtor is not enabled to draw at any one time an amount which, so far as (having regard to section 9 (4)) it represents credit, exceeds the specified amount, or
    (ii) the agreement provides that, if the debit balance rises above a given amount (not exceeding the specified amount), the rate of the total charge for credit increases or any other condition favouring the creditor or his associate comes into operation, or
    (iii) at the time the agreement is made it is probable, having regard to the terms of the agreement and any other relevant considerations, that the debit balance will not at any time rise above the specified amount. [178]

NOTES
Commencement: 1 April 1977.
Commencement order: SI 1977 No 325, art 2(1), and Sch 3, para 1, to this Act.

11. Restricted-use credit and unrestricted-use credit

(1) A restricted-use credit agreement is a regulated consumer credit agreement—

  (a) to finance a transaction between the debtor and the creditor, whether forming part of that agreement or not, or
  (b) to finance a transaction between the debtor and a person (the "supplier") other than the creditor, or
  (c) to refinance any existing indebtedness of the debtor's, whether to the creditor or another person,

and "restricted-use credit" shall be construed accordingly.

(2) An unrestricted-use credit agreement is a regulated consumer credit agreement not falling within subsection (1), and "unrestricted-use credit" shall be construed accordingly.

(3) An agreement does not fall within subsection (1) if the credit is in fact provided in such a way as to leave the debtor free to use it as he chooses, even though certain uses would contravene that or any other agreement.

(4) An agreement may fall within subsection (1) (b) although the identity of the supplier is unknown at the time the agreement is made.

NOTES
Commencement: 1 April 1977.
Commencement order: SI 1977 No 325, art 2(1), and Sch 3, para 1, to this Act.

12. Debtor-creditor-supplier agreements

A debtor-creditor-supplier agreement is a regulated consumer credit agreement being—

  (a) a restricted-use credit agreement which falls within section 11(1) (a), or
  (b) a restricted-use credit agreement which falls within section 11(1) (b) and is made by the creditor under pre-existing arrangements, or in contemplation of future arrangements, between himself and the supplier, or
  (c) an unrestricted-use credit agreement which is made by the creditor under pre-existing arrangements between himself and a person (the "supplier") other than the debtor in the knowledge that the credit is to be used to finance a transaction between the debtor and the supplier.

NOTES
Commencement: 1 April 1977.
Commencement order: SI 1977 No 325, art 2(1), and Sch 3, para 1, to this Act.

13. Debtor-creditor agreements

A debtor-creditor agreement is a regulated consumer credit agreement being—

  (a) a restricted-use credit agreement which falls within section 11(1) (b) but is not made by the creditor under pre-existing arrangements, or in contemplation of future arrangements, between himself and the supplier, or

(b) a restricted-use credit agreement which falls within section 11(1) (c), or
(c) an unrestricted-use credit agreement which is not made by the creditor under pre-existing arrangements between himself and a person (the "supplier") other than the debtor in the knowledge that the credit is to be used to finance a transaction between the debtor and the supplier. **[181]**

NOTES
Commencement: 1 April 1977.
Commencement order: SI 1977 No 325, art 2(1), and Sch 3, para 1, to this Act.

14. Credit-token agreements

(1) A credit-token is a card, check, voucher, coupon, stamp, form, booklet or other document or thing given to an individual by a person carrying on a consumer credit business, who undertakes—
   (a) that on the production of it (whether or not some other action is also required) he will supply cash, goods and services (or any of them) on credit, or
   (b) that where, on the production of it to a third party (whether or not any other action is also required), the third party supplies cash, goods and services (or any of them), he will pay the third party for them (whether or not deducting any discount or commission), in return for payment to him by the individual.

(2) A credit-token agreement is a regulated agreement for the provision of credit in connection with the use of a credit-token.

(3) Without prejudice to the generality of section 9(1), the person who gives to an individual an undertaking falling within subsection (1) (b) shall be taken to provide him with credit drawn on whenever a third party supplies him with cash, goods or services.

(4) For the purposes of subsection (1), use of an object to operate a machine provided by the person giving the object or a third party shall be treated as the production of the object to him. **[182]**

NOTES
Commencement: 1 April 1977.
Commencement order: SI 1977 No 325, art 2(1), and Sch 3, para 1, to this Act.

15. Consumer hire agreements

(1) A consumer hire agreement is an agreement made by a person with an individual (the "hirer") for the bailment or (in Scotland) the hiring of goods to the hirer, being an agreement which—
   (a) is not a hire-purchase agreement, and
   (b) is capable of subsisting for more than three months, and
   (c) does not require the hirer to make payments exceeding [£15,000].

(2) A consumer hire agreement is a regulated agreement if it is not an exempt agreement. **[183]**

NOTES
Commencement: 1 April 1977.
Commencement order: SI 1977 No 325, art 2(1), and Sch 3, para 1, to this Act.
Sub-s (1): amended by SI 1983 No 1878, art 4, Schedule, Part II as from 20 May 1985.

16. Exempt agreements

(1) This Act does not regulate a consumer credit agreement where the creditor is a local authority ..., or a body specified, or of a description specified, in an order made by the Secretary of State, being—

- (*a*) an insurance company,
- (*b*) a friendly society,
- (*c*) an organisation of employers or organisation of workers,
- (*d*) a charity,
- (*e*) a land improvement company, ...
- (*f*) a body corporate named or specifically referred to in any public general Act [, or
- [(*ff*) a body corporate named or specifically referred to in an order made under—

    section 156(4), 444(1) or 447(2)(*a*) of the Housing Act 1985,
    ...
    Article 154(1)(*a*) or 156AA of the Housing (Northern Ireland) Order 1981 or Article 10(6A) of the Housing (Northern Ireland) Order 1983; or]

- (*g*) a building society] [, or
- (*h*) an authorised institution or wholly-owned subsidiary (within the meaning of the Companies Act 1985) of such an institution.]

(2) Subsection (1) applies only where the agreement is—

- (*a*) a debtor-creditor-supplier agreement financing—

    (i) the purchase of land, or
    (ii) the provision of dwellings on any land,
    and secured by a land mortgage on that land, or

- (*b*) a debtor-creditor agreement secured by any land mortgage; or
- (*c*) a debtor-creditor-supplier agreement financing a transaction which is a linked transaction in relation to—

    (i) an agreement falling within paragraph (*a*), or
    (ii) an agreement falling within paragraph (*b*) financing—

    (*aa*) the purchase of any land, or
    (*bb*) the provision of dwellings on any land,

    and secured by a land mortgage on the land referred to in paragraph (*a*) or, as the case may be, the land referred to in subparagraph (ii).

(3) The Secretary of State shall not make, vary or revoke an order—

- (*a*) under subsection (1) (*a*) without consulting the Minister of the Crown responsible for insurance companies,
- (*b*) under subsection (1) (*b*) ... without consulting the Chief Registrar of Friendly Societies,
- (*c*) under subsection (1) (*d*) without consulting the Charity Commissioners,
- (*d*) under subsection (1) (*e*) [, (*f*) or (*ff*)] without consulting any Minister of the Crown with responsibilities concerning the body in question [or
- (*e*) under subsection (1)(*g*) without consulting the Building Societies Commission and the Treasury] [or

(*f*) under subsection (1)(*h*) without consulting the Treasury and the Bank of England.]

(4) An order under subsection (1) relating to a body may be limited so as to apply only to agreements by that body of a description specified in the order.

(5) The Secretary of State may by order provide that this Act shall not regulate other consumer credit agreements where—
   (*a*) the number of payments to be made by the debtor does not exceed the number specified for that purpose in the order, or
   (*b*) the rate of the total charge for credit does not exceed the rate so specified, or
   (*c*) an agreement has a connection with a country outside the United Kingdom.

(6) The Secretary of State may by order provide that this Act shall not regulate consumer hire agreements of a description specified in the order where—
   (*a*) the owner is a body corporate authorised by or under any enactment to supply electricity, gas or water, and
   (*b*) the subject of the agreement is a meter or metering equipment,
[or where the owner is a public telecommunications operator specified in the order].

[(6A) This Act does not regulate a consumer credit agreement where the creditor is a housing authority and the agreement is secured by a land mortgage of a dwelling.

(6B) In subsection (6A) "housing authority" means—
   (*a*) as regards England and Wales, [the Housing Corporation, Housing for Wales and] an authority or body within section 80(1) of the Housing Act 1985 (the landlord condition for secure tenancies), other than a housing association or a housing trust which is a charity;
   (*b*) . . .
   (*c*) as regards Northern Ireland, the Northern Ireland Housing Executive.]

(7) Nothing in this section affects the application of sections 137 to 140 (extortionate credit bargains).

(8) . . .

(9) In the application of this section to Northern Ireland subsection (3) shall have effect as if any reference to a Minister of the Crown were a reference to a Northern Ireland department, any reference to the Chief Registrar of Friendly Societies were a reference to the Registrar of Friendly Societies for Northern Ireland, and any reference to the Charity Commissioners were a reference to the Department of Finance for Northern Ireland.

NOTES
   Commencement: 7 January 1987 (sub-ss (6A), (6B)); 1 April 1977 (remainder).
   Commencement order: SI 1977 No 325, art 2(1), and Sch 3, para 1, to this Act.
   Sub-s (1): words omitted repealed and para (*g*) added by the Building Societies Act 1986, s 120, Sch 18, Part I, para 10(2), Sch 19, Part I, with effect from 1 January 1987; para (*ff*) added by the Housing and Planning Act 1986, s 22(2), (4), with respect to agreements made after 7 January 1987; para (*h*) added by the Banking Act 1987, s 88 in force 10 October 1987. Words omitted apply to Scotland only.
   Sub-s (3): words omitted repealed by the Employment Protection Act 1975, s 125(3), Sch 18; word omitted in para (*c*) repealed and para (*e*) added by the Building Societies Act 1986, s 120, Sch

18, Part I, para 10(3), Sch 19, Part I, with effect from 1 January 1987; para (*d*) amended with respect to agreements made after 7 January 1987 by the Housing and Planning Act 1986, s 22(2), (4); para (*f*) added by the Banking Act 1987, s 88 in force 10 October 1987.

Sub-s (6): amended by the Telecommunications Act 1984, s 109, Sch 4, para 60 from 5 August 1984.

Sub-s (6A): added with respect to agreements made after 7 January 1987 by the Housing and Planning Act 1986, s 22.

Sub-s (6B): added with respect to agreements made after 7 January 1987 by the Housing and Planning Act 1986, s 22; amended by the Housing Act 1988, s 140, Sch 17, Part I from 15 January 1989.

Sub-s (8): applies to Scotland only.

Regulations made under this section are set out below, paras [362]–[370].

17. Small agreements

(1) A small agreement is—

    (*a*) a regulated consumer credit agreement for credit not exceeding [£50], other than a hire-purchase or conditional sale agreement; or

    (*b*) a regulated consumer hire agreement which does not require the hirer to make payments exceeding [£50],

being an agreement which is either unsecured or secured by a guarantee or indemnity only (whether or not the guarantee or indemnity is itself secured).

(2) Section 10(3)(*a*) applies for the purposes of subsection (1) as it applies for the purposes of section 8(2).

(3) Where—

    (*a*) two or more small agreements are made at or about the same time between the same parties, and

    (*b*) it appears probable that they would instead have been made as a single agreement but for the desire to avoid the operation of provisions of this Act which would have applied to that single agreement but, apart from this subsection, are not applicable to the small agreements,

this Act applies to the small agreements as if they were regulated agreements other than small agreements.

(4) If, apart from this subsection, subsection (3) does not apply to any agreements but would apply if, for any party or parties to any of the agreements, there were substituted an associate of that party, or associates of each of those parties, as the case may be, then subsection (3) shall apply to the agreements.

NOTES

Commencement: 1 April 1977.

Commencement order: SI 1977 No 325, art 2(1), and Sch 3, para 1, to this Act.

Sub-s (1): amended by SI 1983 No 1878, art 3, Schedule, Part I from 1 January 1984.

18. Multiple agreements

(1) This section applies to an agreement (a "multiple agreement") if its terms are such as—

    (*a*) to place a part of it within one category of agreement mentioned in this Act, and another part of it within a different category of agreements so mentioned, or within a category of agreement not so mentioned, or

    (*b*) to place it, or a part of it, within two or more categories of agreement so mentioned.

(2) Where a part of an agreement falls within subsection (1), that part shall be treated for the purposes of this Act as a separate agreement.

(3) Where an agreement falls within subsection (1) (*b*), it shall be treated as an agreement in each of the categories in question, and this Act shall apply to it accordingly.

(4) Where under subsection (2) a part of a multiple agreement is to be treated as a separate agreement, the multiple agreement shall (with any necessary modifications) be construed accordingly; and any sum payable under the multiple agreement, if not apportioned by the parties, shall for the purposes of proceedings in any court relating to the multiple agreement be apportioned by the court as may be requisite.

(5) In the case of an agreement for running-account credit, a term of the agreement allowing the credit limit to be exceeded merely temporarily shall not be treated as a separate agreement or as providing fixed-sum credit in respect of the excess.

(6) This Act does not apply to a multiple agreement so far as the agreement relates to goods if under the agreement payments are to be made in respect of the goods in the form of rent (other than a rent-charge) issuing out of land. **[186]**

NOTES
    Commencement: 1 April 1977.
    Commencement order: SI 1977 No 325, art 2(1), and Sch 3, para 1, to this Act.

19. Linked transactions

(1) A transaction entered into by the debtor or hirer, or a relative of his, with any other person ("the other party"), except one for the provision of security, is a linked transaction in relation to an actual or prospective regulated agreement (the "principal agreement") of which it does not form part if—

   (*a*) the transaction is entered into in compliance with a term of the principal agreement; or
   (*b*) the principal agreement is a debtor-creditor-supplier agreement and the transaction is financed, or to be financed, by the principal agreement; or
   (*c*) the other party is a person mentioned in subsection (2), and a person so mentioned initiated the transaction by suggesting it to the debtor or hirer, or his relative, who enters into it—
      (i) to induce the creditor or owner to enter into the principal agreement, or
      (ii) for another purpose related to the principal agreement, or
      (iii) where the principal agreement is a restricted-use credit agreement, for a purpose related to a transaction financed, or to be financed, by the principal agreement.

(2) The persons referred to in subsection (1) (*c*) are—

   (*a*) the creditor or owner, or his associate;
   (*b*) a person who, in the negotiation of the transaction, is represented by a credit-broker who is also a negotiator in antecedent negotiations for the principal agreement;
   (*c*) a person who, at the time the transaction is initiated, knows that the principal agreement has been made or contemplates that it might be made.

(3) A linked transaction entered into before the making of the principal agreement has no effect until such time (if any) as that agreement is made.

(4) Regulations may exclude linked transactions of the prescribed description from the operation of subsection (3). **[187]**

NOTES
Commencement: 1 April 1977 (Sub-ss (1), (2), (4)); 19 May 1985 (sub-s (3)).
Commencement order: SI 1977 No 325, art 2(1), and Sch 3, paras 1–3, to this Act, SI 1983 No 1551.
Regulations under this section: Consumer Credit (Linked Transactions) (Exemptions) Regulations 1983, SI 1983 No 1560.

20. Total charge for credit

(1) The Secretary of State shall make regulations containing such provisions as appear to him appropriate for determining the true cost to the debtor of the credit provided or to be provided under an actual or prospective consumer credit agreement (the "total charge for credit"), and regulations so made shall prescribe—
> (a) what items are to be treated as entering into the total charge for credit, and how their amount is to be ascertained;
> (b) the method of calculating the rate of the total charge for credit.

(2) Regulations under subsection (1) may provide for the whole or part of the amount payable by the debtor or his relative under any linked transaction to be included in the total charge for credit, whether or not the creditor is a party to the transaction or derives benefit from it. **[188]**

NOTES
Commencement: 1 April 1977.
Commencement order: SI 1977 No 325, art 2(1), and Sch 3, paras 1–4, to this Act.
Regulations under this section: Consumer Credit (Total Charge for Credit) Regulations 1980, SI 1980 No 51, amended by SI 1985 No 1192.

PART III

LICENSING OF CREDIT AND HIRE BUSINESSES

Licensing principles

21. Businesses needing a licence

(1) Subject to this section, a licence is required to carry on a consumer credit business or consumer hire business.

(2) A local authority does not need a licence to carry on a business.

(3) A body corporate empowered by a public general Act naming it to carry on a business does not need a licence to do so. **[189]**

NOTES
Commencement: 3 August 1976 - 1 July 1978.
Commencement orders: SI 1975 No 2123, art 2(2), 1977 No 325, art 2(3), 1977 No 2163, art 2, and Sch 3, paras 5,41, to this Act.

22. Standard and group licences

(1) A licence may be—
> (a) a standard licence, that is a licence, issued by the Director to a person named in the licence on an application made by him, which, during

the prescribed period, covers such activities as are described in the licence, or

(b) a group licence, that is a licence, issued by the Director (whether on the application of any person or of his own motion), which, during such period as the Director thinks fit or, if he thinks fit, indefinitely, covers such persons and activities as are described in the licence.

(2) A licence is not assignable or, subject to section 37, transmissible on death or in any other way.

(3) Except in the case of a partnership or an unincorporated body of persons, a standard licence shall not be issued to more than one person.

(4) A standard licence issued to a partnership or an unincorporated body of persons shall be issued in the name of the partnership or body.

(5) The Director may issue a group licence only if it appears to him that the public interest is better served by doing so than by obliging the persons concerned to apply separately for standard licences.

(6) The persons covered by a group licence may be described by general words, whether or not coupled with the exclusion of named persons, or in any other way the Director thinks fit.

(7) The fact that a person is covered by a group licence in respect of certain activities does not prevent a standard licence being issued to him in respect of those activities or any of them.

(8) A group licence issued on the application of any person shall be issued to that person, and general notice shall be given of the issue of any group licence (whether on application or not). **[190]**

NOTES
Commencement: 31 July 1974.
Regulations under this section: Consumer Credit (Period of Standard Licence) Regulations 1975, SI 1975 No 2124, amended by SI 1979 No 796 and SI 1986 No 1016.

23. Authorisation of specific activities

(1) Subject to this section, a licence to carry on a business covers all lawful activities done in the course of that business, whether by the licensee or other persons on his behalf.

(2) A licence may limit the activities it covers, whether by authorising the licensee to enter into certain types of agreement only, or in any other way.

(3) A licence covers the canvassing off trade premises of debtor-creditor-supplier agreements or regulated consumer hire agreements only if, and to the extent that, the licence specifically so provides; and such provision shall not be included in a group licence.

(4) Regulations may be made specifying other activities which, if engaged in by or on behalf of the person carrying on a business, require to be covered by an express term in his licence. **[191]**

NOTES
Commencement: 31 July 1974.

24. Control of name of business

A standard licence authorises the licensee to carry on a business under the name or names specified in the licence, but not under any other name. **[192]**

NOTES
Commencement: 31 July 1974.

25. Licensee to be a fit person

(1) A standard licence shall be granted on the application of any person if he satisfies the Director that—

    (a) he is a fit person to engage in activities covered by the licence, and
    (b) the name or names under which he applies to be licensed is or are not misleading or otherwise undesirable.

(2) In determining whether an applicant for a standard licence is a fit person to engage in any activities, the Director shall have regard to any circumstances appearing to him to be relevant, and in particular any evidence tending to show that the applicant, or any of the applicant's employees, agents or associates (whether past or present) or, where the applicant is a body corporate, any person appearing to the Director to be a controller of the body corporate or an associate of any such person, has—

    (a) committed any offence involving fraud or other dishonesty, or violence,
    (b) contravened any provision made by or under this Act, or by or under any other enactment regulating the provision of credit to individuals or other transactions with individuals,
    (c) practised discrimination on grounds of sex, colour, race or ethnic or national origins in, or in connection with, the carrying on of any business, or
    (d) engaged in business practices appearing to the Director to be deceitful or oppressive, or otherwise unfair or improper (whether unlawful or not).

(3) In subsection (2), "associate", in addition to the persons specified in section 184, includes a business associate. **[193]**

NOTES
Commencement: 31 July 1974.

26. Conduct of business

Regulations may be made as to the conduct by a licensee of his business, and may in particular specify—

    (a) the books and other records to be kept by him, and
    (b) the information to be furnished by him to persons with whom he does business or seeks to do business, and the way it is to be furnished.

[194]

NOTES
Commencement: 31 July 1974.
Regulations under this section: Consumer Credit (Conduct of Business) (Credit References) Regulations 1977, SI 1977 No 330; Consumer Credit (Conduct of Business) (Pawn Records) Regulations 1983, SI 1983 No 1565.

Issue of licences

27. Determination of applications

(1) Unless the Director determines to issue a licence in accordance with an application he shall, before determining the application, by notice—

    (a) inform the applicant, giving his reasons, that, as the case may be, he is minded to refuse the application, or to grant it in terms different from those applied for, describing them, and

    (b) invite the applicant to submit to the Director representations in support of his application in accordance with section 34.

(2) If the Director grants the application in terms different from those applied for then, whether or not the applicant appeals, the Director shall issue the licence in the terms approved by him unless the applicant by notice informs him that he does not desire a licence in those terms. **[195]**

NOTES
    Commencement: 31 July 1974.

28. Exclusion from group licence

Where the Director is minded to issue a group licence (whether on the application of any person or not), and in doing so to exclude any person from the group by name, he shall, before determining the matter,—

    (a) give notice of that fact to the person proposed to be excluded, giving his reasons, and

    (b) invite that person to submit to the Director representations against his exclusion in accordance with section 34. **[196]**

NOTES
    Commencement: 31 July 1974.

Renewal, variation, suspension and revocation of licences

29. Renewal

(1) If the licensee under a standard licence, or the original applicant for, or any licensee under, a group licence of limited duration, wishes the Director to renew the licence, whether on the same terms (except as to expiry) or on varied terms, he must, during the period specified by the Director by general notice or such longer period as the Director may allow, make an application to the Director for its renewal.

(2) The Director may of his own motion renew any group licence.

(3) The preceding provisions of this Part apply to the renewal of a licence as they apply to the issue of a licence, except that section 28 does not apply to a person who was already excluded in the licence up for renewal.

(4) Until the determination of an application under subsection (1) and, where an appeal lies from the determination, until the end of the appeal period, the licence shall continue in force, notwithstanding that apart from this subsection it would expire earlier.

(5) On the refusal of an application under this section, the Director may give directions authorising a licensee to carry into effect agreements made by him before the expiry of the licence.

(6) General notice shall be given of the renewal of a group licence. **[197]**

NOTES
Commencement: 31 July 1974.

30. Variation by request

(1) On an application made by the licensee, the Director may if he thinks fit by notice to the licensee vary a standard licence in accordance with the application.

(2) In the case of a group licence issued on the application of any person, the Director, on an application made by that person, may if he thinks fit by notice to that person vary the terms of the licence in accordance with the application; but the Director shall not vary a group licence under this subsection by excluding a named person, other than the person making the request, unless that named person consents in writing to his exclusion.

(3) In the case of a group licence from which (whether by name or description) a person is excluded, the Director, on an application made by that person, may if he thinks fit, by notice to that person, vary the terms of the licence so as to remove the exclusion.

(4) Unless the Director determines to vary a licence in accordance with an application he shall, before determining the application, by notice—
   (a) inform the applicant, giving his reasons, that he is minded to refuse the application, and
   (b) invite the applicant to submit to the Director representations in support of his application in accordance with section 34.

(5) General notice shall be given that a variation of a group licence has been made under this section. **[198]**

NOTES
Commencement: 31 July 1974.

31. Compulsory variation

(1) Where at a time during the currency of a licence the Director is of the opinion that, if the licence had expired at that time, he would, on an application for its renewal or further renewal on the same terms (except as to expiry), have been minded to grant the application but on different terms, and that therefore the licence should be varied, he shall proceed as follows.

(2) In the case of a standard licence the Director shall, by notice—
   (a) inform the licensee of the variations the Director is minded to make in the terms of the licence, stating his reasons, and
   (b) invite him to submit to the Director representations as to the proposed variations in accordance with section 34.

(3) In the case of a group licence the Director shall—
   (a) give general notice of the variations he is minded to make in the terms of the licence, stating his reasons, and
   (b) in the notice invite any licensee to submit to him representations as to the proposed variations in accordance with section 34.

(4) In the case of a group licence issued on application the Director shall also—

(a) inform the original applicant of the variations the Director is minded to make in the terms of the licence, stating his reasons, and
(b) invite him to submit to the Director representations as to the proposed variations in accordance with section 34.

(5) If the Director is minded to vary a group licence by excluding any person (other than the original applicant) from the group by name the Director shall, in addition, take the like steps under section 28 as are required in the case mentioned in that section.

(6) General notice shall be given that a variation of any group licence has been made under this section.

(7) A variation under this section shall not take effect before the end of the appeal period.

NOTES
Commencement: 31 July 1974.

32. Suspension and revocation

(1) Where at a time during the currency of a licence the Director is of the opinion that if the licence had expired at that time he would have been minded not to renew it, and that therefore it should be revoked or suspended, he shall proceed as follows.

(2) In the case of a standard licence the Director shall, by notice—
(a) inform the licensee that, as the case may be, the Director is minded to revoke the licence, or suspend it until a specified date or indefinitely, stating his reasons, and
(b) invite him to submit representations as to the proposed revocation or suspension in accordance with section 34.

(3) In the case of a group licence the Director shall—
(a) give general notice that, as the case may be, he is minded to revoke the licence, or suspend it until a specified date or indefinitely, stating his reasons, and
(b) in the notice invite any licensee to submit to him representations as to the proposed revocation or suspension in accordance with section 34.

(4) In the case of a group licence issued on application the Director shall also—
(a) inform the original applicant that, as the case may be, the Director is minded to revoke the licence, or suspend it until a specified date or indefinitely, stating his reasons, and
(b) invite him to submit representations as to the proposed revocation or suspension in accordance with section 34.

(5) If he revokes or suspends the licence, the Director may give directions authorising a licensee to carry into effect agreements made by him before the revocation or suspension.

(6) General notice shall be given of the revocation or suspension of a group licence.

(7) A revocation or suspension under this section shall not take effect before the end of the appeal period.

(8) Except for the purposes of section 29, a licensee under a suspended

licence shall be treated, in respect of the period of suspension, as if the licence had not been issued; and where the suspension is not expressed to end on a specified date it may, if the Director thinks fit, be ended by notice given by him to the licensee or, in the case of a group licence, by general notice. **[200]**

NOTES
Commencement: 31 July 1974.

33. Application to end suspension

(1) On an application made by a licensee the Director may, if he thinks fit, by notice to the licensee end the suspension of a licence, whether the suspension was for a fixed or indefinite period.

(2) Unless the Director determines to end the suspension in accordance with the application he shall, before determining the application, by notice—
  (a) inform the applicant, giving his reasons, that he is minded to refuse the application, and
  (b) invite the applicant to submit to the Director representations in support of his application in accordance with section 34.

(3) General notice shall be given that a suspension of a group licence has been ended under this section.

(4) In the case of a group licence issued on application—
  (a) the references in subsection (1) to a licensee include the original applicant;
  (b) the Director shall inform the original applicant that a suspension of a group licence has been ended under this section. **[201]**

NOTES
Commencement: 31 July 1974.

Miscellaneous

34. Representations to Director

(1) Where this section applies to an invitation by the Director to any person to submit representations, the Director shall invite that person, within 21 days after the notice containing the invitation is given to him or published, or such longer period as the Director may allow,—
  (a) to submit his representations in writing to the Director, and
  (b) to give notice to the Director, if he thinks fit, that he wishes to make representations orally,

and where notice is given under paragraph (b) the Director shall arrange for the oral representations to be heard.

(2) In reaching his determination the Director shall take into account any representations submitted or made under this section.

(3) The Director shall give notice of his determination to the persons who were required to be invited to submit representations about it or, where the invitation to submit representations was required to be given by general notice, shall give general notice of the determination. **[202]**

NOTES
Commencement: 31 July 1974.

35. The register

(1) The Director shall establish and maintain a register, in which he shall cause to be kept particulars of—
- (a) applications not yet determined for the issue, variation or renewal of licences, or for ending the suspension of a licence;
- (b) licences which are in force, or have at any time been suspended or revoked, with details of any variation of the terms of a licence;
- (c) decisions given by him under this Act, and any appeal from those decisions; and
- (d) such other matters (if any) as he thinks fit.

(2) The Director shall give general notice of the various matters required to be entered in the register, and of any change in them made under subsection (1) (d).

(3) Any person shall be entitled on payment of the specified fee—
- (a) to inspect the register during ordinary office hours and take copies of any entry, or
- (b) to obtain from the Director a copy, certified by the Director to be correct, of any entry in the register.

(4) The Director may, if he thinks fit, determine that the right conferred by subsection (3) (a) shall be exercisable in relation to a copy of the register instead of, or in addition to, the original.

(5) The Director shall give general notice of the place or places where, and times when, the register or a copy of it may be inspected.

NOTES
Commencement: 2 February 1976.
Commencement order: SI 1975 No 2123, art 2(1), and Sch 3, para 6, to this Act.

36. Duty to notify changes

(1) Within 21 working days after a change takes place in any particulars entered in the register in respect of a standard licence or the licensee under section 35 (1) (d) (not being a change resulting from action taken by the Director), the licensee shall give the Director notice of the change; and the Director shall cause any necessary amendment to be made in the register.

(2) Within 21 working days after—
- (a) any change takes place in the officers of—
  - (i) a body corporate, or an unincorporated body of persons, which is the licensee under a standard licence, or
  - (ii) a body corporate which is a controller of a body corporate which is such a licensee, or
- (b) a body corporate which is such a licensee becomes aware that a person has become or ceased to be a controller of the body corporate, or
- (c) any change takes place in the members of a partnership which is such a licensee (including a change on the amalgamation of the partnership with another firm, or a change whereby the number of partners is reduced to one),

the licensee shall give the Director notice of the change.

(3) Within 14 working days after any change takes place in the officers of a body corporate which is a controller of another body corporate which is a

licensee under a standard licence, the controller shall give the licensee notice of the change.

(4) Within 14 working days after a person becomes or ceases to be a controller of a body corporate which is a licensee under a standard licence, that person shall give the licensee notice of the fact.

(5) Where a change in a partnership has the result that the business ceases be carried on under the name, or any of the names, specified in a standard licence the licence shall cease to have effect.

(6) Where the Director is given notice under subsection (1) or (2) of any change, and subsection (5) does not apply, the Director may by notice require the licensee to furnish him with such information, verified in such manner, as the Director may stipulate. [204]

NOTES
Commencement: 2 February 1976.
Commencement order: SI 1975 No 2123, art 2(1), and Sch 3, para 6, to this Act.

37. Death, bankruptcy etc of licensee

(1) A licence held by one individual terminates if he—
   (a) dies, or
   (b) is adjudged bankrupt, or
   (c) becomes a patient within the meaning of Part VIII of the Mental Health Act 1959.

(2) In relation to a licence held by one individual, or a partnership or other unincorporated body of persons, or a body corporate, regulations may specify other events relating to the licensee on the occurrence of which the licence is to terminate.

(3) Regulations may—
   (a) provide for the termination of a licence by subsection (1), or under subsection (2), to be deferred for a period not exceeding 12 months, and
   (b) authorise the business of the licensee to be carried on under the licence by some other person during the period of deferment, subject to such conditions as may be prescribed.

(4) This section does not apply to group licences. [205]

NOTES
Commencement: 31 July 1974.
Regulations under this section: Consumer Credit (Termination of Licences) Regulations 1976, SI 1976 No 1002, amended by SI 1981 No 614.

NOTES
Section 38, which applies to Scotland and Northern Ireland only, is omitted.

39. Offences against Part III

(1) A person who engages in any activities for which a licence is required when he is not a licensee under a licence covering those activities commits an offence.

(2) A licensee under a standard licence who carries on business under a name not specified in the licence commits an offence.

(3) A person who fails to give the Director or a licensee notice under section 36 within the period required commits an offence. **[206]**

NOTES
Commencement: 31 July 1974.

40. Enforcement of agreements made by unlicensed trader

(1) A regulated agreement, other than a non-commercial agreement, if made when the creditor or owner was unlicensed, is enforceable against the debtor or hirer only where the Director has made an order under this section which applies to the agreement.

(2) Where during any period an unlicensed person (the "trader") was carrying on a consumer credit business or consumer hire business, he or his successor in title may apply to the Director for an order that regulated agreements made by the trader during that period are to be treated as if he had been licensed.

(3) Unless the Director determines to make an order under subsection (2) in accordance with the application, he shall, before determining the application, by notice—
  (a) inform the applicant, giving his reasons, that, as the case may be, he is minded to refuse the application, or to grant it in terms different from those applied for, describing them, and
  (b) invite the applicant to submit to the Director representations in support of his application in accordance with section 34.

(4) In determining whether or not to make an order under subsection (2) in respect of any period the Director shall consider, in addition to any other relevant factors—
  (a) how far, if at all, debtors or hirers under regulated agreements made by the trader during that period were prejudiced by the trader's conduct,
  (b) whether or not the Director would have been likely to grant a licence covering that period on an application by the trader, and
  (c) the degree of culpability for the failure to obtain a licence.

(5) If the Director thinks fit, he may in an order under subsection (2)—
  (a) limit the order to specified agreements, or agreements of a specified description or made at a specified time;
  (b) make the order conditional on the doing of specified acts by the applicant. **[207]**

NOTES
Commencement: 3 August 1976 - 1 July 1978.
Commencement orders: SI 1975 No 2123, art 2(3), 1977 No 325, art 2(3), 1977 No 1263, art 2, and Sch 3, paras 5,7,44, to this Act.

41. Appeals to Secretary of State under Part III

(1) If, in the case of a determination by the Director such as is mentioned in column 1 of the table set out at the end of this section, a person mentioned in relation to that determination in column 2 of the table is aggrieved by the

determination he may, within the prescribed period, and in the prescribed manner, appeal to the Secretary of State.

(2) Regulations may make provision as to the persons by whom (on behalf of the Secretary of State) appeals under this section are to be heard, the manner in which they are to be conducted, and any other matter connected with such appeals.

(3) On an appeal under this section, the Secretary of State may give such directions for disposing of the appeal as he thinks just, including a direction for the payment of costs by any party to the appeal.

(4) A direction under subsection (3) for payment of costs may be made a rule of the High Court on the application of the party in whose favour it is given.

(5) . . .

TABLE

Determination	*Appellant*
Refusal to issue, renew or vary licence in accordance with terms of application.	The applicant.
Exclusion of person from group licence.	The person excluded.
Refusal to give directions in respect of a licensee under section 29(5) or 32(5).	The licensee.
Compulsory variation, or suspension or revocation, of standard licence.	·The licensee.
Compulsory variation, or suspension or revocation, of group licence.	The original applicant or any licensee.
Refusal to end suspension of licence in accordance with terms of application.	The applicant.
Refusal to make order under section 40(2) in accordance with terms of application.	The applicant.

NOTES
Commencement: 31 July 1974.
Sub-s (5): applies to Scotland only.
Regulations under this section: Consumer Credit Licensing (Appeals) Regulations 1976, SI 1976 No 837.

NOTES
Section 42, which amends the Tribunals and Inquiries Act 1971, is omitted.

PART IV

SEEKING BUSINESS

Advertising

43. Advertisements to which Part IV applies

(1) This Part applies to any advertisement, published for the purposes of a business carried on by the advertiser, indicating that he is willing—

(*a*) to provide credit, or

(b) to enter into an agreement for the bailment or (in Scotland) the hiring of goods by him.

(2) An advertisement does not fall within subsection (1) if the advertiser does not carry on—

(a) a consumer credit business or consumer hire business, or
(b) a business in the course of which he provides credit to individuals secured on land, or
(c) a business which comprises or relates to unregulated agreements where—
   (i) the proper law of the agreement is the law of a country outside the United Kingdom, and
   (ii) if the proper law of the agreement were the law of a part of the United Kingdom it would be a regulated agreement.

(3) An advertisement does not fall within subsection (1) (a) if it indicates—

(a) that the credit must exceed [£15,000], and that no security is required, or the security is to consist of property other than land, or
(b) that the credit is available only to a body corporate.

(4) An advertisement does not fall within subsection (1) (b) if it indicates that the advertiser is not willing to enter into a consumer hire agreement.

(5) The Secretary of State may by order provide that this Part shall not apply to other advertisements of a description specified in the order. [209]

NOTES
Commencement: 6 October 1980.
Commencement order: SI 1980 No 50, art 2, and Sch 3, para 8, to this Act.
Sub-s (3): amended by SI 1983 No 1878, art 4, Schedule, Part II as from 20 May 1985.
Regulations under this section: Consumer Credit (Exempt Advertisements) Order 1985, SI 1985 No 621.

44. Form and content of advertisements

(1) The Secretary of State shall make regulations as to the form and content of advertisements to which this Part applies, and the regulations shall contain such provisions as appear to him appropriate with a view to ensuring that, having regard to its subject-matter and the amount of detail included in it, an advertisement conveys a fair and reasonably comprehensive indication of the nature of the credit or hire facilities offered by the advertiser and of their true cost to persons using them.

(2) Regulations under subsection (1) may in particular—

(a) require specified information to be included in the prescribed manner in advertisements, and other specified material to be excluded;
(b) contain requirements to ensure that specified information is clearly brought to the attention of persons to whom advertisements are directed, and that one part of an advertisement is not given insufficient or excessive prominence compared with another. [210]

NOTES
Commencement: 6 October 1980.
Commencement order: SI 1980 No 50, art 2, and Sch 3, para 8, to this Act.
Regulations under this section: Consumer Credit (Advertisement) Regulations 1980, SI 1980 No 54, amended by SI 1980 No 1360, SI 1983 No 110, SI 1983 No 1721, SI 1984 No 1055, SI 1985 No 619.

45. Prohibition of advertisement where goods etc not sold for cash

If an advertisement to which this Part applies indicates that the advertiser is willing to provide credit under a restricted-use credit agreement relating to goods or services to be supplied by any person, but at the time when the advertisement is published that person is not holding himself out as prepared to sell the goods or provide the services (as the case may be) for cash, the advertiser commits an offence. [211]

NOTES
Commencement: 6 October 1980.
Commencement order: SI 1980 No 50, art 2, and Sch 3, para 8, to this Act.

46. False or misleading advertisements

(1) If an advertisement to which this Part applies conveys information which in a material respect is false or misleading the advertiser commits an offence.

(2) Information stating or implying an intention on the advertiser's part which he has not got is false. [212]

NOTES
Commencement: 6 October 1980.
Commencement order: SI 1980 No 50, art 2, and Sch 3, para 8, to this Act.

47. Advertising infringements

(1) Where an advertiser commits an offence against regulations made under section 44 or against section 45 or 46 or would be taken to commit such an offence but for the defence provided by section 168, a like offence is committed by—

  (a) the publisher of the advertisement, and
  (b) any person who, in the course of a business carried on by him, devised the advertisement, or a part of it relevant to the first-mentioned offence, and
  (c) where the advertiser did not procure the publication of the advertisement, the person who did procure it.

(2) In proceedings for an offence under subsection (1) (a) it is a defence for the person charged to prove that—

  (a) the advertisement was published in the course of a business carried on by him, and
  (b) he received the advertisement in the course of that business, and did not know and had no reason to suspect that its publication would be an offence under this Part. [213]

NOTES
Commencement: 6 October 1980.
Commencement order: SI 1980 No 50, art 2, and Sch 3, para 8, to this Act.

Canvassing etc

48. Definition of canvassing off trade premises (regulated agreements)

(1) An individual (the "canvasser") canvasses a regulated agreement off trade premises if he solicits the entry (as debtor or hirer) of another individual (the "consumer") into the agreement by making oral representations to the consumer, or any other individual, during a visit by the canvasser to any place (not

excluded by subsection (2)) where the consumer, or that other individual, as the case may be, is, being a visit—
  (a) carried out for the purpose of making such oral representations to individuals who are at that place, but
  (b) not carried out in response to a request made on a previous occasion.

(2) A place is excluded from subsection (1) if it is a place where a business is carried on (whether on a permanent or temporary basis) by—
  (a) the creditor or owner, or
  (b) a supplier, or
  (c) the canvasser, or the person whose employee or agent the canvasser is, or
  (d) the consumer. [214]

NOTES
Commencement: 31 July 1974.

49. Prohibition of canvassing debtor-creditor agreements off trade premises

(1) It is an offence to canvass debtor-creditor agreements off trade premises.

(2) It is also an offence to solicit the entry of an individual (as debtor) into a debtor-creditor agreement during a visit carried out in response to a request made on a previous occasion, where—
  (a) the request was not in writing signed by or on behalf of the person making it, and
  (b) if no request for the visit had been made, the soliciting would have constituted the canvassing of a debtor-creditor agreement off trade premises.

(3) Subsections (1) and (2) do not apply to any soliciting for an agreement enabling the debtor to overdraw on a current account of any description kept with the creditor, where—
  (a) the Director has determined that current accounts of that description kept with the creditor are excluded from subsections (1) and (2), and
  (b) the debtor already keeps an account with the creditor (whether a current account or not).

(4) A determination under subsection (3) (a)—
  (a) may be made subject to such conditions as the Director thinks fit, and
  (b) shall be made only where the Director is of opinion that it is not against the interests of debtors.

(5) If soliciting is done in breach of a condition imposed under subsection (4) (a), the determination under subsection (3) (a) does not apply to it. [215]

NOTES
Commencement: 1 October 1977.
Commencement order: SI 1977 No 802, art 2(3), and Sch 3, para 9, to this Act.

50. Circulars to minors

(1) A person commits an offence who, with a view to financial gain, sends to a minor any document inviting him to—
  (a) borrow money, or
  (b) obtain goods on credit or hire, or
  (c) obtain services on credit, or

(d) apply for information or advice on borrowing money or otherwise obtaining credit, or hiring goods.

(2) In proceedings under subsection (1) in respect of the sending of a document to a minor, it is a defence for the person charged to prove that he did not know, and had no reasonable cause to suspect, that he was a minor.

(3) Where a document is received by a minor at any school or educational establishment for minors, a person sending it to him at that establishment knowing or suspecting it to be such an establishment shall be taken to have reasonable cause to suspect that he is a minor. [216]

NOTES
Commencement: 1 July 1977.
Commencement order: SI 1977 No 802, art 2(1), and Sch 3, para 10, to this Act.

51. Prohibition of unsolicited credit-tokens

(1) It is an offence to give a person a credit-token if he has not asked for it.

(2) To comply with subsection (1) a request must be contained in a document signed by the person making the request, unless the credit-token agreement is a small debtor-creditor-supplier agreement.

(3) Subsection (1) does not apply to the giving of a credit-token to a person—
 (a) for use under a credit-token agreement already made, or
 (b) in renewal or replacement of a credit-token previously accepted by him under a credit-token agreement which continues in force, whether or not varied. [217]

NOTES
Commencement: 1 July 1977.
Commencement order: SI 1977 No 802, art 2(1), and Sch 3, para 11, to this Act.

Miscellaneous

52. Quotations

(1) Regulations may be made—
 (a) as to the form and content of any document (a "quotation") by which a person who carries on a consumer credit business or consumer hire business, or a business in the course of which he provides credit to individuals secured on land, gives prospective customers information about the terms on which he is prepared to do business;
 (b) requiring a person carrying on such a business to provide quotations to such persons and in such circumstances as are prescribed.

(2) Regulations under subsection (1) (a) may in particular contain provisions relating to quotations such as are set out in relation to advertisements in section 44. [218]

NOTES
Commencement: 31 July 1974.
Regulations under this section: Consumer Credit (Quotations) Regulations 1980, SI 1980 No 55, amended by SI 1980 No 1361, SI 1983 No 110, SI 1983 No 1721, SI 1984 No 1055, SI 1985 No 619.

53. Duty to display information

Regulations may require a person who carries on a consumer credit business or consumer hire business, or a business in the course of which he provides credit to individuals secured on land, to display in the prescribed manner, at any premises where the business is carried on to which the public have access, prescribed information about the business. **[219]**

NOTES
Commencement: 31 July 1974.

54. Conduct of business regulations

Without prejudice to the generality of section 26, regulations under that section may include provisions further regulating the seeking of business by a licensee who carries on a consumer credit business or a consumer hire business. **[220]**

NOTES
Commencement: 31 July 1974.

PART V
ENTRY INTO CREDIT OR HIRE AGREEMENTS
Preliminary matters

55. Disclosure of information

(1) Regulations may require specified information to be disclosed in the prescribed manner to the debtor or hirer before a regulated agreement is made.

(2) A regulated agreement is not properly executed unless regulations under subsection (1) were complied with before the making of the agreement. **[221]**

NOTES
Commencement: 31 July 1974.

56. Antecedent negotiations

(1) In this Act "antecedent negotiations" means any negotiations with the debtor or hirer—
   (a) conducted by the creditor or owner in relation to the making of any regulated agreement, or
   (b) conducted by a credit-broker in relation to goods sold or proposed to be sold by the credit-broker to the creditor before forming the subject-matter of a debtor-creditor-supplier agreement within section 12 (a), or
   (c) conducted by the supplier in relation to a transaction financed or proposed to be financed by a debtor-creditor-supplier agreement within section 12 (b) or (c),

and "negotiator" means the person by whom negotiations are so conducted with the debtor or hirer.

(2) Negotiations with the debtor in a case falling within subsection (1) (b) or (c) shall be deemed to be conducted by the negotiator in the capacity of agent of the creditor as well as in his actual capacity.

(3) An agreement is void if, and to the extent that, it purports in relation to an actual or prospective regulated agreement—

(a) to provide that a person acting as, or on behalf of, a negotiator is to be treated as the agent of the debtor or hirer, or

(b) to relieve a person from liability for acts or omissions of any person acting as, or on behalf of, a negotiator.

(4) For the purposes of this Act, antecedent negotiations shall be taken to begin when the negotiator and the debtor or hirer first enter into communication (including communication by advertisement), and to include any representations made by the negotiator to the debtor or hirer and any other dealings between them. [222]

NOTES
Commencement: 16 May 1977.
Commencement order: SI 1977 No 325, art 2(2), and Sch 3, para 12, to this Act.

57. Withdrawal from prospective agreement

(1) The withdrawal of a party from a prospective regulated agreement shall operate to apply this Part to the agreement, any linked transaction and any other thing done in anticipation of the making of the agreement as it would apply if the agreement were made and then cancelled under section 69.

(2) The giving to a party of a written or oral notice which, however expressed, indicates the intention of the other party to withdraw from a prospective regulated agreement operates as a withdrawal from it.

(3) Each of the following shall be deemed to be the agent of the creditor or owner for the purpose of receiving a notice under subsection (2)—

(a) a credit-broker or supplier who is the negotiator in antecedent negotiations, and

(b) any person who, in the course of a business carried on by him, acts on behalf of the debtor or hirer in any negotiations for the agreement.

(4) Where the agreement, if made, would not be a cancellable agreement, subsection (1) shall nevertheless apply as if the contrary were the case. [223]

NOTES
Commencement: 19 May 1985.
Commencement order: SI 1983 No 1551, and Sch 3, para 13, to this Act.

58. Opportunity for withdrawal from prospective land mortgage

(1) Before sending to the debtor or hirer, for his signature, an unexecuted agreement in a case where the prospective regulated agreement is to be secured on land (the "mortgaged land"), the creditor or owner shall give the debtor or hirer a copy of the unexecuted agreement which contains a notice in the prescribed form indicating the right of the debtor or hirer to withdraw from the prospective agreement, and how and when the right is exercisable, together with a copy of any other document referred to in the unexecuted agreement.

(2) Subsection (1) does not apply to—

(a) a restricted-use credit agreement to finance the purchase of the mortgaged land, or

(b) an agreement for a bridging loan in connection with the purchase of the mortgaged land or other land. [224]

NOTES
Commencement: 19 May 1985.
Commencement order: SI 1983 No 1551, and Sch 3, para 13, to this Act.

59. Agreement to enter future agreement void

(1) An agreement is void if, and to the extent that, it purports to bind a person to enter as debtor or hirer into a prospective regulated agreement.

(2) Regulations may exclude from the operation of subsection (1) agreements such as are described in the regulations. [225]

NOTES
Commencement: 19 May 1985.
Commencement order: SI 1983 No 1551, and Sch 3, para 13, to this Act.
Regulations under this section: Consumer Credit (Agreements to Enter Prospective Agreements) (Exemptions) Regulations 1983, SI 1983 No 1552.

Making the agreement

60. Form and content of agreements

(1) The Secretary of State shall make regulations as to the form and content of documents embodying regulated agreements, and the regulations shall contain such provisions as appear to him appropriate with a view to ensuring that the debtor or hirer is made aware of—

  (a) the rights and duties conferred or imposed on him by the agreement,
  (b) the amount and rate of the total charge for credit (in the case of a consumer credit agreement),
  (c) the protection and remedies available to him under this Act, and
  (d) any other matters which, in the opinion of the Secretary of State, it is desirable for him to know about in connection with the agreement.

(2) Regulations under subsection (1) may in particular—

  (a) require specified information to be included in the prescribed manner in documents, and other specified material to be excluded;
  (b) contain requirements to ensure that specified information is clearly brought to the attention of the debtor or hirer, and that one part of a document is not given insufficient or excessive prominence compared with another.

(3) If, on an application made to the Director by a person carrying on a consumer credit business or a consumer hire business, it appears to the Director impracticable for the applicant to comply with any requirement of regulations under subsection (1) in a particular case, he may, by notice to the applicant, direct that the requirement be waived or varied in relation to such agreements, and subject to such conditions (if any), as he may specify, and this Act and the regulations shall have effect accordingly.

(4) The Director shall give a notice under subsection (3) only if he is satisfied that to do so would not prejudice the interests of debtors or hirers. [226]

NOTES
Commencement: 31 July 1974.

61. Signing of agreement

(1) A regulated agreement is not properly executed unless—

  (a) a document in the prescribed form itself containing all the prescribed terms and conforming to regulations under section 60 (1) is signed in the prescribed manner both by the debtor or hirer and by or on behalf of the creditor or owner, and

(b) the document embodies all the terms of the agreement, other than implied terms, and
(c) the document is, when presented or sent to the debtor or hirer for signature, in such a state that all its terms are readily legible.

(2) In addition, where the agreement is one to which section 58(1) applies, it is not properly executed unless—
(a) the requirements of section 58(1) were complied with, and
(b) the unexecuted agreement was sent, for his signature, to the debtor or hirer by post not less than seven days after a copy of it was given to him under section 58(1), and
(c) during the consideration period, the creditor or owner refrained from approaching the debtor or hirer (whether in person, by telephone or letter, or in any other way) except in response to a specific request made by the debtor or hirer after the beginning of the consideration period, and
(d) no notice of withdrawal by the debtor or hirer was received by the creditor or owner before the sending of the unexecuted agreement.

(3) In subsection (2) (c), "the consideration period" means the period beginning with the giving of the copy under section 58(1) and ending—
(a) at the expiry of seven days after the day on which the unexecuted agreement is sent, for his signature, to the debtor or hirer, or
(b) on its return by the debtor or hirer after signature by him,

whichever first occurs.

(4) Where the debtor or hirer is a partnership or an unincorporated body of persons, subsection (1) (a) shall apply with the substitution for "by the debtor or hirer" of "by or on behalf of the debtor or hirer". [227]

NOTES
Commencement: 19 May 1985.
Commencement order: SI 1983 No 1551, and Sch 3, para 13, to this Act.

62. Duty to supply copy of unexecuted agreement

(1) If the unexecuted agreement is presented personally to the debtor or hirer for his signature, but on the occasion when he signs it the document does not become an executed agreement, a copy of it, and of any other document referred to in it, must be there and then delivered to him.

(2) If the unexecuted agreement is sent to the debtor or hirer for his signature, a copy of it, and of any other document referred to in it, must be sent to him at the same time.

(3) A regulated agreement is not properly executed if the requirements of this section are not observed. [228]

NOTES
Commencement: 19 May 1985.
Commencement order: SI 1983 No 1551, and Sch 3, para 13, to this Act.

63. Duty to supply copy of executed agreement

(1) If the unexecuted agreement is presented personally to the debtor or hirer for his signature, and on the occasion when he signs it the document becomes an executed agreement, a copy of the executed agreement, and of any other document referred to in it, must be there and then delivered to him.

(2) A copy of the executed agreement, and of any other document referred to in it, must be given to the debtor or hirer within the seven days following the making of the agreement unless—

(a) subsection (1) applies, or
(b) the unexecuted agreement was sent to the debtor or hirer for his signature and, on the occasion of his signing it, the document became an executed agreement.

(3) In the case of a cancellable agreement, a copy under subsection (2) must be sent by post.

(4) In the case of a credit-token agreement, a copy under subsection (2) need not be given within the seven days following the making of the agreement if it is given before or at the time when the credit-token is given to the debtor.

(5) A regulated agreement is not properly executed if the requirements of this section are not observed. [229]

NOTES
Commencement: 19 May 1985.
Commencement order: SI 1983 No 1551, and Sch 3, para 13, to this Act.

64. Duty to give notice of cancellation rights

(1) In the case of a cancellable agreement, a notice in the prescribed form indicating the right of the debtor or hirer to cancel the agreement, how and when that right is exercisable, and the name and address of a person to whom notice of cancellation may be given,—

(a) must be included in every copy given to the debtor or hirer under section 62 or 63, and
(b) except where section 63(2) applied, must also be sent by post to the debtor or hirer within the seven days following the making of the agreement.

(2) In the case of a credit-token agreement, a notice under subsection (1) (b) need not be sent by post within the seven days following the making of the agreement if either—

(a) it is sent by post to the debtor or hirer before the credit-token is given to him, or
(b) it is sent by post to him together with the credit-token.

(3) Regulations may provide that except where section 63(2) applied a notice sent under subsection (1) (b) shall be accompanied by a further copy of the executed agreement, and of any other document referred to in it.

(4) Regulations may provide that subsection (1) (b) is not to apply in the case of agreements such as are described in the regulations, being agreements made by a particular person, if—

(a) on an application by that person to the Director, the Director has determined that, having regard to—

(i) the manner in which antecedent negotiations for agreements with the applicant of that description are conducted, and
(ii) the information provided to debtors or hirers before such agreements are made,

the requirement imposed by subsection (1) (b) can be dispensed with without prejudicing the interests of debtors or hirers; and

(b) any conditions imposed by the Director in making the determination are complied with.

(5) A cancellable agreement is not properly executed if the requirements of this section are not observed. [230]

NOTES
Commencement: 19 May 1985.
Commencement order: SI 1983 No 1551, and Sch 3, para 13, to this Act.
Regulations under this section: Consumer Credit (Cancellation Notices and Copies of Documents) Regulations 1983, SI 1983 No 1557, amended by SI 1984 No 1108, SI 1985 No 666, SI 1988 No 2047; Consumer Credit (Notice of Cancellation Rights) (Exemptions) Regulations 1983, SI 1983 No 1558.

65. Consequences of improper execution

(1) An improperly-executed regulated agreement is enforceable against the debtor or hirer on an order of the court only.

(2) A retaking of goods or land to which a regulated agreement relates is an enforcement of the agreement. [231]

NOTES
Commencement: 19 May 1985.
Commencement order: SI 1983 No 1551, and Sch 3, para 13, to this Act.

66. Acceptance of credit-tokens

(1) The debtor shall not be liable under a credit-token agreement for use made of the credit-token by any person unless the debtor had previously accepted the credit-token, or the use constituted an acceptance of it by him.

(2) The debtor accepts a credit-token when—
 (a) it is signed, or
 (b) a receipt for it is signed, or
 (c) it is first used,
either by the debtor himself or by a person who, pursuant to the agreement, is authorised by him to use it. [232]

NOTES
Commencement: 19 May 1985.
Commencement order: SI 1983 No 1551, and Sch 3, para 14, to this Act.

Cancellation of certain agreements within cooling-off period

67. Cancellable agreements

A regulated agreement may be cancelled by the debtor or hirer in accordance with this Part if the antecedent negotiations included oral representations made when in the presence of the debtor or hirer by an individual acting as, or on behalf of, the negotiator, unless—
 (a) the agreement is secured on land, or is a restricted-use credit agreement to finance the purchase of land or is an agreement for a bridging loan in connection with the purchase of land, or
 (b) the unexecuted agreement is signed by the debtor or hirer at premises at which any of the following is carrying on any business (whether on a permanent or temporary basis)—
  (i) the creditor or owner;

(ii) any party to a linked transaction (other than the debtor or hirer or a relative of his);
(iii) the negotiator in any antecedent negotiations. [233]

NOTES
Commencement: 19 May 1985.
Commencement order: SI 1983 No 1551, and Sch 3, para 13, to this Act.

68. Cooling-off period

The debtor or hirer may serve notice of cancellation of a cancellable agreement between his signing of the unexecuted agreement and—

(a) the end of the fifth day following the day on which he received a copy under section 63(2) or a notice under section 64(1) (b), or
(b) if (by virtue of regulations made under section 64(4)) section 64(1) (b) does not apply, the end of the fourteenth day following the day on which he signed the unexecuted agreement. [234]

NOTES
Commencement: 19 May 1985.
Commencement order: SI 1983 No 1551, and Sch 3, para 13, to this Act.

69. Notice of cancellation

(1) If within the period specified in section 68 the debtor or hirer under a cancellable agreement serves on—

(a) the creditor or owner, or
(b) the person specified in the notice under section 64(1), or
(c) a person who (whether by virtue of subsection (6) or otherwise) is the agent of the creditor or owner,

a notice (a "notice of cancellation") which, however expressed and whether or not conforming to the notice given under section 64(1), indicates the intention of the debtor or hirer to withdraw from the agreement, the notice shall operate—

(i) to cancel the agreement, and any linked transaction, and
(ii) to withdraw any offer by the debtor or hirer, or his relative, to enter into a linked transaction.

(2) In the case of a debtor-creditor-supplier agreement for restricted-use credit financing—

(a) the doing of work or supply of goods to meet an emergency, or
(b) the supply of goods which, before service of the notice of cancellation, had by the act of the debtor or his relative become incorporated in any land or thing not comprised in the agreement or any linked transaction,

subsection (1) shall apply with the substitution of the following for paragraph (i)—

"(i) to cancel only such provisions of the agreement and any linked transaction as—

(aa) relate to the provision of credit, or
(bb) require the debtor to pay an item in the total charge for credit, or
(cc) subject the debtor to any obligation other than to pay for the doing of the said work, or the supply of the said goods".

(3) Except so far as is otherwise provided, references in this Act to the

cancellation of an agreement or transaction do not include a case within subsection (2).

(4) Except as otherwise provided by or under this Act, an agreement or transaction cancelled under subsection (1) shall be treated as if it had never been entered into.

(5) Regulations may exclude linked transactions of the prescribed description from subsection (1) (i) or (ii).

(6) Each of the following shall be deemed to be the agent of the creditor or owner for the purpose of receiving a notice of cancellation—

(a) a credit-broker or supplier who is the negotiator in antecedent negotiations, and
(b) any person who, in the course of a business carried on by him, acts on behalf of the debtor or hirer in any negotiations for the agreement.

(7) Whether or not it is actually received by him, a notice of cancellation sent by post to a person shall be deemed to be served on him at the time of posting. [235]

NOTES
Commencement: 19 May 1985.
Commencement order: SI 1983 No 1551, and Sch 3, para 13, to this Act.
Regulations under this section: see note to s 19 ante.

70. Cancellation: recovery of money paid by debtor or hirer

(1) On the cancellation of a regulated agreement, and of any linked transaction,—

(a) any sum paid by the debtor or hirer, or his relative, under or in contemplation of the agreement or transaction, including any item in the total charge for credit, shall become repayable, and
(b) any sum, including any item in the total charge for credit, which but for the cancellation is, or would or might become, payable by the debtor or hirer, or his relative, under the agreement or transaction shall cease to be, or shall not become, so payable, and
(c) in the case of a debtor-creditor-supplier agreement falling within section 12 (b) any sum paid on the debtor's behalf by the creditor to the supplier shall become repayable to the creditor.

(2) If, under the terms of a cancelled agreement or transaction, the debtor or hirer, or his relative, is in possession of any goods, he shall have a lien on them for any sum repayable to him under subsection (1) in respect of that agreement or transaction, or any other linked transaction.

(3) A sum repayable under subsection (1) is repayable by the person to whom it was originally paid, but in the case of a debtor-creditor-supplier agreement falling within section 12(b) the creditor and the supplier shall be under a joint and several liability to repay sums paid by the debtor, or his relative, under the agreement or under a linked transaction falling within section 19(1)(b) and accordingly, in such a case, the creditor shall be entitled, in accordance with rules of court, to have the supplier made a party to any proceedings brought against the creditor to recover any such sums.

(4) Subject to any agreement between them, the creditor shall be entitled to be indemnified by the supplier for loss suffered by the creditor in satisfying his

liability under subsection (3), including costs reasonably incurred by him in defending proceedings instituted by the debtor.

(5) Subsection (1) does not apply to any sum which, if not paid by a debtor, would be payable by virtue of section 71, and applies to a sum paid or payable by a debtor for the issue of a credit-token only where the credit-token has been returned to the creditor or surrendered to a supplier.

(6) If the total charge for credit includes an item in respect of a fee or commission charged by a credit-broker, the amount repayable under subsection (1) in respect of that item shall be the excess over [£3] of the fee or commission.

(7) If the total charge for credit includes any sum payable or paid by the debtor to a credit-broker otherwise than in respect of a fee or commission charged by him, that sum shall for the purposes of subsection (6) be treated as if it were such a fee or commission.

(8) So far only as is necessary to give effect to section 69(2), this section applies to an agreement or transaction within that subsection as it applies to a cancelled agreement or transaction. [236]

NOTES
Commencement: 19 May 1985.
Commencement order: SI 1983 No 1551, and Sch 3, para 13, to this Act.
Sub-s (6): figure in square brackets substituted by the Consumer Credit (Increase of Monetary Amounts) Order 1983, SI 1983 No 1571 from 20 May 1985.

71. Cancellation: repayment of credit

(1) Notwithstanding the cancellation of a regulated consumer credit agreement, other than a debtor-creditor-supplier agreement for restricted-use credit, the agreement shall continue in force so far as it relates to repayment of credit and payment of interest.

(2) If, following the cancellation of a regulated consumer credit agreement, the debtor repays the whole or a portion of a credit—
- (a) before the expiry of one month following service of the notice of cancellation, or
- (b) in the case of a credit repayable by instalments, before the date on which the first instalment is due,

no interest shall be payable on the amount repaid.

(3) If the whole of a credit repayable by instalments is not repaid on or before the date specified in subsection (2) (b), the debtor shall not be liable to repay any of the credit except on receipt of a request in writing in the prescribed form, signed by or on behalf of the creditor, stating the amounts of the remaining instalments (recalculated by the creditor as nearly as may be in accordance with the agreement and without extending the repayment period), but excluding any sum other than principal and interest.

(4) Repayment of a credit, or payment of interest, under a cancelled agreement shall be treated as duly made if it is made to any person on whom, under section 69, a notice of cancellation could have been served, other than a person referred to in section 69 (6) (b). [237]

NOTES
Commencement: 19 May 1985.
Commencement order: SI 1983 No 1551, and Sch 3, para 13, to this Act.
Regulations under this section: Consumer Credit (Repayment of Credit on Cancellation) Regulations 1983, SI 1983 No 1559.

72. Cancellation: return of goods

(1) This section applies where any agreement or transaction relating to goods, being—
   (a) a restricted-use debtor-creditor-supplier agreement, a consumer hire agreement, or a linked transaction to which the debtor or hirer under any regulated agreement is a party, or
   (b) a linked transaction to which a relative of the debtor or hirer under any regulated agreement is a party,

is cancelled after the debtor or hirer (in a case within paragraph (a)) or the relative (in a case within paragraph (b)) has acquired possession of the goods by virtue of the agreement or transaction.

(2) In this section—
   (a) "the possessor" means the person who has acquired possession of the goods as mentioned in subsection (1),
   (b) "the other party" means the person from whom the possessor acquired possession, and
   (c) "the pre-cancellation period" means the period beginning when the possessor acquired possession and ending with the cancellation.

(3) The possessor shall be treated as having been under a duty throughout the pre-cancellation period—
   (a) to retain possession of the goods, and
   (b) to take reasonable care of them.

(4) On the cancellation, the possessor shall be under a duty, subject to any lien, to restore the goods to the other party in accordance with this section, and meanwhile to retain possession of the goods and take reasonable care of them.

(5) The possessor shall not be under any duty to deliver the goods except at his own premises and in pursuance of a request in writing signed by or on behalf of the other party and served on the possessor either before, or at the time when, the goods are collected from those premises.

(6) If the possessor—
   (a) delivers the goods (whether at his own premises or elsewhere) to any person on whom, under section 69, a notice of cancellation could have been served (other than a person referred to in section 69 (6) (b)), or
   (b) sends the goods at his own expense to such a person,

he shall be discharged from any duty to retain the goods or deliver them to any person.

(7) Where the possessor delivers the goods as mentioned in subsection (6) (a) his obligation to take care of the goods shall cease; and if he sends the goods as mentioned in subsection (6) (b), he shall be under a duty to take reasonable care to see that they are received by the other party and not damaged in transit, but in other respects his duty to take care of the goods shall cease.

(8) Where, at any time during the period of 21 days following the cancellation, the possessor receives such a request as is mentioned in subsection

(5), and unreasonably refuses or unreasonably fails to comply with it, his duty to take reasonable care of the goods shall continue until he delivers or sends the goods as mentioned in subsection (6), but if within that period he does not receive such a request his duty to take reasonable care of the goods shall cease at the end of that period.

(9) The preceding provisions of this section do not apply to—
 (a) perishable goods, or
 (b) goods which by their nature are consumed by use and which, before the cancellation, were so consumed, or
 (c) goods supplied to meet an emergency, or
 (d) goods which, before the cancellation had become incorporated in any land or thing not comprised in the cancelled agreement or a linked transaction.

(10) Where the address of the possessor is specified in the executed agreement, references in this section to his own premises are to that address and no other.

(11) Breach of a duty imposed by this section is actionable as a breach of statutory duty. [238]

NOTES
 Commencement: 19 May 1985.
 Commencement order: SI 1983 No 1551, and Sch 3, para 13, to this Act.

73. Cancellation: goods given in part-exchange

(1) This section applies on the cancellation of a regulated agreement where, in antecedent negotiations, the negotiator agreed to take goods in part-exchange (the "part-exchange goods") and those goods have been delivered to him.

(2) Unless, before the end of the period of ten days beginning with the date of cancellation, the part-exchange goods are returned to the debtor or hirer in a condition substantially as good as when they were delivered to the negotiator, the debtor or hirer shall be entitled to recover from the negotiator a sum equal to the part-exchange allowance (as defined in subsection (7) (b)).

(3) In the case of a debtor-creditor-supplier agreement within section 12 (b), the negotiator and the creditor shall be under a joint and several liability to pay to the debtor a sum recoverable under subsection (2).

(4) Subject to any agreement between them, the creditor shall be entitled to be indemnified by the negotiator for loss suffered by the creditor in satisfying his liability under subsection (3), including costs reasonably incurred by him in defending proceedings instituted by the debtor.

(5) During the period of ten days beginning with the date of cancellation, the debtor or hirer, if he is in possession of goods to which the cancelled agreement relates, shall have a lien on them for—
 (a) delivery of the part-exchange goods, in a condition substantially as good as when they were delivered to the negotiator, or
 (b) a sum equal to the part-exchange allowance;
and if the lien continues to the end of that period it shall thereafter subsist only as a lien for a sum equal to the part-exchange allowance.

(6) Where the debtor or hirer recovers from the negotiator or creditor, or both of them jointly, a sum equal to the part-exchange allowance, then, if the

title of the debtor or hirer to the part-exchange goods has not vested in the negotiator, it shall so vest on the recovery of that sum.

(7) For the purposes of this section—
   (a) the negotiator shall be treated as having agreed to take goods in part-exchange if, in pursuance of the antecedent negotiations, he either purchased or agreed to purchase those goods or accepted or agreed to accept them as part of the consideration for the cancelled agreement, and
   (b) the part-exchange allowance shall be the sum agreed as such in the antecedent negotiations or, if no such agreement was arrived at, such sum as it would have been reasonable to allow in respect of the part-exchange goods if no notice of cancellation had been served.

(8) In an action brought against the creditor for a sum recoverable under subsection (2), he shall be entitled, in accordance with rules of court, to have the negotiator made a party to the proceedings.

NOTES
Commencement: 19 May 1985.
Commencement order: SI 1983 No 1551, and Sch 3, para 13, to this Act.

Exclusion of certain agreements from Part V

74. Exclusion of certain agreements from Part V

(1) This Part (except section 56) does not apply to—
   (a) a non-commercial agreement, or
   (b) a debtor-creditor agreement enabling the debtor to overdraw on a current account, or
   (c) a debtor-creditor agreement to finance the making of such payments arising on, or connected with, the death of a person as may be prescribed.

(2) This Part (except sections 55 and 56) does not apply to a small debtor-creditor-supplier agreement for restricted-use credit.

[(2A) In the case of an agreement to which the Consumer Protection (Cancellation of Contracts Concluded away from Business Premises) Regulations 1987 apply the reference in subsection (2) to a small agreement shall be construed as if in section 17(1)(a) and (b) "£35" were substituted for "£50".]

(3) Subsection (1) (b) or (c) applies only where the Director so determines, and such a determination—
   (a) may be made subject to such conditions as the Director thinks fit, and
   (b) shall be made only if the Director is of opinion that it is not against the interests of debtors.

[(3A) Notwithstanding anything in subsection (3) (b) above, in relation to a debtor-creditor agreement under which the creditor is the Bank of England or a bank within the meaning of the Bankers' Books Evidence Act 1879, the Director shall make a determination that subsection (1) (b) above applies unless he considers that it would be against the public interest to do so.]

(4) If any term of an agreement falling within subsection [(1)(c) or (2) is

expressed in writing, regulations under section 60(1) shall apply to that term (subject to section 60(3)) as if the agreement was a regulated agreement not falling within subsection [(1)(c)] or (2). **[240]**

NOTES
Commencement: 1 July 1988 (sub-s (2A)); 1 October 1979 (sub-s (3A)); 31 July 1974 (remainder).
Sub-s (2A): added by SI 1987 No 2117, reg 9, as from 1 July 1988.
Sub-s (3A): added by the Banking Act 1979, s 38(1).
Sub-s (4): amended by the Banking Act 1979, s 38(1).

PART VI

MATTERS ARISING DURING CURRENCY OF CREDIT OR HIRE AGREEMENTS

75. Liability of creditor for breaches by supplier

(1) If the debtor under a debtor-creditor-supplier agreement falling within section 12 (b) or (c) has, in relation to a transaction financed by the agreement, any claim against the supplier in respect of a misrepresentation or breach of contract, he shall have a like claim against the creditor, who, with the supplier, shall accordingly be jointly and severally liable to the debtor.

(2) Subject to any agreement between them, the creditor shall be entitled to be indemnified by the supplier for loss suffered by the creditor in satisfying his liability under subsection (1), including costs reasonably incurred by him in defending proceedings instituted by the debtor.

(3) Subsection (1) does not apply to a claim—
   (a) under a non-commercial agreement, or
   (b) so far as the claim relates to any single item to which the supplier has attached a cash price not exceeding [£100] or more than [£30,000].

(4) This section applies notwithstanding that the debtor, in entering into the transaction, exceeded the credit limit or otherwise contravened any term of the agreement.

(5) In an action brought against the creditor under subsection (1) he shall be entitled, in accordance with rules of court, to have the supplier made a party to the proceedings. **[241]**

NOTES
Commencement: 1 July 1977.
Commencement order: SI 1977 No 802, art 2(2), and Sch 3, para 15, to this Act.
Sub-s (3): first figures in square brackets substituted by SI 1983 No 1878, art 3, Schedule, Part I from 1 January 1984; second figures in square brackets substituted by SI 1983 No 1878, art 4, Schedule, Part II from 20 May 1985.

76. Duty to give notice before taking certain action

(1) The creditor or owner is not entitled to enforce a term of a regulated agreement by—
   (a) demanding earlier payment of any sum, or
   (b) recovering possession of any goods or land, or
   (c) treating any right conferred on the debtor or hirer by the agreement as terminated, restricted or deferred,
except by or after giving the debtor or hirer not less than seven days' notice of intention to do so.

(2) Subsection (1) applies only where—

(a) a period for the duration of the agreement is specified in the agreement, and

(b) that period has not ended when the creditor or owner does an act mentioned in subsection (1),

but so applies notwithstanding that, under the agreement, any party is entitled to terminate it before the end of the period so specified.

(3) A notice under subsection (1) is ineffective if not in the prescribed form.

(4) Subsection (1) does not prevent a creditor from treating the right to draw on any credit as restricted or deferred and taking such steps as may be necessary to make the restriction or deferment effective.

(5) Regulations may provide that subsection (1) is not to apply to agreements described by the regulations.

(6) Subsection (1) does not apply to a right of enforcement arising by reason of any breach by the debtor or hirer of the regulated agreement. [242]

NOTES
Commencement: 19 May 1985.
Commencement order: SI 1983 No 1551, and Sch 3, para 16, to this Act.
Regulations under this section: Consumer Credit (Enforcement, Default and Termination) Regulations 1983, SI 1983 No 1561, amended by SI 1984 No 1109.

77. Duty to give information to debtor under fixed-sum credit agreement

(1) The creditor under a regulated agreement for fixed-sum credit, within the prescribed period after receiving a request in writing to that effect from the debtor and payment of a fee of [50p], shall give the debtor a copy of the executed agreement (if any) and of any other document referred to in it, together with a statement signed by or on behalf of the creditor showing, according to the information to which it is practicable for him to refer,—

(a) the total sum paid under the agreement by the debtor;

(b) the total sum which has become payable under the agreement by the debtor but remains unpaid, and the various amounts comprised in that total sum, with the date when each became due; and

(c) the total sum which is to become payable under the agreement by the debtor, and the various amounts comprised in that total sum, with the date, or mode of determining the date, when each becomes due.

(2) If the creditor possesses insufficient information to enable him to ascertain the amounts and dates mentioned in subsection (1) (c), he shall be taken to comply with that paragraph if his statement under subsection (1) gives the basis on which, under the regulated agreement, they would fall to be ascertained.

(3) Subsection (1) does not apply to—

(a) an agreement under which no sum is, or will or may become, payable by the debtor, or

(b) a request made less than one month after a previous request under that subsection relating to the same agreement was complied with.

(4) If the creditor under an agreement fails to comply with subsection (1)—

(a) he is not entitled, while the default continues, to enforce the agreement; and

(b) if the default continues for one month he commits an offence.

(5) This section does not apply to a non-commercial agreement. [243]

NOTES
Commencement: 19 May 1985.
Commencement order: SI 1983 No 1551, and Sch 3, para 17, to this Act.
Sub-s (1): amended by the Consumer Credit (Increase of Monetary Amounts) Order 1983, SI 1983 No 1571 in force 20 May 1985.
Regulations under this section: Consumer Credit (Prescribed Periods for Giving Information) Regulations 1983, SI 1983 No 1569.

78. Duty to give information to debtor under running-account credit agreement

(1) The creditor under a regulated agreement for running-account credit, within the prescribed period after receiving a request in writing to that effect from the debtor and payment of a fee of [50p], shall give the debtor a copy of the executed agreement (if any) and of any other document referred to in it, together with a statement signed by or on behalf of the creditor showing, according to the information to which it is practicable for him to refer,—
   (a) the state of the account, and
   (b) the amount, if any, currently payable under the agreement by the debtor to the creditor, and
   (c) the amounts and due dates of any payments which, if the debtor does not draw further on the account, will later become payable under the agreement by the debtor to the creditor.

(2) If the creditor possesses insufficient information to enable him to ascertain the amounts and dates mentioned in subsection (1) (c), he shall be taken to comply with that paragraph if his statement under subsection (1) gives the basis on which, under the regulated agreement, they would fall to be ascertained.

(3) Subsection (1) does not apply to—
   (a) an agreement under which no sum is, or will or may become, payable by the debtor, or
   (b) a request made less than one month after a previous request under that subsection relating to the same agreement was complied with.

(4) Where running-account credit is provided under a regulated agreement, the creditor shall give the debtor statements in the prescribed form, and with the prescribed contents—
   (a) showing according to the information to which it is practicable for him to refer, the state of the account at regular intervals of not more than twelve months, and
   (b) where the agreement provides, in relation to specified periods, for the making of payments by the debtor, or the charging against him of interest or any other sum, showing according to the information to which it is practicable for him to refer the state of the account at the end of each of those periods during which there is any movement in the account.

(5) A statement under subsection (4) shall be given within the prescribed period after the end of the period to which the statement relates.

(6) If the creditor under an agreement fails to comply with subsection (1)—
   (a) he is not entitled, while the default continues, to enforce the agreement; and

(b) if the default continues for one month he commits an offence.

(7) This section does not apply to a non-commercial agreement, and subsections (4) and (5) do not apply to a small agreement. **[244]**

NOTES
Commencement: 19 May 1985.
Commencement order: SI 1983 No 1551, and Sch 3, para 17, to this Act.
Sub-s (1): amended by the Consumer Credit (Increase of Monetary Amounts) Order 1983, SI 1983 No 1571 in force 20 May 1985.
Regulations under this section: see note to s 77 ante.

79. Duty to give hirer information

(1) The owner under a regulated consumer hire agreement, within the prescribed period after receiving a request in writing to that effect from the hirer and payment of a fee of [50p], shall give to the hirer a copy of the executed agreement and of any other document referred to in it, together with a statement signed by or on behalf of the owner showing, according to the information to which it is practicable for him to refer, the total sum which has become payable under the agreement by the hirer but remains unpaid and the various amounts comprised in that total sum, with the date when each became due.

(2) Subsection (1) does not apply to—
  (a) an agreement under which no sum is, or will or may become, payable by the hirer, or
  (b) a request made less than one month after a previous request under that subsection relating to the same agreement was complied with.

(3) If the owner under an agreement fails to comply with subsection (1)—
  (a) he is not entitled, while the default continues, to enforce the agreement; and
  (b) if the default continues for one month he commits an offence.

(4) This section does not apply to a non-commercial agreement. **[245]**

NOTES
Commencement: 19 May 1985.
Commencement order: SI 1983 No 1551, and Sch 3, para 17, to this Act.
Sub-s (1): amended by the Consumer Credit (Increase of Monetary Amounts) Order 1983, SI 1983 No 1571 in force 20 May 1985.
Regulations under this section: see note to s 77 ante.

80. Debtor or hirer to give information about goods

(1) Where a regulated agreement, other than a non-commercial agreement, requires the debtor or hirer to keep goods to which the agreement relates in his possession or control, he shall, within seven working days after he has received a request in writing to that effect from the creditor or owner, tell the creditor or owner where the goods are.

(2) If the debtor or hirer fails to comply with subsection (1), and the default continues for 14 days, he commits an offence. **[246]**

NOTES
Commencement: 19 May 1985.
Commencement order: SI 1983 No 1551, and Sch 3, para 17, to this Act.

81. Appropriation of payments

(1) Where a debtor or hirer is liable to make to the same person payments in respect of two or more regulated agreements, he shall be entitled, on making any payment in respect of the agreements which is not sufficient to discharge the total amount then due under all the agreements, to appropriate the sum so paid by him—
- (a) in or towards the satisfaction of the sum due under any one of the agreements, or
- (b) in or towards the satisfaction of the sums due under any two or more of the agreements in such proportions as he thinks fit.

(2) If the debtor or hirer fails to make any such appropriation where one or more of the agreements is—
- (a) a hire-purchase agreement or conditional sale agreement, or
- (b) a consumer hire agreement, or
- (c) an agreement in relation to which any security is provided,

the payment shall be appropriated towards the satisfaction of the sums due under the several agreements respectively in the proportions which those sums bear to one another. [247]

NOTES
Commencement: 19 May 1985.
Commencement order: SI 1983 No 1551, and Sch 3, para 18, to this Act.

82. Variation of agreements

(1) Where, under a power contained in a regulated agreement, the creditor or owner varies the agreement, the variation shall not take effect before notice of it is given to the debtor or hirer in the prescribed manner.

(2) Where an agreement (a "modifying agreement") varies or supplements an earlier agreement, the modifying agreement shall for the purposes of this Act be treated as—
- (a) revoking the earlier agreement, and
- (b) containing provisions reproducing the combined effect of the two agreements,

and obligations outstanding in relation to the earlier agreement shall accordingly be treated as outstanding instead in relation to the modifying agreement.

(3) If the earlier agreement is a regulated agreement but (apart from this subsection) the modifying agreement is not then, unless the modifying agreement is for running-account credit, it shall be treated as a regulated agreement.

(4) If the earlier agreement is a regulated agreement for running-account credit, and by the modifying agreement the creditor allows the credit limit to be exceeded but intends the excess to be merely temporary, Part V (except section 56) shall not apply to the modifying agreement.

(5) If—
- (a) the earlier agreement is a cancellable agreement, and
- (b) the modifying agreement is made within the period applicable under section 68 to the earlier agreement,

then, whether or not the modifying agreement would, apart from this subsection, be a cancellable agreement, it shall be treated as a cancellable agreement in respect of which a notice may be served under section 68 not later than the end of the period applicable under that section to the earlier agreement.

(6) Except under subsection (5), a modifying agreement shall not be treated as a cancellable agreement.

(7) This section does not apply to a non-commercial agreement. [248]

NOTES
Commencement: 1 April 1977.
Commencement order: SI 1977 No 325, art 2(1), and Sch 3, para 19, to this Act.
Regulations under this section: Consumer Credit (Notice of Variation of Agreements) Regulations 1977, SI 1977 No 328, amended by SI 1979 No 661, SI 1979 No 667.

83. Liability for misuse of credit facilities

(1) The debtor under a regulated consumer credit agreement shall not be liable to the creditor for any loss arising from use of the credit facility by another person not acting, or to be treated as acting, as the debtor's agent.

(2) This section does not apply to a non-commercial agreement, or to any loss in so far as it arises from misuse of an instrument to which section 4 of the Cheques Act 1957 applies. [249]

NOTES
Commencement: 19 May 1985.
Commencement order: SI 1983 No 1551, and Sch 3, para 20, to this Act.

84. Misuse of credit-tokens

(1) Section 83 does not prevent the debtor under a credit-token agreement from being made liable to the extent of [£50] (or the credit limit if lower) for loss to the creditor arising from use of the credit-token by other persons during a period beginning when the credit-token ceases to be in the possession of any authorised person and ending when the credit-token is once more in the possession of an authorised person.

(2) Section 83 does not prevent the debtor under a credit-token agreement from being made liable to any extent for loss to the creditor from use of the credit-token by a person who acquired possession of it with the debtor's consent.

(3) Subsections (1) and (2) shall not apply to any use of the credit-token after the creditor has been given oral or written notice that it is lost or stolen, or is for any other reason liable to misuse.

(4) Subsections (1) and (2) shall not apply unless there are contained in the credit-token agreement in the prescribed manner particulars of the name, address and telephone number of a person stated to be the person to whom notice is to be given under subsection (3).

(5) Notice under subsection (3) takes effect when received, but where it is given orally, and the agreement so requires, it shall be treated as not taking effect if not confirmed in writing within seven days.

(6) Any sum paid by the debtor for the issue of the credit-token, to the extent (if any) that it has not been previously offset by use made of the credit token, shall be treated as paid towards satisfaction of any liability under subsection (1) or (2).

(7) The debtor, the creditor, and any person authorised by the debtor to use the credit-token, shall be authorised persons for the purposes of subsection (1).

(8) Where two or more credit-tokens are given under one credit-token agreement, the preceding provisions of this section apply to each credit-token separately. [250]

NOTES
Commencement: 19 May 1985.
Commencement order: SI 1983 No 1551, and Sch 3, para 20, to this Act.
Sub-s (1): figure in square brackets substituted by the Consumer Credit (Increase of Monetary Amounts) Order 1983, SI 1983 No 1571 in force 20 May 1985.
Regulations under this section: Consumer Credit (Credit-Token Agreements) Regulations 1983, SI 1983 No 1555.

85. Duty on issue of new credit-tokens

(1) Whenever, in connection with a credit-token agreement, a credit-token (other than the first) is given by the creditor to the debtor, the creditor shall give the debtor a copy of the executed agreement (if any) and of any other document referred to in it.

(2) If the creditor fails to comply with this section—
    (a) he is not entitled, while the default continues, to enforce the agreement; and
    (b) if the default continues for one month he commits an offence.

(3) This section does not apply to a small agreement. [251]

NOTES
Commencement: 19 May 1985.
Commencement order: SI 1983 No 1551, and Sch 3, para 21, to this Act.

86. Death of debtor or hirer

(1) The creditor or owner under a regulated agreement is not entitled, by reason of the death of the debtor or hirer, to do an act specified in paragraphs (a) to (e) of section 87(1) if at the death the agreement is fully secured.

(2) If at the death of the debtor or hirer a regulated agreement is only partly secured or is unsecured, the creditor or owner is entitled, by reason of the death of the debtor or hirer, to do an act specified in paragraphs (a) to (e) of section 87(1) on an order of the court only.

(3) This section applies in relation to the termination of an agreement only where—
    (a) a period for its duration is specified in the agreement, and
    (b) that period has not ended when the creditor or owner purports to terminate the agreement,
but so applies notwithstanding that, under the agreement, any party is entitled to terminate it before the end of the period so specified.

(4) This section does not prevent the creditor from treating the right to draw on any credit as restricted or deferred, and taking such steps as may be necessary to make the restriction or deferment effective.

(5) This section does not affect the operation of any agreement providing for payment of sums—
    (a) due under the regulated agreement, or
    (b) becoming due under it on the death of the debtor or hirer,
out of the proceeds of a policy of assurance on his life.

(6) For the purposes of this section an act is done by reason of the death of the debtor or hirer if it is done under a power conferred by the agreement which is—

(a) exercisable on his death, or
(b) exercisable at will and exercised at any time after his death. [252]

NOTES
Commencement: 19 May 1985.
Commencement order: SI 1983 No 1551, and Sch 3, para 20, to this Act.

PART VII

DEFAULT AND TERMINATION

Default notices

87. Need for default notice

(1) Service of a notice on the debtor or hirer in accordance with section 88 (a "default notice") is necessary before the creditor or owner can become entitled, by reason of any breach by the debtor or hirer of a regulated agreement,—

(a) to terminate the agreement, or
(b) to demand earlier payment of any sum, or
(c) to recover possession of any goods or land, or
(d) to treat any right conferred on the debtor or hirer by the agreement as terminated, restricted or deferred, or
(e) to enforce any security.

(2) Subsection (1) does not prevent the creditor from treating the right to draw upon any credit as restricted or deferred, and taking such steps as may be necessary to make the restriction or deferment effective.

(3) The doing of an act by which a floating charge becomes fixed is not enforcement of a security.

(4) Regulations may provide that subsection (1) is not to apply to agreements described by the regulations. [253]

NOTES
Commencement: 19 May 1985.
Commencement order: SI 1983 No 1551, and Sch 3, para 23, to this Act.
Regulations under this section: see note to s 76 ante.

88. Contents and effect of default notice

(1) The default notice must be in the prescribed from and specify—

(a) the nature of the alleged breach;
(b) if the breach is capable of remedy, what action is required to remedy it and the date before which that action is to be taken;
(c) if the breach is not capable of remedy, the sum (if any) required to be paid as compensation for the breach, and the date before which it is to be paid.

(2) A date specified under subsection (1) must not be less than seven days after the date of service of the default notice, and the creditor or owner shall not take action such as is mentioned in section 87(1) before the date so specified or (if no requirement is made under subsection (1)) before those seven days have elapsed.

(3) The default notice must not treat as a breach failure to comply with a provision of the agreement which becomes operative only on breach of some other provision, but if the breach of that other provision is not duly remedied or compensation demanded under subsection (1) is not duly paid, or (where no requirement is made under subsection (1)) if the seven days mentioned in subsection (2) have elapsed, the creditor or owner may treat the failure as a breach and section 87(1) shall not apply to it.

(4) The default notice must contain information in the prescribed terms about the consequences of failure to comply with it.

(5) A default notice making a requirement under subsection (1) may include a provision for the taking of action such as is mentioned in section 87(1) at any time after the restriction imposed by subsection (2) will cease, together with a statement that the provision will be ineffective if the breach is duly remedied or the compensation duly paid. [254]

NOTES
Commencement: 19 May 1985.
Commencement order: SI 1983 No 1551, and Sch 3, para 22, to this Act.
Regulations under this section: see note to s 76 ante.

89. Compliance with default notice

If before the date specified for that purpose in the default notice the debtor or hirer takes the action specified under section 88(1)(b) or (c) the breach shall be treated as not having occurred. [255]

NOTES
Commencement: 19 May 1985.
Commencement: SI 1983 No 1551, and Sch 3, para 22, to this Act.

Further restriction of remedies for default

90. Retaking of protected hire-purchase etc goods

(1) At any time when—
 (a) the debtor is in breach of a regulated hire-purchase or a regulated conditional sale agreement relating to goods, and
 (b) the debtor has paid to the creditor one-third or more of the total price of the goods, and
 (c) the property in the goods remains in the creditor,
the creditor is not entitled to recover possession of the goods from the debtor except on an order of the court.

(2) Where under a hire-purchase or conditional sale agreement the creditor is required to carry out any installation and the agreement specifies, as part of the total price, the amount to be paid in respect of the installation (the "installation charge") the reference in subsection (1) (b) to one-third of the total price shall be construed as a reference to the aggregate of the installation charge and one-third of the remainder of the total price.

(3) In a case where—
 (a) subsection (1) (a) is satisfied, but not subsection (1) (b), and
 (b) subsection (1) (b) was satisfied on a previous occasion in relation to an earlier agreement, being a regulated hire-purchase or regulated conditional sale agreement, between the same parties, and relating to

any of the goods comprised in the later agreement (whether or not other goods were also included),

subsection (1) shall apply to the later agreement with the omission of paragraph (b).

(4) If the later agreement is a modifying agreement, subsection (3) shall apply with the substitution, for the second reference to the later agreement, of a reference to the modifying agreement.

(5) Subsection (1) shall not apply, or shall cease to apply, to an agreement if the debtor has terminated, or terminates, the agreement.

(6) Where subsection (1) applies to an agreement at the death of the debtor, it shall continue to apply (in relation to the possessor of the goods) until the grant of probate or administration, or (in Scotland) confirmation (on which the personal representative would fall to be treated as the debtor).

(7) Goods falling within this section are in this Act referred to as "protected goods". [256]

NOTES
Commencement: 19 May 1985.
Commencement order: SI 1983 No 1551, and Sch 3, para 24, to this Act.

91. Consequences of breach of s 90

If goods are recovered by the creditor in contravention of section 90—

(a) the regulated agreement, if not previously terminated, shall terminate, and
(b) the debtor shall be released from all liability under the agreement, and shall be entitled to recover from the creditor all sums paid by the debtor under the agreement. [257]

NOTES
Commencement: 19 May 1985.
Commencement order: SI 1983 No 1551, and Sch 3, para 24, to this Act.

92. Recovery of possession of goods or land

(1) Except under an order of the court, the creditor or owner shall not be entitled to enter any premises to take possession of goods subject to a regulated hire-purchase agreement, regulated conditional sale agreement or regulated consumer hire agreement.

(2) At any time when the debtor is in breach of a regulated conditional sale agreement relating to land, the creditor is entitled to recover possession of the land from the debtor, or any person claiming under him, on an order of the court only.

(3) An entry in contravention of subsection (1) or (2) is actionable as a breach of statutory duty. [258]

NOTES
Commencement: 19 May 1985.
Commencement order: SI 1983 No 1551, and Sch 3, para 25, to this Act.

93. Interest not to be increased on default

The debtor under a regulated consumer credit agreement shall not be obliged to pay interest on sums which, in breach of the agreement, are unpaid by him at a rate—

- (*a*) where the total charge for credit includes an item in respect of interest, exceeding the rate of that interest, or
- (*b*) in any other case, exceeding what would be the rate of the total charge for credit if any items included in the total charge for credit by virtue of section 20(2) were disregarded. **[259]**

NOTES
Commencement: 19 May 1985.
Commencement order: SI 1983 No 1551, and Sch 3, para 26, to this Act.

NOTES
Section 93A, which applies to Scotland only, is omitted.

Early payment by debtor

94. Right to complete payments ahead of time

(1) The debtor under a regulated consumer credit agreement is entitled at any time, by notice to the creditor and the payment to the creditor of all amounts payable by the debtor to him under the agreement (less any rebate allowable under section 95), to discharge the debtor's indebtedness under the agreement.

(2) A notice under subsection (1) may embody the exercise by the debtor of any option to purchase goods conferred on him by the agreement, and deal with any other matter arising on, or in relation to, the termination of the agreement. **[260]**

NOTES
Commencement: 19 May 1985.
Commencement order: SI 1983 No 1551, and Sch 3, para 27, to this Act.

95. Rebate on early settlement

(1) Regulations may provide for the allowance of a rebate of charges for credit to the debtor under a regulated consumer credit agreement where, under section 94, on refinancing, on breach of the agreement, or for any other reason, his indebtedness is discharged or becomes payable before the time fixed by the agreement, or any sum becomes payable by him before the time so fixed.

(2) Regulations under subsection (1) may provide for calculation of the rebate by reference to any sums paid or payable by the debtor or his relative under or in connection with the agreement (whether to the creditor or some other person), including sums under linked transactions and other items in the total charge for credit. **[261]**

NOTES
Commencement: 19 May 1985.
Commencement order: SI 1983 No 1551, and Sch 3, para 27, to this Act.
Regulations under this section: Consumer Credit (Rebate on Early Settlement) Regulations 1983, SI 1983 No 1562.

96. Effect on linked transactions

(1) Where for any reason the indebtedness of the debtor under a regulated consumer credit agreement is discharged before the time fixed by the agreement, he, and any relative of his, shall at the same time be discharged from any liability under a linked transaction, other than a debt which has already become payable.

(2) Subsection (1) does not apply to a linked transaction which is itself an agreement providing the debtor or his relative with credit.

(3) Regulations may exclude linked transactions of the prescribed description from the operation of subsection (1). **[262]**

NOTES
Commencement: 19 May 1985.
Commencement order: SI 1983 No 1551, and Sch 3, para 27, to this Act.
Regulations under this section: see note to s 19 ante.

97. Duty to give information

(1) The creditor under a regulated consumer credit agreement, within the prescribed period after he has received a request in writing to that effect from the debtor, shall give the debtor a statement in the prescribed form indicating, according to the information to which it is practicable for him to refer, the amount of the payment required to discharge the debtor's indebtedness under the agreement, together with the prescribed particulars showing how the amount is arrived at.

(2) Subsection (1) does not apply to a request made less than one month after a previous request under that subsection relating to the same agreement was complied with.

(3) If the creditor fails to comply with subsection (1)—
   (a) he is not entitled, while the default continues, to enforce the agreement; and
   (b) if the default continues for one month he commits an offence. **[263]**

NOTES
Commencement: 19 May 1985.
Commencement order: SI 1983 No 1551, and Sch 3, para 27, to this Act.
Regulations under this section: Consumer Credit (Settlement Information) Regulations 1983, SI 1983 No 1564.

Termination of agreements

98. Duty to give notice of termination (non-default cases)

(1) The creditor or owner is not entitled to terminate a regulated agreement except by or after giving the debtor or hirer not less than seven days' notice of the termination.

(2) Subsection (1) applies only where—
   (a) a period for the duration of the agreement is specified in the agreement, and
   (b) that period has not ended when the creditor or owner does an act mentioned in subsection (1),

but so applies notwithstanding that, under the agreement, any party is entitled to terminate it before the end of the period so specified.

(3) A notice under subsection (1) is ineffective if not in the prescribed form.

(4) Subsection (1) does not prevent a creditor from treating the right to draw on any credit as restricted or deferred and taking such steps as may be necessary to make the restriction or deferment effective.

(5) Regulations may provide that subsection (1) is not to apply to agreements described by the regulations.

(6) Subsection (1) does not apply to the termination of a regulated agreement by reason of any breach by the debtor or hirer of the agreement. [264]

NOTES
    Commencement: 19 May 1985.
    Commencement order: SI 1983 No 1551, and Sch 3, para 28, to this Act.
    Regulations under this section: see note to s 76 ante.

99. Right to terminate hire-purchase etc agreements

(1) At any time before the final payment by the debtor under a regulated hire-purchase or regulated conditional sale agreement falls due, the debtor shall be entitled to terminate the agreement by giving notice to any person entitled or authorised to receive the sums payable under the agreement.

(2) Termination of an agreement under subsection (1) does not affect any liability under the agreement which has accrued before the termination.

(3) Subsection (1) does not apply to a conditional sale agreement relating to land after the title to the land has passed to the debtor.

(4) In the case of a conditional sale agreement relating to goods, where the property in the goods, having become vested in the debtor, is transferred to a person who does not become the debtor under the agreement, the debtor shall not thereafter be entitled to terminate the agreement under subsection (1).

(5) Subject to subsection (4), where a debtor under a conditional sale agreement relating to goods, terminates the agreement under this section after the property in the goods has become vested in him, the property in the goods shall thereupon vest in the person (the "previous owner") in whom it was vested immediately before it became vested in the debtor:

Provided that if the previous owner has died, or any other event has occurred whereby that property, if vested in him immediately before that event, would thereupon have vested in some other person, the property shall be treated as having devolved as if it had been vested in the previous owner immediately before his death or immediately before that event, as the case may be. [265]

NOTES
    Commencement: 19 May 1985.
    Commencement order: SI 1983 No 1551, and Sch 3, para 29, to this Act.

100. Liability of debtor on termination of hire-purchase etc agreement

(1) Where a regulated hire-purchase or regulated conditional sale agreement is terminated under section 99 the debtor shall be liable, unless the agreement provides for a smaller payment, or does not provide for any payment, to pay to the creditor the amount (if any) by which one-half of the total price exceeds the aggregate of the sums paid and the sums due in respect of the total price immediately before the termination.

(2) Where under a hire-purchase or conditional sale agreement the creditor

is required to carry out any installation and the agreement specifies, as part of the total price, the amount to be paid in respect of the installation (the "installation charge") the reference in subsection (1) to one-half of the total price shall be construed as a reference to the aggregate of the installation charge and one-half of the remainder of the total price.

(3) If in any action the court is satisfied that a sum less than the amount specified in subsection (1) would be equal to the loss sustained by the creditor in consequence of the termination of the agreement by the debtor, the court may make an order for the payment of that sum in lieu of the amount specified in subsection (1).

(4) If the debtor has contravened an obligation to take reasonable care of the goods or land, the amount arrived at under subsection (1) shall be increased by the sum required to recompense the creditor for that contravention, and subsection (2) shall have effect accordingly.

(5) Where the debtor, on the termination of the agreement, wrongfully retains possession of goods to which the agreement relates, then, in any action brought by the creditor to recover possession of the goods from the debtor, the court, unless it is satisfied that having regard to the circumstances it would not be just to do so, shall order the goods to be delivered to the creditor without giving the debtor an option to pay the value of the goods. **[266]**

NOTES
Commencement: 19 May 1985.
Commencement order: SI 1983 No 1551, and Sch 3, para 30, to this Act.

101. Right to terminate hire agreement

(1) The hirer under a regulated consumer hire agreement is entitled to terminate the agreement by giving notice to any person entitled or authorised to receive the sums payable under the agreement.

(2) Termination of an agreement under subsection (1) does not affect any liability under the agreement which has accrued before the termination.

(3) A notice under subsection (1) shall not expire earlier than eighteen months after the making of the agreement, but apart from that the minimum period of notice to be given under subsection (1), unless the agreement provides for a shorter period, is as follows.

(4) If the agreement provides for the making of payments by the hirer to the owner at equal intervals, the minimum period of notice is the length of one interval or three months, whichever is less.

(5) If the agreement provides for the making of such payments at differing intervals, the minimum period of notice is the length of the shortest interval or three months, whichever is less.

(6) In any other case, the minimum period of notice is three months.

(7) This section does not apply to—
   (*a*) any agreement which provides for the making by the hirer of payments which in total (and without breach of the agreement) exceed [£900] in any year, or
   (*b*) any agreement where—

> > (i) goods are bailed or (in Scotland) hired to the hirer for the purposes of a business carried on by him, or the hirer holds himself out as requiring the goods for those purposes, and
> > (ii) the goods are selected by the hirer, and acquired by the owner for the purposes of the agreement at the request of the hirer from any person other than the owner's associate, or
>
> (c) any agreement where the hirer requires, or holds himself out as requiring, the goods for the purpose of bailing or hiring them to other persons in the course of a business carried on by him.

(8) If, on an application made to the Director by a person carrying on a consumer hire business, it appears to the Director that it would be in the interest of hirers to do so, he may by notice to the applicant direct that this section shall not apply to consumer hire agreements made by the applicant, and subject to such conditions (if any) as the Director may specify, this Act shall have effect accordingly.

(9) In the case of a modifying agreement subsection (3) shall apply with the substitution, for "the making of the agreement" of "the making of the original agreement". [267]

NOTES
Commencement: 19 May 1985.
Commencement order: SI 1983 No 1551, and Sch 3, para 31, to this Act.
Sub-s (7): figure in square brackets substituted by the Consumer Credit (Increase of Monetary Amounts) Order 1983, SI 1983 No 1571 in force 20 May 1985.

102. Agency for receiving notice of rescission

(1) Where the debtor or hirer under a regulated agreement claims to have a right to rescind the agreement, each of the following shall be deemed to be the agent of the creditor or owner for the purpose of receiving any notice rescinding the agreement which is served by the debtor or hirer—

> (a) a credit-broker or supplier who was the negotiator in antecedent negotiations, and
> (b) any person who, in the course of a business carried on by him, acted on behalf of the debtor or hirer in any negotiations for the agreement.

(2) In subsection (1) "rescind" does not include—

> (a) service of a notice of cancellation, or
> (b) termination of an agreement under section 99 or 101 or by the exercise of a right or power in that behalf expressly conferred by the agreement. [268]

NOTES
Commencement: 19 May 1985.
Commencement order: SI 1983 No 1551, and Sch 3, para 32, to this Act.

103. Termination statements

(1) If an individual (the "customer") serves on any person (the "trader") a notice—

> (a) stating that—
> > (i) the customer was the debtor or hirer under a regulated agreement described in the notice, and the trader was the creditor or owner under the agreement, and

(ii) the customer has discharged his indebtedness to the trader under the agreement, and

(iii) the agreement has ceased to have any operation; and

(b) requiring the trader to give the customer a notice, signed by or on behalf of the trader, confirming that those statements are correct,

the trader shall, within the prescribed period after receiving the notice, either comply with it or serve on the customer a counter-notice stating that, as the case may be, he disputes the correctness of the notice or asserts that the customer is not indebted to him under the agreement.

(2) Where the trader disputes the correctness of the notice he shall give particulars of the way in which he alleges it to be wrong.

(3) Subsection (1) does not apply in relation to any agreement if the trader has previously complied with that subsection on the service of a notice under it with respect to that agreement.

(4) Subsection (1) does not apply to a non-commercial agreement.

(5) If the trader fails to comply with subsection (1), and the default continues for one month, he commits an offence. [269]

NOTES
Commencement: 19 May 1985.
Commencement order: SI 1983 No 1551, and Sch 3, para 33, to this Act.

NOTES
Section 104, which applies to Scotland only, is omitted.

PART VIII

SECURITY

General

105. Form and content of securities

(1) Any security provided in relation to a regulated agreement shall be expressed in writing.

(2) Regulations may prescribe the form and content of documents ("security instruments") to be made in compliance with subsection (1).

(3) Regulations under subsection (2) may in particular—

(a) require specified information to be included in the prescribed manner in documents, and other specified material to be excluded;

(b) contain requirements to ensure that specified information is clearly brought to the attention of the surety, and that one part of a document is not given insufficient or excessive prominence compared with another.

(4) A security instrument is not properly executed unless—

(a) a document in the prescribed form, itself containing all the prescribed terms and conforming to regulations under subsection (2), is signed in the prescribed manner by or on behalf of the surety, and

(b) the document embodies all the terms of the security, other than implied terms, and

(c) the document, when presented or sent for the purpose of being signed by or on behalf of the surety, is in such a state that its terms are readily legible, and

(d) when the document is presented or sent for the purpose of being signed by or on behalf of the surety there is also presented or sent a copy of the document.

(5) A security instrument is not properly executed unless—

(a) where the security is provided after, or at the time when, the regulated agreement is made, a copy of the executed agreement, together with a copy of any other document referred to in it, is given to the surety at the time the security is provided, or

(b) where the security is provided before the regulated agreement is made, a copy of the executed agreement, together with a copy of any other document referred to in it, is given to the surety within seven days after the regulated agreement is made.

(6) Subsection (1) does not apply to a security provided by the debtor or hirer.

(7) If—

(a) in contravention of subsection (1) a security is not expressed in writing, or

(b) a security instrument is improperly executed,

the security, so far as provided in relation to a regulated agreement, is enforceable against the surety on an order of the court only.

(8) If an application for an order under subsection (7) is dismissed (except on technical grounds only) section 106 (ineffective securities) shall apply to the security.

(9) Regulations under section 60(1) shall include provision requiring documents embodying regulated agreements also to embody any security provided in relation to a regulated agreement by the debtor or hirer. **[270]**

NOTES
Commencement: 19 May 1985.
Commencement order: SI 1983 No 1551, and Sch 3, para 36, to this Act.
Regulations under this section: see note to s 60 ante.

106. Ineffective securities

Where, under any provision of this Act, this section is applied to any security provided in relation to a regulated agreement, then, subject to section 177 (saving for registered charges),—

(a) the security, so far as it is so provided, shall be treated as never having effect;

(b) any property lodged with the creditor or owner solely for the purposes of the security as so provided shall be returned by him forthwith;

(c) the creditor or owner shall take any necessary action to remove or cancel an entry in any register, so far as the entry relates to the security as so provided; and

(d) any amount received by the creditor or owner on realisation of the security shall, so far as it is referable to the agreement, be repaid to the surety. **[271]**

NOTES
Commencement: 31 July 1974.

107. Duty to give information to surety under fixed-sum credit agreement

(1) The creditor under a regulated agreement for fixed-sum credit in relation to which security is provided, within the prescribed period after receiving a request in writing to that effect from the surety and payment of a fee of [50p], shall give to the surety (if a different person from the debtor)—

    (a) a copy of the executed agreement (if any) and of any other document referred to in it;
    (b) a copy of the security instrument (if any); and
    (c) a statement signed by or on behalf of the creditor showing, according to the information to which it is practicable for him to refer,—
        (i) the total sum paid under the agreement by the debtor,
        (ii) the total sum which has become payable under the agreement by the debtor but remains unpaid, and the various amounts comprised in that total sum, with the date when each became due, and
        (iii) the total sum which is to become payable under the agreement by the debtor, and the various amounts comprised in that total sum, with the date, or mode of determining the date, when each becomes due.

(2) If the creditor possesses insufficient information to enable him to ascertain the amount and dates mentioned in subsection (1) (c) (iii), he shall be taken to comply with that sub-paragraph if his statement under subsection (1) (c) gives the basis on which, under the regulated agreement, they would fall to be ascertained.

(3) Subsection (1) does not apply to—

    (a) an agreement under which no sum is, or will or may become, payable by the debtor, or
    (b) a request made less than one month after a previous request under that subsection relating to the same agreement was complied with.

(4) If the creditor under an agreement fails to comply with subsection (1)—

    (a) he is not entitled, while the default continues, to enforce the security, so far as provided in relation to the agreement; and
    (b) if the default continues for one month he commits an offence.

(5) This section does not apply to a non-commercial agreement.

NOTES
Commencement: 19 May 1985.
Commencement order: SI 1983 No 1551, and Sch 3, para 37, to this Act.
Sub-s (1): figure in square brackets substituted by the Consumer Credit (Increase of Monetary Amounts) Order 1983, SI 1983 No 1571 in force 20 May 1985.
Regulations under this section: see note to s 77 ante.

108. Duty to give information to surety under running-account credit agreement

(1) The creditor under a regulated agreement for running-account credit in relation to which security is provided, within the prescribed period after receiving a request in writing to that effect from the surety and payment of a fee of [50p], shall give to the surety (if a different person from the debtor)—

(a) a copy of the executed agreement (if any) and of any other document referred to in it;
(b) a copy of the security instrument (if any); and
(c) a statement signed by or on behalf of the creditor showing, according to the information to which it is practicable for him to refer,—
   (i) the state of the account, and
   (ii) the amount, if any, currently payable under the agreement by the debtor to the creditor, and
   (iii) the amounts and due dates of any payments which, if the debtor does not draw further on the account, will later become payable under the agreement by the debtor to the creditor.

(2) If the creditor possesses insufficient information to enable him to ascertain the amounts and dates mentioned in subsection (1) (c) (iii), he shall be taken to comply with that sub-paragraph if his statement under subsection (1) (c) gives the basis on which, under the regulated agreement, they would fall to be ascertained.

(3) Subsection (1) does not apply to—
   (a) an agreement under which no sum is, or will or may become, payable by the debtor, or
   (b) a request made less than one month after a previous request under that subsection relating to the same agreement was complied with.

(4) If the creditor under an agreement fails to comply with subsection (1)—
   (a) he is not entitled, while the default continues, to enforce the security, so far as provided in relation to the agreement; and
   (b) if the default continues for one month he commits an offence.

(5) This section does not apply to a non-commercial agreement. [273]

NOTES
Commencement: 19 May 1985.
Commencement order: SI 1983 No 1551, and Sch 3, para 37, to this Act.
Sub-s (1): figure in square brackets substituted by the Consumer Credit (Increase of Monetary Amounts) Order 1983, SI 1983 No 1571 in force 20 May 1985.

109. Duty to give information to surety under consumer hire agreement

(1) The owner under a regulated consumer hire agreement in relation to which security is provided, within the prescribed period after receiving a request in writing to that effect from the surety and payment of a fee of [50p], shall give to the surety (if a different person from the hirer)—
   (a) a copy of the executed agreement and of any other document referred to in it;
   (b) a copy of the security instrument (if any); and
   (c) a statement signed by or on behalf of the owner showing, according to the information to which it is practicable for him to refer, the total sum which has become payable under the agreement by the hirer but remains unpaid and the various amounts comprised in that total sum, with the date when each became due.

(2) Subsection (1) does not apply to—
   (a) an agreement under which no sum is, or will or may become, payable by the hirer, or
   (b) a request made less than one month after a previous request under that subsection relating to the same agreement was complied with.

(3) If the owner under an agreement fails to comply with subsection (1)—
  (a) he is not entitled, while the default continues, to enforce the security, so far as provided in relation to the agreement; and
  (b) if the default continues for one month he commits an offence.

(4) This section does not apply to a non-commercial agreement. [274]

NOTES
Commencement: 19 May 1985.
Commencement order: SI 1983 No 1551, and Sch 3, para 37, to this Act.
Sub-s (1): figure in square brackets substituted by the Consumer Credit (Increase of Monetary Amounts) Order 1983, SI 1983 No 1571 in force 20 May 1985.

110. Duty to give information to debtor or hirer

(1) The creditor or owner under a regulated agreement, within the prescribed period after receiving a request in writing to that effect from the debtor or hirer and payment of a fee of [50p], shall give the debtor or hirer a copy of any security instrument executed in relation to the agreement after the making of the agreement.

(2) Subsection (1) does not apply to—
  (a) a non-commercial agreement, or
  (b) an agreement under which no sum is, or will or may become, payable by the debtor or hirer, or
  (c) a request made less than one month after a previous request under subsection (1) relating to the same agreement was complied with.

(3) If the creditor or owner under an agreement fails to comply with subsection (1)—
  (a) he is not entitled, while the default continues, to enforce the security (so far as provided in relation to the agreement); and
  (b) if the default continues for one month he commits an offence. [275]

NOTES
Commencement: 19 May 1985.
Commencement order: SI 1983 No 1551, and Sch 3, para 37, to this Act.
Sub-s (1): figure in square brackets substituted by the Consumer Credit (Increase of Monetary Amounts) Order 1983, SI 1983 No 1571 in force 20 May 1985.

111. Duty to give surety copy of default etc notice

(1) When a default notice or a notice under section 76(1) or 98(1) is served on a debtor or hirer, a copy of the notice shall be served by the creditor or owner on any surety (if a different person from the debtor or hirer).

(2) If the creditor or owner fails to comply with subsection (1) in the case of any surety, the security is enforceable against the surety (in respect of the breach or other matter to which the notice relates) on an order of the court only. [276]

NOTES
Commencement: 19 May 1985.
Commencement order: SI 1983 No 1551, and Sch 3, para 38, to this Act.

112. Realisation of securities

Subject to section 121, regulations may provide for any matters relating to the sale or other realisation, by the creditor or owner, of property over which any right has been provided by way of security in relation to an actual or prospective regulated agreement, other than a non-commercial agreement. [277]

NOTES
Commencement: 31 July 1974.
As at 1 May 1989 no regulations had been made under this section.

113. Act not to be evaded by use of security

(1) Where a security is provided in relation to an actual or prospective regulated agreement, the security shall not be enforced so as to benefit the creditor or owner, directly or indirectly, to an extent greater (whether as respects the amount of any payment or the time or manner of its being made) than would be the case if the security were not provided and any obligations of the debtor or hirer, or his relative, under or in relation to the agreement were carried out to the extent (if any) to which they would be enforced under this Act.

(2) In accordance with subsection (1), where a regulated agreement is enforceable on an order of the court or the Director only, any security provided in relation to the agreement is enforceable (so far as provided in relation to the agreement) where such an order has been made in relation to the agreement, but not otherwise.

(3) Where—
   (a) a regulated agreement is cancelled under section 69(1) or becomes subject to section 69(2), or
   (b) a regulated agreement is terminated under section 91, or
   (c) in relation to any agreement an application for an order under section 40(2), 65(1), 124(1) or 149(2) is dismissed (except on technical grounds only), or
   (d) a declaration is made by the court under section 142(1) (refusal of enforcement order) as respects any regulated agreement,
section 106 shall apply to any security provided in relation to the agreement.

(4) Where subsection (3) (d) applies and the declaration relates to a part only of the regulated agreement, section 106 shall apply to the security only so far as it concerns that part.

(5) In the case of a cancelled agreement, the duty imposed on the debtor or hirer by section 71 or 72 shall not be enforceable before the creditor or owner has discharged any duty imposed on him by section 106 (as applied by subsection (3)(a)).

(6) If the security is provided in relation to a prospective agreement or transaction, the security shall be enforceable in relation to the agreement or transaction only after the time (if any) when the agreement is made; and until that time the person providing the security shall be entitled, by notice to the creditor or owner, to require that section 106 shall thereupon apply to the security.

(7) Where an indemnity [or guarantee] is given in a case where the debtor or hirer is a minor, or [an indemnity is given in a case where he] is otherwise not of full capacity, the reference in subsection (1) to the extent to which his obligations would be enforced shall be read in relation to the indemnity [or guarantee] as a reference to the extent to which [those obligations] would be enforced if he were of full capacity.

(8) Subsections (1) to (3) also apply where a security is provided in relation to an actual or prospective linked transaction, and in that case—

(a) references to the agreement shall be read as references to the linked transaction, and
(b) references to the creditor or owner shall be read as references to any person (other than the debtor or hirer, or his relative) who is a party, or prospective party, to the linked transaction. **[278]**

NOTES
Commencement: 31 July 1974.
Sub-s (7): amended by the Minors' Contracts Act 1987, s 4(1) as from 9 June 1987.

Pledges

114. Pawn-receipts

(1) At the time he receives the article, a person who takes any article in pawn under a regulated agreement shall give to the person from whom he receives it a receipt in the prescribed form (a "pawn-receipt").

(2) A person who takes any article in pawn from an individual whom he knows to be, or who appears to be and is, a minor commits an offence.

(3) This section and sections 115 to 122 do not apply to—
(a) a pledge of documents of title [or of bearer bonds], or
(b) a non-commercial agreement. **[279]**

NOTES
Commencement: 19 May 1985.
Commencement order: SI 1983 No 1551, and Sch 3, para 39, to this Act.
Sub-s (3): amended by the Banking Act 1979, s 38(2) in force 1 October 1979.
Regulations under this section: Consumer Credit (Pawn Receipts) Regulations 1983, SI 1983 No 1566; and see note to s 60 ante.

115. Penalty for failure to supply copies of pledge agreement, etc

If the creditor under a regulated agreement to take any article in pawn fails to observe the requirements of sections 62 to 64 or 114(1) in relation to the agreement he commits an offence. **[280]**

NOTES
Commencement: 19 May 1985.
Commencement order: SI 1983 No 1551, and Sch 3, para 39, to this Act.

116. Redemption period

(1) A pawn is redeemable at any time within six months after it was taken.

(2) Subject to subsection (1), the period within which a pawn is redeemable shall be the same as the period fixed by the parties for the duration of the credit secured by the pledge, or such longer period as they may agree.

(3) If the pawn is not redeemed by the end of the period laid down by subsections (1) and (2) (the "redemption period"), it nevertheless remains redeemable until it is realised by the pawnee under section 121 except where under section 120(1) (a) the property in it passes to the pawnee.

(4) No special charge shall be made for redemption of a pawn after the end of the redemption period, and charges in respect of the safe keeping of the pawn shall not be at a higher rate after the end of the redemption period than before.
[281]

NOTES
Commencement: 19 May 1985.
Commencement order: SI 1983 No 1551, and Sch 3, para 39, to this Act.

117. Redemption procedure

(1) On surrender of the pawn-receipt, and payment of the amount owing, at any time when the pawn is redeemable, the pawnee shall deliver the pawn to the bearer of the pawn-receipt.

(2) Subsection (1) does not apply if the pawnee knows or has reasonable cause to suspect that the bearer of the pawn-receipt is neither the owner of the pawn nor authorised by the owner to redeem it.

(3) The pawnee is not liable to any person in tort or delict for delivering the pawn where subsection (1) applies, or refusing to deliver it where the person demanding delivery does not comply with subsection (1) or, by reason of subsection (2), subsection (1) does not apply. [282]

NOTES
Commencement: 19 May 1985.
Commencement order: SI 1983 No 1551, and Sch 3, para 39, to this Act.

118. Loss etc of pawn-receipt

(1) A person (the "claimant") who is not in possession of the pawn-receipt but claims to be the owner of the pawn, or to be otherwise entitled or authorised to redeem it, may do so at any time when it is redeemable by tendering to the pawnee in place of the pawn-receipt—

(a) a statutory declaration made by the claimant in the prescribed form, and with the prescribed contents, or
(b) where the pawn is security for fixed-sum credit not exceeding [£25] or running-account credit on which the credit limit does not exceed [£25], and the pawnee agrees, a statement in writing in the prescribed form, and with the prescribed contents, signed by the claimant.

(2) On compliance by the claimant with subsection (1), section 117 shall apply as if the declaration or statement were the pawn-receipt, and the pawn-receipt itself shall become inoperative for the purposes of section 117. [283]

NOTES
Commencement: 19 May 1985.
Commencement order: SI 1983 No 1551, and Sch 3, para 39, to this Act.
Sub-s (1): figures in square brackets substituted by the Consumer Credit (Increase of Monetary Amounts) Order 1983, SI 1983 No 1571 in force 20 May 1985.
Regulations under this section: Consumer Credit (Loss of Pawn Receipts) Regulations 1983, SI 1983 No 1567.

119. Unreasonable refusal to deliver pawn

(1) If a person who has taken a pawn under a regulated agreement refuses without reasonable cause to allow the pawn to be redeemed, he commits an offence.

(2) On the conviction in England or Wales of a pawnee under subsection (1) where the offence does not amount to theft, section 28 (orders for restitution) of the Theft Act 1968, and any provision of the Theft Act 1968 relating to that section, shall apply as if the pawnee had been convicted of stealing the pawn.

(3) On the conviction in Northern Ireland of a pawnee under subsection (1)

where the offence does not amount to theft, section 27 (orders for restitution) of the Theft Act (Northern Ireland) 1969, and any provision of the Theft Act (Northern Ireland) 1969 relating to that section, shall apply as if the pawnee had been convicted of stealing the pawn. **[284]**

NOTES
Commencement: 19 May 1985.
Commencement order: SI 1983 No 1551, and Sch 3, para 39, to this Act.

120. Consequence of failure to redeem

(1) If at the end of the redemption period the pawn has not been redeemed—

(a) notwithstanding anything in section 113, the property in the pawn passes to the pawnee where the redemption period is six months and the pawn is security for fixed-sum credit not exceeding [£25] or running-account credit on which the credit limit does not exceed [£25]; or

(b) in any other case the pawn becomes realisable by the pawnee.

(2) Where the debtor or hirer is entitled to apply to the court for a time order under section 129, subsection (1) shall apply with the substitution, for "at the end of the redemption period" of "after the expiry of five days following the end of the redemption period". **[285]**

NOTES
Commencement: 19 May 1985.
Commencement order: SI 1983 No 1551, and Sch 3, para 39, to this Act.
Sub-s (1): figures in square brackets substituted by the Consumer Credit (Increase of Monetary Amounts) Order 1983, SI 1983 No 1571 in force 20 May 1985.

121. Realisation of pawn

(1) When a pawn has become realisable by him, the pawnee may sell it, after giving to the pawnor (except in such cases as may be prescribed) not less than the prescribed period of notice of the intention to sell, indicating in the notice the asking price and such other particulars as may be prescribed.

(2) Within the prescribed period after the sale takes place, the pawnee shall give the pawnor the prescribed information in writing as to the sale, its proceeds and expenses.

(3) Where the net proceeds of sale are not less than the sum which, if the pawn had been redeemed on the date of the sale, would have been payable for its redemption, the debt secured by the pawn is discharged and any surplus shall be paid by the pawnee to the pawnor.

(4) Where subsection (3) does not apply, the debt shall be treated as from the date of sale as equal to the amount by which the net proceeds of sale fall short of the sum which would have been payable for the redemption of the pawn on that date.

(5) In this section the "net proceeds of sale" is the amount realised (the "gross amount") less the expenses (if any) of the sale.

(6) If the pawnor alleges that the gross amount is less than the true market value of the pawn on the date of sale, it is for the pawnee to prove that he and any agents employed by him in the sale used reasonable care to ensure that the true market value was obtained, and if he fails to do so subsections (3) and (4)

shall have effect as if the reference in subsection (5) to the gross amount were a reference to the true market value.

(7) If the pawnor alleges that the expenses of the sale were unreasonably high, it is for the pawnee to prove that they were reasonable, and if he fails to do so subsections (3) and (4) shall have effect as if the reference in subsection (5) to expenses were a reference to reasonable expenses. [286]

NOTES
Commencement: 19 May 1985.
Commencement order: SI 1983 No 1551, and Sch 3, para 39, to this Act.
Regulations under this section: Consumer Credit (Realisation of Pawn) Regulations 1983, SI 1983 No 1568.

NOTES
Section 122, which applies to Scotland only, is omitted.

Negotiable instruments

123. Restrictions on taking and negotiating instruments

(1) A creditor or owner shall not take a negotiable instrument, other than a bank note or cheque, in discharge of any sum payable—

(*a*) by the debtor or hirer under a regulated agreement, or
(*b*) by any person as surety in relation to the agreement.

(2) The creditor or owner shall not negotiate a cheque taken by him in discharge of a sum payable as mentioned in subsection (1), except to a banker (within the meaning of the Bills of Exchange Act 1882).

(3) The creditor or owner shall not take a negotiable instrument as security for the discharge of any sum payable as mentioned in subsection (1).

(4) A person takes a negotiable instrument as security for the discharge of a sum if the sum is intended to be paid in some other way, and the negotiable instrument is to be presented for payment only if the sum is not paid in that way.

(5) This section does not apply where the regulated agreement is a non-commercial agreement.

(6) The Secretary of State may by order provide that this section shall not apply where the regulated agreement has a connection with a country outside the United Kingdom. [287]

NOTES
Commencement: 19 May 1985.
Commencement order: SI 1984 No 436.
Regulations under this section: Consumer Credit (Negotiable Instrument) (Exemption) Order 1984, SI 1984 No 435.

124. Consequences of breach of s 123

(1) After any contravention of section 123 has occurred in relation to a sum payable as mentioned in section 123(1) (*a*), the agreement under which the sum is payable is enforceable against the debtor or hirer on an order of the court only.

(2) After any contravention of section 123 has occurred in relation to a sum payable by any surety, the security is enforceable on an order of the court only.

(3) Where an application for an order under subsection (2) is dismissed (except on technical grounds only) section 106 shall apply to the security. **[288]**

NOTES
Commencement: 19 May 1985.
Commencement order: SI 1984 No 436.

125. Holders in due course

(1) A person who takes a negotiable instrument in contravention of section 123(1) or (3) is not a holder in due course, and is not entitled to enforce the instrument.

(2) Where a person negotiates a cheque in contravention of section 123(2), his doing so constitutes a defect in his title within the meaning of the Bills of Exchange Act 1882.

(3) If a person mentioned in section 123(1) (*a*) or (*b*) ("the protected person") becomes liable to a holder in due course of an instrument taken from the protected person in contravention of section 123(1) or (3), or taken from the protected person and negotiated in contravention of section 123(2), the creditor or owner shall indemnify the protected person in respect of that liability.

(4) Nothing in this Act affects the rights of the holder in due course of any negotiable instrument. **[289]**

NOTES
Commencement: 19 May 1985.
Commencement order: SI 1984 No 436.

Land mortgages

126. Enforcement of land mortgages

A land mortgage securing a regulated agreement is enforceable (so far as provided in relation to the agreement) on an order of the court only. **[290]**

NOTES
Commencement: 19 May 1985.
Commencement order: SI 1983 No 1551, and Sch 3, para 41, to this Act.

PART IX
JUDICIAL CONTROL
Enforcement of certain regulated agreements and securities

127. Enforcement orders in cases of infringement

(1) In the case of an application for an enforcement order under—
    (*a*) section 65(1) (improperly executed agreements), or
    (*b*) section 105(7) (*a*) or (*b*) (improperly executed security instruments), or
    (*c*) section 111(2) (failure to serve copy of notice on surety), or
    (*d*) section 124(1) or (2) (taking of negotiable instrument in contravention of section 123),
the court shall dismiss the application if, but (subject to subsections (3) and (4)) only if, it considers it just to do so having regard to—

(i) prejudice caused to any person by the contravention in question, and the degree of culpability for it; and
(ii) the powers conferred on the court by subsection (2) and sections 135 and 136.

(2) If it appears to the court just to do so, it may in an enforcement order reduce or discharge any sum payable by the debtor or hirer, or any surety, so as to compensate him for prejudice suffered as a result of the contravention in question.

(3) The court shall not make an enforcement order under section 65(1) if section 61(1) (*a*) (signing of agreements) was not complied with unless a document (whether or not in the prescribed form and complying with regulations under section 60(1)) itself containing all the prescribed terms of the agreement was signed by the debtor or hirer (whether or not in the prescribed manner).

(4) The court shall not make an enforcement order under section 65(1) in the case of a cancellable agreement if—
   (*a*) a provision of section 62 or 63 was not complied with, and the creditor or owner did not give a copy of the executed agreement, and of any other document referred to in it, to the debtor or hirer before the commencement of the proceedings in which the order is sought, or
   (*b*) section 64(1) was not complied with.

(5) Where an enforcement order is made in a case to which subsection (3) applies, the order may direct that the regulated agreement is to have effect as if it did not include a term omitted from the document signed by the debtor or hirer. [291]

NOTES
Commencement: 19 May 1985.
Commencement order: SI 1983 No 1551, and Sch 3, para 43, to this Act.

128. Enforcement orders on death of debtor or hirer

The court shall make an order under section 86(2) if, but only if, the creditor or owner proves that he has been unable to satisfy himself that the present and future obligations of the debtor or hirer under the agreement are likely to be discharged. [292]

NOTES
Commencement: 19 May 1985.
Commencement: SI 1983 No 1551, and Sch 3, para 43, to this Act.

Extension of time

129. Time orders

(1) [. . .] if it appears to the court just to do so—
   (*a*) on an application for an enforcement order; or
   (*b*) on an application made by a debtor or hirer under this paragraph after service on him of—
      (i) a default notice, or
      (ii) a notice under section 76(1) or 98(1); or
   (*c*) in an action brought by a creditor or owner to enforce a regulated agreement or any security, or recover possession of any goods or land to which a regulated agreement relates,

the court may make an order under this section (a "time order").

(2) A time order shall provide for one or both of the following, as the court considers just—
- (a) the payment by the debtor or hirer or any surety of any sum owed under a regulated agreement or a security by such instalments, payable at such times, as the court, having regard to the means of the debtor or hirer and any surety, considers reasonable;
- (b) the remedying by the debtor or hirer of any breach of a regulated agreement (other than the non-payment of money) within such period as the court may specify.

[(3) . . .]

NOTES
Commencement: 19 May 1985 (sub-ss (1), (2)); to be appointed (sub-s (3)).
Commencement order: SI 1983 No 1551, and Sch 3, para 43, to this Act.
Sub-s (1): words omitted, which apply to Scotland only, added by the Debtors (Scotland) Act 1987, s 108(1), Sch 6, para 17(a), as from 30 November 1988.
Sub-s (3): added by the Debtors (Scotland) Act 1987, s 108(1), Sch 6, para 17(b), as from 30 November 1988.

130. Supplemental provisions about time orders

(1) Where in accordance with rules of court an offer to pay any sum by instalments is made by the debtor or hirer and accepted by the creditor or owner, the court may in accordance with rules of court make a time order under section 129(2) (a) giving effect to the offer without hearing evidence of means.

(2) In the case of a hire-purchase or conditional sale agreement only, a time order under section 129(2) (a) may deal with sums which, although not payable by the debtor at the time the order is made, would if the agreement continued in force become payable under it subsequently.

(3) A time order under section 129(2) (a) shall not be made where the regulated agreement is secured by a pledge if, by virtue of regulations made under section 76(5), 87(4) or 98(5), service of a notice is not necessary for enforcement of the pledge.

(4) Where, following the making of a time order in relation to a regulated hire-purchase or conditional sale agreement or a regulated consumer hire agreement, the debtor or hirer is in possession of the goods, he shall be treated (except in the case of a debtor to whom the creditor's title has passed) as a bailee or (in Scotland) a custodier of the goods under the terms of the agreement, notwithstanding that the agreement has been terminated.

(5) Without prejudice to anything done by the creditor or owner before the commencement of the period specified in a time order made under section 129(2)(b) ("the relevant period"),—
- (a) he shall not while the relevant period subsists take in relation to the agreement any action such as is mentioned in section 87(1);
- (b) where—
  - (i) a provision of the agreement ("the secondary provision") becomes operative only on breach of another provision of the agreement ("the primary provision"), and
  - (ii) the time order provides for the remedying of such a breach of the primary provision within the relevant period,

he shall not treat the secondary provision as operative before the end of that period;

(c) if while the relevant period subsists the breach to which the order relates is remedied it shall be treated as not having occurred.

(6) On the application of any person affected by a time order, the court may vary or revoke the order. [294]

NOTES
Commencement: 19 May 1985.
Commencement order: SI 1983 No 1551, and Sch 3, para 43, to this Act.

Protection of property pending proceedings

131. Protection orders

The court, on the application of the creditor or owner under a regulated agreement, may make such orders as it thinks just for protecting any property of the creditor or owner, or property subject to any security, from damage or depreciation pending the determination of any proceedings under this Act, including orders restricting or prohibiting use of the property or giving directions as to its custody. [295]

NOTES
Commencement: 19 May 1985.
Commencement order: SI 1983 No 1551, and Sch 3, para 43, to this Act.

Hire and hire-purchase etc agreements

132. Financial relief for hirer

(1) Where the owner under a regulated consumer hire agreement recovers possession of goods to which the agreement relates otherwise than by action, the hirer may apply to the court for an order that—

(a) the whole or part of any sum paid by the hirer to the owner in respect of the goods shall be repaid, and

(b) the obligation to pay the whole or part of any sum owed by the hirer to the owner in respect of the goods shall cease,

and if it appears to the court just to do so, having regard to the extent of the enjoyment of the goods by the hirer, the court shall grant the application in full or in part.

(2) Where in proceedings relating to a regulated consumer hire agreement the court makes an order for the delivery to the owner of goods to which the agreement relates the court may include in the order the like provision as may be made in an order under subsection (1). [296]

NOTES
Commencement: 19 May 1985.
Commencement order: SI 1983 No 1551, and Sch 3, para 43, to this Act.

133. Hire-purchase etc agreements: special powers of court

(1) If, in relation to a regulated hire-purchase or conditional sale agreement, it appears to the court just to do so—

(a) on an application for an enforcement order or time order; or

(b) in an action brought by the creditor to recover possession of goods to which the agreement relates,

the court may—

    (i) make an order (a "return order") for the return to the creditor of goods to which the agreement relates;

    (ii) make an order (a "transfer order") for the transfer to the debtor of the creditor's title to certain goods to which the agreement relates ("the transferred goods"), and the return to the creditor of the remainder of the goods.

(2) In determining for the purposes of this section how much of the total price has been paid ("the paid-up sum"), the court may—

    (a) treat any sum paid by the debtor, or owed by the creditor, in relation to the goods as part of the paid-up sum;

    (b) deduct any sum owed by the debtor in relation to the goods (otherwise than as part of the total price) from the paid-up sum,

and make corresponding reductions in amounts so owed.

(3) Where a transfer order is made, the transferred goods shall be such of the goods to which the agreement relates as the court thinks just; but a transfer order shall be made only where the paid-up sum exceeds the part of the total price referable to the transferred goods by an amount equal to at least one-third of the unpaid balance of the total price.

(4) Notwithstanding the making of a return order or transfer order, the debtor may at any time before the goods enter the possession of the creditor, on payment of the balance of the total price and the fulfilment of any other necessary conditions, claim the goods ordered to be returned to the creditor.

(5) When, in pursuance of a time order or under this section, the total price of goods under a regulated hire-purchase agreement or regulated conditional sale agreement is paid and any other necessary conditions are fulfilled, the creditor's title to the goods vests in the debtor.

(6) If, in contravention of a return order or transfer order, any goods to which the order relates are not returned to the creditor, the court, on the application of the creditor, may—

    (a) revoke so much of the order as relates to those goods, and

    (b) order the debtor to pay the creditor the unpaid portion of so much of the total price as is referable to those goods.

(7) For the purposes of this section, the part of the total price referable to any goods is the part assigned to those goods by the agreement or (if no such assignment is made) the part determined by the court to be reasonable.

NOTES
Commencement: 19 May 1985.
Commencement order: SI 1983 No 1551, and Sch 3, para 43, to this Act.

134. Evidence of adverse detention in hire-purchase etc cases

(1) Where goods are comprised in a regulated hire-purchase agreement, regulated conditional sale agreement or regulated consumer hire agreement, and the creditor or owner—

    (a) brings an action or makes an application to enforce a right to recover possession of the goods from the debtor or hirer, and

(b) proves that a demand for the delivery of the goods was included in the default notice under section 88(5), or that, after the right to recover possession of the goods accrued but before the action was begun or the application was made, he made a request in writing to the debtor or hirer to surrender the goods,

then, for the purposes of the claim of the creditor or owner to recover possession of the goods, the possession of them by the debtor or hirer shall be deemed to be adverse to the creditor or owner.

(2) In subsection (1) "the debtor or hirer" includes a person in possession of the goods at any time between the debtor's or hirer's death and the grant of probate or adminstration, or (in Scotland) confirmation.

(3) Nothing in this section affects a claim for damages for conversion or (in Scotland) for delict. **[298]**

NOTES
Commencement: 19 May 1985.
Commencement order: SI 1983 No 1551, and Sch 3, para 43, to this Act.

Supplemental provisions as to orders

135. Power to impose conditions, or suspend operation of order

(1) If it considers it just to do so, the court may in an order made by it in relation to a regulated agreement include provisions—
  (a) making the operation of any term of the order conditional on the doing of specified acts by any party to the proceedings;
  (b) suspending the operation of any term of the order either—
    (i) until such time as the court subsequently directs, or
    (ii) until the occurrence of a specified act or omission.

(2) The court shall not suspend the operation of a term requiring the delivery up of goods by any person unless satisfied that the goods are in his possession or control.

(3) In the case of a consumer hire agreement, the court shall not so use its powers under subsection (1) (b) as to extend the period for which, under the terms of the agreement, the hirer is entitled to possession of the goods to which the agreement relates.

(4) On the application of any person affected by a provision included under subsection (1), the court may vary the provision. **[299]**

NOTES
Commencement: 19 May 1985.
Commencement order: SI 1983 No 1551, and Sch 3, para 43, to this Act.

136. Power to vary agreements and securities

The court may in an order made by it under this Act include such provision as it considers just for amending any agreement or security in consequence of a term of the order. **[300]**

NOTES
Commencement: 19 May 1985.
Commencement order: SI 1983 No 1551, and Sch 3, para 43, to this Act.

Extortionate credit bargains

137. Extortionate credit bargains

(1) If the court finds a credit bargain extortionate it may reopen the credit agreement so as to do justice between the parties.

(2) In this section and sections 138 to 140—

   (a) "credit agreement" means any agreement between an individual (the "debtor") and any other person (the "creditor") by which the creditor provides the debtor with credit of any amount, and
   (b) "credit bargain"—
      (i) where no transaction other than the credit agreement is to be taken into account in computing the total charge for credit, means the credit agreement, or
      (ii) where one or more other transactions are to be so taken into account, means the credit agreement and those other transactions, taken together. [301]

NOTES
Commencement: 16 May 1977.
Commencement order: SI 1977 No 325, art 2(2), and Sch 3, paras 42, 43, to this Act.

138. When bargains are extortionate

(1) A credit bargain is extortionate if it—

   (a) requires the debtor or a relative of his to make payments (whether unconditionally, or on certain contingencies) which are grossly exorbitant, or
   (b) otherwise grossly contravenes ordinary principles of fair dealing.

(2) In determining whether a credit bargain is extortionate, regard shall be had to such evidence as is adduced concerning—

   (a) interest rates prevailing at the time it was made,
   (b) the factors mentioned in subsections (3) to (5), and
   (c) any other relevant considerations.

(3) Factors applicable under subsection (2) in relation to the debtor include—

   (a) his age, experience, business capacity and state of health; and
   (b) the degree to which, at the time of making the credit bargain, he was under financial pressure, and the nature of that pressure.

(4) Factors applicable under subsection (2) in relation to the creditor include—

   (a) the degree of risk accepted by him, having regard to the value of any security provided;
   (b) his relationship to the debtor; and
   (c) whether or not a colourable cash price was quoted for any goods or services included in the credit bargain.

(5) Factors applicable under subsection (2) in relation to a linked transaction include the question how far the transaction was reasonably required for the protection of debtor or creditor, or was in the interest of the debtor. [302]

NOTES
Commencement: 16 May 1977.

Commencement order: SI 1977 No 325, art 2(2), and Sch 3, paras 42, 43, to this Act.

139. Reopening of extortionate agreements

(1) A credit agreement may, if the court thinks just, be reopened on the ground that the credit bargain is extortionate—

    (a) on an application for the purpose made by the debtor or any surety to the High Court, county court or sheriff court; or

    (b) at the instance of the debtor or a surety in any proceedings to which the debtor and creditor are parties, being proceedings to enforce the agreement, any security relating to it, or any linked transaction; or

    (c) at the instance of the debtor or a surety in other proceedings in any court where the amount paid or payable under the credit agreement is relevant.

(2) In reopening the agreement, the court may, for the purpose of relieving the debtor or a surety from payment of any sum in excess of that fairly due and reasonable, by order—

    (a) direct accounts to be taken, or (in Scotland) an accounting to be made, between any persons,

    (b) set aside the whole or part of any obligation imposed on the debtor or surety by the credit bargain or any related agreement,

    (c) require the creditor to repay the whole or part of any sum paid under the credit bargain or any related agreement by the debtor or a surety, whether paid to the creditor or any other person,

    (d) direct the return to the surety of any property provided for the purposes of the security, or

    (e) alter the terms of the credit agreement or any security instrument.

(3) An order may be made under subsection (2) notwithstanding that its effect is to place a burden on the creditor in respect of an advantage unfairly enjoyed by another person who is a party to a linked transaction.

(4) An order under subsection (2) shall not alter the effect of any judgment.

(5) In England and Wales, an application under subsection (1)(a) shall be brought only in the county court in the case of—

    (a) a regulated agreement, or

    (b) an agreement (not being a regulated agreement) under which the creditor provides the debtor with fixed-sum credit not exceeding [the county court limit] or running-account credit on which the credit limit does not exceed [the county court limit].

[(5A) In the preceding subsection "the courty court limit" means the county court limit for the time being specified by an Order in Council under [section 145 of the County Courts Act 1984] as the county court limit for the purposes of that subsection.]

(6) ...

(7) In Northern Ireland an application under subsection (1)(a) may be brought in the county court in the case of—

    (a) a regulated agreement, or

(*b*) an agreement (not being a regulated agreement) under which the creditor provides the debtor with fixed-sum credit not exceeding [£1,000] or running-account credit on which the credit limit does not exceed [£1,000]. [303]

NOTES
Commencement: 1 January 1983 (sub-s (5A)); 16 May 1977 (remainder).
Commencement order: SI 1977 No 325, art 2(2), and Sch 3, paras 42, 43, to this Act.
Sub-s (5): amended by the Administration of Justice Act 1982, s 37, Sch 3, Part II, paras 2, 3.
Sub-s (5A): added by the Administration of Justice Act 1982, s 37, Sch 3, Part II, para 4; amended by the County Courts Act 1984, s 148(1), Sch 2, para 47.
Sub-s (6): applies to Scotland only.
Sub-s (7): amended by the Administration of Justice (Northern Ireland) Order 1975, SI 1975 No 816.

140. Interpretation of sections 137 to 139

Where the credit agreement is not a regulated agreement, expressions used in sections 137 to 139 which, apart from this section, apply only to regulated agreements, shall be construed as nearly as may be as if the credit agreement were a regulated agreement. [304]

NOTES
Commencement: 16 May 1977.
Commencement: SI 1977 No 325, art 2(2), and Sch 3, paras 42, 43, to this Act.

Miscellaneous

141. Jurisdiction and parties

(1) In England and Wales, the county court shall have jurisdiction to hear and determine—

  (*a*) any action by the creditor or owner to enforce a regulated agreement or any security relating to it;
  (*b*) any action to enforce any linked transaction against the debtor or hirer or his relative;

and such an action shall not be brought in any other court.

(2) Where an action or application is brought in the High Court which, by virtue of this Act, ought to have been brought in the county court it shall not be treated as improperly brought, but shall be transferred to the county court.

(3)–(3B) . . .

(4) In Northern Ireland the county court shall have jurisdiction to hear and determine any action or application falling within subsection (1).

(5) Except as may be provided by rules of court, all the parties to a regulated agreement, and any surety, shall be made parties to any proceedings relating to the agreement. [305]

NOTES
Commencement: 19 May 1985.
Commencement: SI 1983 No 1551, and Sch 3, para 43, to this Act.
Sub-ss (3)–(3B): apply to Scotland only.

142. Power to declare rights of parties

(1) Where under any provision of this Act a thing can be done by a creditor or owner on an enforcement order only, and either—

(a) the court dismisses (except on technical grounds only) an application for an enforcement order, or
(b) where no such application has been made or such an application has been dismissed on technical grounds only, an interested party applies to the court for a declaration under this subsection,

the court may if it thinks just make a declaration that the creditor or owner is not entitled to do that thing, and thereafter no application for an enforcement order in respect of it shall be entertained.

(2) Where—
(a) a regulated agreement or linked transaction is cancelled under section 69(1), or becomes subject to section 69(2), or
(b) a regulated agreement is terminated under section 91,

and an interested party applies to the court for a declaration under this subsection, the court may make a declaration to that effect. [306]

NOTES
Commencement: 19 May 1985.
Commencement order: SI 1983 No 1551, and Sch 3, para 43, to this Act.

Northern Ireland

143. Jurisdiction of county court in Northern Ireland

Without prejudice to any provision which may be made by rules of court made in relation to county courts in Northern Ireland such rules may provide—
(a) that any action or application such as is mentioned in section 141(4) which is brought against the debtor or hirer in the county court may be brought in the county court for the division in which the debtor or hirer resided or carried on business at the date on which he last made a payment under the regulated agreement;
(b) that an application by a debtor or hirer or any surety under section 129(1)(b), 132(1), 139(1)(a) or 142(1)(b) which is brought in the county court may be brought in the county court for the division in which the debtor, or, as the case may be, the hirer or surety resides or carries on business;
(c) for service of process on persons outside Northern Ireland. [307]

NOTES
Commencement: 19 May 1985.
Commencement order: SI 1983 No 1551, and Sch 3, para 43, to this Act.

144. Appeal from county court in Northern Ireland

Any person dissatisfied—
(a) with an order, whether adverse to him or in his favour, made by a county court in Northern Ireland in the exercise of any jurisdiction conferred by this Act, or
(b) with the dismissal or refusal by such a county court of any action or application instituted by him under the provisions of this Act,

shall be entitled to appeal from the order or from the dismissal or refusal as if the order, dismissal or refusal had been made in exercise of the jurisdiction conferred by Part III of the County Courts [(Northern Ireland) Order 1980 and the appeal brought under Part VI of that Order and Articles 61 and 62 of that Order shall apply accordingly]. [308]

NOTES
Commencement: 19 May 1985.
Commencement order: SI 1983 No 1551, and Sch 3, para 43, to this Act.
Words in square brackets substituted by the County Courts (Northern Ireland) Order 1980, SI 1980 No 397, art 68(2), Sch 1, Part II.

Part X
Ancillary Credit Business
Definitions

145. Types of ancillary credit business

(1) An ancillary credit business is any business so far as it comprises or relates to—

    (*a*) credit brokerage,
    (*b*) debt-adjusting,
    (*c*) debt-counselling,
    (*d*) debt-collecting, or
    (*e*) the operation of a credit reference agency.

(2) Subject to section 146(5), credit brokerage is the effecting of introductions—

    (*a*) of individuals desiring to obtain credit—

        (i) to persons carrying on businesses to which this sub-paragraph applies, or
        (ii) in the case of an individual desiring to obtain credit to finance the acquisition or provision of a dwelling occupied or to be occupied by himself or his relative, to any person carrying on a business in the course of which he provides credit secured on land, or

    (*b*) of individuals desiring to obtain goods on hire to persons carrying on businesses to which this paragraph applies, or
    (*c*) of individuals desiring to obtain credit, or to obtain goods on hire, to other credit-brokers.

(3) Subsection (2)(*a*)(i) applies to—

    (*a*) a consumer credit business;
    (*b*) a business which comprises or relates to consumer credit agreements being, otherwise than by virtue of section 16(5)(*a*), exempt agreements;
    (*c*) a business which comprises or relates to unregulated agreements where—

        (i) the proper law of the agreement is the law of a country outside the United Kingdom, and
        (ii) if the proper law of the agreement were the law of a part of the United Kingdom it would be a regulated consumer credit agreement.

(4) Subsection (2)(*b*) applies to—

    (*a*) a consumer hire business;

(b) a business which comprises or relates to unregulated agreements where—
  (i) the proper law of the agreement is the law of a country outside the United Kingdom, and
  (ii) if the proper law of the agreement were the law of a part of the United Kingdom it would be a regulated consumer hire agreement.

(5) Subject to section 146(6), debt-adjusting is, in relation to debts due under consumer credit agreements or consumer hire agreements,—
  (a) negotiating with the creditor or owner, on behalf of the debtor or hirer, terms for the discharge of a debt, or
  (b) taking over, in return for payments by the debtor or hirer, his obligation to discharge a debt, or
  (c) any similar activity concerned with the liquidation of a debt.

(6) Subject to section 146(6), debt-counselling is the giving of advice to debtors or hirers about the liquidation of debts due under consumer credit agreements or consumer hire agreements.

(7) Subject to section 146(6), debt-collecting is the taking of steps to procure payment of debts due under consumer credit agreements or consumer hire agreements.

(8) A credit reference agency is a person carrying on a business comprising the furnishing of persons with information relevant to the financial standing of individuals, being information collected by the agency for that purpose.   [309]

NOTES
Commencement: 31 July 1974.

146. Exceptions from section 145

(1) A barrister or advocate acting in that capacity is not to be treated as doing so in the course of any ancillary credit business.

(2) A solicitor engaging in contentious business (as defined in section 86(1) of the Solicitors Act 1957) is not to be treated as doing so in the course of any ancillary credit business.

(3) . . .

(4) A solicitor in Northern Ireland engaging in business done, whether as solicitor or advocate, in or for the purposes of proceedings begun before a court (including the Lands Tribunal for Northern Ireland) or before an arbitrator appointed under the Arbitration Act (Northern Ireland) 1937, not being business [which falls within the definition of non-contentious probate business contained in Article 2(2) of the Administration of Estates (Northern Ireland) Order 1979], is not to be treated as doing so in the course of any ancillary credit business.

(5) For the purposes of section 145(2), introductions effected by an individual by canvassing off trade premises either debtor-creditor-supplier agreements falling within section 12(a) or regulated consumer hire agreements shall be disregarded if—
  (a) the introductions are not effected by him in the capacity of an employee, and

(b) he does not by any other method effect introductions falling within section 145(2).

(6) It is not debt-adjusting, debt-counselling or debt-collecting for a person to do anything in relation to a debt arising under an agreement if—

(a) he is the creditor or owner under the agreement, otherwise than by virtue of an assignment, or
(b) he is the creditor or owner under the agreement by virtue of an assignment made in connection with the transfer to the assignee of any business other than a debt-collecting business, or
(c) he is the supplier in relation to the agreement, or
(d) he is a credit-broker who has acquired the business of the person who was the supplier in relation to the agreement, or
(e) he is a person prevented by subsection (5) from being treated as a credit-broker, and the agreement was made in consequence of an introduction (whether made by him or another person) which, under subsection (5), is to be disregarded. [310]

NOTES
Commencement: 31 July 1974.
Sub-s (3): applies to Scotland only.
Sub-s (4): amended by the Tax, Consumer Credit and Judicature (Northern Ireland Consequential Amendments) Order 1979, SI 1979 No 1576.

Licensing

147. Application of Part III

(1) The provisions of Part III (except section 40) apply to an ancillary credit business as they apply to a consumer credit business.

(2) Without prejudice to the generality of section 26, regulations under that section (as applied by subsection (1)) may include provisions regulating the collection and dissemination of information by credit reference agencies. [311]

NOTES
Commencement: 3 August 1976 - 1 July 1978.
Commencement orders: SI 1975 No 2123, art 2(2), 1977 No 325, 1977 No 2163, art 2, and Sch 3, para 44, to this Act.

148. Agreement for services of unlicensed trader

(1) An agreement for the services of a person carrying on an ancillary credit business (the "trader"), if made when the trader was unlicensed, is enforceable against the other party (the "customer") only where the Director has made an order under subsection (2) which applies to the agreement.

(2) The trader or his successor in title may apply to the Director for an order that agreements within subsection (1) are to be treated as if made when the trader was licensed.

(3) Unless the Director determines to make an order under subsection (2) in accordance with the application, he shall, before determining the application, by notice—

(a) inform the trader, giving his reasons, that, as the case may be, he is minded to refuse the application, or to grant it in terms different from those applied for, describing them, and

(b) invite the trader to submit to the Director representations in support of his application in accordance with section 34.

(4) In determining whether or not to make an order under subsection (2) in respect of any period the Director shall consider, in addition to any other relevant factors,—

(a) how far, if at all, customers under agreements made by the trader during that period were prejudiced by the trader's conduct,
(b) whether or not the Director would have been likely to grant a licence covering that period on an application by the trader, and
(c) the degree of culpability for the failure to obtain a licence.

(5) If the Director thinks fit, he may in an order under subsection (2)—

(a) limit the order to specified agreements, or agreements of a specified description or made at a specified time;
(b) make the order conditional on the doing of specified acts by the trader. [312]

NOTES
Commencement: 3 August 1976 - 1 July 1978.
Commencement orders: SI 1975 No 2123, art 2(2), 1977 No 325, 1977 No 2163, art 2, and Sch 3, para 45, to this Act.

149. Regulated agreements made on introductions by unlicensed credit-broker

(1) A regulated agreement made by a debtor or hirer who, for the purpose of making that agreement, was introduced to the creditor or owner by an unlicensed credit-broker is enforceable against the debtor or hirer only where—

(a) on the application of the credit-broker, the Director has made an order under section 148(2) in respect of a period including the time when the introduction was made, and the order does not (whether in general terms or specifically) exclude the application of this paragraph to the regulated agreement, or
(b) the Director has made an order under subsection (2) which applies to the agreement.

(2) Where during any period individuals were introduced to a person carrying on a consumer credit business or consumer hire business by an unlicensed credit-broker for the purpose of making regulated agreements with the person carrying on that business, that person or his successor in title may apply to the Director for an order that regulated agreements so made are to be treated as if the credit-broker had been licensed at the time of the introduction.

(3) Unless the Director determines to make an order under subsection (2) in accordance with the application, he shall, before determining the application, by notice—

(a) inform the applicant, giving his reasons, that, as the case may be, he is minded to refuse the application, or to grant it in terms different from those applied for, describing them, and
(b) invite the applicant to submit to the Director representations in support of his application in accordance with section 34.

(4) In determining whether or not to make an order under subsection (2) the Director shall consider, in addition to any other relevant factors—

(a) how far, if at all, debtors or hirers under regulated agreements to which the application relates were prejudiced by the credit-broker's conduct, and

(b) the degree of culpability of the applicant in facilitating the carrying on by the credit-broker of his business when unlicensed.

(5) If the Director thinks fit, he may in an order under subsection (2)—

(a) limit the order to specified agreements, or agreements of a specified description or made at a specified time;

(b) make the order conditional on the doing of specified acts by the applicant. [313]

NOTES
Commencement: 1 July 1978.
Commencement order: SI 1977 No 2163, art 2, and Sch 3, para 46, to this Act.

150. Appeals to Secretary of State against licensing decisions

Section 41 (as applied by section 147(1)) shall have effect as if the following entry were included in the table set out at the end—

Determination	*Appellant*
Refusal to make order under section 148(2) or 149(2) in accordance with terms of application	The applicant

[314]

NOTES
Commencement: 31 July 1974.

Seeking business

151. Advertisements

(1) Sections 44 to 47 apply to an advertisement published for the purposes of a business of credit brokerage carried on by any person, whether it advertises the services of that person or the services of persons to whom he effects introductions, as they apply to an advertisement to which Part IV applies.

(2) Sections 44, 46 and 47 apply to an advertisement, published for the purposes of a business carried on by the advertiser, indicating that he is willing to advise on debts, or engage in transactions concerned with the liquidation of debts, as they apply to an advertisement to which Part IV applies.

(3) The Secretary of State may by order provide that an advertisement published for the purposes of a business of credit brokerage, debt-adjusting or debt-counselling shall not fall within subsection (1) or (2) if it is of a description specified in the order.

(4) An advertisement does not fall within subsection (2) if it indicates that the advertiser is not willing to act in relation to consumer credit agreements and consumer hire agreements.

(5) In subsections (1) and (3) "credit brokerage" includes the effecting of introductions of individuals desiring to obtain credit to any person carrying on a business in the course of which he provides credit secured on land. [315]

NOTES
Commencement: 31 July 1974 (sub-ss (3)–(5)); 6 October 1980 (sub-ss (1), (2)).
Commencement order: SI 1980 No 50, art 2, and Sch 3, para 47, to this Act.

Regulations under this section: see note to s 44 ante.

152. Application of sections 52 to 54 to credit brokerage etc

(1) Sections 52 to 54 apply to a business of credit brokerage, debt-adjusting or debt-counselling as they apply to a consumer credit business.

(2) In their application to a business of credit brokerage, sections 52 and 53 shall apply to the giving of quotations and information about the business of any person to whom the credit-broker effects introductions as well as to the giving of quotations and information about his own business. **[316]**

NOTES
Commencement: 31 July 1974.

153. Definition of canvassing off trade premises (agreements for ancillary credit services)

(1) An individual (the "canvasser") canvasses off trade premises the services of a person carrying on an ancillary credit business if he solicits the entry of another individual (the "consumer") into an agreement for the provision to the consumer of those services by making oral representations to the consumer, or any other individual, during a visit by the canvasser to any place (not excluded by subsection (2)) where the consumer, or that other individual, as the case may be, is, being a visit—

    (*a*) carried out for the purpose of making such oral representations to individuals who are at that place, but
    (*b*) not carried out in response to a request made on a previous occasion.

(2) A place is excluded from subsection (1) if it is a place where (whether on a permanent or temporary basis)—

    (*a*) the ancillary credit business is carried on, or
    (*b*) any business is carried on by the canvasser or the person whose employee or agent the canvasser is, or by the consumer. **[317]**

NOTES
Commencement: 31 July 1974.

154. Prohibition of canvassing certain ancillary credit services off trade premises

It is an offence to canvass off trade premises the services of a person carrying on a business of credit brokerage, debt-adjusting or debt-counselling. **[318]**

NOTES
Commencement: 31 July 1974.

155. Right to recover brokerage fees

(1) The excess over [£3] of a fee or commission for his services charged by a credit-broker to an individual to whom this subsection applies shall cease to be payable or, as the case may be, shall be recoverable by the individual if the introduction does not result in his entering into a relevant agreement within the six months following the introduction (disregarding any agreement which is cancelled under section 69(1) or becomes subject to section 69(2)).

(2) Subsection (1) applies to an individual who sought an introduction for a purpose which would have been fulfilled by his entry into—

    (*a*) a regulated agreement, or

(b) in the case of an individual such as is referred to in section 145(2)(a)(ii), an agreement for credit secured on land, or

(c) an agreement such as is referred to in section 145(3)(b) or (c) or (4)(b).

(3) An agreement is a relevant agreement for the purposes of subsection (1) in relation to an individual if it is an agreement such as is referred to in subsection (2) in relation to that individual.

(4) In the case of an individual desiring to obtain credit under a consumer credit agreement, any sum payable or paid by him to a credit-broker otherwise than as a fee or commission for the credit-broker's services shall for the purposes of subsection (1) be treated as such a fee or commission if it enters, or would enter, into the total charge for credit. [319]

NOTES
Commencement: 31 July 1974.
Sub-s (1): amended by the Consumer Credit (Increase of Monetary Amounts) Order 1983, SI 1983 No 1571 from 1 January 1984.

Entry into agreements

156. Entry into agreements

Regulations may make provision, in relation to agreements entered into in the course of a business of credit brokerage, debt-adjusting or debt-counselling, corresponding, with such modifications as the Secretary of State thinks fit, to the provision which is or may be made by or under sections 55, 60, 61, 62, 63, 65, 127, 179 or 180 in relation to agreements to which those sections apply.[320]

NOTES
Commencement: 31 July 1974.
As at 1 May 1989 no regulations had been made under this section.

Credit reference agencies

157. Duty to disclose name etc of agency

(1) A creditor, owner or negotiator, within the prescribed period after receiving a request in writing to that effect from the debtor or hirer, shall give him notice of the name and address of any credit reference agency from which the creditor, owner or negotiator has, during the antecedent negotiations, applied for information about his financial standing.

(2) Subsection (1) does not apply to a request received more than 28 days after the termination of the antecedent negotiations, whether on the making of the regulated agreement or otherwise.

(3) If the creditor, owner or negotiator fails to comply with subsection (1) he commits an offence. [321]

NOTES
Commencement: 16 May 1977.
Commencement order: SI 1977 No 325, art 2(2), and Sch 3, para 48, to this Act.
Regulations under this section: Consumer Credit (Reference Agency) Regulations 1977, SI 1977 No 329.

158. Duty of agency to disclose filed information

(1) A credit reference agency, within the prescribed period after receiving,

(a) a request in writing to that effect from any individual (the "consumer") and
(b) such particulars as the agency may reasonably require to enable them to identify the file, and
(c) a fee of [£1],

shall give the consumer a copy of the file relating to him kept by the agency.

(2) When giving a copy of the file under subsection (1), the agency shall also give the consumer a statement in the prescribed form of his rights under section 159.

(3) If the agency does not keep a file relating to the consumer it shall give him notice of that fact, but need not return any money paid.

(4) If the agency contravenes any provision of this section it commits an offence.

(5) In this Act "file", in relation to an individual, means all the information about him kept by a credit reference agency, regardless of how the information is stored and "copy of the file", as respects information not in plain English, means a transcript reduced into plain English. [322]

NOTES
Commencement: 16 May 1977.
Commencement order: SI 1977 No 325, art 2(2), and Sch 3, para 48, to this Act.
Sub-s (1): amended by the Consumer Credit (Increase of Monetary Amounts) Order 1983, SI 1983 No 1571 from 1 January 1984.
Regulations under this section: see note to s 157 ante.

159. Correction of wrong information

(1) A consumer given information under section 158 who considers that an entry in his file is incorrect, and that if it is not corrected he is likely to be prejudiced, may give notice to the agency requiring it either to remove the entry from the file or amend it.

(2) Within 28 days after receiving a notice under subsection (1), the agency shall by notice inform the consumer that it has—
(a) removed the entry from the file, or
(b) amended the entry, or
(c) taken no action,

and if the notice states that the agency has amended the entry it shall include a copy of the file so far as it comprises the amended entry.

(3) Within 28 days after receiving a notice under subsection (2), or where no such notice was given, within 28 days after the expiry of the period mentioned in subsection (2), the consumer may, unless he has been informed by the agency that it has removed the entry from his file, serve a further notice on the agency requiring it to add to the file an accompanying notice of correction (not exceeding 200 words) drawn up by the consumer and include a copy of it when furnishing information included in or based on that entry.

(4) Within 28 days after receiving a notice under subsection (3), the agency, unless it intends to apply to the Director under subsection (5), shall by notice inform the consumer that it has received the notice under subsection (3) and intends to comply with it.

(5) If—
   (a) the consumer has not received a notice under subsection (4) within the time required, or
   (b) it appears to the agency that it would be improper for it to publish a notice of correction because it is incorrect, or unjustly defames any person, or is frivolous or scandalous, or is for any other reason unsuitable,

the consumer or, as the case may be, the agency may, in the prescribed manner and on payment of the specified fee, apply to the Director, who may make such order on the application as he thinks fit.

(6) If a person to whom an order under this section is directed fails to comply with it within the period specified in the order he commits an offence.

[323]

NOTES
Commencement: 31 July 1974.
Regulations under this section: see note to s 157 ante.

160. Alternative procedure for business consumers

(1) The Director, on an application made by a credit reference agency, may direct that this section shall apply to the agency if he is satisfied—
   (a) that compliance with section 158 in the case of consumers who carry on a business would adversely affect the service provided to its customers by the agency, and
   (b) that, having regard to the methods employed by the agency and to any other relevant factors, it is probable that consumers carrying on a business would not be prejudiced by the making of the direction.

(2) Where an agency to which this section applies receives a request, particulars and a fee under section 158(1) from a consumer who carries on a business, and section 158(3) does not apply, the agency, instead of complying with section 158, may elect to deal with the matter under the following subsections.

(3) Instead of giving the consumer a copy of the file, the agency shall within the prescribed period give notice to the consumer that it is proceeding under this section, and by notice give the consumer such information included in or based on entries in the file as the Director may direct, together with a statement in the prescribed form of the consumer's rights under subsections (4) and (5).

(4) If within 28 days after receiving the information given him under subsection (3), or such longer period as the Director may allow, the consumer—
   (a) gives notice to the Director that he is dissatisfied with the information, and
   (b) satisfies the Director that he has taken such steps in relation to the agency as may be reasonable with a view to removing the cause of his dissatisfaction, and
   (c) pays the Director the specified fee,

the Director may direct the agency to give the Director a copy of the file, and the Director may disclose to the consumer such of the information on the file as the Director thinks fit.

(5) Section 159 applies with any necessary modifications to information

given to the consumer under this section as it applies to information given under section 158.

(6) If an agency making an election under subsection (2) fails to comply with subsection (3) or (4) it commits an offence. [324]

NOTES
Commencement: 31 July 1974.
Regulations under this section: see note to s 157 ante.

Part XI

Enforcement of Act

161. Enforcement authorities

(1) The following authorities ("enforcement authorities") have a duty to enforce this Act and regulations made under it—
   (a) the Director,
   (b) in Great Britain, the local weights and measures authority,
   (c) in Northern Ireland, the Department of Commerce for Northern Ireland.

(2) Where a local weights and measures authority in England or Wales propose to institute proceedings for an offence under this Act (other than an offence under section 162(6), 165(1) or (2) or 174(5)) it shall, as between the authority and the Director, be the duty of the authority to give the Director notice of the intended proceedings, together with a summary of the facts on which the charges are to be founded, and postpone institution of the proceedings until either—
   (a) 28 days have expired since that notice was given, or
   (b) the Director has notified them of receipt of the notice and summary.

(3) Every local weights and measures authority shall, whenever the Director requires, report to him in such form and with such particulars as he requires on the exercise of their functions under this Act.

(4)–(6) ... [325]

NOTES
Commencement: 31 July 1974.
Sub-ss (4)–(6): repealed by the Local Government, Planning and Land Act 1980, s 1(4), Sch 4.

162. Powers of entry and inspection

(1) A duly authorised officer of an enforcement authority, at all reasonable hours and on production, if required, of his credentials, may—
   (a) in order to ascertain whether a breach of any provision of or under this Act has been committed, inspect any goods and enter any premises (other than premises used only as a dwelling);
   (b) if he has reasonable cause to suspect that a breach of any provision of or under this Act has been committed, in order to ascertain whether it has been committed, require any person—
      (i) carrying on, or employed in connection with, a business to produce any books or documents relating to it; or

(ii) having control of any information relating to a business recorded otherwise than in a legible form to provide a document containing a legible reproduction of the whole or any part of the information, and take copies of, or of any entry in, the books or documents;

(c) if he has reasonable cause to believe that a breach of any provision of or under this Act has been committed, seize and detain any goods in order to ascertain (by testing or otherwise) whether such a breach has been committed;

(d) seize and detain any goods, books or documents which he has reason to believe may be required as evidence in proceedings for an offence under this Act;

(e) for the purpose of exercising his powers under this subsection to seize goods, books or documents, but only if and to the extent that it is reasonably necessary for securing that the provisions of this Act and of any regulations made under it are duly observed, require any person having authority to do so to break open any container and, if that person does not comply, break it open himself.

(2) An officer seizing goods, books or documents in exercise of his powers under this section shall not do so without informing the person he seizes them from.

(3) If a justice of the peace, on sworn information in writing, or, in Scotland, a sheriff or a magistrate or justice of the peace, on evidence on oath,—

(a) is satisfied that there is reasonable ground to believe either—

(i) that any goods, books or documents which a duly authorised officer has power to inspect under this section are on any premises and their inspection is likely to disclose evidence of a breach of any provision of or under this Act; or

(ii) that a breach of any provision of or under this Act has been, is being or is about to be committed on any premises; and

(b) is also satisfied either—

(i) that admission to the premises has been or is likely to be refused and that notice of intention to apply for a warrant under this subsection has been given to the occupier; or

(ii) that an application for admission, or the giving of such a notice, would defeat the object of the entry or that the premises are unoccupied or that the occupier is temporarily absent and it might defeat the object of the entry to wait for his return,

the justice or, as the case may be, the sheriff or magistrate may by warrant under his hand, which shall continue in force for a period of one month, authorise an officer of an enforcement authority to enter the premises (by force if need be).

(4) An officer entering premises by virtue of this section may take such other persons and equipment with him as he thinks necessary; and on leaving premises entered by virtue of a warrant under subsection (3) shall, if they are unoccupied or the occupier is temporarily absent, leave them as effectively secured against trespassers as he found them.

(5) Regulations may provide that, in cases described by the regulations, an officer of a local weights and measures authority is not to be taken to be duly authorised for the purposes of this section unless he is authorised by the Director.

(6) A person who is not a duly authorised officer of an enforcement authority, but purports to act as such under this section, commits an offence.

(7) Nothing in this section compels a barrister, advocate or solicitor to produce a document containing a privileged communication made by or to him in that capacity or authorises the seizing of any such document in his possession. [326]

NOTES
Commencement: 31 July 1974.
Regulations under this section: Consumer Credit (Entry and Inspection) Regulations 1977, SI 1977 No 331, amended by SI 1984 No 1046.

163. Compensation for loss

(1) Where, in exercising his powers under section 162, an officer of an enforcement authority seizes and detains goods and their owner suffers loss by reason of—
- (*a*) that seizure, or
- (*b*) the loss, damage or deterioration of the goods during detention,

then, unless the owner is convicted of an offence under this Act committed in relation to the goods, the authority shall compensate him for the loss so suffered.

(2) Any dispute as to the right to or amount of any compensation under subsection (1) shall be determined by arbitration. [327]

NOTES
Commencement: 31 July 1974.

164. Power to make test purchases etc

(1) An enforcement authority may—
- (*a*) make, or authorise any of their officers to make on their behalf, such purchases of goods; and
- (*b*) authorise any of their officers to procure the provision of such services or facilities or to enter into such agreements or other transactions,

as may appear to them expedient for determining whether any provisions made by or under this Act are being complied with.

(2) Any act done by an officer authorised to do it under subsection (1) shall be treated for the purposes of this Act as done by him as an individual on his own behalf.

(3) Any goods seized by an officer under this Act may be tested, and in the event of such a test he shall inform the person mentioned in section 162(2) of the test results.

(4) Where any test leads to proceedings under this Act, the enforcement authority shall—
- (*a*) if the goods were purchased, inform the person they were purchased from of the test results, and
- (*b*) allow any person against whom the proceedings are taken to have the goods tested on his behalf if it is reasonably practicable to do so. [328]

NOTES
Commencement: 31 July 1974.

165. Obstruction of authorised officers

(1) Any person who—
- (a) wilfully obstructs an officer of an enforcement authority acting in pursuance of this Act; or
- (b) wilfully fails to comply with any requirement properly made to him by such an officer under section 162; or
- (c) without reasonable cause fails to give such an officer (so acting) other assistance or information he may reasonably require in performing his functions under this Act,

commits an offence.

(2) If any person, in giving such information as is mentioned in subsection (1)(c), makes any statement which he knows to be false, he commits an offence.

(3) Nothing in this section requires a person to answer any question or give any information if to do so might incriminate that person or (where that person is married) the husband or wife of that person.

NOTES
Commencement: 31 July 1974.

166. Notification of convictions and judgments to Director

Where a person is convicted of an offence or has a judgment given against him by or before any court in the United Kingdom and it appears to the court—
- (a) having regard to the functions of the Director under this Act, that the conviction or judgment should be brought to the Director's attention, and
- (b) that it may not be brought to his attention unless arrangements for that purpose are made by the court,

the court may make such arrangements notwithstanding that the proceedings have been finally disposed of.

NOTES
Commencement: 31 July 1974.

167. Penalties

(1) An offence under a provision of this Act specified in column 1 of Schedule 1 is triable in the mode or modes indicated in column 3, and on conviction is punishable as indicated in column 4 (where a period of time indicates the maximum term of imprisonment, and a monetary amount indicates the maximum fine, for the offence in question).

(2) A person who contravenes any regulations made under section 44, 52, 53, or 112, or made under section 26 by virtue of section 54, commits an offence.

NOTES
Commencement: 31 July 1974.

168. Defences

(1) In any proceedings for an offence under this Act it is a defence for the person charged to prove—

(a) that his act or omission was due to a mistake, or to reliance on information supplied to him, or to an act or omission by another person, or to an accident or some other cause beyond his control, and

(b) that he took all reasonable precautions and exercised all due diligence to avoid such an act or omission by himself or any person under his control.

(2) If in any case the defence provided by subsection (1) involves the allegation that the act or omission was due to an act or omission by another person or to reliance on information supplied by another person, the person charged shall not, without leave of the court, be entitled to rely on that defence unless, within a period ending seven clear days before the hearing, he has served on the prosecutor a notice giving such information identifying or assisting in the identification of that other person as was then in his possession.

NOTES
Commencement: 31 July 1974.

169. Offences by bodies corporate

Where at any time a body corporate commits an offence under this Act with the consent or connivance of, or because of neglect by, any individual, the individual commits the like offence if at that time—

(a) he is a director, manager, secretary or similar officer of the body corporate, or

(b) he is purporting to act as such an officer, or

(c) the body corporate is managed by its members, of whom he is one.

NOTES
Commencement: 31 July 1974.

170. No further sanctions for breach of Act

(1) A breach of any requirement made (otherwise than by any court) by or under this Act shall incur no civil or criminal sanction as being such a breach, except to the extent (if any) expressly provided by or under this Act.

(2) In exercising his functions under this Act the Director may take account of any matter appearing to him to constitute a breach of a requirement made by or under this Act, whether or not any sanction for that breach is provided by or under this Act and, if it is so provided, whether or not proceedings have been brought in respect of the breach.

(3) Subsection (1) does not prevent the grant of an injunction, or the making of an order of certiorari, mandamus or prohibition or as respects Scotland the grant of an interdict or of an order under section 91 of the Court of Session Act 1868 (order for specific performance of statutory duty).

NOTES
Commencement: 31 July 1974.

171. Onus of proof in various proceedings

(1) If an agreement contains a term signifying that in the opinion of the parties section 10(3)(b)(iii) does not apply to the agreement, it shall be taken not to apply unless the contrary is proved.

(2) It shall be assumed in any proceedings, unless the contrary is proved, that when a person initiated a transaction as mentioned in section 19(1)(c) he knew the principal agreement had been made, or contemplated that it might be made.

(3) Regulations under section 44 or 52 may make provision as to the onus of proof in any proceedings to enforce the regulations.

(4) In proceedings brought by the creditor under a credit-token agreement—
    (a) it is for the creditor to prove that the credit-token was lawfully supplied to the debtor, and was accepted by him, and
    (b) if the debtor alleges that any use made of the credit-token was not authorised by him, it is for the creditor to prove either—
        (i) that the use was so authorised, or
        (ii) that the use occurred before the creditor had been given notice under section 84(3).

(5) In proceedings under section 50(1) in respect of a document received by a minor at any school or other educational establishment for minors, it is for the person sending it to him at that establishment to prove that he did not know or suspect it to be such an establishment.

(6) In proceedings under section 119(1) it is for the pawnee to prove that he had reasonable cause to refuse to allow the pawn to be redeemed.

(7) If, in proceedings referred to in section 139(1), the debtor or any surety alleges that the credit bargain is extortionate it is for the creditor to prove the contrary. [335]

NOTES
Commencement: 31 July 1974.

172. Statements by creditor or owner to be binding

(1) A statement by a creditor or owner is binding on him if given under—
    section 77(1),
    section 78(1),
    section 79(1),
    section 97(1),
    section 107(1)(c),
    section 108(1)(c), or
    section 109(1)(c).

(2) Where a trader—
    (a) gives a customer a notice in compliance with section 103(1)(b), or
    (b) gives a customer a notice under section 103(1) asserting that the customer is not indebted to him under an agreement,
the notice is binding on the trader.

(3) Where in proceedings before any court—
    (a) it is sought to rely on a statement or notice given as mentioned in subsection (1) or (2), and
    (b) the statement or notice is shown to be incorrect,
the court may direct such relief (if any) to be given to the creditor or owner from the operation of subsection (1) or (2) as appears to the court to be just. [336]

NOTES
Commencement: 31 July 1974.

173. Contracting-out forbidden

(1) A term contained in a regulated agreement or linked transaction, or in any other agreement relating to an actual or prospective regulated agreement or linked transaction, is void if, and to the extent that, it is inconsistent with a provision for the protection of the debtor or hirer or his relative or any surety contained in this Act or in any regulation made under this Act.

(2) Where a provision specifies the duty or liability of the debtor or hirer or his relative or any surety in certain circumstances, a term is inconsistent with that provision if it purports to impose, directly or indirectly, an additional duty or liability on him in those circumstances.

(3) Notwithstanding subsection (1), a provision of this Act under which a thing may be done in relation to any person on an order of the court or the Director only shall not be taken to prevent its being done at any time with that person's consent given at that time, but the refusal of such consent shall not give rise to any liability. [337]

NOTES
Commencement: 31 July 1974.

PART XII
SUPPLEMENTAL
General

174. Restrictions on disclosure of information

(1) No information obtained under or by virtue of this Act about any individual shall be disclosed without his consent.

(2) No information obtained under or by virtue of this Act about any business shall be disclosed except, so long as the business continues to be carried on, with the consent of the person for the time being carrying it on.

(3) Subsections (1) and (2) do not apply to any disclosure of information made—
   (a) for the purpose of facilitating the performance of any functions under this Act, the Trade Descriptions Act 1968 or Part II or III or section 125 (annual and other reports of Director) of the Fair Trading Act 1973 [or the Estate Agents Act 1979] [or the Competition Act 1980] [or the Telecommunications Act 1984] [or the Gas Act 1986] [or the Airports Act 1986] [or the Consumer Protection Act 1987] [or the Control of Misleading Advertisements Regulations 1988] of the Secretary of State, any other Minister, [the Director General of Telecommunications,] [the Director General of Gas Supply] [the Civil Aviation Authority] any enforcement authority or any Northern Ireland department, or
   (b) in connection with the investigation of any criminal offence or for the purposes of any criminal proceedings, or
   (c) for the purposes of any civil proceedings brought under or by virtue of this Act or under Part III of the Fair Trading Act 1973 [or under the Control of Misleading Advertisements Regulations 1988].

[(3A) Subsections (1) and (2) do not apply to any disclosure of information by the Director to the Bank of England for the purpose of enabling or assisting the Bank to discharge its functions under the Banking Act 1987 or the Director to discharge his functions under this Act.]

(4) Nothing in subsections (1) and (2) shall be construed—
  (a) as limiting the particulars which may be entered in the register; or
  (b) as applying to any information which has been made public as part of the register.

(5) Any person who discloses information in contravention of this section commits an offence. [338]

NOTES
Commencement: 15 July 1987 (sub-s (3A)); 31 July 1974 (remainder).
Sub-s (3): amended by the Estate Agents Act 1979, s 10(4)(b), the Competition Act 1980, s 19(4)(d), the Telecommunications Act 1984, s 109, Sch 4, para 60, the Gas Act 1986, s 67(1), Sch 7, para 19, the Airports Act 1986, s 83(1), Sch 4, para 4, the Consumer Protection Act 1987, s 48, Sch 4 and SI 1988 No 915, reg 7(6)(b)(ii).
Sub-s (3A): added by the Banking Act 1987, s 87.

175. Duty of persons deemed to be agents

Where under this Act a person is deemed to receive a notice or payment as agent of the creditor or owner under a regulated agreement, he shall be deemed to be under a contractual duty to the creditor or owner to transmit the notice, or remit the payment, to him forthwith. [339]

NOTES
Commencement: 31 July 1974.

176. Service of documents

(1) A document to be served under this Act by one person ("the server") on another person ("the subject") is to be treated as properly served on the subject if dealt with as mentioned in the following subsections.

(2) The document may be delivered or sent by post to the subject, or addressed to him by name and left at his proper address.

(3) For the purposes of this Act, a document sent by post to, or left at, the address last known to the server as the address of a person shall be treated as sent by post to, or left at, his proper address.

(4) Where the document is to be served on the subject as being the person having any interest in land, and it is not practicable after reasonable inquiry to ascertain the subject's name or address, the document may be served by—
  (a) addressing it to the subject by the description of the person having that interest in the land (naming it), and
  (b) delivering the document to some responsible person on the land or affixing it, or a copy of it, in a conspicuous position on the land.

(5) Where a document to be served on the subject as being a debtor, hirer or surety, or as having any other capacity relevant for the purposes of this Act, is served at any time on another person who—
  (a) is the person last known to the server as having that capacity, but
  (b) before that time had ceased to have it,
the document shall be treated as having been served at that time on the subject.

(6) Anything done to a document in relation to a person who (whether to the knowledge of the server or not) has died shall be treated for the purposes of subsection (5) as service of the document on that person if it would have been so treated had he not died.

(7) Neither of the following enactments (which provide for the vesting of the estate of an intestate in the Probate Judge) shall be construed as authorising service on the Probate Judge of any document which is to be served under this Act—

section 9 of the Administration of Estates Act 1925;
section 3 of the Administration of Estates Act (Northern Ireland) 1955.

(8) References in the preceding subsections to the serving of a document on a person include the giving of the document to that person. [340]

NOTES
Commencement: 31 July 1974.

177. Saving for registered charges

(1) Nothing in this Act affects the rights of a proprietor of a registered charge (within the meaning of the Land Registration Act 1925), who—
   (a) became the proprietor under a transfer for valuable consideration without notice of any defect in the title arising (apart from this section) by virtue of this Act, or
   (b) derives title from such a proprietor.

(2) Nothing in this Act affects the operation of section 104 of the Law of Property Act 1925 (protection of purchaser where mortgagee exercises power of sale).

(3) Subsection (1) does not apply to a proprietor carrying on a business of debt-collecting.

(4) Where, by virtue of subsection (1), a land mortgage is enforced which apart from this section would be treated as never having effect, the original creditor or owner shall be liable to indemnify the debtor or hirer against any loss thereby suffered by him.

(5) . . .

(6) In the application of this section to Northern Ireland—
   (a) any reference to the proprietor of a registered charge (within the meaning of the Land Registration Act 1925) shall be construed as a reference to the registered owner of a charge under the Local Registration of Title (Ireland) Act 1891 or Part IV of the Land Registration Act (Northern Ireland) 1970, and
   (b) for the reference to section 104 of the Law of Property Act 1925 there shall be substituted a reference to section 21 of the Conveyancing and Law of Property Act 1881 and section 5 of the Conveyancing Act 1911. [341]

NOTES
Commencement: 31 July 1974.
Sub-s (5): applies to Scotland only.

178. Local Acts

The Secretary of State or the Department of Commerce for Northern Ireland may by order make such amendments or repeals of any provision of any local Act as appears to the Secretary of State or, as the case may be, the Department, necessary or expedient in consequence of the replacement by this Act of the enactments relating to pawnbrokers and money-lenders. [342]

NOTES
Commencement: 31 July 1974.
Regulations under this section: Consumer Credit (Local Acts) Order 1984, SI 1984 No 1107.

Regulations, orders, etc

179. Power to prescribe form etc of secondary documents

(1) Regulations may be made as to the form and content of credit-cards, trading-checks, receipts, vouchers and other documents or things issued by creditors, owners or suppliers under or in connection with regulated agreements or by other persons in connection with linked transactions, and may in particular—

  (a) require specified information to be included in the prescribed manner in documents, and other specified material to be excluded;
  (b) contain requirements to ensure that specified information is clearly brought to the attention of the debtor or hirer, or his relative, and that one part of a document is not given insufficient or excessive prominence compared with another.

(2) If a person issues any document or thing in contravention of regulations under subsection (1) then, as from the time of the contravention but without prejudice to anything done before it, this Act shall apply as if the regulated agreement had been improperly executed by reason of a contravention of regulations under section 60(1). [343]

NOTES
Commencement: 31 July 1974.
As at 1 May 1989 no regulations had been made under this section.

180. Power to prescribe form etc of copies

(1) Regulations may be made as to the form and content of documents to be issued as copies of any executed agreement, security instrument or other document referred to in this Act, and may in particular—

  (a) require specified information to be included in the prescribed manner in any copy, and contain requirements to ensure that such information is clearly brought to the attention of a reader of the copy;
  (b) authorise the omission from a copy of certain material contained in the original, or the inclusion of such material in condensed form.

(2) A duty imposed by any provision of this Act (except section 35) to supply a copy of any document—

  (a) is not satisfied unless the copy supplied is in the prescribed form and conforms to the prescribed requirements;
  (b) is not infringed by the omission of any material, or its inclusion in condensed form, if that is authorised by regulations;

and references in this Act to copies shall be construed accordingly.

(3) Regulations may provide that a duty imposed by this Act to supply a copy of a document referred to in an unexecuted agreement or an executed agreement shall not apply to documents of a kind specified in the regulations.

NOTES
Commencement: 31 July 1974.
Regulations under this section: see note to s 58 ante.

181. Power to alter monetary limits etc

(1) The Secretary of State may by order made by statutory instrument amend, or further amend, any of the following provisions of this Act so as to reduce or increase a sum mentioned in that provision, namely, sections 8(2), 15(1)(c), 17(1), 43(3)(a), 70(6), 75(3)(b), 77(1), 78(1), 79(1), 84(1), 101(7)(a), 107(1), 108(1), 109(1), 110(1), 118(1)(b), 120(1)(a), 139(5) and (7), 155(1) and 158(1).

(2) An order under subsection (1) amending section 8(2), 15(1)(c), 17(1), 43(3)(a), 75(3)(b) or 139(5) or (7) shall be of no effect unless a draft of the order has been laid before and approved by each House of Parliament.

NOTES
Commencement: 31 July 1974.
Regulations under this section: Consumer Credit (Increase of Monetary Amounts) Order 1983, SI 1983 No 1571; Consumer Credit (Increase of Monetary Limits) Order 1983, SI 1983 No 1878.

182. Regulations and orders

(1) Any power of the Secretary of State to make regulations or orders under this Act except the power conferred by sections 2(1)(a), 181 and 192 shall be exercisable by statutory instrument subject to annulment in pursuance of a resolution of either House of Parliament.

(2) Where a power to make regulations or orders is exercisable by the Secretary of State by virtue of this Act, regulations or orders made in the exercise of that power may—

(a) make different provision in relation to different cases or classes of case, and
(b) exclude certain cases or classes of case, and
(c) contain such transitional provisions as the Secretary of State thinks fit.

(3) Regulations may provide that specified expressions, when used as described by the regulations, are to be given the prescribed meaning, notwithstanding that another meaning is intended by the person using them.

(4) Any power conferred on the Secretary of State by this Act to make orders includes power to vary or revoke an order so made.

NOTES
Commencement: 31 July 1974.

183. Determinations etc by Director

The Director may vary or revoke any determination or direction made or given by him under this Act (other than Part III, or Part III as applied by section 147).

NOTES
Commencement: 31 July 1974.

Interpretation

184. Associates

(1) A person is an associate of an individual if that person is the individual's husband or wife, or is a relative, or the husband or wife of a relative, of the individual or of the individual's husband or wife.

(2) A person is an associate of any person with whom he is in partnership, and of the husband or wife or a relative of any individual with whom he is in partnership.

(3) A body corporate is an associate of another body corporate—
   (a) if the same person is a controller of both, or a person is a controller of one and persons who are his associates, or he and persons who are his associates, are the controllers of the other; or
   (b) if a group of two or more persons is a controller of each company, and the groups either consist of the same persons or could be regarded as consisting of the same persons by treating (in one or more cases) a member of either group as replaced by a person of whom he is an associate.

(4) A body corporate is an associate of another person if that person is a controller of it or if that person and persons who are his associates together are controllers of it.

(5) In this section "relative" means brother, sister, uncle, aunt, nephew, niece, lineal ancestor or lineal descendant, and references to a husband or wife include a former husband or wife and a reputed husband or wife; and for the purposes of this subsection a relationship shall be established as if any illegitimate child, step-child or adopted child of a person had been a child born to him in wedlock. [348]

NOTES
Commencement: 31 July 1974.

185. Agreement with more than one debtor or hirer

(1) Where an actual or prospective regulated agreement has two or more debtors or hirers (not being a partnership or an unincorporated body of persons)—
   (a) anything required by or under this Act to be done to or in relation to the debtor or hirer shall be done to or in relation to each of them; and
   (b) anything done under this Act by or on behalf of one of them shall have effect as if done by or on behalf of all of them.

(2) Notwithstanding subsection (1)(a), where running-account credit is provided to two or more debtors jointly, any of them may by a notice signed by him (a "dispensing notice") authorise the creditor not to comply in his case with section 78(4) (giving of periodical statement of account); and the dispensing notice shall have effect accordingly until revoked by a further notice given by the debtor to the creditor:

Provided that:

(a) a dispensing notice shall not take effect if previous dispensing notices are operative in the case of the other debtor, or each of the other debtors, as the case may be;
(b) any dispensing notices operative in relation to an agreement shall cease to have effect if any of the debtors dies.
[(c) a dispensing notice which is operative in relation to an agreement shall be operative also in relation to any subsequent agreement which, in relation to the earlier agreement, is a modifying agreement].

(3) Subsection (1)(b) does not apply for the purposes of section 61(1)(a) or 127(3).

(4) Where a regulated agreement has two or more debtors or hirers (not being a partnership or an unincorporated body of persons), section 86 applies to the death of any of them.

(5) An agreement for the provision of credit, or the bailment or (in Scotland) the hiring of goods, to two or more persons jointly where—
(a) one or more of those persons is an individual, and
(b) one or more of them is a body corporate,

is a consumer credit agreement or consumer hire agreement if it would have been one had they all been individuals; and the body corporate or bodies corporate shall accordingly be included among the debtors or hirers under the agreement.

(6) Where subsection (5) applies, references in this Act to the signing of any document by the debtor or hirer shall be construed in relation to a body corporate as referring to a signing on behalf of the body corporate. [349]

NOTES
Commencement: 31 July 1974.
Commencement: Sch 3, para 49, to this Act.
Sub-s (2): amended by the Banking Act 1979, s 38(3) in force 10 October 1979.

186. Agreement with more than one creditor or owner

Where an actual or prospective regulated agreement has two or more creditors or owners, anything required by or under this Act to be done to, or in relation to, or by, the creditor or owner shall be effective if done to, or in relation to, or by, any one of them. [350]

NOTES
Commencement: 31 July 1974.

187. Arrangements between creditor and supplier

(1) A consumer credit agreement shall be treated as entered into under pre-existing arrangements between a creditor and a supplier if it is entered into in accordance with, or in furtherance of, arrangements previously made between persons mentioned in subsection (4)(a), (b) or (c).

(2) A consumer credit agreement shall be treated as entered into in contemplation of future arrangements between a creditor and a supplier if it is entered into in the expectation that arrangements will subsequently be made between persons mentioned in subsection (4)(a), (b) or (c) for the supply of cash, goods and services (or any of them) to be financed by the consumer credit agreement.

(3) Arrangements shall be disregarded for the purposes of subsection (1) or (2) if—

(a) they are arrangements for the making, in specified circumstances, of payments to the supplier by the creditor, and
(b) the creditor holds himself out as willing to make, in such circumstances, payments of the kind to suppliers generally.

[(3A) Arrangements shall also be disregarded for the purposes of subsections (1) and (2) if they are arrangements for the electronic transfer of funds from a current account at a bank within the meaning of the Bankers' Books Evidence Act 1879.]

(4) The persons referred to in subsections (1) and (2) are—

(a) the creditor and the supplier;
(b) one of them and an associate of the other's;
(c) an associate of one and an associate of the other's.

(5) Where the creditor is an associate of the supplier's, the consumer credit agreement shall be treated, unless the contrary is proved, as entered into under pre-existing arrangements between the creditor and the supplier. [351]

NOTES
Commencement: 1 October 1987 (para 3A)); 31 July 1974 (remainder).
Sub-s (3A): added by the Banking Act 1987, s 89.

188. Examples of use of new terminology

(1) Schedule 2 shall have effect for illustrating the use of terminology employed in this Act.

(2) The examples given in Schedule 2 are not exhaustive.

(3) In the case of conflict between Schedule 2 and any other provision of this Act, that other provision shall prevail.

(4) The Secretary of State may by order amend Schedule 2 by adding further examples or in any other way. [352]

NOTES
Commencement: 31 July 1974.
As at 1 May 1989 no regulations had been made under this section.

189. Definitions

(1) In this Act, unless the context otherwise requires—

"advertisement" includes every form of advertising, whether in a publication, by television or radio, by display of notices, signs, labels, showcards or goods, by distribution of samples, circulars, catalogues, price lists or other material, by exhibition of pictures, models or films, or in any other way, and references to the publishing of advertisements shall be construed accordingly;
"advertiser" in relation to an advertisement, means any person indicated by the advertisement as willing to enter into transactions to which the advertisement relates;
"ancillary credit business" has the meaning given by section 145(1);
"antecedent negotiations" has the meaning given by section 56;
"appeal period" means the period beginning on the first day on which an appeal to the Secretary of State may be brought and ending on the last

day on which it may be brought or, if it is brought, ending on its final determination, or abandonment;

. . .

"associate" shall be construed in accordance with section 184;
["authorised institution" means an institution authorised under the Banking Act 1987;]
"bill of sale" has the meaning given by section 4 of the Bills of Sale Act 1878 or, for Northern Ireland, by section 4 of the Bills of Sale (Ireland) Act 1879;
["building society" means a building society within the meaning of the Building Societies Act 1986;]
"business" includes profession or trade, and references to a business apply subject to subsection (2);
"cancellable agreement" means a regulated agreement which, by virtue of section 67, may be cancelled by the debtor or hirer;
"canvass" shall be construed in accordance with sections 48 and 153;
"cash" includes money in any form;
"charity" means as respects England and Wales a charity registered under the Charities Act 1960 or an exempt charity (within the meaning of that Act), and as respects Scotland and Northern Ireland an institution or other organisation established for charitable purposes only ("organisation" including any persons administering a trust and "charitable" being construed in the same way as if it were contained in the Income Tax Acts);
"conditional sale agreement" means an agreement for the sale of goods or land under which the purchase price or part of it is payable by instalments, and the property in the goods or land is to remain in the seller (notwithstanding that the buyer is to be in possession of the goods or land) until such conditions as to the payment of instalments or otherwise as may be specified in the agreement are fulfilled;
"consumer credit agreement" has the meaning given by section 8, and includes a consumer credit agreement which is cancelled under section 69(1), or becomes subject to section 69(2), so far as the agreement remains in force;
"consumer credit business" means any business so far as it comprises or relates to the provision of credit under regulated consumer credit agreements;
"consumer hire agreement" has the meaning given by section 15;
"consumer hire business" means any business so far as it comprises or relates to the bailment or (in Scotland) the hiring of goods under regulated consumer hire agreements;
"controller", in relation to a body corporate, means a person—

(a) in accordance with whose directions or instructions the directors of the body corporate or of another body corporate which is its controller (or any of them) are accustomed to act, or
(b) who, either alone or with any associate or associates, is entitled to exercise or control the exercise of, one third or more of the voting power at any general meeting of the body corporate or of another body corporate which is its controller;

"copy" shall be construed in accordance with section 180;

. . .

"court" means in relation to England and Wales the county court, in relation to Scotland the sheriff court and in relation to Northern Ireland the High Court or the county court;

"credit" shall be construed in accordance with section 9;
"credit-broker" means a person carrying on a business of credit brokerage;
"credit brokerage" has the meaning given by section 145(2);
"credit limit" has the meaning given by section 10(2);
"creditor" means the person providing credit under a consumer credit agreement or the person to whom his rights and duties under the agreement have passed by assignment or operation of law, and in relation to a prospective consumer credit agreement, includes the prospective creditor;
"credit reference agency" has the meaning given by section 145(8);
"credit-sale agreement" means an agreement for the sale of goods, under which the purchase price or part of it is payable by instalments, but which is not a conditional sale agreement;
"credit-token" has the meaning given by section 14(1);
"credit-token agreement" means a regulated agreement for the provision of credit in connection with the use of a credit-token;
"debt-adjusting" has the meaning given by section 145(5);
"debt-collecting" has the meaning given by section 145(7);
"debt-counselling" has the meaning given by section 145(6);
"debtor" means the individual receiving credit under a consumer credit agreement or the person to whom his rights and duties under the agreement have passed by assignment or operation of law, and in relation to a prospective consumer credit agreement includes the prospective debtor;
"debtor-creditor agreement" has the meaning given by section 13;
"debtor-creditor-supplier agreement" has the meaning given by section 12;
"default notice" has the meaning given by section 87(1);
"deposit" means any sum payable by a debtor or hirer by way of deposit or down-payment, or credited or to be credited to him on account of any deposit or down-payment, whether the sum is to be or has been paid to the creditor or owner or any other person, or is to be or has been discharged by a payment of money or a transfer or delivery of goods or by any other means;
"Director" means the Director General of Fair Trading;
"electric line" has the meaning given by the Electric Lighting Act 1882 or, for Northern Ireland, the Electricity Supply (Northern Ireland) Order 1972;
"embodies" and related words shall be construed in accordance with subsection (4);
"enforcement authority" has the meaning given by section 161(1);
"enforcement order" means an order under section 65(1), 105(7)(*a*) or (*b*), 111(2) or 124(1) or (2);
"executed agreement" means a document, signed by or on behalf of the parties, embodying the terms of a regulated agreement, or such of them as have been reduced to writing;
"exempt agreement" means an agreement specified in or under section 16;
"finance" means to finance wholly or partly, and "financed" and "refinanced" shall be construed accordingly;
"file" and "copy of the file" have the meanings given by section 158(5);
"fixed-sum credit" has the meaning given by section 10(1)(*b*);
"friendly society" means a society registered under the Friendly Societies Acts 1896 to 1971 or a society within the meaning of the Friendly Societies Act (Northern Ireland) 1970;
"future arrangements" shall be construed in accordance with section 187;

"general notice" means a notice published by the Director at a time and in a manner appearing to him suitable for securing that the notice is seen within a reasonable time by persons likely to be affected by it;
"give", means, deliver or send by post to;
"goods" has the meaning given by [section 61(1) of the Sale of Goods Act 1979];
"group licence" has the meaning given by section 22(1)(b);
"High Court" means Her Majesty's High Court of Justice, or the Court of Session in Scotland or the High Court of Justice in Northern Ireland;
"hire-purchase agreement" means an agreement, other than a conditional sale agreement, under which—

(a) goods are bailed or (in Scotland) hired in return for periodical payments by the person to whom they are bailed or hired, and
(b) the property in the goods will pass to that person if the terms of the agreement are complied with and one or more of the following occurs—

(i) the exercise of an option to purchase by that person,
(ii) the doing of any other specified act by any party to the agreement,
(iii) the happening of any other specified event;

"hirer" means the individual to whom goods are bailed or (in Scotland) hired under a consumer hire agreement, or the person to whom his rights and duties under the agreement have passed by assignment or operation of law, and in relation to a prospective consumer hire agreement includes the prospective hirer;
"individual" includes a partnership or other unincorporated body of persons not consisting entirely of bodies corporate;
"installation" means—

(a) the installing of any electric line or any gas or water pipe,
(b) the fixing of goods to the premises where they are to be used, and the alteration of premises to enable goods to be used on them,
(c) where it is reasonably necessary that goods should be constructed or erected on the premises where they are to be used, any work carried out for the purpose of constructing or erecting them on those premises;

"insurance company" has the meaning given by [section 96(1) of the Insurance Companies Act 1982], but does not include a friendly society or an organisation of workers or organisation of employers;
"judgment" includes an order or decree made by any court;
"land" includes an interest in land, and in relation to Scotland includes heritable subjects of whatever description;
"land improvement company" means an improvement company as defined by section 7 of the Improvement of Land Act 1899;
"land mortgage" includes any security charged on land;
"licence" means a licence under Part III (including that Part as applied to ancillary credit businesses by section 147);
"licensed", in relation to any act, means authorised by a licence to do the act or cause or permit another person to do it;
"licensee", in the case of a group licence, includes any person covered by the licence;

"linked transaction" has the meaning given by section 19(1);
"local authority", in relation to England and Wales, means ..., a county council, a London borough council, a district council, the Common Council of the City of London, or the Council of Isles of Scilly, and in relation to Scotland, means a regional, islands or district council, and, in relation to Northern Ireland, means a district council;

...

"modifying agreement" has the meaning given by section 82(2);

...

"multiple agreement" has the meaning given by section 18(1);
"negotiator" has the meaning given by section 56(1);
"non-commercial agreement" means a consumer credit agreement or a consumer hire agreement not made by the creditor or owner in the course of a business carried on by him;
"notice" means notice in writing;
"notice of cancellation" has the meaning given by section 69(1);
"owner" means a person who bails or (in Scotland) hires out goods under a consumer hire agreement or the person to whom his rights and duties under the agreement have passed by assignment or operation of law, and in relation to a prospective consumer hire agreement, includes the prospective bailor or persons from whom the goods are to be hired;
"pawn" means any article subject to a pledge;
"pawn-receipt" has the meaning given by section 114;
"pawnee" and "pawnor" include any person to whom the rights and duties of the original pawnee or the original pawnor, as the case may be, have passed by assignment or operation of law;
"payment" includes tender;
"personal credit agreement" has the meaning given by section 8(1);
"pledge" means the pawnee's rights over an article taken in pawn;
"prescribed" means prescribed by regulations made by the Secretary of State;
"pre-existing arrangements" shall be construed in accordance with section 187;
"principal agreement" has the meaning given by section 19(1);
"protected goods" has the meaning given by section 90(7);
"quotation" has the meaning given by section 52(1)(a);
"redemption period" has the meaning given by section 116(3);
"register" means the register kept by the Director under section 35;
"regulated agreement" means a consumer credit agreement, or consumer hire agreement, other than an exempt agreement, and "regulated" and "unregulated" shall be construed accordingly;
"regulations" means regulations made by the Secretary of State;
"relative", except in section 184, means a person who is an associate by virtue of section 184(1);
"representation" includes any condition or warranty, and any other statement or undertaking, whether oral or in writing;
"restricted-use credit agreement" and "restricted-use credit" have the meanings given by section 11(1);
"rules of court", in relation to Northern Ireland means, in relation to the High Court, rules made under section 7 of the Northern Ireland Act 1962, and, in relation to any other court, rules made by the authority having for the time being power to make rules regulating the practice and procedure in that court;
"running-account credit" shall be construed in accordance with section 10;

"security", in relation to an actual or prospective consumer credit agreement or consumer hire agreement, or any linked transaction, means a mortgage, charge, pledge, bond, debenture, indemnity, guarantee, bill, note or other right provided by the debtor or hirer, or at his request (express or implied), to secure the carrying out of the obligations of the debtor or hirer under the agreement;

"security instrument" has the meaning given by section 105(2);

"serve on" means deliver or send by post to;

"signed" shall be construed in accordance with subsection (3);

"small agreement" has the meaning given by section 17(1), and "small" in relation to an agreement within any category shall be construed accordingly;

"specified fee" shall be construed in accordance with section 2(4) and (5);

"standard licence" has the meaning given by section 22(1)(*a*);

"supplier" has the meaning given by section 11(1)(*b*) or 12(*c*) or 13(*c*) or, in relation to an agreement falling within section 11(1)(*a*), means the creditor, and includes a person to whom the rights and duties of a supplier (as so defined) have passed by assignment or operation of law, or (in relation to a prospective agreement) the prospective supplier;

"surety" means the person by whom any security is provided, or the person to whom his rights and duties in relation to the security have passed by assignment or operation of law;

"technical grounds" shall be construed in accordance with subsection (5);

"time order" has the meaning given by section 129(1);

"total charge for credit" means a sum calculated in accordance with regulations under section 20(1);

"total price" means the total sum payable by the debtor under a hire-purchase agreement or a conditional sale agreement, including any sum payable on the exercise of an option to purchase, but excluding any sum payable as a penalty or as compensation or damages for a breach of the agreement;

"unexecuted agreement" means a document embodying the terms of a prospective regulated agreement, or such of them as it is intended to reduce to writing;

"unlicensed" means without a licence but applies only in relation to acts for which a licence is required;

"unrestricted-use credit agreement" and "unrestricted-use credit" have the meanings given by section 11(2);

"working day" means any day other than—

    (*a*) Saturday or Sunday,
    (*b*) Christmas Day or Good Friday,
    (*c*) a bank holiday within the meaning given by section 1 of the Banking and Financial Dealings Act 1971.

(2) A person is not to be treated as carrying on a particular type of business merely because occasionally he enters into transactions belonging to a business of that type.

(3) Any provision of this Act requiring a document to be signed is complied with by a body corporate if the document is sealed by that body.

This subsection does not apply to Scotland.

(4) A document embodies a provision if the provision is set out either in the document itself or in another document referred to in it.

(5) An application dismissed by the court or the Director shall, if the court or the Director (as the case may be) so certifies, be taken to be dismissed on technical grounds only.

(6) Except in so far as the context otherwise requires, any reference in this Act to an enactment shall be construed as a reference to that enactment as amended by or under any other enactment, including this Act.

(7) In this Act, except where otherwise indicated—
- (a) a reference to a numbered Part, section or Schedule is a reference to the Part or section of, or the Schedule to, this Act so numbered, and
- (b) a reference in a section to a numbered subsection is a reference to the subsection of that section so numbered, and
- (c) a reference in a section, subsection or Schedule to a numbered paragraph is a reference to the paragraph of that section, subsection or Schedule so numbered. [353]

NOTES
Commencement: 31 July 1974.

Sub-s (1): words omitted apply to Scotland only; definition "authorised institution" added by the Banking Act 1987, s 88; definition "building society" substituted by the Building Societies Act 1986, s 120, Sch 18, Part I, para 10(4); definition "goods" amended by the Sale of Goods Act 1979, s 63, Sch 2, para 18; definition "insurance company" amended by the Insurance Companies Act 1982, s 99(2), Sch 5, para 14; definition "local authority" amended by the Local Government Act 1985, s 102, Sch 17.

Miscellaneous

190. Financial provisions

(1) There shall be defrayed out of money provided by Parliament—
- (a) all expenses incurred by the Secretary of State in consequence of the provisions of this Act;
- (b) any expenses incurred in consequence of those provisions by any other Minister of the Crown or Government department;
- (c) any increase attributable to this Act in the sums payable out of money so provided under the Superannuation Act 1972 or the Fair Trading Act 1973.

(2) Any fees received by the Director under this Act shall be paid into the Consolidated Fund. [354]

NOTES
Commencement: 31 July 1974.

191. Special provisions as to Northern Ireland

(1) The Director may make arrangements with the Department of Commerce for Northern Ireland for the Department, on his behalf,—
- (a) to receive applications, notices and fees;
- (b) to maintain, and make available for inspection and copying, copies of entries in the register; and
- (c) to provide certified copies of entries in the register,

to the extent that seems to him desirable for the convenience of persons in Northern Ireland.

(2) The Director shall give general notice of any arrangements made under subsection (1).

(3) Nothing in this Act shall authorise any Northern Ireland department to incur any expenses attributable to the provisions of this Act until provision has been made for those expenses to be defrayed out of money appropriated for the purpose.

(4) The power of the Department of Commerce for Northern Ireland to make an order under section 178 shall be exercisable by statutory rule for the purposes of the [Statutory Rules (Northern Ireland) Order 1979], and any such order shall be subject to negative resolution within the meaning of the Interpretation Act (Northern Ireland) 1954 as if it were a statutory instrument within the meaning of that Act.

(5) In this Act "enactment" includes an enactment of the Parliament of Northern Ireland or the Northern Ireland Assembly, and "Act" shall be construed in a corresponding manner; and (without prejudice to section 189(6)) any reference in this Act to such an enactment shall include a reference to any enactment re-enacting it with or without modifications.

(6) Section 38 of the Interpretation Act 1889 (effect of repeals) shall have the same operation in relation to any repeal by this Act of an enactment of the Parliament of Northern Ireland as it has in relation to the repeal of an Act of the Parliament of the United Kingdom, references in that section of the Act of 1889 to Acts and enactments being construed accordingly. **[355]**

NOTES
Commencement: 31 July 1974.
Sub-s (4): amended by the Statutory Rules (Northern Ireland) Order 1979, SI 1979 No 1573, art 11(1), Sch 4, para 15.

192. Transitional and commencement provisions, amendments and repeals

(1) The provisions of Schedule 3 shall have effect for the purposes of this Act.

(2) The appointment of a day for the purposes of any provision of Schedule 3 shall be effected by an order of the Secretary of State made by statutory instrument; and any such order shall include a provision amending Schedule 3 so as to insert an express reference to the day appointed.

(3) Subject to subsection (4)—
  (a) the enactments specified in Schedule 4 shall have effect subject to the amendments specified in that Schedule (being minor amendments or amendments consequential on the preceding provisions of this Act), and
  (b) the enactments specified in Schedule 5 are hereby repealed to the extent shown in column 3 of that Schedule.

(4) The Secretary of State shall by order made by statutory instrument provide for the coming into operation of the amendments contained in Schedule 4 and the repeals contained in Schedule 5, and those amendments and repeals shall have effect only as provided by an order so made. **[356]**

NOTES
Commencement: 31 July 1974.
Regulations under this section: Consumer Credit Act 1974 (Commencement No 1) Order 1975, SI 1975 No 2123; Consumer Credit Act 1974 (Commencement No 2) Order 1977, SI 1977 No 325; Consumer Credit Act 1974 (Commencement No 3) Order 1977, SI 1977 No 802; Consumer Credit Act 1974 (Commencement No 4) Order 1977, SI 1977 No 2163; Consumer Credit Act 1974 (Commencement No 5) Order 1979, SI 1979 No 1685; Consumer Credit Act 1974 (Commencement No 6) Order 1980, SI 1980 No 50; Consumer Credit Act 1974 (Commencement No 7) Order 1981,

SI 1981 No 280; Consumer Credit Act 1974 (Commencement No 8) Order 1983, SI 1983 No 1551; Consumer Credit Act 1974 (Commencement No 9) Order 1984, SI 1984 No 436.

193. Short title and extent

(1) This Act may be cited as the Consumer Credit Act 1974.

(2) This Act extends to Northern Ireland.

NOTES
Commencement: 31 July 1974.

SCHEDULES
SCHEDULE 1

PROSECUTION AND PUNISHMENT OF OFFENCES

Section 167

1 Section	2 Offence	3 Mode of prosecution	4 Imprisonment or fine
7	Knowingly or recklessly giving false information to Director.	(a) Summarily. (b) On indictment.	The prescribed sum. 2 years or a fine or both.
39(1)	Engaging in activities requiring a licence when not a licensee.	(a) Summarily. (b) On indictment.	The prescribed sum. 2 years or a fine or both.
39(2)	Carrying on business under a name not specified in licence.	(a) Summarily. (b) On indictment.	The prescribed sum. 2 years or a fine or both.
39(3)	Failure to notify changes in registered particulars.	(a) Summarily. (b) On indictment.	The prescribed sum. 2 years or a fine or both.
45	Advertising credit where goods etc not available for cash.	(a) Summarily. (b) On indictment.	The prescribed sum. 2 years or a fine or both.
46(1)	False or misleading advertisements.	(a) Summarily. (b) On indictment.	The prescribed sum. 2 years or a fine or both.
47(1)	Advertising infringements.	(a) Summarily. (b) On indictment.	The prescribed sum. 2 years or a fine or both.
49(1)	Canvassing debtor-creditor agreements off trade premises.	(a) Summarily. (b) On indictment.	The prescribed sum. 1 year or a fine or both.
49(2)	Soliciting debtor-creditor agreements during visits made in response to previous oral requests.	(a) Summarily. (b) On indictment.	The prescribed sum. 1 year or a fine or both.
50(1)	Sending circulars to minors.	(a) Summarily. (b) On indictment.	The prescribed sum. 1 year or a fine or both.
51(1)	Supplying unsolicited credit-tokens.	(a) Summarily. (b) On indictment.	The prescribed sum. 2 years or a fine or both.
77(4)	Failure of creditor under fixed-sum credit agreement to supply copies of documents etc.	Summarily.	Level 4 on the standard scale.
78(6)	Failure of creditor under running-account credit agreement to supply copies of documents etc.	Summarily.	Level 4 on the standard scale.
79(3)	Failure of owner under consumer hire agreement to supply copies of documents etc.	Summarily.	Level 4 on the standard scale.
80(2)	Failure to tell creditor or owner whereabouts of goods.	Summarily.	Level 3 on the standard scale.
85(2)	Failure of creditor to supply copy of credit-token agreement.	Summarily.	Level 4 on the standard scale.

97(3)	Failure to supply debtor with statement of amount required to discharge agreement.	Summarily.	Level 3 on the standard scale.
103(5)	Failure to deliver notice relating to discharge of agreements.	Summarily.	Level 3 on the standard scale.
107(4)	Failure of creditor to give information to surety under fixed-sum credit agreement.	Summarily.	Level 4 on the standard scale.
108(4)	Failure of creditor to give information to surety under running-account credit agreement.	Summarily.	Level 4 on the standard scale.
109(3)	Failure to owner to give information to surety under consumer hire agreement.	Summarily.	Level 4 on the standard scale.
110(3)	Failure of creditor or owner to supply a copy of any security instrument to debtor or hirer.	Summarily.	Level 4 on the standard scale.
114(2)	Taking pledges from minors.	(a) Summarily. (b) On indictment.	The prescribed sum. 1 year or a fine or both.
115	Failure to supply copies of a pledge agreement or pawn-receipt.	Summarily.	Level 4 on the standard scale.
119(1)	Unreasonable refusal to allow pawn to be redeemed.	Summarily.	Level 4 on the standard scale.
154	Canvassing ancillary credit services off trade premises.	(a) Summarily. (b) On indictment.	The prescribed sum. 1 year or a fine or both.
157(3)	Refusal to give name etc of credit reference agency.	Summarily.	Level 4 on the standard scale.
158(4)	Failure of credit reference agency to disclose filed information.	Summarily.	Level 4 on the standard scale.
159(6)	Failure of credit reference agency to correct information.	Summarily.	Level 4 on the standard scale.
160(6)	Failure of credit reference agency to comply with section 160(3) or (4).	Summarily.	Level 4 on the standard scale.
162(6)	Impersonation of enforcement authority officers.	(a) Summarily. (b) On indictment.	The prescribed sum. 2 years or a fine or both.
165(1)	Obstruction of enforcement authority officers.	Summarily.	Level 4 on the standard scale.
165(2)	Giving false information to enforcement authority officers.	(a) Summarily. (b) On indictment.	The prescribed sum. 2 years or a fine or both.
167(2)	Contravention of regulations under section 44, 52, 53, 54 or 112.	(a) Summarily. (b) On indictment.	The prescribed sum. 2 years or a fine or both.
174(5)	Wrongful disclosure of information.	(a) Summarily. (b) On indictment.	The prescribed sum. 2 years or a fine or both.

NOTES

Commencement: 31 July 1974.

Amended by the Magistrates' Courts Act 1980, s 32(2); maximum fines for purely summary offences increased and converted to levels on the standard scale by the Criminal Justice Act 1982, ss 37, 38, 46.

SCHEDULE 2

Section 188(1)

Examples of Use of New Terminology

Part I
List of Terms

Term	Defined in section	Illustrated by example(s)
Advertisement	189(1)	2
Advertiser	189(1)	2
Antecedent negotiations	56	1, 2, 3, 4
Cancellable agreement	67	4
Consumer credit agreement	8	5, 6, 7, 15, 19, 21
Consumer hire agreement	15	20, 24
Credit	9	16, 19, 21
Credit-broker	189(1)	2
Credit limit	10(2)	6, 7, 19, 22, 23
Creditor	189(1)	1, 2, 3, 4
Credit-sale agreement	189(1)	5
Credit-token	14	3, 14, 16
Credit-token agreement	14	3, 14, 16, 22
Debtor-creditor agreement	13	8, 16, 17, 18
Debtor-creditor-supplier agreement	12	8, 16
Fixed-sum credit	10	9, 10, 17, 23
Hire-purchase agreement	189(1)	10
Individual	189(1)	19, 24
Linked transaction	19	11
Modifying agreement	82(2)	24
Multiple agreement	18	16, 18
Negotiator	56(1)	1, 2, 3, 4
Personal credit agreement	8(1)	19
Pre-existing arrangements	187	8, 21
Restricted-use credit	11	10, 12, 13, 14, 16
Running-account credit	10	15, 16, 18, 23
Small agreement	17	16, 17, 22
Supplier	189(1)	3, 14
Total charge for credit	20	5, 10
Total price	189(1)	10
Unrestricted-use credit	11	8, 12, 16, 17, 18

NOTES
Commencement: 31 July 1974.

Part II

Examples

Example 1

Facts. Correspondence passes between an employee of a moneylending company (writing on behalf of the company) and an individual about the terms on which the company would grant him a loan under a regulated agreement.

Analysis. The correspondence constitutes antecedent negotiations falling within section 56(1)(*a*), the moneylending company being both creditor and negotiator.

Example 2

Facts. Representations are made about goods in a poster displayed by a shopkeeper near the goods, the goods being selected by a customer who has read the poster and then sold by the shopkeeper to a finance company introduced by him (with whom he has a business relationship). The goods are disposed of by the finance company to the customer under a regulated hire-purchase agreement.

Analysis. The representations in the poster constitute antecedent negotiations falling within section 56(1)(*b*), the shopkeeper being the credit-broker and negotiator and the finance company being the creditor. The poster is an advertisement and the shopkeeper is the advertiser.

EXAMPLE 3

Facts. Discussions take place between a shopkeeper and a customer about goods the customer wishes to buy using a credit-card issued by the D Bank under a regulated agreement.

Analysis. The discussions constitute antecedent negotiations falling within section 56(1)(*c*), the shopkeeper being the supplier and negotiator and the D Bank the creditor. The credit-card is a credit-token as defined in section 14(1), and the regulated agreement under which it was issued is a credit-token agreement as defined in section 14(2).

EXAMPLE 4

Facts. Discussions take place and correspondence passes between a secondhand car dealer and a customer about a car, which is then sold by the dealer to the customer under a regulated conditional sale agreement. Subsequently, on a revocation of that agreement by consent, the car is resold by the dealer to a finance company introduced by him (with whom he has a business relationship), who in turn dispose of it to the same customer under a regulated hire-purchase agreement.

Analysis. The discussions and correspondence constitute antecedent negotiations in relation both to the conditional sale agreement and the hire-purchase agreement. They fall under section 56(1)(*a*) in relation to the conditional sale agreement, the dealer being the creditor and the negotiator. In relation to the hire-purchase agreement they fall within section 56(1)(*b*), the dealer continuing to be treated as the negotiator but the finance company now being the creditor. Both agreements are cancellable if the discussions took place when the individual conducting the negotiations (whether the "negotiator" or his employee or agent) was in the presence of the debtor, unless the unexecuted agreement was signed by the debtor at trade premises (as defined in section 67(*b*)). If the discussions all took place by telephone however, or the unexecuted agreement was signed by the debtor on trade premises (as so defined) the agreements are not cancellable.

EXAMPLE 5

Facts. E agrees to sell to F (an individual) an item of furniture in return for 24 monthly instalments of £10 payable in arrear. The property in the goods passes to F immediately.

Analysis. This is a credit-sale agreement (see definition of "credit-sale agreement" in section 189(1)). The credit provided amounts to £240 less the amount which, according to regulations made under section 20(1), constitutes the total charge for credit. (This amount is required to be deducted by section 9(4).) Accordingly the agreement falls within section 8(2) and is a consumer credit agreement.

EXAMPLE 6

Facts. The G Bank grants H (an individual) an unlimited overdraft, with an increased rate of interest on so much of any debit balance as exceeds £2,000.

Analysis. Although the overdraft purports to be unlimited, the stipulation for increased interest above £2,000 brings the agreement within section 10(3)(*b*)(ii) and it is a consumer credit agreement.

EXAMPLE 7

Facts. J is an individual who owns a small shop which usually carries a stock worth about £1,000. K makes a stocking agreement under which he undertakes to provide on short-term credit the stock needed from time to time by J without any specified limit.

Analysis. Although the agreement appears to provide unlimited credit, it is probable, having regard to the stock usually carried by J, that his indebtedness to K will not at any time rise above £5,000. Accordingly the agreement falls within section 10(3)(*b*)(iii) and is a consumer credit agreement.

EXAMPLE 8

Facts. U, a moneylender, lends £500 to V (an individual) knowing he intends to use it to buy office equipment from W. W introduced V to U, it being his practice to introduce customers needing finance to him. Sometimes U gives W a commission for this and sometimes not. U pays the £500 direct to V.

Analysis. Although this appears to fall under section 11(1)(*b*), it is excluded by section 11(3) and is therefore (by section 11(2)) an unrestricted-use credit agreement. Whether it is a debtor-creditor agreement (by section 13(*c*)) or a debtor-creditor-supplier agreement (by section 12(*c*)) depends on whether the previous dealings between U and W amount to "pre-existing arrangements", that is whether the agreement can be taken to have been entered into "in accordance with, or in furtherance of" arrangements previously made between U and W, as laid down in section 187(1).

EXAMPLE 9

Facts. A agrees to lend B (an individual) £4,500 in nine monthly instalments of £500.

Analysis. This is a cash loan and is a form of credit (see section 9 and definition of "cash" in section 189(1)). Accordingly it falls within section 10(1)(*b*) and is fixed-sum credit amounting to £4,500.

EXAMPLE 10

Facts. C (in England) agrees to bail goods to D (an individual) in return for periodical payments. The agreement provides for the property in the goods to pass to D on payment of a total of £7,500 and the exercise by D of an option to purchase. The sum of £7,500 includes a down-payment of £1,000. It also includes an amount which, according to regulations made under section 20(1), constitutes a total charge for credit of £1,500.

Analysis. This is a hire-purchase agreement with a deposit of £1,000 and a total price of £7,500 (see definitions of "hire-purchase agreement", "deposit" and "total price" in section 189(1)). By section 9(3), it is taken to provide credit amounting to £7,500 - (£1,500 + £1,000), which equals £5,000. Under section 8(2), the agreement is therefore a consumer credit agreement, and under sections 9(3) and 11(1) it is a restricted-use credit agreement for fixed-sum credit. A similar result would follow if the agreement by C had been a hiring agreement in Scotland.

EXAMPLE 11

Facts. X (an individual) borrows £500 from Y (Finance). As a condition of the granting of the loan X is required—
  (*a*) to execute a second mortgage on his house in favour of Y (Finance), and
  (*b*) to take out a policy of insurance on his life with Y (Insurances).

In accordance with the loan agreement, the policy is charged to Y (Finance) as collateral security for the loan. The two companies are associates within the meaning of section 184(3).

Analysis. The second mortgage is a transaction for the provision of security and accordingly does not fall within section 19(1), but the taking out of the insurance policy is a linked transaction falling within section 19(1)(*a*). The charging of the policy is a separate transaction (made between different parties) for the provision of security and again is excluded from section 19(1). The only linked transaction is therefore the taking out of the insurance policy. If X had not been required by the loan agreement to take out the policy, but it had been done at the suggestion of Y (Finance) to induce them to enter into the loan agreement, it would have been a linked transaction under section 19(1)(*c*)(i) by virtue of section 19(2)(*a*).

EXAMPLE 12

Facts. The N Bank agrees to lend O (an individual) £2,000 to buy a car from P. To make sure the loan is used as intended, the N Bank stipulates that the money must be paid by it direct to P.

Analysis. The agreement is a consumer credit agreement by virtue of section 8(2). Since it falls within section 11(1)(*b*), it is a restricted-use credit agreement, P being the supplier. If the N Bank had not stipulated for direct payment to the supplier, section 11(3) would have operated and made the agreement into one for unrestricted-use credit.

EXAMPLE 13

Facts. Q, a debt-adjuster, agrees to pay off debts owed by R (an individual) to various moneylenders. For this purpose the agreement provides for the making of a loan by Q to R in return for R's agreeing to repay the loan by instalments with interest. The loan money is not paid over to R but retained by Q and used to pay off the moneylenders.

Analysis. This is an agreement to refinance existing indebtedness of the debtor's, and if the loan by Q does not exceed £5,000 is a restricted-use credit agreement falling within section 11(1)(*c*).

EXAMPLE 14

Facts. On payment of £1, S issues to T (an individual) a trading check under which T can spend up to £20 at any shop which has agreed, or in future agrees, to accept S's trading checks.

Analysis. The trading check is a credit-token falling within section 14(1) (*b*). The credit-token agreement is a restricted-use credit agreement within section 11(1)(*b*), any shop in which the credit-token is used being the "supplier". The fact that further shops may be added after the issue of the credit-token is irrelevant in view of section 11(4).

EXAMPLE 15

Facts. A retailer, L, agrees with M (an individual) to open an account in M's name and, in return for M's promise to pay a specified minimum sum into the account each month and to pay a monthly charge for credit, agrees to allow to be debited to the account, in respect of purchases made by M from L, such sums as will not increase the debit balance at any time beyond the credit limit, defined in the agreement as a given multiple of the specified minimum sum.

Analysis. This arrangement provides credit falling within the definition of running-account credit in section 10(1)(*a*). Provided the credit limit is not over £5,000, the agreement falls within section 8(2) and is a consumer credit agreement for running-account credit.

EXAMPLE 16

Facts. Under an unsecured agreement, A (Credit), an associate of the A Bank, issues to B (an individual) a credit-card for use in obtaining cash on credit from A (Credit), to be paid by branches of the A Bank (acting as agent of A (Credit)), or goods or cash from suppliers or banks who have agreed to honour credit-cards issued by A (Credit). The credit limit is £30.

Analysis. This is a credit-token agreement falling within section 14(1)(*a*) and (*b*). It is a regulated consumer credit agreement for running-account credit. Since the credit limit does not exceed £30, the agreement is a small agreement. So far as the agreement relates to goods it is a debtor-creditor-supplier agreement within section 12(*b*), since it provides restricted-use credit under section 11(1)(*b*). So far as it relates to cash it is a debtor-creditor agreement within section 13(*c*) and the credit it provides is unrestricted-use credit. This is therefore a multiple agreement. In that the whole agreement falls within several of the categories of agreement mentioned in this Act, it is, by section 18(3), to be treated as an agreement in each of those categories. So far as it is a debtor-creditor-supplier agreement providing restricted-use credit it is, by section 18(2), to be treated as a separate agreement; and similarly so far as it is a debtor-creditor agreement providing unrestricted-used credit. (See also Example 22.)

EXAMPLE 17

Facts. The manager of the C Bank agrees orally with D (an individual) to open a current account in D's name. Nothing is said about overdraft facilities. After maintaining the account in credit for some weeks, D draws a cheque in favour of E for an amount exceeding D's credit balance by £20. E presents the cheque and the Bank pay it.

Analysis. In drawing the cheque D, by implication, requests the Bank to grant him an overdraft of £20 on its usual terms as to interest and other charges. In deciding to honour the cheque, the Bank by implication accepts the offer. This constitutes a regulated small consumer credit agreement for unrestricted-use, fixed-sum credit. It is a debtor-creditor agreement, and falls within section 74(1)(*b*) if covered by a determination under section 74(3). (Compare Example 18.)

EXAMPLE 18

Facts. F (an individual) has had a current account with the G Bank for many years. Although usually in credit, the account has been allowed by the Bank to become overdrawn from time to time. The maximum such overdraft has been is about £1,000. No explicit agreement has ever been made about overdraft facilities. Now, with a credit balance of £500, F draws a cheque for £1,300.

Analysis. It might well be held that the agreement with F (express or implied) under which the Bank operate his account includes an implied term giving him the right to overdraft facilities up to say £1,000. If so, the agreement is a regulated consumer credit agreement for unrestricted-use, running account credit. It is a debtor-creditor agreement, and falls within section 74(1)(*b*) if covered by a direction under section 74(3). It is also a multiple agreement, part of which (ie the part not dealing with the overdraft), as referred to in section 18(1)(*a*), falls within a category of agreement not mentioned in this Act. (Compare Example 17.)

EXAMPLE 19

Facts. H (a finance house) agrees with J (a partnership of individuals) to open an unsecured loan account in J's name on which the debit balance is not to exceed £7,000 (having regard to payments into the account made from time to time by J). Interest is to be payable in advance on this sum, with provision for yearly adjustments. H is entitled to debit the account with interest, a "setting-up" charge, and other charges. Before J has an opportunity to draw on the account it is initially debited with £2,250 for advance interest and other charges.

Analysis. This is a personal running-account credit agreement (see section 8(1) and 10(1)(*a*), and definition of "individual" in section 189(1)). By section 10(2) the credit limit is £7,000. By section 9(4) however the initial debit of £2,250, and any other charges later debited to the account by H, are not to be treated as credit even though time is allowed for their payment. Effect is given to this by section 10(3). Although the credit limit of £7,000 exceeds the amount (£5,000) specified in section 8(2) as the maximum for a consumer credit agreement, so that the agreement is not within section 10(3)(*a*), it is caught by section 10(3)(*b*)(i). At the beginning J can effectively draw (as credit) no more than £4,750, so the agreement is a consumer credit agreement.

EXAMPLE 20

Facts. K (in England) agrees with L (an individual) to bail goods to L for a period of three years certain at £2,000 a year, payable quarterly. The agreement contains no provision for the passing of the property in the goods to L.

Analysis. This is not a hire-purchase agreement (see paragraph (*b*) of the definition of that term in section 189(1)) and is capable of subsisting for more than three months. Paragraphs (*a*) and (*b*) of section 15(1) are therefore satisfied, but paragraph (*c*) is not. The payments by L must exceed £5,000 if he conforms to the agreement. It is true that under section 101 L has a right to terminate the agreement on giving K three months' notice expiring not earlier than eighteen months after the making of the agreement, but that section applies only where the agreement is a regulated consumer hire agreement apart from the section (see subsection (1)). So the agreement is not a consumer hire agreement, though it would be if the hire charge were say £1,500 a year, or there were a "break" clause in it operable by either party before the hire charges exceeded £5,000. A similar result would follow if the agreement by K had been a hiring agreement in Scotland.

Example 21

Facts. The P Bank decides to issue cheque cards to its customers under a scheme whereby the Bank undertakes to honour cheques of up to £30 in every case where the payee has taken the cheque in reliance on the cheque card, whether the customer has funds in his account or not. The P Bank writes to the major retailers advising them of this scheme and also publicises it by advertising. The Bank issues a cheque card to Q (an individual), who uses it to pay by cheque for goods costing £20 bought by Q from R, a major retailer. At the time, Q has £500 in his account at the P Bank.

Analysis. The agreement under which the cheque card is issued to Q is a consumer credit agreement even though at all relevant times Q has more than £30 in his account. This is because Q is free to draw out his whole balance and then use the cheque card, in which case the Bank has bound itself to honour the cheque. In other words the cheque card agreement provides Q with credit, whether he avails himself of it or not. Since the amount of the credit is not subject to any express limit, the cheque card can be used any number of times. It may be presumed however that section 10(3)(*b*)(iii) will apply. The agreement is an unrestricted-use debtor-creditor agreement (by section 13(*c*)). Although the P Bank wrote to R informing R of the P Bank's willingness to honour any cheque taken by R in reliance on a cheque card, this does not constitute pre-existing arrangements as mentioned in section 13 (*c*) because section 187(3) operates to prevent it. The agreement is not a credit-token agreement within section 14(1)(*b*) because payment by the P Bank to R would be a payment of the cheque and not a payment for the goods.

Example 22

Facts. The facts are as in Example 16. On one occasion B uses the credit-card in a way which increases his debit balance with A (Credit) to £40. A (Credit) writes to B agreeing to allow the excess on that occasion only, but stating that it must be paid off within one month.

Analysis. In exceeding his credit limit B, by implication, requests A (Credit) to allow him a temporary excess (compare Example 17). A (Credit) is thus faced by B's action with the choice of treating it as a breach of contract or granting his implied request. They do the latter. If they had done the former, B would be treated as taking credit to which he was not entitled (section 14(3)) and, subject to the terms of his contract with A (Credit), would be liable to damages for breach of contract. As it is, the agreement to allow the excess varies the original credit-token agreement by adding a new term. Under section 10(2), the new term is to be disregarded in arriving at the credit limit, so that the credit-token agreement at no time ceases to be a small agreement. By section 82(2) the later agreement is deemed to revoke the original agreement and contain provisions reproducing the combined effect of the two agreements. By section 82(4), this later agreement is exempted from Part V (except section 56).

Example 23

Facts. Under an oral agreement made on 10 January, X (an individual) has an overdraft on his current account at the Y Bank with a credit limit of £100. On 15 February, when his overdraft standards at £90, X draws a cheque for £25. It is the first time that X has exceeded his credit limit, and on 16 February the bank honours the cheque.

Analysis. The agreement of 10 January is a consumer credit agreement for running-account credit. The agreement of 15—16 February varies the earlier agreement by adding a term allowing the credit limit to be exceeded merely temporarily. By section 82(2) the later agreement is deemed to revoke the earlier agreement and reproduce the combined effect of the two agreements. By section 82(4), Part V of this Act (except section 56) does not apply to the later agreement. By section 18(5), a term allowing a merely temporary excess over the credit limit is not to be treated as a separate agreement, or as providing fixed-sum credit. The whole of the £115 owed to the Bank by X on 16 February is therefore running-account credit.

Example 24

Facts. On 1 March 1975 Z (in England) enters into an agreement with A (an unincorporated body of persons) to bail to A equipment consisting of two components (component P and component Q). The agreement is not a hire-purchase agreement and is for a fixed term of 3 years, so paragraphs (*a*) and (*b*) of section 15(1) are both satisfied.

The rental is payable monthly at a rate of £2,400 a year, but the agreement provides that this is to be reduced to £1,200 a year for the remainder of the agreement if at any time during its currency A returns component Q to the owner Z. On 5 May 1976 A is incorporated as A Ltd., taking over A's assets and liabilities. On 1 March 1977, A Ltd. returns component Q. On 1 January 1978, Z and A Ltd. agree to extend the earlier agreement by one year, increasing the rental for the final year by £250 to £1,450.

Analysis. When entered into on 1 March 1975, the agreement is a consumer hire agreement. A falls within the definition of "individual" in section 189(1) and if A returns component Q before 1 May 1976 the total rental will not exceed £5,000 (see section 15(1)(c)). When this date is passed without component Q having been returned it is obvious that the total rental must now exceed £5,000. Does this mean that the agreement then ceases to be a consumer hire agreement? The answer is no, because there has been no change in the terms of the agreement, and without such a change the agreement cannot move from one category to the other. Similarly, the fact that A's rights and duties under the agreement pass to a body corporate on 5 May 1976 does not cause the agreement to cease to be a consumer hire agreement (see the definition of "hirer" in section 189(1)).

The effect of the modifying agreement of 1 January 1978 is governed by section 82(2), which requires it to be treated as containing provisions reproducing the combined effect of the two actual agreements, that is to say as providing that—

   (a) obligations outstanding on 1 January 1978 are to be treated as outstanding under the modifying agreement;
   (b) the modifying agreement applies at the old rate of hire for the months of January and February 1978, and
   (c) for the year beginning 1 March 1978 A Ltd. will be the bailee of component P at a rental of £1,450.

The total rental under the modifying agreement is £1,850. Accordingly the modifying agreement is a regulated agreement. Even if the total rental under the modifying agreement exceeded £5,000 it would still be regulated because of the provisions of section 82(3). **[360–361]**

NOTES
Commencement: 31 July 1974.

NOTES
Sch 3 (Transitional and Commencement Provisions), Sch 4 (Minor and Consequential Amendments) and Sch 5 (Repeals) are omitted.

CONSUMER CREDIT (EXEMPT AGREEMENTS) (NO 2) ORDER 1985
(SI 1985 No 757)

NOTES
Made: 15 May 1985
Authority: Consumer Credit Act 1974, ss 16(1), (4)-(6), 182(2), (4)
The text incorporates subsequent amendments. Amending instruments are: SI 1985 No 1736; SI 1985 No 1918; SI 1986 No 1105; SI 1986 No 2186; SI 1987 No 1578; SI 1988 No 707 and SI 1988 No 991.

ARRANGEMENT OF ARTICLES

Article		Para
1	Citation, commencement, interpretation and revocation	[362]
2	Exemption of certain consumer credit agreements secured on land	[363]
3	Exemption of certain consumer credit agreements by reference to the number of payments to be made by the debtor	[364]

4	Exemption of certain consumer credit agreements by reference to the rate of the total charge for credit	[365]
5	Exemption of certain consumer credit agreements having a connection with a country outside the United Kingdom	[366]
6	Exemption of certain consumer hire agreements	[367–70]

1. Citation, commencement, interpretation and revocation

(1) This Order may be cited as the Consumer Credit (Exempt Agreements) (No. 2) Order 1985 and shall come into operation on 20 May 1985.

(2) In this Order—

"the Act" means the Consumer Credit Act 1974;
"business premises" means premises for occupation for the purposes of a business (including any activity carried on by a body of persons, whether corporate or unincorporate) or for those and other purposes;

and references to the total charge for credit and the rate thereof are respectively references to the total charge for credit and the rate thereof calculated in accordance with the Consumer Credit (Total Charge for Credit) Regulations 1980.

(3) The Consumer Credit (Exempt Agreements) Order 1980, the Consumer Credit (Exempt Agreements) (Amendment) Order 1981, the Consumer Credit (Exempt Agreements) (Amendment) Order 1982, the Consumer Credit (Exempt Agreements) (Amendment) Order 1984, the Consumer Credit (Exempt Agreements) (Amendment) (No 2) Order 1984 and the Consumer Credit (Exempt Agreements) Order 1985 are hereby revoked. **[362]**

NOTES
Commencement: 20 May 1985.

2. Exemption of certain consumer credit agreements secured on land

(1) The Act shall not regulate a consumer credit agreement which falls within section 16(2) of the Act, being an agreement to which this paragraph applies.

(2) Where the creditor is a body specified in Part I of the Schedule to this Order [or a building society authorised under the Building Societies Act 1986] [or an authorised institution under the Banking Act 1987 or a wholly-owned subsidiary of such an institution], paragraph (1) above applies only to—

(a) a debtor-creditor-supplier agreement falling within section 16(2)(a) [or (c)] of the Act;
(b) a debtor-creditor agreement secured by any land mortgage [to finance]—
    (i) the purchase of land; or
    (ii) the provision of dwellings or business premises on any land; or
    (iii) subject to paragraph (3) below, the alteration, enlarging, repair or improvement of a dwelling or business premises on any land;
(c) a debtor-creditor agreement secured by any land mortgage to refinance any existing indebtedness of the debtor, whether to the creditor or another person, under any agreement by which the debtor was provided with credit for any of the purposes specified in heads (i) to (iii) of sub-paragraph (b) above.
[(d) a debtor-creditor agreement secured by any land mortgage where the creditor is a building society authorised under the Building Societies Act 1986 and its offer to enter into such agreement was made in

writing before 1 January 1987 and the agreement was executed before 1 February 1987.]

(3) Head (iii) of sub-paragraph (b) of paragraph (2) above applies only
[(i)] where the creditor is the creditor under—
    (a) an agreement (whenever made) by which the debtor is provided with credit for any of the purposes specified in head (i) and head (ii) of that sub-paragraph; or
    (b) an agreement (whenever made) refinancing an agreement under which the debtor is provided with credit for any of the said purposes,

being, in either case, an agreement relating to the land referred to in the said head (iii) and secured by a land mortgage on that land.

[or (ii) where a debtor-creditor agreement to finance the alteration, enlarging, repair or improvement of a dwelling, secured by a land mortgage on that dwelling, is made as a result of any such services as are described in section 4(3)(*dd*) of the Housing Associations Act 1985 which are certified as having been provided by—
    (a) a local authority;
    (b) a housing association within the meaning of section 1 of the Housing Associations Act 1985 or Article 114 of the Housing (Northern Ireland) Order 1981;
    (c) a body established by such a housing association for the purpose of providing such services as are described in the said section 4(3)(*dd*);
    (d) a charity;
    (e) the National Home Improvement Council; or
    (f) the Northern Ireland Housing Executive.]

(4) Where the creditor is a body specified in Part II of the Schedule to this Order, paragraph (1) above applies only to an agreement of a description specified in that Part in relation to that body and made pursuant to an enactment or for a purpose so specified. [363]

NOTES
Commencement: 20 May 1985.
Para (2): first amendment made by SI 1986 No 2186, art 2(a); second amendment made by SI 1987 No 1578, art 2(a), other amendments made by SI 1986 No 2186, art 2(a).
Para 3: amended by SI 1988 No 707, art 2.

3. Exemption of certain consumer credit agreements by reference to the number of payments to be made by the debtor

(1) The Act shall not regulate a consumer credit agreement which is an agreement of one of the following descriptions, that is to say,—
    (a) a debtor-creditor-supplier agreement being either—
        (i) an agreement for fixed-sum credit under which the number of payments to be made by the debtor does not exceed four; or
        (ii) an agreement for running-account credit which provides for the making of payments by the debtor in relation to specified periods and requires that the number of payments to be made by the debtor in repayment of the whole amount of the credit provided in each such period shall not exceed one;

not being, in either case, an agreement of a description specified in paragraph (2) below; and in this sub-paragraph, "payment" means a payment comprising an amount in respect of credit with or without any other amount;

(b) a debtor-creditor-supplier agreement financing the purchase of land, being an agreement under which the number of payments to be made by the debtor does not exceed four; and in this sub-paragraph, "payment" means a payment comprising or including an amount in respect of credit or the total charge for credit (if any);
(c) a debtor-creditor-supplier agreement for fixed-sum credit to finance a premium under a contract of insurance relating to any land or to anything thereon where—
   (i) the creditor is the creditor under an agreement secured by a land mortgage on that land which either is an exempt agreement by virtue of section 16(1) of the Act or of Article 2 above or is a personal credit agreement which would be an exempt agreement by virtue of either of those provisions if the credit provided were not to exceed £15,000;
   (ii) the amount of the credit is to be repaid within the period to which the premium relates, not being a period exceeding 12 months; and
   (iii) there is no charge forming part of the total charge for credit under the agreement other than interest at a rate not exceeding the rate of interest from time to time payable under the agreement mentioned in head (i) above,

and the number of payments to be made by the debtor does not exceed twelve; and in this sub-paragraph "payment" has the same meaning as it has in paragraph (1)(b) above; and

(d) a debtor-creditor-supplier agreement for fixed-sum credit where—
   (i) the creditor is the creditor under an agreement secured by a land mortgage on any land which either is an exempt agreement by virtue of section 16(1) of the Act or of Article 2 above or is a personal credit agreement which would be an exempt agreement by virtue of either of those provisions if the credit provided were not to exceed £15,000;
   (ii) the agreement is to finance a premium under a contract of life insurance which provides, in the event of the death before the credit under the agreement referred to in head (1) above has been repaid of the person on whose life the contract is effected, for payment of a sum not exceeding the amount sufficient to defray the sums which, immediately after the credit has been advanced, would be payable to the creditor in respect of that credit and of the total charge for that credit; and
   (iii) there is no charge forming part of the total charge for credit under the agreement other than interest at a rate not exceeding the rate of interest from time to time payable under the agreement referred to in head (i) above,

and the number of payments to be made by the debtor does not exceed twelve; and in this sub-paragraph, "payment" has the same meaning as it has in sub-paragraph (1)(b) above.

(2) The descriptions of agreement referred to in sub-paragraph (a) of paragraph (1) above and to which accordingly that sub-paragraph does not apply are—
   (a) agreements financing the purchase of land;
   (b) agreements which are conditional sale agreements or hire-purchase agreements; and

(c) agreements secured by a pledge (other than a pledge of documents of title or of bearer bonds). [364]

NOTES
Commencement: 20 May 1985.

---

4. Exemption of certain consumer credit agreements by reference to the rate of the total charge for credit

(1) The Act shall not regulate a consumer credit agreement which is an agreement of one of the following descriptions, that is to say—

   (a) subject to paragraphs (2), (3) and (4) below, any debtor-creditor agreement in respect of which the rate of the total charge for credit does not exceed the rate referred to in paragraph (5) below;

   (b) subject to paragraph (4) below, a debtor-creditor-supplier agreement for fixed-sum credit where—

      (i) the creditor is the creditor under an agreement secured by a land mortgage on any land which either is an exempt agreement by virtue of section 16(1) of the Act or of Article 2 above or is a personal credit agreement which would be an exempt agreement by virtue of either of those provisions if the credit provided were not to exceed £15,000;

      (ii) the agreement is to finance a premium under a contract of life insurance which provides, in the event of the death before the credit under the agreement referred to in head (i) above has been repaid of the person on whose life the contract is effected, for payment of a sum not exceeding the amount sufficient to defray the sums which, immediately after that credit has been advanced, would be payable to the creditor in respect of that credit and of the total charge for that credit; and

      (iii) there is no charge forming part of the total charge for credit under the agreement other than interest at a rate not exceeding the rate of interest from time to time payable under the agreement referred to in head (i) above,

and in respect of which the rate of the total charge for credit does not exceed the rate referred to in paragraph (5) below;

   (c) subject to paragraph (4) below, a debtor-creditor agreement in respect of which the only amount included in the total charge for credit is interest which cannot under the agreement at any time exceed the higher of the following, that is to say—

      (i) the sum of one per cent and the highest of any base rates published by the banks named in paragraph (6) below, being the latest rates in operation on the date 28 days before any such time; and

      (ii) 13 per cent;

and for the purposes of this sub-paragraph, "interest" means interest at a rate determined in accordance with the formula set out in paragraph (1) of Regulation 7 of the Consumer Credit (Total Charge for Credit) Regulations 1980, and in that formula as applied by this paragraph "period rate of charge" has the meaning assigned to it in paragraph (2) of that Regulation.

(2) Subject to paragraph (3) below, sub-paragraph (a) of paragraph (1)

above does not apply to agreements which provide for an increase in, or permit the creditor to increase, the rate or amount of any item which—
   (a) is included in the total charge for credit; or
   (b) would fall to be so included, apart from the operation of Regulation 14 of the Consumer Credit (Total Charge for Credit) Regulations 1980,
after the relevant date of the agreement within the meaning of Regulation 1(2) of those Regulations.

(3) Sub-paragraph (a) of paragraph (1) above does apply to agreements—
   (a) in relation to which the debtor [, or any one of two or more debtors where each debtor is a relative of the other debtor or of one of the other debtors,] is an employee of the creditor or of an associate of his and which provide for an increase in, or permit the creditor to increase, the rate or amount of any item such as is mentioned in paragraph (2) above on the termination of [such employment] with the creditor or such associate, as the case may be; or
   (b) under which the rate or amount of any such item falls to be ascertained throughout the duration of the agreement by reference to the level of any index or other factor in accordance with any formula specified in the agreement;
and which do not provide for an increase in, or permit the creditor to increase, the rate or amount of any item mentioned in paragraph (2) above in any way other than those permitted by either or both of sub-paragraphs (a) or (b) of this paragraph.

(4) Paragraph (1) above does not apply to agreements under which the total amount to be repaid by the debtor to discharge his indebtedness in respect of the amount of credit provided may vary according to any formula specified in the agreement having effect by reference to movements in the level of any index or to any other factor.

(5) The rate mentioned in sub-paragraphs (a) and (b) of paragraph (1) above is the higher of the following, that is to say—
   (a) the sum of one per cent and the highest of any base rates published by the banks named in paragraph (6) below, being the latest rates in operation on the date 28 days before the date on which the agreement is made; and
   (b) 13 per cent.

(6) The banks referred to in paragraphs (1)(c) and (5) above are—
   Bank of England
   Bank of Scotland
   Barclays Bank PLC
   Central Trustee Savings Bank Limited
   Clydesdale Bank PLC
   Co-operative Bank Public Limited Company
   Coutts & Co
   Lloyds Bank PLC
   Midland Bank Public Limited Company
   National Westminster Bank Public Limited Company
   The Royal Bank of Scotland PLC

William & Glyn's Bank Public Limited Company. [365]

NOTES
Commencement: 20 May 1985.
Para (3)(*a*): amended by SI 1985 No 1736, art 2(*a*).

5. Exemption of certain consumer credit agreements having a connection with a country outside the United Kingdom

The Act shall not regulate a consumer credit agreement made—

(*a*) in connection with trade in goods or services between the United Kingdom and a country outside the United Kingdom or within a country or between countries outside the United Kingdom, being an agreement under which credit is provided to the debtor in the course of a business carried on by him; or

[(*b*) between a creditor listed in Part III of the Schedule to this Order and a debtor who is—

   (i) a member of any of the armed forces of the United States of America;
   (ii) an employee not habitually resident in the United Kingdom of any of those forces; or
   (iii) any such member's or employee's wife or husband or any other person (whether or not a child of his) whom he wholly or partly maintains and treats as a child of the family.] [366]

NOTES
Commencement: 20 May 1985.
Art 5: para (*b*) substituted by SI 1988 No 991, art 2(*b*), as from 11 July 1988.

6. Exemption of certain consumer hire agreements

The Act shall not regulate a consumer hire agreement where the owner is a body corporate authorised by or under any enactment to supply electricity, gas or water and the subject of the agreement is a meter or metering equipment used or to be used in connection with the supply of electricity, gas or water, as the case may be. [367–370]

NOTES
Commencement: 20 May 1985.

NOTES
The Schedule to this Order, containing a list of bodies whose agreements of the specified descriptions are exempt agreements, is omitted.

SECTION III
CONSUMER PROTECTION

TRADING STAMPS ACT 1964
(c 71)

ARRANGEMENT OF SECTIONS

Section		Para
1	Restrictions on persons who may carry on business as promoters of trading stamp schemes	[371]
2	Statements required on face of trading stamps	[372]
3	Redemption of trading stamps for cash	[373]
4	Warranties to be implied on redemption of trading stamps for goods	[374]
5	Catalogues and stamp books to include name and address of promoter	[375]
6	Advertisements referring to value of trading stamps	[376]
7	Display of information in shops	[377]
8	Offences committed by corporations	[378]
9	Venue in summary proceedings	[379]
10	Interpretation	[380]
11	Short title, extent and commencement	[381]

An Act to make provision with respect to trading stamps, including provision for regulating the issue, use and redemption of trading stamps; to provide for regulating the business of issuing and redeeming trading stamps; and for purposes connected with matters aforesaid [31 July 1964]

1. Restrictions on persons who may carry on business as promoters of trading stamp schemes

(1) No person other than a company or an industrial and provident society shall carry on business as the promoter of a trading stamp scheme.

(2) ...

(3) If a person carries on business in contravention of subsection (1) of this section he shall be liable—

(a) on conviction on indictment to a fine of any amount, and
(b) on summary conviction to a fine not exceeding [the prescribed sum].

(4) In this and the next following section—

"company" means a company formed and registered under the [Companies Act 1985] or an existing company within the meaning of that Act, and "private company" has the same meaning as in that Act;
"industrial and provident society" means a society registered under the Industrial and Provident Societies Act 1893. **[371]**

NOTES
Commencement: 31 January 1965.
Sub-s (2): repealed by the Companies Act 1967, s 130(4), Sch 8, Part VIII.
Sub-s (3): amended by the Magistrate's Courts Act 1980, s 32(2).
Sub-s (4): amended by the Companies Consolidation (Consequential Provisions) Act 1985, s 30, Sch 2.

2. Statements required on face of trading stamps

[(1) No person shall after the coming into force of this section issue any trading stamp, or cause any trading stamp to be issued, or deliver any trading stamp to any person in connection with the sale of any goods, the bailment or (in Scotland) the hiring of any goods under a hire-purchase agreement or the performance of any service, unless such trading stamp bears on its face in clear and legible characters a value expressed in or by reference to current coin of the realm.]

(2) As from the coming into force of this section it shall be the duty of a company or industrial and provident society carrying on business as the promoter of a trading stamp scheme to secure that all trading stamps issued under the scheme bear on their face in clear and legible characters—
- (a) in the case of a company, either the name of the company or a business name registered in respect of the company under the Registration of Business Names Act 1916;
- (b) in the case of an industrial and provident society, the name of the society.

(3) A person guilty of a contravention of subsection (1) of this section or of a failure to comply with subsection (2) of this section shall on summary conviction be liable to a fine not exceeding—
- (a) in the case of an offence by a promoter of a trading stamp scheme, [level 3 on the standard scale], and
- (b) in the case of an offence by some other person, [level 1 on the standard scale]. [372]

NOTES
Commencement: 31 July 1965.
Sub-s (1): amended by the Consumer Credit Act 1974, s 192(3)(a), Sch 4, Part I, para 24.
Sub-s (3): maximum fines increased and converted to levels on the standard scale by the Criminal Justice Act 1982, ss 37, 38, 46.

3. Redemption of trading stamps for cash

(1) If the holder of any number of redeemable trading stamps which have an aggregate cash value of not less than [25p] so requests, the promoter of the trading stamp scheme shall redeem them by paying over their aggregate cash value.

(2) The holder may exercise his right under the foregoing subsection—
- (a) by presenting the stamps at any reasonable time at the promoter's registered office, or
- (b) by sending the stamps by post to that office with sufficient instructions as to the manner in which the cash value is to be paid over,

or in any other manner afforded by the promoter.

(3) The obligation under this section in the case of an aggregate cash value which includes a fraction of a [new penny] shall be arrived at by taking the sum to the nearest [new penny] below the aggregate cash value.

[(4) In this section "redeemable trading stamps" means trading stamps delivered after the coming into force of this section in accordance with a trading stamp scheme on or in connection with either—
- (a) the purchase of any goods,
- (b) the bailment or (in Scotland) the hiring of any goods under a hire-purchase agreement, or
- (c) the obtaining of any services for money,

and "the holder", in relation to such a trading stamp, means the person to whom it was so delivered or any person who holds it without notice of any defect in title.]

(5) Subject to the following subsection this section shall also apply to trading

stamps so delivered before the date of the coming into force of this section if a cash value is stated on their face.

(6) This section shall not apply—
   (a) to trading stamps which have been so delivered before the date of the coming into force of this section and which show on their face that they were so delivered before that date, or
   (b) to trading stamps which have been so delivered not later than six months after the passing of this Act and which show on their face, instead of any reference to any kind of value to the holder, a value indicating the sum paid on the purchase or other transaction in connection with which they were delivered or some other value which, having regard to the terms of the trading stamp scheme, it would be unreasonable to take as their value for the purposes of redemption under this section.

(7) Any agreement under which the rights conferred by this section on holders of redeemable trading stamps are surrendered or modified shall be void. [373]

NOTES
Commencement: 31 July 1965.
Sub-ss (1) and (3): amended by the Decimal Currency Act 1969, s 10(1) and (3), Sch 2, para 22.
Sub-s(4): substituted by the Consumer Credit Act 1974, s 192(3)(a), Sch 4, Part I, para 25.

4. Warranties to be implied on redemption of trading stamps for goods

[(1) In every redemption of trading stamps for goods, notwithstanding any terms to the contrary on which the redemption is made, there is—
   (a) an implied warranty on the part of the promoter of the trading stamp scheme that he has a right to give the goods in exchange;
   (b) an implied warranty that the goods are free from any charge or encumbrance not disclosed or known to the person obtaining the goods before, or at the time of, redemption and that that person will enjoy quiet possession of the goods except so far as it may be disturbed by the owner or other person entitled to the benefit of any charge or encumbrance so disclosed or known;
   (c) an implied warranty that the goods are of merchantable quality, except that there is no such warranty—
      (i) as regards defects specifically drawn to the attention of the person obtaining the goods before or at the time of redemption; or
      (ii) if that person examines the goods before or at the time of redemption, as regards defects which that examination ought to reveal.

(2) Goods of any kind are of merchantable quality within the meaning of this section if they are as fit for the purpose or purposes for which goods of that kind are commonly bought as it is reasonable to expect having regard to any description applied to them and all the other relevant circumstances.

(3) ...] [374]

NOTES
Commencement: 18 May 1973.
Substituted by the Supply of Goods (Implied Terms) Act 1973, s 16(1).
Sub-s (3): applies to Scotland only.

5. Catalogues and stamp books to include name and address of promoter

(1) Every catalogue published by or on behalf of the promoter of a trading stamp scheme which indicates (whether by reference to a stated number of filled stamp books or otherwise) the number of trading stamps required to obtain anything described in the catalogue, and every stamp book published by or on behalf of the promoter of such a scheme, shall contain a prominent statement of the name of the promoter and the address of the promoter's registered office.

(2) If the promoter of a trading stamp scheme publishes, issues or distributes a catalogue or stamp book which fails to comply with any of the requirements of this section, he shall be liable on summary conviction to a fine not exceeding [level 3 on the standard scale]. [375]

NOTES
Commencement: 31 July 1965.
Sub-s (2): maximum fine increased and converted to a level on the standard scale by the Criminal Justice Act 1982, ss 37, 38, 46.

6. Advertisements referring to value of trading stamps

(1) It shall be unlawful for the promoter of a trading stamp scheme, or for any person carrying on a trade or business in which a trading stamp scheme is operated, after the coming into force of this section to issue or publish, or cause to be issued or published, an advertisement in any medium which conveys, or purports to convey, the cash value of any trading stamps—

  (a) by means of a statement which associates the worth of any trading stamps with what the holder pays or may pay to obtain them, or
  (b) in terms which are misleading or deceptive.

(2) A person contravening this section shall be liable on summary conviction to a fine not exceeding [level 3 on the standard scale].

(3) For the purposes of this section an advertisement issued by way of display or exhibition in a public place shall be treated as issued on every day on which it is so displayed or exhibited, but in proceedings brought by virtue of this subsection in a case where the display or exhibition began before the date of the coming into force of this section, it shall be a defence to show that the defendant had taken all reasonable steps to secure that the display or exhibition was terminated before the date. [376]

NOTES
Commencement: 31 July 1965.
Sub-s (2): maximum fine increased and converted to a level on the standard scale by the Criminal Justice Act 1982, ss 37, 38, 46.

7. Display of information in shops

(1) In the case of every shop in which a trading stamp scheme is operated—

  (a) there shall be kept posted a notice stating the cash value of the trading stamps issued under the scheme and giving such particulars as will enable customers readily to ascertain the number of trading stamps, if any, to which they are entitled on any purchase or other transaction, and
  (b) if any current catalogue has been published for the trading stamp scheme by or on behalf of the promoter, a copy of that catalogue shall be kept where it can be conveniently consulted by customers.

(2) A notice under this section shall be posted in such characters and in such a position as to be conveniently read by customers.

(3) If without reasonable excuse any of the foregoing provisions of this section are not complied with in the case of any shop, the occupier or other person having control of the shop shall be liable on summary conviction to a fine not exceeding [level 1 on the standard scale].

(4) If any person pulls down ... any notice posted in pursuance of this section, he shall be liable on summary conviction to a fine not exceeding [level 1 on the standard scale].

(5) In this section "current catalogue" means any such catalogue as is described in section 5 (1) of this Act, being a catalogue which has not been superseded or withdrawn. [377]

NOTES
Commencement: 31 July 1965.
Words omitted repealed by the Criminal Damage Act 1971, s 11(8), Schedule, Part II; maximum fines increased and converted to levels on the standard scale by the Criminal Justice Act 1982, ss 37, 38, 46.

8. Offences committed by corporations

Where any offence under this Act committed by a corporation is proved to have been committed with the consent or connivance of any director, manager, secretary or other officer of the corporation, he, as well as the corporation, shall be deemed to be guilty of that offence and shall be liable to be proceeded against and punished accordingly. [378]

NOTES
Commencement: 31 July 1964.

9. Venue in summary proceedings

Summary proceedings against a person for an offence under this Act may be taken before the court having jurisdiction in the place where that person is for the time being or, in the case of a body corporate, for the time being has a place of business. [379]

NOTES
Commencement: 31 July 1964.

10. Interpretation

(1) In this Act, unless the context otherwise requires, the following expressions have the meanings hereby assigned to them respectively, that is to say—

"cash value" means, in relation to any trading stamp, the value stated on such stamp;
["conditional sale agreement" means an agreement for the sale of goods under which the purchase price or part of it is payable by instalments, and the property in the goods is to remain in the seller (notwithstanding that the buyer is to be in possession of the goods) until such conditions as to the payment of instalments or otherwise as may be specified in the agreement are fulfilled;]
"corporation" means any body corporate, whether incorporated in Great Britain or elsewhere;
"goods" includes vehicles, vessels, aircraft and animals, and generally includes articles and property of any description;

["hire-purchase agreement" means an agreement, other than a conditional sale agreement, under which—
(a) goods are bailed or (in Scotland) hired in return for periodical payments by the person to whom they are bailed or hired, and
(b) the property in the goods will pass to that person if the terms of the agreement are complied with and one or more of the following occurs—

    (i) the exercise of an option to purchase by that person,
    (ii) the doing of any other specified act by any party to the agreement,
    (iii) the happening of any other specified event;]

. . .

"to redeem" means, in relation to any trading stamps, to exchange such stamps (whether by delivering up the stamps or by suffering the same to be cancelled or otherwise howsoever) for money or for goods or for any other benefit, allowance, concession or advantage (but not including the service or repair by the seller or manufacturer of the goods upon or in connection with the purchase of which the stamps are delivered or the replacement of such goods if defective); and the expressions "redeemable" and "redemption" shall be construed accordingly;

"shop" includes any premises, and any vehicle, stall or place other than premises, on or in which any retail trade or business is carried on;

"stamp" means any stamp, coupon, voucher, token or similar device, whether adhesive or not, other than lawful money of the realm;

"stamp book" means a book or similar article in or to which it is intended that trading stamps shall be affixed;

["trading stamp" means a stamp which is, or is intended to be, delivered to any person on or in connection with either—

    (i) the purchase of any goods, or
    (ii) the bailment or (in Scotland) the hiring of any goods under a hire-purchase agreement,

(other than the purchase of a newspaper or other periodical of which the stamp forms part or in which it is contained) and is, or is intended to be, redeemable (whether singly or together with other such stamps) by that or some other person:

Provided that a stamp shall not be deemed to be a trading stamp if—

(a) it is delivered or is intended to be delivered to a person (in this definition called "the purchaser") on or in connection with the purchase of any goods by the purchaser, or the bailment or (in Scotland) the hiring to him of any goods, and
(b) it is intended to be, and is not, redeemable from any person other than—

    (i) the person (in this definition called "the seller") from whom the purchaser purchased those goods, or who bailed or hired those goods to him, or
    (ii) any person from whom the seller (whether directly or indirectly) acquired those goods, and

(c) in the case where a business is carried on by six or more retail establishments, the stamp is one of a kind obtainable at no more than six of those retail establishments, and not obtainable by the public elsewhere, and the arrangements under which it is redeemable are entirely separate from arrangements under which any other stamps, whether trading stamps or not, are redeemable and references in this definition to the purchase of goods include references to the obtaining of services for money;]

"trading stamp scheme" means any arrangements for making trading stamps available for use in shops or elsewhere, together with arrangements for their redemption, and "promoter", in relation to a trading stamp scheme, includes, in a case where a person carrying on a retail trade or business assumes responsibility for the redemption of trading stamps, that person.

(2) For the purposes of this Act, a person shall be deemed to be a director of a corporation if he occupies in relation thereto the position of a director, by whatever name called, or is a person in accordance with whose directions or instructions the directors of the corporation or any of them act:

Provided that a person shall not, by reason only that the directors of a corporation act on advice given by him in a professional capacity, be taken to be a person in accordance with whose directions or instructions those directors act. **[380]**

NOTES
Definitions "conditional sale agreement" and "hire-purchase agreement" inserted, and definition "trading stamp" substituted by the Consumer Credit Act 1974, s 192(3)(a), (b), Sch 4, Part I, para 26, Sch 5, Part I; definition "purchase" repealed by the Consumer Credit Act 1974, s 192(3)(b), Sch 4, Part I.

11. Short title, extent and commencement

(1) This Act may be cited as the Trading Stamps Act 1964.

(2) This Act shall not extend to Northern Ireland.

(3) Section 1 of this Act shall come into force at the expiration of a period of six months beginning with the date of the passing of this Act, and sections 2 to 7 of this Act shall come into force at the expiration of a period of twelve months beginning with that date. **[381]**

TRADE DESCRIPTIONS ACT 1968
(c 29)

ARRANGEMENT OF SECTIONS

PROHIBITION OF FALSE TRADE DESCRIPTIONS

Section		Para
1	Prohibition of false trade descriptions	[382]
2	Trade description	[383]
3	False trade description	[384]
4	Applying a trade description to goods	[385]
5	Trade descriptions used in advertisements	[386]
6	Offer to supply	[387]

POWER TO DEFINE TERMS AND TO REQUIRE DISPLAY, ETC OF INFORMATION

7	Definition orders	[388]
8	Marking orders	[389]

Section		Para
9	Information, etc to be given in advertisements	[390]
10	Provisions supplementary to sections 8 and 9	[391]

MISSTATEMENTS OTHER THAN FALSE TRADE DESCRIPTIONS

11	False or misleading indications as to price of goods	[392]
12	False representations as to royal approval or award, etc	[393]
13	False representations as to supply of goods or services	[394]
14	False or misleading statements as to services, etc	[395]
15	Orders defining terms for purposes of section 14	[396]

PROHIBITION OF IMPORTATION OF CERTAIN GOODS

16	Prohibition of importation of goods bearing false indication of origin	[397]

PROVISIONS AS TO OFFENCES

18	Penalty for offences	[398]
19	Time limit for prosecutions	[399]
20	Offences by corporations	[400]
21	Accessories to offences committed abroad	[401]
22	Restrictions on institution of proceedings and admission of evidence	[402]
23	Offences due to fault of other person	[403]

DEFENCES

24	Defence of mistake, accident, etc	[404]
25	Innocent publication of advertisement	[405]

ENFORCEMENT

26	Enforcing authorities	[406]
27	Power to make test purchases	[407]
28	Power to enter premises and inspect and seize goods and documents	[408]
29	Obstruction of authorised officers	[409]
30	Notice of test and intended prosecution	[410]
31	Evidence by certificate	[411]

MISCELLANEOUS AND SUPPLEMENTAL

32	Power to exempt goods sold for export, etc	[412]
33	Compensation for loss, etc of goods seized under s 28	[413]
34	Trade marks containing trade descriptions	[414]
35	Saving for civil rights	[415]
36	Country of origin	[416]
37	Market research experiments	[417]
38	Orders	[418]
39	Interpretation	[419]
40	Provisions as to Northern Ireland	[420]
43	Short title and commencement	[421]

An Act to replace the Merchandise Marks Acts 1887 to 1953 by fresh provisions prohibiting misdescriptions of goods, services, accommodation and facilities provided in the course of trade; to prohibit false or misleading indications as to the price of goods; to confer power to require information or instructions relating to goods to be marked on or to accompany the goods or to be included in advertisements; to prohibit the unauthorised use of devices or emblems signifying royal awards; to enable the Parliament of Northern Ireland to make laws relating to merchandise marks; and for purposes connected with those matters. [30 May 1968]

GENERAL NOTES
Commencement: 30 November 1968.
This Act applies with modifications to Northern Ireland.

PROHIBITION OF FALSE TRADE DESCRIPTIONS

1. Prohibition of false trade descriptions

(1) Any person who, in the course of a trade or business,—
    (*a*) applies a false trade description to any goods; or
    (*b*) supplies or offers to supply any goods to which a false trade description is applied;
shall, subject to the provisions of this Act, be guilty of an offence.

(2) Sections 2 to 6 of this Act shall have effect for the purposes of this section and for the interpretation of expressions used in this section, wherever they occur in this Act. **[382]**

2. Trade description

(1) A trade description is an indication, direct or indirect, and by whatever means given, of any of the following matters with respect to any goods or parts of goods, that is to say—
    (*a*) quantity, size or gauge;
    (*b*) method of manufacture, production, processing or reconditioning;
    (*c*) composition;
    (*d*) fitness for purpose, strength, performance, behaviour or accuracy;
    (*e*) any physical characteristics not included in the preceding paragraphs;
    (*f*) testing by any person and results thereof;
    (*g*) approval by any person or conformity with a type approved by any person;
    (*h*) place or date of manufacture, production, processing or reconditioning;
    (*i*) person by whom manufactured, produced, processed or reconditioned;
    (*j*) other history, including previous ownership or use.

(2) The matters specified in subsection (1) of this section shall be taken—
    (*a*) in relation to any animal, to include sex, breed or cross, fertility and soundness;
    (*b*) in relation to any semen, to include the identity and characteristics of the animal from which it was taken and measure of dilution.

(3) In this section "quantity" includes length, width, height, area, volume, capacity, weight and number.

(4) Notwithstanding anything in the preceding provisions of this section, the following shall be deemed not to be trade descriptions, that is to say, any description or mark applied in pursuance of—
    (*a*) . . .
    (*b*) section 2 of the Agricultural Produce (Grading and Marking) Act 1928 (as amended by the Agricultural Produce (Grading and Marking)

Amendment Act 1931) or any corresponding enactment of the Parliament of Northern Ireland;
  (c) the Plant Varieties and Seeds Act 1964;
  (d) the Agriculture and Horticulture Act 1964 [or any Community grading rules within the meaning of Part III of that Act];
  (e) the Seeds Act (Northern Ireland) 1965;
  (f) the Horticulture Act (Northern Ireland) 1966;
  [(g) the Consumer Protection Act 1987;]

[any statement made in respect of, or mark applied to, any material in pursuance of Part IV of the Agriculture Act 1970, any name or expression to which a meaning has been assigned under section 70 of that Act when applied to any material in the circumstances specified in that section] . . . any mark prescribed by a system of classification compiled under section 5 of the Agriculture Act 1967 [and any designation, mark or description applied in pursuance of a scheme brought into force under section 6(1) or an order made under section 25(1) of the Agriculture Act 1970].

(5) Notwithstanding anything in the preceding provisions of this section,

  [(a)]where provision is made under the [Food Act 1984], the Food and Drugs (Scotland) Act 1956 or the Food and Drugs Act (Northern Ireland) 1958 [or the Consumer Protection Act 1987] prohibiting the application of a description except to goods in the case of which the requirements specified in that provision are complied with, that description, when applied to such goods, shall be deemed not to be a trade description.
  [(b) where by virtue of any provision made under Part V of the Medicines Act 1968 (or made under any provisions of the said Part V as applied by an order made under section 104 or section 105 of that Act) anything which, in accordance with this Act, constitutes the application of a trade description to goods is subject to any requirements or restrictions imposed by that provision, any particular description specified in that provision, when applied to goods in circumstances to which those requirements or restrictions are applicable, shall be deemed not to be a trade description]. **[383]**

NOTES
  Sub-s (4): para (a) repealed by the European Communities Act 1972, s 4, Sch 3, Part III; para (d) amended by the European Communities Act 1972, s 4, Sch 4, para 4(2); para (g) substituted by the Consumer Protection Act 1987, s 48, Sch 4, para (2); second words omitted repealed and other amendments in square brackets made by the Agriculture Act 1970, ss 6(4), 87(3), 113(3), Sch 5, Part V.
  Sub-s (5): first and final amendments in square brackets made by the Medicines Act 1968, s 135(1), Sch 5, para 16; second amendment in square brackets made by the Food Act 1984, s 134, Sch 10, para 11; third amendment in square brackets made by the Consumer Protection Act 1987, s 48, Sch 4.

3. False trade description

(1) A false trade description is a trade description which is false to a material degree.

(2) A trade description which, though not false, is misleading, that is to say, likely to be taken for such an indication of any of the matters specified in section 2 of this Act as would be false to a material degree, shall be deemed to be a false trade description.

(3) Anything which, though not a trade description, is likely to be taken for

an indication of any of those matters and, as such an indication, would be false to a material degree, shall be deemed to be a false trade description.

(4) A false indication, or anything likely to be taken as an indication which would be false, that any goods comply with a standard specified or recognised by any person or implied by the approval of any person shall be deemed to be a false trade description, if there is no such person or no standard so specified, recognised or implied. **[384]**

4. Applying a trade description to goods

(1) A person applies a trade description to goods if he—

    (*a*) affixes or annexes it to or in any manner marks it on or incorporates it with—

        (i) the goods themselves, or
        (ii) anything in, on or with which the goods are supplied; or

    (*b*) places the goods in, on or with anything which the trade description has been affixed or annexed to, marked on or incorporated with, or places any such thing with the goods; or

    (*c*) uses the trade description in any manner likely to be taken as referring to the goods.

(2) An oral statement may amount to the use of a trade description.

(3) Where goods are supplied in pursuance of a request in which a trade description is used and the circumstances are such as to make it reasonable to infer that the goods are supplied as goods corresponding to that trade description, the person supplying the goods shall be deemed to have applied that trade description to the goods. **[385]**

5. Trade descriptions used in advertisements

(1) The following provisions of this section shall have effect where in an advertisement a trade description is used in relation to any class of goods.

(2) The trade description shall be taken as referring to all goods of the class, whether or not in existence at the time the advertisement is published—

    (*a*) for the purpose of determining whether an offence has been committed under paragraph (*a*) of section 1(1) of this Act; and

    (*b*) where goods of the class are supplied or offered to be supplied by a person publishing or displaying the advertisement, also for the purpose of determining whether an offence has been committed under paragraph (*b*) of the said section 1(1).

(3) In determining for the purposes of this section whether any goods are of a class to which a trade description used in an advertisement relates regard shall be had not only to the form and content of the advertisement but also to the time, place, manner and frequency of its publication and all other matters making it likely or unlikely that a person to whom the goods are supplied would think of the goods as belonging to the class in relation to which the trade description is used in the advertisement. **[386]**

6. Offer to supply

A person exposing goods for supply or having goods in his possession for supply shall be deemed to offer to supply them. **[387]**

POWER TO DEFINE TERMS AND TO REQUIRE DISPLAY, ETC OF INFORMATION

7. Definition orders

Where it appears to the Board of Trade—
- (a) that it would be in the interest of persons to whom any goods are supplied; or
- (b) that it would be in the interest of persons by whom any goods are exported and would not be contrary to the interest of persons to whom such goods are supplied in the United Kingdom;

that any expressions used in relation to the goods should be understood as having definite meanings, the Board may by order assign such meanings either—
- (i) to those expressions when used in the course of a trade or business as, or as part of, a trade description applied to the goods; or
- (ii) to those expressions when so used in such circumstances as may be specified in the order;

and where such a meaning is so assigned to an expression it shall be deemed for the purposes of this Act to have that meaning when used as mentioned in paragraph (i) or, as the case may be, paragraph (ii) of this section. **[388]**

NOTES
No regulations have yet been made under this section.

8. Marking orders

(1) Where it appears to the Board of Trade necessary or expedient in the interest of persons to whom any goods are supplied that the goods should be marked with or accompanied by any information (whether or not amounting to or including a trade description) or instruction relating to the goods, the Board may, subject to the provisions of this Act, by order impose requirements for securing that the goods are so marked or accompanied, and regulate or prohibit the supply of goods with respect to which the requirements are not complied with; and the requirements may extend to the form and manner in which the information or instruction is to be given.

(2) Where an order under this section is in force with respect to goods of any description, any person who, in the course of any trade or business, supplies or offers to supply goods of that description in contravention of the order shall, subject to the provisions of this Act, be guilty of an offence.

(3) An order under this section may make different provision for different circumstances and may, in the case of goods supplied in circumstances where the information or instruction required by the order would not be conveyed until after delivery, require the whole or part thereof to be also displayed near the goods. **[389]**

NOTES
Regulations under this section: Trade Descriptions (Sealskin Goods) Information Order 1980, SI 1980 No 1150; Trade Descriptions (Origin Marking) (Miscellaneous Goods) (Revocation) Order 1986, SI 1986 No 193; Trade Descriptions (Place of Production) (Marking) Order 1988, SI 1988 No 1771.

9. Information, etc to be given in advertisements

(1) Where it appears to the Board of Trade necessary or expedient in the interest of persons to whom any goods are to be supplied that any description of

advertisements of the goods should contain or refer to any information (whether or not amounting to or including a trade description) relating to the goods the Board may, subject to the provisions of this Act, by order impose requirements as to the inclusion of that information, or of an indication of the means by which it may be obtained, in such description of advertisements of the goods as may be specified in the order.

(2) An order under this section may specify the form and manner in which any such information or indication is to be included in advertisements of any description and may make different provision for different circumstances.

(3) Where an advertisement of any goods to be supplied in the course of any trade or business fails to comply with any requirement imposed under this section, any person who publishes the advertisement shall, subject to the provisions of this Act, be guilty of an offence. [390]

NOTES
Regulations under this section: Trade Descriptions (Sealskin Goods) Information Order 1980, SI 1980 No 1150; Trade Descriptions (Origin Marking) (Miscellaneous Goods) (Revocation) Order 1986, SI 1986 No 193.

10. Provisions supplementary to sections 8 and 9

(1) A requirement imposed by an order under section 8 or section 9 of this Act in relation to any goods shall not be confined to goods manufactured or produced in any one country or any one of a number of countries or to goods manufactured or produced outside any one or more countries, unless—

   (a) it is imposed with respect to a description of goods in the case of which the Board of Trade are satisfied that the interest of persons in the United Kingdom to whom goods of that description are supplied will be sufficiently protected if the requirement is so confined; and
   (b) the Board of Trade are satisfied that the order is compatible with the international obligations of the United Kingdom.

(2) Where any requirements with respect to any goods are for the time being imposed by such an order and the Board of Trade are satisfied, on the representation of persons appearing to the Board to have a substantial interest in the matter, that greater hardship would be caused to such persons if the requirements continued to apply than is justified by the interest of persons to whom such goods are supplied, the power of the Board to relax or discontinue the requirements by a further order may be exercised without the consultation and notice required by section 38(3) of this Act. [391]

MISSTATEMENTS OTHER THAN FALSE TRADE DESCRIPTIONS

11. False or misleading indications as to price of goods

... [392]

NOTES
Repealed by the Consumer Protection Act 1987, s 48, Sch 5, from 1 March 1989.

12. False representations as to royal approval or award, etc

(1) If any person, in the course of any trade or business, gives, by whatever means, any false indication, direct or indirect, that any goods or services supplied by him or any methods adopted by him are or are of a kind supplied to

or approved by Her Majesty or any member of the Royal Family, he shall, subject to the provisions of this Act, be guilty of an offence.

(2) If any person, in the course of any trade or business, uses, without the authority of Her Majesty, any device or emblem signifying the Queen's Award to Industry or anything so nearly resembling such a device or emblem as to be likely to deceive, he shall, subject to the provisions of this Act, be guilty of an offence. [393]

13. False representations as to supply of goods or services

If any person, in the course of any trade or business, gives, by whatever means, any false indication, direct or indirect, that any goods or services supplied by him are of a kind supplied to any person he shall, subject to the provisions of this Act, be guilty of an offence. [394]

14. False or misleading statements as to services, etc

(1) It shall be an offence for any person in the course of any trade or business—
   (a) to make a statement which he knows to be false; or
   (b) recklessly to make a statement which is false;

as to any of the following matters, that is to say,—
   (i) the provision in the course of any trade or business of any services, accommodation or facilities;
   (ii) the nature of any services, accommodation or facilities provided in the course of any trade or business;
   (iii) the time at which, manner in which or persons by whom any services, accommodation or facilities are so provided;
   (iv) the examination, approval or evaluation by any person of any services, accommodation or facilities so provided; or
   (v) the location or amenities of any accommodation so provided.

(2) For the purposes of this section—
   (a) anything (whether or not a statement as to any of the matters specified in the preceding subsection) likely to be taken for such a statement as to any of those matters as would be false shall be deemed to be a false statement as to that matter; and
   (b) a statement made regardless of whether it is true or false shall be deemed to be made recklessly, whether or not the person making it had reasons for believing that it might be false.

(3) In relation to any services consisting of or including the application of any treatment or process or the carrying out of any repair, the matters specified in subsection (1) of this section shall be taken to include the effect of the treatment, process or repair.

(4) In this section "false" means false to a material degree and "services" does not include anything done under a contract of service. [395]

15. Orders defining terms for purposes of section 14

Where it appears to the Board of Trade that it would be in the interest of persons for whom any services, accommodation or facilities are provided in the course of any trade or business that any expressions used with respect thereto should be understood as having definite meanings, the Board may by order assign such meanings to those expressions when used as, or as part of, such statements as are mentioned in section 14 of this Act with respect to those services, accommodation or facilities; and where such a meaning is so assigned to an expression it shall be deemed for the purposes of this Act to have that meaning when so used. [396]

NOTES
No regulations have yet been made under this section.

PROHIBITION OF IMPORTATION OF CERTAIN GOODS

16. Prohibition of importation of goods bearing false indication of origin

Where a false trade description is applied to any goods outside the United Kingdom and the false indication, or one of the false indications, given, or likely to be taken as given, thereby is an indication of the place of manufacture, production, processing or reconditioning of the goods or any part thereof, the goods shall not be imported into the United Kingdom. [397]

NOTES
Section 17, which amends the Trade Marks Act 1938, is omitted.

PROVISIONS AS TO OFFENCES

18. Penalty for offences

A person guilty of an offence under this Act for which no other penalty is specified shall be liable—

(a) on summary conviction, to a fine not exceeding [the prescribed sum]; and
(b) on conviction on indictment, to a fine or imprisonment for a term not exceeding two years or both. [398]

NOTES
Amended by the Magistrates' Courts Act 1980, s 32(2).

19. Time limit for prosecutions

(1) No prosecution for an offence under this Act shall be commenced after the expiration of three years from the commission of the offence or one year from its discovery by the prosecutor, whichever is the earlier.

(2) Notwithstanding anything in [section 127(1) of the Magistrates' Courts Act 1980] a magistrates' court may try an information for an offence under this Act if the information was laid at any time within twelve months from the commission of the offence.

(3) . . .

(4) Subsections (2) and (3) of this section do not apply where—

(a) the offence was committed by the making of an oral statement; or
(b) the offence was one of supplying goods to which a false trade description is applied, and the trade description was applied by an oral statement; or
(c) the offence was one where a false trade description is deemed to have been applied to goods by virtue of section 4(3) of this Act and the goods were supplied in pursuance of an oral request. [399]

NOTES
Sub-s (2): amended by the Magistrates' Courts Act 1980, s 154, Sch 7, para 74.
Sub-s (3): applies to Scotland only.

20. Offences by corporations

(1) Where an offence under this Act which has been committed by a body corporate is proved to have been committed with the consent and connivance of, or to be attributable to any neglect on the part of, any director, manager, secretary or other similar officer of the body corporate, or any person who was purporting to act in any such capacity, he as well as the body corporate shall be guilty of that offence and shall be liable to be proceeded against and punished accordingly.

(2) In this section "director", in relation to any body corporate established by or under any enactment for the purpose of carrying on under national ownership any industry or part of an industry or undertaking, being a body corporate whose affairs are managed by the members thereof, means a member of that body corporate. **[400]**

21. Accessories to offences committed abroad

(1) Any person who, in the United Kingdom, assists in or induces the commission in any other country of an act in respect of goods which, if the act were committed in the United Kingdom, would be an offence under section 1 of this Act shall be guilty of an offence, except as provided by subsection (2) of this section, but only if either—

    (a) the false trade description concerned is an indication (or anything likely to be taken as an indication) that the goods or any part thereof were manufactured, produced, processed or reconditioned in the United Kingdom; or

    (b) the false description concerned—

        (i) consists of or comprises an expression (or anything likely to be taken as an expression) to which a meaning is assigned by an order made by virtue of section 7(b) of this Act, and

        (ii) where that meaning is so assigned only in circumstances specfied in the order, the trade description is used in those circumstances.

(2) A person shall not be guilty of an offence under subsection (1) of this section if, by virtue of section 32 of this Act, the act, though committed in the United Kingdom, would not be an offence under section 1 of this Act had the goods been intended for despatch to the other country.

(3) Any person who, in the United Kingdom, assists in or induces the commission outside the United Kingdom of an act which, if committed in the United Kingdom, would be an offence under section 12 of this Act shall be guilty of an offence. **[401]**

22. Restrictions on institution of proceedings and admission of evidence

(1) Where any act or omission constitutes both an offence under this Act and an offence under any provision contained in or having effect by virtue of Part IV of the [Weights and Measures Act 1985] or [Part V of the Weights and Measures (Northern Ireland) Order 1981]—

    (a) proceedings for the offence shall not be instituted under this Act, except by virtue of section 23 thereof, without the service of such a notice as is required by [subsection (3) of section 83 of the said Act of

1985] or, as the case may be, [paragraph (3) of Article 46 of the said Order of 1981], nor after the expiration of the period mentioned in paragraph (c) of that subsection [or, as the case may be, that paragraph]; and

(b) [sections 35, 36 and 37(1) and (2) of the said Act of 1985] or, as the case may be, [of Article 24 of the said Order of 1981], shall, with the necessary modifications, apply as if the offence under this Act were an offence under Part IV of that Act [or, as the case may be, Part V of that Order,] or any instrument made thereunder.

(2) Where any act or omission constitutes both an offence under this Act and an offence under the food and drugs laws, evidence on behalf of the prosecution concerning any sample procured for analysis shall not be admissible in proceedings for the offence under this Act unless the relevant provisions of those laws have been complied with.

In this subsection "the food and drugs laws" means the [Food Act 1984], the Food and Drugs (Scotland) Act 1956, the Food and Drugs Act (Northern Ireland) 1958 [or the Medicines Act 1968] and any instrument made thereunder and "the relevant provisions" means—

(a) in relation to the [said Act of 1984, sections 80 and 84] and Part I of Schedule 7;
(b) in relation to the said Act of 1956, sections 30 and 33; ...
(c) in relation to the said Act of 1958, section 35 and 38; [and
(d) in relation to the said Act of 1968, so much of Schedule 3 to that Act as is applicable to the circumstances in which the sample was procured]

or any provision replacing any of the said provisions by virtue of [section 118 or 119 of the said Act of 1984], section 56 [or 56A] of the said Act of 1956, or section 68 [or 68A] of the said Act of 1958, [or paragraph 27 of Schedule 3 to the said Act of 1968.]

(3) The Board of Trade may by order provide that in proceedings for an offence under this Act in relation to such goods as may be specified in the order (other than proceedings for an offence falling within the preceding provisions of this section) evidence on behalf of the prosecution concerning any sample procured for analysis shall not be admissible unless the sample has been dealt with in such manner as may be specified in the order. **[402]**

NOTES

Sub-s (1): first, third and sixth amendments in square brackets made by the Weights and Measures Act 1985, s 97, Sch 12, para 3; other amendments in square brackets made by the Weights and Measures (Northern Ireland) Order 1981, SI 1981 No 231 (NI 10), art 54(1), Sch 10, para 2.

Sub-s (2): first, third, and sixth amendments in square brackets made by the Food Act 1984, s 134, Sch 10, para 12; second, fourth and final amendments in square brackets and word omitted repealed by the Medicines Act 1968, s 135(1), Sch 5, para 17; fifth and seventh amendments in square brackets made by the European Communities Act 1972, s 4, Sch 4, para 3(2); remaining amendment in square brackets made by the Food and Drugs Order 1975, SR & O (NI) No 373.

23. Offences due to fault of other person

Where the commission by any person of an offence under this Act is due to the act or default of some other person that other person shall be guilty of the offence, and a person may be charged with and convicted of the offence by virtue of this section whether or not proceedings are taken against the first-mentioned person. **[403]**

DEFENCES

24. Defence of mistake, accident, etc

(1) In any proceedings for an offence under this Act it shall, subject to subsection (2) of this section, be a defence for the person charged to prove—

    (*a*) that the commission of the offence was due to a mistake or to reliance on information supplied to him or to the act or default of another person, an accident or some other cause beyond his control; and

    (*b*) that he took all reasonable precautions and exercised all due diligence to avoid the commission of such an offence by himself or any person under his control.

(2) If in any case the defence provided by the last foregoing subsection involves the allegation that the commission of the offence was due to the act or default of another person or to reliance on information supplied by another person, the person charged shall not, without leave of the court, be entitled to rely on that defence unless, within a period ending seven clear days before the hearing, he has served on the prosecutor a notice in writing giving such information identifying or assisting in the identification of that other person as was then in his possession.

(3) In any proceedings for an offence under this Act of supplying or offering to supply goods to which a false trade description is applied it shall be a defence for the person charged to prove that he did not know, and could not with reasonable diligence have ascertained, that the goods did not conform to the description or that the description had been applied to the goods. **[404]**

25. Innocent publication of advertisement

In proceedings for an offence under this Act committed by the publication of an advertisement it shall be a defence for the person charged to prove that he is a person whose business it is to publish or arrange for the publication of advertisements and that he received the advertisement for publication in the ordinary course of business and did not know and had no reason to suspect that its publication would amount to an offence under this Act. **[405]**

ENFORCEMENT

26. Enforcing authorities

(1) It shall be the duty of every local weights and measures authority to enforce within their area the provisions of this Act and of any order made under this Act . . . .

(2) Every local weights and measures authority shall, whenever the Board of Trade so direct, make to the Board a report on the exercise of their functions under this Act in such form and containing such particulars as the Board may direct.

(3)–(5) . . . **[406]**

NOTES
    Sub-s (1): amended by the Weights and Measures Act 1985, s 98, Sch 13, Part I.
    Sub-ss (3), (4): repealed by the Local Government, Planning and Land Act 1980, ss 1(4), 194, Sch 4, para 10, Sch 34, Part IV.
    Sub-s (5): applies to Scotland only.

27. Power to make test purchases

A local weights and measures authority shall have power to make, or to authorise any of their officers to make on their behalf, such purchases of goods, and to authorise any of their officers to secure the provision of such services, accommodation or facilities, as may appear expedient for the purpose of determining whether or not the provisions of this Act and any order made thereunder are being complied with. [407]

28. Power to enter premises and inspect and seize goods and documents

(1) A duly authorised officer of a local weights and measures authority or of a Government department may, at all reasonable hours and on production, if required, of his credentials, exercise the following powers, that is to say,—

- (*a*) he may, for the purpose of ascertaining whether any offence under this Act has been committed, inspect any goods and enter any premises other than premises used only as a dwelling;
- (*b*) if he has reasonable cause to suspect that an offence under this Act has been committed, he may, for the purpose of ascertaining whether it has been committed, require any person carrying on a trade or business or employed in connection with a trade or business to produce any books or documents relating to the trade or business and may take copies of, or of any entry in, any such book or document;
- (*c*) if he has reasonable cause to believe that an offence under this Act has been committed, he may seize and detain any goods for the purpose of ascertaining, by testing or otherwise, whether the offence has been committed;
- (*d*) he may seize and detain any goods or documents which he has reason to believe may be required as evidence in proceedings for an offence under this Act;
- (*e*) he may, for the purpose of exercising his powers under this subsection to seize goods, but only if and to the extent that it is reasonably necessary in order to secure that the provisions of this Act and of any order made thereunder are duly observed, require any person having authority to do so to break open any container or open any vending machine and, if that person does not comply with the requirement, he may do so himself.

(2) An officer seizing any goods or documents in the exercise of his powers under this section shall inform the person from whom they are seized and, in the case of goods seized from a vending machine, the person whose name and address are stated on the machine as being the proprietor's or, if no name and address are so stated, the occupier of the premises on which the machine stands or to which it is affixed.

(3) If a justice of the peace, on sworn information in writing—

- (*a*) is satisfied that there is reasonable ground to believe either—
  - (i) that any goods, books or documents which a duly authorised officer has power under this section to inspect are on any premises and that their inspection is likely to disclose evidence of the commission of an offence under this Act; or
  - (ii) that any offence under this Act has been, is being or is about to be committed on any premises; and
- (*b*) is also satisfied either—

(i) that admission to the premises has been or is likely to be refused and that notice of intention to apply for a warrant under this subsection has been given to the occupier; or
(ii) that an application for admission, or the giving of such a notice, would defeat the object of the entry or that the premises are unoccupied or that the occupier is temporarily absent and it might defeat the object of the entry to await his return,

the justice may by warrant under his hand, which shall continue in force for a period of one month, authorise an officer of a local weights and measures authority or of a Government department to enter the premises, if need be by force.

. . .

(4) An officer entering any premises by virtue of this section may take with him such other persons and such equipment as may appear to him necessary; and on leaving any premises which he has entered by virtue of a warrant under the preceding subsection he shall, if the premises are unoccupied or the occupier is temporarily absent, leave them as effectively secured against trespassers as he found them.

(5) If any person discloses to any person—
   (a) any information with respect to any manufacturing process or trade secret obtained by him in premises which he has entered by virtue of this section; or
   (b) any information obtained by him in pursuance of this Act;

he shall be guilty of an offence unless the disclosure was made in or for the purpose of the performance by him or any other person of functions under this Act.

[(5A) Subsection (5) of this section does not apply to disclosure for a purpose specified in [section 38(2)(a), (b) or (c) of the Consumer Protection Act 1987.]]

(6) If any person who is not a duly authorised officer of a local weights and measures authority or of a Government department purports to act as such under this section he shall be guilty of an offence.

(7) Nothing in this section shall be taken to compel the production by a solicitor of a document containing a privileged communication made by or to him in that capacity or to authorise the taking of possession of any such document which is in his possession. **[408]**

NOTES
Sub-s (3): words omitted apply to Scotland only.
Sub-s (5A): added by the Consumer Credit Act 1974, s 192(3)(a), Sch 4, Part I, para 28; words in square brackets substituted by the Consumer Protection Act 1987, s 48, Sch 4.

29. Obstruction of authorised officers

(1) Any person who—
   (a) wilfully obstructs an officer of a local weights and measures authority or of a Government department acting in pursuance of this Act; or
   (b) wilfully fails to comply with any requirement properly made to him by such an officer under section 28 of this Act; or
   (c) without reasonable cause fails to give such an officer so acting any other assistance or information which he may reasonably require of

him for the purpose of the performance of his functions under this Act,

shall be guilty of an offence and liable, on summary conviction, to a fine not exceeding [level 3 on the standard scale].

(2) If any person, in giving any such information as is mentioned in the preceding subsection, makes any statement which he knows to be false, he shall be guilty of an offence.

(3) Nothing in this section shall be construed as requiring a person to answer any question or give any information if to do so might incriminate him. **[409]**

NOTES
Sub-s (1): maximum fine increased and converted to a level on the standard scale by the Criminal Justice Act 1982, ss 37, 38, 46.

30. Notice of test and intended prosecution

(1) Where any goods seized or purchased by an officer in pursuance of this Act are submitted to a test, then—

    (a) if the goods were seized, the officer shall inform the person mentioned in section 28(2) of this Act of the result of the test;

    (b) if the goods were purchased and the test leads to the institution of proceedings for an offence under this Act, the officer shall inform the person from whom the goods were purchased, or, in the case of goods sold through a vending machine, the person mentioned in section 28(2) of this Act, of the result of the test;

and shall, where as a result of the test proceedings for an offence under this Act are instituted against any person, allow him to have the goods tested on his behalf if it is reasonably practicable to do so.

(2)–(4) . . . **[410]**

NOTES
Words omitted repealed by the Fair Trading Act 1973, ss 130, 139, Sch 13.

31. Evidence by certificate

(1) The Board of Trade may by regulations provide that certificates issued by such persons as may be specified by the regulations in relation to such matters as may be so specified shall, subject to the provisions of this section, be received in evidence of those matters in any proceedings under this Act.

(2) Such a certificate shall not be received in evidence—

    (a) unless the party against whom it is to be given in evidence has been served with a copy thereof not less than seven days before the hearing; or

    (b) if that party has, not less than three days before the hearing, served on the other party a notice requiring the attendance of the person issuing the certificate.

(3) . . .

(4) For the purposes of this section any document purporting to be such a certificate as is mentioned in this section shall be deemed to be such a certificate unless the contrary is shown.

(5) Regulations under this section shall be made by statutory instrument which shall be subject to annulment in pursuance of a resolution of either House of Parliament. **[411]**

NOTES
Sub-s (3): applies to Scotland only.
No regulations have yet been made under this section.

MISCELLANEOUS AND SUPPLEMENTAL

32. Power to exempt goods sold for export, etc

(1) In relation to goods which are intended—
  (a) for despatch to a destination outside the United Kingdom and any designated country within the meaning of [section 24(2)(b) of the Weights and Measures Act 1985] or section 15(5)(b) of the Weights and Measures Act (Northern Ireland) 1967; or
  (b) for use as stores within the meaning of the [Customs and Excise Management Act 1979] in a ship or aircraft on a voyage or flight to an eventual destination outside the United Kingdom; or
  (c) for use by Her Majesty's forces or by a visiting force within the meaning of any of the provisions of Part I of the Visiting Forces Act 1952; or
  [(d) for industrial use within the meaning of the Weights and Measures Act 1985 or for constructional use;]

section 1 of this Act shall apply as if there were omitted from the matters included in section 2(1) of this Act those specified in paragraph (a) thereof; and, if the Board of Trade by order specify any other of those matters for the purposes of this section with respect to any description of goods, the said section 1 shall apply, in relation to goods of that description which are intended for despatch to a destination outside the United Kingdom and such country (if any) as may be specified in the order, as if the matters so specified were also omitted from those included in the said section 2(1).

[(2) In this section "constructional use", in relation to any goods, means the use of those goods in constructional work (or, if the goods are explosives within the meaning of the Explosives Acts 1875 and 1923, in mining, quarrying or demolition work) in the course of the carrying on of a business; **[412]**

NOTES
Commencement: 30 January 1986 (sub-s (2)); before 1 January 1970 (remainder).
Sub-s (1): paras (a),(d) amended by the Weights and Measures Act 1985, s 97, Sch 12, para 4(1); para (b) amended by the Customs and Excise Management Act 1979, s 177(1), Sch 4, para 12, Table, Part I.
Sub-s (2): added by the Weights and Measures Act 1985, s 97, Sch 12, para 4(2).

33. Compensation for loss, etc of goods seized under s 28

(1) Where, in the exercise of his powers under section 28 of this Act, an officer of a local weights and measures authority or of a Government department seizes and detains any goods and their owner suffers loss by reason thereof or by reason that the goods, during the detention, are lost or damaged or deteriorate, then, unless the owner is convicted of an offence under this Act committed in relation to the goods, the authority or department shall be liable to compensate him for the loss so suffered.

(2) Any disputed question as to the right to or the amount of any

compensation payable under this section shall be determined by arbitration and, in Scotland, by a single arbiter appointed, failing agreement between the parties, by the sheriff. [413]

34. Trade marks containing trade descriptions

The fact that a trade description is a trade mark, or part of a trade mark, within the meaning of the Trade Marks Act 1938 does not prevent it from being a false trade description when applied to any goods, except where the following conditions are satisfied, that is to say—
- (*a*) that it could have been lawfully applied to the goods if this Act had not been passed; and
- (*b*) that on the day this Act is passed the trade mark either is registered under the Trade Marks Act 1938 or is in use to indicate a connection in the course of trade between such goods and the proprietor of the trade mark; and
- (*c*) that the trade mark as applied is used to indicate such a connection between the goods and the proprietor of the trade mark or a person registered under section 28 of the Trade Marks Act 1938 as a registered user of the trade mark; and
- (*d*) that the person who is the proprietor of the trade mark is the same person as, or a successor in title of, the proprietor on the day this Act is passed. [414]

35. Saving for civil rights

A contract for the supply of any goods shall not be void or unenforceable by reason only of a contravention of any provision of this Act. [415]

36. Country of origin

(1) For the purposes of this Act goods shall be deemed to have been manufactured or produced in the country in which they last underwent a treatment or process resulting in a substantial change.

(2) The Board of Trade may by order specify—
- (*a*) in relation to any description of goods, what treatment or process is to be regarded for the purposes of this section as resulting or not resulting in a substantial change;
- (*b*) in relation to any description of goods different parts of which were manufactured or produced in different countries, or of goods assembled in a country different from that in which their parts were manufactured or produced, in which of those countries the goods are to be regarded for the purposes of this Act as having been manufactured or produced. [416]

NOTES
    Regulations under this section: Trade Descriptions (Country of Origin) (Cutlery) Order 1981, SI 1981 No 122.

37. Market research experiments

(1) In this section "market research experiment" means any activities conducted for the purpose of ascertaining the opinion of persons (in this section referred to as "participants") of—
- (*a*) any goods; or
- (*b*) anything in, on or with which the goods are supplied; or

(c) the appearance or any other characteristic of the goods or of any such thing; or

(d) the name or description under which the goods are supplied.

(2) This section applies to any market research experiment with respect to which the following conditions are satisfied, that is to say—

(a) that any participant to whom any goods are supplied in the course of the experiment is informed, at or before the time at which they are supplied to him, that they are supplied for such a purpose as is mentioned in subsection (1) of this section, and

(b) that no consideration in money or money's worth is given by a participant for the goods or any goods supplied to him for comparison.

(3) Neither section 1 nor section 8 of this Act shall apply in relation to goods supplied or offered to be supplied, whether to a participant or any other person, in the course of a market research experiment to which this section applies.

[417]

38. Orders

(1) Any power to make an order under the preceding provisions of this Act shall be exercisable by statutory instrument, which shall be subject to annulment in pursuance of a resolution of either House of Parliament, and includes power to vary or revoke such an order by a subsequent order.

(2) Any order under the preceding provisions of this Act which relates to any agricultural, horticultural or fishery produce, whether processed or not, food, feeding stuffs or ingredients of food or feeding stuffs, fertilisers or any goods used as pesticides or for similar purposes shall be made by the Board of Trade acting jointly with the following Ministers, that is to say, if the order extends to England and Wales, the Minister of Agriculture, Fisheries and Food, and if it extends to Scotland or Northern Ireland, the Secretary of State concerned.

(3) The following provisions shall apply to the making of an order under section 7, 8, 9, 15 or 36 of this Act, except in the case mentioned in section 10(2) thereof, that is to say—

(a) before making the order the Board of Trade shall consult with such organisations as appear to them to be representative of interests substantially affected by it and shall publish, in such manner as the Board think appropriate, notice of their intention to make the order and of the place where copies of the proposed order may be obtained; and

(b) the order shall not be made until the expiration of a period of twenty-eight days from the publication of the notice and may then be made with such modifications (if any) as the Board of Trade think appropriate having regard to any representations received by them.

[418]

39. Interpretation

(1) The following provisions shall have effect, in addition to sections 2 to 6 of this Act, for the interpretation in this Act of expressions used therein, that is to say,—

"advertisement" includes a catalogue, a circular and a price list;

"goods" includes ships and aircraft, things attached to land and growing crops;
"premises" includes any place and any stall, vehicle, ship or aircraft; and
"ship" includes any boat and any other description of vessel used in navigation.

(2) For the purposes of this Act, a trade description or statement published in any newspaper, book or periodical or in any film or sound or television broadcast [or in a programme included in a cable programme service] shall not be deemed to be a trade description applied or statement made in the course of a trade or business unless it is or forms part of an advertisement. **[419]**

NOTES
Sub-s (2): amended by the Cable and Broadcasting Act 1984, s 57(1), Sch 5, para 19.

40. Provisions as to Northern Ireland

(1) This Act shall apply to Northern Ireland subject to the following modifications, that is to say—
   (*a*) section 19(2) shall apply as if for the references to [section 127(1) of the Magistrates' Courts Act 1980] and the trial and laying of an information there were substituted respectively references to [Article 19(1) of the Magistrates' Courts (Northern Ireland) Order 1981] and the hearing and determination and making of a complaint;
   (*b*) section 26 and subsections (2) to (4) of section 30 shall not apply but it shall be the duty of the Ministry of Commerce for Northern Ireland to enforce the provisions of this Act and of any order made under it (other than the provisions of section 42 of this Act);
   (*c*) sections 27 to 29 and 33 shall apply as if for references to a local weights and measures authority and any officer of such an authority there were substituted respectively references to the said Ministry and any of its officers.

(2)–(5) . . .

(6) Nothing in this Act shall authorise any department of the Government of Northern Ireland to incur any expenses attributable to the provisions of this Act until provision has been made by the Parliament of Northern Ireland for those expenses to be defrayed out of moneys provided by that Parliament.

(7) . . . **[420]**

NOTES
Sub-s (1): first amendment by the Magistrates' Courts Act 1980, s 154, Sch 7, para 74; second amendment made by the Magistrates' Courts (Northern Ireland) Order 1981, SI 1981 No 1675, art 170(2), Sch 6.
Sub-ss (2)–(4), (7): repealed by the Northern Ireland Constitution Act 1973, s 41(1), Sch 6, Part I.
Sub-s (5): repealed by the Northern Ireland (Modification of Enactments No 1) Order, 1973 No 2163, art 14(2), Sch 6.

NOTES
Section 41 (Consequential amendments and repeals) is omitted.
Section 42 was repealed by the Statute Law (Repeals) Act 1975.

43. Short title and commencement

(1) This Act may be cited as the Trade Descriptions Act 1968.

(2) This Act shall come into force on the expiration of the period of six months beginning with the day on which it is passed. **[421]**

UNSOLICITED GOODS AND SERVICES ACT 1971
(c 30)

ARRANGEMENT OF SECTIONS

Section		Para
1	Rights of recipient of unsolicited goods	[422]
2	Demands and threats regarding payment	[423]
3	Directory entries	[424]
3A	Contents and form of notes of agreement, invoices and similar documents	[425]
4	Unsolicited publications	[426]
5	Offences by corporations	[427]
6	Interpretation	[428]
7	Citation, commencement and extent	[429]

An Act to make provision for the greater protection of persons receiving unsolicited goods, and to amend the law with respect to charges for entries in directories
[12 May 1971]

GENERAL NOTES
This Act does not extend to Northern Ireland.

1. Rights of recipient of unsolicited goods

(1) In the circumstances specified in the following subsection, a person who after the commencement of this Act receives unsolicited goods, may as between himself and the sender, use, deal with or dispose of them as if they were an unconditional gift to him, and any right of the sender to the goods shall be extinguished.

(2) The circumstances referred to in the preceding subsection are that the goods were sent to the recipient with a view to his acquiring them, that the recipient has no reasonable cause to believe that they were sent with a view to their being acquired for the purposes of a trade or business and has neither agreed to acquire nor agreed to return them, and either—

  (a) that during the period of six months beginning with the day on which the recipient received the goods the sender did not take possession of them and the recipient did not unreasonably refuse to permit the sender to do so; or
  (b) that not less than thirty days before the expiration of the period aforesaid the recipient gave notice to the sender in accordance with the following subsection, and that during the period of thirty days beginning with the day on which the notice was given the sender did not take possession of the goods and the recipient did not unreasonably refuse to permit the sender to do so.

(3) A notice in pursuance of the preceding subsection shall be in writing and shall—

  (a) state the recipient's name and address and, if possession of the goods in question may not be taken by the sender at that address, the address at which it may be so taken;
  (b) contain a statement, however expressed, that the goods are unsolicited,

and may be sent by post.

(4) In this section "sender", in relation to any goods, includes any person on whose behalf or with whose consent the goods are sent, and any other person claiming through or under the sender or any such person. **[422]**

NOTES
Commencement: 12 August 1971.

2. Demands and threats regarding payment

(1) A person who, not having reasonable cause to believe there is a right to payment, in the course of any trade or business makes a demand for payment, or asserts a present or prospective right to payment, for what he knows are unsolicited goods sent (after the commencement of this Act) to another person with a view to his acquiring them, shall be guilty of an offence and on summary conviction shall be liable to a fine not exceeding [level 4 on the standard scale].

(2) A person who, not having reasonable cause to believe there is a right to payment, in the course of any trade or business and with a view to obtaining any payment for what he knows are unsolicited goods sent as aforesaid—

(a) threatens to bring any legal proceedings; or
(b) places or causes to be placed the name of any person on a list of defaulters or debtors or threatens to do so; or
(c) invokes or causes to be invoked any other collection procedure or threatens to do so,

shall be guilty of an offence and shall be liable on summary conviction to a fine not exceeding [level 5 on the standard scale]. **[423]**

NOTES
Commencement: 12 August 1971.
Maximum fines increased and converted to levels on the standard scale by the Criminal Justice Act 1982, ss 37, 38, 46.

3. Directory entries

(1) A person shall not be liable to make any payment, and shall be entitled to recover any payment made by him, by way of charge for including or arranging for the inclusion in a directory of an entry relating to that person or his trade or business, unless there has been signed by him or on his behalf an order complying with this section or a note complying with this section of his agreement to the charge and, in the case of a note of agreement to the charge, before the note was signed, a copy of it was supplied, for retention by him, to him or to a person acting on his behalf.

(2) A person shall be guilty of an offence punishable on summary conviction with a fine not exceeding [the prescribed sum] if, in a case where a payment in respect of a charge would, in the absence of an order or note of agreement to the charge complying with this section, be recoverable from him in accordance with the terms of subsection (1) above, he demands payment, or asserts a present or prospective right to payment, of the charge or any part of it, without knowing or having reasonable cause to believe that the entry to which the charge relates was ordered in accordance with this section or a proper note of agreement has been duly signed.

(3) For the purposes of subsection (1) above, an order for an entry in a directory must be made by means of an order form or other stationery belonging to the person to whom, or to whose trade or business, the entry is to relate and bearing, in print, the name and address (or one or more of the addresses) of that

person; and the note required by this section of a person's agreement to a charge *must state the amount of the charge immediately above the place for signature, and*—

(a) must identify the directory or proposed directory, and give the following particulars of it—
   (i) the proposed date of publication of the directory or of the issue in which the entry is to be included and the name and address of the person producing it;
   (ii) if the directory or that issue is to be put on sale, the price at which it is to be offered for sale and the minimum number of copies which are to be available for sale;
   (iii) if the directory or that issue is to be distributed free of charge (whether or not it is also to be put on sale), the minimum number of copies which are to be so distributed; and
(b) must set out or give reasonable particulars of the entry in respect of which the charge would be payable [shall comply with the requirements of regulations under section 3A of this Act applicable thereto].

(4) Nothing in this section shall apply to a payment due under a contract entered into before the commencement of this Act, or entered into by the acceptance of an offer made before that commencement. **[424]**

NOTES
Commencement: 12 August 1971.
Sub-s (2): amended by the Magistrates' Courts Act 1980, s 32(2).
Sub-s (3): words in italics prospectively repealed and words in square brackets prospectively substituted by the Unsolicited Goods and Services (Amendment) Act 1975, s 2(1) as from a day to be appointed.

[3A. Contents and form of notes of agreement, invoices and similar documents

(1) For the purposes of this Act, the Secretary of State may make regulations as to the contents and form of notes of agreement, invoices and similar documents; and, without prejudice to the generality of the foregoing, any such regulations may—

(a) require specified information to be included,
(b) prescribe the manner in which specified information is to be included,
(c) prescribe such other requirements (whether as to presentation, type, size, colour or disposition of lettering, quality or colour of paper or otherwise) as the Secretary of State may consider appropriate for securing that specified information is clearly brought to the attention of the recipient of any note of agreement, invoice or similar document,
(d) make different provision for different classes or descriptions of notes of agreement, invoices and similar documents or for the same class or description in different circumstances,
(e) contain such supplementary and incidental provisions as the Secretary of State may consider appropriate.

(2) Any reference in this section to a note of agreement includes any such copy as is mentioned in section 3(1) of this Act.

(3) Regulations under this section shall be made by statutory instrument and shall be subject to annulment in pursuance of a resolution of either House of Parliament.] **[425]**

NOTES
Commencement: 20 March 1975.
Inserted by the Unsolicited Goods and Services (Amendment) Act 1975, s 1.
Regulations under this section: The Unsolicited Goods and Services (Invoices etc) Regulations 1975, SI 1975 No 732.

4. Unsolicited publications

(1) A person shall be guilty of an offence if he sends or causes to be sent to another person any book, magazine or leaflet (or advertising material for any such publication) which he knows or ought reasonably to know is unsolicited and which describes or illustrates human sexual techniques.

(2) A person found guilty of an offence under this section shall be liable on summary conviction to a fine not exceeding [level 5 on the standard scale].

(3) A prosecution for an offence under this section shall not in England and Wales be instituted except by, or with the consent of, the Director of Public Prosecutions. **[426]**

NOTES
Commencement: 12 August 1971.
Sub-s (2): enhanced penalty on a subsequent conviction abolished, maximum fine on any conviction increased and converted to a level on the standard scale by the Criminal Justice Act 1982, ss 35, 37, 38, 46.

5. Offences by corporations

(1) Where an offence under this Act which has been committed by a body corporate is proved to have been committed with the consent or connivance of, or to be attributable to any neglect on the part of, any director, manager, secretary, or other similar officer of the body corporate, or of any person who was purporting to act in any such capacity, he as well as the body corporate shall be guilty of that offence and shall be liable to be proceeded against and punished accordingly.

(2) Where the affairs of a body corporate are managed by its members, this section shall apply in relation to the acts or defaults of a member in connection with his functions of management as if he were a director of the body corporate. **[427]**

NOTES
Commencement: 12 August 1971.

6. Interpretation

(1) In this Act, unless the context or subject matter otherwise requires,—
"acquire" includes hire;
"send" includes deliver, and "sender" shall be construed accordingly;
"unsolicited" means, in relation to goods sent to any person, that they are sent without any prior request made by him or on his behalf.

[(2) For the purposes of this Act any invoice or similar document stating the amount of any payment and not complying with the requirements of regulations under section 3A of this Act applicable thereto shall be regarded as asserting a right to the payment.] **[428]**

NOTES
Commencement: 12 August 1971.
Sub-s (2): substituted by the Unsolicited Goods and Services (Amendment) Act 1975, s 2(2).

7. Citation, commencement and extent

(1) This Act may be cited as the Unsolicited Goods and Services Act 1971.

(2) This Act shall come into force at the expiration of three months beginning with the day on which it is passed.

(3) This Act does not extend to Northern Ireland. [429]

UNSOLICITED GOODS AND SERVICES (AMENDMENT) ACT 1975
(c 13)

An Act to amend the Unsolicited Goods and Services Act 1971, to enable the Secretary of State to make regulations with respect to the contents and form of notes of agreement, invoices and similar documents and to provide for conviction on indictment in relation to an offence under s 3(2) of the said Act; and for connected matters [20 March 1975]

GENERAL NOTES
This Act does not extend to Northern Ireland.

NOTES
Sections 1 and 2, which modify the Unsolicited Goods and Services Act 1971, are omitted here. The modifications are incorporated in the text of that Act.

3. Provision for offence under section 3(2) of the Act of 1971 to be prosecuted on indictment

(1) An offence under section 3 (2) of the Act of 1971 may be prosecuted on indictment; and a person convicted on indictment of an offence under that section shall be liable to a fine.

(2) This section applies only to offences committed after the coming into operation of this section. [430]

NOTES
Commencement: 20 March 1975.
The Act of 1971: Unsolicited Goods and Services Act 1971.

4. Short title, citation, commencement, transitional provisions and extent

(1) This Act may be cited as the Unsolicited Goods and Services (Amendment) Act 1975 and the Unsolicited Goods and Services Act 1971 and this Act may be cited together as the Unsolicited Goods and Services Act 1971 and 1975.

(2) Sections 1 and 3 of this Act and this section shall come into operation on the passing of this Act but any regulations made by virtue of the said section 1 shall not come into operation before the date appointed by order under subsection (3) below for the coming into operation of section 2 of this Act.

(3) Section 2 of this Act shall come into operation on such date as the Secretary of State may by order made by statutory instrument appoint; and different dates may be appointed by order under this subsection for different provisions of that section.

(4) The amendments made to sections 3 (3) and 6 (2) of the Act of 1971 by section 2 of this Act and any regulations made by virtue of section 1 of this Act

shall not apply to any note of agreement signed, or invoice or similar document sent before the date appointed by order under subsection (3) above for the coming into operation of the said section 2.

(5) This Act shall not extend to Northern Ireland. **[431]**

NOTES
Commencement: 20 March 1975.
The Act of 1971: Unsolicited Goods and Services Act 1971.
Regulations under this section: Unsolicited Goods and Services (Amendment) Act 1975 (Commencement No 1) Order 1975, SI 1975 No 731.

FAIR TRADING ACT 1973
(c 41)

ARRANGEMENT OF SECTIONS

PART I
INTRODUCTORY

Section		Para
1	Director General of Fair Trading	[432]
2	General functions of Director	[433]
3	Consumer Protection Advisory Committee	[434]
4	The Monopolies and Mergers Commission	[435]
5	Principal functions of Commission	[436]
6	Monopoly situation in relation to supply of goods	[437]
7	Monopoly situation in relation to supply of services	[438]
8	Monopoly situation in relation to exports	[439]
9	Monopoly situation limited to part of United Kingdom	[440]
10	Supplementary provisions relating to ss 6 to 9	[441]
11	Meaning of "complex monopoly situation"	[442]
12	Powers of Secretary of State in relation to functions of Director	[443]

PART III
ADDITIONAL FUNCTIONS OF DIRECTOR FOR PROTECTION OF CONSUMERS

34	Action by Director with respect to course of conduct detrimental to interests of consumers	[444]
35	Proceedings before Restrictive Practices Court	[445]
36	Evidence in proceedings under s 35	[446]
37	Order of, or undertaking given to, Court in proceedings under s 35	[447]
38	Provisions as to persons consenting to or conniving at courses of conduct detrimental to interests of consumers	[448]
39	Order of, or undertaking given to, Court in proceedings under s 38	[449]
40	Provisions as to interconnected bodies corporate	[450]
41	Concurrent jurisdiction of other courts in certain cases	[451]
42	Appeals from decisions or orders of courts under Part III	[452]

An Act to provide for the appointment of a Director General of Fair Trading and of a Consumer Protection Advisory Committee, and to confer on the Director General and the Committee so appointed, on the Secretary of State, on the Restrictive Practices Court and on certain other courts new functions for the protection of consumers; to make provisions, in substitution for the Monopolies and Restrictive Practices (Inquiry and Control) Act 1948 and the Monopolies and Mergers Act 1965, for the matters dealt with in those Acts and related matters, including restrictive labour practices; to amend the Restrictive Trade

Practices Act 1956 and the Restrictive Trade Practices Act 1968, to make provision for extending the said Act of 1956 to agreements relating to services, and to transfer to the Director General of Fair Trading the functions of the Registrar of Restrictive Trading Agreements; to make provision with respect to pyramid selling and similar trading schemes; to make new provision in place of section 30(2) to (4) of the Trade Descriptions Act 1968; and for purposes connected with those matters [25 July 1973]

GENERAL NOTES
Parts I and III only of this Act are reproduced here. This Act extends to Northern Ireland.

Part I

Introductory

1. Director General of Fair Trading

(1) The Secretary of State shall appoint an officer to be known as the Director General of Fair Trading (in this Act referred to as "the Director") for the purpose of performing the functions assigned or transferred to the Director by or under this Act.

(2) An appointment of a person to hold office as the Director shall not be for a term exceeding five years; but previous appointment to that office shall not affect eligibility for re-appointment.

(3) The Director may at any time resign his office as the Director by notice in writing addressed to the Secretary of State; and the Secretary of State may remove any person from that office on the ground of incapacity or misbehaviour.

(4) Subject to subsections (2) and (3) of this section, the Director shall hold and vacate office as such in accordance with the terms of his appointment.

(5) The Director may appoint such staff as he may think fit, subject to the approval of the Minister for the Civil Service as to numbers and as to terms and conditions of service.

(6) The provisions of Schedule 1 to this Act shall have effect with respect to the Director.

NOTES
Commencement: 1 November 1973.

2. General functions of Director

(1) Without prejudice to any other functions assigned or transferred to him by or under this Act, it shall be the duty of the Director, so far as appears to him to be practicable from time to time,—

    (*a*) to keep under review the carrying on of commercial activities in the United Kingdom which relate to goods supplied to consumers in the United Kingdom or produced with a view to their being so supplied, or which relate to services supplied for consumers in the United Kingdom, and to collect information with respect to such activities, and the persons by whom they are carried on, with a view to his becoming aware of, and ascertaining the circumstances relating to, practices which may adversely affect the economic interests of consumers in the United Kingdom, and

(b) to receive and collate evidence becoming available to him with respect to such activities as are mentioned in the preceding paragraph and which appears to him to be evidence of practices which may adversely affect the interests (whether they are economic interests or interests with respect to health, safety or other matters) of consumers in the United Kingdom.

(2) It shall also be the duty of the Director, so far as appears to him to be practicable from time to time, to keep under review the carrying on of commercial activities in the United Kingdom, and to collect information with respect to those activities, and the persons by whom they are carried on, with a view to his becoming aware of, and ascertaining the circumstances relating to, monopoly situations or uncompetitive practices.

(3) It shall be the duty of the Director, where either he considers it expedient or he is requested by the Secretary of State to do so,—
- (a) to give information and assistance to the Secretary of State with respect to any of the matters in respect of which the Director has any duties under subsections (1) and (2) of this section, or
- (b) subject to the provisions of Part II of this Act in relation to recommendations under that Part of this Act, to make recommendations to the Secretary of State as to any action which in the opinion of the Director it would be expedient for the Secretary of State or any other Minister to take in relation to any of the matters in respect of which the Director has any such duties.

(4) It shall also be the duty of the Director to have regard to evidence becoming available to him with respect to any course of conduct on the part of a person carrying on a business which appears to be conduct detrimental to the interests of consumers in the United Kingdom and (in accordance with the provisions of Part III of this Act) to be regarded as unfair to them, with a view to considering what action (if any) he should take under Part III of this Act.

(5) It shall be the duty of the Director to have regard to the needs of regional development and to the desirability of dispersing administrative offices from London in making decisions on the location of offices for his staff. **[433]**

NOTES
Commencement: 1 November 1973.

3. Consumer Protection Advisory Committee

(1) There shall be established an advisory committee to be called the Consumer Protection Advisory Committee (in this Act referred to as "the Advisory Committee") for the purpose of performing the functions assigned to that Committee by Part II of this Act.

(2) Subject to subsection (6) of this section, the Advisory Committee shall consist of not less than ten and not more than fifteen members, who shall be appointed by the Secretary of State.

(3) The Secretary of State may appoint persons to the Advisory Committee either as full-time members or as part-time members.

(4) Of the members of the Advisory Committee, the Secretary of State shall appoint one to be chairman and one to be deputy chairman of the Advisory Committee.

(5) In appointing persons to be members of the Advisory Committee, the Secretary of State shall have regard to the need for securing that the Advisory Committee will include—

(a) one or more persons appearing to him to be qualified to advise on practices relating to goods supplied to consumers in the United Kingdom or produced with a view to their being so supplied, or relating to services supplied for consumers in the United Kingdom, by virtue of their knowledge of or experience in the supply (whether to consumers or not) of such goods or by virtue of their knowledge of or experience in the supply of such services;

(b) one or more persons appearing to him to be qualified to advise on such practices as are mentioned in the preceding paragraph by virtue of their knowledge of or experience in the enforcement of the [Weights and Measures Act 1985] or the Trade Descriptions Act 1968 or other similar enactments; and

(c) one or more persons appearing to him to be qualified to advise on such practices by virtue of their knowledge of or experience in organisations established, or activities carried on for the protection of consumers.

(6) The Secretary of State may by order made by statutory instrument increase the maximum number of members of the Advisory Committee to such number as he may think fit.

(7) The provisions of Schedule 2 to this Act shall have effect with respect to the Advisory Committee. [434]

NOTES
Commencement: 1 November 1973.
Amended by the Weights and Measures Act 1985, s 97, Sch 12, para 6.

4. The Monopolies and Mergers Commission

(1) The Commission established under section 1 of the Monopolies and Restrictive Practices (Inquiry and Control) Act 1948 by the name of the Monopolies and Restrictive Practices Commission, and subsequently renamed the Monopolies Commission, shall as from the commencement of this Act be known as the Monopolies and Mergers Commission, and shall continue to exist by that name for the purpose of performing the functions assigned to that Commission (in this Act referred to as "the Commission") by or under this Act.

(2) There shall be not less than ten and (subject to the next following subsection) not more than twenty-five regular members of the Commission, who shall be appointed by the Secretary of State.

(3) The Secretary of State may by order made by statutory instrument increase the maximum number of regular members of the Commission to such number as he may think fit.

(4) The provisions of Schedule 3 to this Act shall have effect with respect to the Commission. [435]

NOTES
Commencement: 1 November 1973.
Regulations under this section: Monopolies and Mergers Commission (Increase in Membership) Order 1982, SI 1982 No 815.

5. Principal functions of Commission

(1) Without prejudice to any other functions assigned to the Commission by or under this Act, it shall be the duty of the Commission, subject to and in accordance with the following provisions of this Act, to investigate and report on any question which may be referred to the Commission under this Act—

 (a) with respect to the existence, or possible existence, of a monopoly situation, or
 (b) with respect to a transfer of a newspaper or of newspaper assets (within the meaning of Part V of this Act), or
 (c) with respect to the creation, or possible creation, of a merger situation qualifying for investigation (within the meaning of Part V of this Act).

(2) It shall be the duty of the Director, for the purpose of assisting the Commission in carrying out an investigation on a reference made to them under this Act, to give to the Commission—

 (a) any information which is in his possession and which relates to matters falling within the scope of the investigation, and which is either requested by the Commission for that purpose or is information which in his opinion it would be appropriate for that purpose to give to the Commission without any such request, and
 (b) any other assistance which the Commission may require, and which it is within his power to give, in relation to any such matters,

and the Commission, for the purpose of carrying out any such investigation, shall take account of any information given to them for that purpose under this subsection.

(3) In this Act "monopoly reference" means any reference to the Commission under this Act which falls within paragraph (a) of subsection (1) of this section; "merger reference" (subject to section 63 of this Act) means any reference to the Commission under this Act which falls within paragraph (b) or paragraph (c) of that subsection; and "monopoly situation" (except in sections 6 to 8 of this Act) means circumstances in which, in accordance with the following provisions of this Part of this Act, a monopoly situation is for the purposes of this Act to be taken to exist in relation to any matters specified in section 6(1), section 7(1) or section 8 of this Act. [436]

NOTES
Commencement: 1 November 1973.

6. Monopoly situation in relation to supply of goods

(1) For the purposes of this Act a monopoly situation shall be taken to exist in relation to the supply of goods of any description in the following cases, that is to say, if—

 (a) at least one-quarter of all the goods of that description which are supplied in the United Kingdom are supplied by one and the same person, or are supplied to one and the same person, or
 (b) at least one-quarter of all the goods of that description which are supplied in the United Kingdom are supplied by members of one and the same group of interconnected bodies corporate, or are supplied to members of one and the same group of interconnected bodies corporate, or
 (c) at least one-quarter of all the goods of that description which are supplied in the United Kingdom are supplied by members of one and

the same group consisting of two or more such persons as are mentioned in subsection (2) of this section, or are supplied to members of one and the same group consisting of two or more such persons, or

(d) one or more agreements are in operation, the result or collective result of which is that goods of that description are not supplied in the United Kingdom at all.

(2) The two or more persons referred to in subsection (1)(c) of this section, in relation to goods of any description, are any two or more persons (not being a group of interconnected bodies corporate) who whether voluntarily or not, and whether by agreement or not, so conduct their respective affairs as in any way to prevent, restrict or distort competition in connection with the production or supply of goods of that description, whether or not they themselves are affected by the competition and whether the competition is between persons interested as producers or suppliers or between persons interested as customers of producers or suppliers. [437]

NOTES
Commencement: 1 November 1973.

7. Monopoly situation in relation to supply of services

(1) For the purposes of this Act a monopoly situation shall be taken to exist in relation to the supply of services of any description in the following cases, that is to say, if—

(a) the supply of services of that description in the United Kingdom is, to the extent of at least one-quarter, supply by one and the same person, or supply for one and the same person, or

(b) the supply of services of that description in the United Kingdom is, to the extent of at least one-quarter, supply by members of one and the same group of interconnected bodies corporate, or supply for members of one and the same group of interconnected bodies corporate, or

(c) the supply of services of that description in the United Kingdom is, to the extent of at least one-quarter, supply by members of one and the same group consisting of two or more such persons as are mentioned in subsection (2) of this section, or supply for members of one and the same group consisting of two or more such persons, or

(d) one or more agreements are in operation, the result or collective result of which is that services of that description are not supplied in the United Kingdom at all.

(2) The two or more persons referred to in subsection (1)(c) of this section, in relation to services of any description, are any two or more persons (not being a group of interconnected bodies corporate) who whether voluntarily or not, and whether by agreement or not, so conduct their respective affairs as in any way to prevent, restrict or distort competition in connection with the supply of services of that description, whether or not they themselves are affected by the competition, and whether the competition is between persons interested as persons by whom, or as persons for whom, services are supplied.

(3) In the application of this section for the purposes of a monopoly reference, the Commission, or the person or persons making the reference, may, to such extent as the Commission, or that person or those persons, think appropriate in the circumstances, treat services as supplied in the United Kingdom if the person supplying the services—

(a) has a place of business in the United Kingdom, or
   (b) controls the relevant activities from the United Kingdom, or
   (c) being a body corporate, is incorporated under the law of Great Britain or of Northern Ireland,

and may do so whether or not those services would otherwise be regarded as supplied in the United Kingdom. **[438]**

NOTES
Commencement: 1 November 1973.

8. Monopoly situation in relation to exports

(1) For the purposes of this Act a monopoly situation shall be taken to exist in relation to exports of goods of any description from the United Kingdom in the following cases, that is to say, if—
   (a) at least one-quarter of all the goods of that description which are produced in the United Kingdom are produced by one and the same person, or
   (b) at least one-quarter of all the goods of that description which are produced in the United Kingdom are produced by members of one and the same group of interconnected bodies corporate;

and in those cases a monopoly situation shall for the purposes of this Act be taken to exist both in relation to exports of goods of that description from the United Kingdom generally and in relation to exports of goods of that description from the United Kingdom to each market taken separately.

(2) In relation to exports of goods of any description from the United Kingdom generally, a monopoly situation shall for the purposes of this Act be taken to exist if—
   (a) one or more agreements are in operation which in any way prevent or restrict, or prevent, restrict or distort competition in relation to, the export of goods of that description from the United Kingdom, and
   (b) that agreement is or (as the case may be) those agreements collectively are operative with respect to at least one-quarter of all the goods of that description which are produced in the United Kingdom.

(3) In relation to exports of goods of any description from the United Kingdom to any particular market, a monopoly situation shall for the purposes of this Act be taken to exist if—
   (a) one or more agreements are in operation which in any way prevent or restrict, or prevent, restrict or distort competition in relation to, the supply of goods of that description (whether from the United Kingdom or not) to that market, and
   (b) that agreement is or (as the case may be) those agreements collectively are operative with respect to at least one-quarter of all the goods of that description which are produced in the United Kingdom. **[439]**

NOTES
Commencement: 1 November 1973.

9. Monopoly situation limited to part of United Kingdom

(1) For the purposes of a monopoly reference, other than a reference relating to exports of goods from the United Kingdom, the person or persons making the reference may, if it appears to him or them to be appropriate in the circumstances

to do so, determine that consideration shall be limited to a part of the United Kingdom.

(2) Where such a determination is made, then for the purposes of that monopoly reference the provisions of sections 6 and 7 of this Act, or such of those provisions as are applicable for those purposes, shall have effect as if, wherever those provisions refer to the United Kingdom, they referred to that part of the United Kingdom to which, in accordance with that determination, consideration is to be limited.

(3) The preceding provisions of this section shall have effect subject to subsection (4) of section 50 of this Act in cases to which that subsection applies. **[440]**

NOTES
Commencement: 1 November 1973.

10. Supplementary provisions relating to ss 6 to 9

(1) In the application of any of the provisions of sections 6 to 9 of this Act for the purposes of a monopoly reference, those provisions shall have effect subject to the following provisions of this section.

(2) No account shall for those purposes be taken of any provisions of an agreement in so far as they are provisions by virtue of which it is an agreement to which [the Act of 1976] applies.

(3) In relation to goods or services of any description which are the subject of different forms of supply—
  (a) references in paragraphs (a) to (d) of subsection (1), and in subsection (2), of section 6 or in section 8(3) of this Act to the supply of goods, or
  (b) references in paragraphs (a) to (d) of subsection (1), and in subsection (2), of section 7 of this Act to the supply of services,

shall for those purposes be construed in whichever of the following ways the Commission, or the person or persons making the monopoly reference, think appropriate in all the circumstances, that is to say, as references to any of those forms of supply taken separately, to all those forms of supply taken together, or to any of those forms of supply taken in groups.

(4) For the purposes of subsection (3) of this section the Commission, or the person or persons making the monopoly reference in question, may treat goods or services as being the subject of different forms of supply whenever the transactions in question differ as to their nature, their parties, their terms or their surrounding circumstances, and the difference is one which, in the opinion of the Commission, or the person or persons making the reference, ought for the purposes of that subsection to be treated as a material difference.

(5) For the purposes of a monopoly reference made by the Director, subsections (3) and (4) of this section shall have effect subject to section 50(3) and (4) of this Act.

(6) In determining, for the purposes of a monopoly reference, whether the proportion of one-quarter mentioned in any provision of section 6, section 7 or section 8 of this Act is fulfilled with respect to goods or services of any description, the Commission, or the person or persons making the reference, shall apply such criterion (whether it be value or cost or price or quantity or capacity or number of workers employed or some other criterion, of whatever

nature) or such combination of criteria as may appear to them or him to be most suitable in all the circumstances.

(7) The criteria for determining when goods or services can be treated, for the purposes of a monopoly reference, as goods or services of a separate description shall be such as the person or persons making the reference may think most suitable in the circumstances.

(8) In construing the provisions of section 7(3) and section 9 of this Act and the provisions of subsections (1) to (7) of this section, the purposes of a monopoly reference shall be taken to include the purpose of enabling the Director, or the Secretary of State or any other Minister, to determine in any particular circumstances—
- (a) whether a monopoly reference could be made under Part IV of this Act, and
- (b) if so, whether in those circumstances such a reference could be made by the Director,

and references in those provisions to the person or persons making a monopoly reference shall be construed accordingly. **[441]**

NOTES
Commencement: 1 November 1973.
Sub-s(2): amended by the Restrictive Trade Practices Act 1976, s 44, Sch 5.
The Act of 1976: Restrictive Trade Practices Act 1976.

11. Meaning of "complex monopoly situation"

(1) In this Act "complex monopoly situation" means circumstances in which, in accordance with the preceding provisions of this Act, a monopoly situation is for the purposes of this Act to be taken to exist in relation to the supply of goods or services of any description, or in relation to exports of goods of any description from the United Kingdom, by reason that the condition specified in paragraph (c) or in paragraph (d) of section 6(1) or of section 7(1) of this Act is fulfilled, or that the conditions specified in subsection (2) or in subsection (3) of section 8 of this Act are fulfilled.

(2) Any reference in the preceding subsection to paragraph (c) or paragraph (d) of section 6(1) or of section 7(1) of this Act shall be construed as including a reference to that paragraph as modified by section 9(2) of this Act. **[442]**

NOTES
Commencement: 1 November 1973.

12. Powers of Secretary of State in relation to functions of Director

(1) The Secretary of State may give general directions indicating considerations to which the Director should have particular regard in determining the order of priority in which—
- (a) matters are to be brought under review in the performance of his duty under section 2(1) of this Act, or
- (b) classes of goods or services are to be brought under review by him for the purpose of considering whether a monopoly situation exists or may exist in relation to them.

(2) The Secretary of State may also give general directions indicating—
- (a) considerations to which in cases where it appears to the Director that a practice may adversely affect the interests of consumers in the

United Kingdom, he should have particular regard in determining whether to make a recommendation to the Secretary of State under section 2(3)(*b*) of this Act, or

(*b*) considerations to which, in cases where it appears to the Director that a consumer trade practice may adversely affect the economic interests of consumers in the United Kingdom, he should have particular regard in determining whether to make a reference to the Advisory Committee under Part II of this Act, or

(*c*) considerations to which, in cases where it appears to the Director that a monopoly situation exists or may exist, he should have particular regard in determining whether to make a monopoly reference to the Commission under Part IV of this Act.

(3) The Secretary of State, on giving any directions under this section, shall arrange for those directions to be published in such manner as the Secretary of State thinks most suitable in the circumstances. [443]

NOTES
Commencement: 1 November 1973.

Part III
Additional Functions of Director for Protection of Consumers

34. Action by Director with respect to course of conduct detrimental to interests of consumers

(1) Where it appears to the Director that the person carrying on a business has in the course of that business persisted in a course of conduct which—

(*a*) is detrimental to the interests of consumers in the United Kingdom, whether those interests are economic interests or interests in respect of health, safety or other matters, and

(*b*) in accordance with the following provisions of this section is to be regarded as unfair to consumers,

the Director shall use his best endeavours, by communication with that person or otherwise, to obtain from him a satisfactory written assurance that he will refrain from continuing that course of conduct and from carrying on any similar course of conduct in the course of that business.

(2) For the purposes of subsection (1)(*b*) of this section a course of conduct shall be regarded as unfair to consumers if it consists of contraventions of one or more enactments which impose duties, prohibitions or restrictions enforceable by criminal proceedings, whether any such duty, prohibition or restriction is imposed in relation to consumers as such or not and whether the person carrying on the business has or has not been convicted of any offence in respect of any such contravention.

(3) A course of conduct on the part of the person carrying on a business shall also be regarded for those purposes as unfair to consumers if it consists of things done, or omitted to be done, in the course of that business in breach of contract or in breach of a duty (other than a contractual duty) owed to any person by virtue of any enactment or rule of law and enforceable by civil proceedings, whether (in any such case) civil proceedings in respect of the breach of contract or breach of duty have been brought or not.

(4) For the purpose of determining whether it appears to him that a person has persisted in such a course of conduct as is mentioned in subsection (1) of

this section, the Director shall have regard to either or both of the following, that is to say—

  (a) complaints received by him, whether from consumers or from other persons;
  (b) any other information collected by or furnished to him, whether by virtue of this Act or otherwise. [444]

NOTES
Commencement: 1 November 1973.

35. Proceedings before Restrictive Practices Court

If, in the circumstances specified in subsection (1) of section 34 of this Act,—

  (a) the Director is unable to obtain from the person in question such an assurance as is mentioned in that subsection, or
  (b) that person has given such an assurance and it appears to the Director that he has failed to observe it,

the Director may bring proceedings against him before the Restrictive Practices Court. [445]

NOTES
Commencement: 1 November 1973.

36. Evidence in proceedings under s 35

(1) For the purposes of section 11 of the Civil Evidence Act 1968, section 10 of the Law Reform (Miscellaneous Provisions) (Scotland) Act 1968 or section 7 of the Civil Evidence Act (Northern Ireland) 1971 (each of which relates to convictions as evidence in civil proceedings), proceedings under section 35 of this Act shall (without prejudice to the generality of the relevant definition) be taken to be civil proceedings within the meaning of the Act in question.

(2) Where in any proceedings under section 35 of this Act the Director alleges such a breach of contract or breach of duty as is mentioned in section 34(3) of this Act, a judgment of any court given in civil proceedings, which includes a finding that the breach of contract or breach of duty in question was committed,—

  (a) shall be admissible in evidence for the purpose of proving the breach of contract or breach of duty, and
  (b) shall, unless the contrary is proved, be taken to be sufficient evidence that the breach of contract or breach of duty was committed.

(3) For the purposes of subsection (2) of this section no account shall be taken of a judgment given in any civil proceedings if it has subsequently been reversed on appeal, or has been varied on appeal so as to negative the finding referred to in that subsection.

(4) In subsection (1) of this section "the relevant definition" means section 18(1) of the Civil Evidence Act 1968, section 17(1) of the Law Reform (Miscellaneous Provisions) (Scotland) Act 1968 or section 14(1) of the Civil Evidence Act (Northern Ireland) 1971, as the case may be. [446]

NOTES
Commencement: 1 November 1973.

37. Order of, or undertaking given to, Court in proceedings under s 35

(1) Where in any proceedings before the Restrictive Practices Court under section 35 of this Act—
- (*a*) the Court finds that the person against whom the proceedings are brought (in this section referred to as "the respondent") has in the course of a business carried on by him persisted in such a course of conduct as is mentioned in section 34(1) of this Act, and
- (*b*) the respondent does not give an undertaking to the Court under subsection (3) of this section which is accepted by the Court, and
- (*c*) it appears to the Court that, unless an order is made against the respondent under this section, he is likely to continue that course of conduct or to carry on a similar course of conduct,

the Court may make an order against the respondent under this section.

(2) An order of the Court under this section shall (with such degree of particularity as appears to the Court to be sufficient for the purposes of the order) indicate the nature of the course of conduct to which the finding of the Court under subsection (1)(*a*) of this section relates, and shall direct the respondent—
- (*a*) to refrain from continuing that course of conduct, and
- (*b*) to refrain from carrying on any similar course of conduct in the course of his business.

(3) Where in any proceedings under section 35 of this Act the Court makes such a finding as is mentioned in subsection (1)(*a*) of this section, and the respondent offers to give to the Court an undertaking either—
- (*a*) to refrain as mentioned in paragraphs (*a*) and (*b*) of subsection (2) of this section, or
- (*b*) to take particular steps which, in the opinion of the Court, would suffice to prevent a continuance of the course of conduct to which the complaint relates and to prevent the carrying on by the respondent of any similar course of conduct in the course of his business,

the Court may, if it thinks fit, accept that undertaking instead of making an order under this section.

NOTES
Commencement: 1 November 1973.

38. Provisions as to persons consenting to or conniving at courses of conduct detrimental to interests of consumers

(1) The provisions of this section shall have effect where it appears to the Director—
- (*a*) that a body corporate has in the course of a business carried on by that body persisted in such a course of conduct as is mentioned in section 34(1) of this Act, and
- (*b*) that the course of conduct in question has been so persisted in with the consent or connivance of a person (in this and the next following section referred to as "the accessory") who at a material time fulfilled the relevant conditions in relation to that body.

(2) For the purposes of this section a person shall be taken to fulfil the relevant conditions in relation to a body corporate at any time if that person either—

(a) is at that time a director, manager, secretary or other similar officer of the body corporate or a person purporting to act in any such capacity, or

(b) whether being an individual or a body of persons, corporate or unincorporate, has at that time a controlling interest in that body corporate.

(3) If, in the circumstances specified in subsection (1) of this section,—

(a) the Director has used his best endeavours to obtain from the accessory such an assurance as is mentioned in the next following subsection and has been unable to obtain such an assurance from him, or

(b) the accessory has given such an assurance to the Director and it appears to the Director that he has failed to observe it,

the Director may bring proceedings against the accessory before the Restrictive Practices Court.

(4) The assurance referred to in subsection (3) of this section is a satisfactory written assurance given by the accessory that he will refrain—

(a) from continuing to consent to or connive at the course of conduct in question;

(b) from carrying on any similar course of conduct in the course of any business which may at any time be carried on by him; and

(c) from consenting to or conniving at the carrying on of any such course of conduct by any other body corporate in relation to which, at any time when that course of conduct is carried on, he fulfils the relevant conditions.

(5) Proceedings may be brought against the accessory under this section whether or not any proceedings are brought under section 35 of this Act against the body corporate referred to in subsection (1) of this section.

(6) Section 36 of this Act shall have effect in relation to proceedings under this section as it has effect in relation to proceedings under section 35 of this Act.

(7) For the purposes of this section a person (whether being an individual or a body of persons, corporate or unincorporate) has a controlling interest in a body corporate if (but only if) that person can, directly or indirectly, determine the manner in which one-half of the votes which could be cast at a general meeting of the body corporate are to be cast on matters, and in circumstances, not of such a description as to bring into play any special voting rights or restrictions on voting rights. **[448]**

NOTES
Commencement: 1 November 1973.

39. Order of, or undertaking given to, Court in proceedings under s 38

(1) Where in any proceedings brought against the accessory before the Restrictive Practices Court under section 38 of this Act—

(a) the Court finds that the conditions specified in paragraphs (a) and (b) of subsection (1) of that section are fulfilled in the case of the accessory, and

(b) the accessory does not give an undertaking to the Court under subsection (3) of this section which is accepted by the Court, and

(c) it appears to the Court that, unless an order is made against the accessory under this section, it is likely that he will not refrain from acting in one or more of the ways mentioned in paragraphs (a) to (c) of subsection (4) of that section,

the Court may make an order against the accessory under this section.

(2) An order of the Court under this section shall (with such degree of particularity as appears to the Court to be sufficient for the purposes of the order) indicate the nature of the course of conduct to which the finding of the Court under subsection (1)(a) of this section relates, and shall direct the accessory, in relation to the course of conduct so indicated, to refrain from acting in any of the ways mentioned in paragraphs (a) to (c) of subsection (4) of section 38 of this Act.

(3) Where in any proceedings under section 38 of this Act the Court makes such a finding as is mentioned in subsection (1)(a) of this section, and the accessory offers to give to the Court an undertaking either—
- (a) to refrain from acting in any of the ways mentioned in paragraphs (a) to (c) of subsection (4) of that section, or
- (b) to take particular steps which, in the opinion of the Court, would suffice to prevent him from acting in any of those ways,

the Court may, if it thinks fit, accept that undertaking instead of making an order under this section.

NOTES
Commencement: 1 November 1973.

40. Provisions as to interconnected bodies corporate

(1) This section applies to any order made under section 37 or section 39 of this Act.

(2) Where an order to which this section applies is made against a body corporate which is a member of a group of interconnected bodies corporate, the Restrictive Practices Court, on making the order, may direct that it shall be binding upon all members of the group as if each of them were the body corporate against which the order is made.

(3) Where an order to which this section applies has been made against a body corporate, and at a time when that order is in force—
- (a) the body corporate becomes a member of a group of interconnected bodies corporate, or
- (b) a group of interconnected bodies corporate of which it is a member is increased by the addition of one or more further members,

the Restrictive Practices Court, on the application of the Director, may direct that the order shall thereafter be binding upon each member of the group as if it were the body corporate against which the order was made.

(4) The power conferred by subsection (3) of this section shall be exercisable—
- (a) whether, at the time when the original order was made, the body corporate against which it was made was a member of a group of interconnected bodies corporate or not, and
- (b) if it was such a member, whether a direction under subsection (2) of this section was given or not.

NOTES
Commencement: 1 November 1973.

41. Concurrent jurisdiction of other courts in certain cases

(1) In any case where—

   (a) the Director could bring proceedings against a person before the Restrictive Practices Court under section 35 or section 38 of this Act, and
   (b) it appears to the Director that the conditions specified in the next following subsection are fulfilled,

the Director may, if he thinks fit, bring those proceedings in an appropriate alternative court instead of bringing them before the Restrictive Practices Court; and, in relation to any proceedings brought by virtue of this section, the appropriate alternative court in which they are brought shall have the like jurisdiction as the Restrictive Practices Court would have had if they had been brought in that Court.

(2) The conditions referred to in the preceding subsection are—

   (a) that neither the person against whom the proceedings are to be brought nor the person against whom any associated proceedings have been or are intended to be brought is a body corporate having a share capital, paid up or credited as paid up, of an amount exceeding £10,000, and
   (b) that neither those proceedings nor any associated proceedings involve or are likely to involve the determination of a question (whether of law or of fact) of such general application as to justify its being reserved for determination by the Restrictive Practices Court.

(3) For the purposes of this section, the following shall be appropriate alternative courts in relation to proceedings in respect of a course of conduct maintained in the course of a business, that is to say, the county court for any district (or, in Northern Ireland, any division) in which, or, in Scotland, any sheriff court within whose jurisdiction, that business is carried on.

(4) In relation to any proceedings brought in an appropriate alternative court by virtue of this section, or to any order made in any such proceedings, any reference in section 37, in section 39 or section 40 of this Act to the Restrictive Practices Court shall be construed as a reference to the appropriate alternative court in which the proceedings are brought.

(5) In this section "associated proceedings"—

   (a) in relation to proceedings under section 35 of this Act, means proceedings under section 38 of this Act against a person as being a person consenting to or conniving at the course of conduct in question, and
   (b) in relation to proceedings under section 38 of this Act, means proceedings under section 35 of this Act against a person as being the person by whom the course of conduct in question has been maintained.

NOTES
Commencement: 1 November 1973.

42. Appeals from decisions or orders of courts under Part III

(1) Notwithstanding anything in any other enactment, an appeal, whether on a question of fact or on a question of law, shall lie from any decision or order of any court in proceedings under Part III of this Act.

(2) Any such appeal shall lie—

(a) in the case of proceedings in England and Wales, to the Court of Appeal;
(b) ...
(c) in the case of proceedings in Northern Ireland, to the Court of Appeal in Northern Ireland. **[452]**

NOTES
Commencement: 1 November 1973.
Sub-s (2): para (b) applies to Scotland only.

CONSUMER PROTECTION ACT 1987
(c 43)

ARRANGEMENT OF SECTIONS

Part I
Product Liability

Section		Para
1	Purpose and construction of Part I	[453]
2	Liability for defective products	[454]
3	Meaning of "defect"	[455]
4	Defences	[456]
5	Damage giving rise to liability	[457]
6	Application of certain enactments etc	[458]
7	Prohibition on exclusions from liability	[459]
8	Power to modify Part I	[460]
9	Application of Part I to Crown	[461]

Part II
Consumer Safety

10	The general safety requirement	[462]
11	Safety regulations	[463]
12	Offences against the safety regulations	[464]
13	Prohibition notices and notices to warn	[465]
14	Suspension notices	[466]
15	Appeals against suspension notices	[467]
16	Forfeiture: England and Wales and Northern Ireland	[468–9]
18	Power to obtain information	[470]
19	Interpretation of Part II	[471]

Part III
Misleading Price Indications

20	Offence of giving misleading indication	[472]
21	Meaning of "misleading"	[473]
22	Application to provision of services and facilities	[474]
23	Application to provision of accommodation etc	[475]
24	Defences	[476]

Section		Para
25	Code of practice	[477]
26	Power to make regulations	[478]

Part IV
Enforcement of Parts II and III

27	Enforcement	[479]
28	Test purchases	[480]
29	Powers of search etc	[481]
30	Provisions supplemental to s 29	[482]
31	Power of customs officer to detain goods	[483]
32	Obstruction of authorised officer	[484]
33	Appeals against detention of goods	[485]
34	Compensation for seizure and detention	[486]
35	Recovery of expenses of enforcement	[487]

Part V
Miscellaneous and Supplemental

36	Amendments of Part I of the Health and Safety at Work etc Act 1974	[488]
37	Power of Commissioners of Customs and Excise to disclose information	[489]
38	Restrictions on disclosure of information	[490]
39	Defence of due diligence	[491]
40	Liability of persons other than principal offender	[492]
41	Civil proceedings	[493]
42	Reports etc	[494]
43	Financial provisions	[495]
44	Service of documents etc	[496]
45	Interpretation	[497]
46	Meaning of "supply"	[498]
47	Savings for certain privileges	[499]
48	Minor and consequential amendments and repeals	[500]
49	Northern Ireland	[501]
50	Short title, commencement and transitional provision	[502]

Schedules

Schedule 1—Limitation of Actions under Part I	
Part I—England and Wales	[503]
Part II—Scotland	[504]
Schedule 2—Prohibition Notices and Notices to Warn	
Part I—Prohibition Notices	[505]
Part II—Notices to warn	[506]
Part III—General	[507–10]

An Act to make provision with respect to the liability of persons for damage caused by defective products; to consolidate with amendments the Consumer Safety Act 1978 and the Consumer Safety (Amendment) Act 1986; to make provision with respect to the giving of price indications; to amend Part I of the Health and Safety at Work etc. Act 1974 and sections 31 and 80 of the Explosives Act 1875; to repeal the Trade Descriptions Act 1972 and the Fabrics (Misdescription) Act 1913; and for connected purposes. [15 May 1987]

Part I
Product Liability

1. Purpose and construction of Part I

(1) This Part shall have effect for the purpose of making such provision as is necessary in order to comply with the product liability Directive and shall be construed accordingly.

(2) In this Part, except in so far as the context otherwise requires—

"agricultural produce" means any produce of the soil, of stock-farming or of fisheries;

"dependant" and "relative" have the same meanings as they have in, respectively, the Fatal Accidents Act 1976 and the Damages (Scotland) Act 1976;

"producer", in relation to a product, means—

(a) the person who manufactured it;
(b) in the case of a substance which has not been manufactured but has been won or abstracted, the person who won or abstracted it;
(c) in the case of a product which has not been manufactured, won or abstracted but essential characteristics of which are attributable to an industrial or other process having been carried out (for example, in relation to agricultural produce), the person who carried out that process;

"product" means any goods or electricity and (subject to subsection (3) below) includes a product which is comprised in another product, whether by virtue of being a component part or raw material or otherwise; and

"the product liability Directive" means the Directive of the Council of the European Communities, dated 25 July 1985, (No 85/374/EEC) on the approximation of the laws, regulations and administrative provisions of the member States concerning liability for defective products.

(3) For the purposes of this Part a person who supplies any product in which products are comprised, whether by virtue of being component parts or raw materials or otherwise, shall not be treated by reason only of his supply of that product as supplying any of the products so comprised. [453]

NOTES
Commencement: 1 March 1988.
Commencement order: SI 1987 No 1680.

2. Liability for defective products

(1) Subject to the following provisions of this Part, where any damage is caused wholly or partly by a defect in a product, every person to whom subsection (2) below applies shall be liable for the damage.

(2) This subsection applies to—

(a) the producer of the product;
(b) any person who, by putting his name on the product or using a trade mark or other distinguishing mark in relation to the product, has held himself out to be the producer of the product;
(c) any person who has imported the product into a member State from a place outside the member States in order, in the course of any business of his, to supply it to another.

(3) Subject as aforesaid, where any damage is caused wholly or partly by a defect in a product, any person who supplied the product (whether to the person who suffered the damage, to the producer of any product in which the product in question is comprised or to any other person) shall be liable for the damage if—

(a) the person who suffered the damage requests the supplier to identify one or more of the persons (whether still in existence or not) to whom subsection (2) above applies in relation to the product;
(b) that request is made within a reasonable period after the damage occurs and at a time when it is not reasonably practicable for the person making the request to identify all those persons; and
(c) the supplier fails, within a reasonable period after receiving the request, either to comply with the request or to identify the person who supplied the product to him.

(4) Neither subsection (2) nor subsection (3) above shall apply to a person in respect of any defect in any game or agricultural produce if the only supply of the game or produce by that person to another was at a time when it had not undergone an industrial process.

(5) Where two or more persons are liable by virtue of this Part for the same damage, their liability shall be joint and several.

(6) This section shall be without prejudice to any liability arising otherwise than by virtue of this Part. [454]

NOTES
Commencement: 1 March 1988.
Commencement order: SI 1987 No 1680.

3. Meaning of "defect"

(1) Subject to the following provisions of this section, there is a defect in a product for the purposes of this Part if the safety of the product is not such as persons generally are entitled to expect; and for those purposes "safety", in relation to a product, shall include safety with respect to products comprised in that product and safety in the context of risks of damage to property, as well as in the context of risks of death or personal injury.

(2) In determining for the purposes of subsection (1) above what persons generally are entitled to expect in relation to a product all the circumstances shall be taken into account, including—
(a) the manner in which, and purposes for which, the product has been marketed, its get-up, the use of any mark in relation to the product and any instructions for, or warnings with respect to, doing or refraining from doing anything with or in relation to the product;
(b) what might reasonably be expected to be done with or in relation to the product; and
(c) the time when the product was supplied by its producer to another;
and nothing in this section shall require a defect to be inferred from the fact alone that the safety of a product which is supplied after that time is greater than the safety of the product in question. [455]

NOTES
Commencement: 1 March 1988.
Commencement order: SI 1987 No 1680.

4. Defences

(1) In any civil proceedings by virtue of this Part against any person ("the person proceeded against") in respect of a defect in a product it shall be a defence for him to show—

(a) that the defect is attributable to compliance with any requirement imposed by or under any enactment or with any Community obligation; or
(b) that the person proceeded against did not at any time supply the product to another, or
(c) that the following conditions are satisfied, that is to say—
   (i) that the only supply of the product to another by the person proceeded against was otherwise than in the course of a business of that person's; and
   (ii) that section 2(2) above does not apply to that person or applies to him by virtue only of things done otherwise than with a view to profit; or
(d) that the defect did not exist in the product at the relevant time; or
(e) that the state of scientific and technical knowledge at the relevant time was not such that a producer of products of the same description as the product in question might be expected to have discovered the defect if it had existed in his products while they were under his control; or
(f) that the defect—
   (i) constituted a defect in a product ("the subsequent product") in which the product in question had been comprised; and
   (ii) was wholly attributable to the design of the subsequent product or to compliance by the producer of the product in question with instructions given by the producer of the subsequent product.

(2) In this section "the relevant time", in relation to electricity, means the time at which it was generated, being a time before it was transmitted or distributed, and in relation to any other product, means—
   (a) if the person proceeded against is a person to whom subsection (2) of section 2 above applies in relation to the product, the time when he supplied the product to another;
   (b) if that subsection does not apply to that person in relation to the product, the time when the product was last supplied by a person to whom that subsection does apply in relation to the product. **[456]**

NOTES
Commencement: 1 March 1988.
Commencement order: SI 1987 No 1680.

5. Damage giving rise to liability

(1) Subject to the following provisions of this section, in this Part "damage" means death or personal injury or any loss of or damage to any property (including land).

(2) A person shall not be liable under section 2 above in respect of any defect in a product for the loss of or any damage to the product itself or for the loss of or any damage to the whole or any part of any product which has been supplied with the product in question comprised in it.

(3) A person shall not be liable under section 2 above for any loss of or damage to any property which, at the time it is lost or damaged, is not—
   (a) of a description of property ordinarily intended for private use, occupation or consumption; and

(b) intended by the person suffering the loss or damage mainly for his own private use, occupation or consumption.

(4) No damages shall be awarded to any person by virtue of this Part in respect of any loss of or damage to any property if the amount which would fall to be so awarded to that person, apart from this subsection and any liability for interest, does not exceed £275.

(5) In determining for the purposes of this Part who has suffered any loss of or damage to property and when any such loss or damage occurred, the loss or damage shall be regarded as having occurred at the earliest time at which a person with an interest in the property had knowledge of the material facts about the loss or damage.

(6) For the purposes of subsection (5) above the material facts about any loss of or damage to any property are such facts about the loss or damage as would lead a reasonable person with an interest in the property to consider the loss or damage sufficiently serious to justify his instituting proceedings for damages against a defendant who did not dispute liability and was able to satisfy a judgment.

(7) For the purposes of subsection (5) above a person's knowledge includes knowledge which he might reasonably have been expected to acquire—
(a) from facts observable or ascertainable by him; or
(b) from facts ascertainable by him with the help of appropriate expert advice which it is reasonable for him to seek;

but a person shall not be taken by virtue of this subsection to have knowledge of a fact ascertainable by him only with the help of expert advice unless he has failed to take all reasonable steps to obtain (and, where appropriate, to act on) that advice.

(8) Subsections (5) to (7) above shall not extend to Scotland. [457]

NOTES
Commencement: 1 March 1988.
Commencement order: SI 1987 No 1680.

6. Application of certain enactments etc

(1) Any damage for which a person is liable under section 2 above shall be deemed to have been caused—
(a) for the purposes of the Fatal Accidents Act 1976, by that person's wrongful act, neglect or default;
(b)–(d) . . .

(2) Where—
(a) a person's death is caused wholly or partly by a defect in a product, or a person dies after suffering damage which has been so caused;
(b) a request such as mentioned in paragraph (a) of subsection (3) of section 2 above is made to a supplier of the product by that person's personal representatives or, in the case of a person whose death is caused wholly or partly by the defect, by any dependant or relative of that person; and
(c) the conditions specified in paragraphs (b) and (c) of that subsection are satisfied in relation to that request,

this Part shall have effect for the purposes of the Law Reform (Miscellaneous Provisions) Act 1934, the Fatal Accidents Act 1976 and the Damages (Scotland)

Act 1976 as if liability of the supplier to that person under that subsection did not depend on that person having requested the supplier to identify certain persons or on the said conditions having been satisfied in relation to a request made by that person.

(3) Section 1 of the Congenital Disabilities (Civil Liability) Act 1976 shall have effect for the purposes of this Part as if—
  (a) a person were answerable to a child in respect of an occurrence caused wholly or partly by a defect in a product if he is or has been liable under section 2 above in respect of any effect of the occurrence on a parent of the child, or would be so liable if the occurrence caused a parent of the child to suffer damage;
  (b) the provisions of this Part relating to liability under section 2 above applied in relation to liability by virtue of paragraph (a) above under the said section 1; and
  (c) subsection (6) of the said section 1 (exclusion of liability) were omitted.

(4) Where any damage is caused partly by a defect in a product and partly by the fault of the person suffering the damage, the Law Reform (Contributory Negligence) Act 1945 and section 5 of the Fatal Accidents Act 1976 (contributory negligence) shall have effect as if the defect were the fault of every person liable by virtue of this Part for the damage caused by the defect.

(5) In subsection (4) above "fault" has the same meaning as in the said Act of 1945.

(6) Schedule 1 to this Act shall have effect for the purpose of amending the Limitation Act 1980 and the Prescription and Limitation (Scotland) Act 1973 in their application in relation to the bringing of actions by virtue of this Part.

(7) It is hereby declared that liability by virtue of this Part is to be treated as liability in tort for the purposes of any enactment conferring jurisdiction on any court with respect to any matter.

(8) Nothing in this Part shall prejudice the operation of section 12 of the Nuclear Installations Act 1965 (rights to compensation for certain breaches of duties confined to rights under that Act). [458]

NOTES
  Commencement: 1 March 1988.
  Commencement order: SI 1987 No 1680.
  Sub-s (1): words omitted apply to Scotland only.

7. Prohibition on exclusions from liability

The liability of a person by virtue of this Part to a person who has suffered damage caused wholly or partly by a defect in a product, or to a dependant or relative of such a person, shall not be limited or excluded by any contract term, by any notice or by any other provision. [459]

NOTES
  Commencement: 1 March 1988.
  Commencement order: SI 1987 No 1680.

8. Power to modify Part I

(1) Her Majesty may by Order in Council make such modifications of this Part and of any other enactment (including an enactment contained in the following Parts of this Act, or in an Act passed after this Act) as appear to Her Majesty in

Council to be necessary or expedient in consequence of any modification of the product liability Directive which is made at any time after the passing of this Act.

(2) An Order in Council under subsection (1) above shall not be submitted to Her Majesty in Council unless a draft of the Order has been laid before, and approved by a resolution of, each House of Parliament. **[460]**

NOTES
Commencement: 1 March 1988.
Commencement order: SI 1987 No 1680.
No order has yet been made under this section.

9. Application of Part I to Crown

(1) Subject to subsection (2) below, this Part shall bind the Crown.

(2) The Crown shall not, as regards the Crown's liability by virtue of this Part, be bound by this Part further than the Crown is made liable in tort or in reparation under the Crown Proceedings Act 1947, as that Act has effect from time to time. **[461]**

NOTES
Commencement: 1 March 1988.
Commencement order: SI 1987 No 1680.

PART II
CONSUMER SAFETY

GENERAL NOTES
Derivation: This Part and Part IV contain a consolidation of provisions which were previously in the Consumer Safety Act 1978 and the Consumer Safety (Amendment) Act 1986. However, it is not purely a consolidation. There are amendments and new provisions.

10. The general safety requirement

(1) A person shall be guilty of an offence if he—
   (a) supplies any consumer goods which fail to comply with the general safety requirement;
   (b) offers or agrees to supply any such goods; or
   (c) exposes or possesses any such goods for supply.

(2) For the purposes of this section consumer goods fail to comply with the general safety requirement if they are not reasonably safe having regard to all the circumstances, including—
   (a) the manner in which, and purposes for which, the goods are being or would be marketed, the get-up of the goods, the use of any mark in relation to the goods and any instructions or warnings which are given or would be given with respect to the keeping, use or consumption of the goods;
   (b) any standards of safety published by any person either for goods of a description which applies to the goods in question or for matters relating to goods of that description; and
   (c) the existence of any means by which it would have been reasonable (taking into account the cost, likelihood and extent of any improvement) for the goods to have been made safer.

(3) For the purposes of this section consumer goods shall not be regarded as failing to comply with the general safety requirement in respect of—
  (a) anything which is shown to be attributable to compliance with any requirement imposed by or under any enactment or with any Community obligation;
  (b) any failure to do more in relation to any matter than is required by—
    (i) any safety regulations imposing requirements with respect to that matter;
    (ii) any standards of safety approved for the purposes of this subsection by or under any such regulations and imposing requirements with respect to that matter;
    (iii) any provision of any enactment or subordinate legislation imposing such requirements with respect to that matter as are designated for the purposes of this subsection by any such regulations.

(4) In any proceedings against any person for an offence under this section in respect of any goods it shall be a defence for that person to show—
  (a) that he reasonably believed that the goods would not be used or consumed in the United Kingdom; or
  (b) that the following conditions are satisfied, that is to say—
    (i) that he supplied the goods, offered or agreed to supply them or, as the case may be, exposed or possessed them for supply in the course of carrying on a retail business; and
    (ii) that, at the time he supplied the goods or offered or agreed to supply them or exposed or possessed them for supply, he neither knew nor had reasonable grounds for believing that the goods failed to comply with the general safety requirement; or
  (c) that the terms on which he supplied the goods or agreed or offered to supply them or, in the case of goods which he exposed or possessed for supply, the terms on which he intended to supply them—
    (i) indicated that the goods were not supplied or to be supplied as new goods; and
    (ii) provided for, or contemplated, the acquisition of an interest in the goods by the persons supplied or to be supplied.

(5) For the purposes of subsection (4)(b) above goods are supplied in the course of carrying on a retail business if—
  (a) whether or not they are themselves acquired for a person's private use or consumption, they are supplied in the course of carrying on a business of making a supply of consumer goods available to persons who generally acquire them for private use or consumption; and
  (b) the descriptions of goods the supply of which is made available in the course of that business do not, to a significant extent, include manufactured or imported goods which have not previously been supplied in the United Kingdom.

(6) A person guilty of an offence under this section shall be liable on summary conviction to imprisonment for a term not exceeding six months or to a fine not exceeding level 5 on the standard scale or to both.

(7) In this section "consumer goods" means any goods which are ordinarily intended for private use or consumption, not being—

(a) growing crops or things comprised in land by virtue of being attached to it;
(b) water, food, feeding stuff or fertiliser;
(c) gas which is, is to be or has been supplied by a person authorised to supply it by or under section 6, 7 or 8 of the Gas Act 1986 (authorisation of supply of gas through pipes);
(d) aircraft (other than hang-gliders) or motor vehicles;
(e) controlled drugs or licensed medicinal products;
(f) tobacco. [462]

NOTES
Commencement: 1 October 1987.
Commencement order: SI 1987 No 1680.

11. Safety regulations

(1) The Secretary of State may by regulations under this section ("safety regulations") make such provision as he considers appropriate for the purposes of section 10(3) above and for the purpose of securing—
(a) that goods to which this section applies are safe;
(b) that goods to which this section applies which are unsafe, or would be unsafe in the hands of persons of a particular description, are not made available to persons generally or, as the case may be, to persons of that description; and
(c) that appropriate information is, and inappropriate information is not, provided in relation to goods to which this section applies.

(2) Without prejudice to the generality of subsection (1) above, safety regulations may contain provision—
(a) with respect to the composition or contents, design, construction, finish or packing of goods to which this section applies, with respect to standards for such goods and with respect to other matters relating to such goods;
(b) with respect to the giving, refusal, alteration or cancellation of approvals of such goods, of descriptions of such goods or of standards for such goods;
(c) with respect to the conditions that may be attached to any approval given under the regulations;
(d) for requiring such fees as may be determined by or under the regulations to be paid on the giving or alteration of any approval under the regulations and on the making of an application for such an approval or alteration;
(e) with respect to appeals against refusals, alterations and cancellations of approvals given under the regulations and against the conditions contained in such approvals;
(f) for requiring goods to which this section applies to be approved under the regulations or to conform to the requirements of the regulations or to descriptions or standards specified in or approved by or under the regulations;
(g) with respect to the testing or inspection of goods to which this section applies (including provision for determining the standards to be applied in carrying out any test or inspection);
(h) with respect to the ways of dealing with goods of which some or all do not satisfy a test required by or under the regulations or a standard connected with a procedure so required;

(i) for requiring a mark, warning or instruction or any other information relating to goods to be put on or to accompany the goods or to be used or provided in some other manner in relation to the goods, and for securing that inappropriate information is not given in relation to goods either by means of misleading marks or otherwise;
(j) for prohibiting persons from supplying, or from offering to supply, agreeing to supply, exposing for supply or possessing for supply, goods to which this section applies and component parts and raw materials for such goods;
(k) for requiring information to be given to any such person as may be determined by or under the regulations for the purpose of enabling that person to exercise any function conferred on him by the regulations.

(3) Without prejudice as aforesaid, safety regulations may contain provision—

(a) for requiring persons on whom functions are conferred by or under section 27 below to have regard, in exercising their functions so far as relating to any provision of safety regulations, to matters specified in a direction issued by the Secretary of State with respect to that provision;
(b) for securing that a person shall not be guilty of an offence under section 12 below unless it is shown that the goods in question do not conform to a particular standard;
(c) for securing that proceedings for such an offence are not brought in England and Wales except by or with the consent of the Secretary of State or the Director of Public Prosecutions;
(d) for securing that proceedings for such an offence are not brought in Northern Ireland except by or with the consent of the Secretary of State or the Director of Public Prosecutions for Northern Ireland;
(e) for enabling a magistrates' court in England and Wales or Northern Ireland to try an information or, in Northern Ireland, a complaint in respect of such an offence if the information was laid or the complaint made within twelve months from the time when the offence was committed;
(f) for enabling summary proceedings for such an offence to be brought in Scotland at any time within twelve months from the time when the offence was committed; and
(g) for determining the persons by whom, and the manner in which, anything required to be done by or under the regulations is to be done.

(4) Safety regulations shall not provide for any contravention of the regulations to be an offence.

(5) Where the Secretary of State proposes to make safety regulations it shall be his duty before he makes them—

(a) to consult such organisations as appear to him to be representative of interests substantially affected by the proposal;
(b) to consult such other persons as he considers appropriate; and
(c) in the case of proposed regulations relating to goods suitable for use at work, to consult the Health and Safety Commission in relation to the application of the proposed regulations to Great Britain;

but the preceding provisions of this subsection shall not apply in the case of regulations which provide for the regulations to cease to have effect at the end of a period of not more than twelve months beginning with the day on which they come into force and which contain a statement that it appears to the Secretary of State that the need to protect the public requires that the regulations should be made without delay.

(6) The power to make safety regulations shall be exercisable by statutory instrument subject to annulment in pursuance of a resolution of either House of Parliament and shall include power—
   (a) to make different provision for different cases; and
   (b) to make such supplemental, consequential and transitional provision as the Secretary of State considers appropriate.

(7) This section applies to any goods other than—
   (a) growing crops and things comprised in land by virtue of being attached to it;
   (b) water, food, feeding stuff and fertiliser;
   (c) gas which is, is to be or has been supplied by a person authorised to supply it by or under section 6, 7 or 8 of the Gas Act 1986 (authorisation of supply of gas through pipes);
   (d) controlled drugs and licensed medicinal products. [463]

NOTES
Commencement: 1 October 1987.
Commencement order: SI 1987 No 1680.
Regulations under this section: Approval of Safety Standards Regulations 1987, SI 1987 No 1911; Cosmetic Products (Safety) (Amendment) Regulations 1987, SI 1987 No 1920; Asbestos Products (Safety) (Amendment) Regulations 1987, SI 1987 No 1979; Benzene in Toys (Safety) Regulations 1979, SI 1987 No 2116; Cosmetic Products (Safety) (Amendment) Regulations 1988, SI 1988 No 802; Furniture and Furnishings (Fire) (Safety) Regulations 1988, SI 1988 No 1324; Ceramic Ware (Safety) Regulations 1988, SI 1988 No 1647; Cosmetic Products (Safety) (Amendment No 2) Regulations 1988, SI 1988 No 2121; Three-Wheeled All-Terrain Motor Vehicles (Safety) Regulations 1988, SI 1988 No 2122; Babies' Dummies (Safety) (Revocation) Regulations 1989, SI 1989 No 141; Gas Cooking Appliances (Safety) Regulations 1989, SI 1989 No 149.

12. Offences against the safety regulations

(1) Where safety regulations prohibit a person from supplying or offering or agreeing to supply any goods or from exposing or possessing any goods for supply, that person shall be guilty of an offence if he contravenes the prohibition.

(2) Where safety regulations require a person who makes or processes any goods in the course of carrying on a business—
   (a) to carry out a particular test or use a particular procedure in connection with the making or processing of the goods with a view to ascertaining whether the goods satisfy any requirements of such regulations; or
   (b) to deal or not to deal in a particular way with a quantity of the goods of which the whole or part does not satisfy such a test or does not satisfy standards connected with such a procedure,
that person shall be guilty of an offence if he does not comply with the requirement.

(3) If a person contravenes a provision of safety regulations which prohibits or requires the provision, by means of a mark or otherwise, of information of a particular kind in relation to goods, he shall be guilty of an offence.

(4) Where safety regulations require any person to give information to another for the purpose of enabling that other to exercise any function, that person shall be guilty of an offence if—
   (a) he fails without reasonable cause to comply with the requirement; or

(b) in giving the information which is required of him—
  (i) he makes any statement which he knows is false in a material particular; or
  (ii) he recklessly makes any statement which is false in a material particular.

(5) A person guilty of an offence under this section shall be liable on summary conviction to imprisonment for a term not exceeding six months or to a fine not exceeding level 5 on the standard scale or to both.

NOTES
Commencement: 1 October 1987.
Commencement order: SI 1987 No 1680.

13. Prohibition notices and notices to warn

(1) The Secretary of State may—
  (a) serve on any person a notice ("a prohibition notice") prohibiting that person, except with the consent of the Secretary of State, from supplying, or from offering to supply, agreeing to supply, exposing for supply or possessing for supply, any relevant goods which the Secretary of State considers are unsafe and which are described in the notice;
  (b) serve on any person a notice ("a notice to warn") requiring that person at his own expense to publish, in a form and manner and on occasions specified in the notice, a warning about any relevant goods which the Secretary of State considers are unsafe, which that person supplies or has supplied and which are described in the notice.

(2) Schedule 2 to this Act shall have effect with respect to prohibition notices and notices to warn; and the Secretary of State may by regulations make provision specifying the manner in which information is to be given to any person under that Schedule.

(3) A consent given by the Secretary of State for the purposes of a prohibition notice may impose such conditions on the doing of anything for which the consent is required as the Secretary of State considers appropriate.

(4) A person who contravenes a prohibition notice or a notice to warn shall be guilty of an offence and liable on summary conviction to imprisonment for a term not exceedings six months or to a fine not exceeding level 5 on the standard scale or to both.

(5) The power to make regulations under subsection (2) above shall be exercisable by statutory instrument subject to annulment in pursuance of a resolution of either House of Parliament and shall include power—
  (a) to make different provision for different cases; and
  (b) to make such supplemental, consequential and transitional provision as the Secretary of State considers appropriate.

(6) In this section "relevant goods" means—
  (a) in relation to a prohibition notice, any goods to which section 11 above applies; and
  (b) in relation to a notice to warn, any goods to which that section applies or any growing crops or things comprised in land by virtue of being attached to it.

NOTES
Commencement: 1 October 1987.
Commencement order: SI 1987 No 1680.
No regulations have yet been made under this section.

14. Suspension notices

(1) Where an enforcement authority has reasonable grounds for suspecting that any safety provision has been contravened in relation to any goods, the authority may serve a notice ("a suspension notice") prohibiting the person on whom it is served, for such period ending not more than six months after the date of the notice as is specified therein, from doing any of the following things without the consent of the authority, that is to say, supplying the goods, offering to supply them, agreeing to supply them or exposing them for supply.

(2) A suspension notice served by an enforcement authority in respect of any goods shall—
   (a) describe the goods in a manner sufficient to identify them;
   (b) set out the grounds on which the authority suspects that a safety provision has been contravened in relation to the goods; and
   (c) state that, and the manner in which, the person on whom the notice is served may appeal against the notice under section 15 below.

(3) A suspension notice served by an enforcement authority for the purpose of prohibiting a person for any period from doing the things mentioned in subsection (1) above in relation to any goods may also require that person to keep the authority informed of the whereabouts throughout that period of any of those goods in which he has an interest.

(4) Where a suspension notice has been served on any person in respect of any goods, no further such notice shall be served on that person in respect of the same goods unless—
   (a) proceedings against that person for an offence in respect of a contravention in relation to the goods of a safety provision (not being an offence under this section); or
   (b) proceedings for the forfeiture of the goods under section 16 or 17 below,
are pending at the end of the period specified in the first-mentioned notice.

(5) A consent given by an enforcement authority for the purposes of subsection (1) above may impose such conditions on the doing of anything for which the consent is required as the authority considers appropriate.

(6) Any person who contravenes a suspension notice shall be guilty of an offence and liable on summary conviction to imprisonment for a term not exceeding six months or to a fine not exceeding level 5 on the standard scale or to both.

(7) Where an enforcement authority serves a suspension notice in respect of any goods, the authority shall be liable to pay compensation to any person having an interest in the goods in respect of any loss or damage caused by reason of the service of the notice if—
   (a) there has been no contravention in relation to the goods of any safety provision; and
   (b) the exercise of the power is not attributable to any neglect or default by that person.

(8) Any disputed question as to the right to or the amount of any compensation payable under this section shall be determined by arbitration or, in Scotland, by a single arbiter appointed, failing agreement between the parties, by the sheriff. **[466]**

NOTES
Commencement: 1 October 1987.
Commencement order: SI 1987 No 1680.

15. Appeals against suspension notices

(1) Any person having an interest in any goods in respect of which a suspension notice is for the time being in force may apply for an order setting aside the notice.

(2) An application under this section may be made—

(a) to any magistrates' court in which proceedings have been brought in England and Wales or Northern Ireland—

  (i) for an offence in respect of a contravention in relation to the goods of any safety provision; or
  (ii) for the forfeiture of the goods under section 16 below;

(b) where no such proceedings have been so brought, by way of complaint to a magistrates' court; or

(c) in Scotland, by summary application to the sheriff.

(3) On an application under this section to a magistrates' court in England and Wales or Northern Ireland the court shall make an order setting aside the suspension notice only if the court is satisfied that there has been no contravention in relation to the goods of any safety provision.

(4) On an application under this section to the sheriff he shall make an order setting aside the suspension notice only if he is satisfied that at the date of making the order—

(a) proceedings for any offence in respect of a contravention in relation to the goods of any safety provision; or

(b) proceedings for the forfeiture of the goods under section 17 below,

have not been brought or, having been brought, have been concluded.

(5) Any person aggrieved by an order made under this section by a magistrates' court in England and Wales or Northern Ireland, or by a decision of such a court not to make such an order, may appeal against that order or decision—

(a) in England and Wales, to the Crown Court;
(b) in Northern Ireland, to the county court;

and an order so made may contain such provision as appears to the court to be appropriate for delaying the coming into force of the order pending the making and determination of any appeal (including any application under section 111 of the Magistrates' Courts Act 1980 or Article 146 of the Magistrates' Courts (Northern Ireland) Order 1981 (statement of case)). **[467]**

NOTES
Commencement: 1 October 1987.
Commencement order: SI 1987 No 1680.

16. Forfeiture: England and Wales and Northern Ireland

(1) An enforcement authority in England and Wales or Northern Ireland may apply under this section for an order for the forfeiture of any goods on the grounds that there has been a contravention in relation to the goods of a safety provision.

(2) An application under this section may be made—
- (a) where proceedings have been brought in a magistrates' court for an offence in respect of a contravention in relation to some or all of the goods of any safety provision, to that court;
- (b) where an application with respect to some or all of the goods has been made to a magistrates' court under section 15 above or section 33 below, to that court; and
- (c) where no application for the forfeiture of the goods has been made under paragraph (a) or (b) above, by way of complaint to a magistrates' court.

(3) On an application under this section the court shall make an order for the forfeiture of any goods only if it is satisfied that there has been a contravention in relation to the goods of a safety provision.

(4) For the avoidance of doubt it is declared that a court may infer for the purposes of this section that there has been a contravention in relation to any goods of a safety provision if it is satisfied that any such provision has been contravened in relation to goods which are representative of those goods (whether by reason of being of the same design or part of the same consignment or batch or otherwise).

(5) Any person aggrieved by an order made under this section by a magistrates' court, or by a decision of such a court not to make such an order, may appeal against that order or decision—
- (a) in England and Wales, to the Crown Court;
- (b) in Northern Ireland, to the county court;

and an order so made may contain such provision as appears to the court to be appropriate for delaying the coming into force of the order pending the making and determination of any appeal (including any application under section 111 of the Magistrates' Courts Act 1980 or Article 146 of the Magistrates' Courts (Northern Ireland) Order 1981 (statement of case)).

(6) Subject to subsection (7) below, where any goods are forfeited under this section they shall be destroyed in accordance with such directions as the court may give.

(7) On making an order under this section a magistrates' court may, if it considers it appropriate to do so, direct that the goods to which the order relates shall (instead of being destroyed) be released, to such person as the court may specify, on condition that that person—
- (a) does not supply those goods to any person otherwise than as mentioned in section 46(7)(a) or (b) below; and
- (b) complies with any order to pay costs or expenses (including any order under section 35 below) which has been made against that person in the proceedings for the order for forfeiture.

NOTES
Commencement: 1 October 1987.
Commencement order: SI 1987 No 1680.

NOTES
Section 17 which applies to Scotland only, is omitted.

18. Power to obtain information

(1) If the Secretary of State considers that, for the purpose of deciding whether—
  (a) to make, vary or revoke any safety regulations; or
  (b) to serve, vary or revoke a prohibition notice; or
  (c) to serve or revoke a notice to warn,
he requires information which another person is likely to be able to furnish, the Secretary of State may serve on the other person a notice under this section.

(2) A notice served on any person under this section may require that person—
  (a) to furnish to the Secretary of State, within a period specified in the notice, such information as is so specified;
  (b) to produce such records as are specified in the notice at a time and place so specified and to permit a person appointed by the Secretary of State for the purpose to take copies of the records at that time and place.

(3) A person shall be guilty of an offence if he—
  (a) fails, without reasonable cause, to comply with a notice served on him under this section; or
  (b) in purporting to comply with a requirement which by virtue of paragraph (a) of subsection (2) above is contained in such a notice—
    (i) furnishes information which he knows is false in a material particular; or
    (ii) recklessly furnishes information which is false in a material particular.

(4) A person guilty of an offence under subsection (3) above shall—
  (a) in the case of an offence under paragraph (a) of that subsection, be liable on summary conviction to a fine not exceeding level 5 on the standard scale; and
  (b) in the case of an offence under paragraph (b) of that subsection be liable—
    (i) on conviction on indictment, to a fine;
    (ii) on summary conviction, to a fine not exceeding the statutory maximum.

NOTES
Commencement: 1 October 1987.
Commencement order: SI 1987 No 1680.

19. Interpretation of Part II

(1) In this Part—
  "controlled drug" means a controlled drug within the meaning of the Misuse of Drugs Act 1971;
  "feeding stuff" and "fertiliser" have the same meanings as in Part IV of the Agriculture Act 1970;

"food" does not include anything containing tobacco but, subject to that, has the same meaning as in the Food Act 1984 or, in relation to Northern Ireland, the same meaning as in the Food and Drugs Act (Northern Ireland) 1958;

"licensed medicinal product" means—

(a) any medicinal product within the meaning of the Medicines Act 1968 in respect of which a product licence within the meaning of that Act is for the time being in force; or

(b) any other article or substance in respect of which any such licence is for the time being in force in pursuance of an order under section 104 or 105 of that Act (application of Act to other articles and substances);

"safe", in relation to any goods, means such that there is no risk, or no risk apart from one reduced to a minimum, that any of the following will (whether immediately or after a definite or indefinite period) cause the death of, or any personal injury to, any person whatsoever, that is to say—

(a) the goods;
(b) the keeping, use or consumption of the goods;
(c) the assembly of any of the goods which are, or are to be, supplied unassembled;
(d) any emission or leakage from the goods or, as a result of the keeping, use or consumption of the goods, from anything else; or
(e) reliance on the accuracy of any measurement, calculation or other reading made by or by means of the goods,

and "safer" and "unsafe" shall be construed accordingly;

"tobacco" includes any tobacco product within the meaning of the Tobacco Products Duty Act 1979 and any article or substance containing tobacco and intended for oral or nasal use.

(2) In the definition of "safe" in subsection (1) above, references to the keeping, use or consumption of any goods are references to—

(a) the keeping, use or consumption of the goods by the persons by whom, and in all or any of the ways or circumstances in which, they might reasonably be expected to be kept, used or consumed; and

(b) the keeping, use or consumption of the goods either alone or in conjunction with other goods in conjunction with which they might reasonably be expected to be kept, used or consumed. **[471]**

NOTES
Commencement: 1 October 1987.
Commencement order: SI 1987 No 1680.

Part III

Misleading Price Indications

20. Offence of giving misleading indication

(1) Subject to the following provisions of this Part, a person shall be guilty of an offence if, in the course of any business of his, he gives (by any means whatever) to any consumers an indication which is misleading as to the price at which any goods, services, accommodation or facilities are available (whether generally or from particular persons).

(2) Subject as aforesaid, a person shall be guilty of an offence if—
   (a) in the course of any business of his, he has given an indication to any consumers which, after it was given, has become misleading as mentioned in subsection (1) above; and
   (b) some or all of those consumers might reasonably be expected to rely on the indication at a time after it has become misleading; and
   (c) he fails to take all such steps as are reasonable to prevent those consumers from relying on the indication.

(3) For the purposes of this section it shall be immaterial—
   (a) whether the person who gives or gave the indication is or was acting on his own behalf or on behalf of another;
   (b) whether or not that person is the person, or included among the persons, from whom the goods, services, accommodation or facilities are available; and
   (c) whether the indication is or has become misleading in relation to all the consumers to whom it is or was given or only in relation to some of them.

(4) A person guilty of an offence under subsection (1) or (2) above shall be liable—
   (a) on conviction on indictment, to a fine;
   (b) on summary conviction, to a fine not exceeding the statutory maximum.

(5) No prosecution for an offence under subsection (1) or (2) above shall be brought after whichever is the earlier of the following, that is to say—
   (a) the end of the period of three years beginning with the day on which the offence was committed; and
   (b) the end of the period of one year beginning with the day on which the person bringing the prosecution discovered that the offence had been committed.

(6) In this Part—

"consumer"—
   (a) in relation to any goods, means any person who might wish to be supplied with the goods for his own private use or consumption;
   (b) in relation to any services or facilities, means any person who might wish to be provided with the services or facilities otherwise than for the purposes of any business of his; and
   (c) in relation to any accommodation, means any person who might wish to occupy the accommodation otherwise than for the purposes of any business of his;

"price", in relation to any goods, services, accommodation or facilities, means—
   (a) the aggregate of the sums required to be paid by a consumer for or otherwise in respect of the supply of the goods or the provision of the services, accommodation or facilities; or
   (b) except in section 21 below, any method which will be or has been applied for the purpose of determining that aggregate.

NOTES
Commencement: 1 March 1989.
Commencement order: SI 1988 No 2076.
See further, in relation to misleading price indications given before 1 June 1989: SI 1988 No 2076, art 3.

21. Meaning of "misleading"

(1) For the purposes of section 20 above an indication given to any consumers is misleading as to a price if what is conveyed by the indication, or what those consumers might reasonably be expected to infer from the indication or any omission from it, includes any of the following, that is to say—

(a) that the price is less than in fact it is;
(b) that the applicability of the price does not depend on facts or circumstances on which its applicability does in fact depend;
(c) that the price covers matters in respect of which an additional charge is in fact made;
(d) that a person who in fact has no such expectation—
  (i) expects the price to be increased or reduced (whether or not at a particular time or by a particular amount); or
  (ii) expects the price, or the price as increased or reduced, to be maintained (whether or not for a particular period); or
(e) that the facts or circumstances by reference to which the consumers might reasonably be expected to judge the validity of any relevant comparison made or implied by the indication are not what in fact they are.

(2) For the purposes of section 20 above, an indication given to any consumers is misleading as to a method of determining a price if what is conveyed by the indication, or what those consumers might reasonably be expected to infer from the indication or any omission from it, includes any of the following, that is to say—

(a) that the method is not what in fact it is;
(b) that the applicability of the method does not depend on facts or circumstances on which its applicability does in fact depend;
(c) that the method takes into account matters in respect of which an additional charge will in fact be made;
(d) that a person who in fact has no such expectation—
  (i) expects the method to be altered (whether or not at a particular time or in a particular respect); or
  (ii) expects the method, or that method as altered, to remain unaltered (whether or not for a particular period); or
(e) that the facts or circumstances by reference to which the consumers might reasonably be expected to judge the validity of any relevant comparison made or implied by the indication are not what in fact they are.

(3) For the purposes of subsections (1)(e) and (2)(e) above a comparison is a relevant comparison in relation to a price or method of determining a price if it is made between that price or that method, or any price which has been or may be determined by that method, and—

(a) any price or value which is stated or implied to be, to have been or to be likely to be attributed or attributable to the goods, services, accommodation or facilities in question or to any other goods, services, accommodation or facilities; or

(b) any method, or other method, which is stated or implied to be, to have been or to be likely to be applied or applicable for the determination of the price or value of the goods, services, accommodation or facilities in question or of the price or value of any other goods, services, accommodation or facilities. **[473]**

NOTES
Commencement: 1 March 1989.
Commencement order: SI 1988 No 2076.

22. Application to provision of services and facilities

(1) Subject to the following provisions of this section, references in this Part to services or facilities are references to any services or facilities whatever including, in particular—

  (a) the provision of credit or of banking or insurance services and the provision of facilities incidental to the provision of such services;
  (b) the purchase or sale of foreign currency;
  (c) the supply of electricity;
  (d) the provision of a place, other than on a highway, for the parking of a motor vehicle;
  (e) the making of arrangements for a person to put or keep a caravan on any land other than arrangements by virtue of which that person may occupy the caravan as his only or main residence.

(2) References in this Part to services shall not include references to services provided to an employer under a contract of employment.

(3) References in this Part to services or facilities shall not include references to services or facilities which are provided by an authorised person or appointed representative in the course of the carrying on of an investment business.

(4) In relation to a service consisting in the purchase or sale of foreign currency, references in this Part to the method by which the price of the service is determined shall include references to the rate of exchange.

(5) In this section—

"appointed representative", "authorised person" and "investment business" have the same meanings as in the Financial Services Act 1986;
"caravan" has the same meaning as in the Caravan Sites and Control of Development Act 1960;
"contract of employment" and "employer" have the same meanings as in the Employment Protection (Consolidation) Act 1978;
"credit" has the same meaning as in the Consumer Credit Act 1974. **[474]**

NOTES
Commencement: 1 March 1989.
Commencement order: SI 1988 No 2076.

23. Application to provision of accommodation etc

(1) Subject to subsection (2) below, references in this Part to accommodation or facilities being available shall not include references to accommodation or facilities being available to be provided by means of the creation or disposal of an interest in land except where—

  (a) the person who is to create or dispose of the interest will do so in the course of any business of his; and

(b) the interest to be created or disposed of is a relevant interest in a new dwelling and is to be created or disposed of for the purpose of enabling that dwelling to be occupied as a residence, or one of the residences, of the person acquiring the interest.

(2) Subsection (1) above shall not prevent the application of any provision of this Part in relation to—
  (a) the supply of any goods as part of the same transaction as any creation or disposal of an interest in land; or
  (b) the provision of any services or facilities for the purposes of, or in connection with, any transaction for the creation or disposal of such an interest.

(3) In this section—
  "new dwelling" means any building or part of a building in Great Britain which—
    (a) has been constructed or adapted to be occupied as a residence; and
    (b) has not previously been so occupied or has been so occupied only with other premises or as more than one residence,
and includes any yard, garden, out-houses or appurtenances which belong to that building or part or are to be enjoyed with it;
  "relevant interest"—
    (a) in relation to a new dwelling in England and Wales, means the freehold estate in the dwelling or a leasehold interest in the dwelling for a term of years absolute of more than twenty-one years, not being a term of which twenty-one years or less remains unexpired;
    (b) in relation to a new dwelling in Scotland, means the *dominium utile* of the land comprising the dwelling, or a leasehold interest in the dwelling where twenty-one years or more remains unexpired. **[475]**

NOTES
  Commencement: 1 March 1989.
  Commencement order: SI 1988 No 2076.

24. Defences

(1) In any proceedings against a person for an offence under subsection (1) or (2) of section 20 above in respect of any indication it shall be a defence for that person to show that his acts or omissions were authorised for the purposes of this subsection by regulations made under section 26 below.

(2) In proceedings against a person for an offence under subsection (1) or (2) of section 20 above in respect of an indication published in a book, newspaper, magazine, film or radio or television broadcast or in a programme included in a cable programme service, it shall be a defence for that person to show that the indication was not contained in an advertisement.

(3) In proceedings against a person for an offence under subsection (1) or (2) of section 20 above in respect of an indication published in an advertisement it shall be a defence for that person to show that—
  (a) he is a person who carries on a business of publishing or arranging for the publication of advertisements;

(b) he received the advertisement for publication in the ordinary course of that business; and
(c) at the time of publication he did not know and had no grounds for suspecting that the publication would involve the commission of the offence.

(4) In any proceedings against a person for an offence under subsection (1) of section 20 above in respect of any indication, it shall be a defence for that person to show that—

(a) the indication did not relate to the availability from him of any goods, services, accommodation or facilities;
(b) a price had been recommended to every person from whom the goods, services, accommodation or facilities were indicated as being available;
(c) the indication related to that price and was misleading as to that price only by reason of a failure by any person to follow the recommendation; and
(d) it was reasonable for the person who gave the indication to assume that the recommendation was for the most part being followed.

(5) The provisions of this section are without prejudice to the provisions of section 39 below.

(6) In this section—

"advertisement" includes a catalogue, a circular and a price list;
"cable programme service" has the same meaning as in the Cable and Broadcasting Act 1984.

NOTES
Commencement: 1 March 1989.
Commencement order: SI 1988 No 2076.

25. Code of practice

(1) The Secretary of State may, after consulting the Director General of Fair Trading and such other persons as the Secretary of State considers it appropriate to consult, by order approve any code of practice issued (whether by the Secretary of State or another person) for the purpose of—

(a) giving practical guidance with respect to any of the requirements of section 20 above; and
(b) promoting what appear to the Secretary of State to be desirable practices as to the circumstances and manner in which any person gives an indication as to the price at which any goods, services, accommodation or facilities are available or indicates any other matter in respect of which any such indication may be misleading.

(2) A contravention of a code of practice approved under this section shall not of itself give rise to any criminal or civil liability, but in any proceedings against any person for an offence under section 20(1) or (2) above—

(a) any contravention by that person of such a code may be relied on in relation to any matter for the purpose of establishing that that person committed the offence or of negativing any defence; and
(b) compliance by that person with such a code may be relied on in relation to any matter for the purpose of showing that the commission of the offence by that person has not been established or that that person has a defence.

(3) Where the Secretary of State approves a code of practice under this section he may, after such consultation as is mentioned in subsection (1) above, at any time by order—

(a) approve any modification of the code; or
(b) withdraw his approval;

and references in subsection (2) above to a code of practice approved under this section shall be construed accordingly.

(4) The power to make an order under this section shall be exercisable by statutory instrument subject to annulment in pursuance of a resolution of either House of Parliament. [477]

NOTES
Commencement: 1 March 1989.
Commencement order: SI 1988 No 2076.
Regulations under this section: Consumer Protection (Code of Practice for Traders on Price Indication) Approval Order 1988, SI 1988 No 2078.

26. Power to make regulations

(1) The Secretary of State may, after consulting the Director General of Fair Trading and such other persons as the Secretary of State considers it appropriate to consult, by regulations make provision—

(a) for the purpose of regulating the circumstances and manner in which any person—

　(i) gives any indication as to the price at which any goods, services, accommodation or facilities will be or are available or have been supplied or provided; or
　(ii) indicates any other matter in respect of which any such indication may be misleading;

(b) for the purpose of facilitating the enforcement of the provisions of section 20 above or of any regulations made under this section.

(2) The Secretary of State shall not make regulations by virtue of subsection (1)(a) above except in relation to—

(a) indications given by persons in the course of business; and
(b) such indications given otherwise than in the course of business as—

　(i) are given by or on behalf of persons by whom accommodation is provided to others by means of leases or licences; and
　(ii) relate to goods, services or facilities supplied or provided to those others in connection with the provision of the accommodation.

(3) Without prejudice to the generality of subsection (1) above, regulations under this section may—

(a) prohibit an indication as to a price from referring to such matters as may be prescribed by the regulations;
(b) require an indication as to a price or other matter to be accompanied or supplemented by such explanation or such additional information as may be prescribed by the regulations;
(c) require information or explanations with respect to a price or other matter to be given to an officer of an enforcement authority and to authorise such an officer to require such information or explanations to be given;

(d) require any information or explanation provided for the purposes of any regulations made by virtue of paragraph (b) or (c) above to be accurate;

(e) prohibit the inclusion in indications as to a price or other matter of statements that the indications are not to be relied upon;

(f) provide that expressions used in any indication as to a price or other matter shall be construed in a particular way for the purposes of this Part;

(g) provide that a contravention of any provision of the regulations shall constitute a criminal offence punishable—

    (i) on conviction on indictment, by a fine;

    (ii) on summary conviction, by a fine not exceeding the statutory maximum;

(h) apply any provision of this Act which relates to a criminal offence to an offence created by virtue of paragraph (g) above.

(4) The power to make regulations under this section shall be exercisable by statutory instrument subject to annulment in pursuance of a resolution of either House of Parliament and shall include power—

(a) to make different provision for different cases; and

(b) to make such supplemental, consequential and transitional provision as the Secretary of State considers appropriate.

(5) In this section "lease" includes a sub-lease and an agreement for a lease and a statutory tenancy (within the meaning of the Landlord and Tenant Act 1985 or the Rent (Scotland) Act 1984). **[478]**

NOTES
    Commencement: 1 March 1989.
    Commencement order: SI 1988 No 2076.
    No regulations have yet been made under this section.

Part IV

Enforcement of Parts II and III

27. Enforcement

(1) Subject to the following provisions of this section—

(a) it shall be the duty of every weights and measures authority in Great Britain to enforce within their area the safety provisions and the provisions made by or under Part III of this Act; and

(b) it shall be the duty of every district council in Northern Ireland to enforce within their area the safety provisions.

(2) The Secretary of State may by regulations—

(a) wholly or partly transfer any duty imposed by subsection (1) above on a weights and measures authority or a district council in Northern Ireland to such other person who has agreed to the transfer as is specified in the regulations;

(b) relieve such an authority or council of any such duty so far as it is exercisable in relation to such goods as may be described in the regulations.

(3) The power to make regulations under subsection (2) above shall be

exercisable by statutory instrument subject to annulment in pursuance of a resolution of either House of Parliament and shall include power—

    (a) to make different provision for different cases; and
    (b) to make such supplemental, consequential and transitional provision as the Secretary of State considers appropriate.

(4) Nothing in this section shall authorise any weights and measures authority, or any person on whom functions are conferred by regulations under subsection (2) above, to bring proceedings in Scotland for an offence. **[479]**

NOTES
Commencement: 1 October 1987 (in relation to Part II); 1 March 1989 (otherwise).
Commencement orders: SI 1987 No 1680, 1988 No 2076.
No regulations have yet been made under this section.

28. Test purchases

(1) An enforcement authority shall have power, for the purpose of ascertaining whether any safety provision or any provision made by or under Part III of this Act has been contravened in relation to any goods, services, accommodation or facilities—

    (a) to make, or to authorise an officer of the authority to make, any purchase of any goods; or
    (b) to secure, or to authorise an officer of the authority to secure, the provision of any services, accommodation or facilities.

(2) Where—

    (a) any goods purchased under this section by or on behalf of an enforcement authority are submitted to a test; and
    (b) the test leads to—
        (i) the bringing of proceedings for an offence in respect of a contravention in relation to the goods of any safety provision or of any provision made by or under Part III of this Act or for the forfeiture of the goods under section 16 or 17 above; or
        (ii) the serving of a suspension notice in respect of any goods; and
    (c) the authority is requested to do so and it is practicable for the authority to comply with the request,

the authority shall allow the person from whom the goods were purchased or any person who is a party to the proceedings or has an interest in any goods to which the notice relates to have the goods tested.

(3) The Secretary of State may by regulations provide that any test of goods purchased under this section by or on behalf of an enforcement authority shall—

    (a) be carried out at the expense of the authority in a manner and by a person prescribed by or determined under the regulations; or
    (b) be carried out either as mentioned in paragraph (a) above or by the authority in a manner prescribed by the regulations.

(4) The power to make regulations under subsection (3) above shall be exercisable by statutory instrument subject to annulment in pursuance of a resolution of either House of Parliament and shall include power—

    (a) to make different provision for different cases; and

(b) to make such supplemental, consequential and transitional provision as the Secretary of State considers appropriate.

(5) Nothing in this section shall authorise the acquisition by or on behalf of an enforcement authority of any interest in land. **[480]**

NOTES
Commencement: see note to s 27.
Commencement orders: SI 1987 No 1680, SI 1988 No 2076.
No regulations have yet been made under this section.

29. Powers of search etc

(1) Subject to the following provisions of this Part, a duly authorised officer of an enforcement authority may at any reasonable hour and on production, if required, of his credentials exercise any of the powers conferred by the following provisions of this section.

(2) The officer may, for the purpose of ascertaining whether there has been any contravention of any safety provision or of any provision made by or under Part III of this Act, inspect any goods and enter any premises other than premises occupied only as a person's residence.

(3) The officer may, for the purpose of ascertaining whether there has been any contravention of any safety provision, examine any procedure (including any arrangements for carrying out a test) connected with the production of any goods.

(4) If the officer has reasonable grounds for suspecting that any goods are manufactured or imported goods which have not been supplied in the United Kingdom since they were manufactured or imported he may—
- (a) for the purpose of ascertaining whether there has been any contravention of any safety provision in relation to the goods, require any person carrying on a business, or employed in connection with a business, to produce any records relating to the business;
- (b) for the purpose of ascertaining (by testing or otherwise) whether there has been any such contravention, seize and detain the goods;
- (c) take copies of, or of any entry in, any records produced by virtue of paragraph (a) above.

(5) If the officer has reasonable grounds for suspecting that there has been a contravention in relation to any goods of any safety provision or of any provision made by or under Part III of this Act, he may—
- (a) for the purpose of ascertaining whether there has been any such contravention, require any person carrying on a business, or employed in connection with a business, to produce any records relating to the business;
- (b) for the purpose of ascertaining (by testing or otherwise) whether there has been any such contravention, seize and detain the goods;
- (c) take copies of, or of any entry in, any records produced by virtue of paragraph (a) above.

(6) The officer may seize and detain—
- (a) any goods or records which he has reasonable grounds for believing may be required as evidence in proceedings for an offence in respect of a contravention of any safety provision or of any provision made by or under Part III of this Act;

(b) any goods which he has reasonable grounds for suspecting may be liable to be forfeited under section 16 or 17 above.

(7) If and to the extent that it is reasonably necessary to do so to prevent a contravention of any safety provision or of any provision made by or under Part III of this Act, the officer may, for the purpose of exercising his power under subsection (4), (5) or (6) above to seize any goods or records—

    (a) require any person having authority to do so to open any container or to open any vending machine; and

    (b) himself open or break open any such container or machine where a requirement made under paragraph (a) above in relation to the container or machine has not been complied with. **[481]**

NOTES
Commencement: see note to s 27.
Commencement orders: SI 1987 No 1680, 1988 No 2076.

30. Provisions supplemental to s 29

(1) An officer seizing any goods or records under section 29 above shall inform the following persons that the goods or records have been so seized, that is to say—

    (a) the person from whom they are seized; and

    (b) in the case of imported goods seized on any premises under the control of the Commissioners of Customs and Excise, the importer of those goods (within the meaning of the Customs and Excise Management Act 1979).

(2) If a justice of the peace—

    (a) is satisfied by any written information on oath that there are reasonable grounds for believing either—

        (i) that any goods or records which any officer has power to inspect under section 29 above are on any premises and that their inspection is likely to disclose evidence that there has been a contravention of any safety provision or of any provision made by or under Part III of this Act; or

        (ii) that such a contravention has taken place, is taking place or is about to take place on any premises; and

    (b) is also satisfied by any such information either—

        (i) that admission to the premises has been or is likely to be refused and that notice of intention to apply for a warrant under this subsection has been given to the occupier; or

        (ii) that an application for admission, or the giving of such a notice, would defeat the object of the entry or that the premises are unoccupied or that the occupier is temporarily absent and it might defeat the object of the entry to await his return,

the justice may by warrant under his hand, which shall continue in force for a period of one month, authorise any officer of an enforcement authority to enter the premises, if need be by force.

(3) An officer entering any premises by virtue of section 29 above or a warrant under subsection (2) above may take with him such other persons and such equipment as may appear to him necessary.

(4) On leaving any premises which a person is authorised to enter by a

warrant under subsection (2) above, that person shall, if the premises are unoccupied or the occupier is temporarily absent, leave the premises as effectively secured against trespassers as he found them.

(5) If any person who is not an officer of an enforcement authority purports to act as such under section 29 above or this section he shall be guilty of an offence and liable on summary conviction to a fine not exceeding level 5 on the standard scale.

(6) Where any goods seized by an officer under section 29 above are submitted to a test, the officer shall inform the persons mentioned in subsection (1) above of the result of the test and, if—

    (a) proceedings are brought for an offence in respect of a contravention in relation to the goods of any safety provision or of any provision made by or under Part III of this Act or for the forfeiture of the goods under section 16 or 17 above, or a suspension notice is served in respect of any goods; and

    (b) the officer is requested to do so and it is practicable to comply with the request,

the officer shall allow any person who is a party to the proceedings or, as the case may be, has an interest in the goods to which the notice relates to have the goods tested.

(7) The Secretary of State may by regulations provide that any test of goods seized under section 29 above by an officer of an enforcement authority shall—

    (a) be carried out at the expense of the authority in a manner and by a person prescribed by or determined under the regulations; or

    (b) be carried out either as mentioned in paragraph (a) above or by the authority in a manner prescribed by the regulations.

(8) The power to make regulations under subsection (7) above shall be exercisable by statutory instrument subject to annulment in pursuance of a resolution of either House of Parliament and shall include power—

    (a) to make different provision for different cases; and

    (b) to make such supplemental, consequential and transitional provision as the Secretary of State considers appropriate.

(9) In the application of this section to Scotland; the reference in subsection (2) above to a justice of the peace shall include a reference to a sheriff and the references to written information on oath shall be construed as references to evidence on oath.

(10) In the application of this section to Northern Ireland, the references in subsection (2) above to any information on oath shall be construed as references to any complaint on oath.

NOTES
    Commencement: see note to s 27.
    Commencement orders: SI 1987 No 1680, 1988 No 2076.
    No regulations have yet been made under this section.

31. Power of customs officer to detain goods

(1) A customs officer may, for the purpose of facilitating the exercise by an enforcement authority or officer of such an authority of any functions conferred on the authority or officer by or under Part II of this Act, or by or under this

Part in its application for the purposes of the safety provisions, seize any imported goods and detain them for not more than two working days.

(2) Anything seized and detained under this section shall be dealt with during the period of its detention in such manner as the Commissioners of Customs and Excise may direct.

(3) In subsection (1) above the reference to two working days is a reference to a period of forty-eight hours calculated from the time when the goods in question are seized but disregarding so much of any period as falls on a Saturday or Sunday or on Christmas Day, Good Friday or a day which is a bank holiday under the Banking and Financial Dealings Act 1971 in the part of the United Kingdom where the goods are seized.

(4) In this section and section 32 below "customs officer" means any officer within the meaning of the Customs and Excise Management Act 1979. [483]

NOTES
Commencement: see note to s 27.
Commencement orders: SI 1987 No 1680, 1988 No 2076.

32. Obstruction of authorised officer

(1) Any person who—
    (*a*) intentionally obstructs any officer of an enforcement authority who is acting in pursuance of any provision of this Part or any customs officer who is so acting; or
    (*b*) intentionally fails to comply with any requirement made of him by any officer of an enforcement authority under any provision of this Part; or
    (*c*) without reasonable cause fails to give any officer of an enforcement authority who is so acting any other assistance or information which the officer may reasonably require of him for the purposes of the exercise of the officer's functions under any provision of this Part,

shall be guilty of an offence and liable on summary conviction to a fine not exceeding level 5 on the standard scale.

(2) A person shall be guilty of an offence if, in giving any information which is required of him by virtue of subsection (1)(*c*) above—
    (*a*) he makes any statement which he knows is false in a material particular; or
    (*b*) he recklessly makes a statement which is false in a material particular.

(3) A person guilty of an offence under subsection (2) above shall be liable—
    (*a*) on conviction on indictment, to a fine;
    (*b*) on summary conviction, to a fine not exceeding the statutory maximum. [484]

NOTES
Commencement: see note to s 27.
Commencement orders: SI 1987 No 1680, 1988 No 2076.

33. Appeals against detention of goods

(1) Any person having an interest in any goods which are for the time being detained under any provision of this Part by an enforcement authority or by an officer of such an authority may apply for an order requiring the goods to be released to him or to another person.

(2) An application under this section may be made—

    (a) to any magistrates' court in which proceedings have been brought in England and Wales or Northern Ireland—

        (i) for an offence in respect of a contravention in relation to the goods of any safety provision or of any provision made by or under Part III of this Act; or

        (ii) for the forfeiture of the goods under section 16 above;

    (b) where no such proceedings have been so brought, by way of complaint to a magistrates' court; or

    (c) in Scotland, by summary application to the sheriff.

(3) On an application under this section to a magistrates' court or to the sheriff, an order requiring goods to be released shall be made only if the court or sheriff is satisfied—

    (a) that proceedings—

        (i) for an offence in respect of a contravention in relation to the goods of any safety provision or of any provision made by or under Part III of this Act; or

        (ii) for the forfeiture of the goods under section 16 or 17 above,

have not been brought or, having been brought, have been concluded without the goods being forfeited; and

    (b) where no such proceedings have been brought, that more than six months have elapsed since the goods were seized.

(4) Any person aggrieved by an order made under this section by a magistrates' court in England and Wales or Northern Ireland, or by a decision of such a court not to make such an order, may appeal against that order or decision—

    (a) in England and Wales, to the Crown Court;

    (b) in Northern Ireland, to the county court;

and an order so made may contain such provision as appears to the court to be appropriate for delaying the coming into force of the order pending the making and determination of any appeal (including any application under section 111 of the Magistrates' Courts Act 1980 or Article 146 of the Magistrates' Courts (Northern Ireland) Order 1981 (statement of case)). **[485]**

NOTES

Commencement: see note to s 27.

Commencement orders SI 1987 No 1680, 1988 No 2076.

34. Compensation for seizure and detention

(1) Where an officer of an enforcement authority exercises any power under section 29 above to seize and detain goods, the enforcement authority shall be liable to pay compensation to any person having an interest in the goods in respect of any loss or damage caused by reason of the exercise of the power if—

    (a) there has been no contravention in relation to the goods of any safety provision or of any provision made by or under Part III of this Act; and

    (b) the exercise of the power is not attributable to any neglect or default by that person.

(2) Any disputed question as to the right to or the amount of any

compensation payable under this section shall be determined by arbitration or, in Scotland, by a single arbiter appointed, failing agreement between the parties, by the sheriff. **[486]**

NOTES
Commencement: see note to s 27.
Commencement orders: SI 1987 No 1680, 1988 No 2076.

35. Recovery of expenses of enforcement

(1) This section shall apply where a court—
- (*a*) convicts a person of an offence in respect of a contravention in relation to any goods of any safety provision or of any provision made by or under Part III of this Act; or
- (*b*) makes an order under section 16 or 17 above for the forfeiture of any goods.

(2) The court may (in addition to any other order it may make as to costs or expenses) order the person convicted or, as the case may be, any person having an interest in the goods to reimburse an enforcement authority for any expenditure which has been or may be incurred by that authority—
- (*a*) in connection with any seizure or detention of the goods by or on behalf of the authority; or
- (*b*) in connection with any compliance by the authority with directions given by the court for the purposes of any order for the forfeiture of the goods. **[487]**

NOTES
Commencement: see note to s 27.
Commencement orders: SI 1987 No 1680, 1988 No 2076.

Part V

Miscellaneous and Supplemental

36. Amendments of Part I of the Health and Safety at Work etc Act 1974

Part I of the Health and Safety at Work etc Act 1974 (which includes provision with respect to the safety of certain articles and substances) shall have effect with the amendments specified in Schedule 3 to this Act; and, accordingly, the general purposes of that Part of that Act shall include the purpose of protecting persons from the risks protection from which would not be afforded by virtue of that Part but for those amendments. **[488]**

NOTES
Commencement: 1 March 1988.
Commencement orders: SI 1987 No 1680.

37. Power of Commissioners of Customs and Excise to disclose information

(1) If they think it appropriate to do so for the purpose of facilitating the exercise by any person to whom subsection (2) below applies of any functions conferred on that person by or under Part II of this Act, or by or under Part IV of this Act in its application for the purposes of the safety provisions, the Commissioners of Customs and Excise may authorise the disclosure to that person of any information obtained for the purposes of the exercise by the Commissioners of their functions in relation to imported goods.

(2) This subsection applies to an enforcement authority and to any officer of an enforcement authority.

(3) A disclosure of information made to any person under subsection (1) above shall be made in such manner as may be directed by the Commissioners of Customs and Excise and may be made through such persons acting on behalf of that person as may be so directed.

(4) Information may be disclosed to a person under subsection (1) above whether or not the disclosure of the information has been requested by or on behalf of that person. **[489]**

NOTES
Commencement: 1 October 1987 (in relation to Part II); 1 March 1989 (otherwise).
Commencement orders: SI 1987 No 1680, 1988 No 2076.

38. Restrictions on disclosure of information

(1) Subject to the following provisions of this section, a person shall be guilty of an offence if he discloses any information—

- (a) which was obtained by him in consequence of its being given to any person in compliance with any requirement imposed by safety regulations or regulations under section 26 above;
- (b) which consists in a secret manufacturing process or a trade secret and was obtained by him in consequence of the inclusion of the information—
   - (i) in written or oral representations made for the purposes of Part I or II of Schedule 2 to this Act; or
   - (ii) in a statement of a witness in connection with any such oral representations;
- (c) which was obtained by him in consequence of the exercise by the Secretary of State of the power conferred by section 18 above;
- (d) which was obtained by him in consequence of the exercise by any person of any power conferred by Part IV of this Act; or
- (e) which was disclosed to or through him under section 37 above.

(2) Subsection (1) above shall not apply to a disclosure of information if the information is publicised information or the disclosure is made—

- (a) for the purpose of facilitating the exercise of a relevant person's functions under this Act or any enactment or subordinate legislation mentioned in subsection (3) below;
- (b) for the purposes of compliance with a Community obligation; or
- (c) in connection with the investigation of any criminal offence or for the purposes of any civil or criminal proceedings.

(3) The enactments and subordinate legislation referred to in subsection (2)(a) above are—

- (a) the Trade Descriptions Act 1968;
- (b) Parts II and III and section 125 of the Fair Trading Act 1973;
- (c) the relevant statutory provisions within the meaning of Part I of the Health and Safety at Work etc Act 1974 or within the meaning of the Health and Safety at Work (Northern Ireland) Order 1978;
- (d) the Consumer Credit Act 1974;
- (e) the Restrictive Trade Practices Act 1976;
- (f) the Resale Prices Act 1976;
- (g) the Estate Agents Act 1979;

(h) the Competition Act 1980;
(i) the Telecommunications Act 1984;
(j) the Airports Act 1986;
(k) the Gas Act 1986;
(l) any subordinate legislation made (whether before or after the passing of this Act) for the purpose of securing compliance with the Directive of the Council of the European Communities, dated 10 September 1984 (No 84/450/EEC) on the approximation of the laws, regulations and administrative provisions of the member States concerning misleading advertising.

(4) In subsection (2)(a) above the reference to a person's functions shall include a reference to any function of making, amending or revoking any regulations or order.

(5) A person guilty of an offence under this section shall be liable—

(a) on summary conviction, to a fine not exceeding the statutory maximum;
(b) on conviction on indictment, to imprisonment for a term not exceeding two years or to a fine or to both.

(6) In this section—

"publicised information" means any information which has been disclosed in any civil or criminal proceedings or is or has been required to be contained in a warning published in pursuance of a notice to warn; and

"relevant person" means any of the following, that is to say—

(a) a Minister of the Crown, Government department or Northern Ireland department;
(b) the Monopolies and Mergers Commission, the Director General of Fair Trading, the Director General of Telecommunications or the Director General of Gas Supply;
(c) the Civil Aviation Authority;
(d) any weights and measures authority, any district council in Northern Ireland or any person on whom functions are conferred by regulations under section 27(2) above;
(e) any person who is an enforcing authority for the purposes of Part I of the Health and Safety at Work etc Act 1974 or for the purposes of Part II of the Health and Safety at Work (Northern Ireland) Order 1978. **[490]**

NOTES
Commencement: see note to s 37.
Commencement orders: SI 1987 No 1680, SI 1988 No 2076.

39. Defence of due diligence

(1) Subject to the following provisions of this section, in proceedings against any person for an offence to which this section applies it shall be a defence for that person to show that he took all reasonable steps and exercised all due diligence to avoid committing the offence.

(2) Where in any proceedings against any person for such an offence the defence provided by subsection (1) above involves an allegation that the commission of the offence was due—

(a) to the act or default of another; or

(b) to reliance on information given by another,

that person shall not, without the leave of the court, be entitled to rely on the defence unless, not less than seven clear days before the hearing of the proceedings, he has served a notice under subsection (3) below on the person bringing the proceedings.

(3) A notice under this subsection shall give such information identifying or assisting in the identification of the person who committed the act or default or gave the information as is in the possession of the person serving the notice at the time he serves it.

(4) It is hereby declared that a person shall not be entitled to rely on the defence provided by subsection (1) above by reason of his reliance on information supplied by another, unless he shows that it was reasonable in all the circumstances for him to have relied on the information, having regard in particular—

(a) to the steps which he took, and those which might reasonably have been taken, for the purpose of verifying the information; and
(b) to whether he had any reason to disbelieve the information.

(5) This section shall apply to an offence under section 10, 12(1), (2) or (3), 13(4), 14(6) or 20(1) above.

NOTES
Commencement: see note to s 37.
Commencement orders: SI 1987 No 1680, 1988 No 2076.

40. Liability of persons other than principal offender

(1) Where the commission by any person of an offence to which section 39 above applies is due to an act or default committed by some other person in the course of any business of his, the other person shall be guilty of the offence and may be proceeded against and punished by virtue of this subsection whether or not proceedings are taken against the first-mentioned person.

(2) Where a body corporate is guilty of an offence under this Act (including where it is so guilty by virtue of subsection (1) above) in respect of any act or default which is shown to have been committed with the consent or connivance of, or to be attributable to any neglect on the part of, any director, manager, secretary or other similar officer of the body corporate or any person who was purporting to act in any such capacity he, as well as the body corporate, shall be guilty of that offence and shall be liable to be proceeded against and punished accordingly.

(3) Where the affairs of a body corporate are managed by its members, subsection (2) above shall apply in relation to the acts and defaults of a member in connection with his functions of management as if he were a director of the body corporate.

NOTES
Commencement: see note to s 37.
Commencement orders: SI 1987 No 1680, 1988 No 2076.

41. Civil proceedings

(1) An obligation imposed by safety regulations shall be a duty owed to any person who may be affected by a contravention of the obligation and, subject to any provision to the contrary in the regulations and to the defences and other

incidents applying to actions for breach of statutory duty, a contravention of any such obligation shall be actionable accordingly.

(2) This Act shall not be construed as conferring any other right of action in civil proceedings, apart from the right conferred by virtue of Part I of this Act, in respect of any loss or damage suffered in consequence of a contravention of a safety provision or of a provision made by or under Part III of this Act.

(3) Subject to any provision to the contrary in the agreement itself, an agreement shall not be void or unenforceable by reason only of a contravention of a safety provision or of a provision made by or under Part III of this Act.

(4) Liability by virtue of subsection (1) above shall not be limited or excluded by any contract term, by any notice or (subject to the power contained in subsection (1) above to limit or exclude it in safety regulations) by any other provision.

(5) Nothing in subsection (1) above shall prejudice the operation of section 12 of the Nuclear Installations Act 1965 (rights to compensation for certain breaches of duties confined to rights under that Act).

(6) In this section "damage" includes personal injury and death. [493]

NOTES
Commencement: 1 October 1987 (in relation to Part II); 1 March 1989 (otherwise) (sub-ss (1), (3)–(5); 1 March 1988 (otherwise) (sub-ss (2) and (6)).
Commencement orders: SI 1987 No 1680, 1988 No 2076.

42. Reports etc

(1) It shall be the duty of the Secretary of State at least once in every five years to lay before each House of Parliament a report on the exercise during the period to which the report relates of the functions which under Part II of this Act, or under Part IV of this Act in its application for the purposes of the safety provisions, are exercisable by the Secretary of State, weights and measures authorities, district councils in Northern Ireland and persons on whom functions are conferred by regulations made under section 27(2) above.

(2) The Secretary of State may from time to time prepare and lay before each House of Parliament such other reports on the exercise of those functions as he considers appropriate.

(3) Every weights and measures authority, every district council in Northern Ireland and every person on whom functions are conferred by regulations under subsection (2) of section 27 above shall, whenever the Secretary of State so directs, make a report to the Secretary of State on the exercise of the functions exercisable by that authority or council under that section or by that person by virtue of any such regulations.

(4) A report under subsection (3) above shall be in such form and shall contain such particulars as are specified in the direction of the Secretary of State.

(5) The first report under subsection (1) above shall be laid before each House of Parliament not more than five years after the laying of the last report under section 8(2) of the Consumer Safety Act 1978. [494]

NOTES
Commencement: see note to s 37.
Commencement orders: SI 1987 No 1680, 1988 No 2076.

43. Financial provisions

(1) There shall be paid out of money provided by Parliament—

  (a) any expenses incurred or compensation payable by a Minister of the Crown or Government department in consequence of any provision of this Act; and

  (b) any increase attributable to this Act in the sums payable out of money so provided under any other Act.

(2) Any sums received by a Minister of the Crown or Government department by virtue of this Act shall be paid into the Consolidated Fund. [495]

NOTES
Commencement: see note to s 37.
Commencement orders: SI 1987 No 1680, 1988 No 2076.

44. Service of documents etc

(1) Any document required or authorised by virtue of this Act to be served on a person may be so served—

  (a) by delivering it to him or by leaving it at his proper address or by sending it by post to him at that address; or

  (b) if the person is a body corporate, by serving it in accordance with paragraph (a) above on the secretary or clerk of that body; or

  (c) if the person is a partnership, by serving it in accordance with that paragraph on a partner or on a person having control or management of the partnership business.

(2) For the purposes of subsection (1) above, and for the purposes of section 7 of the Interpretation Act 1978 (which relates to the service of documents by post) in its application to that subsection, the proper address of any person on whom a document is to be served by virtue of this Act shall be his last known address except that—

  (a) in the case of service on a body corporate or its secretary or clerk, it shall be the address of the registered or principal office of the body corporate;

  (b) in the case of service on a partnership or a partner or a person having the control or management of a partnership business, it shall be the principal office of the partnership;

and for the purposes of this subsection the principal office of a company registered outside the United Kingdom or of a partnership carrying on business outside the United Kingdom is its principal office within the United Kingdom.

(3) The Secretary of State may by regulations make provision for the manner in which any information is to be given to any person under any provision of Part IV of this Act.

(4) Without prejudice to the generality of subsection (3) above regulations made by the Secretary of State may prescribe the person, or manner of determining the person, who is to be treated for the purposes of section 28(2) or 30 above as the person from whom any goods were purchased or seized where the goods were purchased or seized from a vending machine.

(5) The power to make regulations under subsection (3) or (4) above shall be exercisable by statutory instrument subject to annulment in pursuance of a resolution of either House of Parliament and shall include power—

  (a) to make different provision for different cases; and

(b) to make such supplemental, consequential and transitional provision as the Secretary of State considers appropriate. [496]

NOTES
Commencement: see note to s 37.
Commencement orders: SI 1987 No 1680, 1988 No 2076.
No regulations have yet been made under this section.

45. Interpretation

(1) In this Act, except in so far as the context otherwise requires—

"aircraft" includes gliders, balloons and hovercraft;

"business" includes a trade or profession and the activities of a professional or trade association or of a local authority or other public authority;

"conditional sale agreement", "credit-sale agreement" and "hire-purchase agreement" have the same meanings as in the Consumer Credit Act 1974 but as if in the definitions in that Act "goods" had the same meaning as in this Act;

"contravention" includes a failure to comply and cognate expressions shall be construed accordingly;

"enforcement authority" means the Secretary of State, any other Minister of the Crown in charge of a Government department, any such department and any authority, council or other person on whom functions under this Act are conferred by or under section 27 above;

"gas" has the same meaning as in Part I of the Gas Act 1986;

"goods" includes substances, growing crops and things comprised in land by virtue of being attached to it and any ship, aircraft or vehicle;

"information" includes accounts, estimates and returns;

"magistrates' court", in relation to Northern Ireland, means a court of summary jurisdiction;

"mark" and "trade mark" have the same meanings as in the Trade Marks Act 1938;

"modifications" includes additions, alterations and omissions, and cognate expressions shall be construed accordingly;

"motor vehicle" has the same meaning as in [the Road Traffic Act 1988];

"notice" means a notice in writing;

"notice to warn" means a notice under section 13(1)(b) above;

"officer", in relation to an enforcement authority, means a person authorised in writing to assist the authority in carrying out its functions under or for the purposes of the enforcement of any of the safety provisions or of any of the provisions made by or under Part III of this Act;

"personal injury" includes any disease and any other impairment of a person's physical or mental condition;

"premises" includes any place and any ship, aircraft or vehicle;

"prohibition notice" means a notice under section 13(1)(a) above;

"records" includes any books or documents and any records in non-documentary form;

"safety provision" means the general safety requirement in section 10 above or any provision of safety regulations, a prohibition notice or a suspension notice;

"safety regulations" means regulations under section 11 above;

"ship" includes any boat and any other description of vessel used in navigation;

"subordinate legislation" has the same meaning as in the Interpretation Act 1978;

"substance" means any natural or artificial substance, whether in solid, liquid or gaseous form or in the form of a vapour, and includes substances that are comprised in or mixed with other goods;
"supply" and cognate expressions shall be construed in accordance with section 46 below;
"suspension notice" means a notice under section 14 above.

(2) Except in so far as the context otherwise requires, references in this Act to a contravention of a safety provision shall, in relation to any goods, include references to anything which would constitute such a contravention if the goods were supplied to any person.

(3) References in this Act to any goods in relation to which any safety provision has been or may have been contravened shall include references to any goods which it is not reasonably practicable to separate from any such goods.

(4) Section 68(2) of the Trade Marks Act 1938 (construction of references to use of a mark) shall apply for the purposes of this Act as it applies for the purposes of that Act.

(5) . . .

[497]

NOTES
Commencement: 1 October 1987 (in relation to Part II); 1 March 1988 (in relation to Part I); 1 March 1989 (otherwise).
Commencement orders: SI 1987 No 1680, 1988 No 2076.
Sub-s (1): in definition "motor vehicle", words in square brackets substituted by the Road Traffic (Consequential Provisions) Act 1988, s 4, Sch 3, para 35.
Sub-s (5), which applies to Scotland only, is omitted.

46. Meaning of "supply"

(1) Subject to the following provisions of this section, references in this Act to supplying goods shall be construed as references to doing any of the following, whether as principal or agent, that is to say—

- (a) selling, hiring out or lending the goods;
- (b) entering into a hire-purchase agreement to furnish the goods;
- (c) the performance of any contract for work and materials to furnish the goods;
- (d) providing the goods in exchange for any consideration (including trading stamps) other than money;
- (e) providing the goods in or in connection with the performance of any statutory function; or
- (f) giving the goods as a prize or otherwise making a gift of the goods;

and, in relation to gas or water, those references shall be construed as including references to providing the service by which the gas or water is made available for use.

(2) For the purposes of any reference in this Act to supplying goods, where a person ("the ostensible supplier") supplies goods to another person ("the customer") under a hire-purchase agreement, conditional sale agreement or credit-sale agreement or under an agreement for the hiring of goods (other than a hire-purchase agreement) and the ostensible supplier—

- (a) carries on the business of financing the provision of goods for others by means of such agreements; and

(b) in the course of that business acquired his interest in the goods supplied to the customer as a means of financing the provision of them for the customer by a further person ("the effective supplier"),

the effective supplier and not the ostensible supplier shall be treated as supplying the goods to the customer.

(3) Subject to subsection (4) below, the performance of any contract by the erection of any building or structure on any land or by the carrying out of any other building works shall be treated for the purposes of this Act as a supply of goods in so far as, but only in so far as, it involves the provision of any goods to any person by means of their incorporation into the building, structure or works.

(4) Except for the purposes of, and in relation to, notices to warn or any provision made by or under Part III of this Act, references in this Act to supplying goods shall not include references to supplying goods comprised in land where the supply is effected by the creation or disposal of an interest in the land.

(5) Except in Part I of this Act references in this Act to a person's supplying goods shall be confined to references to that person's supplying goods in the course of a business of his, but for the purposes of this subsection it shall be immaterial whether the business is a business of dealing in the goods.

(6) For the purposes of subsection (5) above goods shall not be treated as supplied in the course of a business if they are supplied, in pursuance of an obligation arising under or in connection with the insurance of the goods, to the person with whom they were insured.

(7) Except for the purposes of, and in relation to, prohibition notices or suspension notices, references in Parts II to IV of this Act to supplying goods shall not include—

(a) references to supplying goods where the person supplied carries on a business of buying goods of the same description as those goods and repairing or reconditioning them;
(b) references to supplying goods by a sale of articles as scrap (that is to say, for the value of materials included in the articles rather than for the value of the articles themselves).

(8) Where any goods have at any time been supplied by being hired out or lent to any person, neither a continuation or renewal of the hire or loan (whether on the same or different terms) nor any transaction for the transfer after that time of any interest in the goods to the person to whom they were hired or lent shall be treated for the purposes of this Act as a further supply of the goods to that person.

(9) A ship, aircraft or motor vehicle shall not be treated for the purposes of this Act as supplied to any person by reason only that services consisting in the carriage of goods or passengers in that ship, aircraft or vehicle, or in its use for any other purpose, are provided to that person in pursuance of an agreement relating to the use of the ship, aircraft or vehicle for a particular period or for particular voyages, flights or journeys. [498]

NOTES
Commencement: see note to s 45.
Commencement orders: SI 1987 No 1680, 1988 No 2076.

47. Savings for certain privileges

(1) Nothing in this Act shall be taken as requiring any person to produce any records if he would be entitled to refuse to produce those records in any proceedings in any court on the grounds that they are the subject of legal professional privilege or, in Scotland, that they contain a confidential communication made by or to an advocate or solicitor in that capacity, or as authorising any person to take possession of any records which are in the possession of a person who would be so entitled.

(2) Nothing in this Act shall be construed as requiring a person to answer any question or give any information if to do so would incriminate that person or that person's spouse. [499]

NOTES
Commencement: see note to s 37.
Commencement orders: SI 1987 No 1680, 1988 No 2076.

48. Minor and consequential amendments and repeals

(1) The enactments mentioned in Schedule 4 to this Act shall have effect subject to the amendments specified in that Schedule (being minor amendments and amendments consequential on the provisions of this Act).

(2) The following Acts shall cease to have effect, that is to say—
   (a) the Trade Descriptions Act 1972; and
   (b) the Fabrics (Misdescription) Act 1913.

(3) The enactments mentioned in Schedule 5 to this Act are hereby repealed to the extent specified in the third column of that Schedule. [500]

NOTES
Commencement: sub-ss (1) and (3): 1 October 1987 (certain purposes), 1 March 1989 (remaining purposes). Sub-s (2)(a): 31 December 1988; sub-s (2)(b): 1 October 1987.
Commencement orders: SI 1987 No 1680, 1988 No 2041, 1988 No 2076.

49. Northern Ireland

(1) This Act shall extend to Northern Ireland with the exception of—
   (a) the provisions of Parts I and III;
   (b) any provision amending or repealing an enactment which does not so extend; and
   (c) any other provision so far as it has effect for the purposes of, or in relation to, a provision falling within paragraph (a) or (b) above.

(2) Subject to any Order in Council made by virtue of subsection (1)(a) of section 3 of the Northern Ireland Constitution Act 1973, consumer safety shall not be a transferred matter for the purposes of that Act but shall for the purposes of subsection (2) of that section be treated as specified in Schedule 3 to that Act.

(3) An Order in Council under paragraph 1(1)(b) of Schedule 1 to the Northern Ireland Act 1974 (exercise of legislative functions for Northern Ireland) which states that it is made only for purposes corresponding to any of the provisions of this Act mentioned in subsection (1)(a) to (c) above—
   (a) shall not be subject to paragraph 1(4) and (5) of that Schedule (affirmative resolution procedure and procedure in cases of urgency); but

(b) shall be subject to annulment in pursuance of a resolution of either House of Parliament. **[501]**

NOTES
Commencement: 1 March 1988.
Commencement order: SI 1987 No 1680.

50. Short title, commencement and transitional provision

(1) This Act may be cited as the Consumer Protection Act 1987.

(2) This Act shall come into force on such day as the Secretary of State may by order made by statutory instrument appoint, and different days may be so appointed for different provisions or for different purposes.

(3) The Secretary of State shall not make an order under subsection (2) above bringing into force the repeal of the Trade Descriptions Act 1972, a repeal of any provision of that Act or a repeal of that Act or of any provision of it for any purposes, unless a draft of the order has been laid before, and approved by a resolution of, each House of Parliament.

(4) An order under subsection (2) above bringing a provision into force may contain such transitional provision in connection with the coming into force of that provision as the Secretary of State considers appropriate.

(5) Without prejudice to the generality of the power conferred by subsection (4) above, the Secretary of State may by order provide for any regulations made under the Consumer Protection Act 1961 or the Consumer Protection Act (Northern Ireland) 1965 to have effect as if made under section 11 above and for any such regulations to have effect with such modifications as he considers appropriate for that purpose.

(6) The power of the Secretary of State by order to make such provision as is mentioned in subsection (5) above, shall, in so far as it is not exercised by an order under subsection (2) above, be exercisable by statutory instrument subject to annulment in pursuance of a resolution of either House of Parliament.

(7) Nothing in this Act or in any order under subsection (2) above shall make any person liable by virtue of Part I of this Act for any damage caused wholly or partly by a defect in a product which was supplied to any person by its producer before the coming into force of Part I of this Act.

(8) Expressions used in subsection (7) above and in Part I of this Act have the same meanings in that subsection as in that Part. **[502]**

NOTES
Commencement: 1 October 1987.
Commencement order: SI 1987 No 1680.
Regulations under this section: Consumer Protection Act 1987 (Commencement No 1) Order 1987, SI 1987 No 1680; Consumer Protection Act 1987 (Commencement No 2) Order 1988, SI 1988 No 2041; Consumer Protection Act 1987 (Commencement No 3) Order 1988, SI 1988 No 2076.

SCHEDULES
SCHEDULE 1

Section 6

LIMITATION OF ACTIONS UNDER PART I

PART I
England and Wales

...

NOTES
Commencement: 1 March 1988.
Commencement order: SI 1987 No 1680.
This Part amends the Limitation Act 1980, ss 12, 14, 28, 32, 33 and adds s 11A.

PART II
Scotland

...

NOTES
Commencement: 1 March 1988.
Commencement order: SI 1987 No 1680.
This Part amends the Prescription and Limitation (Scotland) Act 1973, s 7, Sch 2, adds ss 16A, 22A, 22B, 22C, 22D and repeals s 23 with savings.

SCHEDULE 2

Section 13

PROHIBITION NOTICES AND NOTICES TO WARN

PART I
Prohibition Notices

1. A prohibition notice in respect of any goods shall—

   (*a*) state that the Secretary of State considers that the goods are unsafe;
   (*b*) set out the reasons why the Secretary of State considers that the goods are unsafe;
   (*c*) specify the day on which the notice is to come into force; and
   (*d*) state that the trader may at any time make representations in writing to the Secretary of State for the purpose of establishing that the goods are safe.

2.—(1) If representations in writing about a prohibition notice are made by the trader to the Secretary of State, it shall be the duty of the Secretary of State to consider whether to revoke the notice and—

   (*a*) if he decides to revoke it, to do so;
   (*b*) in any other case, to appoint a person to consider those representations, any further representations made (whether in writing or orally) by the trader about the notice and the statements of any witnesses examined under this Part of this Schedule.

(2) Where the Secretary of State has appointed a person to consider representations about a prohibition notice, he shall serve a notification on the trader which—

   (*a*) states that the trader may make oral representations to the appointed person for the purpose of establishing that the goods to which the notice relates are safe; and
   (*b*) specifies the place and time at which the oral representations may be made.

(3) The time specified in a notification served under sub-paragraph (2) above shall not be before the end of the period of twenty-one days beginning with the day on which the notification is served, unless the trader otherwise agrees.

(4) A person on whom a notification has been served under sub-paragraph (2) above or his representative may, at the place and time specified in the notification—

(a) make oral representations to the appointed person for the purpose of establishing that the goods in question are safe; and
(b) call and examine witnesses in connection with the representations.

3.—(1) Where representations in writing about a prohibition notice are made by the trader to the Secretary of State at any time after a person has been appointed to consider representations about that notice, then, whether or not the appointed person has made a report to the Secretary of State, the following provisions of this paragraph shall apply instead of paragraph 2 above.

(2) The Secretary of State shall, before the end of the period of one month beginning with the day on which he receives the representations, serve a notification on the trader which states—

(a) that the Secretary of State has decided to revoke the notice, has decided to vary it or, as the case may be, has decided neither to revoke nor to vary it; or
(b) that, a person having been appointed to consider representations about the notice, the trader may, at a place and time specified in the notification, make oral representations to the appointed person for the purpose of establishing that the goods to which the notice relates are safe.

(3) The time specified in a notification served for the purposes of sub-paragraph (2)(b) above shall not be before the end of the period of twenty-one days beginning with the day on which the notification is served, unless the trader otherwise agrees or the time is the time already specified for the purposes of paragraph 2(2)(b) above.

(4) A person on whom a notification has been served for the purposes of sub-paragraph (2)(b) above or his representative may, at the place and time specified in the notification—

(a) make oral representations to the appointed person for the purpose of establishing that the goods in question are safe; and
(b) call and examine witnesses in connection with the representations.

4.—(1) Where a person is appointed to consider representations about a prohibition notice, it shall be his duty to consider—

(a) any written representations made by the trader about the notice, other than those in respect of which a notification is served under paragraph 3(2)(a) above;
(b) any oral representations made under paragraph 2(4) or 3(4) above; and
(c) any statements made by witnesses in connection with the oral representations,

and, after considering any matters under this paragraph, to make a report (including recommendations) to the Secretary of State about the matters considered by him and the notice.

(2) It shall be the duty of the Secretary of State to consider any report made to him under sub-paragraph (1) above and, after considering the report, to inform the trader of his decision with respect to the prohibition notice to which the report relates.

5.—(1) The Secretary of State may revoke or vary a prohibition notice by serving on the trader a notification stating that the notice is revoked or, as the case may be, is varied as specified in the notification.

(2) The Secretary of State shall not vary a prohibition notice so as to make the effect of the notice more restrictive for the trader.

(3) Without prejudice to the power conferred by section 13(2) of this Act, the service of a notification under sub-paragraph (1) above shall be sufficient to satisfy the requirement of paragraph 4(2) above that the trader shall be informed of the Secretary of State's decision.

NOTES
Commencement: 1 October 1987.
Commencement order: SI 1987 No 1680.

Part II

Notices to warn

6.—(1) If the Secretary of State proposes to serve a notice to warn on any person in respect of any goods, the Secretary of State, before he serves the notice, shall serve on that person a notification which—

(a) contains a draft of the proposed notice;
(b) states that the Secretary of State proposes to serve a notice in the form of the draft on that person;
(c) states that the Secretary of State considers that the goods described in the draft are unsafe;
(d) sets out the reasons why the Secretary of State considers that those goods are unsafe; and
(e) states that that person may make representations to the Secretary of State for the purpose of establishing that the goods are safe if, before the end of the period of fourteen days beginning with the day on which the notification is served, he informs the Secretary of State—
  (i) of his intention to make representations; and
  (ii) whether the representations will be made only in writing or both in writing and orally.

(2) Where the Secretary of State has served a notification containing a draft of a proposed notice to warn on any person, he shall not serve a notice to warn on that person in respect of the goods to which the proposed notice relates unless—

(a) the period of fourteen days beginning with the day on which the notification was served expires without the Secretary of State being informed as mentioned in sub-paragraph (1)(e) above;
(b) the period of twenty-eight days beginning with that day expires without any written representations being made by that person to the Secretary of State about the proposed notice; or
(c) the Secretary of State has considered a report about the proposed notice by a person appointed under paragraph 7(1) below.

7.—(1) Where a person on whom a notification containing a draft of a proposed notice to warn has been served—

(a) informs the Secretary of State as mentioned in paragraph 6(1)(e) above before the end of the period of fourteen days beginning with the day on which the notification was served; and
(b) makes written representations to the Secretary of State about the proposed notice before the end of the period of twenty-eight days beginning with that day,

the Secretary of State shall appoint a person to consider those representations, any further representations made by that person about the draft notice and the statements of any witnesses examined under this Part of this Schedule.

(2) Where—

(a) the Secretary of State has appointed a person to consider representations about a proposed notice to warn; and
(b) the person whose representations are to be considered has informed the Secretary of State for the purposes of paragraph 6(1)(e) above that the representations he intends to make will include oral representations,

the Secretary of State shall inform the person intending to make the representations of the place and time at which oral representations may be made to the appointed person.

(3) Where a person on whom a notification containing a draft of a proposed notice to warn has been served is informed of a time for the purposes of sub-paragraph (2) above, that time shall not be—

  (a) before the end of the period of twenty-eight days beginning with the day on which the notification was served; or
  (b) before the end of the period of seven days beginning with the day on which that person is informed of the time.

(4) A person who has been informed of a place and time for the purposes of sub-paragraph (2) above or his representative may, at that place and time—

  (a) make oral representations to the appointed person for the purpose of establishing that the goods to which the proposed notice relates are safe; and
  (b) call and examine witnesses in connection with the representations.

8.—(1) Where a person is appointed to consider representations about a proposed notice to warn, it shall be his duty to consider—

  (a) any written representations made by the person on whom it is proposed to serve the notice; and
  (b) in a case where a place and time has been appointed under paragraph 7(2) above for oral representations to be made by that person or his representative, any representations so made and any statements made by witnesses in connection with those representations,

and, after considering those matters, to make a report (including recommendations) to the Secretary of State about the matters considered by him and the proposal to serve the notice.

(2) It shall be the duty of the Secretary of State to consider any report made to him under sub-paragraph (1) above and, after considering the report, to inform the person on whom it was proposed that a notice to warn should be served of his decision with respect to the proposal.

(3) If at any time after serving a notification on a person under paragraph 6 above the Secretary of State decides not to serve on that person either the proposed notice to warn or that notice with modifications, the Secretary of State shall inform that person of the decision; and nothing done for the purposes of any of the preceding provisions of this Part of this Schedule before that person was so informed shall—

  (a) entitle the Secretary of State subsequently to serve the proposed notice or that notice with modifications; or
  (b) require the Secretary of State, or any person appointed to consider representations about the proposed notice, subsequently to do anything in respect of, or in consequence of, any such representations.

(4) Where a notification containing a draft of a proposed notice to warn is served on a person in respect of any goods, a notice to warn served on him in consequence of a decision made under sub-paragraph (2) above shall either be in the form of the draft or shall be less onerous than the draft.

9. The Secretary of State may revoke a notice to warn by serving on the person on whom the notice was served a notification stating that the notice is revoked. [506]

NOTES
Commencement: 1 October 1987.
Commencement order: SI 1987 No 1680.

PART III

General

10.—(1) Where in a notification served on any person under this Schedule the Secretary of State has appointed a time for the making of oral representations or the examination of witnesses, he may, by giving that person such notification as the Secretary of State considers appropriate, change that time to a later time or appoint further times at which further representations may be made or the examination of witnesses may be continued; and paragraphs 2(4), 3(4) and 7(4) above shall have effect accordingly.

(2) For the purposes of this Schedule the Secretary of State may appoint a person (instead of the appointed person) to consider any representations or statements, if the person originally appointed, or last appointed under this sub-paragraph, to consider those representations or statements has died or appears to the Secretary of State to be otherwise unable to act.

11. In this Schedule—

"the appointed person" in relation to a prohibition notice or a proposal to serve a notice to warn, means the person for the time being appointed under this Schedule to consider representations about the notice or, as the case may be, about the proposed notice;
"notification" means a notification in writing;
"trader", in relation to a prohibition notice, means the person on whom the notice is or was served. [507–510]

NOTES
Commencement: 1 October 1987.
Commencement order: SI 1987 No 1680.

NOTES
Sch 3 (Amendments to Health and Safety at Work etc Act 1974), Sch 4 (Minor and consequential amendments) and Sch 5 (Repeals) are omitted.

CONSUMER ARBITRATION AGREEMENTS ACT 1988
(c 21)

ARRANGEMENT OF SECTIONS

ENGLAND, WALES AND NORTHERN IRELAND

Section		Para
1	Arbitration agreements	[511]
2	Exclusions	[512]
3	Contracting "as a consumer"	[513]
4	Power of court to disapply section 1 where no detriment to consumer	[514]
5	Orders adding to the causes of action to which section 1 applies	[515–8]

SUPPLEMENTARY

9	Short title, commencement, interpretation and extent	[519]

An Act to extend to consumers certain rights as regards agreements to refer future differences to arbitration and for purposes connected therewith

[28 June 1988]

ENGLAND, WALES AND NORTHERN IRELAND

1. Arbitration agreements

(1) Where a person (referred to in section 4 below as "the consumer") enters into a contract as a consumer, an agreement that future differences arising between parties to the contract are to be referred to arbitration cannot be

enforced against him in respect of any cause of action so arising to which this section applies except—

(a) with his written consent signified after the differences in question have arisen; or
(b) where he has submitted to arbitration in pursuance of the agreement, whether in respect of those or any other differences; or
(c) where the court makes an order under section 4 below in respect of that cause of action.

(2) This section applies to a cause of action—

(a) if proceedings in respect of it would be within the jurisdiction of a county court; or
(b) if it satisfies such other conditions as may be prescribed for the purposes of this paragraph in an order under section 5 below.

(3) Neither section 4(1) of the Arbitration Act 1950 nor section 4 of the Arbitration Act (Northern Ireland) 1937 (which provide for the staying of court proceedings where an arbitration agreement is in force) shall apply to an arbitration agreement to the extent that it cannot be enforced by virtue of this section. [511]

NOTES
Commencement: 28 June 1988.
Appointed day order: this section to have effect in relation to contracts made on or after 1 October 1988, by virtue of the Consumer Arbitration Agreements Act 1988 (Appointed Day No 1) Order 1988, SI 1988 No 1598.

2. Exclusions

Section 1 above does not affect—

(a) the enforcement of an arbitration agreement to which section 1 of the Arbitration Act 1975 applies, that is, an arbitration agreement other than a domestic arbitration agreement within the meaning of that section;
(b) the resolution of differences arising under any contract so far as it is, by virtue of section 1(2) of, and Schedule 1 to, the Unfair Contract Terms Act 1977 ("the Act of 1977"), excluded from the operation of section 2, 3, 4 or 7 of that Act. [512]

NOTES
Commencement: 28 June 1988.
Appointed day order: this section to have effect in relation to contracts made on or after 1 October 1988, by virtue of the Consumer Arbitration Agreements Act 1988 (Appointed Day No 1) Order 1988, SI 1988 No 1598.

3. Contracting "as a consumer"

(1) For the purposes of section 1 above a person enters into a contract "as a consumer" if—

(a) he neither makes the contract in the course of a business nor holds himself out as doing so; and
(b) the other party makes the contract in the course of a business; and
(c) in the case of a contract governed by the law of sale of goods or hire-purchase, or by section 7 of the Act of 1977, the goods passing under or in pursuance of the contract are of a type ordinarily supplied for private use or consumption;

but on a sale by auction or by competitive tender the buyer is not in any circumstances to be regarded as entering into the contract as a consumer.

(2) In subsection (1) above—

"business" includes a profession and the activities of any government department, Northern Ireland department or local or public authority; and

"goods" has the same meaning as in the Sale of Goods Act 1979.

(3) It is for those claiming that a person entered into a contract otherwise than as a consumer to show that he did so. [513]

NOTES
Commencement: 28 June 1988.
Appointed day order: this section to have effect in relation to contracts made on or after 1 October 1988, by virtue of the Consumer Arbitration Agreements Act 1988 (Appointed Day No 1) Order 1988, SI 1988 No 1598.

4. Power of court to disapply section 1 where no detriment to consumer

(1) The High Court or a county court may, on an application made after the differences in question have arisen, order that a cause of action to which this section applies shall be treated as one to which section 1 above does not apply.

(2) Before making an order under this section the court must be satisfied that it is not detrimental to the interests of the consumer for the differences in question to be referred to arbitration in pursuance of the arbitration agreement instead of being determined by proceedings before a court.

(3) In determining for the purposes of subsection (2) above whether a reference to arbitration is or is not detrimental to the interests of the consumer, the court shall have regard to all factors appearing to be relevant, including, in particular, the availability of legal aid and the relative amount of any expense which may result to him—

(a) if the differences in question are referred to arbitration in pursuance of the arbitration agreement; and
(b) if they are determined by proceedings before a court.

(4) This section applies to a cause of action—

(a) if proceedings in respect of it would be within the jurisdiction of a county court and would not fall within the small claims limit; or
(b) if it satisfies the conditions referred to in section 1(2)(b) above and the order under section 5 below prescribing the conditions in question provides for this section to apply to causes of action which satisfy them.

(5) For the purposes of subsection (4)(a) above proceedings "fall within the small claims limit"—

(a) in England and Wales, if in a county court they would stand referred to arbitration (without any order of the court) under rules made by virtue of section 64(1)(a) of the County Courts Act 1984;
(b) in Northern Ireland, if in a county court the action would be dealt with by way of arbitration by a circuit registrar by virtue of Article 30(3) of the County Courts (Northern Ireland) Order 1980.

(6) Where the consumer submits to arbitration in consequence of an order

under this section, he shall not be regarded for the purposes of section 1(1)(*b*) above as submitting to arbitration in pursuance of the agreement there mentioned. **[514]**

NOTES
Commencement: 28 June 1988.
Appointed day order: this section to have effect in relation to contracts made on or after 1 October 1988, by virtue of the Consumer Arbitration Agreements Act 1988 (Appointed Day No 1) Order 1988, SI 1988 No 1598.

5. Orders adding to the causes of action to which section 1 applies

(1) Orders under this section may prescribe the conditions referred to in section 1(2)(*b*) above; and any such order may provide that section 4 above shall apply to a cause of action which satisfies the conditions so prescribed.

(2) Orders under this section may make different provision for different cases and for different purposes.

(3) The power to make orders under this section for England and Wales shall be exercisable by statutory instrument made by the Secretary of State with the concurrence of the Lord Chancellor; but no such order shall be made unless a draft of it has been laid before and approved by resolution of, each House of Parliament.

(4) The power to make orders under this section for Northern Ireland shall be exercisable by the Department of Economic Development for Northern Ireland with the concurrence of the Lord Chancellor; and any such order—
    (*a*) shall be a statutory rule for the purposes of the Statutory Rules (Northern Ireland) Order 1979; and
    (*b*) shall be subject to affirmative resolution, within the meaning of section 41(4) of the Interpretation Act (Northern Ireland) 1954.

[515–518]

NOTES
Commencement: 28 June 1988.
Appointed day order: this section to have effect in relation to contracts made on or after 1 October 1988, by virtue of the Consumer Arbitration Agreements Act 1988 (Appointed Day No 1) Order 1988, SI 1988 No 1598.
No orders have yet been made under this section.

NOTES
Sections 6–8, which apply to Scotland only, are omitted.

Supplementary

9. Short title, commencement, interpretation and extent

(1) This Act may be cited as the Consumer Arbitration Agreements Act 1988.

(2) This Act shall have effect in relation to contracts made on or after such day as the Secretary of State may by order made by statutory instrument appoint; and different days may be so appointed for different provisions and different purposes.

(3) In this Act "the Act of 1977" means the Unfair Contract Terms Act 1977.

(4) Sections 1 to 5 above do not extend to Scotland, sections 6 to 8 extend to Scotland only, and this Act, apart from sections 6 to 8, extends to Northern Ireland.

NOTES
Commencement: 28 June 1988.

CONSUMER TRANSACTIONS (RESTRICTIONS ON STATEMENTS) ORDER 1976
(SI 1976 No 1813)

NOTES
Made: 1 November 1976
Authority: Fair Trading Act 1973, s 22

1. This Order may be cited as the Consumer Transactions (Restrictions on Statements) Order 1976, and shall come into operation as respects—

(a) this Article, Article 2 and Article 3(a), at the expiry of the period of 1 month beginning with the date on which this Order is made;

(b) the remainder of Article 3, at the expiry of the period of 12 months beginning with that date; and

(c) the remainder of this Order, at the expiry of the period of 2 years beginning with that date.

NOTES
Commencement: 1 December 1976.

2. (1) In this Order—

"advertisement" includes a catalogue and a circular;

"consumer" means a person acquiring goods otherwise than in the course of a business but does not include a person who holds himself out as acquiring them in the course of a business;

"consumer transaction" means—

[(a) a consumer sale, that is a sale of goods (other than an excepted sale) by a seller where the goods—

(i) are of a type ordinarily bought for private use or consumption, and

(ii) are sold to a person who does not buy or hold himself out as buying them in the course of a business.

For the purposes of this paragraph an excepted sale is a sale by auction, a sale by competitive tender and a sale arising by virtue of a contract for the international sale of goods as originally defined in section 62(1) of the Sale of Goods Act 1893 as amended by the Supply of Goods (Implied Terms) Act 1973;

(b) a hire-purchase agreement (within the meaning of section 189(1) of the Consumer Credit Act 1974) where the owner makes the agreement in the course of a business and the goods to which the agreement relates—

(i) are of a type ordinarily supplied for private use or consumption, and

(ii) are hired to a person who does not hire or hold himself out as hiring them in the course of a business;]
(c) an agreement for the redemption of trading stamps under a trading stamp scheme within section 10(1) of the Trading Stamps Act 1964 or, as the case may be, within section 9 of the Trading Stamps Act (Northern Ireland) 1965;

"container" includes any form of packaging of goods whether by way of wholly or partly enclosing the goods or by way of attaching the goods to, or winding the goods round, some other article, and in particular includes a wrapper or confining band;

"statutory rights" means the rights arising by virtue of sections 13 to 15 of the Sale of Goods Act 1893 as amended by the Act of 1973, sections 9 to 11 of the Act of 1973, or section 4(1)(c) of the Trading Stamps Act 1964 or section 4(1)(c) of the Trading Stamps Act (Northern Ireland) 1965 both as amended by the Act of 1973.

(2) The Interpretation Act 1889 shall apply for the interpretation of this Order as it applies for the interpretation of an Act of Parliament. [521]

NOTES
Commencement: 1 December 1976.
Amended by SI 1978 No 127.
The Act of 1973: Supply of Goods (Implied Terms) Act 1973.

3. A person shall not, in the course of a business—
   (a) display, at any place where consumer transactions are effected (whether wholly or partly), a notice containing a statement which purports to apply, in relation to consumer transactions effected there, a term which would—
      [(i) be void by virtue of section 6 or 20 of the Unfair Contract Terms Act 1977,] or
      (ii) be inconsistent with a warranty (in Scotland a stipulation) implied by section 4(1)(c) of the Trading Stamps Act 1964 or section 4(1)(c) of the Trading Stamps Act (Northern Ireland) 1965 both as amended by the Act of 1973,
      if applied to some or all such consumer transactions;
   (b) publish or cause to be published any advertisement which is intended to induce persons to enter into consumer transactions and which contains a statement purporting to apply in relation to such consumer transactions such a term as is mentioned in paragraph (a)(i) or (ii), being a term which would be void by virtue of, or as the case may be, inconsistent with, the provisions so mentioned if applied to some or all of those transactions;
   (c) supply to a consumer pursuant to a consumer transaction goods bearing, or goods in a container bearing, a statement which is a term of that consumer transaction and which is void by virtue of, or inconsistent with, the said provisions, or if it were a term of that transaction, would be so void or inconsistent;
   (d) furnish to a consumer in connection with the carrying out of a consumer transaction or to a person likely, as a consumer, to enter into such a transaction, a document which includes a statement which is a term of that transaction and is void or inconsistent as aforesaid, or, if it were a term of that transaction or were to become a term of a prospective transaction, would be so void or inconsistent. [522]

NOTES
Commencement: 1 December 1976 (para (a)), 1 November 1977 (remainder).
Amended by SI 1978 No 127.
The Act of 1973: Supply of Goods (Implied Terms) Act 1973.

4. A person shall not in the course of a business—

(i) supply to a consumer pursuant to a consumer transaction goods bearing, or goods in a container bearing, a statement about the rights that the consumer has against that person or about the obligations to the consumer accepted by that person in relation to the goods (whether legally enforceable or not), being rights or obligations that arise if the goods are defective or are not fit for a purpose or do not correspond with a description;

(ii) furnish to a consumer in connection with the carrying out of a consumer transaction or to a person likely, as a consumer, to enter into such a transaction with him or through his agency a document containing a statement about such rights and obligations,

unless there is in close proximity to any such statement another statement which is clear and conspicuous and to the effect that the first mentioned statement does not or will not affect the statutory rights of a consumer. [523]

NOTES
Commencement: 1 November 1978.

5. (1) This Article applies to goods which are supplied in the course of a business by one person ("the supplier") to another where, at the time of the supply, the goods were intended by the supplier to be, or might reasonably be expected by him to be, the subject of a subsequent consumer transaction.

(2) A supplier shall not—

(a) supply goods to which this Article applies if the goods bear, or are in a container bearing, a statement which sets out or describes or limits obligations (whether legally enforceable or not) accepted or to be accepted by him in relation to the goods; or

(b) furnish a document in relation to the goods which contains such a statement,

unless there is in close proximity to any such statement another statement which is clear and conspicuous and to the effect that the first mentioned statement does not or will not affect the statutory rights of a consumer.

(3) A person does not contravene paragraph (2) above—

(i) in a case to which sub-paragraph (a) of that paragraph applies, unless the goods have become the subject of a consumer transaction;

(ii) in a case to which sub-paragraph (b) applies, unless the document has been furnished to a consumer in relation to goods which were the subject of a consumer transaction, or to a person likely to become a consumer pursuant to such a transaction; or

(iii) by virtue of any statement if before the date on which this Article comes into operation the document containing, or the goods or container bearing, the statement has ceased to be in his possession. [524]

NOTES
Commencement: 1 November 1978.

CONSUMER PROTECTION (CANCELLATION OF CONTRACTS CONCLUDED AWAY FROM BUSINESS PREMISES) REGULATIONS 1987
(SI 1987 No 2117)

NOTES
Made: 7 December 1987
Authority: European Communities Act 1972, s 2(2)

ARRANGEMENT OF REGULATIONS

Regulation	Para
1 Citation and commencement	[525]
2 Interpretation	[526]
3 Contracts to which the Regulations apply	[527]
4 Cancellation of Contract	[528]
5 Recovery of money paid by consumer	[529]
6 Repayment of credit	[530]
7 Return of goods by consumer after cancellation	[531]
8 Goods given in part-exchange	[532]
9 Amendment of the Consumer Credit Act 1974	[533]
10 No contracting-out	[534]
11 Service of documents	[535]

Schedule—
Part I—Information to be Contained in Notice of Cancellation Rights .. [536]
Part II—Cancellation Form to be Included in Notice of Cancellation Rights .. [537]

GENERAL NOTES
These regulations were introduced to implement the EEC Directive (85/577/EEC) to protect the consumer in respect of contracts negotiated away from business premises. The text of the Directive is at paragraph [788] below.

1. Citation and commencement

These Regulations may be cited as the Consumer Protection (Cancellation of Contracts Concluded away from Business Premises) Regulations 1987 and shall come into force on 1 July 1988. **[525]**

NOTES
Commencement: 1 July 1988.

2. Interpretation

(1) In these Regulations—

"business" includes a trade or profession;
"consumer" means a person, other than a body corporate, who, in making a contract to which these Regulations apply, is acting for purposes which can be regarded as outside his business;
"goods" has the meaning given by section 61(1) of the Sale of Goods Act 1979;
"land mortgage" includes any security charged on land and in relation to Scotland includes any heritable security;
"notice of cancellation" has the meaning given by regulation 4(5) below;

"security" in relation to a contract means a mortgage, charge, pledge, bond, debenture, indemnity, guarantee, bill, note or other right provided by the consumer, or at his request (express or implied), to secure the carrying out of his obligations under the contract;
"signed" has the same meaning as in the Consumer Credit Act 1974; and
"trader" means a person who, in making a contract to which these Regulations apply, is acting for the purposes of his business, and anyone acting in the name or on behalf of such a person.

(2) ... [526]

NOTES
Commencement: 1 July 1988.
Para (2): applies to Scotland only.

3. Contracts to which the Regulations apply

(1) These Regulations apply to a contract, other than an excepted contract, for the supply by a trader of goods or services to a consumer which is made—

    (*a*) during an unsolicited visit by a trader—

        (i) to the consumer's home or to the home of another person; or
        (ii) to the consumer's place of work;

    (*b*) during a visit by a trader as mentioned in paragraph (*a*)(i) or (ii) above at the express request of the consumer where the goods or services to which the contract relates are other than those concerning which the consumer requested the visit of the trader, provided that when the visit was requested the consumer did not know, or could not reasonably have known, that the supply of those other goods or services formed part of the trader's business activities;

    (*c*) after an offer was made by the consumer in respect of the supply by a trader of the goods or services in the circumstances mentioned in paragraph (a) or (b) above or (d) below; or

    (*d*) during an excursion organised by the trader away from premises on which he is carrying on any business (whether on a permanent or temporary basis).

(2) For the purposes of this regulation an excepted contract means

    (*a*) any contract—

        (i) for the sale or other disposition of land, or for a lease or land mortgage;
        (ii) to finance the purchase of land;
        (iii) for a bridging loan in connection with the purchase of land; or
        (iv) for the construction or extension of a building or other erection on land:

    Provided that these Regulations shall apply to a contract for the supply of goods and their incorporation in any land or a contract for the repair or improvement of a building or other erection on land, where the contract is not financed by a loan secured by a land mortgage;

    (*b*) any contract for the supply of food, drink or other goods intended for current consumption by use in the household and supplied by regular roundsmen;

    (*c*) any contract for the supply of goods or services which satisfies all the following conditions, namely—

(i) terms of the contract are contained in a trader's catalogue which is readily available to the consumer to read in the absence of the trader or his representative before the conclusion of the contract;
(ii) the parties to the contract intend that there shall be maintained continuity of contact between the trader or his representative and the consumer in relation to the transaction in question or any subsequent transaction; and
(iii) both the catalogue and the contract contain or are accompanied by a prominent notice indicating that the consumer has a right to return to the trader or his representative goods supplied to him within the period of not less than 7 days from the day on which the goods are received by the consumer and otherwise to cancel the contract within that period without the consumer incurring any liability, other than any liability which may arise from the failure of the consumer to take reasonable care of the goods while they are in his possession;

(d) contracts of insurance to which the Insurance Companies Act 1982 applies;
(e) investment agreements within the meaning of the Financial Services Act 1986, and agreements for the making of deposits within the meaning of the Banking Act 1987 in respect of which Regulations have been made for regulating the making of unsolicited calls under section 34 of that Act;
(f) any contract not falling within sub-paragraph (g) below under which the total payments to be made by the consumer do not exceed £35; and
(g) any contract under which credit within the meaning of the Consumer Credit Act 1974 is provided not exceeding £35 other than a hire-purchase or conditional sale agreement.

(3) In this regulation "unsolicited visit" means a visit by a trader, whether or not he is the trader who supplies the goods or services, which does not take place at the express request of the consumer and includes a visit which takes place after a trader telephones the consumer (otherwise than at his express request) indicating expressly or by implication that he is willing to visit the consumer. **[527]**

NOTES
Commencement: 1 July 1988.

4. Cancellation of Contract

(1) No contract to which these Regulations apply shall be enforceable against the consumer unless the trader has delivered to the consumer notice in writing in accordance with paragraphs (3) and (4) below indicating the right of the consumer to cancel the contract within the period of 7 days mentioned in paragraph (5) below containing both the information set out in Part I of the Schedule to these Regulations and a Cancellation Form in the form set out in Part II of the Schedule and completed in accordance with the footnotes.

(2) Paragraph (1) above does not apply to a cancellable agreement within the meaning of the Consumer Credit Act 1974 or to an agreement which may be cancelled by the consumer in accordance with terms of the agreement conferring upon him similar rights as if the agreement were such a cancellable agreement.

(3) The information to be contained in the notice under paragraph (1) above shall be easily legible and if incorporated in the contract or other document shall be afforded no less prominence than that given to any other information in the document apart from the heading to the document and the names of the parties to the contract and any information inserted in handwriting.

(4) The notice shall be dated and delivered to the consumer—
    (a) in the cases mentioned in regulation 3(1)(a), (b) and (d) above, at the time of the making of the contract; and
    (b) in the case mentioned in regulation 3(1)(c) above, at the time of the making of the offer by the consumer.

(5) If within the period of 7 days following the making of the contract the consumer serves a notice in writing (a "notice of cancellation") on the trader or any other person specified in a notice referred to in paragraph (1) above as a person to whom notice of cancellation may be given which, however expressed and whether or not conforming to the cancellation form set out in Part II of the Schedule to these Regulations, indicates the intention of the consumer to cancel the contract, the notice of cancellation shall operate to cancel the contract.

(6) Except as otherwise provided under these Regulations, a contract cancelled under paragraph (5) above shall be treated as if it had never been entered into by the consumer.

(7) Notwithstanding anything in section 7 of the Interpretation Act 1978, a notice of cancellation sent by post by a consumer shall be deemed to have been served at the time of posting, whether or not it is actually received. **[528]**

NOTES
Commencement: 1 July 1988.

5. Recovery of money paid by consumer

(1) Subject to regulation 7(2) below, on the cancellation of a contract under regulation 4 above, any sum paid by or on behalf of the consumer under or in contemplation of the contract shall become repayable.

(2) If under the terms of the cancelled contract the consumer or any person on his behalf is in possession of any goods, he shall have a lien on them for any sum repayable to him under paragraph (1) above.

(3) Where any security has been provided in relation to the cancelled contract, the security, so far as it is so provided, shall be treated as never having had effect and any property lodged with the trader solely for the purposes of the security as so provided shall be returned by him forthwith. **[529]**

NOTES
Commencement: 1 July 1988.

6. Repayment of credit

(1) Notwithstanding the cancellation of a contract under regulation 4 above under which credit is provided, the contract shall continue in force so far as it relates to repayment of credit and payment of interest.

(2) If, following the cancellation of the contract, the consumer repays the whole or a portion of the credit—
    (a) before the expiry of one month following service of the notice of cancellation, or

(b) in the case of a credit repayable by instalments, before the date on which the first instalment is due,

no interest shall be payable on the amount repaid.

(3) If the whole of a credit repayable by instalments is not repaid on or before the date specified in paragraph (2)(b) above, the consumer shall not be liable to repay any of the credit except on receipt of a request in writing signed by the trader stating the amounts of the remaining instalments (recalculated by the trader as nearly as may be in accordance with the contract and without extending the repayment period), but excluding any sum other than principal and interest.

(4) Repayment of a credit, or payment of interest, under a cancelled contract shall be treated as duly made if it is made to any person on whom, under regulation 4(5) above, a notice of cancellation could have been served.

(5) Where any security has been provided in relation to the contract, the duty imposed on the consumer by this regulation shall not be enforceable before the trader has discharged any duty imposed on him by regulation 5(3) above.

[(6) In this regulation, the following expressions have the meanings hereby assigned to them:—

"cash" includes money in any form;

"credit" means a cash loan and any facility enabling the consumer to overdraw on a current account;

"current account" means an account under which the customer may, by means of cheques or similar orders payable to himself or to any other person, obtain or have the use of money held or made available by the person with whom the account is kept and which records alterations in the financial relationship between the said person and the customer; and

"repayment", in relation to credit, means the repayment of money—
    (a) paid to a consumer before the cancellation of the contract; or
    (b) to the extent that he has overdrawn on his current account before the cancellation.] [530]

NOTES
  Commencement: 1 July 1988.
  Para (6): substituted by SI 1988 No 958, reg 2.

7. Return of goods by consumer after cancellation

(1) Subject to paragraph (2) below, a consumer who has before cancelling a contract under regulation 4 above acquired possession of any goods by virtue of the contract shall be under a duty, subject to any lien, on the cancellation to restore the goods to the trader in accordance with this regulation, and meanwhile to retain possession of the goods and take reasonable care of them.

(2) The consumer shall not be under a duty to restore—
    (i) perishable goods;
    (ii) goods which by their nature are consumed by use and which, before the cancellation, were so consumed;
    (iii) goods supplied to meet an emergency; or
    (iv) goods which, before the cancellation, had become incorporated in any land or thing not comprised in the cancelled contract,

but he shall be under a duty to pay in accordance with the cancelled contract for the supply of the goods and for the provision of any services in connection with the supply of the goods before the cancellation.

(3) The consumer shall not be under any duty to deliver the goods except at his own premises and in pursuance of a request in writing signed by the trader and served on the consumer either before, or at the time when, the goods are collected from those premises.

(4) If the consumer—
    (i) delivers the goods (whether at his own premises or elsewhere) to any person on whom, under regulation 4(5) above, a notice of cancellation could have been served; or
    (ii) sends the goods at his own expense to such a person,
he shall be discharged from any duty to retain possession of the goods or restore them to the trader.

(5) Where the consumer delivers the goods as mentioned in paragraph (4)(i) above, his obligation to take care of the goods shall cease; and if he send the goods as mentioned in paragraph (4)(ii) above, he shall be under a duty to take reasonable care to see that they are received by the trader and not damaged in transit, but in other respects his duty to take care of the goods shall cease.

(6) Where, at any time during the period of 21 days following the cancellation, the consumer receives such a request as is mentioned in paragraph (3) above and unreasonably refuses or unreasonably fails to comply with it, his duty to retain possession and take reasonable care of the goods shall continue until he delivers or sends the goods as mentioned in paragraph (4) above, but if within that period he does not receive such a request his duty to take reasonable care of the goods shall cease at the end of that period.

(7) Where any security has been provided in relation to the cancelled contract, the duty imposed on the consumer to restore goods by this regulation shall not be enforceable before the trader has discharged any duty imposed on him by regulation 5(3) above.

(8) Breach of a duty imposed by this regulation on a consumer is actionable as a breach of statutory duty.

NOTES
Commencement: 1 July 1988.

8. Goods given in part-exchange

(1) This regulation applies on the cancellation of a contract under regulation 4 above where the trader agreed to take goods in part-exchange (the "part-exchange goods") and those goods have been delivered to him.

(2) Unless, before the end of the period of ten days beginning with the date of cancellation, the part-exchange goods are returned to the consumer in a condition substantially as good as when they were delivered to the trader, the consumer shall be entitled to recover from the trader a sum equal to the part-exchange allowance.

(3) During the period of ten days beginning with the date of cancellation, the consumer, if he is in possession of goods to which the cancelled contract relates, shall have a lien on them for—

(a) delivery of the part-exchange goods in a condition substantially as good as when they were delivered to the trader; or

(b) a sum equal to the part-exchange allowance;

and if the lien continues to the end of that period it shall thereafter subsist only as a lien for a sum equal to the part-exchange allowance.

(4) In this regulation the part-exchange allowance means the sum agreed as such in the cancelled contract, or if no such sum was agreed, such sum as it would have been reasonable to allow in respect of the part-exchange goods if no notice of cancellation had been served. [532]

NOTES
Commencement: 1 July 1988.

9. Amendment of the Consumer Credit Act 1974

. . . [533]

NOTES
Commencement: 1 July 1988.
This regulation adds the Consumer Credit Act 1974, s 74(2A) paragraph [240] ante.

10. No contracting-out

(1) A term contained in a contract to which these Regulations apply is void if, and to the extent that, it is inconsistent with a provision for the protection of the consumer contained in these Regulations.

(2) Where a provision of these Regulations specifies the duty or liability of the consumer in certain circumstances a term contained in a contract to which these Regulations apply is inconsistent with that provision if it purports to impose, directly or indirectly, an additional duty or liability on him in those cicrcumstances. [534]

NOTES
Commencement: 1 July 1988.

11. Service of documents

(1) A document to be served under these Regulations on a person may be so served—

(a) by delivering it to him, or by sending it by post to him, or by leaving it with him, at his proper address addressed to him by name;

(b) if the person is a body corporate, by serving it in accordance with paragraph (a) above on the secretary or clerk of that body; or

(c) if the person is a partnership, by serving it in accordance with paragraph (a) above on a partner or on a person having the control or management of the partnership business.

(2) For the purposes of these Regulations, a document sent by post to, or left at, the address last known to the server of the document as the address of a person shall be treated as sent by post to, or left at, his proper address. [535]

NOTES
Commencement: 1 July 1988.

Regulation 4(1)

SCHEDULE

Part I

Information to be Contained in Notice of Cancellation Rights

1. The name of the trader.

2. The trader's reference number, code or other details to enable the contract or offer to be identified.

3. A statement that the consumer has a right to cancel the contract if he wishes and that this right can be exercised by sending or taking a written notice of cancellation to the person mentioned in paragraph 4 within the period of 7 days following the making of the contract.

4. The name and address of a person to whom notice of cancellation may be given.

5. A statement that the consumer can use the cancellation form provided if he wishes.

[536]

NOTES
Commencement: 1 July 1988.

Part II

Cancellation Form to be Included in Notice of Cancellation Rights

(Complete, detach and return this form ONLY IF YOU WISH TO CANCEL THE CONTRACT.)

To: 1

I/We* hereby give notice that I/we* wish to cancel my/our* contract 2

Signed

Date

*Delete as appropriate

Notes:

1. Trader to insert name and address of person to whom notice may be given.

2. Trader to insert reference number, code or other details to enable the contract or offer to be identified. He may also insert the name and address of the consumer. [537]

NOTES
Commencement: 1 July 1988.

CONTROL OF MISLEADING ADVERTISEMENTS REGULATIONS 1988
(SI 1988 No 915)

NOTES
Made: 23 May 1988
Authority: European Communities Act 1972, s 2(2)

ARRANGEMENT OF REGULATIONS

Regulation	Para
1 Citation and commencement	[538]
2 Interpretation	[539]
3 Application	[540]
4 Complaints to the Director	[541]

5	Applications to the Court by the Director	[542]
6	Functions of the Court	[543]
7	Powers of the Director to obtain and disclose information and disclosure of information generally	[544]
8	Complaints to the IBA	[545]
9	Control by the IBA of misleading advertisements	[546]
10	Complaints to the Cable Authority	[547]
11	Control by the Cable Authority of misleading advertisements	[548]

GENERAL NOTES

These regulations were introduced to implement the EEC Directive (84/450/EEC) on the approximation of the laws of Member States concerning misleading advertising. The text of the Directive is at paragraph [755] below.

1. Citation and commencement

These Regulations may be cited as the Control of Misleading Advertisements Regulations 1988 and shall come into force on 20 June 1988. [538]

NOTES
Commencement: 20 June 1988.

2. Interpretation

(1) In these Regulations—

"advertisement" means any form of representation which is made in connection with a trade, business, craft or profession in order to promote the supply or transfer of goods or services, immovable property, rights or obligations;

"broadcast advertisement" means any advertisement included or proposed to be included in any programme or teletext transmission broadcast by the IBA and includes any advertisement included or proposed to be included in a licensed service by the reception and immediate re-transmission of broadcasts made by the IBA;

"Cable Authority" means the authority mentioned in section 1(1) of the Cable and Broadcasting Act 1984;

"court", in relation to England and Wales and Northern Ireland, means the High Court, and, in relation to Scotland, the Court of Session;

"Director" means the Director General of Fair Trading;

"IBA" means the Independent Broadcasting Authority mentioned in section 1(1) of the Broadcasting Act 1981;

"licensable service" has the meaning given by section 2(2) of the Cable and Broadcasting Act 1984;

"licensed service" means a licensable service in respect of which the Cable Authority has granted a licence pursuant to section 4 of the Cable and Broadcasting Act 1984;

"publication" in relation to an advertisement means the dissemination of that advertisement whether to an individual person or a number of persons and whether orally or in writing or in any other way whatsoever, and "publish" shall be construed accordingly.

(2) For the purposes of these Regulations an advertisement is misleading if in any way, including its presentation, it deceives or is likely to deceive the persons to whom it is addressed or whom it reaches and if, by reason of its deceptive nature, it is likely to affect their economic behaviour or, for those reasons, injures or is likely to injure a competitor of the person whose interests the advertisement seeks to promote.

(3) In the application of these Regulations to Scotland for references to an injunction or an interlocutory injunction there shall be substituted references to an interdict or an interim interdict respectively. **[539]**

NOTES
Commencement: 20 June 1988.

3. Application

(1) These Regulations do not apply to—
  (a) the following advertisements issued or caused to be issued by or on behalf of an authorised person or appointed representative, that is to say—
    (i) investment advertisements; and
    (ii) any other advertisements in respect of investment business,
    except where any such advertisements relate exclusively to any matter in relation to which the authorised person in question is an exempted person; and
  (b) advertisements of a description referred to in section 58(1)(d) of the Financial Services Act 1986, except where any such advertisements consist of or any part of the matters referred to in section 58(1)(d)(ii) of that Act as being required or permitted to be published by an approved exchange under Part V of that Act.

(2) In this regulation "appointed representative", "approved exchange", "authorised person", "exempted person", "investment advertisement" and "investment business" have the same meanings as in the Financial Services Act 1986. **[540]**

NOTES
Commencement: 20 June 1988.

4. Complaints to the Director

(1) Subject to paragraphs (2) and (3) below, it shall be the duty of the Director to consider any complaint made to him that an advertisement is misleading, unless the complaint appears to the Director to be frivolous or vexatious.

(2) The Director shall not consider any complaint which these Regulations require or would require, leaving aside any question as to the frivolous or vexatious nature of the complaint, the IBA or the Cable Authority to consider.

(3) Before considering any complaint under paragraph (1) above the Director may require the person making the complaint to satisfy him that—
  (a) there have been invoked in relation to the same or substantially the same complaint about the advertisement in question such established means of dealing with such complaints as the Director may consider appropriate, having regard to all the circumstances of the particular case;
  (b) a reasonable opportunity has been allowed for those means to deal with the complaint in question; and
  (c) those means have not dealt with the complaint adequately.

(4) In exercising the powers conferred on him by these Regulations the Director shall have regard to—
  (a) all the interests involved and in particular the public interest; and

(b) the desirability of encouraging the control, by self-regulatory bodies, of advertisements. **[541]**

NOTES
Commencement: 20 June 1988.

5. Applications to the Court by the Director

(1) If, having considered a complaint about an advertisement pursuant to regulation 4(1) above, he considers that the advertisement is misleading, the Director may, if he thinks it appropriate to do so, bring proceedings for an injunction (in which proceedings he may also apply for an interlocutory injuction) against any person appearing to him to be concerned or likely to be concerned with the publication of the advertisement.

(2) The Director shall give reasons for his decision to apply or not to apply, as the case may be, for an injunction in relation to any complaint which these Regulations require him to consider. **[542]**

NOTES
Commencement: 20 June 1988.

6. Functions of the Court

(1) The court on an application by the Director may grant an injunction on such terms as it may think fit but (except where it grants an interlocutory injunction) only if the court is satisfied that the advertisement to which the application relates is misleading. Before granting an injunction the court shall have regard to all the interests involved and in particular the public interest.

(2) An injunction may relate not only to a particular advertisement but to any advertisement in similar terms or likely to convey a similar impression.

(3) In considering an application for an injunction the court may, whether or not on the application of any party to the proceedings, require any person appearing to the court to be responsible for the publication of the advertisement to which the application relates to furnish the court with evidence of the accuracy of any factual claim made in the advertisement. The court shall not make such a requirement unless it appears to the court to be appropriate in the circumstances of the particular case, having regard to the legitimate interests of the person who would be the subject of or affected by the requirement and of any other person concerned with the advertisement.

(4) If such evidence is not furnished to it following a requirement made by it under paragraph (3) above or if it considers such evidence inadequate, the court may decline to consider the factual claim mentioned in that paragraph accurate.

(5) The court shall not refuse to grant an injunction for lack of evidence that—

(a) the publication of the advertisement in question has given rise to loss or damage to any person; or
(b) the person responsible for the advertisement intended it to be misleading or failed to exercise proper care to prevent its being misleading.

(6) An injunction may prohibit the publication or the continued or further publication of an advertisement. **[543]**

NOTES
Commencement: 20 June 1988.

7. Powers of the Director to obtain and disclose information and disclosure of information generally

(1) For the purpose of facilitating the exercise by him of any functions conferred on him by these Regulations, the Director may, by notice in writing signed by him or on his behalf, require any person to furnish to him such information as may be specified or described in the notice or to produce to him any documents so specified or described.

(2) A notice under paragraph (1) above may—
   (*a*) specify the way in which and the time within which it is to be complied with; and
   (*b*) be varied or revoked by a subsequent notice.

(3) Nothing in this regulation compels the production or furnishing by any person of a document or of information which he would in an action in a court be entitled to refuse to produce or furnish on grounds of legal professional privilege or, in Scotland, on the grounds of confidentiality as between client and professional legal adviser.

(4) If a person makes default in complying with a notice under paragraph (1) above the court may, on the application of the Director, make such order as the court thinks fit for requiring the default to be made good, and any such order may provide that all the costs or expenses of and incidental to the application shall be borne by the person in default or by any officers of a company or other association who are responsible for its default.

(5) Subject to any provision to the contrary made by or under any enactment, where the Director considers it appropriate to do so for the purpose of controlling misleading advertisements, he may refer to any person any complaint (including any related documentation) about an advertisement or disclose to any person any information (whether or not obtained by means of the exercise of the power conferred by paragraph (1) above).

(6) ...

(7) Subject to paragraph (5) above, any person who knowingly discloses, otherwise than for the purposes of any legal proceedings or of a report of such proceedings or the investigation of any criminal offence, any information obtained by means of the exercise of the power conferred by paragraph (1) above without the consent either of the person to whom the information relates, or, if the information relates to a business, the consent of the person for the time being carrying on that business, shall be guilty of an offence and liable on summary conviction to imprisonment for a term not exceeding 3 months or to a fine not exceeding £2,000 or to both.

(8) The Director may arrange for the dissemination in such form and manner as he considers appropriate of such information and advise concerning the operation of these Regulations as may appear to him to be expedient to give to the public and to all persons likely to be affected by these Regulations.

NOTES
Commencement: 20 June 1988.
Para (6): contains amendments only.

8. Complaints to the IBA

(1) It shall be the duty of the IBA to consider any complaint made to it that a broadcast advertisement is misleading, unless the complaint appears to the IBA to be frivolous or vexatious.

(2) The IBA shall give reasons for its decisions.

(3) In exercising the powers conferred on it by these Regulations the IBA shall have regard to all the interests involved and in particular the public interest. **[545]**

NOTES
Commencement: 20 June 1988.

9. Control by the IBA of misleading advertisements

(1) If, having considered a complaint about a broadcast advertisement pursuant to regulation 8(1) above, it considers that the advertisement is misleading, the IBA may, if it thinks it appropriate to do so, refuse to broadcast the advertisement.

(2) The IBA may require any person appearing to it to be responsible for a broadcast advertisement which the IBA believes may be misleading to furnish it with evidence as to the accuracy of any factual claim made in the advertisement. In deciding whether or not to make such a requirement the IBA shall have regard to the legitimate interests of any person who would be the subject of or affected by the requirement.

(3) If such evidence is not furnished to it following a requirement made by it under paragraph (2) above or if it considers such evidence inadequate, the IBA may consider the factual claim inaccurate. **[546]**

NOTES
Commencement: 20 June 1988.

10. Complaints to the Cable Authority

(1) Subject to paragraph (2) below, it shall be the duty of the Cable Authority to consider any complaint made to it that any advertisement included or proposed to be included in a licensed service is misleading, unless the complaint appears to the Authority to be frivolous or vexatious.

(2) The Cable Authority shall not consider any complaint about an advertisement included or proposed to be included in a licensed service by the reception and immediate re-transmission of broadcasts made by the IBA or the British Broadcasting Corporation.

(3) In exercising the powers conferred on it by these Regulations the Cable Authority shall have regard to all the interests involved and in particular the public interest. **[547]**

NOTES
Commencement: 20 June 1988.

11. Control by the Cable Authority of misleading advertisements

(1) If, having considered a complaint about an advertisement pursuant to regulation 10(1) above, it considers that the advertisement is misleading, the Authority may, if it thinks it appropriate to do so, exercise the power conferred

on it by section 15(1) of the Cable and Broadcasting Act 1984 (power to give directions) in relation to the advertisement.

(2) The Authority shall give reasons for its decision to give or not to give, as the case may be, a direction in accordance with paragraph (1) above in any particular case.

(3) The Authority may require any person appearing to it to be responsible for an advertisement which the Authority believes may be misleading to furnish it with evidence as to the accuracy of any factual claim made in the advertisement. In deciding whether or not to make such a requirement the Authority shall have regard to the legitimate interests of any person who would be the subject of or affected by the requirement.

(4) If such evidence is not furnished to it following a requirement made by it under paragraph (3) above or if it considers such evidence inadequate, the Authority may consider the factual claim inaccurate. **[548]**

NOTES
Commencement: 20 June 1988.

SECTION IV
INTERNATIONAL TRADE

BILLS OF LADING ACT 1855
(c 111)

ARRANGEMENT OF SECTIONS

	Para
Preamble	[549]
Section	
1 Rights under bills of lading to vest in consignee or endorsee	[550]
2 Not to affect right of stoppage in transitu or claims for freight	[551]
3 Bill of Lading in hands of consignee, etc, conclusive evidence of shipment as against master, etc—Proviso	[552]

An Act to amend the Law relating to Bills of Lading [14 August 1855]

GENERAL NOTES
This Act applies to Northern Ireland. It came into force on 14 August 1855.

Preamble

Whereas, by the custom of merchants, a bill of lading of goods being transferable by endorsement, the property in the goods may thereby pass to the endorsee, but nevertheless all rights in respect of the contract contained in the bill of lading continue in the original shipper or owner; and it is expedient that such rights should pass with the property: And whereas it frequently happens that the goods in respect of which bills of lading purport to be signed have not been laden on board, and it is proper that such bills of lading in the hands of a bona fide holder for value should not be questioned by the master or other person signing the same on the ground of the goods not having been laden as aforesaid: **[549]**

1. Rights under bills of lading to vest in consignee or endorsee

Every consignee of goods named in a bill of lading, and every endorsee of a bill of lading, to whom the property in the goods therein mentioned shall pass upon or by reason of such consignment or endorsement, shall have transferred to and vested in him all rights of suit, and be subject to the same liabilities in respect of such goods as if the contract contained in the bill of lading had been made with himself. **[550]**

2. Not to affect right of stoppage in transitu or claims for freight

Nothing herein contained shall prejudice or affect any right of stoppage in transitu, or any right to claim freight against the original shipper or owner, or any liability of the consignee or endorsee by reason or in consequence of his being such consignee or endorsee, or of his receipt of the goods by reason or in consequence of such consignment or endorsement. **[551]**

3. Bill of Lading in hands of consignee, etc, conclusive evidence of shipment as against master, etc—Proviso

Every bill of lading in the hands of a consignee or endorsee for valuable consideration, representing goods to have been shipped on board a vessel, shall be conclusive evidence of such shipment as against the master or other person signing the same, notwithstanding that such goods or some part thereof may not have been so shipped, unless such holder of the bill of lading shall have had actual notice at the time of receiving the same that the goods had not been in fact laden on board; Provided, that the master or other person so signing may exonerate himself in respect of such misrepresentation by showing that it was caused without any default on his part, and wholly by the fraud of the shipper, or of the holder, or some person under whom the holder claims. **[552]**

MARINE INSURANCE ACT 1906
(c 41)

ARRANGEMENT OF SECTIONS

Marine Insurance

Section		Para
1	Marine insurance defined	[553]
2	Mixed sea and land risks	[554]
3	Marine adventure and maritime perils defined	[555]

Insurable Interest

4	Avoidance of wagering or gaming contracts	[556]
5	Insurable interest defined	[557]
6	When interest must attach	[558]
7	Defeasible or contingent interest	[559]
8	Partial interest	[560]
9	Re-insurance	[561]
10	Bottomry	[562]
11	Master's and seamen's wages	[563]
12	Advance freight	[564]
13	Charges of insurance	[565]
14	Quantum of interest	[566]
15	Assignment of interest	[567]

Insurable Value

16	Measure of insurable value	[568]

Disclosure and Representations

17	Insurance is uberrimae fidei	[569]
18	Disclosure by assured	[570]
19	Disclosure by agent effecting insurance	[571]
20	Representations pending negotiation of contract	[572]
21	When contract is deemed to be concluded	[573]

The Policy

22	Contract must be embodied in policy	[574]
23	What policy must specify	[575]
24	Signature of insurer	[576]
25	Voyage and time policies	[577]
26	Designation of subject-matter	[578]
27	Valued policy	[579]
28	Unvalued policy	[580]
29	Floating policy by ship or ships	[581]
30	Construction of terms in policy	[582]
31	Premium to be arranged	[583]

Marine Insurance Act 1906

Section		Para
	DOUBLE INSURANCE	
32	Double insurance	[584]
	WARRANTIES, ETC	
33	Nature of warranty	[585]
34	When breach of warranty excused	[586]
35	Express warranties	[587]
36	Warranty of neutrality	[588]
37	No implied warranty of nationality	[589]
38	Warranty of good safety	[590]
39	Warranty of seaworthiness of ship	[591]
40	No implied warranty that goods are seaworthy	[592]
41	Warranty of legality	[593]
	THE VOYAGE	
42	Implied condition as to commencement of risk	[594]
43	Alteration of port of departure	[595]
44	Sailing for different destination	[596]
45	Change of voyage	[597]
46	Deviation	[598]
47	Several ports of discharge	[599]
48	Delay in voyage	[600]
49	Excuses for deviation or delay	[601]
	ASSIGNMENT OF POLICY	
50	When and how policy is assignable	[602]
51	Assured who has no interest cannot assign	[603]
	THE PREMIUM	
52	When premium payable	[604]
53	Policy effected through broker	[605]
54	Effect of receipt on policy	[606]
	LOSS AND ABANDONMENT	
55	Included and excluded losses	[607]
56	Partial and total loss	[608]
57	Actual total loss	[609]
58	Missing ship	[610]
59	Effect of transhipment, etc	[611]
60	Constructive total loss defined	[612]
61	Effect of constructive total loss	[613]
62	Notice of abandonment	[614]
63	Effect of abandonment	[615]
	PARTIAL LOSSES (INCLUDING SALVAGE AND GENERAL AVERAGE AND PARTICULAR CHARGES)	
64	Particular average loss	[616]
65	Salvage charges	[617]
66	General average loss	[618]
	MEASURE OF INDEMNITY	
67	Extent of liability of insurer for loss	[619]
68	Total loss	[620]
69	Partial loss of ship	[621]

Section		Para
70	Partial loss of freight	[622]
71	Partial loss of goods, merchandise, etc	[623]
72	Apportionment of valuation	[624]
73	General average contributions and salvage charges	[625]
74	Liabilities to third parties	[626]
75	General provisions as to measure of indemnity	[627]
76	Particular average warranties	[628]
77	Successive losses	[629]
78	Suing and labouring clause	[630]

RIGHTS OF INSURER ON PAYMENT

79	Right of subrogation	[631]
80	Right of contribution	[632]
81	Effect of under insurance	[633]

RETURN OF PREMIUM

82	Enforcement of return	[634]
83	Return by agreement	[635]
84	Return for failure of consideration	[636]

MUTUAL INSURANCE

85	Modification of Act in case of mutual insurance	[637]

SUPPLEMENTAL

86	Ratification by assured	[638]
87	Implied obligations varied by agreement or usage	[639]
88	Reasonable time, etc, a question of fact	[640]
89	Slip as evidence	[641]
90	Interpretation of terms	[642]
91	Savings	[643]
94	Short title	[644]

SCHEDULES

Schedule 1—	[645]

An Act to codify the Law relating to Marine Insurance [21 December 1906]

GENERAL NOTES
This Act applies to Northern Ireland.
Commencement: 21 December 1906.
The application of this Act is extended to hovercraft by virtue of the Hovercraft (Application of Enactments) Order 1972, SI 1972 No 971.

MARINE INSURANCE

1. Marine insurance defined

A contract of marine insurance is a contract whereby the insurer undertakes to indemnify the assured, in manner and to the extent thereby agreed, against marine losses, that is to say, the losses incident to marine adventure. **[553]**

2. Mixed sea and land risks

(1) A contract of marine insurance may, by its express terms, or by usage of trade, be extended so as to protect the assured against losses on inland waters or on any land risk which may be incidental to any sea voyage.

(2) Where a ship in course of building, or the launch of a ship, or any adventure analogous to a marine adventure, is covered by a policy in the form of a marine policy, the provisions of this Act, in so far as applicable, shall apply thereto; but, except as by this section provided, nothing in this Act shall alter or affect any rule of law applicable to any contract of insurance other than a contract of marine insurance as by this Act defined. [554]

3. Marine adventure and maritime perils defined

(1) Subject to the provisions of this Act, every lawful marine adventure may be the subject of a contract of marine insurance.

(2) In particular there is a marine adventure where—
   (a) Any ship goods or other moveables are exposed to maritime perils. Such property is in this Act referred to as "insurable property";
   (b) The earning or acquisition of any freight, passage money, commission, profit, or other pecuniary benefit, or the security for any advances, loan, or disbursements, is endangered by the exposure of insurable property to maritime perils;
   (c) Any liability to a third party may be incurred by the owner of, or other person interested in or responsible for, insurable property, by reason of maritime perils.

"Maritime perils" means the perils consequent on, or incidental to, the navigation of the sea, that is to say, perils of the seas, fire, war perils, pirates, rovers, thieves, captures, seisures, restraints, and detainments of princes and peoples, jettisons, barratry, and any other perils, either of the like kind or which may be designated by the policy. [555]

INSURABLE INTEREST

4. Avoidance of wagering or gaming contracts

(1) Every contract of marine insurance by way of gaming or wagering is void.

(2) A contract of marine insurance is deemed to be a gaming or wagering contract—
   (a) Where the assured has not an insurable interest as defined by this Act, and the contract is entered into with no expectation of acquiring such an interest; or
   (b) Where the policy is made "interest or no interest," or "without further proof of interest than the policy itself," or "without benefit of salvage to the insurer," or subject to any other like term:

Provided that, where there is no possibility of salvage, a policy may be effected without benefit of salvage to the insurer. [556]

5. Insurable interest defined

(1) Subject to the provisions of this Act, every person has an insurable interest who is interested in a marine adventure.

(2) In particular a person is interested in a marine adventure where he stands in any legal or equitable relation to the adventure or to any insurable property at risk therein, in consequence of which he may benefit by the safety or due arrival of insurable property, or may be prejudiced by its loss, or damage thereto, or by the detention thereof, or may incur liability in respect thereof.
[557]

6. When interest must attach

(1) The assured must be interested in the subject-matter insured at the time of the loss though he need not be interested when the insurance is effected:

Provided that where the subject-matter is insured "lost or not lost," the assured may recover although he may not have acquired his interest until after the loss, unless at the time of effecting the contract of insurance the assured was aware of the loss, and the insurer was not.

(2) Where the assured has no interest at the time of the loss, he cannot acquire interest by any act or election after he is aware of the loss. [558]

7. Defeasible or contingent interest

(1) A defeasible interest is insurable, as also is a contingent interest.

(2) In particular, where the buyer of goods has insured them, he has an insurable interest, notwithstanding that he might, at his election, have rejected the goods, or have treated them as at the seller's risk, by reason of the latter's delay in making delivery or otherwise. [559]

8. Partial interest

A partial interest of any nature is insurable. [560]

9. Re-insurance

(1) The insurer under a contract of marine insurance has an insurable interest in his risk, and may re-insure in respect of it.

(2) Unless the policy otherwise provides, the original assured has no right or interest in respect of such re-insurance. [561]

10. Bottomry

The lender of money on bottomry or respondentia has an insurable interest in respect of the loan. [562]

11. Master's and seamen's wages

The master or any member of the crew of a ship has an insurable interest in respect of his wages. [563]

12. Advance freight

In the case of advance freight, the person advancing the freight has an insurable interest, in so far as such freight is not repayable in case of loss. [564]

13. Charges of insurance

The assured has an insurable interest in the charges of any insurance which he may effect. [565]

14. Quantum of interest

(1) Where the subject-matter insured is mortgaged, the mortgagor has an insurable interest in the full value thereof, and the mortgagee has an insurable interest in respect of any sum due or to become due under the mortgage.

(2) A mortgagee, consignee, or other person having an interest in the subject-matter insured may insure on behalf and for the benefit of other persons interested as well as for his own benefit.

(3) The owner of insurable property has an insurable interest in respect of the full value thereof, notwithstanding that some third person may have agreed, or be liable, to indemnify him in case of loss. [566]

15. Assignment of interest

Where the assured assigns or otherwise parts with his interest in the subject-matter insured, he does not thereby transfer to the assignee his rights under the contract of insurance, unless there be an express or implied agreement with the assignee to that effect.

But the provisions of this section do not affect a transmission of interest by operation of law. [567]

INSURABLE VALUE

16. Measure of insurable value

Subject to any express provision or valuation in the policy, the insurable value of the subject-matter insured must be ascertained as follows:—

(1) In insurance on ship, the insurable value is the value, at the commencement of the risk, of the ship, including her outfit, provisions and stores for the officers and crew, money advanced for seamen's wages, and other disbursements (if any) incurred to make the ship fit for the voyage or adventure contemplated by the policy, plus the charges of insurance upon the whole:

The insurable value, in the case of a steamship, includes also the machinery, boilers, and coals and engine stores if owned by the assured, and, in the case of a ship engaged in a special trade, the ordinary fittings requisite for that trade:

(2) In insurance on freight, whether paid in advance or otherwise, the insurable value is the gross amount of the freight at the risk of the assured, plus the charges of insurance:

(3) In insurance on goods or merchandise, the insurable value is the prime cost of the property insured, plus the expenses of and incidental to shipping and the charges of insurance upon the whole:

(4) In insurance on any other subject-matter, the insurable value is the amount at the risk of the assured when the policy attaches, plus the charges of insurance. [568]

Disclosure and Representations

17. Insurance is uberrimae fidei

A contract of marine insurance is a contract based upon the utmost good faith, and, if the utmost good faith be not observed by either party, the contract may be avoided by the other party. [569]

18. Disclosure by assured

(1) Subject to the provisions of this section, the assured must disclose to the insurer, before the contract is concluded, every material circumstance which is known to the assured, and the assured is deemed to know every circumstance which, in the ordinary course of business, ought to be known by him. If the assured fails to make such disclosure, the insurer may avoid the contract.

(2) Every circumstance is material which would influence the judgment of a prudent insurer in fixing the premium, or determining whether he will take the risk.

(3) In the absence of inquiry the following circumstances need not be disclosed, namely:—
- (a) Any circumstance which diminishes the risk;
- (b) Any circumstance which is known or presumed to be known to the insurer. The insurer is presumed to know matters of common notoriety or knowledge, and matters which an insurer in the ordinary course of his business, as such, ought to know;
- (c) Any circumstance as to which information is waived by the insurer;
- (d) Any circumstance which it is superfluous to disclose by reason of any express or implied warranty.

(4) Whether any particular circumstance, which is not disclosed, be material or not is, in each case, a question of fact.

(5) The term "circumstance" includes any communication made to, or information received by, the assured. [570]

19. Disclosure by agent effecting insurance

Subject to the provisions of the preceding section as to circumstances which need not be disclosed, where an insurance is effected for the assured by an agent, the agent must disclose to the insurer—
- (a) Every material circumstance which is known to himself, and an agent to insure is deemed to know every circumstance which in the ordinary course of business ought to be known by, or to have been communicated to, him; and
- (b) Every material circumstance which the assured is bound to disclose, unless it come to his knowledge too late to communicate it to the agent. [571]

20. Representations pending negotiation of contract

(1) Every material representation made by the assured or his agent to the insurer during the negotiations for the contract, and before the contract is concluded, must be true. If it be untrue the insurer may avoid the contract.

(2) A representation is material which would influence the judgment of a

prudent insurer in fixing the premium, or determining whether he will take the risk.

(3) A representation may be either a representation as to a matter of fact, or as to a matter of expectation or belief.

(4) A representation as to matter of fact is true, if it be substantially correct, that is to say, if the difference between what is represented and what is actually correct would not be considered material by a prudent insurer.

(5) A representation as to a matter of expectation or belief is true if it be made in good faith.

(6) A representation may be withdrawn or corrected before the contract is concluded.

(7) Whether a particular representation be material or not is, in each case, a question of fact. [572]

21. When contract is deemed to be concluded

A contract of marine insurance is deemed to be concluded when the proposal of the assured is accepted by the insurer, whether the policy be then issued or not; and, for the purpose of showing when the proposal was accepted, reference may be made to the slip or covering note or other customary memorandum of the contract, ... [573]

NOTES
Words omitted repealed by the Finance Act 1959, s 37(5), Sch 8, Part II.

THE POLICY

22. Contract must be embodied in policy

Subject to the provisions of any statute, a contract of marine insurance is inadmissible in evidence unless it is embodied in a marine policy in accordance with this Act. The policy may be executed and issued either at the time when the contract is concluded, or afterwards. [574]

23. What policy must specify

A marine policy must specify—

(1) The name of the assured, or of some person who effects the insurance on his behalf:

(2)–(5) ... [575]

NOTES
Words omitted repealed by the Finance Act 1959, ss 30(5), (7), 37(5), Sch 8, Part II.

24. Signature of insurer

(1) A marine policy must be signed by or on behalf of the insurer, provided that in the case of a corporation the corporate seal may be sufficient, but nothing in this section shall be construed as requiring the subscription of a corporation to be under seal.

(2) Where a policy is subscribed by or on behalf of two or more insurers, each subscription, unless the contrary be expressed, constitutes a distinct contract with the assured. [576]

25. Voyage and time policies

(1) Where the contract is to insure the subject-matter "at and from", or from one place to another or others, the policy is called a "voyage policy", and where the contract is to insure the subject-matter for a definite period of time the policy is called a "time policy". A contract for both voyage and time may be included in the same policy.

(2) ... [577]

NOTES
Sub-s (2): repealed by the Finance Act 1959, ss 30(5), (7), 37(5), Sch 8, Part II.

26. Designation of subject-matter

(1) The subject-matter insured must be designated in a marine policy with reasonable certainty.

(2) The nature and extent of the interest of the assured in the subject-matter insured need not be specified in the policy.

(3) Where the policy designates the subject-matter insured in general terms, it shall be construed to apply to the interest intended by the assured to be covered.

(4) In the application of this section regard shall be had to any usage regulating the designation of the subject-matter insured. [578]

27. Valued policy

(1) A policy may be either valued or unvalued.

(2) A valued policy is a policy which specifies the agreed value of the subject-matter insured.

(3) Subject to the provisions of this Act, and in the absence of fraud, the value fixed by the policy is, as between the insurer and assured, conclusive of the insurable value of the subject intended to be insured, whether the loss be total or partial.

(4) Unless the policy otherwise provides, the value fixed by the policy is not conclusive for the purpose of determining whether there has been a constructive total loss. [579]

28. Unvalued policy

An unvalued policy is a policy which does not specify the value of the subject-matter insured, but, subject to the limit of the sum insured, leaves the insurable value to be subsequently ascertained, in the manner herein-before specified.
[580]

29. Floating policy by ship or ships

(1) A floating policy is a policy which describes the insurance in general terms, and leaves the name of the ship or ships and other particulars to be defined by subsequent declaration.

(2) The subsequent declaration or declarations may be made by indorsement on the policy, or in other customary manner.

(3) Unless the policy otherwise provides, the declarations must be made in the order of dispatch or shipment. They must, in the case of goods, comprise all consignments within the terms of the policy, and the value of the goods or other property must be honestly stated, but an omission or erroneous declaration may be rectified even after loss or arrival, provided the omission or declaration was made in good faith.

(4) Unless the policy otherwise provides, where a declaration of value is not made until after notice of loss or arrival, the policy must be treated as an unvalued policy as regards the subject-matter of that declaration. **[581]**

30. Construction of terms in policy

(1) A policy may be in the form in the First Schedule to this Act.

(2) Subject to the provisions of this Act, and unless the context of the policy otherwise requires, the terms and expressions mentioned in the First Schedule to this Act shall be construed as having the scope and meaning in that schedule assigned to them. **[582]**

31. Premium to be arranged

(1) Where an insurance is effected at a premium to be arranged, and no arrangement is made, a reasonable premium is payable.

(2) Where an insurance is effected on the terms that an additional premium is to be arranged in a given event, and that event happens but no arrangement is made, then a reasonable additional premium is payable. **[583]**

DOUBLE INSURANCE

32. Double insurance

(1) Where two or more policies are effected by or on behalf of the assured on the same adventure and interest or any part thereof, and the sums insured exceed the indemnity allowed by this Act, the assured is said to be over-insured by double insurance.

(2) Where the assured is over-insured by double insurance—
  (a) The assured, unless the policy otherwise provides, may claim payment from the insurers in such order as he may think fit, provided that he is not entitled to receive any sum in excess of the indemnity allowed by this Act;
  (b) Where the policy under which the assured claims is a valued policy, the assured must give credit as against the valuation for any sum received by him under any other policy without regard to the actual value of the subject-matter insured;
  (c) Where the policy under which the assured claims is an unvalued policy he must give credit, as against the full insurable value, for any sum received by him under any other policy;
  (d) Where the assured receives any sum in excess of the indemnity allowed by this Act, he is deemed to hold such sum in trust for the insurers, according to their right of contribution among themselves.
[584]

WARRANTIES, ETC

33. Nature of warranty

(1) A warranty, in the following sections relating to warranties, means a promissory warranty, that is to say, a warranty by which the assured undertakes that some particular thing shall or shall not be done, or that some condition shall be fulfilled, or whereby he affirms or negatives the existence of a particular state of facts.

(2) A warranty may be express or implied.

(3) A warranty, as above defined, is a condition which must be exactly complied with, whether it be material to the risk or not. If it be not so complied with, then, subject to any express provision in the policy, the insurer is discharged from liability as from the date of the breach of warranty, but without prejudice to any liability incurred by him before that date. [585]

34. When breach of warranty excused

(1) Non-compliance with a warranty is excused when, by reason of a change of circumstances, the warranty ceases to be applicable to the circumstances of the contract, or when compliance with the warranty is rendered unlawful by any subsequent law.

(2) Where a warranty is broken, the assured cannot avail himself of the defence that the breach has been remedied, and the warranty complied with, before loss.

(3) A breach of warranty may be waived by the insurer. [586]

35. Express warranties

(1) An express warranty may be in any form of words from which the intention to warrant is to be inferred.

(2) An express warranty must be included in, or written upon, the policy, or must be contained in some document incorporated by reference into the policy.

(3) An express warranty does not exclude an implied warranty, unless it be inconsistent therewith. [587]

36. Warranty of neutrality

(1) Where insurable property, whether ship or goods, is expressly warranted neutral, there is an implied condition that the property shall have a neutral character at the commencement of the risk, and that, so far as the assured can control the matter, its neutral character shall be preserved during the risk.

(2) Where a ship is expressly warranted "neutral" there is also an implied condition that, so far as the assured can control the matter, she shall be properly documented, that is to say, that she shall carry the necessary papers to establish her neutrality, and that she shall not falsify or suppress her papers, or use simulated papers. If any loss occurs through breach of this condition, the insurer may avoid the contract. [588]

37. No implied warranty of nationality

There is no implied warranty as to the nationality of a ship, or that her nationality shall not be changed during the risk. [589]

38. Warranty of good safety

Where the subject-matter insured is warranted "well" or "in good safety" on a particular day, it is sufficient if it be safe at any time during that day. [590]

39. Warranty of seaworthiness of ship

(1) In a voyage policy there is an implied warranty that at the commencement of the voyage the ship shall be seaworthy for the purpose of the particular adventure insured.

(2) Where the policy attaches while the ship is in port, there is also an implied warranty that she shall, at the commencement of the risk, be reasonably fit to encounter the ordinary perils of the port.

(3) Where the policy relates to a voyage which is performed in different stages, during which the ship requires different kinds of or further preparation or equipment, there is an implied warranty that at the commencement of each stage the ship is seaworthy in respect of such preparation or equipment for the purposes of that stage.

(4) A ship is deemed to be seaworthy when she is reasonably fit in all respects to encounter the ordinary perils of the seas of the adventure insured.

(5) In a time policy there is no implied warranty that the ship shall be seaworthy at any stage of the adventure, but where, with the privity of the assured, the ship is sent to sea in an unseaworthy state, the insurer is not liable for any loss attributable to unseaworthiness. [591]

40. No implied warranty that goods are seaworthy

(1) In a policy on goods or other moveables there is no implied warranty that the goods or moveables are seaworthy.

(2) In a voyage policy on goods or other moveables there is an implied warranty that at the commencement of the voyage the ship is not only seaworthy as a ship, but also that she is reasonably fit to carry the goods or other moveables to the destination contemplated by the policy. [592]

41. Warranty of legality

There is an implied warranty that the adventure insured is a lawful one, and that, so far as the assured can control the matter, the adventure shall be carried out in a lawful manner. [593]

The Voyage

42. Implied condition as to commencement of risk

(1) Where the subject-matter is insured by a voyage policy "at and from" or "from" a particular place, it is not necessary that the ship should be at that place when the contract is concluded, but there is an implied condition that the adventure shall be commenced within a reasonable time, and that if the adventure be not so commenced the insurer may avoid the contract.

(2) The implied condition may be negatived by showing that the delay was caused by circumstances known to the insurer before the contract was concluded, or by showing that he waived the condition. [594]

43. Alteration of port of departure

Where the place of departure is specified by the policy, and the ship instead of sailing from that place sails from any other place, the risk does not attach. **[595]**

44. Sailing for different destination

Where the destination is specified in the policy, and the ship, instead of sailing for that destination, sails for any other destination, the risk does not attach.
[596]

45. Change of voyage

(1) Where, after the commencement of the risk, the destination of the ship is voluntarily changed from the destination contemplated by the policy, there is said to be a change of voyage.

(2) Unless the policy otherwise provides, where there is a change of voyage, the insurer is discharged from liability as from the time of change, that is to say, as from the time when the determination to change it is manifested; and it is immaterial that the ship may not in fact have left the course of voyage contemplated by the policy when the loss occurs. **[597]**

46. Deviation

(1) Where a ship, without lawful excuse, deviates from the voyage contemplated by the policy, the insurer is discharged from liability as from the time of deviation, and it is immaterial that the ship may have regained her route before any loss occurs.

(2) There is a deviation from the voyage contemplated by the policy—
   (a) Where the course of the voyage is specifically designated by the policy, and that course is departed from; or
   (b) Where the course of the voyage is not specifically designated by the policy, but the usual and customary course is departed from.

(3) The intention to deviate is immaterial; there must be a deviation in fact to discharge the insurer from his liability under the contract. **[598]**

47. Several ports of discharge

(1) Where several ports of discharge are specified by the policy, the ship may proceed to all or any of them, but, in the absence of any usage or sufficient cause to the contrary, she must proceed to them, or such of them as she goes to, in the order designated by the policy. If she does not there is a deviation.

(2) Where the policy is to "ports of discharge", within a given area, which are not named, the ship must, in the absence of any usage or sufficient cause to the contrary, proceed to them, or such of them as she goes to, in their geographical order. If she does not there is a deviation. **[599]**

48. Delay in voyage

In the case of a voyage policy, the adventure insured must be prosecuted throughout its course with reasonable dispatch, and, if without lawful excuse it is not so prosecuted, the insurer is discharged from liability as from the time when the delay became unreasonable. **[600]**

49. Excuses for deviation or delay

(1) Deviation or delay in prosecuting the voyage contemplated by the policy is excused—
- (*a*) Where authorised by any special term in the policy; or
- (*b*) Where caused by circumstances beyond the control of the master and his employer; or
- (*c*) Where reasonably necessary in order to comply with an express or implied warranty; or
- (*d*) Where reasonably necessary for the safety of the ship or subject-matter insured; or
- (*e*) For the purpose of saving human life, or aiding a ship in distress where human life may be in danger; or
- (*f*) Where reasonably necessary for the purpose of obtaining medical or surgical aid for any person on board the ship; or
- (*g*) Where caused by the barratrous conduct of the master or crew, if barratry be one of the perils insured against.

(2) When the cause excusing the deviation or delay ceases to operate, the ship must resume her course, and prosecute her voyage, with reasonable dispatch. **[601]**

ASSIGNMENT OF POLICY

50. When and how policy is assignable

(1) A marine policy is assignable unless it contains terms expressly prohibiting assignment. It may be assigned either before or after loss.

(2) Where a marine policy has been assigned so as to pass the beneficial interest in such policy, the assignee of the policy is entitled to sue thereon in his own name; and the defendant is entitled to make any defence arising out of the contract which he would have been entitled to make if the action had been brought in the name of the person by or on behalf of whom the policy was effected.

(3) A marine policy may be assigned by indorsement thereon or in other customary manner. **[602]**

51. Assured who has no interest cannot assign

Where the assured has parted with or lost his interest in the subject-matter insured, and has not, before or at the time of so doing, expressly or impliedly agreed to assign the policy, any subsequent assignment of the policy is inoperative:

Provided that nothing in this section affects the assignment of a policy after loss. **[603]**

THE PREMIUM

52. When premium payable

Unless otherwise agreed, the duty of the assured or his agent to pay the premium, and the duty of the insurer to issue the policy to the assured or his agent, are concurrent conditions, and the insurer is not bound to issue the policy until payment or tender of the premium. **[604]**

53. Policy effected through broker

(1) Unless otherwise agreed, where a marine policy is effected on behalf of the assured by a broker, the broker is directly responsible to the insurer for the premium, and the insurer is directly responsible to the assured for the amount which may be payable in respect of losses, or in respect of returnable premium.

(2) Unless otherwise agreed, the broker has, as against the assured, a lien upon the policy for the amount of the premium and his charges in respect of effecting the policy; and, where he has dealt with the person who employs him as a principal, he has also a lien on the policy in respect of any balance on any insurance account which may be due to him from such person, unless when the debt was incurred he had reason to believe that such person was only an agent.

54. Effect of receipt on policy

Where a marine policy effected on behalf of the assured by a broker acknowledges the receipt of the premium, such acknowledgment is, in the absence of fraud, conclusive as between the insurer and the assured, but not as between the insurer and broker.

LOSS AND ABANDONMENT

55. Included and excluded losses

(1) Subject to the provisions of this Act, and unless the policy otherwise provides, the insurer is liable for any loss proximately caused by a peril insured against, but, subject as aforesaid, he is not liable for any loss which is not proximately caused by a peril insured against.

(2) In particular,—
   (a) The insurer is not liable for any loss attributable to the wilful misconduct of the assured, but, unless the policy otherwise provides, he is liable for any loss proximately caused by a peril insured against, even though the loss would not have happened but for the misconduct or negligence of the master or crew;
   (b) Unless the policy otherwise provides, the insurer on ship or goods is not liable for any loss proximately caused by delay, although the delay be caused by a peril insured against;
   (c) Unless the policy otherwise provides, the insurer is not liable for ordinary wear and tear, ordinary leakage and breakage, inherent vice or nature of the subject-matter insured, or for any loss proximately caused by rats or vermin, or for any injury to machinery not proximately caused by maritime perils.

56. Partial and total loss

(1) A loss may be either total or partial. Any loss other than a total loss, as hereinafter defined, is a partial loss.

(2) A total loss may be either an actual total loss, or a constructive total loss.

(3) Unless a different intention appears from the terms of the policy, an insurance against total loss includes a constructive, as well as an actual, total loss.

(4) Where the assured brings an action for a total loss and the evidence

proves only a partial loss, he may, unless the policy otherwise provides, recover for a partial loss.

(5) Where goods reach their destination in specie, but by reason of obliteration of marks, or otherwise, they are incapable of identification, the loss, if any, is partial, and not total. [608]

57. Actual total loss

(1) Where the subject-matter insured is destroyed, or so damaged as to cease to be a thing of the kind insured, or where the assured is irretrievably deprived thereof, there is an actual total loss.

(2) In the case of an actual total loss no notice of abandonment need be given. [609]

58. Missing ship

Where the ship concerned in the adventure is missing, and after the lapse of a reasonable time no news of her has been received, an actual total loss may be presumed. [610]

59. Effect of transhipment, etc

Where, by a peril insured against, the voyage is interrupted at an intermediate port or place, under such circumstances as, apart from any special stipulation in the contract of affreightment, to justify the master in landing and re-shipping the goods or other moveables, or in transhipping them, and sending them on to their destination, the liability of the insurer continues, notwithstanding the landing or transhipment. [611]

60. Constructive total loss defined

(1) Subject to any express provision in the policy, there is a constructive total loss where the subject-matter insured is reasonably abandoned on account of its actual total loss appearing to be unavoidable, or because it could not be preserved from actual total loss without an expenditure which would exceed its value when the expenditure had been incurred.

(2) In particular, there is a constructive total loss—
   (i) Where the assured is deprived of the possession of his ship or goods by a peril insured against, and (*a*) it is unlikely that he can recover the ship or goods, as the case may be, or (*b*) the cost of recovering the ship or goods, as the case may be, would exceed their value when recovered; or
   (ii) In the case of damage to a ship, where she is so damaged by a peril insured against that the cost of repairing the damage would exceed the value of the ship when repaired.

   In estimating the cost of repairs, no deduction is to be made in respect of general average contributions to those repairs payable by other interests, but account is to be taken of the expense of future salvage operations and of any future general average contributions to which the ship would be liable if repaired; or
   (iii) In the case of damage to goods, where the cost of repairing the damage and forwarding the goods to their destination would exceed their value on arrival. [612]

61. Effect of constructive total loss

Where there is a constructive total loss the assured may either treat the loss as a partial loss, or abandon the subject-matter insured to the insurer and treat the loss as if it were an actual total loss. **[613]**

62. Notice of abandonment

(1) Subject to the provisions of this section, where the assured elects to abandon the subject-matter insured to the insurer, he must give notice of abandonment. If he fails to do so the loss can only be treated as a partial loss.

(2) Notice of abandonment may be given in writing, or by word of mouth, or partly in writing and partly by word of mouth, and may be given in terms which indicate the intention of the assured to abandon his insured interest in the subject-matter insured unconditionally to the insurer.

(3) Notice of abandonment must be given with reasonable diligence after the receipt of reliable information of the loss, but where the information is of a doubtful character the assured is entitled to a reasonable time to make inquiry.

(4) Where notice of abandonment is properly given, the rights of the assured are not prejudiced by the fact that the insurer refuses to accept the abandonment.

(5) The acceptance of an abandonment may be either express or implied from the conduct of the insurer. The mere silence of the insurer after notice is not an acceptance.

(6) Where a notice of abandonment is accepted the abandonment is irrevocable. The acceptance of the notice conclusively admits liability for the loss and the sufficiency of the notice.

(7) Notice of abandonment is unnecessary where, at the time when the assured receives information of the loss, there would be no possibility of benefit to the insurer if notice were given to him.

(8) Notice of abandonment may be waived by the insurer.

(9) Where an insurer has re-insured his risk, no notice of abandonment need be given by him. **[614]**

63. Effect of abandonment

(1) Where there is a valid abandonment the insurer is entitled to take over the interest of the assured in whatever may remain of the subject-matter insured, and all proprietary rights incidental thereto.

(2) Upon the abandonment of a ship, the insurer thereof is entitled to any freight in course of being earned, and which is earned by her subsequent to the casualty causing the loss, less the expenses of earning it incurred after the casualty; and, where the ship is carrying the owner's goods, the insurer is entitled to a reasonable remuneration for the carriage of them subsequent to the casualty causing the loss. **[615]**

Partial Losses (including Salvage and General Average and Particular Charges)

64. Particular average loss

(1) A particular average loss is a partial loss of the subject-matter insured, caused by a peril insured against, and which is not a general average loss.

(2) Expenses incurred by or on behalf of the assured for the safety or preservation of the subject-matter insured, other than general average and salvage charges, are called particular charges. Particular charges are not included in particular average. [616]

65. Salvage charges

(1) Subject to any express provision in the policy, salvage charges incurred in preventing a loss by perils insured against may be recovered as a loss by those perils.

(2) "Salvage charges" means the charges recoverable under maritime law by a salvor independently of contract. They do not include the expenses of services in the nature of salvage rendered by the assured or his agents, or any person employed for hire by them, for the purpose of averting a peril insured against. Such expenses, where properly incurred, may be recovered as particular charges or as a general average loss, according to the circumstances under which they were incurred. [617]

66. General average loss

(1) A general average loss is a loss caused by or directly consequential on a general average act. It includes a general average expenditure as well as a general average sacrifice.

(2) There is a general average act where any extraordinary sacrifice or expenditure is voluntarily and reasonably made or incurred in time of peril for the purpose of preserving the property imperilled in the common adventure.

(3) Where there is a general average loss, the party on whom it falls is entitled, subject to the conditions imposed by maritime law, to a rateable contribution from the other parties interested, and such contribution is called a general average contribution.

(4) Subject to any express provision in the policy, where the assured has incurred a general average expenditure, he may recover from the insurer in respect of the proportion of the loss which falls upon him; and, in the case of a general average sacrifice, he may recover from the insurer in respect of the whole loss without having enforced his right of contribution from the other parties liable to contribute.

(5) Subject to any express provision in the policy, where the assured has paid, or is liable to pay, a general average contribution in respect of the subject insured, he may recover therefor from the insurer.

(6) In the absence of express stipulation, the insurer is not liable for any general average loss or contribution where the loss was not incurred for the purpose of avoiding, or in connexion with the avoidance of, a peril insured against.

(7) Where ship, freight, and cargo, or any two of those interests, are owned

by the same assured, the liability of the insurer in respect of general average losses or contributions is to be determined as if those subjects were owned by different persons. [618]

MEASURE OF INDEMNITY

67. Extent of liability of insurer for loss

(1) The sum which the assured can recover in respect of a loss on a policy by which he is insured, in the case of an unvalued policy to the full extent of the insurable value, or, in the case of a valued policy to the full extent of the value fixed by the policy, is called the measure of indemnity.

(2) Where there is a loss recoverable under the policy, the insurer, or each insurer if there be more than one, is liable for such proportion of the measure of indemnity as the amount of his subscription bears to the value fixed by the policy in the case of a valued policy, or to the insurable value in the case of an unvalued policy. [619]

68. Total loss

Subject to the provisions of this Act and to any express provision in the policy, where there is a total loss of the subject-matter insured,—

(1) If the policy be a valued policy, the measure of indemnity is the sum fixed by the policy:

(2) If the policy be an unvalued policy, the measure of indemnity is the insurable value of the subject-matter insured. [620]

69. Partial loss of ship

Where a ship is damaged, but is not totally lost, the measure of indemnity, subject to any express provision in the policy, is as follows:—

(1) Where the ship has been repaired, the assured is entitled to the reasonable cost of the repairs, less the customary deductions, but not exceeding the sum insured in respect of any one casualty:

(2) Where the ship has been only partially repaired, the assured is entitled to the reasonable cost of such repairs, computed as above, and also to be indemnified for the reasonable depreciation, if any, arising from the unrepaired damage, provided that the aggregate amount shall not exceed the cost of repairing the whole damage, computed as above:

(3) Where the ship has not been repaired, and has not been sold in her damaged state during the risk, the assured is entitled to be indemnified for the reasonable depreciation arising from the unrepaired damage, but not exceeding the reasonable cost of repairing such damage, computed as above. [621]

70. Partial loss of freight

Subject to any express provision in the policy, where there is a partial loss of freight, the measure of indemnity is such proportion of the sum fixed by the policy in the case of a valued policy, or of the insurable value in the case of an unvalued policy, as the proportion of freight lost by the assured bears to the whole freight at the risk of the assured under the policy. [622]

71. Partial loss of goods, merchandise, etc

Where there is a partial loss of goods, merchandise, or other moveables, the measure of indemnity, subject to any express provision in the policy, is as follows:—

(1) Where part of the goods, merchandise or other moveables insured by a valued policy is totally lost, the measure of indemnity is such proportion of the sum fixed by the policy as the insurable value of the part lost bears to the insurable value of the whole, ascertained as in the case of an unvalued policy:

(2) Where part of the goods, merchandise, or other moveables insured by an unvalued policy is totally lost, the measure of indemnity is the insurable value of the part lost, ascertained as in case of total loss:

(3) Where the whole or any part of the goods or merchandise insured has been delivered damaged at its destination, the measure of indemnity is such proportion of the sum fixed by the policy in the case of a valued policy, or of the insurable value in the case of an unvalued policy, as the difference between the gross sound and damaged values at the place of arrival bears to the gross sound value:

(4) "Gross value" means the wholesale price or, if there be no such price, the estimated value, with, in either case, freight, landing charges, and duty paid beforehand; provided that, in the case of goods or merchandise customarily sold in bond, the bonded price is deemed to be the gross value. "Gross proceeds" means the actual price obtained at a sale where all charges on sale are paid by the sellers. **[623]**

72. Apportionment of valuation

(1) Where different species of property are insured under a single valuation, the valuation must be apportioned over the different species in proportion to their respective insurable values, as in the case of an unvalued policy. The insured value of any part of a species is such proportion of the total insured value of the same as the insurable value of the part bears to the insurable value of the whole, ascertained in both cases as provided by this Act.

(2) Where a valuation has to be apportioned, and particulars of the prime cost of each separate species, quality, or description of goods cannot be ascertained, the division of the valuation may be made over the net arrived sound values of the different species, qualities, or descriptions of goods. **[624]**

73. General average contributions and salvage charges

(1) Subject to any express provision in the policy, where the assured has paid, or is liable for, any general average contribution, the measure of indemnity is the full amount of such contribution, if the subject-matter liable to contribution is insured for its full contributory value; but, if such subject-matter be not insured for its full contributory value, or if only part of it be insured, the indemnity payable by the insurer must be reduced in proportion to the under insurance, and where there has been a particular average loss which constitutes a deduction from the contributory value, and for which the insurer is liable, that amount must be deducted from the insured value in order to ascertain what the insurer is liable to contribute.

(2) Where the insurer is liable for salvage charges the extent of his liability must be determined on the like principle. **[625]**

74. Liabilities to third parties

Where the assured has effected an insurance in express terms against any liability to a third party, the measure of indemnity, subject to any express provision in the policy, is the amount paid or payable by him to such third party in respect of such liability. **[626]**

75. General provisions as to measure of indemnity

(1) Where there has been a loss in respect of any subject-matter not expressly provided for in the foregoing provisions of this Act, the measure of indemnity shall be ascertained, as nearly as may be, in accordance with those provisions, in so far as applicable to the particular case.

(2) Nothing in the provisions of this Act relating to the measure of indemnity shall affect the rules relating to double insurance, or prohibit the insurer from disproving interest wholly or in part, or from showing that at the time of the loss the whole or any part of the subject-matter insured was not at risk under the policy. **[627]**

76. Particular average warranties

(1) Where the subject-matter insured is warranted free from particular average, the assured cannot recover for a loss of part, other than a loss incurred by a general average sacrifice unless the contract contained in the policy be apportionable; but, if the contract be apportionable, the assured may recover for a total loss of any apportionable part.

(2) Where the subject-matter insured is warranted free from particular average, either wholly or under a certain percentage, the insurer is nevertheless liable for salvage charges, and for particular charges and other expenses properly incurred pursuant to the provisions of the suing and labouring clause in order to avert a loss insured against.

(3) Unless the policy otherwise provides, where the subject-matter insured is warranted free from particular average under a specified percentage, a general average loss cannot be added to a particular average loss to make up the specified percentage.

(4) For the purpose of ascertaining whether the specified percentage has been reached, regard shall be had only to the actual loss suffered by the subject-matter insured. Particular charges and the expenses of and incidental to ascertaining and proving the loss must be excluded. **[628]**

77. Successive losses

(1) Unless the policy otherwise provides, and subject to the provisions of this Act, the insurer is liable for successive losses, even though the total amount of such losses may exceed the sum insured.

(2) Where, under the same policy, a partial loss, which has not been repaired or otherwise made good, is followed by a total loss, the assured can only recover in respect of the total loss:

Provided that nothing in this section shall affect the liability of the insurer under the suing and labouring clause. **[629]**

78. Suing and labouring clause

(1) Where the policy contains a suing and labouring clause, the engagement thereby entered into is deemed to be supplementary to the contract of insurance, and the assured may recover from the insurer any expenses properly incurred pursuant to the clause, notwithstanding that the insurer may have paid for a total loss, or that the subject-matter may have been warranted free from particular average, either wholly or under a certain percentage.

(2) General average losses and contributions and salvage charges, as defined by this Act, are not recoverable under the suing and labouring clause.

(3) Expenses incurred for the purpose of averting or diminishing any loss not covered by the policy are not recoverable under the suing and labouring clause.

(4) It is the duty of the assured and his agents, in all cases, to take such measures as may be reasonable for the purpose of averting or minimising a loss. [630]

RIGHTS OF INSURER ON PAYMENT

79. Right of subrogation

(1) Where the insurer pays for a total loss, either of the whole, or in the case of goods of any apportionable part, of the subject-matter insured, he thereupon becomes entitled to take over the interest of the assured in whatever may remain of the subject-matter so paid for, and he is thereby subrogated to all the rights and remedies of the assured in and in respect of that subject-matter as from the time of the casualty causing the loss.

(2) Subject to the foregoing provisions, where the insurer pays for a partial loss, he acquires no title to the subject-matter insured, or such part of it as may remain, but he is thereupon subrogated to all rights and remedies of the assured in and in respect of the subject-matter insured as from the time of the casualty causing the loss, in so far as the assured has been indemnified, according to this Act, by such payment for the loss. [631]

80. Right of contribution

(1) Where the assured is over-insured by double insurance, each insurer is bound, as between himself and the other insurers, to contribute rateably to the loss in proportion to the amount for which he is liable under his contract.

(2) If any insurer pays more than his proportion of the loss, he is entitled to maintain an action for contribution against the other insurers, and is entitled to the like remedies as a surety who has paid more than his proportion of the debt. [632]

81. Effect of under insurance

Where the assured is insured for an amount less than the insurable value or, in the case of a valued policy, for an amount less than the policy valuation, he is deemed to be his own insurer in respect of the uninsured balance. [633]

RETURN OF PREMIUM

82. Enforcement of return

Where the premium or a proportionate part thereof is, by this Act, declared to be returnable,—
  (a) If already paid, it may be recovered by the assured from the insurer; and
  (b) If unpaid, it may be retained by the assured or his agent. [634]

83. Return by agreement

Where the policy contains a stipulation for the return of the premium, or a proportionate part thereof, on the happening of a certain event, and that event happens, the premium, or, as the case may be, the proportionate part thereof, is thereupon returnable to the assured. [635]

84. Return for failure of consideration

(1) Where the consideration for the payment of the premium totally fails, and there has been no fraud or illegality on the part of the assured or his agents, the premium is thereupon returnable to the assured.

(2) Where the consideration for the payment of the premium is apportionable and there is a total failure of any apportionable part of the consideration, a proportionate part of the premium is, under the like conditions, thereupon returnable to the assured.

  (3) In particular—
  (a) Where the policy is void, or is avoided by the insurer as from the commencement of the risk, the premium is returnable, provided that there has been no fraud or illegality on the part of the assured; but if the risk is not apportionable, and has once attached, the premium is not returnable;
  (b) Where the subject-matter insured, or part thereof, has never been imperilled, the premium, or, as the case may be, a proportionate part thereof, is returnable:
    Provided that where the subject-matter has been insured "lost or not lost" and has arrived in safety at the time when the contract is concluded, the premium is not returnable unless, at such time, the insurer knew of the safe arrival.
  (c) Where the assured has no insurable interest throughout the currency of the risk, the premium is returnable, provided that this rule does not apply to a policy effected by way of gaming or wagering;
  (d) Where the assured has a defeasible interest which is terminated during the currency of the risk, the premium is not returnable;
  (e) Where the assured has over-insured under an unvalued policy, a proportionate part of the premium is returnable;
  (f) Subject to the foregoing provisions, where the assured has over-insured by double insurance, a proportionate part of the several premiums is returnable:
    Provided that, if the policies are effected at different times, and any earlier policy has at any time borne the entire risk, or if a claim has been paid on the policy in respect of the full sum insured thereby, no

premium is returnable in respect of that policy, and when the double insurance is effected knowingly by the assured no premium is returnable. [636]

MUTUAL INSURANCE

85. Modification of Act in case of mutual insurance

(1) Where two or more persons mutually agree to insure each other against marine losses there is said to be a mutual insurance.

(2) The provisions of this Act relating to the premium do not apply to mutual insurance, but a guarantee, or such other arrangement as may be agreed upon, may be substituted for the premium.

(3) The provisions of this Act, in so far as they may be modified by the agreement of the parties, may in the case of mutual insurance be modified by the terms of the policies issued by the association, or by the rules and regulations of the association.

(4) Subject to the exceptions mentioned in this section, the provisions of this Act apply to a mutual insurance. [637]

SUPPLEMENTAL

86. Ratification by assured

Where a contract of marine insurance is in good faith effected by one person on behalf of another, the person on whose behalf it is effected may ratify the contract even after he is aware of a loss. [638]

87. Implied obligations varied by agreement or usage

(1) Where any right, duty, or liability would arise under a contract of marine insurance by implication of law, it may be negatived or varied by express agreement, or by usage, if the usage be such as to bind both parties to the contract.

(2) The provisions of this section extend to any right, duty, or liability declared by this Act which may be lawfully modified by agreement. [639]

88. Reasonable time, etc, a question of fact

Where by this Act any reference is made to reasonable time, reasonable premium, or reasonable diligence, the question what is reasonable is a question of fact. [640]

89. Slip as evidence

Where there is a duly stamped policy, reference may be made, as heretofore, to the slip or covering note, in any legal proceeding. [641]

90. Interpretation of terms

In this Act, unless the context or subject-matter otherwise requires,—

"Action" includes counter-claim and set off:
"Freight" includes the profit derivable by a shipowner from the employment of his ship to carry his own goods or moveables, as well

as freight payable by a third party, but does not include passage money:

"Moveables" means any moveable tangible property, other than the ship, and includes money, valuable securities, and other documents:

"Policy" means a marine policy.

91. Savings

(1) Nothing in this Act, or in any repeal effected thereby, shall affect—
- (a) The provisions of the Stamp Act 1891, or any enactment for the time being in force relating to the revenue;
- (b) The provisions of the Companies Act 1862, or any enactment amending or substituted for the same;
- (c) The provisions of any statute not expressly repealed by this Act.

(2) The rules of the common law including the law merchant, save in so far as they are inconsistent with the express provisions of this Act, shall continue to apply to contracts of marine insurance.

NOTES

Sections 92 and 93 were repealed by the Statute Law Revision Act 1927.

94. Short title

This Act may be cited as the Marine Insurance Act 1906.

SCHEDULES

SCHEDULE 1

Section 30

FORM OF POLICY

. . .

NOTES

The Form of Policy is omitted.

RULES FOR CONSTRUCTION OF POLICY

The following are the rules referred to by this Act for the construction of a policy in the above or other like form, where the context does not otherwise require:—

1. Where the subject-matter is insured "lost or not lost," and the loss has occurred before the contract is concluded, the risk attaches unless, at such time the assured was aware of the loss, and the insurer was not.

2. Where the subject-matter is insured "from" a particular place, the risk does not attach until the ship starts on the voyage insured.

3.—(a) Where a ship is insured "at and from" a particular place, and she is at that place in good safety when the contract is concluded, the risk attaches immediately.

- (b) If she be not at that place when the contract is concluded, the risk attaches as soon as she arrives there in good safety, and, unless the policy otherwise provides, it is immaterial that she is covered by another policy for a specified time after arrival.
- (c) Where chartered freight is insured "at and from" a particular place, and the ship is at that place in good safety when the contract is concluded the risk

attaches immediately. If she be not there when the contract is concluded, the risk attaches as soon as she arrives there in good safety.

(d) Where freight, other than chartered freight, is payable without special conditions and is insured "at and from" a particular place, the risk attaches pro rata as the goods or merchandise are shipped; provided that if there be cargo in readiness which belongs to the shipowner, or which some other person has contracted with him to ship, the risk attaches as soon as the ship is ready to receive such cargo.

4. Where goods or other moveables are insured "from the loading thereof," the risk does not attach until such goods or moveables are actually on board, and the insurer is not liable for them while in transit from the shore to ship.

5. Where the risk on goods or other moveables continues until they are "safely landed," they must be landed in the customary manner and within a reasonable time after arrival at the port of discharge, and if they are not so landed the risk ceases.

6. In the absence of any further license or usage, the liberty to touch and stay "at any port or place whatsoever" does not authorise the ship to depart from the course of her voyage from the port of departure to the port of destination.

7. The term "perils of the seas" refers only to fortuitous accidents or casualties of the seas. It does not include the ordinary action of the winds and waves.

8. The term "pirates" includes passengers who mutiny and rioters who attack the ship from the shore.

9. The term "thieves" does not cover clandestine theft or a theft committed by any one of the ship's company, whether crew or passengers.

10. The term "arrests, etc, of kings, princes, and people" refers to political or executive acts, and does not include a loss caused by riot or by ordinary judicial process.

11. The term "barratry" includes every wrongful act wilfully committed by the master or crew to the prejudice of the owner, or, as the case may be, the charterer.

12. The term "all other perils" includes only perils similar in kind to the perils specifically mentioned in the policy.

13. The term "average unless general" means a partial loss of the subject-matter insured other than a general average loss, and does not include "particular charges."

14. Where the ship has stranded, the insurer is liable for the excepted losses, although the loss is not attributable to the stranding, provided that when the stranding takes place the risk has attached and, if the policy be on goods, that the damaged goods are on board.

15. The term "ship" includes the hull, materials and outfit, stores and provisions for the officers and crew, and, in the case of vessels engaged in a special trade, the ordinary fittings requisite for the trade, and also, in the case of a steamship, the machinery, boilers, and coals and engine stores, if owned by the assured.

16. The term "freight" includes the profit derivable by a shipowner from the employment of his ship to carry his own goods or moveables, as well as freight payable by a third party, but does not include passage money.

17. The term "goods" means goods in the nature of merchandise, and does not include personal effects or provisions and stores for use on board.

In the absence of any usage to the contrary, deck cargo and living animals must be insured specifically, and not under the general denomination of goods.

NOTES
Schedule 2 was repealed by the Statute Law Revision Act 1927.

UNIFORM LAWS ON INTERNATIONAL SALES ACT 1967
(c 45)

ARRANGEMENT OF SECTIONS

Section		Para
1	Application of Uniform Law on the International Sale of Goods	[646]
2	Application of Uniform Law on the Formation of Contracts for the International Sale of Goods	[647]
3	Revision of Uniform Laws	[648]
4	Application to Isle of Man and Channel Islands	[649]
5	Short title	[650]

SCHEDULES

		Para
Schedule 1—The Uniform Law on the International Sale of Goods		
Chapter I Sphere of Application of the Law		[651]
Chapter II General Provisions		[652]
Chapter III Obligations of the Seller		[653]
Chapter IV Obligations of the Buyer		[654]
Chapter V Provisions Common to the Obligations of the Seller and of the Buyer		[655]
Chapter VI Passing of the Risk		[656]
Schedule 2—The Uniform Law on the Formation of Contracts for the International Sale of Goods		[657]

An Act to give effect to two Conventions with respect to the international sale of goods; and for purposes connected therewith [14 July 1967]

GENERAL NOTES
Commencement: 14 July 1967.
This Act applies to Northern Ireland.

---

1. Application of Uniform Law on the International Sale of Goods

(1) In this Act "the Uniform Law on Sales" means the Uniform Law on the International Sale of Goods forming the Annex to the First Convention and set out, with the modification provided for by Article III of that Convention, in Schedule 1 to this Act; and "the First Convention" means the Convention relating to a Uniform Law on the International Sale of Goods done at The Hague on 1 July 1964.

(2) The Uniform Law on Sales shall, subject to the following provisions of this section, have the force of law in the United Kingdom.

(3) While an Order of Her Majesty in Council is in force declaring that a declaration by the United Kingdom under Article V of the First Convention (application only by choice of parties) has been made and not withdrawn the Uniform Law on Sales shall apply to a contract of sale only if it has been chosen by the parties to the contract as the law of the contract.

[(4) In determining the extent of the application of the Uniform Law on Sales by virtue of Article 4 thereof (choice of parties)—
  (a) in relation to a contract made before 18 May 1973, no provision of the law of any part of the United Kingdom shall be regarded as a mandatory provision within the meaning of that Article;
  (b) in relation to a contract made on or after 18 May 1973 and before 1 February 1978, no provision of that law shall be so regarded except sections 12 to 15, 55 and 56 of the Sale of Goods Act 1979;

(c) in relation to a contract made on or after 1 February 1978, no provision of that law shall be so regarded except sections 12 to 15 of the Sale of Goods Act 1979.]

(5) If Her Majesty by Order in Council declares what States are Contracting States and in respect of what territories or what declarations under Article II of the First Convention are for the time being in force, the Order shall, while in force, be conclusive for the purposes of paragraph 1 or, as the case may be, paragraph 5 of Article 1 of the Uniform Law on Sales; but any Order in Council under this subsection may be varied or revoked by a subsequent Order in Council.

(6) The Uniform Law on Sales shall not apply to contracts concluded before such date as Her Majesty may by Order in Council declare to be the date on which the First Convention comes into force in respect of the United Kingdom.

(7) Any Order in Council under the preceding provisions of this section shall be laid before Parliament after being made.

(8) An Order in Council made under subsection (3) of this section may be revoked by a subsequent Order in Council; but no recommendation shall be made to Her Majesty in Council to make an Order under this subsection unless a draft thereof has been laid before and approved by each House of Parliament. **[646]**

NOTES
Sub-s (4): substituted by the Sale of Goods Act 1979, s 63, Sch 2, para 15.
Order in Council under this section: Uniform Laws on International Sales Order 1972, SI 1972 No 973, as amended by SI 1987 No 2061.

2. Application of Uniform Law on the Formation of Contracts for the International Sale of Goods

(1) In this Act "the Uniform Law on Formation" means the Law forming Annex I to the Second Convention as set out, with the modifications provided for by paragraph 3 of Article I of that Convention, in Schedule 2 to this Act; and "the Second Convention" means the Convention relating to a Uniform Law on the Formation of Contracts for the International Sale of Goods done at the Hague on 1 July 1964.

(2) Subject to subsection (3) of this section the Uniform Law on Formation shall have the force of law in the United Kingdom.

(3) The Uniform Law on Formation shall not apply to offers, replies and acceptances made before such date as Her Majesty may by Order in Council declare to be the date on which the Second Convention comes into force in respect of the United Kingdom.

(4) An Order in Council under this section shall be laid before Parliament after being made. **[647]**

NOTES
Order in Council under this Section: Uniform Laws on International Sales Order 1972, SI 1972 No 973, as amended by SI 1987 No 2061.

3. Revision of Uniform Laws

(1) If by any international Convention the Uniform Law on Sales or the Uniform Law on Formation is amended Her Majesty may by Order in Council

modify the Schedules to this Act in such manner as appears to Her necessary for the purpose of giving effect to the Convention.

(2) No recommendation shall be made to Her Majesty in Council to make an Order under this section unless a draft thereof has been laid before and approved by each House of Parliament. **[648]**

NOTES
No Order in Council has yet been made under this section.

4. Application to Isle of Man and Channel Islands

Her Majesty may by Order in Council direct that the provisions of this Act shall extend, with such exceptions, adaptations and modifications as may be specified in the Order, to the Isle of Man or any of the Channel Islands; and an Order in Council under this section may be varied or revoked by a subsequent Order in Council. **[649]**

NOTES
No Order in Council has yet been made under this section.

5. Short title

This Act may be cited as the Uniform Laws on International Sales Act 1967.
[650]

SCHEDULES
SCHEDULE 1

Section 1

THE UNIFORM LAW ON THE INTERNATIONAL SALE OF GOODS

CHAPTER I—SPHERE OF APPLICATION OF THE LAW

ARTICLE 1

1. The present Law shall apply to contracts of sale of goods entered into by parties whose places of business are in the territories of different Contracting States, in each of the following cases:
   (a) where the contract involves the sale of goods which are at the time of the conclusion of the contract in the course of carriage or will be carried from the territory of one State to the territory of another;
   (b) where the acts constituting the offer and the acceptance have been effected in the territories of different States;
   (c) where delivery of the goods is to be made in the territory of a State other than that within whose territory the acts constituting the offer and the acceptance have been effected.

2. Where a party to the contract does not have a place of business, reference shall be made to his habitual residence.

3. The application of the present Law shall not depend on the nationality of the parties.

4. In the case of contracts by correspondence, offer and acceptance shall be considered to have been effected in the territory of the same State only if the letters, telegrams or other documentary communications which contain them have been sent and received in the territory of that State.

5. For the purpose of determining whether the parties have their places of business or habitual residences in "different States", any two or more States shall not be considered to be "different States" if a valid declaration to that effect made under Article II of the

Convention dated the 1st day of July 1964 relating to a Uniform Law on the International Sale of Goods is in force in respect of them.

ARTICLE 2

Rules of private international law shall be excluded for the purposes of the application of the present Law, subject to any provision to the contrary in the said Law.

ARTICLE 3

The parties to a contract of sale shall be free to exclude the application thereto of the present Law either entirely or partially. Such exclusion may be express or implied.

ARTICLE 4

The present Law shall also apply where it has been chosen as the law of the contract by the parties, whether or not their places of business or their habitual residences are in different States and whether or not such States are Parties to the Convention dated the 1st day of July 1964 relating to the Uniform Law on the International Sale of Goods, to the extent that it does not affect the application of any mandatory provisions of law which would have been applicable if the parties had not chosen the Uniform Law.

ARTICLE 5

1. The present Law shall not apply to sales:

    (a) of stocks, shares, investment securities, negotiable instruments or money;
    (b) of any ship, vessel or aircraft, which is or will be subject to registration;
    (c) of electricity;
    (d) by authority of law or on execution or distress.

2. The present Law shall not affect the application of any mandatory provision of national law for the protection of a party to a contract which contemplates the purchase of goods by that party by payment of the price by instalments.

ARTICLE 6

Contracts for the supply of goods to be manufactured or produced shall be considered to be sales within the meaning of the present Law, unless the party who orders the goods undertakes to supply an essential and substantial part of the materials necessary for such manufacture or production.

ARTICLE 7

The present Law shall apply to sales regardless of the commercial or civil character of the parties or of the contracts.

ARTICLE 8

The present Law shall govern only the obligations of the seller and the buyer arising from a contract of sale. In particular, the present Law shall not, except as otherwise expressly provided therein, be concerned with the formation of the contract, nor with the effect which the contract may have on the property in the goods sold, nor with the validity of the contract or of any of its provisions or of any usage. **[651]**

Chapter II—General Provisions

ARTICLE 9

1. The parties shall be bound by any usage which they have expressly or impliedly made applicable to their contract and by any practices which they have established between themselves.

2. They shall also be bound by usages which reasonable persons in the same situation as the parties usually consider to be applicable to their contract. In the event of conflict with the present Law, the usages shall prevail unless otherwise agreed by the parties.

3. Where expressions, provisions or forms of contract commonly used in commercial practice are employed, they shall be interpreted according to the meaning usually given to them in the trade concerned.

ARTICLE 10

For the purposes of the present Law, a breach of contract shall be regarded as fundamental wherever the party in breach knew, or ought to have known, at the time of the conclusion of the contract, that a reasonable person in the same situation as the other party would not have entered into the contract if he had foreseen the breach and its effects.

ARTICLE 11

Where under the present Law an act is required to be performed "promptly", it shall be performed within as short a period as possible, in the circumstances, from the moment when the act could reasonably be performed.

ARTICLE 12

For the purposes of the present Law, the expression "current price" means a price based upon an official market quotation, or, in the absence of such a quotation, upon those factors which, according to the usage of the market, serve to determine the price.

ARTICLE 13

For the purposes of the present Law, the expression "a party knew or ought to have known", or any similar expression, refers to what should have been known to a reasonable person in the same situation.

ARTICLE 14

Communications provided for by the present Law shall be made by the means usual in the circumstances.

ARTICLE 15

A contract of sale need not be evidenced by writing and shall not be subject to any other requirements as to form. In particular, it may be proved by means of witnesses.

ARTICLE 16

Where under the provisions of the present Law one party to a contract of sale is entitled to require performance of any obligation by the other party, a court shall not be bound to enter or enforce a judgment providing for specific performance except in accordance with the provisions of Article VII of the Convention dated the 1st day of July 1964 relating to a Uniform Law on the International Sale of Goods.

ARTICLE 17

Questions concerning matters governed by the present Law which are not expressly settled therein shall be settled in conformity with the general principles on which the present Law is based.

CHAPTER III—OBLIGATIONS OF THE SELLER

ARTICLE 18

The seller shall effect delivery of the goods, hand over any documents relating thereto and transfer the property in the goods, as required by the contract and the present Law.

Section I.—Delivery of the Goods

ARTICLE 19

1. Delivery consists in the handing over of goods which conform with the contract.

2. Where the contract of sale involves carriage of the goods and no other place for delivery has been agreed upon, delivery shall be effected by handing over the goods to the carrier for transmission to the buyer.

3. Where the goods handed over to the carrier are not clearly appropriated to performance of the contract by being marked with an address or by some other means, the seller shall, in addition to handing over the goods, send to the buyer notice of the consignment and, if necessary, some document specifying the goods.

Sub-section 1.—Obligations of the Seller as Regards the Date and Place of Delivery

A.—Date of Delivery

ARTICLE 20

Where the parties have agreed upon a date for delivery or where such date is fixed by usage, the seller shall, without the need for any other formality, be bound to deliver the goods at that date, provided that the date thus fixed is determined or determinable by the calendar or is fixed in relation to a definite event, the date of which can be ascertained by the parties.

ARTICLE 21

Where by agreement of the parties or by usage delivery shall be effected within a certain period (such as a particular month or season), the seller may fix the precise date of delivery, unless the circumstances indicate that the fixing of the date was reserved to the buyer.

ARTICLE 22

Where the date of delivery has not been determined in accordance with the provisions of Articles 20 or 21, the seller shall be bound to deliver the goods within a reasonable time after the conclusion of the contract, regard being had to the nature of the goods and to the circumstances.

B.—Place of Delivery

ARTICLE 23

1. Where the contract of sale does not involve carriage of the goods, the seller shall deliver the goods at the place where he carried on business at the time of the conclusion of the contract, or, in the absence of a place of business, at his habitual residence.

2. If the sale relates to specific goods and the parties knew that the goods were at a certain place at the time of the conclusion of the contract, the seller shall deliver the goods at that place. The same rule shall apply if the goods sold are unascertained goods to be taken from a specified stock or if they are to be manufactured or produced at a place known to the parties at the time of the conclusion of the contract.

C.—Remedies for the seller's failure to perform his obligations as regards the date and place of delivery

ARTICLE 24

1. Where the seller fails to perform his obligations as regards the date or the place of delivery, the buyer may, as provided in Articles 25 to 32:

   (*a*) require performance of the contract by the seller;

(b) declare the contract avoided.

2. The buyer may also claim damages as provided in Article 82 or in Articles 84 to 87.

3. In no case shall the seller be entitled to apply to a court or arbitral tribunal to grant him a period of grace.

ARTICLE 25

The buyer shall not be entitled to require performance of the contract by the seller, if it is in conformity with usage and reasonably possible for the buyer to purchase goods to replace those to which the contract relates. In this case the contract shall be *ipso facto* avoided as from the time when such purchase should be effected.

(a) Remedies as regards the date of delivery

ARTICLE 26

1. Where the failure to deliver the goods at the date fixed amounts to a fundamental breach of the contract, the buyer may either require performance by the seller or declare the contract avoided. He shall inform the seller of his decision within a reasonable time; otherwise the contract shall be *ipso facto* avoided.

2. If the seller requests the buyer to make known his decision under paragraph 1 of this Article and the buyer does not comply promptly, the contract shall be *ipso facto* avoided.

3. If the seller has effected delivery before the buyer has made known his decision under paragraph 1 of this Article and the buyer does not exercise promptly his right to declare the contract avoided, the contract cannot be avoided.

4. Where the buyer has chosen performance of the contract and does not obtain it within a reasonable time, he may declare the contract avoided.

ARTICLE 27

1. Where failure to deliver the goods at the date fixed does not amount to a fundamental breach of the contract, the seller shall retain the right to effect delivery and the buyer shall retain the right to require performance of the contract by the seller.

2. The buyer may however grant the seller an additional period of time of reasonable length. Failure to deliver within this period shall amount to a fundamental breach of the contract.

ARTICLE 28

Failure to deliver the goods at the date fixed shall amount to a fundamental breach of the contract whenever a price for such goods is quoted on a market where the buyer can obtain them.

ARTICLE 29

Where the seller tenders delivery of the goods before the date fixed, the buyer may accept or reject delivery; if he accepts, he may reserve the right to claim damages in accordance with Article 82.

(b) Remedies as regards the place of delivery

ARTICLE 30

1. Where failure to deliver the goods at the place fixed amounts to a fundamental breach of the contract, and failure to deliver the goods at the date fixed would also amount to a fundamental breach, the buyer may either require performance of the contract by the seller or declare the contract avoided. The buyer shall inform the seller of his decision within a reasonable time; otherwise the contract shall be *ipso facto* avoided.

2. If the seller requests the buyer to make known his decision under paragraph 1 of

this Article and the buyer does not comply promptly, the contract shall be *ipso facto* avoided.

3. If the seller has transported the goods to the place fixed before the buyer has made known his decision under paragraph 1 of this Article and the buyer does not exercise promptly his right to declare the contract avoided, the contract cannot be avoided.

ARTICLE 31

1. In cases not provided for in Article 30, the seller shall retain the right to effect delivery at the place fixed and the buyer shall retain the right to require performance of the contract by the seller.

2. The buyer may however grant the seller an additional period of time of reasonable length. Failure to deliver within this period at the place fixed shall amount to a fundamental breach of the contract.

ARTICLE 32

1. If delivery is to be effected by handing over the goods to a carrier and the goods have been handed over at a place other than that fixed, the buyer may declare the contract avoided, whenever the failure to deliver the goods at the place fixed amounts to a fundamental breach of the contract. He shall lose this right if he has not promptly declared the contract avoided.

2. The buyer shall have the same right, in the circumstances and on the conditions provided in paragraph 1 of this Article, if the goods have been despatched to some place other than that fixed.

3. If despatch from a place or to a place other than that fixed does not amount to a fundamental breach of the contract, the buyer may only claim damages in accordance with Article 82.

Sub-section 2.—Obligations of the Seller as Regards the Conformity of the Goods

A.—Lack of conformity

ARTICLE 33

1. The seller shall not have fulfilled his obligation to deliver the goods, where he has handed over:
   (*a*) part only of the goods sold or a larger or a smaller quantity of the goods than he contracted to sell;
   (*b*) goods which are not those to which the contract relates or goods of a different kind;
   (*c*) goods which lack the qualities of a sample or model which the seller has handed over or sent to the buyer, unless the seller has submitted it without any express or implied undertaking that the goods would conform therewith;
   (*d*) goods which do not possess the qualities necessary for their ordinary or commercial use;
   (*e*) goods which do not possess the qualities for some particular purpose expressly or impliedly contemplated by the contract;
   (*f*) in general, goods which do not possess the qualities and characteristics expressly or impliedly contemplated by the contract.

2. No difference in quantity, lack of part of the goods or absence of any quality or characteristic shall be taken into consideration where it is not material.

ARTICLE 34

In the cases to which Article 33 relates, the rights conferred on the buyer by the present Law exclude all other remedies based on lack of conformity of the goods.

ARTICLE 35

1. Whether the goods are in conformity with the contract shall be determined by their condition at the time when risk passes. However, if risk does not pass because of a

declaration of avoidance of the contract or of a demand for other goods in replacement, the conformity of the goods with the contract shall be determined by their condition at the time when risk would have passed had they been in conformity with the contract.

2. The seller shall be liable for the consequences of any lack of conformity occurring after the time fixed in paragraph 1 of this Article if it was due to an act of the seller or of a person for whose conduct he is responsible.

ARTICLE 36

The seller shall not be liable for the consequences of any lack of conformity of the kind referred to in sub-paragraphs (*d*), (*e*) or (*f*) of paragraph 1 of Article 33, if at the time of the conclusion of the contract the buyer knew, or could not have been unaware of, such lack of conformity.

ARTICLE 37

If the seller has handed over goods before the date fixed for delivery he may, up to that date, deliver any missing part or quantity of the goods or deliver other goods which are in conformity with the contract or remedy any defects in the goods handed over, provided that the exercise of this right does not cause the buyer either unreasonable inconvenience or unreasonable expense.

B.—*Ascertainment and notification of lack of conformity*

ARTICLE 38

1. The buyer shall examine the goods, or cause them to be examined, promptly.

2. In case of carriage of the goods the buyer shall examine them at the place of destination.

3. If the goods are redespatched by the buyer without transhipment and the seller knew or ought to have known, at the time when the contract was concluded, of the possibility of such redespatch, examination of the goods may be deferred until they arrive at the new destination.

4. The methods of examination shall be governed by the agreement of the parties or, in the absence of such agreement, by the law or usage of the place where the examination is to be effected.

ARTICLE 39

1. The buyer shall lose the right to rely on a lack of conformity of the goods if he has not given the seller notice thereof promptly after he has discovered the lack of conformity or ought to have discovered it. If a defect which could not have been revealed by the examination of the goods provided for in Article 38 is found later, the buyer may nonetheless rely on that defect, provided that he gives the seller notice thereof promptly after its discovery. In any event, the buyer shall lose the right to rely on a lack of conformity of the goods if he has not given notice thereof to the seller within a period of two years from the date on which the goods were handed over, unless the lack of conformity constituted a breach of a guarantee covering a longer period.

2. In giving notice to the seller of any lack of conformity, the buyer shall specify its nature and invite the seller to examine the goods or to cause them to be examined by his agent.

3. Where any notice referred to in paragraph 1 of this Article has been sent by letter, telegram or other appropriate means, the fact that such notice is delayed or fails to arrive at its destination shall not deprive the buyer of the right to rely thereon.

ARTICLE 40

The seller shall not be entitled to rely on the provisions of Articles 38 and 39 if the lack of conformity relates to facts of which he knew, or of which he could not have been unaware, and which he did not disclose.

C.—*Remedies for lack of conformity*

ARTICLE 41

1. Where the buyer has given due notice to the seller of the failure of the goods to conform with the contract, the buyer may, as provided in Articles 42 to 46:

    (*a*) require performance of the contract by the seller;
    (*b*) declare the contract avoided;
    (*c*) reduce the price.

2. The buyer may also claim damages as provided in Article 82 or in Articles 84 to 87.

ARTICLE 42

1. The buyer may require the seller to perform the contract:

    (*a*) if the sale relates to goods to be produced or manufactured by the seller, by remedying defects in the goods, provided the seller is in a position to remedy the defects;
    (*b*) if the sale relates to specific goods, by delivering the goods to which the contract refers or the missing part thereof;
    (*c*) if the sale relates to unascertained goods, by delivering other goods which are in conformity with the contract or by delivering the missing part or quantity, except where the purchase of goods in replacement is in conformity with usage and reasonably possible.

2. If the buyer does not obtain performance of the contract by the seller within a reasonable time, he shall retain the rights provided in Articles 43 to 46.

ARTICLE 43

The buyer may declare the contract avoided if the failure of the goods to conform to the contract and also the failure to deliver on the date fixed amount to fundamental breaches of the contract. The buyer shall lose his right to declare the contract avoided if he does not exercise it promptly after giving the seller notice of the lack of conformity or, in the case to which paragraph 2 of Article 42 applies, after the expiration of the period referred to in that paragraph.

ARTICLE 44

1. In cases not provided for in Article 43, the seller shall retain, after the date fixed for the delivery of the goods, the right to deliver any missing part or quantity of the goods or to deliver other goods which are in conformity with the contract or to remedy any defect in the goods handed over, provided that the exercise of this right does not cause the buyer either unreasonable inconvenience or unreasonable expense.

2. The buyer may however fix an additional period of time of reasonable length for the further delivery or for the remedying of the defect. If at the expiration of the additional period the seller has not delivered the goods or remedied the defect, the buyer may choose between requiring the performance of the contract or reducing the price in accordance with Article 46 or, provided that he does so promptly, declare the contract avoided.

ARTICLE 45

1. Where the seller has handed over part only of the goods or an insufficient quantity or where part only of the goods handed over is in conformity with the contract, the provisions of Articles 43 and 44 shall apply in respect of the part or quantity which is missing or which does not conform with the contract.

2. The buyer may declare the contract avoided in its entirety only if the failure to effect delivery completely and in conformity with the contract amounts to a fundamental breach of the contract.

ARTICLE 46

Where the buyer has neither obtained performance of the contract by the seller nor declared the contract avoided, the buyer may reduce the price in the same proportion as the value of the goods at the time of the conclusion of the contract has been diminished because of their lack of conformity with the contract.

ARTICLE 47

Where the seller has proffered to the buyer a quantity of unascertained goods greater than that provided for in the contract, the buyer may reject or accept the excess quantity. If the buyer rejects the excess quantity, the seller shall be liable only for damages in accordance with Article 82. If the buyer accepts the whole or part of the excess quantity, he shall pay for it at the contract rate.

ARTICLE 48

The buyer may exercise the rights provided in Articles 43 to 46, even before the time fixed for delivery, if it is clear that goods which would be handed over would not be in conformity with the contract.

ARTICLE 49

1. The buyer shall lose his right to rely on lack of conformity with the contract at the expiration of a period of one year after he has given notice as provided in Article 39, unless he has been prevented from exercising his right because of fraud on the part of the seller.

2. After the expiration of this period, the buyer shall not be entitled to rely on the lack of conformity, even by way of defence to an action. Nevertheless, if the buyer has not paid for the goods and provided that he has given due notice of the lack of conformity promptly, as provided in Article 39, he may advance as a defence to a claim for payment of the price a claim for a reduction in the price or for damages.

Section II.—Handing over of documents

ARTICLE 50

Where the seller is bound to hand over to the buyer any documents relating to the goods, he shall do so at the time and place fixed by the contract or by usage.

ARTICLE 51

If the seller fails to hand over documents as provided in Article 50 at the time and place fixed or if he hands over documents which are not in conformity with those which he was bound to hand over, the buyer shall have the same rights as those provided under Articles 24 to 32 or under Articles 41 to 49, as the case may be.

Section III.—Transfer of property

ARTICLE 52

1. Where the goods are subject to a right or claim of a third person, the buyer, unless he agreed to take the goods subject to such right or claim, shall notify the seller of such right or claim, unless the seller already knows thereof, and request that the goods should be freed therefrom within reasonable time or that other goods free from all rights and claims of third persons be delivered to him by the seller.

2. If the seller complies with a request made under paragraph 1 of this Article and the buyer nevertheless suffers a loss, the buyer may claim damages in accordance with Article 82.

3. If the seller fails to comply with a request made under paragraph 1 of this Article and a fundamental breach of the contract results thereby, the buyer may declare the contract avoided and claim damages in accordance with Articles 84 to 87. If the buyer

does not declare the contract avoided or if there is no fundamental breach of the contract, the buyer shall have the right to claim damages in accordance with Article 82.

4. The buyer shall lose his right to declare the contract avoided if he fails to act in accordance with paragraph 1 of this Article within a reasonable time from the moment when he became aware or ought to have become aware of the right or claim of the third person in respect of the goods.

ARTICLE 53

The rights conferred on the buyer by Article 52 exclude all other remedies based on the fact that the seller has failed to perform his obligation to transfer the property in the goods or that the goods are subject to a right or claim of a third person.

Section IV.—Other obligations of the seller

ARTICLE 54

1. If the seller is bound to despatch the goods to the buyer, he shall make, in the usual way and on the usual terms, such contracts as are necessary for the carriage of the goods to the place fixed.

2. If the seller is not bound by the contract to effect insurance in respect of the carriage of the goods, he shall provide the buyer, at his request, with all information necessary to enable him to effect such insurance.

ARTICLE 55

1. If the seller fails to perform any obligation other than those referred to in Articles 20 to 53, the buyer may:
   (*a*) where such failure amounts to a fundamental breach of the contract, declare the contract avoided, provided that he does so promptly, and claim damages in accordance with Articles 84 to 87, or
   (*b*) in any other case, claim damages in accordance with Article 82.

2. The buyer may also require performance by the seller of his obligation, unless the contract is avoided. [653]

CHAPTER IV—OBLIGATIONS OF THE BUYER

ARTICLE 56

The buyer shall pay the price for the goods and take delivery of them, as required by the contract and the present law.

Section I.—Payment of the price

A.—Fixing the price

ARTICLE 57

Where a contract has been concluded but does not state a price or make provision for the determination of the price, the buyer shall be bound to pay the price generally charged by the seller at the time of the conclusion of the contract.

ARTICLE 58

Where the price is fixed according to the weight of the goods, it shall, in case of doubt, be determined by the net weight.

B.—Place and date of payment

ARTICLE 59

1. The buyer shall pay the price to the seller at the seller's place of business or, if he does not have a place of business, at his habitual residence, or, where the payment is to be

made against the handing over of the goods or of documents, at the place where such handing over takes place.

2. Where, in consequence of a change in the place of business or habitual residence of the seller subsequent to the conclusion of the contract, the expenses incidental to payment are increased, such increase shall be borne by the seller.

ARTICLE 60

Where the parties have agreed upon a date for the payment of the price or where such date is fixed by usage, the buyer shall, without the need for any other formality, pay the price at that date.

C.—Remedies for non-payment

ARTICLE 61

1. If the buyer fails to pay the price in accordance with the contract and with the present law, the seller may require the buyer to perform his obligation.

2. The seller shall not be entitled to require payment of the price by the buyer if it is in conformity with usage and reasonably possible for the seller to resell the goods. In that case the contract shall be *ipso facto* avoided as from the time when such resale should be effected.

ARTICLE 62

1. Where the failure to pay the price at the date fixed amounts to a fundamental breach of the contract, the seller may either require the buyer to pay the price or declare the contract avoided. He shall inform the buyer of his decision within a reasonable time; otherwise the contract shall be *ipso facto* avoided.

2. Where the failure to pay the price at the date fixed does not amount to a fundamental breach of the contract, the seller may grant to the buyer an additional period of time of reasonable length. If the buyer has not paid the price at the expiration of the additional period, the seller may either require the payment of the price by the buyer or, provided that he does so promptly, declare the contract avoided.

ARTICLE 63

1. Where the contract is avoided because of failure to pay the price, the seller shall have the right to claim damages in accordance with Articles 84 to 87.

2. Where the contract is not avoided, the seller shall have the right to claim damages in accordance with Articles 82 and 83.

ARTICLE 64

In no case shall the buyer be entitled to apply to a court or arbitral tribunal to grant him a period of grace for the payment of the price.

Section II.—Taking delivery

ARTICLE 65

Taking delivery consists in the buyer's doing all such acts as are necessary in order to enable the seller to hand over the goods and actually taking them over.

ARTICLE 66

1. Where the buyer's failure to take delivery of the goods in accordance with the contract amounts to a fundamental breach of the contract or gives the seller good grounds for fearing that the buyer will not pay the price, the seller may declare the contract avoided.

2. Where the failure to take delivery of the goods does not amount to a fundamental breach of the contract, the seller may grant to the buyer an additional period of time of reasonable length. If the buyer has not taken delivery of the goods at the expiration of

the additional period, the seller may declare the contract avoided, provided that he does so promptly.

ARTICLE 67

1. If the contract reserves to the buyer the right subsequently to determine the form, measurement or other features of the goods (sale by specification) and he fails to make such specification either on the date expressly or impliedly agreed upon or within a reasonable time after receipt of a request from the seller, the seller may declare the contract avoided, provided that he does so promptly, or make the specification himself in accordance with the requirements of the buyer in so far as these are known to him.

2. If the seller makes the specification himself, he shall inform the buyer of the details thereof and shall fix a reasonable period of time within which the buyer may submit a different specification. If the buyer fails to do so the specification made by the seller shall be binding.

ARTICLE 68

1. Where the contract is avoided because of the failure of the buyer to accept delivery of the goods or to make a specification, the seller shall have the right to claim damages in accordance with Articles 84 to 87.

2. Where the contract is not avoided, the seller shall have the right to claim damages in accordance with Article 82.

Section III.—Other obligations of the buyer

ARTICLE 69

The buyer shall take the steps provided for in the contract, by usage or by laws and regulations in force, for the purpose of making provision for or guaranteeing payment of the price, such as the acceptance of a bill of exchange, the opening of a documentary credit or the giving of a banker's guarantee.

ARTICLE 70

1. If the buyer fails to perform any obligation other than those referred to in Sections I and II of this Chapter, the seller may:
   (a) where such failure amounts to a fundamental breach of the contract, declare the contract avoided, provided that he does so promptly, and claim damages in accordance with Articles 84 to 87; or
   (b) in any other case, claim damages in accordance with Article 82.

2. The seller may also require performance by the buyer of his obligation, unless the contract is avoided.

CHAPTER V—PROVISIONS COMMON TO THE OBLIGATIONS OF THE SELLER AND OF THE BUYER

Section I.—Concurrence between delivery of the goods and payment of the price

ARTICLE 71

Except as otherwise provided in Article 72, delivery of the goods and payment of the price shall be concurrent conditions. Nevertheless, the buyer shall not be obliged to pay the price until he has had an opportunity to examine the goods.

ARTICLE 72

1. Where the contract involves carriage of the goods and where delivery is, by virtue of paragraph 2 of Article 19, effected by handing over the goods to the carrier, the seller may either postpone despatch of the goods until he receives payment or proceed to despatch them on terms that reserve to himself the right of disposal of the goods during transit. In the latter case, he may require that the goods shall not be handed over to the

buyer at the place of destination except against payment of the price and the buyer shall not be bound to pay the price until he has had an opportunity to examine the goods.

2. Nevertheless, when the contract requires payment against documents, the buyer shall not be entitled to refuse payment of the price on the ground that he has not had the opportunity to examine the goods.

ARTICLE 73

1. Each party may suspend the performance of his obligations whenever, after the conclusion of the contract, the economic situation of the other party appears to have become so difficult that there is good reason to fear that he will not perform a material part of his obligations.

2. If the seller has already despatched the goods before the economic situation of the buyer described in paragraph 1 of this Article becomes evident, he may prevent the handing over of the goods to the buyer even if the latter holds a document which entitles him to obtain them.

3. Nevertheless, the seller shall not be entitled to prevent the handing over of the goods if they are claimed by a third person who is a lawful holder of a document which entitles him to obtain the goods, unless the document contains a reservation concerning the effects of its transfer or unless the seller can prove that the holder of the document, when he acquired it, knowingly acted to the detriment of the seller.

Section II.—Exemptions

ARTICLE 74

1. Where one of the parties has not performed one of his obligations, he shall not be liable for such non-performance if he can prove that it was due to circumstances which, according to the intention of the parties at the time of the conclusion of the contract, he was not bound to take into account or to avoid or to overcome; in the absence of any expression of the intention of the parties, regard shall be had to what reasonable persons in the same situation would have intended.

2. Where the circumstances which gave rise to the non-performance of the obligation constituted only a temporary impediment to performance, the party in default shall nevertheless be permanently relieved of his obligation if, by reason of the delay, performance would be so radically changed as to amount to the performance of an obligation quite different from that contemplated by the contract.

3. The relief provided by this Article for one of the parties shall not include the avoidance of the contract under some other provision of the present Law or deprive the other party of any right which he has under the present Law to reduce the price, unless the circumstances which entitled the first party to relief were caused by the act of the other party or of some person for whose conduct he was responsible.

Section III.—Supplementary rules concerning the avoidance of the contract

A.—Supplementary grounds for avoidance

ARTICLE 75

1. Where, in the case of contracts for delivery of goods by instalments, by reason of any failure by one party to perform any of his obligations under the contract in respect of any instalment, the other party has good reason to fear failure of performance in respect of future instalments, he may declare the contract avoided for the future, provided that he does so promptly.

2. The buyer may also, provided that he does so promptly, declare the contract avoided in respect of future deliveries or in respect of deliveries already made or both, if by reason of their interdependence such deliveries would be worthless to him.

ARTICLE 76

Where prior to the date fixed for performance of the contract it is clear that one of the parties will commit a fundamental breach of the contract, the other party shall have the right to declare the contract avoided.

ARTICLE 77

Where the contract has been avoided under Article 75 or Article 76, the party declaring the contract avoided may claim damages in accordance with Articles 84 to 87.

B.—*Effects of avoidance*

ARTICLE 78

1. Avoidance of the contract releases both parties from their obligations thereunder, subject to any damages which may be due.

2. If one party has performed the contract either wholly or in part, he may claim the return of whatever he has supplied or paid under the contract. If both parties are required to make restitution, they shall do so concurrently.

ARTICLE 79

1. The buyer shall lose his right to declare the contract avoided where it is impossible for him to return the goods in the condition in which he received them.

2. Nevertheless, the buyer may declare the contract avoided:
   (*a*) if the goods or part of the goods have perished or deteriorated as a result of the defect which justifies the avoidance;
   (*b*) if the goods or part of the goods have perished or deteriorated as a result of the examination prescribed in Article 38;
   (*c*) if part of the goods have been consumed or transformed by the buyer in the course of normal use before the lack of conformity with the contract was discovered;
   (*d*) if the impossibility of returning the goods or of returning them in the condition in which they were received is not due to the act of the buyer or of some other person for whose conduct he is responsible;
   (*e*) if the deterioration or transformation of the goods is unimportant.

ARTICLE 80

The buyer who has lost the right to declare the contract avoided by virtue of Article 79 shall retain all the other rights conferred on him by the present Law.

ARTICLE 81

1. Where the seller is under an obligation to refund the price, he shall also be liable for the interest thereon at the rate fixed by Article 83, as from the date of payment.

2. The buyer shall be liable to account to the seller for all benefits which he has derived from the goods or part of them, as the case may be:
   (*a*) where he is under an obligation to return the goods or part of them,
   (*b*) where it is impossible for him to return the goods or part of them, but the contract is nevertheless avoided.

Section IV.—*Supplementary rules concerning damages*

A.—*Damages where the contract is not avoided*

ARTICLE 82

Where the contract is not avoided, damages for a breach of contract by one party shall consist of a sum equal to the loss, including loss of profit, suffered by the other party. Such damages shall not exceed the loss which the party in breach ought to have foreseen at the time of the conclusion of the contract, in the light of the facts and matters which then were known or ought to have been known to him, as a possible consequence of the breach of the contract.

ARTICLE 83

Where the breach of contract consists of delay in the payment of the price, the seller shall in any event be entitled to interest on such sum as is in arrear at a rate equal to the official discount rate in the country where he has his place of business or, if he has no place of business, his habitual residence, plus 1 per cent.

B.—Damages where the contract is avoided

ARTICLE 84

1. In case of avoidance of the contract, where there is a current price for the goods, damages shall be equal to the difference between the price fixed by the contract and the current price on the date on which the contract is avoided.

2. In calculating the amount of damages under paragraph 1 of this Article, the current price to be taken into account shall be that prevailing in the market in which the transaction took place or, if there is no such current price or if its application is inappropriate, the price in a market which serves as a reasonable substitute, making due allowance for differences in the cost of transporting the goods.

ARTICLE 85

If the buyer has bought goods in replacement or the seller has resold goods in a reasonable manner, he may recover the difference between the contract price and the price paid for the goods bought in replacement or that obtained by the resale.

ARTICLE 86

The damages referred to in Articles 84 and 85 may be increased by the amount of any reasonable expenses incurred as a result of the breach or up to the amount of any loss, including loss of profit, which should have been foreseen by the party in breach, at the time of the conclusion of the contract, in the light of the facts and matters which were known or ought to have been known to him, as a possible consequence of the breach of the contract.

ARTICLE 87

If there is no current price for the goods, damages shall be calculated on the same basis as that provided in Article 82.

C.—General provisions concerning damages

ARTICLE 88

The party who relies on a breach of the contract shall adopt all reasonable measures to mitigate the loss resulting from the breach. If he fails to adopt such measures, the party in breach may claim a reduction in the damages.

ARTICLE 89

In case of fraud, damages shall be determined by the rules applicable in respect of contracts of sale not governed by the present law.

Section V.—Expenses

ARTICLE 90

The expenses of delivery shall be borne by the seller; all expenses after delivery shall be borne by the buyer.

Section VI.—Preservation of the Goods

ARTICLE 91

Where the buyer is in delay in taking delivery of the goods or in paying the price, the seller shall take reasonable steps to preserve the goods; he shall have the right to retain them until he has been reimbursed his reasonable expenses by the buyer.

ARTICLE 92

1. Where the goods have been received by the buyer, he shall take reasonable steps to preserve them if he intends to reject them; he shall have the right to retain them until he has been reimbursed his reasonable expenses by the seller.

2. Where goods despatched to the buyer have been put at his disposal at their place of destination and he exercises the right to reject them, he shall be bound to take possession of them on behalf of the seller, provided that this may be done without payment of the price and without unreasonable inconvenience or unreasonable expense. This provision shall not apply where the seller or a person authorised to take charge of the goods on his behalf is present at such destination.

ARTICLE 93

The party who is under an obligation to take steps to preserve the goods may deposit them in the warehouse of a third person at the expense of the other party provided that the expense incurred is not unreasonable.

ARTICLE 94

1. The party who, in the cases to which Articles 91 and 92 apply, is under an obligation to take steps to preserve the goods may sell them by any appropriate means, provided that there has been unreasonable delay by the other party in accepting them or taking them back or in paying the costs of preservation and provided that due notice has been given to the other party of the intention to sell.

2. The party selling the goods shall have the right to retain out of the proceeds of sale an amount equal to the reasonable costs of preserving the goods and of selling them and shall transmit the balance to the other party.

ARTICLE 95

Where, in the cases to which Articles 91 and 92 apply, the goods are subject to loss or rapid deterioration or their preservation would involve unreasonable expense, the party under the duty to preserve them is bound to sell them in accordance with Article 94.

CHAPTER VI—PASSING OF THE RISK

ARTICLE 96

Where the risk has passed to the buyer, he shall pay the price notwithstanding the loss or deterioration of the goods, unless this is due to the act of the seller or of some other person for whose conduct the seller is responsible.

ARTICLE 97

1. The risk shall pass to the buyer when delivery of the goods is effected in accordance with the provisions of the contract and the present Law.

2. In the case of the handing over of goods which are not in conformity with the contract, the risk shall pass to the buyer from the moment when the handing over has, apart from the lack of conformity, been effected in accordance with the provisions of the contract and of the present Law, where the buyer has neither declared the contract avoided nor required goods in replacement.

ARTICLE 98

1. Where the handing over of the goods is delayed owing to the breach of an obligation of the buyer, the risk shall pass to the buyer as from the last date when, apart from such breach, the handing over could have been made in accordance with the contract.

2. Where the contract relates to a sale of unascertained goods, delay on the part of the buyer shall cause the risk to pass only when the seller has set aside goods manifestly appropriated to the contract and has notified the buyer that this has been done.

3. Where unascertained goods are of such a kind that the seller cannot set aside a part of them until the buyer takes delivery, it shall be sufficient for the seller to do all acts necessary to enable the buyer to take delivery.

ARTICLE 99

1. Where the sale is of goods in transit by sea, the risk shall be borne by the buyer as from the time at which the goods were handed over to the carrier.

2. Where the seller, at the time of the conclusion of the contract, knew or ought to have known that the goods had been lost or had deteriorated, the risk shall remain with him until the time of the conclusion of the contract.

ARTICLE 100

If, in a case to which paragraph 3 of Article 19 applies, the seller, at the time of sending the notice or other document referred to in that paragraph knew or ought to have known that the goods had been lost or had deteriorated after they were handed over to the carrier, the risk shall remain with the seller until the time of sending such notice or document.

ARTICLE 101

The passing of the risk shall not necessarily be determined by the provisions of the contract concerning expenses.

SCHEDULE 2

Section 2

The Uniform Law on the Formation of Contracts for the International Sale of Goods

ARTICLE 1

The present Law shall apply to the formation of contracts of sale of goods which, if they were concluded, would be governed by the Uniform Law on the International Sale of Goods.

ARTICLE 2

1. The provisions of the following Articles shall apply except to the extent that it appears from the preliminary negotiations, the offer, the reply, the practices which the parties have established between themselves or usage, that other rules apply.

2. However, a term of the offer stipulating that silence shall amount to acceptance is invalid.

ARTICLE 3

An offer or an acceptance need not be evidenced by writing and shall not be subject to any other requirement as to form. In particular, they may be proved by means of witnesses.

ARTICLE 4

1. The communication which one person addresses to one or more specific persons with the object of concluding a contract of sale shall not constitute an offer unless it is

sufficiently definite to permit the conclusion of the contract by acceptance and indicates the intention of the offeror to be bound.

2. This communication may be interpreted by reference to and supplemented by the preliminary negotiations, any practices which the parties have established between themselves, usage and the provisions of the Uniform Law on the International Sale of Goods.

ARTICLE 5

1. The offer shall not bind the offeror until it has been communicated to the offeree; it shall lapse if its withdrawal is communicated to the offeree before or at the same time as the offer.

2. After an offer has been communicated to the offeree it can be revoked unless the revocation is not made in good faith or in conformity with fair dealing or unless the offer states a fixed time for acceptance or otherwise indicates that it is firm or irrevocable.

3. An indication that the offer is firm or irrevocable may be express or implied from the circumstances, the preliminary negotiations, any practices which the parties have established between themselves or usage.

4. A revocation of an offer shall only have effect if it has been communicated to the offeree before he has despatched his acceptance or has done any act treated as acceptance under paragraph 2 of Article 6.

ARTICLE 6

1. Acceptance of an offer consists of a declaration by any means whatsoever to the offeror.

2. Acceptance may also consist of the despatch of the goods or of the price or of any other act which may be considered to be equivalent to the declaration referred to in paragraph 1 of this Article either by virtue of the offer or as a result of practices which the parties have established between themselves or usage.

ARTICLE 7

1. An acceptance containing additions, limitations or other modifications shall be a rejection of the offer and shall constitute a counter-offer.

2. However, a reply to an offer which purports to be an acceptance but which contains additional or different terms which do not materially alter the terms of the offer shall constitute an acceptance unless the offeror promptly objects to the discrepancy; if he does not so object, the terms of the contract shall be the terms of the offer with the modifications contained in the acceptance.

ARTICLE 8

1. A declaration of acceptance of an offer shall have effect only if it is communicated to the offeror within the time he has fixed or, if no such time is fixed, within a reasonable time, due account being taken of the circumstances of the transaction, including the rapidity of the means of communication employed by the offeror, and usage. In the case of an oral offer, the acceptance shall be immediate, if the circumstances do not show that the offeree shall have time for reflection.

2. If a time for acceptance is fixed by an offeror in a letter or in a telegram, it shall be presumed to begin to run from the day the letter was dated or the hour of the day the telegram was handed in for despatch.

3. If an acceptance consists of an act referred to in paragraph 2 of Article 6, the act shall have effect only if it is done within the period laid down in paragraph 1 of the present Article.

ARTICLE 9

1. If the acceptance is late, the offeror may nevertheless consider it to have arrived in due time on condition that he promptly so informs the acceptor orally or by despatch of a notice.

2. If however the acceptance is communicated late, it shall be considered to have been communicated in due time, if the letter or document which contains the acceptance shows that it has been sent in such circumstances that if its transmission had been normal it would have been communicated in due time; this provision shall not however apply if the offeror has promptly informed the acceptor orally or by despatch of a notice that he considers his offer as having lapsed.

ARTICLE 10

An acceptance cannot be revoked except by a revocation which is communicated to the offeror before or at the same time as the acceptance.

ARTICLE 11

The formation of the contract is not affected by the death of one of the parties or by his becoming incapable of contracting before acceptance unless the contrary results from the intention of the parties, usage or the nature of the transaction.

ARTICLE 12

1. For the purposes of the present Law, the expression "to be communicated" means to be delivered at the address of the person to whom the communication is directed.

2. Communications provided for by the present Law shall be made by the means usual in the circumstances.

ARTICLE 13

1. "Usage" means any practice or method of dealing which reasonable persons in the same situation as the parties usually consider to be applicable to the formation of their contract.

2. Where expressions, provisions or forms of contract commonly used in commercial practice are employed, they shall be interpreted according to the meaning usually given to them in the trade concerned.

CARRIAGE OF GOODS BY SEA ACT 1971
(c 19)

ARRANGEMENT OF SECTIONS

Section		Para
1	Application of Hague Rules as amended	[658]
2	Contracting States, etc	[659]
3	Absolute warranty of seaworthiness not to be implied in contracts to which Rules apply	[660]
4	Application of Act to British possessions, etc	[661]
5	Extension of application of Rules to carriage from ports in British possessions, etc	[662]
6	Supplemental	[663]
	Schedule—The Hague Rules as amended by the Brussels Protocol 1968	[664]

An Act to amend the law with respect to the carriage of goods by sea

[8 April 1971]

GENERAL NOTES
  This Act applies to Northern Ireland.
  This Act applies, with modifications, to hovercraft by virtue of the Hovercraft (Civil Liability) Order 1986, SI 1986 No 1305, arts 4, 5, 10, Sch 2, Sch 4.

1. Application of Hague Rules as amended

(1) In this Act, "the Rules" means the International Convention for the unification of certain rules of law relating to bills of lading signed at Brussels on 25 August 1924, as amended by the Protocol signed at Brussels on 23 February 1968 [and by the Protocol signed at Brussels on 21 December 1979].

(2) The provisions of the Rules, as set out in the Schedule to this Act, shall have the force of law.

(3) Without prejudice to subsection (2) above, the said provisions shall have effect (and have the force of law) in relation to and in connection with the carriage of goods by sea in ships where the port of shipment is a port in the United Kingdom, whether or not the carriage is between ports in two different States within the meaning of Article X of the Rules.

(4) Subject to subsection (6) below, nothing in this section shall be taken as applying anything in the Rules to any contract for the carriage of goods by sea, unless the contract expressly or by implication provides for the issue of a bill of lading or any similar document of title.

(5) ...

(6) Without prejudice to Article X (c) of the Rules, the Rules shall have the force of law in relation to—

(a) any bill of lading if the contract contained in or evidenced by it expressly provides that the Rules shall govern the contract, and
(b) any receipt which is a non-negotiable document marked as such if the contract contained in or evidenced by it is a contract for the carriage of goods by sea which expressly provides that the Rules are to govern the contract as if the receipt were a bill of lading,

but subject, where paragraph (b) applies, to any necessary modifications and in particular with the omission in Article III of the Rules of the second sentence of paragraph 4 and of paragraph 7.

(7) If and so far as the contract contained in or evidenced by a bill of lading or receipt within paragraph (a) or (b) of subsection (6) above applies to deck cargo or live animals, the Rules as given the force of law by that subsection shall have effect as if Article I (c) did not exclude deck cargo and live animals.

In this subsection "deck cargo" means cargo which by the contract of carriage is stated as being carried on deck and is so carried.

NOTES
Commencement: 23 June 1977.
Commencement order: SI 1977 No 981.
Sub-s (1): amended by the Merchant Shipping Act 1981, s 2(1).
Sub-s (5): repealed by the Merchant Shipping Act 1981, s 5(3), Schedule.

2. Contracting States, etc

(1) If Her Majesty by Order in Council certifies to the following effect, that is to say, that for the purposes of the Rules—

(a) a State specified in the Order is a contracting State, or is a contracting State in respect of any place or territory so specified; or
(b) any place or territory specified in the Order forms part of a State so specified (whether a contracting State or not),

the Order shall, except so far as it has been superseded by a subsequent Order, be conclusive evidence of the matters so certified.

(2) An Order in Council under this section may be varied or revoked by a subsequent Order in Council. **[659]**

NOTES
Commencement: 23 June 1977.
Commencement order: SI 1977 No 981.
Order in Council under this section: Carriage of Goods by Sea (Parties to Convention) Order 1985, SI 1985 No 443.

3. Absolute warranty of seaworthiness not to be implied in contracts to which Rules apply

There shall not be implied in any contract for the carriage of goods by sea to which the Rules apply by virtue of this Act any absolute undertaking by the carrier of the goods to provide a seaworthy ship. **[660]**

NOTES
Commencement: 23 June 1977.
Commencement order: SI 1977 No 981.

4. Application of Act to British possessions, etc

(1) Her Majesty may by Order in Council direct that this Act shall extend, subject to such exceptions, adaptations and modifications as may be specified in the Order, to all or any of the following territories, that is—

    (*a*) any colony (not being a colony for whose external relations a country other than the United Kingdom is responsible),

    (*b*) any country outside Her Majesty's dominions in which Her Majesty has jurisdiction in right of Her Majesty's Government of the United Kingdom.

(2) An Order in Council under this section may contain such transitional and other consequential and incidental provisions as appear to Her Majesty to be expedient, including provisions amending or repealing any legislation about the carriage of goods by sea forming part of the law of any of the territories mentioned in paragraphs (*a*) and (*b*) above.

(3) An Order in Council under this section may be varied or revoked by a subsequent Order in Council. **[661]**

NOTES
Commencement: 23 June 1977.
Commencement order: SI 1977 No 981.
Orders in Council under this section: Carriage of Goods by Sea (Bermuda) Order 1980, SI 1980 No 1507; Carriage of Goods by Sea (Hong Kong) Order 1980, SI 1980 No 1508, amended by SI 1980 No 1954; Carriage of Goods by Sea (Bermuda) Order 1982, SI 1982 No 1662; Carriage of Goods by Sea (Hong Kong) Order 1982, SI 1982 No 1663; Carriage of Goods by Sea (Overseas territories) Order 1982, SI 1982 No 1664.

5. Extension of application of Rules to carriage from ports in British possessions, etc

(1) Her Majesty may by Order in Council provide that section 1(3) of this Act shall have effect as if the reference therein to the United Kingdom included a reference to all or any of the following territories, that is—

    (*a*) the Isle of Man;

    (*b*) any of the Channel Islands specified in the Order;

(c) any colony specified in the Order (not being a colony for whose external relations a country other than the United Kingdom is responsible);
(d) any associated state (as defined by section 1 (3) of the West Indies Act 1967) specified in the Order;
(e) any country specified in the Order, being a country outside Her Majesty's dominions in which Her Majesty has jurisdiction in right of Her Majesty's Government of the United Kingdom.

(2) An Order in Council under this section may be varied or revoked by a subsequent Order in Council. [662]

NOTES
Commencement: 23 June 1977.
Commencement order: SI 1977 No 981.
No Orders in Council have yet been made under this section.

6. Supplemental

(1) This Act may be cited as the Carriage of Goods by Sea Act 1971.

(2) It is hereby declared that this Act extends to Northern Ireland.

(3) The following enactments shall be repealed, that is—
(a) the Carriage of Goods by Sea Act 1924,
(b) section 12(4)(a) of the Nuclear Installations Act 1965,

and without prejudice to section 38(1) of the Interpretation Act 1889, the reference to the said Act of 1924 in section 1(1)(i)(ii) of the Hovercraft Act 1968 shall include a reference to this Act.

(4) It is hereby declared that for the purposes of Article VIII of the Rules [section 18 of the Merchant Shipping Act 1979 (which] entirely exempts shipowners and others in certain circumstances from liability for loss of, or damage to, goods) is a provision relating to limitation of liability.

(5) This Act shall come into force on such day as Her Majesty may by Order in Council appoint, and, for the purposes of the transition from the law in force immediately before the day appointed under this subsection to the provisions of this Act, the Order appointing the day may provide that those provisions shall have effect subject to such transitional provisions as may be contained in the Order. [663]

NOTES
Commencement: 23 June 1977.
Commencement order: SI 1977 No 981.
Sub-s (4): words in square brackets substituted with savings by the Merchant Shipping Act 1979, s 19, Sch 5, as from 1 December 1986.
Order in Council under this section: Carriage of Goods by Sea 1971 (Commencement) Order 1977, SI 1977 No 981.

SCHEDULE

The Hague Rules as amended by the Brussels Protocol 1968

ARTICLE I

In these Rules the following words are employed, with the meanings set out below:—
(a) "Carrier" includes the owner or the charterer who enters into a contract of carriage with a shipper.

(b) "Contract of carriage" applies only to contracts of carriage covered by a bill of lading or any similar document of title, in so far as such document relates to the carriage of goods by sea, including any bill of lading or any similar document as aforesaid issued under or pursuant to a charter party from the moment at which such bill of lading or similar document of title regulates the relations between a carrier and a holder of the same.

(c) "Goods" includes goods, wares, merchandise, and articles of every kind whatsoever except live animals and cargo which by the contract of carriage is stated as being carried on deck and is so carried.

(d) "Ship" means any vessel used for the carriage of goods by sea.

(e) "Carriage of goods" covers the period from the time when the goods are loaded on to the time they are discharged from the ship.

ARTICLE II

Subject to the provisions of Article VI, under every contract of carriage of goods by sea the carrier, in relation to the loading, handling, stowage, carriage, custody, care and discharge of such goods, shall be subject to the responsibilities and liabilities, and entitled to the rights and immunities hereinafter set forth.

ARTICLE III

1. The carrier shall be bound before and at the beginning of the voyage to exercise due diligence to—

    (a) Make the ship seaworthy.
    (b) Properly man, equip and supply the ship.
    (c) Make the holds, refrigerating and cool chambers, and all other parts of the ship in which goods are carried, fit and safe for their reception, carriage and preservation.

2. Subject to the provisions of Article IV, the carrier shall properly and carefully load, handle, stow, carry, keep, care for, and discharge the goods carried.

3. After receiving the goods into his charge the carrier or the master or agent of the carrier shall, on demand of the shipper, issue to the shipper a bill of lading showing among other things—

    (a) The leading marks necessary for identification of the goods as the same are furnished in writing by the shipper before the loading of such goods starts, provided such marks are stamped or otherwise shown clearly upon the goods if uncovered, or on the cases or coverings in which such goods are contained, in such a manner as should ordinarily remain legible until the end of the voyage.
    (b) Either the number of packages or pieces, or the quantity, or weight, as the case may be, as furnished in writing by the shipper.
    (c) The apparent order and condition of the goods.

    Provided that no carrier, master or agent of the carrier shall be bound to state or show in the bill of lading any marks, number, quantity, or weight which he has reasonable ground for suspecting not accurately to represent the goods actually received, or which he has had no reasonable means of checking.

4. Such a bill of lading shall be prima facie evidence of the receipt by the carrier of the goods as therein described in accordance with paragraph 3 (a), (b) and (c). However, proof to the contrary shall not be admissible when the bill of lading has been transferred to a third party acting in good faith.

5. The shipper shall be deemed to have guaranteed to the carrier the accuracy at the time of shipment of the marks, number, quantity and weight, as furnished by him, and the shipper shall indemnify the carrier against all loss, damages and expenses arising or resulting from inaccuracies in such particulars. The right of the carrier to such indemnity shall in no way limit his responsibility and liability under the contract of carriage to any person other than the shipper.

6. Unless notice of loss or damage and the general nature of such loss or damage be given in writing to the carrier or his agent at the port of discharge before or at the time

of the removal of the goods into the custody of the person entitled to delivery thereof under the contract of carriage, or, if the loss or damage be not apparent, within three days, such removal shall be prima facie evidence of the delivery by the carrier of the goods as described in the bill of lading.

The notice in writing need not be given if the state of the goods has, at the time of their receipt, been the subject of joint survey or inspection.

Subject to paragraph 6*bis* the carrier and the ship shall in any event be discharged from all liability whatsoever in respect of the goods, unless suit is brought within one year of their delivery or of the date when they should have been delivered. This period may, however, be extended if the parties so agree after the cause of action has arisen.

In the case of any actual or apprehended loss or damage the carrier and the receiver shall give all reasonable facilities to each other for inspecting and tallying the goods.

6*bis*. An action for indemnity against a third person may be brought even after the expiration of the year provided for in the preceding paragraph if brought within the time allowed by the law of the Court seized of the case. However, the time allowed shall be not less than three months, commencing from the day when the person bringing such action for indemnity has settled the claim or has been served with process in the action against himself.

7. After the goods are loaded the bill of lading to be issued by the carrier, master, or agent of the carrier, to the shipper shall, if the shipper so demands, be a "shipped" bill of lading, provided that if the shipper shall have previously taken up any document of title to such goods, he shall surrender the same as against the issue of the "shipped" bill of lading, but at the option of the carrier such document of title may be noted at the port of shipment by the carrier, master, or agent with the name or names of the ship or ships upon which the goods have been shipped and the date or dates of shipment, and when so noted, if it shows the particulars mentioned in paragraph 3 of Article III, shall for the purpose of this article be deemed to constitute a "shipped" bill of lading.

8. Any clause, covenant, or agreement in a contract of carriage relieving the carrier or the ship from liability for loss or damage to, or in connection with, goods arising from negligence, fault, or failure in the duties and obligations provided in this article or lessening such liability otherwise than as provided in these Rules, shall be null and void and of no effect. A benefit of insurance in favour of the carrier or similar clause shall be deemed to be a clause relieving the carrier from liability.

ARTICLE IV

1. Neither the carrier nor the ship shall be liable for loss or damage arising or resulting from unseaworthiness unless caused by want of due diligence on the part of the carrier to make the ship seaworthy, and to secure that the ship is properly manned, equipped and supplied, and to make the holds, refrigerating and cool chambers and all other parts of the ship in which goods are carried fit and safe for their reception, carriage and preservation in accordance with the provisions of paragraph 1 of Article III. Whenever loss or damage has resulted from unseaworthiness the burden of proving the exercise of due diligence shall be on the carrier or other person claiming exemption under this article.

2. Neither the carrier nor the ship shall be responsible for loss or damage arising or resulting from—
    (*a*) Act, neglect, or default of the master, mariner, pilot, or the servants of the carrier in the navigation or in the management of the ship.
    (*b*) Fire, unless caused by the actual fault or privity of the carrier.
    (*c*) Perils, dangers and accidents of the sea or other navigable waters.
    (*d*) Act of God.
    (*e*) Act of war.
    (*f*) Act of public enemies.
    (*g*) Arrest or restraint of princes, rulers or people, or seizure under legal process.
    (*h*) Quarantine restrictions.
    (*i*) Act or omission of the shipper or owner of the goods, his agent or representative.

(j) Strikes or lockouts or stoppage or restraint of labour from whatever cause, whether partial or general.
(k) Riots and civil commotions.
(l) Saving or attempting to save life or property at sea.
(m) Wastage in bulk or weight or any other loss or damage arising from inherent defect, quality or vice of the goods.
(n) Insufficiency of packing.
(o) Insufficiency or inadequacy of marks.
(p) Latent defects not discoverable by due diligence.
(q) Any other cause arising without the actual fault or privity of the carrier, or without the fault or neglect of the agents or servants of the carrier, but the burden of proof shall be on the person claiming the benefit of this exception to show that neither the actual fault or privity of the carrier nor the fault or neglect of the agents or servants of the carrier contributed to the loss or damage.

3. The shipper shall not be responsible for loss or damage sustained by the carrier or the ship arising or resulting from any cause without the act, fault or neglect of the shipper, his agents or his servants.

4. Any deviation in saving or attempting to save life or property at sea or any reasonable deviation shall not be deemed to be an infringement or breach of these Rules or of the contract of carriage, and the carrier shall not be liable for any loss or damage resulting therefrom.

5. (a) Unless the nature and value of such goods have been declared by the shipper before shipment and inserted in the bill of lading, neither the carrier nor the ship shall in any event be or become liable for any loss or damage to or in connection with the goods in an amount exceeding [666.67 units of account] per package or unit or [2 units of account per kilogramme] of gross weight of the goods lost or damaged, whichever is the higher.

(b) The total amount recoverable shall be calculated by reference to the value of such goods at the place and time at which the goods are discharged from the ship in accordance with the contract or should have been so discharged.

The value of the goods shall be fixed according to the commodity exchange price, or, if there be no such price, according to the current market price, or, if there be no commodity exchange price or current market price, by reference to the normal value of goods of the same kind and quality.

(c) Where a container, pallet or similar article of transport is used to consolidate goods, the number of packages or units enumerated in the bill of lading as packed in such article of transport shall be deemed the number of packages or units for the purpose of this paragraph as far as these packages or units are concerned. Except as aforesaid such article of transport shall be considered the package or unit.

[(d) The unit of account mentioned in this Article is the special drawing right as defined by the International Monetary Fund. The amounts mentioned in sub-paragraph (a) of this paragraph shall be converted into national currency on the basis of the value of that currency on a date to be determined by the law of the Court seized of the case.]

(e) Neither the carrier nor the ship shall be entitled to the benefit of the limitation of liability provided for in this paragraph if it is proved that the damage resulted from an act or omission of the carrier done with intent to cause damage, or recklessly and with knowledge that damage would probably result.

(f) The declaration mentioned in sub-paragraph (a) of this paragraph, if embodied in the bill of lading, shall be prima facie evidence, but shall not be binding or conclusive on the carrier.

(g) By agreement between the carrier, master or agent of the carrier and the shipper other maximum amounts than those mentioned in sub-paragraph (a) of this paragraph may be fixed, provided that no maximum amount so fixed shall be less than the appropriate maximum mentioned in that sub-paragraph.

(h) Neither the carrier nor the ship shall be responsible in any event for loss or damage to, or in connection with, goods if the nature or value thereof has been knowingly mis-stated by the shipper in the bill of lading.

6. Goods of an inflammable, explosive or dangerous nature to the shipment whereof the carrier, master or agent of the carrier has not consented with knowledge of their nature and character, may at any time before discharge be landed at any place, or destroyed or rendered innocuous by the carrier without compensation and the shipper of such goods shall be liable for all damages and expenses directly or indirectly arising out of or resulting from such shipment. If any such goods shipped with such knowledge and consent shall become a danger to the ship or cargo, they may in like manner be landed at any place, or destroyed or rendered innocuous by the carrier without liability on the part of the carrier except to general average, if any.

ARTICLE IV BIS

1. The defences and limits of liability provided for in these Rules shall apply in any action against the carrier in respect of loss or damage to goods covered by a contract of carriage whether the action be founded in contract or in tort.

2. If such an action is brought against a servant or agent of the carrier (such servant or agent not being an independent contractor), such servant or agent shall be entitled to avail himself of the defences and limits of liability which the carrier is entitled to invoke under these Rules.

3. The aggregate of the amounts recoverable from the carrier, and such servants and agents, shall in no case exceed the limit provided for in these Rules.

4. Nevertheless, a servant or agent of the carrier shall not be entitled to avail himself of the provisions of this article, if it is proved that the damage resulted from an act or omission of the servant or agent done with intent to cause damage or recklessly and with knowledge that damage would probably result.

ARTICLE V

A carrier shall be at liberty to surrender in whole or in part all or any of his rights and immunities or to increase any of his responsibilities and obligations under these Rules, provided such surrender or increase shall be embodied in the bill of lading issued to the shipper. The provisions of these Rules shall not be applicable to charter parties, but if bills of lading are issued in the case of a ship under a charter party they shall comply with the terms of these Rules. Nothing in these Rules shall be held to prevent the insertion in a bill of lading of any lawful provision regarding general average.

ARTICLE VI

Notwithstanding the provisions of the preceding articles, a carrier, master or agent of the carrier and a shipper shall in regard to any particular goods be at liberty to enter into any agreement in any terms as to the responsibility and liability of the carrier for such goods, and as to the rights and immunities of the carrier in respect of such goods, or his obligation as to seaworthiness, so far as this stipulation is not contrary to public policy, or the care or diligence of his servants or agents in regard to the loading, handling, stowage, carriage, custody, care and discharge of the goods carried by sea, provided that in this case no bill of lading has been or shall be issued and that the terms agreed shall be embodied in a receipt which shall be a non-negotiable document and shall be marked as such.

Any agreement so entered into shall have full legal effect.

Provided that this article shall not apply to ordinary commercial shipments made in the ordinary course of trade, but only to other shipments where the character or condition of the property to be carried or the circumstances, terms and conditions under which the carriage is to be performed are such as reasonably to justify a special agreement.

ARTICLE VII

Nothing herein contained shall prevent a carrier or a shipper from entering into any agreement, stipulation, condition, reservation or exemption as to the responsibility and liability of the carrier or the ship for the loss or damage to, or in connection with, the custody and care and handling of goods prior to the loading on, and subsequent to the discharge from, the ship on which the goods are carried by sea.

ARTICLE VIII

The provisions of these Rules shall not affect the rights and obligations of the carrier under any statute for the time being in force relating to the limitation of the liability of owners of sea-going vessels.

ARTICLE IX

These Rules shall not affect the provisions of any international Convention or national law governing liability for nuclear damage.

ARTICLE X

The provisions of these Rules shall apply to every bill of lading relating to the carriage of goods between ports in two different States if:
  (a) the bill of lading is issued in a contracting State, or
  (b) the carriage is from a port in a contracting State, or
  (c) the contract contained in or evidenced by the bill of lading provides that these Rules or legislation of any State giving effect to them are to govern the contract,
whatever may be the nationality of the ship, the carrier, the shipper, the consignee, or any other interested person.

[*The last two paragraphs of this article are not reproduced. They require contracting States to apply the Rules to bills of lading mentioned in the article and authorise them to apply the Rules to other bills of lading.*]

[*Articles 11 to 16 of the International Convention for the unification of certain rules of law relating to bills of lading signed at Brussels on 25th August 1924 are not reproduced. They deal with the coming into force of the Convention, procedure for ratification, accession and denunciation, and the right to call for a fresh conference to consider amendments to the Rules contained in the Convention.*] **[664]**

NOTES
Commencement: 23 June 1977.
Commencement order: SI 1977 No 981.
The words in italics in square brackets are as set out in the Queen's Printer's version of the Act.
Article IV para 5: amended by the Merchant Shipping Act 1981, s 2(3), (4).

CIVIL JURISDICTION AND JUDGMENTS ACT 1982
(c 27)

ARRANGEMENT OF SECTIONS

Part I

Implementation of the Conventions

Main implementing provisions

Section		Para
1	Interpretation of references to the Conventions and Contracting States	[665]
2	The Conventions to have the force of law	[666]
3	Interpretation of the Conventions	[667]

Supplementary provisions as to recognition and enforcement of judgments

4	Enforcement of judgments other than maintenance orders	[668]
5	Recognition and enforcement of maintenance orders	[669]
6	Appeals under Article 37, second paragraph and Article 41	[670]

Section		Para
7	Interest on registered judgments	[671]
8	Currency of payment under registered maintenance orders	[672]

Other supplementary provisions

9	Provisions supplementary to Title VII of 1968 Convention	[673]
10	Allocation within UK of jurisdiction with respect to trusts and consumer contracts	[674]
11	Proof and admissibility of certain judgments and related documents	[675]
12	Provision for issue of copies of, and certificates in connection with, UK judgments	[676]
13	Modifications to cover authentic instruments and court settlements	[677]
14	Modifications consequential on revision of the Conventions	[678]
15	Interpretation of Part I and consequential Amendments	[679]

Part II

Jurisdiction, and Recognition and Enforcement of Judgments, within United Kingdom

16	Allocation within UK of jurisdiction in certain civil proceedings	[680]
17	Exclusion of certain proceedings from Schedule 4	[681]
18	Enforcement of UK judgments in other parts of UK	[682]
19	Recognition of UK judgments in other parts of UK	[683–7]

Part IV

Miscellaneous Provisions

Provisions relating to jurisdiction

24	Interim relief and protective measures in cases of doubtful jurisdiction	[688]
25	Interim relief in England and Wales and Northern Ireland in the absence of substantive proceedings	[689]
26	Security in Admiralty proceedings in England and Wales or Northern Ireland in case of stay, etc	[690–2]
29	Service of county court process outside Northern Ireland	[693]
30	Proceedings in England and Wales or Northern Ireland for torts to immovable property	[694]

Provisions relating to recognition and enforcement of judgments

31	Overseas judgments given against states, etc	[695]
32	Overseas judgments given in proceedings brought in breach of agreement for settlement of disputes	[696]
33	Certain steps not to amount to submission to jurisdiction of overseas court	[697]
34	Certain judgments a bar to further proceedings on the same cause of action	[698]
35	Minor amendments relating to overseas judgments	[699]
36	Registration of maintenance orders in Northern Ireland	[700]
37	Minor amendments relating to maintenance orders	[701]
38	Overseas judgments counteracting an award of multiple damages	[702]

Jurisdiction, and recognition and enforcement of judgments, as between United Kingdom and certain territories

39	Application of provisions corresponding to 1968 Convention in relation to certain territories	[703]

Legal aid

40	Power to modify enactments relating to legal aid etc	[704]

Part V

Supplementary and General Provisions

Domicile

41	Domicile of individuals	[705]
42	Domicile and seat of corporation or association	[706]
43	Seat of corporation or association for purposes of Article 16(2) and related provisions	[707]
44	Persons deemed to be domiciled in the United Kingdom for certain purposes	[708]

Section		Para
45	Domicile of trusts	[709]
46	Domicile and seat of the Crown	[710]

Other supplementary provisions

47	Modifications occasioned by decisions of European Court as to meaning or effect of Conventions	[711]
48	Matters for which rules of court may provide	[712]
49	Saving for powers to stay, sist, strike out or dismiss proceedings	[713]

General

50	Interpretation: general	[714]
51	Application to Crown	[715]
52	Extent	[716]
53	Commencement, transitional provisions and savings	[717]
54	Repeals	[718]
55	Short title	[719]

SCHEDULES

Schedule 1—Text of 1968 Convention, as Amended		[720]
Schedule 2—Text of 1971 Protocol, as Amended		[721]
Schedule 3—Text of Titles V and VI of Accession Convention		[722–34]

An Act to make further provision about the jurisdiction of courts and tribunals in the United Kingdom and certain other territories and about the recognition and enforcement of judgments given in the United Kingdom or elsewhere; to provide for the modification of certain provisions relating to legal aid; and for connected purposes. [13 July 1982]

GENERAL NOTES
This Act applies to Northern Ireland.

PART I

IMPLEMENTATION OF THE CONVENTIONS

Main implementing provisions

1. Interpretation of references to the Conventions and Contracting States

(1) In this Act—

"the 1968 Convention" means the Convention on jurisdiction and the enforcement of judgments in civil and commercial matters (including the Protocol annexed to that Convention), signed at Brussels on 27 September 1968;

"the 1971 Protocol" means the Protocol on the interpretation of the 1968 Convention by the European Court, signed at Luxembourg on 3 June 1971;

"the Accession Convention" means the Convention on the accession to the 1968 Convention and the 1971 Protocol of Denmark, the Republic of Ireland and the United Kingdom, signed at Luxembourg on 9 October 1978;

"the Conventions" means the 1968 Convention, the 1971 Protocol and the Accession Convention.

(2) In this Act, unless the context otherwise requires—

(a) references to, or to any provision of, the 1968 Convention or the 1971 Protocol are references to that Convention, Protocol or provision as amended by the Accession Convention; and
(b) any reference to a numbered Article is a reference to the Article so numbered of the 1968 Convention, and any reference to a sub-division of a numbered Article shall be construed accordingly.

(3) In this Act "Contracting State" means—
(a) one of the original parties to the 1968 Convention (Belgium, the Federal Republic of Germany, France, Italy, Luxembourg and the Netherlands); or
(b) one of the parties acceding to that Convention under the Accession Convention (Denmark, the Republic of Ireland and the United Kingdom),

being a state in respect of which the Accession Convention has entered into force in accordance with Article 39 of that Convention. [665]

NOTES
Commencement: 1 January 1987.
Commencement order: SI 1986 No 2044.

2. The Conventions to have the force of law

(1) The Conventions shall have the force of law in the United Kingdom, and judicial notice shall be taken of them.

(2) For convenience of reference there are set out in Schedules 1, 2 and 3 respectively the English texts of—
(a) the 1968 Convention as amended by Titles II and III of the Accession Convention;
(b) the 1971 Protocol as amended by Title IV of the Accession Convention; and
(c) Titles V and VI of the Accession Convention (transitional and final provisions),

being texts prepared from the authentic English texts referred to in Articles 37 and 41 of the Accession Convention. [666]

NOTES
Commencement: 1 January 1987.
Commencement order: SI 1986 No 2044.

3. Interpretation of the Conventions

(1) Any question as to the meaning or effect of any provision of the Conventions shall, if not referred to the European Court in accordance with the 1971 Protocol, be determined in accordance with the principles laid down by and any relevant decision of the European Court.

(2) Judicial notice shall be taken of any decision of, or expression of opinion by, the European Court on any such question.

(3) Without prejudice to the generality of subsection (1), the following reports (which are reproduced in the Official Journal of the Communities), namely—
(a) the reports by Mr. P. Jenard on the 1968 Convention and the 1971 Protocol; and

(b) the report by Professor Peter Schlosser on the Accession Convention,

may be considered in ascertaining the meaning or effect of any provision of the Conventions and shall be given such weight as is appropriate in the circumstances. [667]

NOTES
Commencement: 1 January 1987.
Commencement order: SI 1986 No 2044.

Supplementary provisions as to recognition and enforcement of judgments

4. Enforcement of judgments other than maintenance orders

(1) A judgment, other than a maintenance order, which is the subject of an application under Article 31 for its enforcement in any part of the United Kingdom shall, to the extent that its enforcement is authorised by the appropriate court, be registered in the prescribed manner in that court.

In this subsection "the appropriate court" means the court to which the application is made in pursuance of Article 32 (that is to say, the High Court or the Court of Session).

(2) Where a judgment is registered under this section, the reasonable costs or expenses of and incidental to its registration shall be recoverable as if they were sums recoverable under the judgment.

(3) A judgment registered under this section shall, for the purposes of its enforcement, be of the same force and effect, the registering court shall have in relation to its enforcement the same powers, and proceedings for or with respect to its enforcement may be taken, as if the judgment had been originally given by the registering court and had (where relevant) been entered.

(4) Subsection (3) is subject to Article 39 (restriction on enforcement where appeal pending or time for appeal unexpired), to section 7 and to any provision made by rules of court as to the manner in which and conditions subject to which a judgment registered under this section may be enforced. [668]

NOTES
Commencement: 1 January 1987.
Commencement order: SI 1986 No 2044.

5. Recognition and enforcement of maintenance orders

(1) The function of transmitting to the appropriate court an application under Article 31 for the recognition or enforcement in the United Kingdom of a maintenance order shall be discharged—

(a) as respects England and Wales and Scotland, by the Secretary of State;
(b) as respects Northern Ireland, by the Lord Chancellor.

In this subsection "the appropriate court" means the magistrates' court or sheriff court having jurisdiction in the matter in accordance with the second paragraph of Article 32.

(2) Such an application shall be determined in the first instance by the prescribed officer of that court.

(3) Where on such an application the enforcement of the order is authorised

to any extent, the order shall to that extent be registered in the prescribed manner in that court.

(4) A maintenance order registered under this section shall, for the purposes of its enforcement, be of the same force and effect, the registering court shall have in relation to its enforcement the same powers, and proceedings for or with respect to its enforcement may be taken, as if the order had been originally made by the registering court.

(5) Subsection (4) is subject to Article 39 (restriction on enforcement where appeal pending or time for appeal unexpired), to section 7 and to any provision made by rules of court as to the manner in which and conditions subject to which an order registered under this section may be enforced.

[(5A) A maintenance order which by virtue of this section is enforceable by a magistrates' court in England and Wales shall be enforceable in the same manner as a magistrates' court maintenance order made by that court.

In this subsection "magistrates' court maintenance order" has the same meaning as in section 150(1) of the Magistrates' Courts Act 1980.]

(6) A maintenance order which by virtue of this section is enforceable by a magistrates' court in *England and Wales or* Northern Ireland shall be enforceable in the same manner as an affiliation order made by that court.

(7) The payer under a maintenance order registered under this section in a magistrates' court in England and Wales or Northern Ireland shall give notice of any change of address to the clerk of that court.

A person who without reasonable excuse fails to comply with this subsection shall be guilty of an offence and liable on summary conviction to a fine not exceeding [level 2 on the standard scale]. **[669]**

NOTES
Commencement: 1 January 1987 (sub-ss (1)-(5), (6)-(7)); to be appointed (remainder).
Commencement order: SI 1986 No 2044.
Sub-s (5A): added by the Family Law Reform Act 1987, s 33(1), Sch 2, para 89(2) as from 1 April 1989 (SI 1989 No 382).
Sub-s (6): words in italics repealed by the Family Law Reform Act 1987, s 33(1), Sch 2, para 89(3) as from 1 April 1989 (SI 1989 No 382).
Sub-s (7): maximum fine converted to a level on the standard scale by the Criminal Justice Act 1982, ss 37, 46.

6. Appeals under Article 37, second paragraph and Article 41

(1) The single further appeal on a point of law referred to in Article 37, second paragraph and Article 41 in relation to the recognition or enforcement of a judgment other than a maintenance order lies—

    (*a*) in England and Wales or Northern Ireland, to the Court of Appeal or to the House of Lords in accordance with Part II of the Administration of Justice Act 1969 (appeals direct fom the High Court to the House of Lords);

    (*b*) in Scotland, to the Inner House of the Court of Session.

(2) Paragraph (*a*) of subsection (1) has effect notwithstanding section 15(2) of the Administration of Justice Act 1969 (exclusion of direct appeal to the House of Lords in cases where no appeal to that House lies from a decision of the Court of Appeal).

(3) The single further appeal on a point of law referred to in Article 37,

second paragraph and Article 41 in relation to the recognition or enforcement of a maintenance order lies—

    (*a*) in England and Wales, to the High Court by way of case stated in accordance with section 111 of the Magistrates' Courts Act 1980;
    (*b*) in Scotland, to the Inner House of the Court of Session;
    (*c*) in Northern Ireland, to the Court of Appeal.

NOTES
Commencement: 1 January 1987.
Commencement order: SI 1986 No 2044.

7. Interest on registered judgments

(1) Subject to subsection (4), where in connection with an application for registration of a judgment under section 4 or 5 the applicant shows—

    (*a*) that the judgment provides for the payment of a sum of money; and
    (*b*) that in accordance with the law of the Contracting State in which the judgment was given interest on that sum is recoverable under the judgment from a particular date or time,

the rate of interest and the date or time from which it is so recoverable shall be registered with the judgment and, subject to any provision made under subsection (2), the debt resulting, apart from section 4(2), from the registration of the judgment shall carry interest in accordance with the registered particulars.

(2) Provision may be made by rules of court as to the manner in which and the periods by reference to which any interest payable by virtue of subsection (1) is to be calculated and paid, including provision for such interest to cease to accrue as from a prescribed date.

(3) Costs or expenses recoverable by virtue of section 4(2) shall carry interest as if they were the subject of an order for the payment of costs or expenses made by the registering court on the date of registration.

(4) Interest on arrears of sums payable under a maintenance order registered under section 5 in a magistrates' court in England and Wales or Northern Ireland shall not be recoverable in that court, but without prejudice to the operation in relation to any such order of section 2A of the Maintenance Orders Act 1958 or section 11A of the Maintenance and Affiliation Orders Act (Northern Ireland) 1966 (which enable interest to be recovered if the order is re-registered for enforcement in the High Court).

(5) Except as mentioned in subsection (4), debts under judgments registered under section 4 or 5 shall carry interest only as provided by this section.

NOTES
Commencement: 1 January 1987.
Commencement order: SI 1986 No 2044.

8. Currency of payment under registered maintenance orders

(1) Sums payable in the United Kingdom under a maintenance order by virtue of its registration under section 5, including any arrears so payable, shall be paid in the currency of the United Kingdom.

(2) Where the order is expressed in any other currency, the amounts shall be converted on the basis of the exchange rate prevailing on the date of registration of the order.

(3) For the purposes of this section, a written certificate purporting to be signed by an officer of any bank in the United Kingdom and stating the exchange rate prevailing on a specified date shall be evidence, and in Scotland sufficient evidence, of the facts stated. [672]

NOTES
Commencement: 1 January 1987.
Commencement order: SI 1986 No 2044.

Other supplementary provisions

9. Provisions supplementary to Title VII of 1968 Convention

(1) The provisions of Title VII of the 1968 Convention (relationship between that convention and other conventions to which Contracting States are or may become parties) shall have effect in relation to—

   (a) any statutory provision, whenever passed or made, implementing any such other convention in the United Kingdom; and
   (b) any rule of law so far as it has the effect of so implementing any such other convention,

as they have effect in relation to that other convention itself.

(2) Her Majesty may by Order in Council declare a provision of a convention entered into by the United Kingdom to be a provision whereby the United Kingdom assumed an obligation of a kind provided for in Article 59 (which allows a Contracting State to agree with a third State to withhold recognition in certain cases from a judgment given by a court in another Contracting State which took jurisdiction on one of the grounds mentioned in the second paragraph of Article 3). [673]

NOTES
Commencement: 1 January 1987.
Commencement order: SI 1986 No 2044.
Orders in Council under this section: The Reciprocal Enforcement of Foreign Judgments (Canada) Order 1987, SI 1987 No 468, is made in part under this section.

10. Allocation within UK of jurisdiction with respect to trusts and consumer contracts

(1) The provisions of this section have effect for the purpose of allocating within the United Kingdom jurisdiction in certain proceedings in respect of which the 1968 Convention confers jurisdiction on the courts of the United Kingdom generally and to which section 16 does not apply.

(2) Any proceedings which by virtue of Article 5(6) (trusts) are brought in the United Kingdom shall be brought in the courts of the part of the United Kingdom in which the trust is domiciled.

(3) Any proceedings which by virtue of the first paragraph of Article 14 (consumer contracts) are brought in the United Kingdom by a consumer on the ground that he is himself domiciled there shall be brought in the courts of the part of the United Kingdom in which he is domiciled. [674]

NOTES
Commencement: 1 January 1987.
Commencement order: SI 1986 No 2044.

11. Proof and admissibility of certain judgments and related documents

(1) For the purposes of the 1968 Convention—

   (a) a document, duly authenticated, which purports to be a copy of a judgment given by a court of a Contracting State other than the United Kingdom shall without further proof be deemed to be a true copy, unless the contrary is shown; and

   (b) the original or a copy of any such document as is mentioned in Article 46(2) or 47 (supporting documents to be produced by a party seeking recognition or enforcement of a judgment) shall be evidence, and in Scotland sufficient evidence, of any matter to which it relates.

(2) A document purporting to be a copy of a judgment given by any such court as is mentioned in subsection (1)(a) is duly authenticated for the purposes of this section if it purports—

   (a) to bear the seal of that court; or

   (b) to be certified by any person in his capacity as a judge or officer of that court to be a true copy of a judgment given by that court.

(3) Nothing in this section shall prejudice the admission in evidence of any document which is admissible apart from this section. **[675]**

NOTES
Commencement: 1 January 1987.
Commencement order: SI 1986 No 2044.

12. Provision for issue of copies of, and certificates in connection with, UK judgments

Rules of court may make provision for enabling any interested party wishing to secure under the 1968 Convention the recognition or enforcement in another Contracting State of a judgment given by a court in the United Kingdom to obtain, subject to any conditions specified in the rules—

   (a) a copy of the judgment; and

   (b) a certificate giving particulars relating to the judgment and the proceedings in which it was given. **[676]**

NOTES
Commencement: 1 January 1987.
Commencement order: SI 1986 No 2044.
Regulations under this section. The Magistrates' Courts (Civil Jurisdiction and Judgments Act 1982) Rules 1986, SI 1986 No 1962, are in part made under this section.

13. Modifications to cover authentic instruments and court settlements

(1) Her Majesty may by Order in Council provide that—

   (a) any provision of this Act relating to the recognition or enforcement in the United Kingdom or elsewhere of judgments to which the 1968 Convention applies; and

   (b) any other statutory provision, whenever passed or made, so relating,

shall apply, with such modifications as may be specified in the Order, in relation to documents and settlements within Title IV of the 1968 Convention (authentic instruments and court settlements enforceable in the same manner as judgments) as if they were judgments to which that Convention applies.

(2) An Order in Council under this section may make different provision in relation to different descriptions of documents and settlements.

(3) Any Order in Council under this section shall be subject to annulment in pursuance of a resolution of either House of Parliament. [677]

NOTES
Commencement: 1 January 1987.
Commencement order: No Order in Council has yet been made under this section.

14. Modifications consequential on revision of the Conventions

(1) If at any time it appears to Her Majesty in Council that Her Majesty's Government in the United Kingdom have agreed to a revision of any of the Conventions, including in particular any revision connected with the accession to the 1968 Convention of one or more further states, Her Majesty may by Order in Council make such modifications of this Act or any other statutory provision, whenever passed or made, as Her Majesty considers appropriate in consequence of the revision.

(2) An Order in Council under this section shall not be made unless a draft of the Order has been laid before Parliament and approved by a resolution of each House of Parliament.

(3) In this section "revision" means an omission from, addition to or alteration of any of the Conventions and includes replacement of any of the Conventions to any extent by another convention, protocol or other description of international agreement. [678]

NOTES
Commencement: 1 January 1987.
Commencement order: No Order in Council has yet been made under this section.

15. Interpretation of Part I and consequential Amendments

(1) In this Part, unless the context otherwise requires—
- "judgment" has the meaning given by Article 25;
- "maintenance order" means a maintenance judgment within the meaning of the 1968 Convention;
- "payer", in relation to a maintenance order, means the person liable to make the payments for which the order provides;
- "prescribed" means prescribed by rules of court.

(2) References in this Part to a judgment registered under section 4 or 5 include, to the extent of its registration, references to a judgment so registered to a limited extent only.

(3) Anything authorised or required by the 1968 Convention or this Part to be done by, to or before a particular magistrates' court may be done by, to or before any magistrates' court acting for the same petty sessions area (or, in Northern Ireland, petty sessions district) as that court.

(4) The enactments specified in Part I of Schedule 12 shall have effect with the amendments specified there, being amendments consequential on this Part. [679]

NOTES
Commencement: 1 January 1987.
Commencement order: SI 1986 No 2044.

Part II

JURISDICTION, AND RECOGNITION AND ENFORCEMENT OF JUDGMENTS, WITHIN UNITED KINGDOM

16. Allocation within UK of jurisdiction in certain civil proceedings

(1) The provisions set out in Schedule 4 (which contains a modified version of Title II of the 1968 Convention) shall have effect for determining, for each part of the United Kingdom, whether the courts of law of that part, or any particular court of law in that part, have or has jurisdiction in proceedings where—
   (a) the subject-matter of the proceedings is within the scope of the 1968 Convention as determined by Article 1 (whether or not the Convention has effect in relation to the proceedings); and
   (b) the defendant or defender is domiciled in the United Kingdom or the proceedings are of a kind mentioned in Article 16 (exclusive jurisdiction regardless of domicile).

(2) In Schedule 4 modifications of Title II of the 1968 Convention are indicated as follows—
   (a) modifications by way of omission are indicated by dots; and
   (b) within each Article words resulting from modifications by way of addition or substitution are printed in heavy type.

(3) In determining any question as to the meaning or effect of any provision contained in Schedule 4—
   (a) regard shall be had to any relevant principles laid down by the European Court in connection with Title II of the 1968 Convention and to any relevant decision of that court as to the meaning or effect of any provision of that Title; and
   (b) without prejudice to the generality of paragraph (a), the reports mentioned in section 3(3) may be considered and shall, so far as relevant, be given such weight as is appropriate in the circumstances.

(4) The provisions of this section and Schedule 4 shall have effect subject to the 1968 Convention and to the provisions of section 17.

(5) ...

NOTES
Commencement: 1 January 1987.
Commencement order: SI 1986 No 2044.
Sub-s (5): amends the Maintenance Orders Act 1950, s 15(1)(a).

17. Exclusion of certain proceedings from Schedule 4

(1) Schedule 4 shall not apply to proceedings of any description listed in Schedule 5 or to proceedings in Scotland under any enactment which confers jurisdiction on a Scottish court in respect of a specific subject-matter on specific grounds.

(2) Her Majesty may by Order in Council—
   (a) add to the list in Schedule 5 any description of proceedings in any part of the United Kingdom; and
   (b) remove from that list any description of proceedings in any part of the United Kingdom (whether included in the list as originally enacted or added by virtue of this subsection).

(3) An Order in Council under subsection (2)—
  (a) may make different provisions for different descriptions of proceedings, for the same description of proceedings in different courts or for different parts of the United Kingdom; and
  (b) may contain such transitional and other incidental provisions as appear to Her Majesty to be appropriate.

(4) An Order in Council under subsection (2) shall not be made unless a draft of the Order has been laid before Parliament and approved by a resolution of each House of Parliament. [681]

NOTES
Commencement: 1 January 1987.
Commencement order: SI 1986 No 2044.
No Order in Council has yet been made under this section.

18. Enforcement of UK judgments in other parts of UK

(1) In relation to any judgment to which this section applies—
  (a) Schedule 6 shall have effect for the purpose of enabling any money provisions contained in the judgment to be enforced in a part of the United Kingdom other than the part in which the judgment was given; and
  (b) Schedule 7 shall have effect for the purpose of enabling any non-money provisions so contained to be so enforced.

(2) In this section "judgment" means any of the following (references to the giving of a judgment being construed accordingly)—
  (a) any judgment or order (by whatever name called) given or made by a court of law in the United Kingdom;
  (b) any judgment or order not within paragraph (a) which has been entered in England and Wales or Northern Ireland in the High Court or a county court;
  (c) any document which in Scotland has been registered for execution in the Books of Council and Session or in the sheriff court books kept for any sheriffdom;
  (d) any award or order made by a tribunal in any part of the United Kingdom which is enforceable in that part without an order of a court of law;
  (e) an arbitration award which has become enforceable in the part of the United Kingdom in which it was given in the same manner as a judgment given by a court of law in that part;
and, subject to the following provisions of this section, this section applies to all such judgments.

(3) Subject to subsection (4), this section does not apply to—
  (a) a judgment given in proceedings in a magistrates' court in England and Wales or Northern Ireland;
  (b) a judgment given in proceedings other than civil proceedings;
  [(ba) a judgment given in the exercise of jurisdiction in relation to insolvency law, within the meaning of section [426 of the Insolvency Act 1986];]
  (c) a judgment given in proceedings relating to—
    (i), (ii) . . .

(iii) the obtaining of title to administer the estate of a deceased person.

(4) This section applies, whatever the nature of the proceedings in which it is made, to—
   (a) a decree issued under section 13 of the Court of Exchequer (Scotland) Act 1856 (recovery of certain rentcharges and penalties by process of the Court of Session);
   (b) an order which is enforceable in the same manner as a judgment of the High Court in England and Wales by virtue of section 16 of the Contempt of Court Act 1981 or section 140 of the Supreme Court Act 1981 (which relate to fines for contempt of court and forfeiture of recognisances).

[(4A) This section does not apply as respects the enforcement in Scotland of orders made by the High Court in England and Wales under or for the purposes of the Drug Trafficking Offences Act 1986 [or Part VI of the Criminal Justice Act 1988 (confiscation of the proceeds of offences)] [; or as respects the enforcement in England and Wales of orders made by the Court of Session under or for the purposes of Part I of the Criminal Justice (Scotland) Act 1987].]

(5) This section does not apply to so much of any judgment as—
   (a) is an order to which section 16 of the Maintenance Orders Act 1950 applies (and is therefore an order for whose enforcement in another part of the United Kingdom provision is made by Part II of that Act);
   (b) concerns the status or legal capacity of an individual;
   (c) relates to the management of the affairs of a person not capable of managing his own affairs;
   (d) is a provisional (including protective) measure other than an order for the making of an interim payment;
and except where otherwise stated references to a judgment to which this section applies are to such a judgment exclusive of any such provisions.

(6) The following are within subsection (5)(b), but without prejudice to the generality of that provision—
   (a) a decree of judicial separation or of separation;
   (b) any provision relating to guardianship or custody.

(7) This section does not apply to a judgment of a court outside the United Kingdom which falls to be treated for the purposes of its enforcement as a judgment of a court of law in the United Kingdom by virtue of registration under Part II of the Administration of Justice Act 1920, Part I of the Foreign Judgments (Reciprocal Enforcement) Act 1933, Part I of the Maintenance Orders (Reciprocal Enforcement) Act 1972 or section 4 or 5 of this Act.

(8) A judgment to which this section applies, other than a judgment within paragraph (e) of subsection (2), shall not be enforced in another part of the United Kingdom except by way of registration under Schedule 6 or 7.

NOTES
Commencement: 1 April 1988 (sub-s (4A) certain purposes); 12 January 1987 (sub-s (4A) remaining purposes); 1 January 1987 (remainder).
Commencement orders: SI 1986 No 2044, 1986 No 2145.
Sub-s (3): para (ba) added by the Insolvency Act 1985, s 235, Sch 8, para 36 and the Insolvency Act 1986, s 437, Sch 11, words in square brackets substituted by the Insolvency Act 1986, s 439(2), Sch 14; in para (c) words omitted repealed by the Insolvency Act 1985, s 235, Sch 10, Part IV and the Insolvency Act 1986, s 437, Sch 11.

Sub-s (4A): added by the Drug Trafficking Offences Act 1986, s 39(4); first amendment made by the Criminal Justice Act 1988, s 170(1), Sch 15, para 82; final amendment made by the Criminal Justice (Scotland) Act 1987, s 45(3).

19. Recognition of UK judgments in other parts of UK

(1) A judgment to which this section applies given in one part of the United Kingdom shall not be refused recognition in another part of the United Kingdom solely on the ground that, in relation to that judgment, the court which gave it was not a court of competent jurisdiction according to the rules of private international law in force in that other part.

(2) Subject to subsection (3), this section applies to any judgment to which section 18 applies.

(3) This section does not apply to—
    (a) the documents mentioned in paragraph (c) of the definition of "judgment" in section 18(2);
    (b) the awards and orders mentioned in paragraphs (d) and (e) of that definition;
    (c) the decrees and orders referred to in section 18(4). **[683–687]**

NOTES
Commencement: 1 January 1987.
Commencement order: SI 1986 No 2044.

NOTES
Part III of this Act (ss 20–23), which applies to Scotland only, is omitted.

PART IV

MISCELLANEOUS PROVISIONS

Provisions relating to jurisdiction

24. Interim relief and protective measures in cases of doubtful jurisdiction

(1) Any power of a court in England and Wales or Northern Ireland to grant interim relief pending trial or pending the determination of an appeal shall extend to a case where—
    (a) the issue to be tried, or which is the subject of the appeal, relates to the jurisdiction of the court to entertain the proceedings; or
    (b) the proceedings involve the reference of any matter to the European Court under the 1971 Protocol.

(2) ...

(3) Subsections (1) and (2) shall not be construed as restricting any power to grant interim relief or protective measures which a court may have apart from this section. **[688]**

NOTES
Commencement: 1 January 1987 (sub-ss (1)(b), (2)(b)); 24 August 1982 (remainder).
Commencement order: SI 1986 No 2044.
Sub-s (2): applies to Scotland only.

25. Interim relief in England and Wales and Northern Ireland in the absence of substantive proceedings

(1) The High Court in England and Wales or Northern Ireland shall have power to grant interim relief where—

(a) proceedings have been or are to be commenced in a Contracting State other than the United Kingdom or in a part of the United Kingdom other than that in which the High Court in question exercises jurisdiction; and
(b) they are or will be proceedings whose subject-matter is within the scope of the 1968 Convention as determined by Article 1 (whether or not the Convention has effect in relation to the proceedings).

(2) On an application for any interim relief under subsection (1) the court may refuse to grant that relief if, in the opinion of the court, the fact that the court has no jurisdiction apart from this section in relation to the subject-matter of the proceedings in question makes it inexpedient for the court to grant it.

(3) Her Majesty may by Order in Council extend the power to grant interim relief conferred by subsection (1) so as to make it exercisable in relation to proceedings of any of the following descriptions, namely—
(a) proceedings commenced or to be commenced otherwise than in a Contracting State;
(b) proceedings whose subject-matter is not within the scope of the 1968 Convention as determined by Article 1;
(c) arbitration proceedings.

(4) An Order in Council under subsection (3)—
(a) may confer power to grant only specified descriptions of interim relief;
(b) may make different provision for different classes of proceedings, for proceedings pending in different countries or courts outside the United Kingdom or in different parts of the United Kingdom, and for other different circumstances; and
(c) may impose conditions or restrictions on the exercise of any power conferred by the Order.

(5) An Order in Council under subsection (3) which confers power to grant interim relief in relation to arbitration proceedings may provide for the repeal of any provision of section 12(6) of the Arbitration Act 1950 or section 21(1) of the Arbitration Act (Nothern Ireland) 1937 to the extent that it is superseded by the provisions of the Order.

(6) Any Order in Council under subsection (3) shall be subject to annulment in pursuance of a resolution of either House of Parliament.

(7) In this section "interim relief", in relation to the High Court in England and Wales or Northern Ireland, means interim relief of any kind which that court has power to grant in proceedings relating to matters within its jurisdiction, other than—
(a) a warrant for the arrest of property; or
(b) provision for obtaining evidence.   [689]

NOTES
Commencement: 1 January 1987.
Commencement order: SI 1986 No 2044.
No Order in Council has yet been made under this section.

26. Security in Admiralty proceedings in England and Wales or Northern Ireland in case of stay, etc

(1) Where in England and Wales or Northern Ireland a court stays or dismisses Admiralty proceedings on the ground that the dispute in question should be

submitted to arbitration or to the determination of the courts of another part of the United Kingdom or of an overseas country, the court may, if in those proceedings property has been arrested or bail or other security has been given to prevent or obtain release from arrest—

(a) order that the property arrested be retained as security for the satisfaction of any award or judgment which—
  (i) is given in respect of the dispute in the arbitration or legal proceedings in favour of which those proceedings are stayed or dismissed; and
  (ii) is enforceable in England and Wales or, as the case may be, in Northern Ireland; or
(b) order that the stay or dismissal of those proceedings be conditional on the provision of equivalent security for the satisfaction of any such award or judgment.

(2) Where a court makes an order under subsection (1), it may attach such conditions to the order as it thinks fit, in particular conditions with respect to the institution or prosecution of the relevant arbitration or legal proceedings.

(3) Subject to any provision made by rules of court and to any necessary modifications, the same law and practice shall apply in relation to property retained in pursuance of an order made by a court under subsection (1) as would apply if it were held for the purposes of proceedings in that court. [690–692]

NOTES
Commencement: 1 November 1984.
Commencement order: SI 1984 No 1553.

NOTES
Sections 27 and 28, which apply to Scotland only, are omitted.

29. Service of county court process outside Northern Ireland

The County Court Rules Committee established by Article 46 of the County Courts (Northern Ireland) Order 1980 may make county court rules with respect to the service of process outside Northern Ireland and the conditions subject to which process may be so served; ... [693]

NOTES
Commencement: 24 August 1982.
Words omitted amend the County Courts (Northern Ireland) Order 1980, SI 1980 No 397, art 48.

30. Proceedings in England and Wales or Northern Ireland for torts to immovable property

(1) The jurisdiction of any court in England and Wales or Northern Ireland to entertain proceedings for trespass to, or any other tort affecting, immovable property shall extend to cases in which the property in question is situated outside that part of the United Kingdom unless the proceedings are principally concerned with a question of the title to, or the right to possession of, that property.

(2) Subsection (1) has effect subject to the 1968 Convention and to the provisions set out in Schedule 4. [694]

NOTES
Commencement: 24 August 1982: Sch 13, para 2.

Provisions relating to recognition and enforcement of judgments

31. Overseas judgments given against states, etc

(1) A judgment given by a court of an overseas country against a state other than the United Kingdom or the state to which that court belongs shall be recognised and enforced in the United Kingdom if, and only if—
- (a) it would be so recognised and enforced if it had not been given against a state; and
- (b) that court would have had jurisdiction in the matter if it had applied rules corresponding to those applicable to such matters in the United Kingdom in accordance with sections 2 to 11 of the State Immunity Act 1978.

(2) References in subsection (1) to a judgment given against a state include references to judgments of any of the following descriptions given in relation to a state—
- (a) judgments against the government, or a department of the government, of the state but not (except as mentioned in paragraph (c)) judgments against an entity which is distinct from the executive organs of government;
- (b) judgments against the sovereign or head of state in his public capacity;
- (c) judgments against any such separate entity as is mentioned in paragraph (a) given in proceedings relating to anything done by it in the exercise of the sovereign authority of the state.

(3) Nothing in subsection (1) shall affect the recognition or enforcement in the United Kingdom of a judgment to which Part I of the Foreign Judgments (Reciprocal Enforcement) Act 1933 applies by virtue of section 4 of the Carriage of Goods by Road Act 1965, section 17(4) of the Nuclear Installations Act 1965, section 13(3) of the Merchant Shipping (Oil Pollution) Act 1971, [section 6 of the International Transport Conventions Act 1983] or section 5 of the Carriage of Passengers by Road Act 1974.

(4) Sections 12, 13 and 14(3) and (4) of the State Immunity Act 1978 (service of process and procedural privileges) shall apply to proceedings for the recognition or enforcement in the United Kingdom of a judgment given by a court of an overseas country (whether or not that judgment is within subsection (1) of this section) as they apply to other proceedings.

(5) In this section "state", in the case of a federal state, includes any of its constituent territories.

NOTES
Commencement: 24 August 1982: Sch 13, para 2.
Sub-s (3): amended by the International Transport Conventions Act 1983, s 11.

32. Overseas judgments given in proceedings brought in breach of agreement for settlement of disputes

(1) Subject to the following provisions of this section, a judgment given by a court of an overseas country in any proceedings shall not be recognised or enforced in the United Kingdom if—
- (a) the bringing of those proceedings in that court was contrary to an agreement under which the dispute in question was to be settled otherwise than by proceedings in the courts of that country; and

(b) those proceedings were not brought in that court by, or with the agreement of, the person against whom the judgment was given; and
(c) that person did not counterclaim in the proceedings or otherwise submit to the jurisdiction of that court.

(2) Subsection (1) does not apply where the agreement referred to in paragraph (a) of that subsection was illegal, void or unenforceable or was incapable of being performed for reasons not attributable to the fault of the party bringing the proceedings in which the judgment was given.

(3) In determining whether a judgment given by a court of an overseas country should be recognised or enforced in the United Kingdom, a court in the United Kingdom shall not be bound by any decision of the overseas court relating to any of the matters mentioned in subsection (1) or (2).

(4) Nothing in subsection (1) shall affect the recognition or enforcement in the United Kingdom of—
  (a) a judgment which is required to be recognised or enforced there under the 1968 Convention;
  (b) a judgment to which Part I of the Foreign Judgments (Reciprocal Enforcement) Act 1933 applies by virtue of section 4 of the Carriage of Goods by Road Act 1965, section 17(4) of the Nuclear Installations Act 1965, section 13(3) of the Merchant Shipping (Oil Pollution) Act 1971, [section 6 of the International Transport Conventions Act 1983], section 5 of the Carriage of Passengers by Road Act 1974 or section 6(4) of the Merchant Shipping Act 1974. **[696]**

NOTES
Commencement: 24 August 1982: Sch 13 para 2.
Sub-s (4): amended by the International Transport Convention Act 1983, s 11.

33. Certain steps not to amount to submission to jurisdiction of overseas court

(1) For the purposes of determining whether a judgment given by a court of an overseas country should be recognised or enforced in England and Wales or Northern Ireland, the person against whom the judgment was given shall not be regarded as having submitted to the jurisdiction of the court by reason only of the fact that he appeared (conditionally or otherwise) in the proceedings for all or any one or more of the following purposes, namely—
  (a) to contest the jurisdiction of the court;
  (b) to ask the court to dismiss or stay the proceedings on the ground that the dispute in question should be submitted to arbitration or to the determination of the courts of another country;
  (c) to protect, or obtain the release of, property seized or threatened with seizure in the proceedings.

(2) Nothing in this section shall affect the recognition or enforcement in England and Wales or Northern Ireland of a judgment which is required to be recognised or enforced there under the 1968 Convention. **[697]**

NOTES
Commencement: 24 August 1982: Sch 13 para 2.

34. Certain judgments a bar to further proceedings on the same cause of action

No proceedings may be brought by a person in England and Wales or Northern Ireland on a cause of action in respect of which a judgment has been given in his favour in proceedings between the same parties, or their privies, in a court in another part of the United Kingdom or in a court of an overseas country, unless that judgment is not enforceable or entitled to recognition in England and Wales or, as the case may be, in Northern Ireland. **[698]**

NOTES
Commencement: 24 August 1982: Sch 13 para 2.

35. Minor amendments relating to overseas judgments

(1) The Foreign Judgments (Reciprocal Enforcement) Act 1933 shall have effect with the amendments specified in Schedule 10, being amendments whose main purpose is to enable Part I of that Act to be applied to judgments of courts other than superior courts, to judgments providing for interim payments and to certain arbitration awards.

(2), (3) . . . **[699]**

NOTES
Commencement: 14 November 1986 (sub-s (1)); 1 January 1987 (sub-s (2)); 24 August 1982 (remainder).
Commencement orders: SI 1986 No 1781, 1986 No 2044.
Sub-s (2): substitutes the Administration of Justice Act 1920, s 10.
Sub-s (3): amends the Administration of Justice Act 1920, s 14.

36. Registration of maintenance orders in Northern Ireland

(1) Where—
   (a) a High Court order or a Court of Session order has been registered in the High Court of Justice in Northern Ireland ("the Northern Ireland High Court") under Part II of the Maintenance Orders Act 1950; or
   (b) a county court order, a magistrates' court order or a sheriff court order has been registered in a court of summary jurisdiction in Northern Ireland under that Part,

an application may be made to the original court for the registration of the order in, respectively, a court of summary jurisdiction in Northern Ireland or the Northern Ireland High Court.

(2) In subsection (1) "the original court", in relation to an order, means the court by which the order was made.

(3) Section 2 (except subsection (6A)) and section 2A of the Maintenance Orders Act 1958 shall have effect for the purposes of an application under subsection (1), and subsections (2), (3), (4) and (4A) of section 5 of that Act shall have effect for the purposes of the cancellation of a registration made on such an application, as if—
   (a) "registration" in those provisions included registration in the appropriate Northern Ireland court ("registered" being construed accordingly);
   (b) any reference in those provisions to a High Court order or a magistrates' court order included, respectively, a Court of Session order or a sheriff court order; and
   (c) any other reference in those provisions to the High Court or a magistrates' court included the Northern Ireland High Court or a court of summary jurisdiction in Northern Ireland.

(4) Where an order is registered in Northern Ireland under this section, Part II of the Maintenance and Affiliation Orders Act (Northern Ireland) 1966,

except sections 11, 11A and 14(2) and (3), shall apply as if the order had been registered in accordance with the provisions of that Part.

(5) A court of summary jurisdiction in Northern Ireland shall have jurisdiction to hear a complaint by or against a person residing outside Northern Ireland for the discharge or variation of an order registered in Northern Ireland under this section; and where such a complaint is made against a person residing outside Northern Ireland, then, if he resides in England and Wales or Scotland, section 15 of the Maintenance Orders Act 1950 (which relates to the service of process on persons residing in those countries) shall have effect in relation to the complaint as it has effect in relation to the proceedings therein mentioned.

(6) The enactments specified in Part III of Schedule 12 shall have effect with the amendments specified there, being amendments consequential on this section. [700]

NOTES
Commencement: 1 January 1987.
Commencement order: SI 1986 No 2044.

37. Minor amendments relating to maintenance orders

(1) The enactments specified in Schedule 11 shall have effect with the amendments specified there, being amendments whose main purpose is as follows—

> Part I—to extend certain enforcement provisions to lump sum maintenance orders;
> Part II—to provide for the recovery of interest according to the law of the country of origin in the case of maintenance orders made in other jurisdictions and registered in the High Court;
> Part III—to extend the Maintenance Orders (Reciprocal Enforcement) Act 1972 to cases where the payer under a maintenance order is not resident within the jurisdiction but has assets there.

(2) ... [701]

NOTES
Commencement: 1 January 1987.
Commencement order: SI 1986 No 2044.
Sub-s (2): amends the Maintenance Orders (Reciprocal Enforcement) Act 1972, s 27(1).

38. Overseas judgments counteracting an award of multiple damages

... [702]

NOTES
Commencement: 24 August 1982.
This section amends the Protection of Trading Interests Act 1980, s 7.

Jurisdiction, and recognition and enforcement of judgments, as between United Kingdom and certain territories

39. Application of provisions corresponding to 1968 Convention in relation to certain territories

(1) Her Majesty may by Order in Council make provision corresponding to the provision made by the 1968 Convention as between the Contracting States to that Convention, with such modifications as appear to Her Majesty to be

appropriate, for regulating, as between the United Kingdom and any of the territories mentioned in subsection (2), the jurisdiction of courts and the recognition and enforcement of judgments.

(2) The territories referred to in subsection (1) are—
  (a) the Isle of Man;
  (b) any of the Channel Islands;
  (c) Gibraltar;
  (d) the Sovereign Base Areas of Akrotiri and Dhekelia (that is to say the areas mentioned in section 2(1) of the Cyprus Act 1960).

(3) An Order in Council under this section may contain such supplementary and incidental provisions as appear to Her Majesty to be necessary or expedient, including in particular provisions corresponding to or applying any of the provisions of Part I with such modifications as may be specified in the Order.

(4) Any Order in Council under this section shall be subject to annulment in pursuance of a resolution of either House of Parliament. [703]

NOTES
Commencement: 1 January 1987.
Commencement order: SI 1986 No 2044.
No Order in Council has yet been made under this section

Legal aid

40. Power to modify enactments relating to legal aid etc

. . . [704]

NOTES
Commencement: 24 August 1982.
This section amends the Legal Aid Act 1974, s 20, the Legal Aid (Scotland) Act 1967, s 15, and the Legal Aid, Advice and Assistance (Northern Ireland) Order 1981, SI 1981 No 228, art 22.
Repealed in part by the Legal Aid Act 1988, s 45, Sch 6.

PART V

SUPPLEMENTARY AND GENERAL PROVISONS

Domicile

41. Domicile of individuals

(1) Subject to Article 52 (which contains provisions for determining whether a party is domiciled in a Contracting State), the following provisions of this section determine, for the purposes of the 1968 Convention and this Act, whether an individual is domiciled in the United Kingdom or in a particular part of, or place in, the United Kingdom or in a state other than a Contracting State.

(2) An individual is domiciled in the United Kingdom if and only if—
  (a) he is resident in the United Kingdom; and
  (b) the nature and circumstances of his residence indicate that he has a substantial connection with the United Kingdom.

(3) Subject to subsection (5), an individual is domiciled in a particular part of the United Kingdom if and only if—
  (a) he is resident in that part; and

(b) the nature and circumstances of his residence indicate that he has a substantial connection with that part.

(4) An individual is domiciled in a particular place in the United Kingdom if and only if he—
   (a) is domiciled in the part of the United Kingdom in which that place is situated; and
   (b) is resident in that place.

(5) An individual who is domiciled in the United Kingdom but in whose case the requirements of subsection (3)(b) are not satisified in relation to any particular part of the United Kingdom shall be treated as domiciled in the part of the United Kingdom in which he is resident.

(6) In the case of an individual who—
   (a) is resident in the United Kingdom, or in a particular part of the United Kingdom; and
   (b) has been so resident for the last three months or more,
the requirements of subsection (2)(b) or, as the case may be, subsection (3)(b) shall be presumed to be fulfilled unless the contrary is proved.

(7) An individual is domiciled in a state other than a Contracting State if and only if—
   (a) he is resident in that state; and
   (b) the nature and circumstances of his residence indicate that he has a substantial connection with that state. **[705]**

NOTES
   Commencement: 1 January 1987.
   Commencement order: SI 1986 No 2044.

42. Domicile and seat of corporation or association

(1) For the purposes of this Act the seat of a corporation or association (as determined by this section) shall be treated as its domicile.

(2) The following provisions of this section determine where a corporation or association has its seat—
   (a) for the purpose of Article 53 (which for the purposes of the 1968 Convention equates the domicile of such a body with its seat); and
   (b) for the purposes of this Act other than the provisions mentioned in section 43(1)(b) and (c).

(3) A corporation or association has its seat in the United Kingdom if and only if—
   (a) it was incorporated or formed under the law of a part of the United Kingdom and has its registered office or some other official address in the United Kingdom; or
   (b) its central management and control is exercised in the United Kingdom.

(4) A corporation or association has its seat in a particular part of the United Kingdom if and only if it has its seat in the United Kingdom and—
   (a) it has its registered office or some other official address in that part; or
   (b) its central management and control is exercised in that part; or

(c) it has a place of business in that part.

(5) A corporation or association has its seat in a particular place in the United Kingdom if and only if it has its seat in the part of the United Kingdom in which that place is situated and—
- (a) it has its registered office or some other official address in that place; or
- (b) its central management and control is exercised in that place; or
- (c) it has a place of business in that place.

(6) Subject to subsection (7), a corporation or association has its seat in a state other than the United Kingdom if and only if—
- (a) it was incorporated or formed under the law of that state and has its registered office or some other official address there; or
- (b) its central management and control is exercised in that state.

(7) A corporation or association shall not be regarded as having its seat in a Contracting State other than the United Kingdom if it is shown that the courts of that state would not regard it as having its seat there.

(8) In this section—
"business" includes any activity carried on by a corporation or association, and "place of business" shall be construed accordingly;
"official address", in relation to a corporation or association, means an address which it is required by law to register, notify or maintain for the purpose of receiving notices or other communications. [706]

NOTES
Commencement: 1 January 1987.
Commencement order: SI 1986 No 2044.

43. Seat of corporation or association for purposes of Article 16(2) and related provisions

(1) The following provisions of this section determine where a corporation or association has its seat for the purposes of—
- (a) Article 16(2) (which confers exclusive jurisdiction over proceedings relating to the formation or dissolution of such bodies, or to the decisions of their organs);
- (b) Articles 5A and 16(2) in Schedule 4; and
- (c) Rules 2(12) and 4(1)(b) in Schedule 8.

(2) A corporation or association has its seat in the United Kingdom if and only if—
- (a) it was incorporated or formed under the law of a part of the United Kingdom; or
- (b) its central management and control is exercised in the United Kingdom.

(3) A corporation or association has its seat in a particular part of the United Kingdom if and only if it has its seat in the United Kingdom and—
- (a) subject to subsection (5), it was incorporated or formed under the law of that part; or
- (b) being incorporated or formed under the law of a state other than the United Kingdom, its central management and control is exercised in that part.

(4) A corporation or association has its seat in a particular place in Scotland if and only if it has its seat in Scotland and—
- (a) it has its registered office or some other official address in that place; or
- (b) it has no registered office or other official address in Scotland, but its central management and control is exercised in that place.

(5) A corporation or association incorporated or formed under—
- (a) an enactment forming part of the law of more than one part of the United Kingdom; or
- (b) an instrument having effect in the domestic law of more than one part of the United Kingdom,

shall, if it has a registered office, be taken to have its seat in the part of the United Kingdom in which that office is situated, and not in any other part of the United Kingdom.

(6) Subject to subsection (7), a corporation or association has its seat in a Contracting State other than the United Kingdom if and only if—
- (a) it was incorporated or formed under the law of that state; or
- (b) its central management and control is exercised in that state.

(7) A corporation or association shall not be regarded as having its seat in a Contracting State other than the United Kingdom if—
- (a) it has its seat in the United Kingdom by virtue of subsection (2)(a); or
- (b) it is shown that the courts of that other state would not regard it for the purposes of Article 16(2) as having its seat there.

(8) In this section "official address" has the same meaning as in section 42.

NOTES
Commencement: 1 January 1987.
Commencement order: SI 1986 No 2044.

44. Persons deemed to be domiciled in the United Kingdom for certain purposes

(1) This section applies to—
- (a) proceedings within Section 3 of Title II of the 1968 Convention (insurance contracts), and
- (b) proceedings within Section 4 of that Title (consumer contracts).

(2) A person who, for the purposes of proceedings to which this section applies arising out of the operations of a branch, agency or other establishment in the United Kingdom, is deemed for the purposes of the 1968 Convention to be domiciled in the United Kingdom by virtue of—
- (a) Article 8, second paragraph (insurers); or
- (b) Article 13, second paragraph (suppliers of goods, services or credit to consumers),

shall, for the purposes of those proceedings, be treated for the purposes of this Act as so domiciled and as domiciled in the part of the United Kingdom in which the branch, agency or establishment in question is situated.

NOTES
Commencement: 1 January 1987.
Commencement order: SI 1986 No 2044.

45. Domicile of trusts

(1) The following provisions of this section determine, for the purposes of the 1968 Convention and this Act, where a trust is domiciled.

(2) A trust is domiciled in the United Kingdom if and only if it is by virtue of subsection (3) domiciled in a part of the United Kingdom.

(3) A trust is domiciled in a part of the United Kingdom if and only if the system of law of that part is the system of law with which the trust has its closest and most real connection.

NOTES
Commencement: 1 January 1987.
Commencement order: SI 1986 No 2044.

46. Domicile and seat of the Crown

(1) For the purposes of this Act the seat of the Crown (as determined by this section) shall be treated as its domicile.

(2) The following provisions of this section determine where the Crown has its seat—

    (a) for the purposes of the 1968 Convention (in which Article 53 equates the domicile of a legal person with its seat); and
    (b) for the purposes of this Act.

(3) Subect to the provisions of any Order in Council for the time being in force under subsection (4)—

    (a) the Crown in right of Her Majesty's government in the United Kingdom has its seat in every part of, and every place in, the United Kingdom; and
    (b) the Crown in right of Her Majesty's government in Northern Ireland has its seat in, and in every place in, Northern Ireland.

(4) Her Majesty may by Order in Council provide that, in the case of proceedings of any specified description against the Crown in right of Her Majesty's government in the United Kingdom, the Crown shall be treated for the purposes of the 1968 Convention and this Act as having its seat in, and in every place in, a specified part of the United Kingdom and not in any other part of the United Kingdom.

(5) An Order in Council under subsection (4) may frame a description of proceedings in any way, and in particular may do so by reference to the government department or officer of the Crown against which or against whom they fall to be instituted.

(6) Any Order in Council made under this section shall be subject to annulment in pursuance of a resolution of either House of Parliament.

(7) Nothing in this section applies to the Crown otherwise than in right of Her Majesty's government in the United Kingdom or Her Majesty's government in Northern Ireland.

NOTES
Commencement: 1 January 1987.
Commencement order: SI 1986 No 2044.
No Order in Council has yet been made under this section.

Other supplementary provisions

47. Modifications occasioned by decisions of European Court as to meaning or effect of Conventions

(1) Her Majesty may by Order in Council—
  (*a*) make such provision as Her Majesty considers appropriate for the purpose of bringing the law of any part of the United Kingdom into accord with the Conventions as affected by any principle laid down by the European Court in connection with the Conventions or by any decision of that court as to the meaning or effect of any provision of the Conventions; or
  (*b*) make such modifications of Schedule 4 or Schedule 8, or of any other statutory provision affected by any provision of either of those Schedules, as Her Majesty considers appropriate in view of any principle laid down by the European Court in connection with Title II of the 1968 Convention or of any decision of that court as to the meaning or effect of any provision of that Title.

(2) The provision which may be made by virtue of paragraph (*a*) of subsection (1) includes such modifications of this Act or any other statutory provision, whenever passed or made, as Her Majesty considers appropriate for the purpose mentioned in that paragraph.

(3) The modifications which may be made by virtue of paragraph (*b*) of subsection (1) include modifications designed to produce divergence between any provision of Schedule 4 or Schedule 8 and a corresponding provision of Title II of the 1968 Convention as affected by any such principle or decision as is mentioned in that paragraph.

(4) An Order in Council under this section shall not be made unless a draft of the Order has been laid before Parliament and approved by a resolution of each House of Parliament. [711]

NOTES
Commencement: 1 January 1987.
Commencement order: SI 1986 No 2044.
No Order in Council has yet been made under this section.

48. Matters for which rules of court may provide

(1) Rules of court may make provision for regulating the procedure to be followed in any court in connection with any provision of this Act or the Conventions.

(2) Rules of court may make provision as to the manner in which and the conditions subject to which a certificate or judgment registered in any court under any provision of this Act may be enforced, including provision for enabling the court or, in Northern Ireland the Enforcement of Judgments Office, subject to any conditions specified in the rules, to give directions about such matters.

(3) Without prejudice to the generality of subsections (1) and (2), the power to make rules of court for magistrates' courts, and in Northern Ireland the power to make Judgment Enforcement Rules, shall include power to make such provision as the rule-making authority considers necessary or expedient for the purposes of the provisions of the Conventions and this Act relating to maintenance proceedings and the recognition and enforcement of maintenance

orders, and shall in particular include power to make provision as to any of the following matters—
- (a) authorising the service in another Contracting State of process issued by or for the purposes of a magistrates' court and the service and execution in England and Wales or Northern Ireland of process issued in another Contracting State;
- (b) requesting courts in other parts of the United Kingdom or in other Contracting States to take evidence there for the purposes of proceedings in England and Wales or Northern Ireland;
- (c) the taking of evidence in England and Wales or Northern Ireland in response to similar requests received from such courts;
- (d) the circumstances in which and the conditions subject to which any powers conferred under paragraphs (a) to (c) are to be exercised;
- (e) the admission in evidence, subject to such conditions as may be prescribed in the rules, of statements contained in documents purporting to be made or authenticated by a court in another part of the United Kingdom or in another Contracting State, or by a judge or official of such a court, which purport—
    - (i) to set out or summarise evidence given in proceedings in that court or to be documents received in evidence in such proceedings or copies of such documents; or
    - (ii) to set out or summarise evidence taken for the purposes of proceedings in England and Wales or Northern Ireland, whether or not in response to any such request as is mentioned in paragraph (b); or
    - (iii) to record information relating to the payments made under an order of that court;
- (f) the circumstances and manner in which a magistrates' court may or must vary or revoke a maintenance order registered in that court, cancel the registration of, or refrain from enforcing, such an order or transmit such an order for enforcement in another part of the United Kingdom;
- (g) the cases and manner in which courts in other parts of the United Kingdom or in other Contracting States are to be informed of orders made, or other things done, by or for the purposes of a magistrates' court;
- (h) the circumstances and manner in which a magistrates' court may communicate for other purposes with such courts;
- (i) the giving of notice of such matters as may be prescribed in the rules to such persons as may be so prescribed and the manner in which such notice is to be given.

(4) Nothing in this section shall be taken as derogating from the generality of any power to make rules of court conferred by any other enactment. [712]

NOTES
Commencement: 1 January 1987.
Commencement order: SI 1986 No 2044.
Regulation under this section: see note to s 12 ante.

49. Saving for powers to stay, sist, strike out or dismiss proceedings

Nothing in this Act shall prevent any court in the United Kingdom from staying, sisting, striking out or dismissing any proceedings before it, on the ground of *forum non conveniens* or otherwise, where to do so in not inconsistent with the 1968 Convention.

NOTES
Commencement: 24 August 1982: Sch 13 para 2.

General

50. Interpretation: general

In this Act, unless the context otherwise requires—

"the Accession Convention" has the meaning given by section 1(1);

"Article" and references to sub-divisions of numbered Articles are to be construed in accordance with section 1(2)(*b*);

"association" means an unincorporated body of persons;

"Contracting State" has the meaning given by section 1(3);

"the 1968 Convention" has the meaning given by section 1(1), and references to that Convention and to provisions of it are to be construed in accordance with section 1(2)(*a*);

"the Conventions" has the meaning given by section 1(1);

"corporation" means a body corporate, and includes a partnership subsisting under the law of Scotland;

"court", without more, includes a tribunal;

"court of law", in relation to the United Kingdom, means any of the following courts, namely—
  (*a*) the House of Lords,
  (*b*) in England and Wales or Northern Ireland, the Court of Appeal, the High Court, the Crown Court, a county court and a magistrates' court,
  (*c*) in Scotland, the Court of Session and a sheriff court;

"the Crown" is to be construed in accordance with section 51(2);

"enactment" includes an enactment comprised in Northern Ireland legislation;

"judgment", subject to sections 15(1) and 18(2) and to paragraph 1 of Schedules 6 and 7, means any judgment or order (by whatever name called) given or made by a court in any civil proceedings;

"magistrates' court", in relation to Northern Ireland, means a court of summary jurisdiction;

"modifications" includes additions, omissions and alterations;

"overseas country" means any country or territory outside the United Kingdom;

"part of the United Kingdom" means England and Wales, Scotland or Northern Ireland;

"the 1971 Protocol" has the meaning given by section 1(1), and references to that Protocol and to provisions of it are to be construed in accordance with section 1(2)(*a*);

"rules of court", in relation to any court, means rules, orders or regulations made by the authority having power to make rules, orders or regulations regulating the procedure of that court, and includes—
  (*a*) in Scotland, Acts of Sederunt;
  (*b*) in Northern Ireland, Judgment Enforcement Rules;

"statutory provision" means any provision contained in an Act, or in any Northern Ireland legislation, or in—
  (*a*) subordinate legislation (as defined in section 21(1) of the Interpretation Act 1978); or
  (*b*) any instrument of a legislative character made under any Northern Ireland legislation;

"tribunal"—
  (a) means a tribunal of any description other than a court of law;
  (b) in relation to an overseas country, includes, as regards matters relating to maintenance within the meaning of the 1968 Convention, any authority having power to give, enforce, vary or revoke a maintenance order. **[714]**

NOTES
Commencement: 24 August 1982: Sch 13 para 2.

51. Application to Crown

(1) This Act binds the Crown.

(2) In this section and elsewhere in this Act references to the Crown do not include references to Her Majesty in Her private capacity or to Her Majesty in right of Her Duchy of Lancaster or to the Duke of Cornwall. **[715]**

NOTES
Commencement: 24 August 1982: Sch 13 para 2.

52. Extent

(1) This Act extends to Northern Ireland.

(2) Without prejudice to the power conferred by section 39, Her Majesty may by Order in Council direct that all or any of the provisions of this Act apart from that section shall extend, subject to such modifications as may be specified in the Order, to any of the following territories, that is to say—
  (a) the Isle of Man;
  (b) any of the Channel Islands;
  (c) Gibraltar;
  (d) the Sovereign Base Areas of Akrotiri and Dhekelia (that is to say the areas mentioned in section 2(1) of the Cyprus Act 1960). **[716]**

NOTES
Commencement: 24 August 1982: Sch 13 para 2.
Orders in Council under this section: Protection of Trading Interests Act 1980 (Isle of Man) Order 1980, SI 1983 No 1704, the Protection of Trading Interests Act 1980 (Guernsey) Order 1983, SI 1983 No 1703 and the Protection of Trading Interests Act 1980 (Jersey) Order 1983, SI 1983 No 607 are in part made under this section.

53. Commencement, transitional provisions and savings

(1) This Act shall come into force in accordance with the provisions of Part I of Schedule 13.

(2) The transitional provisions and savings contained in Part II of that Schedule shall have effect in relation to the commencement of the provisions of this Act mentioned in that Part. **[717]**

NOTES
Commencement: 1 January 1987 — 13 July 1982.
Commencement orders: SI 1984 No 1553, SI 1986 No 2044.

54. Repeals

The enactments mentioned in Schedule 14 are hereby repealed to the extent specified in the third column of that Schedule. [718]

NOTES
Commencement: 1 January 1987 (in part); 24 August 1982 (remainder).
Commencement order: SI 1986 No 2044.

55. Short title
This Act may be cited as the Civil Jurisdiction and Judgments Act 1982. [719]

NOTES
Commencement: 13 July 1982.

SCHEDULES

SCHEDULE 1

Section 2(2)

TEXT OF 1968 CONVENTION, AS AMENDED

ARRANGEMENT OF PROVISIONS

TITLE I. SCOPE (Article 1).
TITLE II. JURISDICTION
  Section 1. General provisions (Articles 2–4).
  Section 2. Special jurisdiction (Articles 5–6A).
  Section 3. Jurisdiction in matters relating to insurance (Articles 7–12A).
  Section 4. Jurisdiction over consumer contracts (Articles 13–15).
  Section 5. Exclusive jurisdiction (Article 16).
  Section 6. Prorogation of jurisdiction (Articles 17 and 18).
  Section 7. Examination as to jurisdiction and admissibility (Articles 19–20).
  Section 8. Lis pendens—Related actions (Articles 21–23).
  Section 9. Provisional, including protective, measures (Article 24).
TITLE III. RECOGNITION AND ENFORCEMENT
  Definition of "judgment" (Articles 25)
  Section 1. Recognition (Articles 26–30)
  Section 2. Enforcement (Articles 31–45)
  Section 3. Common provisions (Articles 46–49)
TITLE IV. AUTHENTIC INSTRUMENTS AND COURT SETTLEMENTS (Articles 50–51)
TITLE V. GENERAL PROVISIONS (Articles 52–53)
TITLE VI. TRANSITIONAL PROVISIONS (Article 54)
TITLE VII. RELATIONSHIP TO OTHER CONVENTIONS (Articles 55–59)
TITLE VIII. FINAL PROVISIONS (Articles 60–68)

CONVENTION ON JURISDICTION AND THE ENFORCEMENT OF JUDGMENTS IN CIVIL AND COMMERCIAL MATTERS

Preamble

The High Contracting Parties to the Treaty establishing the European Economic Community,

Desiring to implement the provisions of Article 220 of that Treaty by virtue of which they undertook to secure the simplification of formalities governing the reciprocal recognition and enforcement of judgments of courts or tribunals;

Anxious to strengthen in the Community the legal protection of persons therein established;

Considering that it is necessary for this purpose to determine the international jurisdiction of their courts, to facilitate recognition and to introduce an expeditious procedure for securing the enforcement of judgments, authentic instruments and court settlements;

Have decided to conclude this Convention and to this end have designated as their Plenipotentiaries:

(Designations of Plenipotentiaries of the original six Contracting States)

Who, meeting within the Council, having exchanged their Full Powers, found in good and due form,

Have agreed as follows:

TITLE I

SCOPE

ARTICLE 1

This Convention shall apply in civil and commercial matters whatever the nature of the court or tribunal. It shall not extend, in particular, to revenue, customs or administrative matters.

The Convention shall not apply to:
(1) the status or legal capacity of natural persons, rights in property arising out of a matrimonial relationship, wills and succession;
(2) bankruptcy, proceedings relating to the winding-up of insolvent companies or other legal persons, judicial arrangements, compositions and analogous proceedings;
(3) social security;
(4) arbitration.

TITLE II

JURISDICTION

Section 1

General provisions

ARTICLE 2

Subject to the provisions of this Convention, persons domiciled in a Contracting State shall, whatever their nationality, be sued in the courts of that State.

Persons who are not nationals of the State in which they are domiciled shall be governed by the rules of jurisdiction applicable to nationals of that State.

ARTICLE 3

Persons domiciled in a Contracting State may be sued in the courts of another Contracting State only by virtue of the rules set out in Sections 2 to 6 of this Title.

In particular the following provisions shall not be applicable as against them:

—in Belgium:	Article 15 of the civil code (*Code civil—Burgerlijk Wetboek*) and Article 638 of the Judicial code (*Code judiciaire—Gerechtelijk Wetboek*);
—in Denmark:	Article 248(2) of the law on civil procedure (*Lov om rettens pleje*) and Chapter 3, Article 3 of the Greenland law on civil procedure (*Lov for Grønland om rettens pleje*);
—in the Federal Republic of Germany:	Article 23 of the code of civil procedure (*Zivilprozessordnung*);
—in France:	Articles 14 and 15 of the civil code (*Code civil*);
—in Ireland:	the rules which enable jurisdiction to be founded on the document instituting the proceedings having been served on the defendant during his temporary presence in Ireland:

—in Italy: Article 2 and Article 4, Nos 1 and 2 of the code of civil procedure (*Codice di procedura civile*);
—in Luxembourg: Articles 14 and 15 of the civil code (*Code civil*);
—in the Netherlands: Article 126(3) and Article 127 of the code of civil procedure (*Wetboek van Burgerlijke Rechtsvordering*);
—in the United Kingdom: the rules which enable jurisdiction to be founded on:
   (a) the document instituting the proceedings having been served on the defendant during his temporary presence in the United Kingdom; or
   (b) the presence within the United Kingdom of property belonging to the defendant; or
   (c) the seizure by the plaintiff of property situated in the United Kingdom.

Article 4

If the defendant is not domiciled in a Contracting State, the jurisdiction of the courts of each Contracting State shall, subject to the provisions of Article 16, be determined by the law of that State.

As against such a defendant, any person domiciled in a Contracting State may, whatever his nationality, avail himself in that State of the rules of jurisdiction there in force, and in particular those specified in the second paragraph of Article 3, in the same way as the nationals of that State.

Section 2

Special jurisdiction

Article 5

A person domiciled in a Contracting State may, in another Contracting State, be sued:
   (1) in matters relating to a contract, in the courts for the place of performance of the obligation in question;
   (2) in matters relating to maintenance, in the courts for the place where the maintenance creditor is domiciled or habitually resident or, if the matter is ancillary to proceedings concerning the status of a person, in the court which, according to its own law, has jurisdiction to entertain those proceedings, unless that jurisdiction is based solely on the nationality of one of the parties;
   (3) in matters relating to tort, delict or quasi-delict, in the courts for the place where the harmful event occurred;
   (4) as regards a civil claim for damages or restitution which is based on an act giving rise to criminal proceedings, in the court seised of those proceedings, to the extent that that court has jurisdiction under its own law to entertain civil proceedings;
   (5) as regards a dispute arising out of the operations of a branch, agency or other establishment, in the courts for the place in which the branch, agency or other establishment is situated;
   (6) in his capacity as settlor, trustee or beneficiary of a trust created by the operation of a statute, or by a written instrument, or created orally and evidenced in writing, in the courts of the Contracting State in which the trust is domiciled;
   (7) as regards a dispute concerning the payment of remuneration claimed in respect of the salvage of a cargo or freight, in the court under the authority of which the cargo or freight in question:
      (a) has been arrested to secure such payment, or

(b) could have been so arrested, but bail or other security has been given; provided that this provision shall apply only if it is claimed that the defendant has an interest in the cargo or freight or had such an interest at the time of salvage.

ARTICLE 6

A person domiciled in a Contracting State may also be sued:
  (1) where he is one of a number of defendants, in the courts for the place where any one of them is domiciled;
  (2) as a third party in an action on a warranty or guarantee or in any other third party proceedings, in the court seised of the original proceedings, unless these were instituted solely with the object of removing him from the jurisdiction of the court which would be competent in his case;
  (3) on a counterclaim arising from the same contract or facts on which the original claim was based, in the court in which the original claim is pending.

ARTICLE 6A

Where by virtue of this Convention a court of a Contracting State has jurisdiction in actions relating to liability arising from the use or operation of a ship, that court, or any other court substituted for this purpose by the internal law of that State, shall also have jurisdiction over claims for limitation of such liability.

Section 3

Jurisdiction in matters relating to insurance

ARTICLE 7

In matters relating to insurance, jurisdiction shall be determined by this Section, without prejudice to the provisions of Articles 4 and 5(5).

ARTICLE 8

An insurer domiciled in a Contracting State may be sued:
  (1) in the courts of the State where he is domiciled, or
  (2) in another Contracting State, in the courts for the place where the policy-holder is domiciled, or
  (3) if he is a co-insurer, in the courts of a Contracting State in which proceedings are brought against the leading insurer.

An insurer who is not domiciled in a Contracting State but has a branch, agency or other establishment in one of the Contracting States shall, in disputes arising out of the operations of the branch, agency or establishment, be deemed to be domiciled in that State.

ARTICLE 9

In respect of liability insurance or insurance of immovable property, the insurer may in addition be sued in the courts for the place where the harmful event occurred. The same applies if movable and immovable property are covered by the same insurance policy and both are adversely affected by the same contingency.

ARTICLE 10

In respect of liability insurance, the insurer may also, if the law of the court permits it, be joined in proceedings which the injured party has brought against the insured.

The provisions of Articles 7, 8 and 9 shall apply to actions brought by the injured party directly against the insurer, where such direct actions are permitted.

If the law governing such direct actions provides that the policy-holder or the insured may be joined as a party to the action, the same court shall have jurisdiction over them.

ARTICLE 11

Without prejudice to the provisions of the third paragraph of Article 10, an insurer may bring proceedings only in the courts of the Contracting State in which the defendant is domiciled, irrespective of whether he is the policy-holder, the insured or a beneficiary.

The provisions of this Section shall not affect the right to bring a counterclaim in the court in which, in accordance with this Section, the original claim is pending.

ARTICLE 12

The provisions of this Section may be departed from only by an agreement on jurisdiction:
  (1) which is entered into after the dispute has arisen, or
  (2) which allows the policy-holder, the insured or a beneficiary to bring proceedings in courts other than those indicated in this Section, or
  (3) which is concluded between a policy-holder and an insurer, both of whom are at the time of conclusion of the contract domiciled or habitually resident in the same Contracting State, and which has the effect of conferring jurisdiction on the courts of that State even if the harmful event were to occur abroad, provided that such an agreement is not contrary to the law of that State, or
  (4) which is concluded with a policy-holder who is not domiciled in a Contracting State, except in so far as the insurance is compulsory or relates to immovable property in a Contracting State, or
  (5) which relates to a contract of insurance in so far as it covers one or more of the risks set out in Article 12A.

ARTICLE 12A

The following are the risks referred to in Article 12(5):
  (1) Any loss of or damage to
    (a) sea-going ships, installations situated offshore or on the high seas, or aircraft, arising from perils which relate to their use for commercial purposes,
    (b) goods in transit other than passengers' baggage where the transit consists of or includes carriage by such ships or aircraft;
  (2) Any liability, other than for bodily injury to passengers or loss of or damage to their baggage,
    (a) arising out of the use or operation of ships, installations or aircraft as referred to in (1)(a) above in so far as the law of the Contracting State in which such aircraft are registered does not prohibit agreements on jurisdiction regarding insurance of such risks,
    (b) for loss or damage caused by goods in transit as described in (1)(b) above;
  (3) Any financial loss connected with the use or operation of ships, installations or aircraft as referred to in (1)(a) above, in particular loss of freight or charter-hire;
  (4) Any risk or interest connected with any of those referred to in (1) to (3) above.

Section 4

Jurisdiction over consumer contracts

ARTICLE 13

In proceedings concerning a contract concluded by a person for a purpose which can be regarded as being outside his trade or profession, hereinafter called the "consumer", jurisdiction shall be determined by this Section, without prejudice to the provisions of Articles 4 and 5(5), if it is:
  (1) a contract for the sale of goods on instalment credit terms, or

(2) a contract for a loan repayable by instalments, or for any other form of credit, made to finance the sale of goods, or
(3) any other contract for the supply of goods or a contract for the supply of services and
   (a) in the State of the consumer's domicile the conclusion of the contract was preceded by a specific invitation addressed to him or by advertising, and
   (b) the consumer took in that State the steps necessary for the conclusion of the contract.

Where a consumer enters into a contract with a party who is not domiciled in a Contracting State but has a branch, agency or other establishment in one of the Contracting States, that party shall, in disputes arising out of the operations of the branch, agency or establishment, be deemed to be domiciled in that State.

This Section shall not apply to contracts of transport.

Article 14

A consumer may bring proceedings against the other party to a contract either in the courts of the Contracting State in which that party is domiciled or in the courts of the Contracting State in which he is himself domiciled.

Proceedings may be brought against a consumer by the other party to the contract only in the courts of the Contracting State in which the consumer is domiciled.

These provisions shall not affect the right to bring a counterclaim in the court in which, in accordance with this Section, the original claim is pending.

Article 15

The provisions of this Section may be departed from only by an agreement:
(1) which is entered into after the dispute has arisen, or
(2) which allows the consumer to bring proceedings in courts other than those indicated in this Section, or
(3) which is entered into by the consumer and the other party to the contract, both of whom are at the time of conclusion of the contract domiciled or habitually resident in the same Contracting State, and which confers jurisdiction on the courts of that State, provided that such an agreement is not contrary to the law of that State.

Section 5

Exclusive jurisdiction

Article 16

The following courts shall have exclusive jurisdiction, regardless of domicile:
(1) in proceedings which have as their object rights *in rem* in, or tenancies of, immovable property, the courts of the Contracting State in which the property is situated;
(2) in proceedings which have as their object the validity of the constitution, the nullity or the dissolution of companies or other legal persons or associations of natural or legal persons, or the decisions of their organs, the courts of the Contracting State in which the company, legal person or association has its seat;
(3) in proceedings which have as their object the validity of entries in public registers, the courts of the Contracting State in which the register is kept;
(4) in proceedings concerned with the registration or validity of patents, trade marks, designs, or other similar rights required to be deposited or registered, the courts of the Contracting State in which the deposit or registration has been applied for, has taken place or is under the terms of an international convention deemed to have taken place;

(5) in proceedings concerned with the enforcement of judgments, the courts of the Contracting State in which the judgment has been or is to be enforced.

Section 6

Prorogation of jurisdiction

ARTICLE 17

If the parties, one or more of whom is domiciled in a Contracting State, have agreed that a court or the courts of a Contracting State are to have jurisdiction to settle any disputes which have arisen or which may arise in connection with a particular legal relationship, that court or those courts shall have exclusive jurisdiction. Such an agreement conferring jurisdiction shall be either in writing or evidenced in writing or, in international trade or commerce, in a form which accords with practices in that trade or commerce of which the parties are or ought to have been aware. Where such an agreement is concluded by parties, none of whom is domiciled in a Contracting State, the courts of other Contracting States shall have no jurisdiction over their disputes unless the court or courts chosen have declined jurisdiction.

The court or courts of a Contracting State on which a trust instrument has conferred jurisdiction shall have exclusive jurisdiction in any proceedings brought against a settlor, trustee or beneficiary, if relations between these persons or their rights or obligations under the trust are involved.

Agreements or provisions of a trust instrument conferring jurisdiction shall have no legal force if they are contrary to the provisions of Articles 12 or 15, or if the courts whose jurisdiction they purport to exclude have exclusive jurisdiction by virtue of Article 16.

If an agreement conferring jurisdiction was concluded for the benefit of only one of the parties, that party shall retain the right to bring proceedings in any other court which has jurisdiction by virtue of this Convention.

ARTICLE 18

Apart from jurisdiction derived from other provisions of this Convention, a court of a Contracting State before whom a defendant enters an appearance shall have jurisdiction. This rule shall not apply where appearance was entered solely to contest the jurisdiction, or where another court has exclusive jurisdiction by virtue of Article 16.

Section 7

Examination as to jurisdiction and admissibility

ARTICLE 19

Where a court of a Contracting State is seised of a claim which is principally concerned with a matter over which the courts of another Contracting State have exclusive jurisdiction by virtue of Article 16, it shall declare of its own motion that it has no jurisdiction.

ARTICLE 20

Where a defendant domiciled in one Contracting State is sued in a court of another Contracting State and does not enter an appearance, the court shall declare of its own motion that it has no jurisdiction unless its jurisdiction is derived from the provisions of this Convention.

The court shall stay the proceedings so long as it is not shown that the defendant has been able to receive the document instituting the proceedings or an equivalent document in sufficient time to enable him to arrange for his defence, or that all necessary steps have been taken to this end.

The provisions of the foregoing paragraph shall be replaced by those of Article 15 of the Hague Convention of 15 November 1965 on the Service Abroad of Judicial and

Extrajudicial Documents in Civil or Commercial Matters, if the document instituting the proceedings or notice thereof had to be transmitted abroad in accordance with that Convention.

Section 8

Lis Pendens—Related actions

ARTICLE 21

Where proceedings involving the same cause of action and between the same parties are brought in the courts of different Contracting States, any court other than the court first seised shall of its own motion decline jurisdiction in favour of that court.

A court which would be required to decline jurisdiction may stay its proceedings if the jurisdiction of the other court is contested.

ARTICLE 22

Where related actions are brought in the courts of different Contracting States, any court other than the court first seised may, while the actions are pending at first instance, stay its proceedings.

A court other than the court first seised may also, on the application of one of the parties, decline jurisdiction if the law of that court permits the consolidation of related actions and the court first seised has jurisdiction over both actions.

For the purposes of this Article, actions are deemed to be related where they are so closely connected that it is expedient to hear and determine them together to avoid the risk of irreconcilable judgments resulting from separate proceedings.

ARTICLE 23

Where actions come within the exclusive jurisdiction of several courts, any court other than the court first seised shall decline jurisdiction in favour of that court.

Section 9

Provisional, including protective, measures

ARTICLE 24

Application may be made to the courts of a Contracting State for such provisional, including protective, measures as may be available under the law of that State, even if, under this Convention, the courts of another Contracting State have jurisdiction as to the substance of the matter.

TITLE III

RECOGNITION AND ENFORCEMENT

ARTICLE 25

For the purposes of this Convention, "judgment" means any judgment given by a court or tribunal of a Contracting State, whatever the judgment may be called, including a decree, order, decision or writ of execution, as well as the determination of costs or expenses by an officer of the court.

Section 1

Recognition

ARTICLE 26

A judgment given in a Contracting State shall be recognised in the other Contracting States without any special procedure being required.

Any interested party who raises the recognition of a judgment as the principal issue in a dispute may, in accordance with the procedures provided for in Sections 2 and 3 of this Title, apply for a decision that the judgment be recognised.

If the outcome of proceedings in a court of a Contracting State depends on the determination of an incidental question of recognition that court shall have jurisdiction over that question.

ARTICLE 27

A judgment shall not be recognised:
(1) if such recognition is contrary to public policy in the State in which recognition is sought;
(2) where it was given in default of appearance, if the defendant was not duly served with the document which instituted the proceedings or with an equivalent document in sufficient time to enable him to arrange for his defence;
(3) if the judgment is irreconcilable with a judgment given in a dispute between the same parties in the State in which recognition is sought;
(4) if the court of the State in which the judgment was given, in order to arrive at its judgment, has decided a preliminary question concerning the status or legal capacity of natural persons, rights in property arising out of a matrimonial relationship, wills or succession in a way that conflicts with a rule of the private international law of the State in which the recognition is sought, unless the same result would have been reached by the application of the rules of private international law of that State;
(5) if the judgment is irreconcilable with an earlier judgment given in a non-Contracting State involving the same cause of action and between the same parties, provided that this latter judgment fulfils the conditions necessary for its recognition in the State addressed.

ARTICLE 28

Moreover, a judgment shall not be recognised if it conflicts with the provisions of Sections 3, 4 or 5 of Title II, or in a case provided for in Article 59.

In its examination of the grounds of jurisdiction referred to in the foregoing paragraph, the court or authority applied to shall be bound by the findings of fact on which the court of the State in which the judgment was given based its jurisdiction.

Subject to the provisions of the first paragraph, the jurisdiction of the court of the State in which the judgment was given may not be reviewed; the test of public policy referred to in Article 27(1) may not be applied to the rules relating to jurisdiction.

ARTICLE 29

Under no circumstances may a foreign judgment be reviewed as to its substance.

ARTICLE 30

A court of a Contracting State in which recognition is sought of a judgment given in another Contracting State may stay the proceedings if an ordinary appeal against the judgment has been lodged.

A court of a Contracting State in which recognition is sought of a judgment given in Ireland or the United Kingdom may stay the proceedings if enforcement is suspended in the State in which the judgment was given by reason of an appeal.

Section 2

Enforcement

ARTICLE 31

A judgment given in a Contracting State and enforceable in that State shall be enforced in another Contracting State when, on the application of any interested party, the order for its enforcement has been issued there.

However, in the United Kingdom, such a judgment shall be enforced in England and Wales, in Scotland, or in Northern Ireland when, on the application of any interested party, it has been registered for enforcement in that part of the United Kingdom.

ARTICLE 32

The application shall be submitted:

—in Belgium, to the *tribunal de première instance* or *rechtbank van eerste aanleg*;

—in Denmark, to the *underret*;

—in the Federal Republic of Germany, to the presiding judge of a chamber of the *Landgericht*:

—in France, to the presiding judge of the *tribunal de grande instance*;

—in Ireland, to the High Court;

—in Italy, to the *corte d'appello*;

—in Luxembourg, to the presiding judge of the *tribunal d'arrondissement*;

—in the Netherlands, to the presiding judge of the *arrondissementsrechtbank*;

—in the United Kingdom;
   (1) in England and Wales, to the High Court of Justice, or in the case of a maintenance judgment to the Magistrates' Court on transmission by the Secretary of State;
   (2) in Scotland, to the Court of Session, or in the case of a maintenance judgment to the Sheriff Court on transmission by the Secretary of State;
   (3) in Northern Ireland, to the High Court of Justice, or in the case of a maintenance judgment to the Magistrates' Court on transmission by the Secretary of State.

The jurisdiction of local courts shall be determined by reference to the place of domicile of the party against whom enforcement is sought. If he is not domiciled in the State in which enforcement is sought, it shall be determined by reference to the place of enforcement.

ARTICLE 33

The procedure for making the application shall be governed by the law of the State in which enforcement is sought.

The applicant must give an address for service of process within the area of jurisdiction of the court applied to. However, if the law of the State in which enforcement is sought does not provide for the furnishing of such an address, the applicant shall appoint a representative *ad litem*.

The documents referred to in Articles 46 and 47 shall be attached to the application.

ARTICLE 34

The court applied to shall give its decision without delay; the party against whom enforcement is sought shall not at this stage of the proceedings be entitled to make any submissions on the application.

The application may be refused only for one of the reasons specified in Articles 27 and 38.

Under no circumstances may the foreign judgment be reviewed as to its substance.

Article 35

The appropriate officer of the court shall without delay bring the decision given on the application to the notice of the applicant in accordance with the procedure laid down by the law of the State in which enforcement is sought.

Article 36

If enforcement is authorised, the party against whom enforcement is sought may appeal against the decision within one month of service thereof.

If that party is domiciled in a Contracting State other than that in which the decision authorising enforcement was given, the time for appealing shall be two months and shall run from the date of service, either on him in person or at his residence. No extension of time may be granted on account of distance.

Article 37

An appeal against the decision authorising enforcement shall be lodged in accordance with the rules governing procedure in contentious matters:

—in Belgium, with the *tribunal de première instance* or *rechtbank van eerste aanleg*;

—in Denmark, with the *landsret*;

—in the Federal Republic of Germany, with the *Oberlandesgericht*;

—in France, with the *cour d'appel*;

—in Ireland, with the High Court;

—in Italy, with the *corte d'appello*;

—in Luxembourg, with the *Cour supérieure de Justice* sitting as a court of civil appeal;

—in the Netherlands, with the *arrondissementsrechtbank*;

—in the United Kingsom:
  (1) in England and Wales, with the High Court of Justice or in the case of a maintenance judgment with the Magistrates' Court;
  (2) in Scotland, with the Court of Session, or in the case of a maintenance judgment with the Sheriff Court;
  (3) in Northern Ireland, with the High Court of Justice, or in the case of a maintenance judgment with the Magistrates' Court.

The judgment given on the appeal may be contested only:

—in Belgium, France, Italy, Luxembourg and the Netherlands, by an appeal in cassation;

—in Denmark, by an appeal to the *hojesteret*, with the leave of the Minister of Justice;

—in the Federal Republic of Germany, by a *Rechtsbeschwerde*;

—in Ireland, by an appeal on a point of law to the Supreme Court;

—in the United Kingdom, by a single further appeal on a point of law.

Article 38

The court with which the appeal under the first paragraph of Article 37 is lodged may, on the application of the appellant, stay the proceedings if an ordinary appeal has been lodged against the judgment in the State in which that judgment was given or if the time for such an appeal has not yet expired; in the latter case, the court may specify the time within which such an appeal is to be lodged.

Where the judgment was given in Ireland or the United Kingdom, any form of appeal available in the State in which it was given shall be treated as an ordinary appeal for the purposes of the first paragraph.

The court may also make enforcement conditional on the provision of such security as it shall determine.

ARTICLE 39

During the time specified for an appeal pursuant to Article 36 and until any such appeal has been determined, no measures of enforcement may be taken other than protective measures taken against the property of the party against whom enforcement is sought.

The decision authorising enforcement shall carry with it the power to proceed to any such protective measures.

ARTICLE 40

If the application for enforcement is refused, the applicant may appeal;

—in Belgium, to the *cour d'appel* or *hof van beroep*;

—in Denmark, to the *landsret*;

—in the Federal Republic of Germany, to the *Oberlandesgericht*;

—in France, to the *cour d'appel*;

—in Ireland, to the High Court;

—in Italy, to the *corte d'appello*;

—in Luxembourg, to the *Cour supérieure de Justice* sitting as a court of civil appeal;

—in the Netherlands, to the *gerechtshof*;

—in the United Kingdom:
  (1) in England and Wales, to the High Court of Justice, or in the case of a maintenance judgment to the Magistrates' Court;
  (2) in Scotland, to the Court of Session, or in the case of a maintenance judgment to the Sheriff Court;
  (3) in Northern Ireland, to the High Court of Justice, or in the case of a maintenance judgment to the Magistrates' Court.

The party against whom enforcement is sought shall be summoned to appear before the appellate court. If he fails to appear, the provisions of the second and third paragraphs of Article 20 shall apply even where he is not domiciled in any of the Contracting States.

ARTICLE 41

A judgment given on an appeal provided for in Article 40 may be contested only:

—in Belgium, France, Italy, Luxembourg and the Netherlands, by an appeal in cassation;

—in Denmark, by an appeal to the *højesteret*, with the leave of the Minister of Justice;

—in the Federal Republic of Germany, by a *Rechtsbeschwerde*;

—in Ireland, by an appeal on a point of law to the Supreme Court;

—in the United Kingdom, by a single further appeal on a point of law.

Article 42

Where a foreign judgment has been given in respect of several matters and enforcement cannot be authorised for all of them, the court shall authorise enforcement for one or more of them.

An applicant may request partial enforcement of a judgment.

Article 43

A foreign judgment which orders a periodic payment by way of a penalty shall be enforceable in the State in which enforcement is sought only if the amount of the payment has been finally determined by the courts of the State in which the judgment was given.

Article 44

An applicant who, in the State in which the judgment was given, has benefited from complete or partial legal aid or exemption from costs or expenses, shall be entitled, in the procedures provided for in Articles 32 to 35, to benefit from the most favourable legal aid or the most extensive exemption from costs or expenses provided for by the law of the State addressed.

An applicant who requests the enforcement of a decision given by an administrative authority in Denmark in respect of a maintenance order may, in the State addressed, claim the benefits referred to in the first paragraph if he presents a statement from the Danish Ministry of Justice to the effect that he fulfils the economic requirements to qualify for the grant of complete or partial legal aid or exemption from costs or expenses.

Article 45

No security, bond or deposit, however described, shall be required of a party who in one Contracting State applies for enforcement of a judgment given in another Contracting State on the ground that he is a foreign national or that he is not domiciled or resident in the State in which enforcement is sought.

Section 3

Common provisions

Article 46

A party seeking recognition or applying for enforcement of a judgment shall produce:
(1) a copy of the judgment which satisfies the conditions necessary to establish its authenticity;
(2) in the case of a judgment given in default, the original or a certified true copy of the document which establishes that the party in default was served with the document instituting the proceedings or with an equivalent document.

Article 47

A party applying for enforcement shall also produce:
(1) documents which establish that, according to the law of the State in which it has been given, the judgment is enforceable and has been served;
(2) where appropriate, a document showing that the applicant is in receipt of legal aid in the State in which the judgment was given.

Article 48

If the documents specified in Article 46(2) and Article 47(2) are not produced, the court may specify a time for their production, accept equivalent documents or, if it considers that it has sufficient information before it, dispense with their production.

If the court so requires, a translation of the documents shall be produced; the translation shall be certified by a person qualified to do so in one of the Contracting States.

ARTICLE 49

No legalisation or other similar formality shall be required in respect of the documents referred to in Articles 46 or 47 or the second paragraph of Article 48, or in respect of a document appointing a representative *ad litem*.

TITLE IV

AUTHENTIC INSTRUMENTS AND COURT SETTLEMENTS

ARTICLE 50

A document which has been formally drawn up or registered as an authentic instrument and is enforceable in one Contracting State shall, in another Contracting State, have an order for its enforcement issued there, on application made in accordance with the procedures provided for in Article 31 *et seq*. The application may be refused only if enforcement of the instrument is contrary to public policy in the State in which enforcement is sought.

The instrument produced must satisfy the conditions necessary to establish its authenticity in the State of origin.

The provisions of Section 3 of Title III shall apply as appropriate.

ARTICLE 51

A settlement which has been approved by a court in the course of proceedings and is enforceable in the State in which it was concluded shall be enforceable in the State in which enforcement is sought under the same conditions as authentic instruments.

TITLE V

GENERAL PROVISIONS

ARTICLE 52

In order to determine whether a party is domiciled in the Contracting State whose courts are seised of the matter, the court shall apply its internal law.

If a party is not domiciled in the State whose courts are seised of the matter, then, in order to determine whether the party is domiciled in another Contracting State, the court shall apply the law of that State.

The domicile of a party shall, however, be determined in accordance with his national law if, by that law, his domicile depends on that of another person or on the seat of an authority.

ARTICLE 53

For the purposes of this Convention, the seat of a company or other legal person or association of natural or legal persons shall be treated as its domicile. However, in order to determine that seat, the court shall apply its rules of private international law.

In order to determine whether a trust is domiciled in the Contracting State whose courts are seised of the matter, the court shall apply its rules of private international law.

TITLE VI

TRANSITIONAL PROVISIONS

Article 54

The provisions of this Convention shall apply only to legal proceedings instituted and to documents formally drawn up or registered as authentic instruments after its entry into force.

However, judgments given after the date of entry into force of this Convention in proceedings instituted before that date shall be recognised and enforced in accordance with the provisions of Title III if jurisdiction was founded upon rules which accorded with those provided for either in Title II of this Convention or in a convention concluded between the State of origin and the State addressed which was in force when the proceedings were instituted.

TITLE VII

RELATIONSHIP TO OTHER CONVENTIONS

Article 55

. . .

NOTES
Article 55, which lists Conventions superseded by this Convention, is omitted.

Article 56

The Treaty and the conventions referred to in Article 55 shall continue to have effect in relation to matters to which this Convention does not apply.

They shall continue to have effect in respect of judgments given and documents formally drawn up or registered as authentic instruments before the entry into force of this Convention.

Article 57

This Convention shall not affect any conventions to which the Contracting States are or will be parties and which, in relation to particular matters, govern jurisdiction or the recognition or enforcement of judgments.

This Convention shall not affect the application of provisions which, in relation to particular matters, govern jurisdiction or the recognition or enforcement of judgments and which are or will be contained in acts of the Institutions of the European Communities or in national laws harmonised in implementation of such acts.

(Article 25(2) of the Accession Convention provides:

"With a view to its uniform interpretation, paragraph 1 of Article 57 shall be applied in the following manner:
  (a) The 1968 Convention as amended shall not prevent a court of a Contracting State which is a party to a convention on a particular matter from assuming jurisdiction in accordance with that convention, even where the defendant is domiciled in another Contracting State which is not a party to that convention. The court shall, in any event, apply Article 20 of the 1968 Convention as amended.
  (b) A judgment given in a Contracting State in the exercise of jurisdiction provided for in a convention on a particular matter shall be recognised and enforced in the other Contracting States in accordance with the 1968 Convention as amended.
  Where a convention on a particular matter to which both the State of origin and the State addressed are parties lays down conditions for the recognition or enforcement of judgments, those conditions shall apply.

In any event, the provisions of the 1968 Convention as amended which concern the procedures for recognition and enforcement of judgments may be applied.")

ARTICLE 58

This Convention shall not affect the rights granted to Swiss nationals by the Convention concluded on 15 June 1869 between France and the Swiss Confederation on Jurisdiction and the Enforcement of Judgments in Civil Matters.

ARTICLE 59

This Convention shall not prevent a Contracting State from assuming, in a convention on the recognition and enforcement of judgments, an obligation towards a third State not to recognise judgments given in other Contracting States against defendants domiciled or habitually resident in the third State where, in cases provided for in Article 4, the judgment could only be founded on a ground of jurisdiction specified in the second paragraph of Article 3.

However, a Contracting State may not assume an obligation towards a third State not to recognise a judgment given in another Contracting State by a court basing its jurisdiction on the presence within that State of property belonging to the defendant, or the seizure by the plaintiff of property situated there:

(1) if the action is brought to assert or declare proprietary or possessory rights in that property, seeks to obtain authority to dispose of it, or arises from another issue relating to such property, or

(2) if the property constitutes the security for a debt which is the subject-matter of the action.

TITLE VIII

FINAL PROVISIONS

ARTICLE 60

This Convention shall apply to the European territories of the Contracting States, including Greenland, to the French overseas departments and territories, and to Mayotte.

The Kingdom of the Netherlands may declare at the time of signing or ratifying this Convention or at any later time, by notifying the Secretary-General of the Council of the European Communities, that this Convention shall be applicable to the Netherlands Antilles. In the absence of such declaration, proceedings taking place in the European territory of the Kingdom as a result of an appeal in cassation from the judgment of a court in the Netherlands Antilles shall be deemed to be proceedings taking place in the latter court.

Notwithstanding the first paragraph, this Convention shall not apply to:

(1) the Faroe Islands, unless the Kingdom of Denmark makes a declaration to the contrary,

(2) any European territory situated outside the United Kingdom for the international relations of which the United Kingdom is responsible, unless the United Kingdom makes a declaration to the contrary in respect of any such territory.

Such declarations may be made at any time by notifying the Secretary-General of the Council of the European Communities.

Proceedings brought in the United Kingdom on appeal from courts in one of the territories referred to in subparagraph (2) of the third paragraph shall be deemed to be proceedings taking place in those courts.

Proceedings which in the Kingdom of Denmark are dealt with under the law on civil procedure for the Faroe Islands (*lov for Faeroerne om rettens pleje*) shall be deemed to be proceedings taking place in the courts of the Faroe Islands.

Article 61

This Convention shall be ratified by the signatory States. The instruments of ratification shall be deposited with the Secretary-General of the Council of the European Communities.

Article 62

This Convention shall enter into force on the first day of the third month following the deposit of the instrument of ratification by the last signatory State to take this step.

Article 63

The Contracting States recognise that any State which becomes a member of the European Economic Community shall be required to accept this Convention as a basis for the negotiations between the Contracting States and that State necessary to ensure the implementation of the last paragraph of Article 220 of the Treaty establishing the European Economic Community.

The necessary adjustments may be the subject of a special convention between the Contracting State of the one part and the new Member State of the other part.

Article 64

The Secretary-General of the Council of the European Communities shall notify the signatory States of:
  (a) the deposit of each instrument of ratification;
  (b) the date of entry into force of this Convention;
  (c) any declaration received pursuant to Article 60;
  (d) any declaration received pursuant to Article IV of the Protocol;
  (e) any communication made pursuant to Article VI of the Protocol.

Article 65

The Protocol annexed to this Convention by common accord of the Contracting States shall form an integral part thereof.

Article 66

This Convention is concluded for an unlimited period.

Article 67

Any Contracting State may request the revision of this Convention. In this event, a revision conference shall be convened by the President of the Council of the European Communities.

Article 68

This Convention, drawn up in a single original in the Dutch, French, German and Italian languages, all four texts being equally authentic, shall be deposited in the archives of the Secretariat of the Council of the European Communities. The Secretary-General shall transmit a certified copy to the Government of each signatory State.

(Signatures of Plenipotentiaries of the original six Contracting States)

ANNEXED PROTOCOL

Article I

Any person domiciled in Luxembourg who is sued in a court of another Contracting State pursuant to Article 5(1) may refuse to submit to the jurisdiction of that court. If the defendant does not enter an appearance the court shall declare of its own motion that it has no jurisdiction.

An agreement conferring jurisdiction, within the meaning of Article 17, shall be valid with respect to a person domiciled in Luxembourg only if that person has expressly and specifically so agreed.

ARTICLE II

Without prejudice to any more favourable provisions of national laws, persons domiciled in a Contracting State who are being prosecuted in the criminal courts of another Contracting State of which they are not nationals for an offence which was not intentionally committed may be defended by persons qualified to do so, even if they do not appear in person.

However, the court seised of the matter may order appearance in person; in the case of failure to appear, a judgment given in the civil action without the person concerned having had the opportunity to arrange for his defence need not be recognised or enforced in the other Contracting States.

ARTICLE III

In proceedings for the issue of an order for enforcement, no charge, duty or fee calculated by reference to the value of the matter in issue may be levied in the State in which enforcement is sought.

ARTICLE IV

Judicial and extrajudicial documents drawn up in one Contracting State which have to be served on persons in another Contracting State shall be transmitted in accordance with the procedures laid down in the conventions and agreements concluded between the Contracting States.

Unless the State in which service is to take place objects by declaration to the Secretary-General of the Council of the European Communities, such documents may also be sent by the appropriate public officers of the State in which the document has been drawn up directly to the appropriate public officers of the State in which the addressee is to be found. In this case the officer of the State of origin shall send a copy of the document to the officer of the State addressed who is competent to forward it to the addressee. The document shall be forwarded in the manner specified by the law of the State addressed. The forwarding shall be recorded by a certificate sent directly to the officer of the State of origin.

ARTICLE V

The jurisdiction specified in Article 6(2) and Article 10 in actions on a warranty or guarantee or in any other third party proceedings may not be resorted to in the Federal Republic of Germany. In that State, any person domiciled in another Contracting State may be sued in the courts in pursuance of Articles 68, 72, 73 and 74 of the code of civil procedure (*Zivilprozessordnung*) concerning third-party notices.

Judgments given in the other Contracting State by virtue of Article 6(2) or Article 10 shall be recognised and enforced in the Federal Republic of Germany in accordance with Title III. Any effects which judgments given in that State may have on third parties by application of Articles 68, 72, 73 and 74 of the code of civil procedure (*Zivilprozessordnung*) shall also be recognised in the other Contracting States.

ARTICLE V A

In matters relating to maintenance, the expression "court" includes the Danish administrative authorities.

ARTICLE V B

In proceedings involving a dispute between the master and a member of the crew of a sea-going ship registered in Denmark or in Ireland, concerning remuneration or other conditions of service, a court in a Contracting State shall establish whether the diplomatic or consular officer responsible for the ship has been notified of the dispute. It shall stay the proceedings so long as he has not been notified. It shall of its own motion decline jurisdiction if the officer, having been duly notified, has exercised the powers accorded to him in the matter by a consular convention, or in the absence of such a convention, has, within the time allowed, raised any objection to the exercise of such jurisdiction.

ARTICLE V C

Articles 52 and 53 of this Convention shall, when applied by Article 69(5) of the Convention for the European Patent for the Common Market, signed at Luxembourg on 15 December 1975, to the provisions relating to "residence" in the English text of that Convention, operate as if "residence" in that text were the same as "domicile" in Articles 52 and 53.

ARTICLE V D

Without prejudice to the jurisdiction of the European Patent Office under the Convention on the Grant of European Patents, signed at Munich on 5 October 1973, the courts of each Contracting State shall have exclusive jurisdiction, regardless of domicile, in proceedings concerned with the registration or validity of any European patent granted for that State which is not a Community patent by virtue of the provisions of Article 86 of the Convention for the European Patent for the Common Market, signed at Luxembourg on 15 December 1975.

ARTICLE VI

The Contracting States shall communicate to the Secretary-General of the Council of the European Communities the text of any provisions of their laws which amend either those articles of their laws mentioned in the Convention or the lists of courts specified in Section 2 of Title III of the Convention. **[720]**

NOTES
 Commencement: 1 January 1987.
 Commencement order: SI 1986 No 2044.

SCHEDULE 2

Section 2(2)

TEXT OF 1971 PROTOCOL, AS AMENDED

ARTICLE 1

The Court of Justice of the European Communities shall have jurisdiction to give rulings on the interpretation of the Convention on Jurisdiction and the Enforcement of Judgments in Civil and Commercial Matters and of the Protocol annexed to that Convention, signed at Brussels on 27 September 1968, and also on the interpretation of the present Protocol.

The Court of Justice of the European Communities shall also have jurisdiction to give rulings on the interpretation of the Convention on the Accession of the Kingdom of Denmark, Ireland and the United Kingdom of Great Britain and Northern Ireland to the Convention of 27 September 1968 and to this Protocol.

ARTICLE 2

The following courts may request the Court of Justice to give preliminary rulings on questions of interpretation:

(1) - in Belgium: *la Cour de Cassation - het Hof van Cassatie* and *le Conseil d'Etat - de Raad van State,*

 - in Denmark: *højesteret,*

 - in the Federal Republic of Germany: *die obersten Gerichtshöfe des Bundes,*

 - in France: *la Cour de Cassation* and *le Conseil d'Etat,*

 - in Ireland: the Supreme Court,

- in Italy: *la Corte Suprema di Cassazione,*

- in Luxembourg: *la cour supérieure de Justice* when sitting as *Cour de Cassation,*

- in the Netherlands: *de Hoge Raad,*

- in the United Kingdom: the House of Lords and courts to which application has been made under the second paragraph of Article 37 or under Article 41 of the Convention;

(2) the courts of the Contracting States when they are sitting in an appellate capacity;

(3) in the cases provided for in Article 37 of the Convention, the courts referred to in that Article.

Article 3

(1) Where a question of interpretation of the Convention or of one of the other instruments referred to in Article 1 is raised in a case pending before one of the courts listed in Article 2(1), that court shall, if it considers that a decision on the question is necessary to enable it to give judgment, request the Court of Justice to give a ruling thereon.

(2) Where such a question is raised before any court referred to in Article 2(2) or (3), that court may, under the conditions laid down in paragraph (1), request the Court of Justice to give a ruling thereon.

Article 4

(1) The competent authority of a Contracting State may request the Court of Justice to give a ruling on a question of interpretation of the Convention or of one of the other instruments referred to in Article 1 if judgments given by courts of that State conflict with the interpretation given either by the Court of Justice or in a judgment of one of the courts of another Contracting State referred to in Article 2(1) or (2). The provisions of this paragraph shall apply only to judgments which have become *res judicata*.

(2) The interpretation given by the Court of Justice in response to such a request shall not affect the judgments which gave rise to the request for interpretation.

(3) The Procurators-General of the Courts of Cassation of the Contracting States, or any other authority designated by a Contracting State, shall be entitled to request the Court of Justice for a ruling on interpretation in accordance with paragraph (1).

(4) The Registrar of the Court of Justice shall give notice of the request to the Contracting States, to the Commission and to the Council of the European Communities; they shall then be entitled within two months of the notification to submit statements of case or written observations to the Court.

(5) No fees shall be levied or any costs or expenses awarded in respect of the proceedings provided for in this Article.

Article 5

(1) Except where this Protocol otherwise provides, the provisions of the Treaty establishing the European Economic Community and those of the Protocol on the Statute of the Court of Justice annexed thereto, which are applicable when the Court is requested to give a preliminary ruling, shall also apply to any proceedings for the interpretation of the Convention and the other instruments referred to in Article 1.

(2) The Rules of Procedure of the Court of Justice shall, if necessary, be adjusted and supplemented in accordance with Article 188 of the Treaty establishing the European Economic Community.

Article 6

This Protocol shall apply to the European territories of the Contracting States, including Greenland, to the French overseas departments and territories, and to Mayotte.

The Kingdom of the Netherlands may declare at the time of signing or ratifying this Protocol or at any later time, by notifying the Secretary-General of the Council of the European Communities, that this Protocol shall be applicable to the Netherlands Antilles.

Notwithstanding the first paragraph, this Protocol shall not apply to:

(1) the Faroe Islands, unless the Kingdom of Denmark makes a declaration to the contrary,

(2) any European territory situated outside the United Kingdom for the international relations of which the United Kingdom is responsible, unless the United Kingdom makes a declaration to the contrary in respect of any such territory.

Such declarations may be made at any time by notifying the Secretary-General of the Council of the European Communities.

Article 7

This Protocol shall be ratified by the signatory States. The instruments of ratification shall be deposited with the Secretary-General of the Council of the European Communities.

Article 8

This Protocol shall enter into force on the first day of the third month following the deposit of the instrument of ratification by the last signatory State to take this step; provided that it shall at the earliest enter into force at the same time as the Convention of 27 September 1968 on Jurisdiction and the Enforcement of Judgments in Civil and Commercial Matters.

Article 9

The Contracting States recognise that any State which becomes a member of the European Economic Community, and to which Article 63 of the Convention on Jurisdiction and the Enforcement of Judgments in Civil and Commercial Matters applies, must accept the provisions of this Protocol, subject to such adjustments as may be required.

Article 10

The Secretary-General of the Council of the European Communities shall notify the signatory States of:
 (a) the deposit of each instrument of ratification;
 (b) the date of entry into force of this Protocol;
 (c) any designation received pursuant to Article 4(3);
 (d) any declaration received pursuant to Article 6.

Article 11

The Contracting States shall communicate to the Secretary-General of the Council of the European Communities the texts of any provisions of their laws which necessitate an amendment to the list of courts in Article 2(1).

Article 12

This Protocol is concluded for an unlimited period.

Article 13

Any Contracting State may request the revision of this Protocol. In this event, a revision conference shall be convened by the President of the Council of the European Communities.

Article 14

This Protocol, drawn up in a single original in the Dutch, French, German and Italian languages, all four texts being equally authentic, shall be deposited in the archives of the Secretariat of the Council of the European Communities. The Secretary-General shall transmit a certified copy to the Government of each signatory State. [721]

NOTES
Commencement: 1 January 1987.
Commencement order: SI 1986 No 2044.

SCHEDULE 3

Section 2(2)

Text of Titles V and VI of Accession Convention

TITLE V

TRANSITIONAL PROVISIONS

Article 34

(1) The 1968 Convention and the 1971 Protocol, with the amendments made by this Convention, shall apply only to legal proceedings instituted and to authentic instruments formally drawn up or registered after the entry into force of this Convention in the State of origin and, where recognition or enforcement of a judgment or authentic instrument is sought, in the State addressed.

(2) However, as between the six Contracting States to the 1968 Convention, judgments given after the date of entry into force of this Convention in proceedings instituted before that date shall be recognised and enforced in accordance with the provisions of Title III of the 1968 Convention as amended.

(3) Moreover, as between the six Contracting States to the 1968 Convention and the three States mentioned in Article 1 of this Convention, and as between those three States, judgments given after the date of entry into force of this Convention between the State of origin and the State addressed in proceedings instituted before that date shall also be recognised and enforced in accordance with the provisions of Title III of the 1968 Convention as amended if jurisdiction was founded upon rules which accorded with the provisions of Title II, as amended, or with provisions of a convention concluded between the State of origin and the State addressed which was in force when the proceedings were instituted.

Article 35

If the parties to a dispute concerning a contract had agreed in writing before the entry into force of this Convention that the contract was to be governed by the law of Ireland or of a part of the United Kingdom, the courts of Ireland or of that part of the United Kingdom shall retain the right to exercise jurisdiction in the dispute.

Article 36

For a period of three years from the entry into force of the 1968 Convention for the Kingdom of Denmark and Ireland respectively, jurisdiction in maritime matters shall be determined in these States not only in accordance with the provisions of that Convention but also in accordance with the provisions of paragraphs (1) to (6) following. However, upon the entry into force of the International Convention relating to the Arrest of Sea-going Ships, signed at Brussels on 10 May 1952, for one of these States, these provisions shall cease to have effect for that State.

(1) A person who is domiciled in a Contracting State may be sued in the courts of one of the States mentioned above in respect of a maritime claim if the ship to which the claim relates or any other ship owned by him has been arrested by judicial process within the territory of the latter State to secure the claim, or could have been so arrested there but bail or other security has been given, and either:

(a) the claimant is domiciled in the latter State; or
(b) the claim arose in the latter State; or
(c) the claim concerns the voyage during which the arrest was made or could have been made; or
(d) the claim arises out of a collision or out of damage caused by a ship to another ship or to goods or persons on board either ship, either by the execution or non-execution of a manoeuvre or by the non-observance of regulations; or
(e) the claim is for salvage; or
(f) the claim is in respect of a mortgage or hypothecation of the ship arrested.

(2) A claimant may arrest either the particular ship to which the maritime claim relates, or any other ship which is owned by the person who was, at the time when the maritime claim arose, the owner of the particular ship. However, only the particular ship to which the maritime claim relates may be arrested in respect of the maritime claims set out in subparagraphs (o), (p) or (q) of paragraph (5) of this Article.

(3) Ships shall be deemed to be in the same ownership when all the shares therein are owned by the same person or persons.

(4) When in the case of a charter by demise of a ship the charterer alone is liable in respect of a maritime claim relating to that ship, the claimant may arrest that ship or any other ship owned by the charterer, but no other ship owned by the owner may be arrested in respect of such claim. The same shall apply to any case in which a person other than the owner of a ship is liable in respect of a maritime claim relating to that ship.

(5) The expression "maritime claim" means a claim arising out of one or more of the following:
(a) damage caused by any ship either in collision or otherwise;
(b) loss of life or personal injury caused by any ship or occurring in connection with the operation of any ship;
(c) salvage;
(d) agreement relating to the use or hire of any ship whether by charterparty or otherwise;
(e) agreement relating to the carriage of goods in any ship whether by charterparty or otherwise;
(f) loss of or damage to goods including baggage carried in any ship;
(g) general average;
(h) bottomry;
(i) towage;
(j) pilotage;
(k) goods or materials wherever supplied to a ship for her operation or maintenance;
(l) construction, repair or equipment of any ship or dock charges and dues;
(m) wages of masters, officers or crew;
(n) master's disbursements, including disbursements made by shippers, charterers or agents on behalf of a ship or her owner;
(o) dispute as to the title to or ownership of any ship;
(p) disputes between co-owners of any ship as to the ownership, possession employment or earnings of that ship;
(q) the mortgage or hypothecation of any ship.

(6) In Denmark, the expression "arrest" shall be deemed as regards the maritime claims referred to in subparagraphs (o) and (p) of paragraph (5) of this Article, to include a *forbud*, where that is the only procedure allowed in respect of such a claim under Articles 646 to 653 of the law on civil procedure (*lov om rettens pleje*).

TITLE VI

FINAL PROVISIONS

ARTICLE 37

The Secretary-General of the Council of the European Communities shall transmit a certified copy of the 1968 Convention and of the 1971 Protocol in the Dutch, French,

German and Italian languages to the Governments of the Kingdom of Denmark, Ireland and the United Kingdom of Great Britain and Northern Ireland.

The texts of the 1968 Convention and the 1971 Protocol, drawn up in the Danish, English and Irish languages, shall be annexed to this Convention. The texts drawn up in the Danish, English and Irish languages shall be authentic under the same conditions as the original texts of the 1968 Convention and the 1971 Protocol.

Article 38

This Convention shall be ratified by the signatory States. The instruments of ratification shall be deposited with the Secretary-General of the Council of the European Communities.

Article 39

This Convention shall enter into force, as between the States which shall have ratified it, on the first day of the third month following the deposit of the last instrument of ratification by the original Member States of the Community and one new Member State.

It shall enter into force for each new Member State which subsequently ratifies it on the first day of the third month following the deposit of its instrument of ratification.

Article 40

The Secretary-General of the Council of the European Communities shall notify the signatory States of:

(a) the deposit of each instrument of ratification,
(b) the dates of entry into force of this Convention for the Contracting States.

Article 41

This Convention, drawn up in a single original in the Danish, Dutch, English, French, German, Irish and Italian languages, all seven texts being equally authentic, shall be deposited in the archives of the Secretariat of the Council of the European Communities. The Secretary-General shall transmit a certified copy to the Government of each signatory State. [722–734]

NOTES
Commencement: 1 January 1987.
Commencement order: SI 1986 No 2044.

NOTES
Schedules 4–14 are omitted.

SECTION V
EUROPEAN MATERIALS

COUNCIL OF EUROPE: EUROPEAN CONVENTION ON PRODUCTS LIABILITY IN REGARD TO PERSONAL INJURY AND DEATH
[Done at Strasbourg, 27 January 1977]

GENERAL NOTES
On the occasion of the 59th Session of the Committee of Ministers of the Council of Europe, the Convention was opened to signature on 27 January 1977. It was signed by the plenipotentiaries of Belgium, France, and Luxembourg.

EUROPEAN CONVENTION ON PRODUCTS LIABILITY IN REGARD TO PERSONAL INJURY AND DEATH

The member States of the Council of Europe, signatory hereto,

Considering that the aim of the Council of Europe is to achieve a greater unity between its Members;

Considering the development of case law in the majority of member States extending liability of producers prompted by a desire to protect consumers taking into account the new production techniques and marketing and sales methods;

Desiring to ensure better protection of the public and, at the same time, to take producers' legitimate interests into account;

Considering that priority should be given to compensation for personal injury and death;

Aware of the importance of introducing special rules on the liability of producers at European level,

Have agreed as follows:

Article 1

1. Each Contracting State shall make its national law conform with the provisions of this Convention not later than the date of the entry into force of the Convention in respect of that State.

2. Each Contracting State shall communicate to the Secretary General of the Council of Europe, not later than the date of the entry into force of the Convention in respect of that State, any text adopted or a statement of the contents of the existing law which it relies on to implement the Convention.

Article 2

For the purpose of this Convention:
  (a) the term "product" indicates all movables, natural or industrial, whether raw or manufactured, even though incorporated into another movable or into an immovable;
  (b) the term "producer" indicates the manufacturers of finished products or of component parts and the producers of natural products;
  (c) a product has a "defect" when it does not provide the safety which a person is entitled to expect, having regard to all the circumstances including the presentation of the product;
  (d) a product has been "put into circulation" when the producer has delivered it to another person.

Article 3

1. The producer shall be liable to pay compensation for death or personal injuries caused by a defect in his product.

2. Any person who has imported a product for putting it into circulation in the course of a business and any person who has presented a product as his product by causing his name, trademark or other distinguishing feature to appear on the product, shall be deemed to be producers for the purpose of this Convention and shall be liable as such.

3. When the product does not indicate the identity of any of the persons liable under paragraphs 1 and 2 of this Article, each supplier shall be deemed to be a producer for the purpose of this Convention and liable as such, unless he discloses, within a reasonable time, at the request of the claimant, the identity of the producer or of the person who supplied him with the product. The same shall apply, in the case of an imported product, if this product does not indicate the identity of the importer referred to in paragraph 2, even if the name of the producer is indicated.

4. In the case of damage caused by a defect in a product incorporated into another product, the producer of the incorporated product and the producer incorporating that product shall be liable.

5. Where several persons are liable under this Convention for the same damage, each shall be liable in full (*in solidum*).

Article 4

1. If the injured person or the person entitled to claim compensation has by his own fault contributed to the damage, the compensation may be reduced or disallowed having regard to all the circumstances.

2. The same shall apply if a person, for whom the injured person or the person entitled to claim compensation is responsible under national law, has contributed to the damage by his fault.

Article 5

1. A producer shall not be liable under this Convention if he proves:
   - (*a*) that the product has not been put into circulation by him; or
   - (*b*) that, having regard to the circumstances, it is probable that the defect which caused the damage did not exist at the time when the product was put into circulation by him or that this defect came into being afterwards; or
   - (*c*) that the product was neither manufactured for sale, hire or any other form of distribution for the economic purposes of the producer nor manufactured or distributed in the course of his business.

2. The liability of a producer shall not be reduced when the damage is caused both by a defect in the product and by the act or by omission of a third party.

Article 6

Proceedings for the recovery of the damages shall be subject to a limitation period of three years from the day the claimant became aware or should reasonably have been aware of the damage, the defect and the identity of the producer.

Article 7

The right to compensation under this Convention against a producer shall be extinguished if an action is not brought within ten years from the date on which the producer put into circulation the individual product which causes the damage. [741]

Article 8

The liability of the producer under this Convention cannot be excluded or limited by any exemption or exoneration clause. [742]

Article 9

This Convention shall not apply to:
  (a) the liability of producers *inter se* and their rights of recourse against third parties;
  (b) nuclear damage. [743]

Article 10

Contracting States shall not adopt rules derogating from this Convention, even if these rules are more favourable to the victim. [744]

Article 11

States may replace the liability of the producer, in a principal or subsidiary way, wholly or in part, in a general way, or for certain risks only, by the liability of a guarantee fund or other form of collective guarantee, provided that the victim shall receive protection at least equivalent to the protection he would have had under the liability scheme provided for by this Convention. [745]

Article 12

This Convention shall not affect any rights which a person suffering damage may have according to the ordinary rules of the law of contractual and extra-contractual liability including any rules concerning the duties of a seller who sells goods in the course of his business. [746]

Article 13

1. This Convention shall be open to signature by the member States of the Council of Europe. It shall be subject to ratification, acceptance or approval. Instruments of ratification, acceptance or approval shall be deposited with the Secretary General of the Council of Europe.

2. This Convention shall enter into force on the first day of the month following the expiration of a period of six months after the date of deposit of the third instrument of ratification, acceptance or approval.

3. In respect of a signatory State ratifying, accepting or approving subsequently, the Convention shall come into force on the first day of the month following the expiration of a period of six months after the date of the deposit of its instrument of ratification, acceptance or approval. [747]

Article 14

1. After the entry into force of this Convention, the Committee of Ministers of the Council of Europe may invite any non-member State to accede thereto.

2. Such accession shall be effected by depositing with the Secretary General of the Council of Europe an instrument of accession which shall take effect on the first day of the month following the expiration of a period of six months after the date of its deposit. **[748]**

Article 15

1. Any State may, at the time of signature or when depositing its instrument of ratification, acceptance, approval or accession, specify the territory or territories to which this Convention shall apply.

2. Any State may, when depositing its instrument of ratification, acceptance, approval or accession or at any later date, by declaration addressed to the Secretary General of the Council of Europe, extend this Convention to any other territory or territories specified in the declaration and for whose international relations it is responsible or on whose behalf it is authorised to give undertakings.

3. Any declaration made in pursuance of the preceding paragraph may, in respect of any territory mentioned in such declaration, be withdrawn by means of a notification addressed to the Secretary General of the Council of Europe. Such withdrawal shall take effect on the first day of the month following the expiration of a period of six months after the date of receipt by the Secretary General of the Council of Europe of the declaration of withdrawal. **[749]**

Article 16

1. Any State may, at the time of signature or when depositing its instrument of ratification, acceptance, approval or accession, or at any later date, by notification addressed to the Secretary General of the Council of Europe, declare that, in pursuance of an international agreement to which it is a Party, it will not consider imports from one or more specified States also Parties to that agreement as imports for the purpose of paragraphs 2 and 3 of Article 3; in this case the person importing the products into any of these States from another State shall be deemed to be an importer for all the State Parties to this agreement.

2. Any declaration made in pursuance of the preceding paragraph may be withdrawn by means of a notification addressed to the Secretary General of the Council of Europe. Such withdrawal shall take effect the first day of the month following the expiration of a period of one month after the date of receipt by the Secretary General of the Council of Europe of the declaration of withdrawal. **[750]**

Article 17

1. No reservation shall be made to the provisions of this Convention except those mentioned in the Annex to this Convention.

2. The Contracting State which has made one of the reservations mentioned in the Annex to this Convention may withdraw it by means of a declaration addressed to the Secretary General of the Council of Europe which shall become effective the first day of the month following the expiration of a period of one month after the date of its receipt by the Secretary General. **[751]**

Article 18

1. Any Contracting State may, in so far as it is concerned, denounce this Convention by means of a notification addressed to the Secretary General of the Council of Europe.

2. Such denunciation shall take effect on the first day of the month following the expiration of a period of six months after the date of receipt by the Secretary General of such notification.

Article 19

The Secretary General of the Council of Europe shall notify the member States of the Council and any State which has acceded to this Convention of:

(a) any signature;
(b) any deposit of an instrument of ratification, acceptance, approval or accession;
(c) any date of entry into force of this Convention in accordance with Article 13 thereof;
(d) any reservation made in pursuance of the provisions of Article 17, paragraph 1;
(e) withdrawal of any reservation carried out in pursuance of the provisions of Article 17, paragraph 2;
(f) any communication or notification received in pursuance of the provisions of Article 1, paragraph 2, Article 15, paragraphs 2 and 3 and Article 16, paragraphs 1 and 2;
(g) any notification received in pursuance of the provisions of Article 18 and the date on which denunciation takes effect.

In witness whereof, the undersigned, being duly authorised thereto, have signed this Convention.

Done at Strasbourg, this day of January 1977, in English and in French, both texts being equally authoritative, in a single copy which shall remain deposited in the archives of the Council of Europe. The Secretary General of the Council of Europe shall transmit certified copies of each of the signatory and acceding Parties.

APPENDIX

Each State may declare, at the moment of signature or at the moment of the deposit of its instrument of ratification, acceptance, approval or accession, that it reserves the right:

1. to apply its ordinary law, in place of the provisions of Article 4, in so far as such law provides that compensation may be reduced or disallowed only in case of gross negligence or intentional conduct by the injured person or the person entitled to claim compensation;

2. to limit, by provisions of its national law, the amount of compensation to be paid by a producer under this national law in compliance with the present Convention. However, this limit shall not be less than:

(a) the sum in national currency corresponding to 70,000 Special Drawing Rights as defined by the International Monetary Fund at the time of the ratification, for each deceased person or person suffering personal injury;
(b) the sum in national currency corresponding to 10 million Special Drawing Rights as defined by the International Monetary Fund at the time of ratification, for all damage caused by identical products having the same defect.

3. to exclude the retailer of primary agricultural products from liability under the terms of paragraph 3 of Article 3 providing he discloses to the claimant all information in his possession concerning the identity of the persons mentioned in Article 3.

COUNCIL DIRECTIVE
of 10 September 1984
relating to the approximation of the laws, regulations and administrative provisions of the Member States concerning misleading advertising

(84/450/EEC)

GENERAL NOTES
The Directive has been implemented in the UK by the Control of Misleading Advertisements Regulations 1988, SI 1988 No 915, para [538] ante.

THE COUNCIL OF THE EUROPEAN COMMUNITIES,
Having regard to the Treaty establishing the European Economic Community, and in particular Article 100 thereof,

Having regard to the proposal from the Commission,

Having regard to the opinion of the European Parliament,

Having regard to the opinion of the Economic and Social Committee,

Whereas the laws against misleading advertising now in force in the Member States differ widely ; whereas, since advertising reaches beyond the frontiers of individual Member States, it has a direct effect on the establishment and the functioning of the common market;

Whereas misleading advertising can lead to distortion of competition within the common market ;

Whereas advertising, whether or not it induces a contract, affects the economic welfare of consumers ;

Whereas misleading advertising may cause a consumer to take decisions prejudicial to him when acquiring goods or other property, or using services, and the differences between the laws of the Member States not only lead, in many cases, to inadequate levels of consumer protection, but also hinder the execution of advertising campaigns beyond national boundaries and thus affect the free circulation of goods and provision of services ;

Whereas the second programme of the European Economic Community for a consumer protection and information policy provides for appropriate action for the protection of consumers against misleading and unfair advertising ;

Whereas it is in the interest of the public in general, as well as that of consumers and all those who, in competition with one another, carry on a trade, business, craft or profession, in the common market, to harmonise in the first instance national provisions against misleading advertising and that, at a second stage, unfair advertising and, as far as necessary, comparative advertisng should be dealt with, on the basis of appropriate Commission proposals;

Whereas minimum and objective criteria for determining whether advertising is misleading should be established for this purpose ;

Whereas the laws to be adopted by Member States against misleading advertising must be adequate and effective ;

Whereas persons or organisations regarded under national law as having a legitimate interest in the matter must have facilities for initiating proceedings against misleading advertising, either before a court or before an administrative authority which is competent to decide upon complaints or to initiate appropriate legal proceedings;

Whereas it should be for each Member State to decide whether to enable the courts or administrative authorities to require prior recourse to other established means of dealing with the complaint;

Whereas the courts or administrative authorities must have powers enabling them to order or obtain the cessation of misleading advertising;

Whereas in certain cases it may be desirable to prohibit misleading advertising even before it is published; whereas, however, this in no way implies that Member States are under an obligation to introduce rules requiring the systematic prior vetting of advertising;

Whereas provision should be made for accelerated procedures under which measures with interim or definitive effect can be taken;

Whereas it may be desirable to order the publication of decisions made by courts or administrative authorities or of corrective statements in order to eliminate any continuing effects of misleading advertising;

Whereas administrative authorities must be impartial and the exercise of their powers must be subject to judicial review;

Whereas the voluntary control exercised by self-regulatory bodies to eliminate misleading advertising may avoid recourse to administrative or judicial action and ought therefore to be encouraged;

Whereas the advertiser should be able to prove, by appropriate means, the material accuracy of the factual claims he makes in his advertising, and may in appropriate cases be required to do so by the court or administrative authority;

Whereas this Directive must not preclude Member States from retaining or adopting provisions with a view to ensuring more extensive protection of consumers, persons carrying on a trade, business, craft or profession, and the general public,

HAS ADOPTED THIS DIRECTIVE:

Article 1

The purpose of this Directive is to protect consumers, persons carrying on a trade or business or practising a craft or profession and the interests of the public in general against misleading advertising and the unfair consequences thereof.

Article 2

For the purposes of this Directive:

1. 'advertising' means the making of a representation in any form in connection with a trade, business, craft or profession in order to promote the supply of goods or services, including immovable property, rights and obligations;

2. 'misleading advertising' means any advertising which in any way, including its presentation, deceives or is likely to deceive the persons to whom it is addressed or whom it reaches and which, by reason of its deceptive nature, is likely to affect their economic behaviour or which, for those reasons, injures or is likely to injure a competitor;

3. 'person' means any natural or legal person. [757]

Article 3

In determining whether advertising is misleading, account shall be taken of all its features, and in particular of any information it contains concerning :
> (a) the characteristics of goods or services, such as their availability, nature, execution, composition, method and date of manufacture or provision, fitness for purpose, uses, quantity, specification, geographical or commercial origin or the results to be expected from their use, or the results and material features of tests or checks carried out on the goods or services ;
> (b) the price or the manner in which the price is calculated, and the conditions on which the goods are supplied or the services provided ;
> (c) the nature, attributes and rights of the advertiser, such as his identity and assets, his qualifications and ownership of industrial, commercial or intellectual property rights or his awards and distinctions. [758]

Article 4

1. Member States shall ensure that adequate and effective means exist for the control of misleading advertising in the interests of consumers as well as competitors and the general public.

Such means shall include legal provisions under which persons or organisations regarded under national law as having a legitimate interest in prohibiting misleading advertising may :
> (a) take legal action against such advertising ; and/or
> (b) bring such advertising before an administrative authority competent either to decide on complaints or to initiate appropriate legal proceedings.

It shall be for each Member State to decide which of these facilities shall be available and whether to enable the courts or administrative authorities to require prior recourse to other established means of dealing with complaints, including those referred to in Article 5

2. Under the legal provisions referred to in paragraph 1, Member States shall confer upon the courts or administrative authorities powers enabling them, in cases they deem such measures to be necessary taking into account all the interests involved and in particular the public interest :
> —to order the cessation of, or to institute appropriate legal proceedings for an order for the cessation of, misleading advertising, or
> —if misleading advertising has not yet been published but publication is imminent, to order the prohibition of, or to institute appropriate legal proceedings for an order for the prohibition of, such publication,

even without proof of actual loss or damage or of intention or negligence on the part of the advertiser.

Member States shall also make provision for the measures referred to in the first paragraph to be taken under an accelerated procedure:
> —either with interim effect, or
> —with definitive effect,

on the understanding that it is for each Member State to decide which of the two options to select.

Furthermore, Member States may confer upon the courts or administrative

authorities powers enabling them, with a view to eliminating the continuing effects of misleading advertising the cessation of which has been ordered by a final decision:
—to require publication of that decision in full or in part and in such form as they deem adequate,
—to require in addition the publication of a corrective statement.

3. The administrative authorities referred to in paragraph 1 must:
   (a) be composed so as not to cast doubt on their impartiality;
   (b) have adequate powers, where they decide on complaints, to monitor and enforce the observance of their decisions effectively;
   (c) normally give their reasons for their decisions.

Where the powers referred to in paragraph 2 are exercised exclusively by an administrative authority, reasons for its decisions shall always be given. Furthermore in this case, provision must be made for procedures whereby improper or unreasonable exercise of its powers by the administrative authority or improper or unreasonable failure to exercise the said powers can be the subject of judicial review. [759]

Article 5

This Directive does not exclude the voluntary control of misleading advertising by self-regulatory bodies and recourse to such bodies by the persons or organisations referred to in Article 4 if proceedings before such bodies are in addition to the court or administrative proceedings referred to in that Article. [760]

Article 6

Member States shall confer upon the courts or administrative authorities powers enabling them in the civil or administrative proceedings provided for in Article 4:
   (a) to require the advertiser to furnish evidence as to the accuracy of factual claims in advertising if, taking into account the legitimate interests of the advertiser and any other party to the proceedings, such a requirement appears appropriate on the basis of the circumstances of the particular case; and
   (b) to consider factual claims as inaccurate if the evidence demanded in accordance with (a) is not furnished or is deemed insufficient by the court or administrative authority. [761]

Article 7

This Directive shall not preclude Member States from retaining or adopting provisions with a view to ensuring more extensive protection for consumers, persons carrying on a trade, business, craft or profession, and the general public. [762]

Article 8

Member States shall bring into force the measures necessary to comply with this Directive by 1 October 1986 at the latest. They shall inform the Commission thereof.

Member States shall communicate to the Commission the text of all provisions of national law which they adopt in the field covered by this Directive. [763]

Article 9
This Directive is addressed to Member States.

Done at Brussels, 10 September 1984.

COUNCIL DIRECTIVE
of 25 July 1985
on the approximation of the laws, regulations and administrative provisions of the Member States concerning liability for defective products

(85/374/EEC)

GENERAL NOTES
   The Directive has been implemented in the UK by the Consumer Protection Act 1987 Part I, para [453] ante.

THE COUNCIL OF THE EUROPEAN COMMUNITIES,

Having regard to the Treaty establishing the European Economic Community, and in particular Article 100 thereof,

Having regard to the proposal from the Commission,

Having regard to the opinion of the European Parliament,

Having regard to the opinion of the Economic and Social Committee,

Whereas approximation of the laws of the Member States concerning the liability of the producer for damage caused by the defectiveness of his products is necessary because the existing divergences may distort competition and affect the movement of goods within the common market and entail a differing degree of protection of the consumer against damage caused by a defective product to his health or property;

Whereas liability without fault on the part of the producer is the sole means of adequately solving the problem, peculiar to our age of increasing technicality, of a fair apportionment of the risks inherent in modern technological production;

Whereas liability without fault should apply only to movables which have been industrially produced; whereas, as a result, it is appropriate to exclude liability for agricultural products and game, except where they have undergone a processing of an industrial nature which could cause a defect in these products; whereas the liability provided for in this Directive should also apply to movables which are used in the construction of immovables or are installed in immovables;

Whereas protection of the consumer requires that all producers involved in the production process should be made liable, in so far as their finished product, component part or any raw material supplied by them was defective; whereas, for the same reason, liability should extend to importers of products into the Community and to persons who present themselves as producers by affixing their name, trade mark or other distinguishing feature or who supply a product the producer of which cannot be identified;

Whereas, in situations where several persons are liable for the same damage, the protection of the consumer requires that the injured person should be able to claim full compensation for the damage from any one of them;

Whereas, to protect the physical well-being and property of the consumer, the defectiveness of the product should be determined by reference not to its fitness for use but to the lack of the safety which the public at large is entitled to expect; whereas the safety is assessed by excluding any misuse of the product not reasonable under the circumstances;

Whereas a fair apportionment of risk between the injured person and the producer implies that the producer should be able to free himself from liability if he furnishes proof as to the existence of certain exonerating circumstances;

Whereas the protection of the consumer requires that the liability of the producer remains unaffected by acts or omissions of other persons having contributed to cause the damage; whereas, however, the contributory negligence of the injured person may be taken into account to reduce or disallow such liability;

Whereas the protection of the consumer requires compensation for death and personal injury as well as compensation for damage to property; whereas the latter should nevertheless be limited to goods for private use or consumption and be subject to a deduction of a lower threshold of a fixed amount in order to avoid litigation in an excessive number of cases; whereas this Directive should not prejudice compensation for pain and suffering and other non-material damages payable, where appropriate, under the law applicable to the case;

Whereas a uniform period of limitation for the bringing of an action for compensation is in the interests both of the injured person and of the producer;

Whereas products age in the course of time, higher safety standards are developed and the state of science and technology progresses; whereas, therefore, it would not be reasonable to make the producer liable for an unlimited period for the defectiveness of his product; whereas, therefore, liability should expire after a reasonable length of time, without prejudice to claims pending at law;

Whereas, to achieve effective protection of consumers, no contractual derogation should be permitted as regards the liability of the producer in relation to the injured person;

Whereas under the legal systems of the Member States an injured party may have a claim for damages based on grounds of contractual liability or on grounds of non-contractual liability other than that provided for in this Directive; in so far as these provisions also serve to attain the objective of effective protection of consumers, they should remain unaffected by this Directive; whereas, in so far as effective protection of consumers in the sector of pharmaceutical products is already also attained in a Member State under a special liability system, claims based on this system should similarly remain possible;

Whereas, to the extent that liability for nuclear injury or damage is already covered in all Member States by adequate special rules, it has been possible to exclude damage of this type from the scope of this Directive;

Whereas, since the exclusion of primary agricultural products and game from the scope of this Directive may be felt, in certain Member States, in view of what is expected for the protection of consumers, to restrict unduly such protection, it should be possible for a Member State to extend liability to such products;

Whereas, for similar reasons, the possibility offered to a producer to free himself from liability if he proves that the state of scientific and technical knowledge at the time when he put the product into circulation was not such as to enable the existence of a defect to be discovered may be felt in certain Member States to restrict unduly the protection of the consumer; whereas it should therefore be possible for a Member State to maintain in its legislation or to provide by new legislation that this exonerating circumstance is not admitted;

whereas, in the case of new legislation, making use of this derogation should, however, be subject to a Community stand-still procedure, in order to raise, if possible, the level of protection in a uniform manner throughout the Community;

Whereas, taking into account the legal traditions in most of the Member States, it is inappropriate to set any financial ceiling on the producer's liability without fault; whereas, in so far as there are, however, differing traditions, it seems possible to admit that a Member State may derogate from the principle of unlimited liability by providing a limit for the total liability of the producer for damage resulting from a death or personal injury and caused by identical items with the same defect, provided that this limit is established at a level sufficiently high to guarantee adequate protection of the consumer and the correct functioning of the common market;

Whereas the harmonisation resulting from this cannot be total at the present stage, but opens the way towards greater harmonisation; whereas it is therefore necessary that the Council receive at regular intervals, reports from the Commission on the application of this Directive, accompanied, as the case may be, by appropriate proposals;

Whereas it is particularly important in this respect that a re-examination be carried out of those parts of the Directive relating to the derogations open to the Member States, at the expiry of sufficient length to gather practical experience on the effects of these derogations on the protection of consumers and on the functioning of the common market,

HAS ADOPTED THIS DIRECTIVE:

Article 1

The producer shall be liable for damage caused by a defect in his product.

Article 2

For the purpose of this Directive "product" means all movables, with the exception of primary agricultural products and game, even though incorporated into another movable or into an immovable. "Primary agricultural products" means the products of the soil, of stock-farming and of fisheries, excluding products which have undergone initial processing. "Product" includes electricity.

Article 3

1. "Producer" means the manufacturer of a finished product, the producer of any raw material or the manufacturer of a component part and any person who, by putting his name, trade mark or other distinguishing feature on the product presents himself as its producer.

2. Without prejudice to the liability of the producer, any person who imports into the Community a product for sale, hire, leasing or any form of distribution in the course of his business shall be deemed to be a producer within the meaning of this Directive and shall be responsible as a producer.

3. Where the producer of the product cannot be identified, each supplier of the product shall be treated as its producer unless he informs the injured person, within a reasonable time, of the identity of the producer or of the person who supplied him with the product. The same shall apply, in the case of an imported product, if this product does not indicate the identity of the importer referred to in paragraph 2, even if the name of the producer is indicated.

Article 4

The injured person shall be required to prove the damage, the defect and the causal relationship between defect and damage. [769]

Article 5

Where, as a result of the provisions of this Directive, two or more persons are liable for the same damage, they shall be liable jointly and severally, without prejudice to the provisions of national law concerning the rights of contribution or recourse. [770]

Article 6

1. A product is defective when it does not provide the safety which a person is entitled to expect, taking all circumstances into account, including:
   (a) the presentation of the product;
   (b) the use to which it could reasonably be expected that the product would be put;
   (c) the time when the product was put into circulation.

2. A product shall not be considered defective for the sole reason that a better product is subsequently put into circulation. [771]

Article 7

The producer shall not be liable as a result of this Directive if he proves:
   (a) that he did not put the product into circulation; or
   (b) that, having regard to the circumstances, it is probable that the defect which caused the damage did not exist at the time when the product was put into circulation by him or that this defect came into being afterwards; or
   (c) that the product was neither manufactured by him for sale or any form of distribution for economic purpose nor manufactured or distributed by him in the course of his business; or
   (d) that the defect is due to compliance of the product with mandatory regulations issued by the public authorities; or
   (e) that the state of scientific and technical knowledge at the time when he put the product into circulation was not such as to enable the existence of the defect to be discovered; or
   (f) in the case of a manufacturer of a component, that the defect is attributable to the design of the product in which the component has been fitted or to the instructions given by the manufacturer of the product. [772]

Article 8

1. Without prejudice to the provisions of national law concerning the right of contribution or recourse, the liability of the producer shall not be reduced when the damage is caused both by a defect in product and by the act or omission of a third party.

2. The liability of the producer may be reduced or disallowed when, having regard to all the circumstances, the damage is caused both by a defect in the product and by the fault of the injured person or any person for whom the injured person is responsible. [773]

Article 9

For the purpose of Article 1, "damage" means:
    (a) damage caused by death or by personal injuries;
    (b) damage to, or destruction of, any item of property other than the defective product itself, with a lower threshold of 500 ECU, provided that the item of property:
        (i) is of a type ordinarily intended for private use or consumption; and
        (ii) was used by the injured person mainly for his own private use or consumption.

This Article shall be without prejudice to national provisions relating to non-material damage.

Article 10

1. Member States shall provide in their legislation that a limitation period of three years shall apply to proceedings for the recovery of damages as provided for in this Directive. The limitation period shall begin to run from the day on which the plaintiff became aware, or should reasonably have become aware, of the damage, the defect and the identity of the producer.

2. The laws of the Member States regulating suspension or interruption of the limitation period shall not be affected by this Directive.

Article 11

Member States shall provide in their legislation that the rights conferred upon the injured person pursuant to this Directive shall be extinguished upon the expiry of a period of 10 years from the date on which the producer put into circulation the actual product which caused the damage, unless the injured person has in the meantime instituted proceedings against the producer.

Article 12

The liability of the producer arising from this Directive may not, in relation to the injured person, be limited or excluded by a provision limiting his liability or exempting him from liability.

Article 13

This Directive shall not affect any rights which an injured person may have according to the rules of the law of contractual or non-contractual liability or a special liability system existing at the moment when this Directive is notified.

Article 14

This Directive shall not apply to injury or damage arising from nuclear accidents and covered by international conventions ratified by the Member States.

Article 15

1. Each Member State may:
    (a) by way of derogation from Article 2, provide in its legislation that within the meaning of Article 1 of this Directive "product" also means primary agricultural products and game;

(b) by way of derogation from Article 7 (e), maintain or, subject to the procedure set out in paragraph 2 of this Article, provide in this legislation that the producer shall be liable even if he proves that the state of scientific and technical knowledge at the time when he put the product into circulation was not such as to enable the defect to be discovered.

2. A Member State wishing to introduce the measure specified in paragraph 1 (b) shall communicate the text of the proposed measure to the Commission. The Commission shall inform the other Member States thereof.

The Member State concerned shall hold the proposed measure in abeyance for nine months after the Commission is informed and provided that in the meantime the Commission has not submitted to the Council a proposal amending this Directive on the relevant matter. However, if within three months of receiving the said information, the Commission does not inform the Member State concerned that it intends submitting such a proposal to the Council, the Member State may take the proposed measure immediately.

If the Commission does submit to the Council such a proposal amending this Directive within the aforementioned nine months, the Member State concerned shall hold the proposed measure in abeyance for a further period of 18 months from the date on which the proposal is submitted.

3. Ten years after the date of notification of this Directive, the Commission shall submit to the Council a report on the effect that rulings by the courts as to the application of Article 7 (e) and of paragraph 1 (b) of this Article have on consumer protection and the functioning of the common market. In the light of this report the Council, acting on a proposal from the Commission and pursuant to the terms of Article 100 of the Treaty, shall decide whether to repeal Article 7 (e). **[780]**

Article 16

1. Any Member State may provide that a producer's total liability for damage resulting from a death or personal injury and caused by identical items with the same defect shall be limited to an amount which may not be less than 70 million ECU.

2. Ten years after the date of notification of this Directive, the Commission shall submit to the Council a report on the effect on consumer protection and the functioning of the common market of the implementation of the financial limit on liability by those Member States which have used the option provided for in paragraph 1. In the light of this report the Council, acting on a proposal from the Commission and pursuant to the terms of Article 100 of the Treaty, shall decide whether to repeal paragraph 1. **[781]**

Article 17

This Directive shall not apply to products put into circulation before the date on which the provisions referred to in Article 19 enter into force. **[782]**

Article 18

1. For the purposes of this Directive, the ECU shall be that defined by Regulation (EEC) No 3180/78, as amended by Regulation (EEC) No 2626/84. The equivalent in national currency shall initially be calculated at the rate obtaining on the date of adoption of this Directive.

2. Every five years the Council, acting on a proposal from the Commission, shall examine and, if need be, revise the amounts in this Directive, in the light of economic and monetary trends in the Community.

Article 19

1. Member States shall bring into force, not later than three years from the notification of this Directive, the laws, regulations and administrative provisions necessary to comply with this Directive. They shall forthwith inform the Commission thereof.

2. The procedure set out in Article 15 (2) shall apply from the date of notification of this Directive.

Article 20

Member States shall communicate to the Commission the texts of the main provisions of national law which they subsequently adopt in the field governed by this Directive.

Article 21

Every five years the Commission shall present a report to the Council on the application of this Directive and, if necessary, shall submit appropriate proposals to it.

Article 22

This Directive is addressed to the Member States.

Done at Brussels, 25 July 1985.

COUNCIL DIRECTIVE
of 20 December 1985
to protect the consumer in respect of contracts negotiated away from business premises

(85/577/EEC)

GENERAL NOTES
The Directive has been implemented in the UK by the Consumer Protection (Cancellation of Contracts Concluded away from Business Premises) Regulations 1987, SI 1987 No 2117, para [525] ante.

THE COUNCIL OF THE EUROPEAN COMMUNITIES,

Having regard to the Treaty establishing the European Economic Community, and in particular Article 100 thereof,

Having regard to the proposal from the Commission,

Having regard to the opinion of the European Parliament,

Having regard to the opinion of the Economic and Social Committee,

Whereas it is a common form of commercial practice in the Member States for the conclusion of a contract or a unilateral engagement between a trader and consumer to be made away from the business premises of the trader, and whereas such contracts and engagements are the subject of legislation which differs from one Member State to another;

Whereas any disparity between such legislation may directly affect the functioning of the common market; whereas it is therefore necessary to approximate laws in this field;

Whereas the preliminary programme of the European Economic Community for a consumer protection and information policy provides *inter alia*, under paragraphs 24 and 25, that appropriate measures be taken to protect consumers against unfair commercial practices in respect of doorstep selling; whereas the second programme of the European Economic Community for a consumer protection and information policy confirmed that the action and priorities defined in the preliminary programme would be pursued;

Whereas the special feature of contracts concluded away from the business premises of the trader is that as a rule it is the trader who initiates the contract negotiations, for which the consumer is unprepared or which he does not expect; whereas the consumer is often unable to compare the quality and price of the offer with other offers; whereas this surprise element generally exists not only in contracts made at the doorstep but also in other forms of contract concluded by the trader away from his business premises;

Whereas the consumer should be given a right of cancellation over a period of at least seven days in order to enable him to assess the obligations arising under the contract;

Whereas appropriate measures should be taken to ensure that the consumer is informed in writing of this period for reflection;

Whereas the freedom of the Member States to maintain or introduce a total or partial prohibition on the conclusion of contracts away from business premises, inasmuch as they consider this to be in the interest of consumers, must not be affected;

HAS ADOPTED THIS DIRECTIVE:

Article 1

1. This Directive shall apply to contracts under which a trader supplies goods or services to a consumer and which are concluded :
—during an excursion organised by the trader away from his business premises, or
—during a visit by a trader
  (i) to the consumer's home or to that of another consumer;
  (ii) to the consumer's place of work;
where the visit does not take place at the express request of the consumer.

2. This Directive shall also apply to contracts for the supply of goods or services other than those concerning which the consumer requested the visit of the trader, provided that when he requested the visit the consumer did not know, or could not reasonably have known, that the supply of those other goods or services formed part of the trader's commercial or professional activities.

3. This Directive shall also apply to contracts in respect of which an offer was made by the consumer under conditions similar to those described in paragraph 1 or paragraph 2 although the consumer was not bound by that offer before its acceptance by the trader.

4. This Directive shall also apply to offers made contractually by the consumer under conditions similar to those described in paragraph 1 or paragraph 2 where the consumer is bound by his offer.

Article 2

For the purposes of this Directive :

"consumer" means a natural person who, in transactions covered by this Directive, is acting for purposes which can be regarded as outside his trade or profession;

"trader" means a natural or legal person who, for the transaction in question, acts in his commercial or professional capacity, and anyone acting in the name or on behalf of a trader.

Article 3

1. The Member States may decide that this Directive shall apply only to contracts for which the payment to be made by the consumer exceeds a specified amount. This amount may not exceed 60 ECU.

The Council, acting on a proposal from the Commission, shall examine and, if necessary, revise this amount for the first time no later than four years after the notification of the Directive and thereafter every two years, taking into account economic and monetary developments in the Community.

2. This Directive shall not apply to:
  (a) contracts for the construction, sale and rental of immovable property or contracts for repairing immovable property or contracts concerning other rights relating to immovable property.

Contracts for the supply of goods and for their incorporation in immovable property or contracts for repairing immovable property shall fall within the scope of this Directive;

    (b) contracts for the supply of foodstuffs or beverages or other goods intended for current consumption in the household and supplied by regular roundsmen;

    (c) contracts for the supply of goods or services, provided that all three of the following conditions are met:
  - (i) the contract is concluded on the basis of a trader's catalogue which the consumer has a proper opportunity of reading in the absence of the trader's representative,
  - (ii) there is intended to be continuity of contract between the trader's representative and the consumer in relation to that or any subsequent transaction,
  - (iii) both the catalogue and the contract clearly inform the consumer of his right to return goods to the supplier within a period of not less than seven days of receipt or otherwise to cancel the contract within that period without obligation of any kind other than to take reasonable care of the goods;

    (d) insurance contracts;
    (e) contracts for securities.

3. By way of derogation from Article 1(2), member States may refrain from applying this Directive to contracts for the supply of goods or services having a direct connection with the goods or service concerning which the consumer requested the visit of the trader.

Article 4

In the case of transactions within the scope of Article 1, traders shall be required to give consumers written notice of their right of cancellation within the period laid down in Article 5, together with the name and address of a person against whom that right may be exercised.

Such notice shall be dated and shall state particulars enabling the contract to be identified. It shall be given to the consumer :
  - (a) in the case of Article 1(1), at the time of conclusion of the contract;
  - (b) in the case of Article 1(2), not later than the time of conclusion of the contract;
  - (c) in the case of Article 1(3) and 1(4), when the offer is made by the consumer.

Member States shall ensure that their national legislation lays down appropriate consumer protection measures in cases where the information referred to in this Article is not supplied.

Article 5

1. The consumer shall have the right to renounce the effects of his undertaking by sending notice within a period of not less than seven days from receipt by the consumer of the notice referred to in Article 4, in accordance with the procedure laid down by national law. It shall be sufficient if the notice is dispatched before the end of such period.

2. The giving of the notice shall have effect of releasing the consumer from any obligations under the cancelled contract.

Article 6

The consumer may not waive the rights conferred on him by this Directive.
[794]

Article 7

If the consumer exercises his right of renunciation, the legal effects shall be governed by national laws, particularly regarding reimbursement of payments for goods and services provided and the return of goods received. [795]

Article 8

This Directive shall not prevent Member States from adopting or maintaining more favourable provisions to protect consumers in the field in which it covers.
[796]

Article 9

1. Member States shall take the measures necessary to comply with this Directive within 24 months of its notification. They shall forthwith inform the Commission thereof.

2. Member States shall ensure that the texts of the main provisions of national law which they adopt in the field covered by this Directive are communicated to the Commission. [797]

Article 10

This Directive is addressed to Member States. [798]

Done at Brussels, 20 December 1985.

COUNCIL DIRECTIVE
of 22 December 1986
for the approximation of the laws, regulations and administrative provisions of the Member States concerning consumer credit

(87/102/EEC)

THE COUNCIL OF THE EUROPEAN COMMUNITIES,

Having regard to the Treaty establishing the European Economic Community, and in particular Article 100 thereof,

Having regard to the proposal from the Commission,

Having regard to the opinion of the European Parliament,

Having regard to the opinion of the Economic and Social Committee,

Whereas wide differences exist in the laws of the Member States in the field of consumer credit;

Whereas these differences of law can lead to distortions of competition between grantors of credit in the common market;

Whereas these differences limit the opportunities the consumer has to obtain credit in other Member States; whereas they affect the volume and the nature of the credit sought, and also the purchase of goods and services;

Whereas, as a result, these differences have an influence on the free movement of goods and services obtainable by consumers on credit and thus directly affect the functioning of the common market;

Whereas, given the increasing volume of credit granted in the Community to consumers, the establishment of a common market in consumer credit would benefit alike consumers, grantors of credit, manufacturers, wholesalers and retailers of goods and providers of services;

Whereas the programmes of the European Economic Community for a consumer protection and information policy provide, *inter alia*, that the consumer should be protected against unfair credit terms and that a harmonization of the general conditions governing consumer credit should be undertaken as a priority;

Whereas differences of law and practice result in unequal consumer protection in the field of consumer credit from one Member State to another;

Whereas there has been much change in recent years in the types of credit available to and used by consumers; whereas new forms of consumer credit have emerged and continue to develop;

Whereas the consumer should receive adequate information on the conditions and cost of credit and on his obligations; whereas this information should include, *inter alia*, the annual percentage rate of charge for credit, or, failing that, the total amount that the consumer must pay for credit; whereas, pending a decision on a Community method or methods the annual percentage rate of charge, Member States should be able to retain existing methods or practices for calculating this rate, or, failing that, should establish provisions for indicating the total cost of the credit to the consumer;

Whereas the terms of the credit may be disadvantageous to the consumer;

whereas better protection of the consumer can be achieved by adopting certain requirements which are to apply to all forms of credit;

Whereas, having regard to the character of certain credit agreements or types of transaction, these agreements or transactions should be partly or entirely excluded from the field of application of this Directive;

Whereas it should be possible for Member States, in consultation with the Commission, to exempt from the Directive certain forms of credit of a non-commercial character granted under particular conditions;

Whereas the practices existing in some Member States in respect of authentic acts drawn up before a notary or judge are such as to render the application of certain provisions of this Directive unnecessary in the case of such acts; whereas it should therefore be possible for Member States to exempt such acts from those provisions;

Whereas credit agreements for very large financial amounts tend to differ from the usual consumer credit agreements; whereas the application of the provisions of this Directive to agreements for very small amounts could create unnecessary administrative burdens both for consumers and grantors of credit; whereas therefore, agreements above or below specified financial limits should be excluded from the Directive;

Whereas the provision of information on the cost of credit in advertising and at the business premises of the creditor or credit broker can make it easier for the consumer to compare different offers;

Whereas consumer protection is further improved if credit agreements are made in writing and contain certain minimum particulars concerning the contractual terms;

Whereas, in the case of credit granted for the acquisition of goods, Member States should lay down the conditions in which goods may be repossessed, particularly if the consumer has not given his consent; whereas the account between the parties should upon repossession be made up in such manner as to ensure that the repossession does not entail any unjustified enrichment;

Whereas the consumer should be allowed to discharge his obligations before the due date; whereas the consumer should then be entitled to an equitable reduction in the total cost of the credit;

Whereas the assignment of the creditors rights arising under a credit agreement should not be allowed to weaken the position of the consumer;

Whereas the Member States which permit consumers to use bills of exchange, promissory notes or cheques in connection with credit agreements should ensure that the consumer is suitably protected when so using such instruments;

Whereas, as regards goods or services which the consumer has contracted to acquire on credit, the consumer should, at least in the circumstances defined below, have rights *vis-à-vis* the grantor of credit which are in addition to his normal contractual rights against him and against the supplier of the goods or services; whereas the circumstances referred to above are those where the grantor of credit and the supplier of goods or services have a pre-existing agreement whereunder credit is made available exclusively by that grantor of credit to customers of that supplier for the purpose of enabling the customer to acquire goods or services from the latter;

Whereas the ECU is as defined in Council Regulation (EEC) No 3180/78, as last amended by Regulation (EEC) No 2626/84; whereas Member States should to a limited extent be at liberty to round off the amounts in national currency resulting from the conversion of amounts of this Directive expressed in ECU; whereas the amounts in this Directive should be periodically re-examined in the light of economic and monetary trends in the Community, and, if need be, revised;

Whereas suitable measures should be adopted by Member States for authorizing persons offering credit or offering to arrange credit agreements or for inspecting or monitoring the activities of persons granting credit or arranging for credit to be granted or for enabling consumers to complain about credit agreements or credit conditions;

Whereas credit agreements should not derogate, to the detriment of the consumer, from the provisions adopted in implementation of this Directive or corresponding to its provisions; whereas those provisions should not be circumvented as a result of the way in which agreements are formulated;

Whereas, since this Directive provides for a certain degree of approximation of the laws, regulations and administrative provisions of the Member States concerning consumer credit and for a certain level of consumer protection, Member States should not be prevented from retaining or adopting more stringent measures to protect the consumer, with due regard for their obligations under the Treaty;

Whereas, not later than 1 January 1995, the Commission should present to the Council a report concerning the operation of this Directive,

HAS ADOPTED THIS DIRECTIVE:

Article 1

1. This Directive applies to credit agreements.

    2. For the purpose of this Directive:
        (a) "consumer" means a natural person who, in transactions covered by this Directive, is acting for purposes which can be regarded as outside his trade or profession;
        (b) "creditor" means a natural or legal person who grants credit in the course of his trade, business or profession, or a group of such persons;
        (c) "credit agreement" means an agreement whereby a creditor grants or promises to grant to a consumer a credit in the form of a deferred payment, a loan or other similar financial accommodation.

        Agreements for the provision on a continuing basis of a service or a utility, where the consumer has the right to pay for them, for the duration of their provision, by means of instalments, are not deemed to be credit agreements for the purpose of this Directive;
        (d) "total cost of the credit to the consumer" means all the costs of the credit including interest and other charges directly connected with the credit agreement, determined in accordance with the provisions or practices existing in, or to be established by, the Member States;
        (e) "annual percentage rate of charge" means the total cost of the credit to the consumer expressed as an annual percentage of the amount of the credit granted and calculated according to existing methods of the Member States.

Article 2

1. This Directive shall not apply to:
    (a) credit agreements or agreements promising to grant credit:
    —intended primarily for the purpose of acquiring or retaining property rights in land or in an existing or projected building,
    —intended for the purpose of renovating or improving a building as such;
    (b) hiring agreements except where these provide that the title will pass ultimately to the hirer;
    (c) credit granted or made available without payment of interest or any other charge;
    (d) credit agreements under which no interest is charged provided the consumer agrees to repay the credit in a single payment;
    (e) credit in the form of advances on a current account granted by a credit institution or financial institution other than on credit card accounts. Nevertheless, the provisions of Article 6 shall apply to such credits;
    (f) credit agreements involving amounts of less than 200 ECU or more than 20,000 ECU;
    (g) credit agreements under which the consumer is required to repay the credit:
    —either, within a period not exceeding three months,
    —or, by a maximum number of four payments within a period not exceeding 12 months.

2. A Member State may, in consultation with the Commission, exempt from the application of this Directive certain types of credit which fulfil the following conditions:
    —they are granted at rates of charge below those prevailing in the market, and
    —they are not offered to the public generally.

3. The provisions of Article 4 and of Articles 6 to 12 shall not apply to credit agreements or agreements promising to grant credit, secured by mortgage on immovable property, in so far as these are not already excluded from the Directive under paragraph 1 (a) of this Article.

4. Member States may exempt from the provisions of Articles 6 to 12 credit agreements in the form of an authentic act signed before a notary or judge.

Article 3

Without prejudice to Council Directive 84/450/EEC of 10 September 1984 relating to the approximation of the laws, regulations and administrative provisions of the Member States concerning misleading advertising, and to the rules and principles applicable to unfair advertising, any advertisement, or any offer which is displayed at business premises, in which a person offers credit or offers to arrange a credit agreement and in which a rate of interest or any figures relating to the cost of the credit are indicated, shall also include a statement of the annual percentage rate of charge, by means of a representative example if no other means is practicable.

Article 4

1. Credit agreements shall be made in writing. The consumer shall receive a copy of the written agreement.

2. The written agreement shall include:
   (a) a statement of the annual percentage rate of charge;
   (b) a statement of the conditions under which the annual percentage rate of charge may be amended.
   In cases where it is not possible to state the annual percentage rate of charge, the consumer shall be provided with adequate information in the written agreement. This information shall at least include the information provided for in the second indent of Article 6 (1).

3. The written agreement shall further include the other essential terms of the contract.

By way of illustration, the Annex to this Directive contains a list of terms which Member States may require to be included in the written agreement as being essential. [803]

Article 5

By way of derogation from Article 3 and 4 (2), and pending a decision on the introduction of a Community method or methods of calculating the annual percentage rate of charge, those Member States which, at the time of notification of this Directive, do not require the annual percentage rate of charge to be shown or which do not have an established method for its calculation, shall at least require the total cost of the credit to the consumer to be indicated. [804]

Article 6

1. Notwithstanding the exclusion provided for in Article 2 (1) (e), where there is an agreement between a credit institution and a consumer for the granting of credit in the form of an advance on a current account, other than on credit card accounts, the consumer shall be informed at the time or before the agreement is concluded:
   —of the credit limit, if any,
   —of the annual rate of interest and the charges applicable from the time when the agreement is concluded and the conditions under which these may be amended,
   —of the procedure for terminating the agreement.

This information shall be confirmed in writing.

2. Furthermore, during the period of the agreement, the consumer shall be informed of any change in the annual rate of interest or in the relevant charges at the time it occurs. Such information may be given in a statement of account or in any other manner acceptable to the Member States.

3. In Member States where tacitly accepted overdrafts are permissible, the Member States concerned shall ensure that the consumer is informed of the annual rate of interest and the charges applicable, and of any amendment thereof, where the overdraft extends beyond a period of three months. [805]

Article 7

In the case of credit granted for the acquisition of goods, Member States shall lay down the conditions under which goods may be repossessed, in particular if the consumer has not given his consent. They shall further ensure that where the creditor recovers possession of the goods the account between the parties shall be made up so as to ensure that the repossession does not entail any unjustified enrichment. [806]

Article 8

The Consumer shall be entitled to discharge his obligations under a credit agreement before the time fixed by the agreement. In this event, in accordance with the rules laid down by the Member States, the consumer shall be entitled to an equitable reduction in the total cost of the credit.

Article 9

Where the creditor's rights under a credit agreement are assigned to a third person, the consumer shall be entitled to plead against that third person any defence which was available to him against the original creditor, including set-off where the latter is permitted in the Member States concerned.

Article 10

The Member States which, in connection with credit agreements, permit the consumer:

(a) to make payment by bills of exchange including promissory notes;
(b) to give security by means of bills of exchange including promissory notes and cheques,

shall ensure that the consumer is suitably protected when using these instruments in those ways.

Article 11

1. Member States shall ensure that the existence of a credit agreement shall not in any way affect the rights of the consumer against the supplier of goods or services purchased by means of such an agreement in cases where the goods or services are not supplied or are otherwise not in conformity with the contract for their supply.

2. Where:
   (a) in order to buy goods or obtain services the consumer enters into a credit agreement with a person other than the supplier of them; and
   (b) the grantor of the credit and the supplier of the goods or services have a pre-existing agreement whereunder credit is made available exclusively by that grantor of credit to customers of that supplier for the acquisition of goods or services from that supplier; and
   (c) the consumer referred to in subparagraph (a) obtains his credit pursuant to that pre-existing agreement; and
   (d) the goods or services covered by the credit agreement are not supplied, or are supplied only in part, or are not in conformity with the contract for supply of them; and
   (e) the consumer has pursued his remedies against the supplier but has failed to obtain the satisfaction to which he is entitled,

the consumer shall have the right to pursue remedies against the grantor of credit. Member States shall determine to what extent and under what conditions these remedies shall be exercisable.

3. Paragraph 2 shall not apply where the individual transaction in question is for an amount less than the equivalent of 200 ECU.

Article 12

1. Member States shall:

(a) ensure that persons offering credit or offering to arrange credit agreements shall obtain official authorization to do so, either specifically or as suppliers of goods and services; or
(b) ensure that persons granting credit or arranging for credit to be granted shall be subject to inspection or monitoring of their activities by an institution or official body; or
(c) promote the establishment of appropriate bodies to receive complaints concerning credit agreements or credit conditions and to provide relevant information or advice to consumers regarding them.

2. Member States may provide that the authorization referred to in paragraph 1 (a) shall not be required where persons offering to conclude or arrange credit agreements satisfy the definition in Article 1 of the first Council Directive of 12 December 1977 on the coordination of laws, regulations and administrative provisions relating to the taking up and pursuit of the business of credit institutions and are authorized in accordance with the provisions of the Directive.

Where persons granting credit or arranging for credit to be granted have been authorized both specifically, under the provisions of paragraph 1 (a) and also under the provisions of the aforementioned Directive, but the latter authorization is subsequently withdrawn, the competent authority responsible for issuing the specific authorization to grant credit under paragraph 1 (a) shall be informed and shall decide whether the persons concerned may continue to grant credit, or arrange for credit to be granted, or whether the specific authorization granted under paragraph 1 (a) should be withdrawn. **[811]**

Article 13

1. For the purposes of this Directive, the ECU shall be that defined by Regulation (EEC) No 3180/78, as amended by Regulation (EEC) 2626/84. The equivalent in national currency shall initially be calculated at the rate obtaining on the date of the adoption of this Directive.

Member States may round off the amounts in national currency resulting from the conversion of the amounts in ECU provided that such rounding off does not exceed 10 ECU.

2. Every five years, and for the first time in 1995, the Council, acting on a proposal from the Commission, shall examine, and, if need be, revise the amounts in this Directive, in the light of economic and monetary trends in the Community. **[812]**

Article 14

1. Member States shall ensure that credit agreements shall not derogate, to the detriment of the consumer, from the provisions of national law implementing or corresponding to this Directive.

2. Member States shall further ensure that the provisions which they adopt in implementation of this directive are not circumvented as a result of the way in which agreements are formulated, in particular by the device of distributing the amount of credit over several agreements. **[813]**

Article 15

This Directive shall not preclude Member States from retaining or adopting more stringent provisions to protect consumers consistent with their obligations under the Treaty. **[814]**

Article 16

1. Member States shall bring into force the measures necessary to comply with this Directive not later than 1 January 1990 and shall forthwith inform the Commission thereof.

2. Member States shall communicate to the Commission the texts of the main provisions of a national law which they adopt in the field covered by this Directive. [815]

Article 17

Not later than 1 January 1995 the Commission shall present a report to the Council concerning the operation of this Directive. [816]

Article 18

This Directive is addressed to the Member States. [817]

Done at Brussels, 22 December 1986.

ANNEX
LIST OF TERMS REFERRED TO IN ARTICLE 4 (3)

1. **Credit agreements for financing the supply of particular goods or services:**
(i) a description of the goods or services covered by the agreement;
(ii) the cash price and the price payable under the credit agreement;
(iii) the amount of the deposit, if any, the number and amount of instalments and the dates on which they fall due, or the method of ascertaining any of the same if unknown at the time the agreement is concluded;
(iv) an indication that the consumer will be entitled, as provided in Article 8, to a reduction if he repays early;
(v) who owns the goods (if ownership does not pass immediately to the consumer) and the terms on which the consumer becomes the owner of them;
(vi) a description of the security required, if any;
(vii) the cooling-off period, if any;
(viii) an indication of the insurance (s) required, if any, and, when the choice of insurer is not left to the consumer, an indication of the cost thereof.

2. **Credit agreements operated by credit cards:**
(i) the amount of the credit limit, if any;
(ii) the terms of repayment or the means of determining them;
(iii) the cooling-off period, if any;

3. **Credit agreements operated by running account which are not otherwise covered by the Directive:**
(i) the amount of the credit limit, if any, or the method of determining it;
(ii) the terms of use and repayment;
(iii) the cooling-off period, if any.

4. **Other credit agreements covered by the Directive:**
(i) the amount of the credit limit, if any;
(ii) an indication of the security required, if any;
(iii) the terms of repayment;

(iv) the cooling-off period, if any;
(v) an indication that the consumer will be entitled, as provided in Article 8, to a reduction if he repays early.

INDEX
References are to paragraph number

A

ADMIRALTY PROCEEDINGS
security in case of stay, [690]

ADVERTISEMENTS, [538]–[548]
ancillary credit business, [315]
consumer credit, [209]–[213]. *See also* Consumer credit
definition, [353], [539]
information to be given in, [390]
misleading, [538]–[548]. *See also* Misleading advertisements
EEC Directive [755]–[764]
trade description used in, [386]

APPEALS
civil jurisdiction and judgments, and, [670]
detention of goods, against, [485]
Restrictive Practices Court, from, [452]
suspension notice, against, [467]

ARBITRATION, [511]–[519]. *See also* Arbitration agreements; Consumer arbitration

ARBITRATION AGREEMENTS, [511]
contracting "as a consumer", [513]
exclusions, [512]
orders adding to causes of action, [515]
powers of court, and, [514]
Scotland, [516]–[518]

ASSOCIATE
meaning, [348]

ASSOCIATION
domicile of, [706], [707]

AUCTION SALES, [141]

B

BAILEE
definitions, [167]
power of sale, [47]

BAILOR
definition, [167]

BILLS OF LADING, [549]–[552]
consignees empowered to sue, [550]
endorsees empowered to sue, [550]
evidence, as, [552]
stoppage in transit, and, [551]

BREACH OF CONTRACT
avoidance of liability, [58]
sale of goods, and, [133]–[138]. *See also* Sale of goods

BROADCAST ADVERTISEMENT
meaning, [539]

BUSINESS
definitions, [33], [68], [144], [167], [353], [497]

BUSINESS PREMISES
contracts negotiated away from EEC Directive, [788]–[798]

BUYER
definition, [33], [144]
disposition by, [8]

C

CABLE AUTHORITY
misleading advertisements, and [547], [548]

CANCELLATION OF CONTRACTS, [525]–[537]
application of Regulations, [527]
concluded away from business premises, [525]–[537]
contracting-out, [534]
form to be included in notice of rights, [537]
goods given in part-exchange, and, [532]
information to be contained in notice of rights, [536]
recovery of money paid by consumer, [529]
repayment of credit, [530]
return of goods by consumer after, [531]
service of documents, [535]

CANVASSING OFF TRADE PREMISES
definition, [317], [318]

CARRIAGE OF GOODS BY SEA, [658]–[664]. *See also* Hague Rules
application of Act of 1971 to British possessions, [661]

CHARITY
definition, [353]

CIVIL JURISDICTION AND JUDGMENTS, [665]–[734]
admissibility of judgments, [675]
allocation within UK, [680], [681]
amendments relating to overseas judgments, [699]
appeals, [670]
application of Act of 1982 to Crown, [715]
application of s 1, Administration of Justice (Scotland) Act 1972, [692]
authentic instruments, [677]
consumer contracts, [674]
Conventions to have force of law, [666]
court settlements, [677]
domicile. *See* Domicile
enforcement of judgments other than maintenance orders, [668]
enforcement of UK judgments in other parts of UK, [682]
interest on registered judgments, [671]
interim relief in absence of substantive proceedings, [689]
interim relief in cases of doubtful jurisdiction, [688]
interpretation of Conventions, [667]
interpretation of references to Conventions and Contracting States, [665]

CIVIL JURISDICTION AND JUDGMENTS—*continued*
  issue of copies and certificates, [677]
  judgments a bar to further proceedings on same cause of action, [698]
  legal aid, [704]
  matters for which rules of court may provide, [712]
  modifications consequential on revision of Conventions, [678]
  modifications occasioned by decisions of European Court as to meaning or effect of Conventions, [711]
  overseas judgments counteracting award of multiple damages, [702]
  overseas judgments given against states, [695]
  overseas judgments in proceedings brought in breach of agreement for settlement of disputes, [696]
  powers to stay, sist, strike out or dismiss proceedings, [713]
  proceedings in England and Wales or Northern Ireland for torts to immovable property, [694]
  proof of judgments, [675]
  protective measures in cases of doubtful jurisdiction, [688]
  provisions supplementary to Title VII, 1968 Convention, [673]
  recognition of UK judgments in other parts of UK, [683]
  registration of maintenance orders in Northern Ireland, [700]
  Scotland, [684]-[687]. *See also* Scotland
  security in Admiralty proceedings in case of stay, [690]
  service of county court process outside Northern Ireland, [693]
  steps not amounting to submission to jurisdiction of overseas court, [697]
  trusts, [674]
  United Kingdom and certain territories, as between, [703]

COMPLEX MONOPOLY SITUATION
  meaning, [442]

CONDITION
  definition, [33]
  sale of goods, and, [95]-[99]

CONDITIONAL SALE AGREEMENT
  definitions, [21], [33], [353], [380]
  implied terms, and, [32]

CONSIDERATION
  implied term about
    supply of services, and, [164]

CONSUMER
  meaning, [526], [790], [800]

CONSUMER ARBITRATION, [511]-[519]. *See also* Arbitration

CONSUMER CONTRACTS
  allocation within UK of jurisdiction, [674]

CONSUMER CREDIT, [171]-[361]. *See also* Credit
  Act of 1974
    commencement provisions, [361]
    transitional provisions, [361]
  advertising, [209]-[213]
    content, [210]
    false, [212]
    form, [210]
    infringements, [213]
    misleadng, [212]
    prohibition where goods not sold for cash, [211]
  agreement with more than one creditor or owner, [350]
  agreement with more than one debtor or hirer, [349]
  agreements secured on land, [363]
  ancillary business, [309]-[310]
    advertisements, [315]
    canvassing off trade premises, [317], [318]
    entry into agreements, [320]
    right to recover brokerage fees, [319]
  appeal from county court in Northern Ireland, [307]
  arrangements between creditor and supplier, [351]
  associates, [348]
  canvassing, [214]-[217]
  circulars to minors, [216]
  conduct of business regulations, [220]
  contracting-out forbidden, [337]
  copies, form of, [344]
  defences, [332]
  determinations by Director, [347]
  duty of persons deemed to be agents, [339]
  duty to display information, [219]
  EEC Directive, [799]-[818]
  enforcement authorities, [325]
    compensation for loss, [327]
  enforcement orders, [291], [292]
  exempt agreements, [184], [362]-[370]
    bodies, list of, [368]-[370]
    connection with country outside United Kingdom, [366]
    consumer hire agreements, [367]
    number of payments to be made by debtor, and, [364]
    rate of total charge for credit, by reference to, [365]
  extension of time, [293], [294]
  financial provisions of Act of 1974, [354]
  judicial control, [291]-[308]
  jurisdiction, [305]
  jurisdiction of county court in Northern Ireland, [307]
  licensing, [311]-[314]
    appeals to Secretary of State, [314]
  linked transactions, [187]
  local Acts, [342]
  monetary limits, power to alter, [345]
  multiple agreements, [186]
  Northern Ireland, [355]
  notification of convictions and judgments to Director, [330]
  obstruction of authorised officers, [329]
  offences, [358]
  offences by bodies corporate, [333]
  onus of proof in proceedings, [335]

CONSUMER CREDIT—continued
orders, [299], [300], [346]
orders on death of debtor or hirer, [292]
parties, [305]
penalties, [331]
power of enforcement authority to make test purchases, [328]
power to declare rights of parties, [306]
powers of entry and inspection, [326]
protection orders, [295]
quotations, [218]
registered charges, and, [341]
regulations, [346]
restrictions on disclosure of information, [338]
sanctions for breach of Act of 1974, [334]
secondary documents, form of, [343]
security, [270]-[278]
  Act not to be evaded by use of, [278]
  content, [270]
  duty to give information to debtor or hirer, [275]
  duty to give information to surety, [272]-[274]
  duty to give surety copy of default notice, [276]
  form, [270]
  ineffective, [271]
  realisation, [277]
seeking business, [209]-[220]
service of documents, [340]
small agreements, [185]
statements by creditor or owner to be binding, [336]
terminology, [352], [359], [360]
unlimited trader, [312], [313]
unsolicited credit-tokens, [217]

CONSUMER CREDIT AGREEMENTS, [176]

CONSUMER CREDIT BUSINESS
definition, [353]
licensing of, [189]-[208]
  appeals to Secretary of State, [208]
  authorisation of specific activities, [191]
  bankruptcy of licensee, [205]
  conduct of business, [194]
  control of name of business, [192]
  enforcement of agreements made by unlicensed trader, [207]
  death of licensee, [205]
  duty to notify changes, [204]
  group, [190]
  issue of licences, [195], [196]
  licensee to be fit person, [193]
  offences, [206]
  register, [203]
  renewal, [197]
  representations to Director, [202]
  revocation, [200]
  standard, [190]
  suspension, [200], [201]
  variation, [198], [199]

CONSUMER GOODS
guarantee of, [60]

CONSUMER HIRE AGREEMENTS, [183]

CONSUMER HIRE BUSINESS
licensing of, [189]-[208]
  appeals to Secretary of State, [208]
  authorisation of specific activities, [191]
  bankruptcy of licensee, [205]
  conduct of business, [194]
  control of name of business, [192]
  death of licensee, [205]
  duty to notify changes, [204]
  enforcement of agrements made by unlicensed trader, [207]
  group, [190]
  issue of licences, [195], [196]
  licensee to be fit person, [193]
  offences, [206]
  register, [203]
  renewal, [197]
  representations to Director, [202]
  revocation, [200]
  standard, [190]
  suspension, [200], [201]
  variation, [198], [199]

CONSUMER PROTECTION
appeals against detention of goods, [485]
cancellation contracts. *See* Cancellation of contracts
civil proceedings, [493]
compensation of seizure and detention, [486]
due diligence, defence of, [491]
enforcement of Act of 1987, [479]-[487]
financial provisions of Act of 1987, [495]
liability of persons other than principal offender, [492]
Northern Ireland, [501]
obstruction of authorised officer, [484]
power of Commissioners of Customs and Excise to disclose information, [489]
powers of search, [481], [482]
privileges, savings for, [499]
recovery of expenses of enforcement, [487]
reports by Secretary of State, [494]
restrictions on disclosure of information, [490]
service documents, [496]
test purchases, [480]

CONSUMER PROTECTION ADVISORY COMMITTEE, [434]

CONSUMER SAFETY, [462]-[471]. *See also* Consumer protection
forfeiture, [468], [469]
general requirement, [462]
notices to warn, [465], [506]
power of Secretary of State to obtain information, [470]
prohibition notices, [465], [505]
regulations, [463]
  offences against, [464]
suspension notices, [466]
  appeals against, [467]

CONSUMER TRANSACTIONS
restrictions on statments, [520]-[524]

CONTRACT
cancellation of. *See* Cancellation of contracts

CONTRACTS
negotiated away from business premises
  EEC Directive, [788]-[798]

CONTRIBUTION, [77]–[85]
  assessment of, [78]
  Crown, and, [81]
  entitlement to, [77]
  proceedings against persons jointly liable for same debt or damage, [79]
  successive actions against persons liable for same damage, [80]

CONTROLLER
  definition, [353]

CONVENTION ON JURISDICTION AND THE ENFORCEMENT OF JUDGMENTS IN CIVIL AND COMMERCIAL MATTERS, [720]. *See also* Civil jurisdiction and judgments
  Annexed Protocol, [720]
  authentic instruments, [720]
  court settlements, [720]
  enforcement, [720]
  final provisions, [720]
  general provisions, [720]
  jurisdiction, [720]
  recognition, [720]
  relationship to other Conventions, [720]
  scope, [720]
  text of 1971 protocol, [721]
  text of Titles V and VI of Accession Convention, [722]
  transitional provisions, [720]

CONVERSION, [45], [46]

CORPORATION
  domicile of, [706], [707]

COUNTY COURT
  appeal from
    Northern Ireland, in, [307]
  jurisdiction in Northern Ireland, [307]
  service of process outside Northern Ireland, [693]

COURT
  sale authorised by, [48]

COURT OF LAW
  definition, 714

CREDIT. *See also* Consumer credit
  fixed-sum, [178]
  meaning, [177]
  restricted-use, [179]
  running-account, [178]
  total charge for, [188]
  unrestricted-use, [179]

CREDIT AGREEMENTS, [221]–[240]. *See also* Hire agreements
  acceptance of credit-tokens, [232]
  agreement to enter future agreement void, [225]
  antecedent negotiations, [222]
  appropriation of payments, [247]
  business consumers, and, [324]
  cancellation within cooling-off period, [233]–[239]
  correction of wrong information, [323]
  content, [226]
  cooling-off period, [234]
  death of debtor, [252]
  default notice, [253]–[255]

CREDIT AGREEMENTS—*continued*
  disclosure of information, [221]
  duty of agency to disclose filed information, [322]
  duty of negotiator to disclose name, [321]
  duty to give information, [263]
  duty to give notice before taking action, [242]
  duty to give notice of cancellation rights, [230]
  duty to give information to debtor, [243], [244]
  duty to supply copy, [228], [229]
  early payment by debtor
    effect on linked transactions, [262]
  exclusion of certain agreements from Act of 1974, [240]
  form, [226]
  improper execution, [231]
  interest not to be increased on default, [259]
  liability of creditor for breaches by supplier, [241]
  misuse of credit facilities, [249]
  new credit-tokens, duty on issue of, [251]
  notice of rescission, and, [268]
  opportunity for withdrawal from prospective land mortgage, [224]
  power to vary, [300]
  rebate on early settlement, [261]
  retaking of protected goods, [256]–[258]
  right to complete payments ahead of time, [260]
  signing, [227]
  termination, [264]–[269]
    statements, [269]
  variations, [248]
  withdrawal from prospective agreement, [223]

CREDIT-BROKER
  definition, [144], [167]

CREDIT BROKERAGE
  definition, [167]

CREDIT REFERENCE AGENCIES, [321]–[324]

CREDIT-SALE AGREEMENT
  definition, [353]

CREDIT-TOKEN AGREEMENTS, [182]

CREDITOR
  definition, [21], [33], [353], [791]

CROWN
  application of Civil Jurisdiction and Judgments Act 1982, [715]
  contribution, and, [81]
  domicile of, [710]
  product liability, and, [461]

CUSTOMS OFFICER
  power to detain goods, [483]

D

DAMAGES
  interference with goods. *See* Interference with goods
  misrepresentation, for, [23]
  multiple
    overseas judgments counteracting, [702]
  non-acceptance of goods, for [134]

Index

DEALING AS CONSUMER
definition, [66]

DEATH
European Convention on Products Liability in regard to, [735]–[754]

DEBTOR
definition, [353]

DEBTOR-CREDITOR AGREEMENTS, [181]

DEBTOR-CREDITOR-SUPPLIER AGREEMENTS, [180]

DEFECT
meaning, [736]

DEFECTIVE PRODUCTS
EEC Directive, [765]–[787]

DELIVERY
definition, [144]

DEPOSIT
definition, [353]

DETENTION OF GOODS, [37]–[39]
form of judgment, [38]
interlocutory relief, [39]

DETINUE
abolition, [37]

DIRECTOR GENERAL OF FAIR TRADING, [171]–[175], [432]
action with respect to course of conduct detrimental to interests of consumers, [444]
dissemination of information and advice, [173]
form of application, [174]
functions, [433]
general functions, [171]
jurisdiction of courts, and, [451]
penalty for false information, [175]
persons consenting to or conniving at courses of conduct detrimental to interests of consumers, [448]
powers of Secretary of State in relation to, [172, 443]
proceedings before Restrictive Practices Court, [445]
evidence in, [446]
register, [203]
representations to, [202]

DISPOSITION
definition, [21]

DOCUMENT OF TITLE
definition, 1
mode of transfer, 11
transfer, effect of, 10

DOMICILE, [705]–[710]
association, of, [706], [707]
corporation, of, [706], [707]
Crown, of, [710]
individuals, of, [705]
persons deemed domiciled in United Kingdom, [708]
trusts, of, [709]

E

EEC
Directive on consumer credit, [799]–[818]
Directive on defective products, [765]–[787]
Directive relating to misleading advertising, [755]–[764]
Directive to protect consumer in respect of contracts negotiated away from business premises, [788]–[798]
European Convention on Products Liability in regard to personal injury and death, [735]–[754]

EUROPEAN COURT
decisions of
Conventions, and, [711]

EXECUTED AGREEMENT
definition, [353]

EXEMPTED CLAUSE
varieties of, [67]

EXTORTIONATE CREDIT BARGAINS, [301]–[304]
reopening, [303]

F

FALSE TRADE DESCRIPTIONS, [382] *et seq*
meaning, [384]
prohibition, [382]

FOOD
meaning, [471]

FREIGHT
meaning, 642

FRUSTRATION OF CONTRACT, [16]–[18]
adjustment of rights and liabilities of parties, [16]–[18]

FUTURE GOODS
definition, [144]

G

GOODS
definition, [1], [144], [167], [497]

GUARANTEE
consumer goods, of, [60]

H

HAGUE RULES, [658], [664]
contracting states, [659]
extension of application to carriage from ports in British possessions, [662]
warranty of seaworthiness, [660]

HEALTH AND SAFETY AT WORK ETC ACT 1974
amendments, 488

HIRE AGREEMENTS, [221]–[240]. *See also* credit agreements
acceptance of credit-tokens, 232
agreement to enter future agreement void, [225]
antecedent negotiations, [222]
appropriation of payments, [247]

HIRE AGREEMENTS—*continued*
  cancellation within cooling-off period, [233]–[239]
  content, 226
  cooling-off period, 234
  credit-tokens, misuse of, [250]
  death of hirer, [252]
  default notice, [253]–[255]
  disclosure of information, [221]
  duty to give information to hirer, [245], [246]
  duty to give notice before taking action, [242]
  duty to give notice of cancellation rights, [230]
  duty to supply copy, [228], [229]
  exclusion of certain agreements from Act of 1974, [240]
  form, [226]
  improper execution, [231]
  liability of creditor for breaches by supplier, [241]
  notice of rescission, and, [268]
  opportunity for withdrawal from prospective land mortgage, [224]
  power to vary, [300]
  signing, [227]
  termination, [264]–[269]
    statements, [269]
  variation, [248]
  withdrawal from prospective agreement, [223]

HIRE OF GOODS, CONTRACT FOR, [155]–[160]
  implied terms
    exclusion, [160]
  implied terms about quality or fitness, [158]
  implied terms about right to transfer possession, [156]
  implied terms where hire by description, [157]
  implied terms where hire by sample, [159]
  meaning, [155]

HIRE-PURCHASE, [19]–[21]
  implied terms. *See* Implied terms
  unfair contract terms, [61]

HIRE-PURCHASE AGREEMENTS
  definitions, [21], [33], [353], [380]
  evidence of adverse detention, [298]
  financial relief for hirer, [296]
  special powers of court, [297]

HIRER
  definition, [353]

I

IMMOVABLE PROPERTY
  tort to
    proceedings in England and Wales or Northern Ireland, [694]

IMPLIED TERMS, [27]–[35]
  bailing by description, [28]
  care and skill, about, [162]
  conditional sale agreements, and, [32]
  consideration, about
    supply of services, and, [164]
  exclusion, [31], [139]
    supply of services, and, [165]
  hire, and, [160]
  hire by description, where, [157]
  hire by sample, where, [159]

IMPLIED TERMS—*continued*
  hire-purchase, and, [27]–[33]
  hiring by description, [28]
  quality or fitness, as to, [29], [9], [153]
    hire, and, [158]
  right to transfer possession, as to, [156]
  samples, [30]
  time for performance, about
    supply of services, and, [163]
  title, as to, [27], [97], [151]
  transfer of goods by description, where, [152]
  transfer of goods by sample, and, [154]

INDEMNITY CLAUSE
  unreasonable, [59]

INDEPENDENT BROADCASTING AUTHORITY
  complaints to, [545], [546]

INSTALLATION
  definition, [353]

INSURANCE
  marine. *See* Marine insurance

INTERFERENCE WITH GOODS, [36]–[55]
  competing rights to goods, [43]
  concurrent actions, [44]
  damages, [40], [41]
    allowance for improvement of goods, [41]
    extinction of title on satisfaction of claim for, [40]
  definition, [36]
  detention of goods, [37]–[39]
  double liability, [42]
  liability to two or more claimants, [42]–[44]

L

LAND
  consumer credit agreements secured on, [363]

LAND MORTGAGES, [290]

LEGAL AID, [704]

LICENSED MEDICINAL PRODUCT
  meaning, [471]

LIEN
  unpaid seller, of, [125]–[127]
    part delivery, [126]
    termination, [127]

M

MAINTENANCE ORDER
  amendment of legislation relating to, [701]
  enforcement, [669]
  meaning, [679]
  recognition, [669]
  registered
    currency of payment under, [672]
  registration
    Northern Ireland, in, [700]

MARINE INSURANCE, [553]–[644]
  abandonment, [614], [615]
  alteration of port of departure, [595]
  assignment of policy, [602], [603]
  avoidance of wagering or gaming contracts, [556]

Index

MARINE INSURANCE—*continued*
  change of voyage, [597]
  contrast deemed to be concluded, [573]
  contribution, right of, [632]
  definition, [553]
  delay in voyage, [600]
    excuses for, [601]
  deviation, [598]
    excuses for, [601]
  disclosure, [569]–[571]
  double insurance, [584]
  form of policy, [645]
  implied condition as to commencement of risk, [594]
  implied obligations varied by agreement or usage, [639]
  insurable interest, [556]–[567]
    advance freight, [564]
    assignment of, [567]
    bottomry, [562]
    charges of insurance, [565]
    contingent, [559]
    defeasible, [559]
    definition, [557]
    master's and seamen's wages, [563]
    partial, [560]
    quantum of, [566]
    re-insurance, [561]
    when interest must attach, [558]
  insurance value, [568]
  interpretation of terms, [642]
  losses, [607]–[613], [616]–[618]
    actual total, [609]
    constructive total, [612], [613]
    excluded, [607]
    general average, [618]
    included, [607]
    missing ship, [610]
    partial, [608]
    particular average, [616]
    salvage charges, [617]
    total, [608]
    transhipment, effect of, [611]
  marine adventure, [555]
  maritime perils, [555]
  measure of indemnity, [619]–[630]
    apportionment of valuation, [624]
    extent of liability of insurer for loss, [619]
    general average contributions, [625]
    general provisions, [627]
    partial loss, [621], [622], [623]
    particular average warranties, [628]
    salvage charges, [625]
    successive losses, [629]
    suing and labouring clause, [630]
    third parties, liabilities to, [626]
    total loss, [620]
  mixed sea and land risks, [554]
  mutual insurance, [637]
  policy, [574]–[583]
    construction of terms in, [582]
    contents, [575]
    contract embodied in, [574]
    designation of subject-matter, [578]
    floating policy by ship or ships, [581]
    premium to be arranged, [583]
    signature of insurer, [576]
    time policies, [577]
    unvalued, [580]

MARINE INSURANCE—*continued*
  policy—*continued*
    valued, [579]
    voyage policies, [577]
  premium, [604]–[606]
  ratification by assured, [638]
  reasonable time
    question of fact, [640]
  representations, [572]
  return of premium, [634]–[636]
    agreement, by, [635]
    enforcement, [634]
    failure of consideration, for, [636]
  rights of insurer on payment, [631]–[633]
  rules for construction of policy, [645]
  sailing for different destination, [596]
  several ports of discharge, [599]
  slip as evidence, [641]
  subrogation, right of, [631]
  under insurance, effect of, [633]
  voyage, [594]–[601]
  warranties, [585]–[593]
    breach excused, when, [586]
    express, [587]
    good safety, [590]
    legality, [593]
    nationality, [589]
    nature of, [585]
    neutrality, of, [588]
    seaworthiness, [591], [592]

MARKET RESEARCH EXPERIMENTS
  meaning, [417]
  trade descriptions, and, [417]

MERCANTILE AGENTS, [2]–[7]
  agreements through clerks, [6]
  common law powers, [13]
  consignees, provisions, as to, [7]
  consignors, provisions as to, [7]
  definition, [1], [111]
  powers with respect to disposition of goods, [2]
  rights acquired by exchange of goods or documents, [5]
  rights of the owner, and, [12]

MINORS
  consumer credit canvassing, and, [216]

MISLEADING ADVERTISEMENTS, [538]–[548]
  applications to High Court by Director-General of Fair Trading, [542]
  Cable Authority, and, [547], [548]
  complaints to Director-General of Fair Trading, [541]
  functions of court, [543]
  IBA, and, [545], [546]
  powers of Director to obtain and disclose information, [544]

MISLEADING PRICE INDICATIONS, [472]–[478]
  code of practice, [477]
  defences, [476]
  facilities, and, [474]
  misleading, meaning, [473]
  offence, [472]
  power to make regulations, [478]
  provision of accommodation, and, [475]
  services, and, [474]

MISREPRESENTATION, [22]–[26]
  avoidance of provisions excluding liability for, [24]
  damages for, [23]
  rescission, and, [22]
MONOPOLIES AND MERGERS COMMISSION, [435]
  functions, [436]
MONOPOLY SITUATION, [437]–[442]
  complex, [442]
  exports, in relation to, [439]
  limited to part of United Kingdom, [440]
  meaning, [437]–[440]
  supply of goods, in relation to, [437]
  supply of services, in relation to, [438]
MORTGAGE
  land. *See* Land mortgages
  opportunity for withdrawal from, [224]
MOTOR VEHICLE
  definition, [21]
  presumptions relating to dealings with, [20]
  protection of purchasers, [19]
MOVEABLES
  meaning, [642]

N

NEGLIGENCE
  avoidance of liability, [57]
  meaning, [56]
NEGOTIABLE INSTRUMENTS, [287]–[289]
  holders in due course, [289]
  restrictions on taking and negotiating, [287], [288]
NORTHERN IRELAND
  appeal from county court, [307]
  consumer credit, [355]
  Consumer Protection Act 1987, and, [501]
  jurisdiction of county court, [307]
  registration of maintenance orders, [700]
  trade descriptions, provisions as to, [420]
NOTICE
  definition, [68]

O

OVERSEAS JUDGMENTS. *See* Civil jurisdiction and judgments
OWNER
  definition, [353]

P

PAWN-RECEIPTS 279. *See also* Pledges
  loss of, [283]
PERSONAL INJURY
  definition, [68]
  European Convention on Products Liability in regard to, [735]–[754]

PLAINTIFF
  definition, [144]
PLEDGES [279]–[286]. *See also* Pawn-receipt
  antecedent debt, for, [4]
  consequence of failure to redeem, [285]
  definition, [1]
  document of title, of
    effect of, [3]
  penalty for failure to supply copies of agreement, [280]
  realisation of pawn, [286]
  redemption period, [281]
  redemption procedure, [282]
  unreasonable refusal to deliver pawn, [284]
PRICE OF GOODS
  false or misleading indications as to, [392]
PRODUCER
  meaning, [453], [736], [768]
PRODUCT
  meaning, [453], [736], [767]
PRODUCT LIABILITY, [453]–[461]
  application of enactments, [458]
  Crown, and, [461]
  damage giving rise to, [457]
  "defect", meaning of, [455]
  defective products, liability for, [454]
  defences, [456]
  European Convention, [735]–[754]
  prohibition on exclusions from liability, [459]
PROPERTY
  definition, [144], [167]
PUBLICATION
  meaning, [539]

Q

QUALITY
  definition, [144], [167]
QUALITY OR FITNESS
  implied terms about, [99], [153]
  hire, and, [158]

R

REDEEM
  definition, [380]
REDEMPTION
  definition, [167]
RESCISSION
  misrepresentation, and, [22]
  notice of, [268]
  unpaid seller, and, [132]
RESTRICTIVE PRACTICES COURT
  appeals from, [452]
  interconnected bodies corporate, and, [450]
  order of, [447], [449]
  proceedings by Director-General of Fair Trading, [445]
    evidence in, [446]
  undertaking given to, [447], [449]
ROYAL APPEAL
  false representations as to, [393]

RULES OF COURT
definition, [714]

S

SAFE
meaning, [471]

SALE
definition, [144]
unfair contract terms, [61]

SALE OF GOODS, [86]–[149]
acceptance of goods, [120]
actions for breach of contract, [133]–[138]
    action for price, [133]
    buyer's remedies, [135]–[137]
    damages for non-acceptance, [134]
    interest, [138]
    non-delivery, damages for, [135]
    remedy for breach of warranty, [137]
    specific performance, [136]
agreement to sell at valuation, [94]
auction sales, [141]
buyer not bound to return rejected goods, [121]
buyer's liability for not taking delivery, [122]
capacity to buy and sell, [88]
conditions, [95]–[99]
conflict of laws, [140]
contract of sale, [87]
contracts to which Act of 1979 applies, [86]
delivery, [114]
    buyer's right of examining goods, [119]
    carrier, to, [117]
    instalment, [116]
    risk where goods are delivered at distant place, [118]
    wrong quantity, [115]
duties of seller and buyer, [112]
effects of contract, [101]–[111]
existing goods, [90]
formalities of contract, [89]
future goods, [90]
implied terms
    exclusion, [139]
implied terms about quality or fitness, [99]
implied terms about title, [97]
modification of Act of 1979 for certain contracts, [148]
payment and delivery concurrent conditions, [113]
performance of contract, [112]–[122]
perished goods, [91], [92]
price, [93], [94]
reasonable time a question of fact, [142]
rights enforceable by action, [143]
rights of unpaid seller against goods, [123]–[132]
    lien, [125]–[127]
    re-sale by buyer, [131]
    rescission, [132]
    stoppage in transit, [128]–[130]. *See also* Stoppage in transit
sale by description, [98]
sale by sample, [100]
time, stipulations as to, [95]
transfer of property as between seller and buyer, [101]–[105]
    goods must be ascertained, [101]

SALE OF GOODS—*continued*
transfer of property as between seller and buyer—*continued*
    property passes when intended to pass, [102]
    reservation of right of disposal, [104]
    risk prima facie passes with property, [105]
    rules for ascertaining intention, [103]
transfer of title, [106]–[111]
    buyer in possession after sale, [110]
    market overt, [107]
    sale by person not owner, [106]
    sale under voidable title, [108]
    seller in possession after sale, [109]
warranties, [95]–[99]

SAMPLES
implied terms, and, [30]

SCOTLAND
application of s 1, Administration of Justice (Scotland) Act 1972, [692]
arbitration agreements, [516]–[518]
jurisdiction in [684]–[687]
provisional and protective measures in absence of substantive proceedings, [691]

SEARCH, POWER OF
consumer protection, and, [481], [482]

SECURITY
definition, [353], [526]

SELLER
definition, [33], [144]
disposition by, [8]

SERVICES
false or misleading statements as to, [395], [396]

SPECIFIC PERFORMANCE
breach of contract to deliver goods, and, [136]

SPECIFIED GOODS
definition, [144]

STATEMENTS
restrictions on, [520]–[524]

STOPPAGE IN TRANSIT, [128]–[130]
bills of lading, and, [551]
effect of transfer of document of title on, [10]
unpaid seller, rights of, [128]–[130]
    duration of transit, [129]
    how effected, [130]

SUBSTANCE
definition, [497]

SUPPLY
meaning, [498]

SUPPLY OF GOODS, [150]–[160]
contracts for transfer of property in goods, [150]
false representations as to, [394]
implied terms about title, [151]
implied terms where transfer is by description, [152]

SUPPLY OF SERVICES, [161]–[165]
care and skill, implied term about, [162]
consideration, implied term about, [164]
contracts concerned, [161]

SUPPLY OF SERVICES—*continued*
  implied terms
    exclusion of, [165]
    time for performance, implied term about, [163]
SURETY
  definition, [353]

T

THE CONVENTIONS
  meaning, [665]
TITLE
  implied terms as to, [97], [151]
TOBACCO
  meaning, [471]
TORT
  immovable property, to
    proceedings in England and Wales or Northern Ireland, [694]
TOTAL PRICE
  definition, [353]
TRADE DESCRIPTIONS
  accessories to offences committed abroad, [401]
  accident, defence of, [404]
  advertisements, used in, [386]
  application to goods, [385]
  civil rights, and, [415]
  compensation for loss of goods seized, [413]
  country of origin, [416]
  defences, [404], [405]
  definition orders, [388]
  enforcement, [406]–[411]
  enforcing authorities, [406]
  entry of premises, [408]
  evidence by certificate, [411]
  false. *See* False trade descriptions
  false or misleading statements as to services, [395], [396]
  false representations as to royal approval or award, [393]
  false representations as to supply of goods or services, [394]
  innocent publication of advertisement, [405]
  inspection of goods and documents, [408]
  market research experiments, [417]
  marking orders, [389], [391]
  meaning, [383]
  mistake, defence of, [404]
  Northern Ireland, provisions as to, [420]
  notice of intended prosecution, [410]
  notice of test, [410]
  obstruction of authorised offices, [409]
  offences, [398]
  offences by corporations, [400]
  offences due to fault of other person, [403]
  offer to supply, and, [387]
  orders, [418]
  power to exempt goods, sold for export, [412]
  prohibition of importation of goods bearing false indication of origin, [397]
  restriction on admission of evidence, [402]
  restriction on institution of proceedings, [402]
  seizure of goods and documents, [408]
  test purchases, [407]

TRADE DESCRIPTIONS—*continued*
  time limit for prosecutions, [399]
  trade marks containing, [414]
TRADE MARKS
  trade descriptions, containing, [414]
TRADER
  meaning, [526], [758]
TRADING STAMPS, [371]–[381]
  advertisements referring to value of, [376]
  books to include name and address of promoter, [375]
  catalogues to include name and address of promoter, [375]
  definition, [167], [380]
  display of information in shops, [377]
  offences committed by corporations, [378]
  promoters of schemes
    restrictions on persons carrying on business, [371]
  redemption for cash, [373]
  statements required on face, [372]
  venue in summary proceedings, [379]
  warranties to be implied on redemption for goods, [374]
TRANSFEREE
  definition, [167]
TRANSFEROR
  definition, [167]
TRESPASS TO GOODS, [45], [46]
TRIBUNAL
  definition, [714]
TRUSTS
  allocation within UK of jurisdiction, [674]
  domicile of, [709]

U

UNCOLLECTED GOODS, [47], [48], [53]
UNFAIR CONTRACT TERMS, [56]–[76]
  breach of contract, and, [63]
  choice of law clauses, [70]
  contract liability, [58]
  "dealing as consumer", [66]
  evasion by means of secondary contract, [64]
  "guarantee" of consumer goods, [60]
  hire-purchase, [61]
  international supply contracts, [69]
  miscellaneous contracts under which goods pass, [62]
  negligence liability, [57]
  "reasonableness" test, [65]
  sale, [61]
  scope of statute, [75], [76]
  temporary provision for sea carriage of passengers, [71]
  unreasonable indemnity clauses, [59]
UNIFORM LAW ON FORMATION OF CONTRACTS FOR INTERNATIONAL SALE OF GOODS, [647], [657]
  revision of [648]

UNIFORM LAW ON INTERNATIONAL SALE OF GOODS, [646]
  application of, [651]
  delivery of goods, [653]
  general provisions, [652]
  obligations of buyer, [653]
  obligations of seller, [653]
  obligations of seller as regards conformity of goods, [653]
  passing of risk, [656]
  provisions common to obligations of seller and of buyer, [655]
  revision of, [648]

UNPAID SELLER
  definition, [123]

UNREASONABLE INDEMNITY CLAUSE, [59]

UNSOLICITED
  definition, [428]

UNSOLICITED GOODS, [422]–[431]
  demands and threats regarding payment, [423]
  directing entries, [424]

UNSOLICITED GOODS—*continued*
  invoices, form and content of, [425]
  notes of agreement, form and content of, [425]
  offence prosecuted on indictment, [430]
  offences by corporations, [427]
  publications, [426]
  rights of recipient, [422]

V

VENDOR'S LIEN
  effect of trnsfer of document of title on, [10]

W

WARRANTY
  breach, remedy for, [137]
  definition, [33], [144]
  marine insurance. *See* Marine insurance
  sale of goods, and, [95]–[99]

WRONGFUL INTERFERENCE WITH GOODS
  definition, [36]